June 2007 Supplement

Is It Admissible?

by Ashley S. Lipson, Esq.

HIGHLIGHTS

This annual update to Ashley Lipson's popular book will help you continue to quickly determine admissibility. New case law has been added throughout the book, and the following sections have been modified or added in both the looseleaf office book and the softcover courtroom guide:

- Argumentative Questions: Legal Analysis. *§1.300*
- Hearsay Rule: Legal Analysis. *§5.300*
- Lawyer-Client Privilege. *§9.500*
- *Daubert vs. Dow. §11.603*
- Basics: Hearsay Rule. *§20.500*
- Automobile Accident Reports. *§21.401(b)*
- Private Sector Business Records. *§22.100*
- Opposition Checklist. *§22.300*
- Bills and Statements of Account. *§22.403*
- Letters of Explanation. *§22.408(b)*
- Nurses' Notes. *§22.420(d)*
- Ambulance Call Report. *§22.420(e)*
- Personal Resume. *§23.416*
- Care and Handling. *§30.300*
- Computer-Generated Animation and Graphics. *§47.600*

You continue to receive the following for each item of evidence discussed in the book:

- A quick explanation of the rule
- Strategies for admission and exclusion
- Pattern foundation questions
- Model objection language with responses
- State and federal statute and case citations

Don't overlook the book's dozens of novel arguments, proven strategies, memory aids, and successful shortcuts. *Is It Admissible?* reveals:

- The four magic words that tell you how to propose and oppose every type of evidence. *Page 0-2*
- The 12 basic objections and when to use them. *Page 0-7*
- For each objection, short lists of trigger words indicating an objectionable question. *Page 3-2*
- Model objection language, with potential responses. *Page 3-4*
- A simple guide to admission of the average piece of evidence. *Page 0-10*
- The 12 ways to oppose ordinary business records. *Page 22-5*

James Publishing, Inc.

(Rev. 9, 6/07)

We are confident that you will not want to be without this valuable update. You may, however, return the supplement within 30 days for full credit. Please include the enclosed invoice, and check the reason for the return on the back of the invoice.

If you have any suggestions for improvement, or any criticisms of *Is It Admissible?*,
please contact Jim Pawell at:

jimpawell@jamespublishing.com
714-755-5472

James Publishing, Inc.
Attn: Jim Pawell
3505 Cadillac Ave., Suite H
Costa Mesa, CA 92626

www.JamesPublishing.com
(714) 755-5450

Abbreviated Contents

Is It Admissible?

Ashley S. Lipson, Esq.

JAMES PUBLISHING

Contact us at (800) 440-4780 or www. jamespublishing.com

(Rev. 9, 6/07)

ISBN 1-58012-024-5

We view the publication of this work as the beginning of a dialogue with our readers. Periodic revisions to it will give us the opportunity to incorporate your suggested changes. Call us at (714) 755-5450 or send your comments to:

Revision Editor
James Publishing, Inc.
3505 Cadillac Ave., Suite H
Costa Mesa, CA 92626

SUPPLEMENT STAFF

Editor: Michael Margol
Production: Kristen Sachs

CD-ROM Guide

Enclosed with your copy of *Is It Admissible?* is a CD-ROM, a tremendous bonus added to this publication at no additional cost to you. The CD-ROM includes a search program that allows you to search the text of the entire book. We feel this CD-ROM will be a welcome addition to your practice for several reasons:

- **Easy to use** – Some search programs have a significant learning curve before you can start to get results. That's not the case with the enclosed James Publishing Search program. You can be up and running in no time at all.

- **No installation** – We have made it easy for you to get started right away. Pop the CD into your computer, start the search program and you are ready. No installation required.

- **Use it like a book** – Using the James Publishing Search program, you can browse each part of the publication, chapter by chapter or section by section. The CD is a second copy of the book – use it on your laptop when out of the office.

- **Search the entire book in seconds** – The James Publishing Search program allows you to search the book better than any index ever could. Using standard Boolean-searching commands, you can quickly and easily search through the entire book instantly. Find exactly what you are looking for with ease.

How to Use This CD-ROM:

For Windows NT, 2000 & XP Users:

You have three options on how you can use the contents of this CD-ROM:
- Search the entire contents of the book using the search software
- Use the text of the book in your word processor
- View the images in Adobe Acrobat

To search the entire contents of the book, please do the following:
1. Place the CD-ROM into your CD-ROM drive.
2. Select START then RUN from the Taskbar.
3. Type D:\search.exe (Replace D with the letter of your CD-ROM drive if necessary).
4. Click OK or press the Enter key.
5. The James Publishing Search program will then start.

To learn more about the James Publishing Search software, please refer to the following:
- The Help function in the program itself.
- James Publishing Search Tour within the blue pages at the front of your book

To use the text of the book in your word processor, follow these steps:
1. Place the CD-ROM into your CD-ROM drive.
2. Open the word processing program of your choice.
3. From the File menu, select Open.
4. Choose your CD-ROM drive and double-click that icon (this is usually the D: drive).
5. A directory of the contents of the CD will appear. Double click on the folder labeled **Text**.
6. The contents of the folder will appear.

7. Select the section of the book you wish to view and click OK.

For Windows ME, 3.1, 95, 98 and Macintosh Users:

Unfortunately, the James Publishing Search program is not compatible with Windows ME, 3.1, 95, 98 or Macintosh systems. Users of these systems can only view the contents of the book and the images found on this CD-ROM through their word processors and Adobe Acrobat Reader.

To use the text of the book in your word processor, follow these steps:

1. Place the CD-ROM into your CD-ROM drive.
2. Open the word processing program of your choice.
3. From the File menu, select Open.
4. Choose your CD-ROM drive and double-click that icon (this is usually the D: drive).
5. A directory of the contents of the CD will appear. Double-click on the folder labeled **Text**.
6. The contents of the folder will appear.
7. Select the section of the book you wish to view and click OK.

James Publishing Search Tour

The James Publishing Search program is a powerful application utilizing the Alchemy Search software. This tour should point you in the right direction during your use of the James Publishing Search program.

For more information regarding the use of the James Publishing Search program, please refer to the Help Menu within the program. To access this feature, click on Help menu and select Contents.

Getting Started

When you first start the James Publishing Search program, a window will open which contains three distinct sections. On the far left is the Tree View, which allows you to see all of the documents available for your search. On the top right of the window is the Viewer. The Viewer allows you to see any document you are interested in. The bottom right section features the Profile of each document. While both the Tree View and Viewer are essential, the Profile section is not as valuable. You can easily remove the Profile section from the window by deselecting it under the View menu.

Along the top, under the menu bar, is a strip of buttons for the most commonly used functions. As you move the pointer over these buttons, James Publishing Search displays a short description in the balloon help and also on the status line at the bottom left of the window.

Buttons

The buttons found here are some of the most used functions.

Change View

These three buttons allow you to select which of the three viewing tools you would like to have active. The buttons, from left to right, represent the Tree View, Viewer and Profile, respectively.

Print Current Document

Clicking this button will print the document currently displayed in the Viewer or selected in the Tree View. Be careful with this tool since some documents are much longer than others.

Launch Application

The Launch Application feature opens files in their native application. This is ideal for files that cannot be viewed in the James Publishing Search program, or when the program's built-in viewer is not sufficient.

Search

Clicking on the Search function opens up the search dialog window. Once you have opened the Search function, you have the option of performing an Advanced Search or a Simple Search by toggling in between the two by clicking on the binocular icon at the top left of the Search window. For most users, the Simple Search will be sufficient.

Previous and Next Document

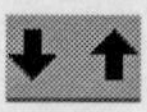

These buttons allow you to go to the previous or next document according to the list in the Tree View.

Back and Forward

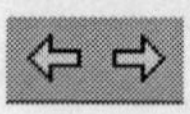

Just as with your Internet browser, these buttons allow you to go to back and forth between documents in your viewed document list.

Settings

The settings function allows you to customize the program to your preferences on a number of different items.

Frequently Asked Questions:

Can I copy the files on the CD-ROM to my hard drive?
Yes, but you don't need to do so. The CD-ROM serves as a library from which you may select the files you need. Copying them to your hard drive may occupy too much of your hard drive space and we advise against copying all the files to your hard drive for that reason.

Can I share this CD-ROM with other people?
This CD-ROM and its contents are copyrighted by James Publishing, Inc. This CD-ROM is a single-user disk. No duplication of this CD-ROM or any portion thereof for republication or distribution is permitted. This CD-ROM is licensed to the book purchaser for his or her single-screen use only.

Why can't I see a database when I open the Search program?
If no database appears in the Search program, simply click on "File" in the menu along the top of the window, then choose "Open Database." Click on "Browse," select "File System" and select the CD-ROM drive. Then select the database titled "ia.ald" which has a small CD icon next to it and click "Open."

Why am I having formatting problems?
Please be aware that not all computers and printers are set up the same way, and we have tried to accommodate how the majority of these systems operate. We cannot anticipate every configuration that may occur, though. Therefore, how the documents print may be slightly different than how they appear on screen. You may need to insert or remove page breaks as necessary to suit your particular printing needs.

I'm still having trouble. Is there someone I can contact for technical support?
If you still have questions after reading the entire contents of the blue pages, you may contact us with any questions. Call us at (714) 755-5450 or send a detailed email to us at techsupport@jamespublishing.com. Please be very specific about the problem you are having.

Disclaimer: When running the Search program, first-time users might encounter a prompt regarding an installation of files onto your computer. Please note that the program is simply updating existing files on your computer in order for the search feature to function properly. The program will not be installed on your computer.

(This page intentionally left blank.)

About the Author

The author (and creator/programmer of the game *OBJECTION!*) has been a practicing lawyer for more than 25 years. In addition to several leading books on evidence,[1] Ashley Lipson has published many articles and has lectured and taught evidence throughout the country; he is presently an Adjunct Professor of Law. He is also the author of *Law Office Automation for Paralegals, Administrators and Legal Secretaries*,[2] a book which provides a computer-oriented filing system for use in law offices.

Mr. Lipson received his B.A. degree from Michigan State University in 1966, and his J.D. degree from St. John's University in 1970 (along with awards for excellence in the study of jurisprudence); his education continued, as evidenced by his masters degrees in mathematics (M.A., 1975) and tax law (LL.M., 1978), both from Wayne State University. He has also completed two undergraduate degrees in computer science, and studied physics at the University of Michigan.

Mr. Lipson had been the managing partner of the law firm of Coleman, Lipson and Bradford, P.C., of Farmington Hills, Michigan, for over sixteen years. He is a member of the California and Michigan bar associations and is certified to practice law by the New York Committee of Bar Examiners. He is also licensed before various federal bars, including Tax Court and the U.S. Supreme Court. His other professional memberships include the American Bar Association, American Trial Lawyers Association, Mensa Lawyers, Volunteer Lawyers for the Arts, the College of Computer Lawyers, and the National Platform Association.

1 *Documentary Evidence* (1986) and *Demonstrative Evidence* (1988), both published by Matthew Bender & Co.

2 Prentice Hall, Inc. (1989).

Introduction

This book is designed to explain just what you need to know in order to try cases, i.e., how to propose and oppose virtually every form of evidence. It is written for all of those harried practitioners and busy students of the law who want fast answers and solid principles without having to wade through over-broad topics and pragmatically irrelevant theories.

We start with the proposition that the entire universe of evidence is divided into four and only four major types:

(1) Testimonial Evidence
(2) Documentary Evidence
(3) Real Evidence
(4) Demonstrative Evidence

The division is logical, economical, and pragmatic, since the elements of each type share some very important foundational traits.

When it comes to Testimonial Evidence (Part I), no lawyer should *ever* set foot into a courtroom without a firm grasp of the **Twelve Primary Objections**. Questions falling into their pigeonholes pop up during most trials. Yet, if you were to pick up virtually any book on evidence, you would only find vague references to *many* of them; and those references would be intertwined between lengthy discussions concerning the Dead Man's Statute and other esoteric matters.

A well known and highly respected law school casebook devotes a **total** of seven pages (out of 1,532) to "Leading Questions, Misleading Questions, Argumentative Questions, and Narratives." That means that less than one half of one percent of the entire text is allocated to matters that could realistically comprise a majority of questions at any real-world trial. Often, lawyers know when a question is wrong, but they can't seem to find the right pigeonhole for an objection. This guide is designed to help solve that problem. Each of the twelve universally recognized objections has its own chapter. In most trial situations, perhaps as many as 98% of all objectionable questions will fall neatly into one of the twelve slots. For rapid reference, the objections and their corresponding chapters are alphabetically arranged. Each chapter provides discussions, examples, and supporting cases, all arranged for quick access.

The need for a ready-reference is not limited to testimony. For Documentary Evidence (Part II), we take a unique "type of document" approach to the structure and presentation. It is based on the simple premise that someone seeking to admit or oppose a specific type of document does not want to wade through generic indexes and then lengthy dissertations in hopes of finding mention of his or her document buried amidst talk of the hearsay or best evidence rules. Of course, we do provide an academic basis for those rules (see Chapter 20). But in the five chapters that follow, we also provide a simple alphabetical structure that permits the immediate location of virtually every type of document.

Consider, for example, the simple birth certificate; assume that you want to determine the basis for admitting one into evidence. As an experiment, measure the time that it takes you to locate and dig through your state or federal rules for an answer. Then flip to our Part II Table of Contents and start a comparative search. Notice that we have covered virtually every type of document from police reports to discarded garbage, and notice the time that it takes to locate them.

For the remaining materials, Real Evidence (Part III) and Demonstrative Evidence (Part IV), we take an "object oriented" approach. In this arena, it is the type or form of the "object" (i.e., videotape, model, mouse, etc.) that most often determines the strategy for admissibility and opposition.

In summary, the topics are individually arranged for rapid, intuitive access. The most important aspects of every evidentiary presentation are included. The materials will show you how to lay and oppose foundations for virtually every type, shape, and form of evidence.

Summary Table of Contents

Overview

Table of Contents

Overview

Part I - Testimonial Evidence

Chapter 1
Argumentative Questions

Chapter 2
Best Evidence Rule

Chapter 3
Questions Calling for a Conclusion

Chapter 4
Questions That Assume Unproven Facts

Chapter 5
Hearsay Rule

Chapter 6
Irrelevant or Immaterial Questions

Chapter 7
Leading Questions

Chapter 8
Multiple Questions

Chapter 9
Privilege

Chapter 10
Repetitive Questions

Chapter 11
Speculative Questions

Chapter 12
Vague Questions

Chapters 13-19
Reserved for Supplementation

PART II - DOCUMENTARY EVIDENCE

Chapter 20
Basics of Documentary Evidence

Chapter 21
Governmental Documents

Chapter 22
Private Sector Business Records

Chapter 23
Personal Documents

Chapter 24
Published Writings

Chapter 25
Legal Documents

Chapters 26-29
Reserved for Supplementation

PART III - REAL EVIDENCE

Chapter 30
Basics of Real Evidence

Chapter 31
Physical Objects

Chapter 32
Samples

Chapter 33
People

Chapter 34
Animals

Chapter 35
Views

Chapter 36
On-Site Recordings

Chapters 37-39
Reserved for Supplementation

PART IV - DEMONSTRATIVE EVIDENCE

Chapter 40
Basics of Demonstrative Evidence

Chapter 41
Models

Chapter 42
Maps, Charts, Graphs and Diagrams

Chapter 43
Documents

Chapter 44
Photographs, Slides, Films and Videos

Chapter 45
Audiotapes

Chapter 46
Finger, Foot, and Palm Prints

Chapter 47
Computer-Generated Materials

Chapter 48
Live Demonstrations

Chapter 49
Internal Pictures

Appendix A
Responding to Objections at a Glance

Overview

What Is Evidence?

Factual disagreements and claims can be resolved in a number of ways. In the streets of the Old West, when someone said "prove it," gun play would decide who was right. And for the loser, perhaps, that's where we got the expression "dead wrong." It wasn't the most accurate system, but it was very final.

Today, judges and juries (instead of undertakers) have the job of sifting truth from fiction, and the "prove it" is now left to lawyers. The courts base their verdicts upon the words, documents, demonstrations, and objects that are presented by living witnesses. We call these presentations "evidence." To put it another way, "evidence" is the method by which litigants prosecute or defend their cases in court.

There are four types of evidence. They are referred to as: Testimonial Evidence, Documentary Evidence, Real Evidence and Demonstrative Evidence.[1]

Testimonial (Oral) Evidence is the most fundamental and indispensable type. Even when the other forms of evidence are used, testimony is needed to establish required foundations for them. To properly *give* testimony, liars and truth-sayers (both called "witnesses") take the stand and testify as to matters that they personally observed. For example—"I *saw* Staggerlee pick up the gun and point it at Billy; I *heard* the shot; I *smel't* the smoke; I *saw* Billy drop; and then I *felt* the warm, wet blood oozing from his chest." Each of the senses (seeing, hearing, smelling and touching) provides an example of a *personal observation.*

Documentary Evidence involves bills, notes, records, contracts and virtually every form of writing or "document." But business records, medical reports, letters, and handwritten pages ripped from diaries are not the *only* forms of documentary evidence. Microfilm, photocopies, and other secondary storage media may also be considered as "documentary." Often perplexing is the fact that electronic and optical impulses that comprise digitized computer data (fancy talk for "computer files") may constitute documentary evidence *even though* an actual printout or "hard copy" has yet to be created. In other words, the electronic and optical impulses *themselves* may constitute a "document."

Real Evidence is a physical part or component of the controversy itself, but *not* photographs or other demonstrative images of that component. Consider, for example, the actual gun that shot Billy, *not* a photo or replica. A photo or replica would be demonstrative. But the gun itself would be "real." Samples or portions are also considered as "real," such as a small drop or two of the *same* corn liquor that was used to poison Uncle Jake.

Demonstrative Evidence is the fastest growing type of evidence, and the most chic. It is often described as a self-serving presentation which appeals directly to the senses by a means other than testimony or verbal descriptions. Technically speaking, however, it is a derivative presentation designed to clarify one or more of the preceding three types of evidence. Photos, videos, maps, charts, models, films, tape recordings, and demonstrations are commonly thought of as forms of Demonstrative Evidence. For example, consider a chart showing the path of Staggerlee's bullet, or a tape recording that simulates the sounds of Billy gurgling out one last verse of *Don't Take Your Guns to Town* as his

1 The term "tangible" has been used to describe the last two types. But, not all forms of demonstrative evidence can be touched. So the term "tangible" has served to confuse the subject matter, and would, therefore, best be forgotten.

face hits the floor. Both items would be demonstrative. However, even though it may be "visual," a videotape showing L.A. police clubbing Staggerlee would be considered as real, not demonstrative evidence (assuming that it had been taken by a disinterested onlooker).

Foundations - A Single Word to the Wise

There does not seem to be a set of rules or standard terms concerning foundations followed by every jurisdiction; even judges and courts within a given state announce standards that vary from case to case.[2] But there are some common threads. And although the foundation "buzz-words" may be different, the underlying principles seem consistent, and will be considered later in more detail. For now, at the risk of gross over-simplification, here is a set of one-word foundation elements for each of the four major types of evidence:

- Testimonial - Knowledge
- Documentary - Authenticity
- Real - Identity
- Demonstrative - Clarification

Scientific Evidence

Where does so-called scientific evidence fit into the scheme? Everywhere! Consider a fiber, hair, blood stain, or spent bullet; all are *real.* The tests performed on them result in a written lab report (i.e., *documents*). The experts who must lay foundations for their admissibility use *testimonial* evidence, and often employ graphs, charts, and other *"demonstratives"* for enhancement. Since the lab report is the final embodiment of the evidence (the demonstratives are optional), it logically suits our purpose to place scientific evidence into the *DOCUMENTARY* pigeonhole.

For new or unestablished science, or "junk science," Chapter 11 (dealing with *SPECULATIVE* evidence), is the place to go.

Proper Evidence

Questions and answers start the show and make it run. Those two elements fashion "testimony," which is required to present facts or to lay foundations for the other three forms of evidence.

The "best" question will often follow the rule of the five W's used by journalists. In particular, they will start with one of these interrogatories: Who, What, When, Why or Where. Of course, other types of questions can also be proper. In any event, questions should seek information that flows directly from the witness' personal observations.

A proper question thus seeks to elicit information obtained from the witness' memory, a memory based on the use of his or her *own* senses (seeing, hearing, touching, smelling, tasting) instead of facts provided by someone else (second-hand). Fed. R. Evid. 602[3] sums it up like this:

> A witness may *not* testify to a matter unless evidence is introduced sufficient to support a finding that the witness has *personal knowledge* of the matter. Evidence to prove personal knowledge may, but need not, consist of the witness' own testimony. This rule is subject to the provisions of rule 703, relating to opinion testimony by expert witnesses (emphasis supplied).

2 There is no formal rule of evidence requiring a foundation. According to *A.I. Credit Corp., v. Legion Insurance Corp.,* 265 F.3d 630 (7th Cir., Ind., 2001), "foundation" is a loose term attached to preliminary questions designed to establish that evidence is admissible.

3 We shall frequently refer to the Federal Rules of Evidence because of the uniformity they have created. Of 101 jurisdictions (i.e. 50 federal, 50 state, plus the Military), 85 have adapted the Rules; and, remaining states have certainly been influenced by them.

This is a somewhat long-winded way of saying that witnesses should only testify concerning things that they know about. Testimony that is not based upon such first-hand knowledge will often draw any one of a number of objections that we are going to consider in the chapters that follow.

The rule requiring personal knowledge does have an important exception, which is specifically mentioned in the last sentence of Fed. R. Evid. 602. That exception involves the opinions and testimony of "experts," a term loosely used to refer to professionals in virtually any field. Mechanics, coroners, document examiners, doctors, and engineers might all be classified as "experts" within their particular fields. However, palm readers, ball gazers, astrologists, graphologists, and other mystic endeavors are generally excluded.

Because experts are normally hired *after* something, terrible or otherwise, has already happened, they must be able to base their opinions on information provided to them, since they will have no first-hand knowledge. A ballistics expert, for example, can testify about the path of a murderous bullet, even though he never witnessed the shooting. But his testimony must, nevertheless, be based upon facts that he observed and tests that he conducted or properly relied upon. Consider the previously mentioned Fed. R. Evid. 703:

> The facts or data in the particular case upon which an expert bases an opinion or inference may be those perceived by or made known to the expert at or before the hearing. If of a type reasonably relied upon by experts in the particular field in forming opinions or inferences upon the subject, the facts or data need not be admissible in evidence.

Admissibility

The universal test for determining the admissibility of every type of evidence, testimonial or otherwise, is three-pronged. It must be *relevant*, *material*, and *competent* in order to be admissible, or used for any purpose.

And, in the last analysis, it is the trial court that must decide these issues of admissibility.[4] The trial judge's decision in that regard will not be reversed unless there is an error of law or an abuse of that discretion,[5] and there is an

---

4 *Rush v. Jostock*, 710 N.W.2d 570 (Minn.App., 2006). Absent an erroneous interpretation of the law, the admissibility of evidence falls within the court's discretion. *In re Conservatorship of Smith,* 655 N.W.2d 814 (Minn. App., 2003); *Barnes v. Everett,* 95 S.W.3d 740, 351 Ark. 479 (2003); *Oxford Presbyterian Church v. Weil-McLain Co., Inc.,* 815 A.2d 1094 (Pa. Super., 2003); *State ex rel S.A.K.,* 67 P.3d 1037 (Utah App. 2003); *Hancock v. Shook,* 100 S.W.3d 786 (Mo., 2003); *Beto v. Stewart,* 582 S.E.2d 802, 213 W.Va. 355 (2003); *Kurczy v. St. Joseph Veterans Association, Inc.,* 820 A.2d 929 (R.I., 2003); *Frazier v. Havens,* 102 S.W.3d 406 (Tex.App., 2003); *In re Marriage of Nies and Cooper,* 68 P.3d 697, 315 Mont. 260 (2003); *Mowen v. Holland,* 270 Ill.Dec 605, 783 N.E.2d 180, 336 Ill.App.3d 368 (2003); *Joyce v. State Department of Corrections,* 64 P.3d 1266 (Wash.App. 2003); *MCN Energy Enterprises v. Omagro de Columbia, L.D.C.,* 98 S.W.3d 766 (Tex. App., 2003); *In re Juvenile 2002-209,* 825 A.2d 476 (N.H., 2003).

5 *City of Chicago v. Old Colony Partners*, 364 Ill.App.3d 806, 847 N.E.2d 565, 301 Ill.Dec. 555 (2006). A trial court's decision to admit evidence will not be disturbed absent an abuse of discretion.

Magill v. Edd Kirby Chevrolet, 627 S.E.2d 207 (Ga.App., 2006). Decisions pertaining to the admissibility of evidence fall within the court's discretion and will not be reversed absent an abuse of that discretion.

State of Connecticut v. Irizarry, 95 Conn.App. 224, 896 A.2d 828 (2006). When reviewing a trial court's determinations as to the relevancy of evidence and the scope of cross-examination, every reasonable presumption should be made in favor of the correctness of the trial court's ruling in determining whether or not there has been an abuse of discretion.

Alberswerth v. Alberswerth, 184 S.W.3d 81 (Mo.App., 2006) took the trouble to define "abuse of discretion" as an action that occurs when the court's ruling is so unreasonable and arbitrary that it shocks our sense of justice and is clearly contrary to the logic of the surrounding circumstances. The case of *Kaiser v. University Physicians Clinic*, 724 N.W.2d 186, 2006 SD 95 (2006) provided some additional clarification by stating that the trial court's

(Footnote 5 continued on page 0-4.)

implied, if not expressed requirement that, in order to warrant a reversal, there must be a showing of prejudice.[6] A variety of adjectives have been used to describe the extensive range of discretion that the trial judge possesses with respect to determining the admissibility of evidence, in general. It might, therefore, be stated that the trial judge has the following: wide discretion,[7] sound discretion,[8] broad discretion,[9] significant discretion,[10] great discretion,[11] and

---

5 (Continued from page 0-3.) evidentiary rulings are presumed correct and will not be reversed absent a clear abuse of discretion; such an abuse refers to a discretion that is exercised to an end or purpose that is not justified by the evidence, and is clearly against both reason and the evidence. With regard to interpreting the rules of evidence, an abuse of discretion occurs when a trial court misapplies a rule of evidence, not when it merely allows or refuses to allow questionable evidence.

See also *Crawford v. Dammann*, 626 S.E.2d 632, 277 Ga.App. 442 (2006); *Williams v. Black Rock Yacht Club, Inc.*, 877 A.2d 849, 90 Conn.App. 27 (2005); *Floyd v. Floyd*, 615 S.E.2d 465, 365 S.C. 56 (2005); *Zak v. Riffel*, 115 P.3d 165, 34 Kan.App.2d 93 (2005); *Burgard v. Allstate Insurance Company*, 904 So.2d 867 (La.App., 2005); *Michigan Department of Transportation v. Haggerty Corridor Partners, L.P.*, 700 N.W.2d 380, 473 Mich. 124 (2005); *Sheehan & Sheehan v. Nelson Malley and Company*, 117 P.3d 219 (Nevada, 2005); *Seabrook v. Berger*, 616 S.E.2d 431, 365 S.C. 234 (2005); *Musgrove Construction, Inc. v. Malley*, 912 So.2d 227 (Ala.Civ.App., 2005); *In re L.F.*, 121 P.3d 267 (Colo.App., 2005); *Badillo v. Mid Century Insurance Company*, 121 P.3d 1080 (Okla., 2005); *Oxford Presbyterian Church v. Weil-McLain Co., Inc.*, 815 A.2d 1094 (Pa.Super., 2003); *Thornhill v. Midwest Physician Center of Orland Park*, 272 Ill. Dec. 432, 787 N.E.2d 247 (2003); *State ex rel S.A.K.*, 67 P.3d 1037 (Utah App., 2003); *Kurczy v. St. Joseph Veterans Association, Inc.*, 820 A.2d 929 (R.I., 2003); *In re Marriage of Nies and Cooper*, 68 P.3d 697, 315 Mont. 260 (2003); *Mowen v. Holland*, 270 Ill. Dec 605, 783 N.E.2d 180, 336 Ill.App.3d 368 (2003); *Peterson v. BASF Corp.*, 657 N.W.2d 853 (Minn.App. 2003); *Abrams v. Marlin Firearms Co.*, 838 So.2d 925 (Miss., 2003); *Thoma Opticians, Inc. v Barnes, Dennig & Co.*, 784 N.E.2d 1207, 151 Ohio.App.3d 566 (2003).

6 *Lake Superior Center Authority v. Hammel, Green & Abrahamson, Inc.*, 715 N.W.2d 458 (Minn.App., 2006). Absent an erroneous interpretation of the law, the question of whether or not to admit evidence is within the district court's discretion. Entitlement to a new trial on the grounds of improper evidentiary rulings rests upon the complaining party's ability to demonstrate prejudicial error. *Pirolo v. DeJesus*, 905 A.2d 1210, 97 Conn.App. 585 (2006). An evidentiary ruling will result in a new trial only if the ruling was both wrong and harmful. Before a party is entitled to a new trial because of an erroneous evidentiary ruling, he or she has the burden of demonstrating that the error was harmful. And, when determining whether an erroneous evidentiary ruling in a civil case was harmful such as to warrant a new trial, the standard to be used is whether or not the erroneous ruling would have likely affected the result. See also *Greene v. Bryant*, 626 S.E.2d 185 (Ga.App., 2006); *Barnes v. Everett*, 95 S.W.3d 740, 351 Ark. 479 (2003).

7 *Hooker v. Wal-Mart Stores, Inc.*, 867 So.2d 869 (La. App. 2d Cir. March 3, 2004); *Rittenour v. Gibson*, 656 N.W.2d 691, 2003 (2003); *State v. Sanchez*, 815 A.2d 242, 75 Conn. App. 223 (2003); *State v. Francis D.*, 815 A.2d 191, 75 Conn. App. 1 (2003); *State v. Jolley*, 656 N.W.2d 305 (2003).

8 *Caulfield v. Stark*, 893 A.2d 970 (D.C., 2006); *Phoenix Services Limited Partnership v. Johns Hopkins Hospital*, 892 A.2d 1185, 167 Md.App. 327 (2006); *Parrish v. Groathouse Construction, Inc.*, 130 P.3d 502, 2006 WY 33 (2006); *Zak v. Riffel*, 115 P.3d 165, 34 Kan.App.2d 93 (2005); *Brown v. Hove*, 603 S.E.2d 63 (Ga. App., 2004); *Care & Treatment of Wadleigh v. State*, 145 S.W.3d 434 (Mo. Ct. App., 2004); *Madison v. Barnett*, 601 S.E.2d 704 (Ga. App., 2004); *Bader v. Dallas Central Appraisal District*, 139 S.W.3d 778 (Tex. App. Dallas 2004); *Jackson v. State Farm Mut. Auto. Insurance Co.*, 600 S.E.2d 346, 215 W.Va. 634 (2004).

9 *National Pub. Co. v. Hartford Fire Ins. Co.*, 892 A.2d 261, 94 Conn.App. 234 (2006). See also *Jone v. Coleman Corp.*, 183 S.W.3d 600 (Mo.App., 2006); *Williams v. Black Rock Yacht Club, Inc.*, 877 A.2d 849, 90 Conn.App. 27 (2005); *Sheehan & Sheehan v. Nelson Malley and Company*, 117 P.3d 219 (Nevada, 2005); *Seabrook v. Berger*, 616 S.E.2d 431, 365 S.C. 234 (2005); *Price v. Freeland*, 832 N.E.2d 1036 (Ind.App., 2005); *Porter v. Director of Revenue*, 168 S.W.3d 147 (Mo.App., 2005); *Hooker v. State Farm Fire and Casualty Co.*, 880 A.2d 70 (Pa.Cmnwlth., 2005); *Wasson v. Wasson*, 881 A.2d 356, 91 Conn.App. 149 (2005); *Karlson v. Harris*, 97 P.3d 428 (Idaho 2004); *Payne v. Knutson*, 99 P.3d 200, 323 Mont. 165 (2004); *Rice v. C.I. Lanning*, 97 P.3d 580, 322 Mont. 487 (2004); *Roberts v. Owens-Corning Fiberglas Corp.*, 878 So.2d 631 (La. App. 1 Cir. Apr. 2, 2004); *Glacier Tennis Club at the Summit, L.L.C. v. Treweek Construction Co.*, 87 P.3d 431, 320 Mont. 351 (2004).

10 *Green v. Charleston Area Medical Center, Inc.*, 600 S.E.2d 340, 215 W.Va. 628 (2004).

11 *Burgard v. Allstate Insurance Company*, 904 So.2d 867 (La.App., 2005); *Medine v. Roniger*, 879 So.2d 706 (La. July 2, 2004).

even plain old brown wrapper "for the trial court to decide" discretion.[12] Take your pick.

RELEVANCE is the easiest test to satisfy; if the evidence has the smallest tendency to suggest that some related fact is true or untrue, then it will satisfy the relevance test. Fed. R. Evid. 401 defines relevant evidence as that evidence "having any tendency to make the existence of any fact, that is of consequence to the determination of the action, more probable or less probable than it would be without the evidence." By requiring the "fact" to be "of consequence to the determination," the federal definition of relevance seems to encompass materiality.

MATERIALITY is often confused with relevance. It should not be, for there is a distinction. In order for evidence to be both relevant and material, it must not only tend to suggest some fact that is of interest to the proceedings (this satisfies "relevance"), but it must also tend to prove a fact that is determinative of the outcome of the case (to satisfy materiality). Consider for example, a defendant on trial for murder. The prosecutor would love to show that he was arrested and charged with a string of prior rapes and pillages; such a showing would tend to paint the defendant as a bad person, so the evidence would be relevant. But according to the law, prior arrests should not be used against a defendant to prove the instant crime; so such evidence is immaterial. By mixing "relevance" with "materiality," however, the court might simply hold that such evidence is "irrelevant." Fed. R. Evid. 401 creates such a mixture.

This mixture often occurs during personal injury trials limited to damages (where liability is admitted). The plaintiff's attempts to enter testimony concerning "fault" will often be considered as immaterial. Such evidence is, of course, relevant because it concerns the facts involved in the case; but it would be immaterial because the "negligence" of the defending party would no longer be in issue.

COMPETENCE is a negative requirement. In particular, the concept suggests that even if evidence is both relevant and material, it must be checked further to make sure that it does *not* violate some specific exclusionary rule; and, of course, there are many.

If you're a little concerned about having to wade through mountains of books in search of all of the exclusionary rules, cheer up. There is an easier way to determine a "proper" question. Think of a competent question as one that does *not* violate any of the twelve rules conveniently listed in the next section; each violation corresponds to a chapter of this book for those who want more information.

Exclusionary rule problems **other** than those listed as "the twelve" have an overwhelming chance of falling into a very few special cases. For criminal cases, the most common is the rule that prohibits the use of evidence obtained by police as the result of an illegal search or seizure.

For civil cases, there are rules which exclude evidence that a defective object was repaired or corrected following an injury. The absence of such a rule would discourage repairs and that would be contrary to public policy.

For both civil and criminal cases, all evidence of attempts to compromise or settle the material disputes should be excluded. The lack of such a rule would inhibit free discussions concerning settlement negotiations, which, in turn, would inhibit the settlement process. And that would violate the public policy favoring the pretrial resolution of disputes.

Objectionable Questions

Objections are offensive noises that we lawyers make when we think that questions are improper. If you're a fan of the original Perry Mason series, you may recall that most of his objections had the familiar ring: "Your Honor, I object because the question is irrelevant, incom-

12 *Brown v. Bright Clouds Ministries, Inc.*, 891 A.2d 999, 94 Conn.App. 181 (2006); *Burr v. Mississippi Baptist Medical Center*, 909 So.2d 721 (Miss., 2005); *Dixon Dairy Farms, Inc. v. Purina Mills, Inc.*, 601 S.E.2d 152, 267 Ga. App. 738 (2004); *Independent Trust Corp. v. Hurwick*, 286 Ill. Dec. 669, 814 N.E.2d 895 (Ill. App. Ct., 2004).

petent and immaterial." That generic approach certainly covered all bases, but it was really too general[13] for ruling judges, if not for the television audiences of the 50s. In actual trials, more specificity is required.

The fundamental purpose of voicing an objection is to bring to the court's attention potentially inadmissible evidence so that it can make a ruling about the propriety of the subject question. Without **specific** notice as to the nature of the objection, the court might be left guessing about its underlying basis. Fed. R. Evid. 103(a)(1) encompasses a two-pronged test for a proper objection:

> Objection. In case the ruling is one admitting evidence, a *timely* objection or motion to strike appears of record, stating the *specific ground* of objection, if the specific ground was not apparent from the context...

If you fail to make an objection to bad evidence, you waive your right to exclude it.[14] And the failure to object to improper evidence (even hearsay) may constitute a waiver of your right to raise that objection on appeal.[15]

Generally, an objection should be presented each specific time that the opposition attempts to present improper evidence or testimony. This is certainly the safest course, even if the court permits so-called "running objections."[16]

Speed and specificity are paramount, as Fed. R. Evid. 103 suggests. The time lapse between the end of a question and the beginning of a witness' answer is often less than one second. It takes a quick objection to head off the answer; for, once the answer has been spoken, the cat is out of the bag. A judge can always instruct the jury to disregard the answer, but that is like trying to "unring" a bell.[17]

A speedy specific objection is an authoritative one. Speed and authority tend to disarm the opponent. Such an objection also tends to signal a drifting judge that you mean business. So keep the twelve objections, set forth below, close by. Knowing how and when to use them is half the battle.

---

13 Such an objection is really no objection at all unless the underlying question is so far off base that it is inadmissible for all purposes, *Leonard v. Boston Ry. Co.*, 125 N.E. 593, 234 Mass. 480 (1920); *Wimer v. Hinkle*, 379 S.E.2d 383 (W.Va., 1989).

14 *Benchoff v. Morgan*, 394 S.E.2d 19 (S.C. App., 1990). *Diversified Telecom Services, Inc. v. Clevinger,* 683 N.W.2d 338, 268 Neb. 388 (2004). If inadmissible evidence is offered and the party against whom it is offered consents to its introduction, or fails to object or to insist upon a ruling on an objection to its introduction, or otherwise fails to raise a question as to its admissibility, he is considered to have waived whatever objection he may have had thereto, and the evidence is in the record for consideration the same as other evidence.

15 *R.W. v. Schrein*, 652 N.W.2d 574, 264 Neb. 818 (2002) suggests that sometimes you may have to do more than merely object in order to preserve your appeal. In particular, if the objection happens to be ignored, the failure to insist upon a ruling can be deemed a waiver. *Creger v. Robertson*, 542 So.2d 1090 (La. App. 2 Cir. 1989).

16 *Spurgeon v. Mruz*, 832 N.E.2d 321, 358 Ill.App.3d 358, 832 N.E.2d 321, 295 Ill.Dec. 170 (2005). A party must make a timely objection to preserve an issue for appellate review. Timeliness requires that objections to evidence be made at the time the evidence is offered or as soon as the grounds for the objection become apparent. A party who, prior to trial, unsuccessfully moves to bar certain evidence must object again to the evidence when it is offered. The "running objection" is exception to general rule that party must continue to object and get ruling for each individual instance of inadmissible testimony. *In re A.P.,* 42 S.W.3d 248 (Tex. App., 2001). Such objections generally apply only to similar portions of testimony by same witness. Nevertheless, objection must be entered, at very least, each time new witness testifies, even if that objection is on same grounds as continuing objection to testimony of prior witness. *In re Estate of Peters*, 765 A.2d 468 (VT., 2000).

17 *Coho Resources, Inc. v. McCarthy*, 829 So.2d 1 (Miss. 2002). An aggrieved party must make a timely objection to any allegedly improper remark. *Grandstaff v. Hawks,* 36 S.W.3d 482 (Tenn.App., 2000). Objections to introduction of evidence must be timely and specific.

It is the ability to select the best *specific* objection, *fast*, that is important. Here are your universally recognized objections:

Universally Recognized Objections

1. The question is ARGUMENTATIVE.
2. The question violates the BEST EVIDENCE (or PAROL EVIDENCE) RULE.
3. The question calls for a CONCLUSION.
4. The question assumes FACTS not in evidence.
5. The question calls for HEARSAY.
6. The question is IRRELEVANT or IMMATERIAL.
7. The question is LEADING.
8. The question is MULTIPLE or COMPOUND.
9. The question violates PRIVILEGE.
10. The question is REPETITIVE.
11. The question is SPECULATIVE.
12. The question is VAGUE.

First we're going to examine each of the twelve objections in depth (Part I). The chapters that follow will provide some quick explanations for those who don't enjoy reading, some examples for game players, and some detailed explanations for those who may need to defend their objections before a judge.

After considering testimonial evidence, we will then consider the three remaining types: documentary evidence, real evidence, and demonstrative evidence. Particular emphasis will placed on the methods for establishing and opposing foundations for every type and form of evidence.

Maneuvering Through the Federal Rules

Where do I start? And, in which direction do I head? The skeletal outline that runs from here to the end of this chapter is designed to answer only those two questions. In later chapters we will analyze the details. The hearsay rule and its exceptions, like the principles pertaining to privilege, are examples of "details" to be covered later.

As you glance into your book of federal rules, logic would seem to suggest that there should be a noticeable starting point for laying a general foundation, followed by a set of consecutive steps and procedures, in some type of order. But that is not the case. If in doubt, try to name the starting point. Or try to find it. If you can't, don't worry; this book will provide a relatively simple road map for tracing the federal rules as they relate to the setting of a foundation.

Straight from the Federal Rules of Evidence, here are the technical requirements that the court must follow with respect to the foundation process. We've stripped away all of the subsections that apply to special cases so that our outline can provide a clearer picture of how the rules should flow for a "generic" piece of evidence. Key parts are in boldface. With the foregoing in mind, Rule 104 is the first point:

STEP 1: Rule 104(a) & (b) Is Titled "Preliminary Questions"

(a) *Questions of admissibility generally.* Preliminary questions concerning the qualification of a person to be a witness, the existence of a privilege, or the admissibility of evidence shall be determined by the court, subject to the provisions of subdivision (b). In making its determination it is not bound by the rules of evidence except those with respect to privileges.

(b) *Relevancy conditioned on fact.* When the relevancy of evidence depends upon the fulfillment of a condition of fact, the court shall admit it upon, or subject to, the introduction of evidence sufficient to support a finding of the fulfillment of the condition.

Notice that under 104(a), the court is not bound by the rules of evidence when it comes to establishing a particular foundation element. An unopposed affidavit or even a notation on a photograph (both are hearsay) might be used, for example, to establish the identity of a piece of evidence. That "identity" element along with others would hopefully build the foundation of "relevance."

STEP 2: Rules 401, 402, 403 Pertain to "Relevance & Prejudice"[18]

401 "Relevant evidence" means evidence having any tendency to make the existence of any fact that is of consequence to the determination of the action more probable or less probable than it would be without the evidence.

402 All relevant evidence is admissible, except as otherwise provided by the Constitution of the United States, by Act of Congress, by these rules, or by other rules prescribed by the Supreme Court pursuant to statutory authority. Evidence which is not relevant is not admissible.

403 Although relevant, evidence may be excluded if its probative value is substantially outweighed by the danger of unfair prejudice, confusion of the issues, or misleading the jury, or by considerations of undue delay, waste of time, or needless presentation of cumulative evidence.

Rule 402 is a gross oversimplification, not to be taken literally. But it does provide a good starting point once the elements of relevance have been established.[19] Once relevancy is established, you should go to rules 901 and 902 to determine if "authentication" is required.

Notice the manner in which Rule 403 presents a modest shopping list of methods for opposing evidence. Most significant, however, is the fact that this list can be used to oppose all four types of evidence (i.e., Testimonial, Documentary, Real and Demonstrative), unlike The Big Twelve, which pertains primarily to Testimonial Evidence.

STEP 3: Rules 901 & 902 Pertain to "Authentication"

901 (a) General provision. The requirement of authentication or identification as a condition precedent to admissibility is satisfied by evidence sufficient to support a finding that the matter in question is what its proponent claims.

(b) Illustrations. By way of illustration only, and not by way of limitation, the following are examples of authentication or identification conforming with the requirements of this rule:

(1) Testimony of witness with knowledge.
(2) Nonexpert opinion on handwriting.
(3) Comparison by trier or expert witness.
(4) Distinctive characteristics and the like.
(5) Voice identification.
(6) Telephone conversations.
(7) Public records or reports.
(8) Ancient documents or data compilation.
(9) Process or system.
(10) Methods provided by statute or rule.

---

18 Rule 401 provides a basic definition. The "+" suggests that Rule 402 is a provision that facilitates or favors the introduction of evidence, while the "-" in front of Rule 403 suggests that it is used to oppose admissibility.

19 See generally, Chapter 6.

902 Extrinsic evidence of authenticity as a condition precedent to admissibility is not required with respect to the following:

(1) Domestic public documents under seal.
(2) Domestic public documents not under seal.
(3) Foreign public documents.
(4) Certified copies of public records.
(5) Official publications.
(6) Newspapers and periodicals.
(7) Trade inscriptions.
(8) Acknowledged documents.
(9) Commercial paper.
(10) Presumption under Act of Congress.

From the above points, we travel to rule 602 to test whether or not the witness knows what he or she is talking about.

STEP 4: Rule 602 Pertains to a "Lack of Personal Knowledge"

A witness may not testify to a matter unless evidence is introduced sufficient to support a finding that **the witness has personal knowledge of the matter**. Evidence to prove personal knowledge may, but need not, consist of the witness' own testimony. This rule is subject to the provisions of rule 703, relating to opinion testimony by expert witnesses.

A good distinction to draw between steps 4 and 5 is that of fact versus opinion. Rule 602 seems to address personal knowledge of "relevant facts." The committee notes are consistent with this notion. Rules 701, 702 and 703, however, are directed squarely at opinions and conclusions.[20]

STEP 5: Rule 701 Pertains to Laypersons, Rules 702 & 703 to Experts

701 If the witness is **not** testifying as an expert, the witness' testimony in the form of opinions or inferences is limited to those opinions or inferences which are (a) rationally based on the perception of the witness and (b) helpful to a clear understanding of the witness' testimony or the determination of a fact in issue.

702 If scientific, technical, or other specialized knowledge will assist the trier of fact to understand the evidence or to determine a fact in issue, a witness qualified as an expert by knowledge, skill, experience, training, or education, may testify thereto in the form of an opinion or otherwise.

703 The facts or data in the particular case upon which an expert bases an opinion or inference may be those perceived by or made known to the expert at or before the hearing. If of a type reasonably relied upon by experts in the particular field in forming opinions or inferences upon the subject, the facts or data need not be admissible in evidence.[21]

The Federal Rules of Evidence, instead of providing a clear guide for the evidence admission process, delivers a non-consecutive set of statements, and, as with most statutes, drifts off into special cases, thereby losing those readers who just want a simple guide for an "average" piece of evidence, if there is such an animal. The preceding outline tries to provide that guide. Here is an even more "skeletal" guide:

20 See generally, Chapter 3.

21 During March, 1999, a Proposed Amendment to Rule 703 (156 F.3d p.Ct.R-136) was submitted for public coment by the Advisory Committee, directed to the admissibility of the underlying data; it provides: "If the facts or data are otherwise inadmissible, they shall not be disclosed to the jury by the proponent of the opinion or inference unless their probative value substantially outweighs their prejudicial effect." Subject to Supreme Court and congressional approval, the change takes effect December 1, 2000.

1. Are there preliminary foundation questions?
   (A) YES—See Fed. R. Evid. 104, then GOTO #2
   (B) NO—GOTO #2
2. Are you proposing the evidence?
   (A) YES—Read Fed. R. Evid. 402 (first sentence), then GOTO #7
   (B) NO—GOTO #3
3. Are you opposing the evidence?
   (A) YES—See Fed. R. Evid. 402 (last sentence), then read Fed. R. Evid. 403, then GOTO #4 (B)
   (B) NO—What the heck are you doing here? GOTO #2
4. Are you still opposing the evidence?
   (A) NO—I can't decide, GOTO LUNCH.
   (B) YES—Is hearsay involved?
   NO—GOTO #5
   YES—See Fed. R. Evid. 802 (hearsay rule), then GOTO #5
5. Are documents involved?
   (A) NO—GOTO #6
   (B) YES—See Fed. R. Evid. 802 (hearsay rule) and 1002 (best evidence rule, Chapter 2), determine genuineness, then GOTO #6
6. To improve your opposition—check out: Fed. R. Evid. 602, to attack the proponent's personal knowledge, then GOTO #8
7. To enhance your admission—check out:
   (A) Fed. R. Evid. 803 and 804 if you have hearsay problems; these are exceptions.
   (B) Fed. R. Evid. 902 for a select list of assistance
   (C) For best evidence problems, see Fed. R. Evid. 1003-1006
8. Is expert testimony involved?
   (A) YES—read Fed. R. Evid. 702 and 703
   (B) NO—look up Fed. R. Evid. 701

Determining Admissibility

While this book deals primarily with substantive admissibility issues, it is worth our while to briefly consider the procedural aspects before we get started. They are often a source of confusion for practitioners even though there are only a few methods by which admissibility is procedurally determined:[22]

[1] BY STIPULATION:

It may come as a surprise to law students but not experienced practitioners—most of the evidence that appears during the course of a trial has been admitted without a shot being fired. Pursuant to pre-trial orders, opposing counsel must meet, confer and stipulate to those facts and items of evidence for which there is no legitimate dispute. Business records provide the most common example of stipulated evidence.

A word of caution is warranted. Experience has shown that far too much evidence is unopposed. Before conceding to the admission of any of the opposition's evidence, you should first consult the applicable *Opposition Checklist* in the chapters that follow. For *Documentary Evidence*, opposition points are contained within an item by item analysis (as opposed to a general checklist).

CAUTION!-
Most Common Mistake

Do not be among the majority of attorneys who are far too quick to concede the admissibility of "business

22 In last analysis, decision whether or not to admit evidence is within trial court's broad discretion. *Turner v. Board of Aviation Commissioners,* 743 N.E.2d 1153 (Ind.App. 2001); *Hasney v. Allstate Insurance Company,* 781 So.2d 598 (La.App. 2001); *Miller v. Hensley*, 624 N.W.2d 582, 244 Mich.App. 528 (2001). That discretion will only be considered as abused if trial court improperly deprives party of fair trial. *Kotvan v. Kirk,* 254 Ill.Dec. 633, 747 N.E.2d 1045, 321 Ill.App.3d 733 (2001); *In re Robb,* 622 N.W.2d 564 (Minn.App. 2001).

records." Those mesmerizing two-words foster the misconception that such documents are automatically admissible. They are not. A proper foundation must be laid, similar to other hearsay exceptions; and, there are many points of attack. See §22.300 (*Opposition Checklist*).

[2] BY JUDICIAL NOTICE:

Judicial notice is a method by which the court, upon proper request, will take notice of certain facts, statutes, and the authenticity of certain documents. Be sure to check your applicable court rules. There is no point assembling evidence that you don't need. Judicial Notice is not "evidence." On the contrary, it is a substitute for evidence. There is no need to "formally" introduce any evidence to support an point that has been judicially noticed. The court, however, may require supporting documentation or information prior to determining whether or not notice is warranted.

CAUTION!- Most Common Mistake

Judicial notice is not "automatic," even for so-called "matters of common knowledge." Always bring supporting information (cases or statutes, or encyclopedias where applicable) to advise and inform the court. Do not expect the judge to have facts, figures, or even statutes "at his or her fingertips."

[3] BY MOTION DURING TRIAL:

The riskiest method of admitting evidence involves the classic introduction process whereby: (1) witnesses lay a foundation for the evidence, (2) the evidence is offered to the court and (3) to opposing counsel for inspection; then (4) a motion in the form of a simple request is made to the court seeking formal admission of the evidence. (Note that foundation information is provided throughout the book.)

CAUTION!

Objections during the course of trial must be quick and specific. There is normally less than a single second between the time opposing counsel completes a question and the witness starts to answer.

[4] BY MOTION IN LIMINE:

The Motion in Limine is becoming a very common method for obtaining admissibility rulings in advance of trial. It is a highly favored practice because it:

- Permits attorneys to better prepare cases by narrowing and reducing the number of admissibility related battles
- Saves time at trial
- Focuses on, and permits the correction of, any foundational deficiencies prior to trial
- Avoids putting judges "on the spot" in the midst of trial.

For these reasons, some added discussion about the *Motion in Limine* is warranted at this juncture.

Keep in mind that there are three basic types of Motions in Limine:

1. *Affirmative Motions*, designed to obtain a ruling that the proposed evidence is admissible
2. *Prohibitive Motions*, designed to exclude evidence and any mention of it in front of a jury
3. *Conditional Motions*, intended to require that the opposition establish certain foundational elements before introducing or mentioning the evidence in front of a jury.

Motions in Limine should be presented in writing in accordance with the court's rules. Some courts permit oral motions.

CAUTION!- Mistake Concerning Preservation

If your motion in limine is denied, **do not assume** that your rights of appeal are preserved. Play it safe, renew your objection (or motion to admit the evidence) during trial. There are many conflicting rules and cases pertaining to whether or not the court makes a "definitive" ruling with respect to motions in limine, and whether or not it should, therefore, be unnecessary to renew the motion at trial. Common sense, however, suggests—Don't guess and don't rely on appellate decisions. Just renew your motion at trial and be safe!

The following forms are designed to provide a structure along with a list of potential supporting allegations and arguments. Those allegations should be weighed by the practitioner for their potential benefits and detriments prior to considering such a motion. Use the information contained in the forms for oral or written motions:

Sample Language For:

[1]

MOTION IN LIMINE TO EXCLUDE EVIDENCE

The Plaintiff, by and through its attorneys, hereby moves that this honorable court exclude from the trial of this cause, and further prohibit the publication, presentation or mention to the jury, the following evidence for the reasons herein: [Description of Evidence]

1. Plaintiff (Motions in Limine can made by any party) is informed and does believe that Defendant intends to seek the admission of the subject evidence for the following reasons [State Reasons].
2. The subject evidence is inadmissible for the following reasons [The reasons should be supported by an accompanying Statement of Points and Authorities or Brief, subject to the applicable court rules.].
3. The court should address this motion and rule upon the admissibility of the subject evidence prior to trial for the following reasons:
   A. Excluding the evidence now, instead of at trial, would avoid the an inevitable prejudicial effect upon the jury as the improper evidence is proposed during the course of trial.
   B. Excluding the evidence now, as opposed to later at trial, will enable all of the parties to better prepare their respective cases for presentation at trial. Parties will be better able to determine which witnesses might be eliminated before they are issued subpoenas or placed on call. Delays and adjournments to accommodate unnecessary witnesses can thereby be averted.
   C. Excluding the evidence now will avoid the otherwise inevitable waste of time that the introduction process normally entails and would also enable the court more time within which to provide an opinion, without delaying trial.
   D. Excluding the evidence now will avoid potential problems with respect to other trial presentations that may have been contingent upon the outcome of an admissibility ruling. In particular, the parties will be less likely to make foundational errors or errors with respect to related evidence if they are not "taken by surprise" at trial.

WHEREFORE, The Plaintiff respectfully requests that this honorable court issue its order excluding from the trial of this cause, the subject evidence and any mention of that evidence in the presence of the jury.

[2]

MOTION IN LIMINE TO ADMIT EVIDENCE

The Plaintiff, by and through its attorneys, hereby moves that this honorable court issue a ruling that would permit the Plaintiff to formally admit into evidence, and accordingly use during trial, the following evidence, for the reasons stated herein: [Description of Evidence]

1. Plaintiff intends to use the subject evidence at trial for the following reasons [State Reasons].
2. The subject evidence is relevant and competent, and therefore admissible. Plaintiff believes, however, that the admissibility will be challenged for the following reasons [State Reasons].
3. The challenge would be without merit for the following reasons [The reasons should be supported by an accompanying Statement of Points and Authorities or Brief, subject to the applicable court rules.].
4. The court should address this motion and rule upon the admissibility of the subject evidence prior to trial for the following reasons:
   A. Admitting the evidence now, as opposed to later at trial, will enable all of the parties to better prepare their respective cases for presentation at trial. Parties will be better able to determine which witnesses might be eliminated before they are issued subpoenas or placed on call. Delays and adjournments to accommodate unnecessary witnesses can thereby be averted. By the same token, witnesses who are "definitely" going to testify can be so informed.
   B. Admitting the evidence now will avoid the otherwise inevitable waste of time that the introduction process normally entails and would also enable the court more time within which to provide an opinion, without delaying trial.
   C. Admitting the evidence now will avoid potential problems with respect to other trial presentations that may be contingent upon the outcome of an admissibility ruling. In particular, the parties will be less likely to make foundational errors or errors with respect to related evidence if they are not "taken by surprise" at trial.

WHEREFORE, The Plaintiff respectfully requests that this honorable court issue its order admitting for use at the trial of this cause, the subject evidence.

[3]

MOTION IN LIMINE TO EXCLUDE EVIDENCE SUBJECT TO ESTABLISHMENT OF PROPER FOUNDATION

The Plaintiff, by and through its attorneys, hereby moves that this honorable court exclude from the trial of this cause, and further prohibit the publication, presentation or mention to the jury, of the following evidence for the reasons herein: [Description of Evidence]

1. Plaintiff is informed and does believe that Defendant intends to seek the admission of the subject evidence for the following reasons [State Reasons].
2. The subject evidence is inadmissible because, upon information and belief, the Defendant will not be able to properly establish the required foundation for the following reasons [The foundation elements should be clearly and precisely stated along with the reasons why Defendant would not be able to satisfy one or more of them. The position should be supported by an accompanying Statement of Points and Authorities or Brief, subject to the applicable court rules.].

3. The court should address this motion and rule upon the admissibility of the subject evidence prior to trial for the following reasons:
   A. Excluding the evidence now, instead of at trial, would avoid the an inevitable prejudicial effect upon the jury as the inadmissible evidence is proposed during the course of trial.
   B. Excluding the evidence now, as opposed to later at trial, will enable all of the parties to better prepare their respective cases for presentation at trial. Parties will be better able to determine which witnesses might be eliminated before they are issued subpoenas or placed on call. Delays and adjournments to accommodate unnecessary witnesses can be averted.
   C. Excluding the evidence now will avoid an inevitable waste of time as an incomplete foundation, at best, would otherwise be presented.
   D. Excluding the evidence now will avoid potential problems with respect to other trial presentations that may have been contingent upon the outcome of an admissibility ruling. In particular, the parties will be less likely to make foundational errors or errors with respect to related evidence if they are warned in advance.
4. Defendant will be no more likely to establish the required foundation elements for the subject evidence at trial than at the present time.

WHEREFORE, The Plaintiff respectfully requests that this honorable court issue its order excluding from the trial of this cause, the subject evidence and any mention of that evidence in front of the jury, unless the Defendant, at the hearing on this motion is able to demonstrate for this honorable court that a proper foundation for the subject evidence exists.

The *Conditional Motion In Limine* is particularly helpful where expert witnesses are involved. The conditional motion might be used to challenge their qualifications or any new scientific evidence (Under *Rule* 702 of the *Federal Rules of Evidence*) that has not been generally accepted.

[5] BY MOTION TO SUPPRESS:

The motion to suppress illegally obtained evidence is a very common device used in criminal cases. It is the criminal-case equivalent to the civil-based *Prohibitive Motion In Limine.* The Motion To Suppress became standard fare following the landmark, *Mapp v. Ohio,* 367 U.S. 643 (1961), wherein the United States Supreme Court clarified and applied the "Exclusionary Rule," upon which the motion is based.

CAUTION!

The Motion To Suppress is a key defense weapon that should carefully be considered for most criminal cases.

Part I - Testimonial Evidence

Table of Contents

Chapter 1
Argumentative Questions

Chapter 2
Best Evidence Rule

Chapter 3
Questions Calling for a Conclusion

Chapter 4
Questions That Assume Unproven Facts

Chapter 5
Hearsay Rule

Chapter 6
Irrelevant or Immaterial Questions

Chapter 7
Leading Questions

Chapter 8
Multiple Questions

Chapter 9
Privilege

Chapter 10
Repetitive Questions

Chapter 11
Speculative Questions

Chapter 12
Vague Questions

Chapters 13-19
Reserved for Supplementation

(This page intentionally left blank.)

Chapter 1

Argumentative Questions

§1.100 Introduction

When conducting direct examination or cross-examination, it is never proper to engage in name-calling. Insults and disparaging comments are for the movies, not the courtroom. Questions that degrade, harass, embarrass, or humiliate the witness, rather than obtain information, run the risk of being deemed "argumentative" and, therefore, objectionable.

§1.200 Quick Explanation

A lawyer can always attempt to show that a witness is biased or lying, but he or she must do so by asking proper questions. Humiliation and disgrace are not proper tools of interrogation. And, despite popular belief, it is not a lawyer's inalienable right to degrade witnesses during cross-examination. The primary purpose for testimony should always be the presentation of facts that relate to the issues of the case, not the presentation of insults.

EXAMPLES OF ARGUMENTATIVE QUESTIONS:

1. Have you been lying since you took the stand?
2. Your last answer was a crock, wasn't it?
3. Do you really believe that (in reference to witness' last answer)?

WHAT TO LOOK FOR:

Questions that would insult *you*, if you were on the stand.

OBJECT AND RESPOND

OBJECTION:

"Counsel is arguing with the witness."

POTENTIAL RESPONSES TO OBJECTION:

A. "My question, your Honor, was supported by this witness' prior inconsistent testimony.
B. "If the witness would merely answer the question, there would be no need to argue."
C. "Very well. This witness' testimony speaks for itself."

§1.300 General Legal Analysis

Start with the general proposition that a court has broad discretion to limit examinations that are unduly harassing or argumentative.

Questions that per se imply that the witness is dishonest, corrupt, or of questionable character, are all candidates for an "argumentative" objection.[1] For female witnesses, suggestions of sexual activity may fall within this ilk.[2]

Often, the determination of whether or not such a question is objectionable may be a judgment call. And, for close calls, it might help to draw a distinction between direct examination and cross-examination.

With respect to direct examination, it is rarely proper for a lawyer to attack his own witness, unless that witness has executed a sudden about-

1 *U.S. v. Saunders,* 166 F.3d 907 (7th Cir. Ill 1999); *State v. Bettencourt*, 723 A.2d 1101 (RI. 1999); *People v. Prevo,* 235 Ill.Dec. 950, 706 N.E.2d 505, 302 Ill.App.3d 1038 (1999). The trial court properly uses its discretion when it restricts the scope of cross-examination on order to preclude repetitive or unduly harassing testimony. *People v. Johnson,* 683 N.Y.S.2d 681 (1998).

2 Questions implying that a female is promiscuous or active sexually can often be considered to be insulting. But, consider *U.S. v. Buchanan*, 891 F.2d 1436 (10th Cir. 1989), involving a prosecution for fire-bombing the home of a mother-in-law. The defense was properly permitted to question the defendant's former wife about her romantic involvement with the investigator for the Bureau of Alcohol, Tobacco, and Firearms, to show her bias in favor of the government.

face during trial by testifying differently than was reasonably anticipated,[3] or unless he has otherwise been declared a hostile witness.[4] Absent such a turnabout, there is a greater likelihood that a nasty question will be considered as argumentative if it happens to be directed to one's own witness. Opposing counsel may interpose: "Objection! Counsel is not only argumentative, but he's also trying to impeach his own witness."

For cross-examination, there is room for a little more leeway, since an opposing witness is involved.[5] It is proper, through impeachment, to make the witness look like a liar, but it is not proper to call a witness a "liar" or "perjurer."[6] The trick, therefore, is to degrade and humiliate an opposing witness without using derogatory words.

The Federal Rules of Evidence, particularly Rule 611, make no effort to draw a specific distinction between direct and cross-examination. The cases interpreting that rule, however, fall into line with the preceding comments. Rule 611(a), which acts as a model for many states, provides:

---

3 *State v. Duran*, 762 P.2d 890 (N.M. 1988); See also *United States v. Rivera*, 513 F.2d 519 (2d Cir. 1975). *Moore v. State*, 755 So.2d 1276 (Miss.App. 2000). A party may only impeach its own witness after a genuine showing of (1) surprise and (2) unexpected hostility. *Walker v. State,* 818 A.2d 1078, 375 Md. 360 (2003). The state may impeach its own witness's testimony where there has been a showing of surprise, but calling a witness as a subterfuge for impeachment evidence should not be permitted.

4 See *Sidenstricker v. Miller Pavement Maintenance, Inc.*, 815 N.E.2d 736, 158 Ohio App.3d.

5 *McGowan v. State*, 188 S.W.3d 239 (Tex.App., 2006). Wide latitude should be permitted for cross-examination in criminal cases. Reasons to limit the scope of cross-examination include the prevention of harassment, prejudice and repetitive questions.

State v. Rice, 184 S.W.3d 646 (Tenn., 2006). Although the trial court retains discretion regarding the exercise of the right to examine witnesses for bias, any undue restriction on that right may violate a defendant's right to confrontation under state and federal constitutions. To show a violation of the right, the defendant must demonstrate that he was prohibited from engaging in otherwise appropriate cross-examination designed to show bias on the part of the witness, thereby exposing to the jury to facts from which jurors could appropriately draw inferences relating to the reliability of the witnesses.

People v. Chatman, 38 Cal.4th 344, 133 P.3d 534, 42 Cal.Rptr.3d 621 (2006). The permissible scope of cross-examination of a criminal defendant is generally broad.

James v. State, 580 S.E.2d 334, 260 Ga.App. 536 (2003) held that, as a general rule, it is better that cross-examination should be too free than too restricted; see also *Lugo v. State,* 845 So.2d 74 (Fla., 2003) noting that each defendant in a trial is entitled to engage in vigorous cross-examination of the witnesses presented against him.*Commonwealth v. Gagnon*, 557 N.E.2d 728, 408 Mass. 185 (1990). An accused in a criminal case should be given wide latitude when cross-examining a witness for the prosecution. See *In re W.D.*, 141 Ill. Dec. 364, 551 N.E.2d 357, 194 Ill.App.3d 686 (1990). *Allen v. K-Mart*, 528 S.E.2d 60 (N.C.App. 2000). Cross-examination of opposing witness for purpose of showing his bias or interest is substantial legal right which trial judge can neither abrogate nor abridge. *Clayborne v. U.S.*, 751 A.2d 956 (D.C. 2000). Bias or testimonial motivation is always a proper subject of cross-examination. *Hodo v. State*, 528 S.E.2d 250, 272 Ga. 272 (2000). Cross-examination of a witness is a matter of right, and one of the permissible purposes of cross-examination is to attempt to elicit facts demonstrating that witness's testimony is either unbelievable, biased, or partial.

6 *Jensen v. State of Wyoming*, 116 P.3d 1088 (Wyoming, 2005). A prosecutor engaged in misconduct during the cross-examination of a defendant when he repeatedly asked the defendant if he believed that the victim or an investigating officer was lying in their testimony. Moreover, it is error and misconduct for the prosecutor to cross-examine a defendant using the "lying" or "not telling the truth" or "mistaken" technique. Rather, the proper approach is ask the defendant what other witnesses had to say, allow the jury to draw its own conclusions and then make a proper closing argument based on the testimony. But see *People v. Baugh*, 832 N.E.2d 903, 358 Ill.App.3d 718 (2005). A prosecutor's improper question during the cross-examination of the defendant (asking the defendant whether an officer lied) was not reversible error. The prosecutor asked defendant the improper question only once, the question was directed at the defendant's specific testimony denying that he made an admission to the officer, and the prosecutor did not ask the defendant's opinion as to the general veracity of the officer's testimony.

> The court shall exercise reasonable control over the mode and order of interrogating witnesses... and protect witnesses from harassment or undue embarrassment.

The notes of the Advisory Committee for the 1972 amendments make it clear that Rule 611(a) should not be used to prevent the impeachment of a witness. Impeachment is, of course, a key purpose of cross-examination.

Evidence designed to *show* that a witness has provided false or biased testimony, is always admissible.[7] Thus, while the trial judge should protect the witness from questions that "go beyond the bounds of proper cross-examination merely to harass, annoy, or humiliate,"[8] such protection should not foreclose efforts to discredit a witness.[9] Fed. R. Evid. 607 seems to add some weight to this proposition by providing:

> The credibility of a witness may be attacked by any party, including the party calling the witness.

Notice that Rule 607 tends to diminish our prior distinction between direct and cross-examination, at least in the federal realm. The notes of the Advisory Committee for the 1972 amendments make it clear that the "traditional rule" against impeaching one's own witness should be abandoned.[10]

Regardless of whom is to be impeached, the attack must be made by way of factual questions, not insulting innuendoes or arguments. And, the trial judge has wide latitude to impose reasonable limits on cross-examination to avoid harassment and prejudice, even in criminal cases where the defendant's rights of confrontation are constitutionally guaranteed.[11] Consider, for example, a case where a prosecutor cross-examined a convict who was serving a life sentence, by asking:

---

7 *State v. Yang*, 712 N.W.2d 400, 2006 WI App 48 (2006). Inquiring into a witness' bias is always material and relevant.

Baker v. Kammerer, 187 S.W.3d 292 (Ky., 2006). The admissibility of evidence relating to bias is always favored.

State v. Jacobs, 616 S.E.2d 306 (N.C., 2005). The cross-examination of an opposing witness for the purpose of showing his bias or interest is a substantial legal right. *Snelson v. Kamm,* 272 Ill.Dec. 610, 787 N.E.2d 796 (2003). Generally, during cross-examination, opposing counsel may probe bias, partnership or financial interests of the witness.

8 *People v. Baugh*, 832 N.E.2d 903, 358 Ill.App.3d 718 (2005). While it is permissible to cross-examine a witness in order to explain, modify or discredit what he said on direct examination, cross-examination that is designed to harass, annoy or humiliate a witness should not be tolerated. See also *Adams v. Unites States*, 883 A.2d 76 (D.C., 2005) and *State v. Oliveira*, 882 A.2d 1097 (R.I., 2005). *U.S. v. Beverly,* 369 F.3d 516 (6th Cir. Ohio 2004); *Kaczmarek v. State*, 91 P.3d 16 (Nev. 2004); *City of Champaign v. Sides,* 284 Ill. Dec. 634, 810 N.E.2d 287 (Ill. App. Ct., 2004). *Commonwealth v. Murphy,* 784 N.E.2d 1144, 57 Mass.App.Ct 586 (2003); *Vance v. Vance,* 784 N.E.2d 172, 151 Ohio.App.3d 391(2003).

9 *ARB Construction, LLC v. Pinney Construction Corp.,* 815 A.2d 705, 75 Conn.App. 151 (2003). Even in civil actions, cross-examination is an absolute right afforded to the parties. In determining whether or not the trial court unduly restricted a defendant's right of cross-examination, the appellate court should consider: (1) The nature of the excluded inquiry, (2) whether or not the field of inquiry was adequately covered by other questions and answers, and (3) the overall quality of the cross- examination when viewed in relation to the issues actually litigated during trial.

See also *Daeda v. State,* 841 So.2d 632 (Fla.App., 2003). *Alford v. United States*, 282 U.S. 687, 51 S.Ct. 218, 75 L.Ed. 624 (1931).

10 See also *U.S. v. Schatzle*, 901 F.2d 252 (2d Cir. 1990).

11 *Adams v. U.S.,* 883 A.2d 76 (D.C., 2005). Although the Sixth Amendment guarantees to a defendant in a criminal prosecution the right to be confronted by the witnesses against him, which includes the opportunity to cross-examine the government's witnesses, this right is not without reasonable limitation. The extent of cross-examination of a witness with respect to an appropriate subject of inquiry is within the sound discretion of the trial court, and the trial court may always limit cross to preclude repetitive and unduly harassing interrogations, or to prevent inquiry into matters having little relevance or probative value to the issues raised at trial. See also *State v. Oliveira*, 882 A.2d 1097 (R.I., 2005).

(Footnote 11 continued on page 1-5.)

"It wouldn't bother you any, to come in here and lie from the time you started to the time you stopped, would it?" That precise question was properly held to be argumentative.[12]

In another case, a similar ruling resulted from the question: "As a matter of fact, you drove the car that was parked outside the liquor store when he went in and stole some liquor; is that not a fact?"[13] Both of the prior examples involved questions that implied wrongdoing on the part of the witness.[14]

Let's contemplate a prosecution for mayhem. The following question (paraphrased) was asked: "Isn't it a fact that defen-dant's mouth is so small that he could not get it opened wide enough to get the victim's ear in there?" Because both the ear and the mouth were visible to the jury, the question was held to be "argumentative."[15] Personally, I disagree; the question is certainly leading (see Chapter 7). But upon cross-examination, it would seem to be fair game, *particularly* since the accused mouth and the said ear were both in court.

The most common episodes of "being argumentative" involve repeated exchanges between the interrogator and a witness. The scenario often arises where the lawyer questioning the witness simply refuses to take "no" for an answer. In *Berger v. United States*,[16] the U.S. Supreme Court found that the government's prosecuting attorney had overstepped the bounds of "propriety and fairness" by committing a litany of misdeeds, not the least of which was "bullying and arguing with witnesses." Here was a typical exchange:

Q. Now Mr. Berger, do you remember yesterday when the court recessed for a few minutes and you saw me out in the hall; do you remember that?
A. I do, Mr. Singer.
Q. You talked to me out in the hall?
A. I talked to you?
Q. Yes.
A. No.
Q. You say you didn't say to me, out in the hall yesterday, 'You wait until I take the stand and I will take care of you?' You didn't say that yesterday?
A. No. I didn't, Mr. Singer; you are lying.
Q. I am lying, you are right! You didn't say that at all?
A. No.
Q. You didn't speak to me out in the hall?

---

11 (Continued from page 1-4.) *People v. Love,* 762 N.Y.S.2d 162 (N.Y.A.D., 2003). The trial courts have broad discretion and wide latitude to limit cross-examination on collateral matters that are designed solely to impeach a victim's credibility. *Matchett v. State*, 941 S.W.2d 922 (Tex. Crim. Ct. App.,1996); *Elliott v. U.S.*, 633 A.2d 27 (D.C.,1993); *State v. Harris*, 839 S.W.2d 54 (Tenn. 1992); *People v. Frieberg*, 168 Ill. Dec. 108, 589 N.E.2d 508, 147 Ill. 2d 326 (1992); *Shaw v. State*, 411 S.E.2d 537, 201 Ga.App. 456 (1991); *U.S. v. Casoni,* 950 F.2d 893 (3rd Cir. 1991); *People v. Sammons*, 478 N.W.2d 901, *appeal denied* ,480 N.W.2d 103 (Mich. Ct. App. 1991); *Recer v. State*, 821 S.W.2d 715 (Tex. Ct. App. 1991). In the last analysis, the trial judge has broad discretion to preclude repetitive and unduly harassing interrogation. *U.S. v. Saunders*, 166 F.3d 907 (C.A.7, Ill.,1999); *State v. Green,* 609 N.E.2d 1253, 66 Ohio St.3d 141 (1993). But see *State v. Flynn*, 855 A.2d 1254 (2004) holding that although a trial court has broad discretion in determining the scope of cross-examination, it may not completely deny a defendant the right to cross-examine a witness on a proper matter of inquiry.

12 *United States v. Micklus*, 581 F.2d 612 (7th Cir. 1978).

13 *United States v. Cash*, 499 F.2d 26 (9th Cir. 1974). As a side note, the judge acted promptly, sustaining the objection before it was made, directing the witness not to answer. But before the ruling could take effect, the witness had already answered with a denial.

14 Compare the case of *Pilkington v. Peking Chinese Restaurant, Inc.*, 596 So.2d 586 (Ala. 1992), a negligence action involving a minor plaintiff; the trial court was held not to have abused its discretion by overruling plaintiff's objection to defendant's sarcastic question implying that the parent was contributorily negligent.

15 *White v. State,* 22 Okla. Crim. 131, 210 P.313 (1922).

16 295 U.S., 78, 55 S. Ct. 629, 79 L. Ed. 1314 (1935).

A. I never did speak to you outside since this case started, except the day I was in your office, when you questioned me.
Q. I said yesterday.
A. No, Mr. Singer.
Q. Do you mean that seriously?
A. I said no.
Q. That never happened?
A. No, Mr. Singer, it did not.
Q. You did not say that to me?
A. I did not.
Q. Of course, I have just made that up?
A. What do you want me to answer you?
Q. I want you to tell me I am lying, is that so?

[No effort was ever made by Singer to prove, by competent evidence, that such a statement had ever been made.]

Although the principles used to determine argumentative questions do not draw separate definitions for civil and criminal proceedings, a prosecutor in a criminal case has a specific burden to refrain from improper questions that could conceivably produce a wrongful conviction.[17] From this, it is fair to conclude that repeated argumentative questioning is more likely to produce a mistrial in the criminal realm than in the civil arena.

In the last analysis, whether or not a question is deemed to be argumentative must depend upon the particular circumstances of each case. The more *subjective* the nature of the objection, the more *discretion* the court possesses.[18] But practically speaking, experience teaches that there is a more powerful unwritten rule, one that transcends the distinctions between direct and cross-examination, and civil versus criminal matters. It might be termed the "Rule of Proportional Slimy Behavior." Its principle simply states that the amount of harassment and argument that will be allowed is directly proportional to the established sliminess of the witness. If the judge perceives the witness to be a liar, much leeway will be allowed while the witness is attacked.[19] But skill must be employed. Establishing that the witness is slimy must be accomplished, first, through the employment of factual references, not innuendoes or insults.

§1.400 Selected State Rules and Cases

Essentially, "argumentative questions" are argumentative regardless of the jurisdiction or the particular labels attached by that forum (i.e., "harassment," "torment," "humiliation," "degradation," etc.). Moreover, determining whether or not a question is argumentative depends more heavily upon the unique events and circumstances surrounding that question, and less upon established rules.

CALIFORNIA:

Most states employ the terminology of Fed. R. Evid. 611(a), if not its exact words (*see supra*). In place of the term "argumentative," the California Evidence Code ("CEC") uses the "611 terms": "harassment" and "embarrassment." For our purposes, one might treat all three words as being synonymous. With respect to the italicized portion cited below, CEC 765 is substantially identical to Fed. R. Evid. 611(a). CEC 765(a) provides that:

17 *Berger v. United States*, 295 U.S. 78, 55 S. Ct. 629, 79 L. Ed. 1314 (1935); See *United States v. Spain*, 536 F.2d 170 (7th Cir. 1976) concerning argumentative comments before the jury.

18 For other cases involving argumentative questions, see *Pettus v. Louisville & N.R. Co.*, 214 Ala. 187, 106 So. 807 (1925); and *Johnson v. Wilmington City Ry. Co.*, 23 Del. 5, 76 A. 961 (1905). Trial judge has discretion during cross-examination to ban unreasonable, repetitious and argumentative questions and matters of tenuous relevance. *State v. Hatcher*, 524 S.E.2d 815 (N.C.App. 2000).

19 *Haffey v. Generac Portable Products, LLC.*, 171 S.W.3d 805 (Mo.App., 2005). Where a witness' prior inconsistent statement relates specifically to a paramount issue in the case, the trial court does not have discretion to prevent the impeachment of the witness through the use of that statement. In utilizing such statements, the form of the prior inconsistent statement does not matter. Also, a prior inconsistent statement of a witness who is available for cross-examination may be used as substantive evidence in a civil trial.

> The court shall exercise reasonable control over the mode of interrogation of a witness so as to make such interrogation as rapid, as distinct, and as effective for the ascertainment of the truth, as may be, and *to protect the witness from undue harassment or embarrassment.*

Notice that the stated aim of the "argumentative objection" is to protect the witness. That makes it somewhat unique, since the other ones (excepting the "privilege" objection) are designed primarily to protect the integrity of the evidence. In particular, the exclusion of improper evidence is the focus of most other objections.

As an established proposition, in California as elsewhere, witnesses who appear to testify in court are entitled to protection from "unjustified character assassination" and "vilification" by attorneys. *Hallinan v. U.S.*, 182 F.2d 880, *cert. denied*, 71 S. Ct. 1010, 341 U.S. 952, 95 L. Ed. 1375, *reh'g denied*, 72 S. Ct. 623, 342 U.S. 956, 96 L. Ed. 710, *reh'g denied* 72 S. Ct. 756, 343 U.S. 931, 96 L. Ed. 1341 (Cal. App. 1950).

Moreover, a witness should not be subjected to public insult simply to satisfy the feelings of a party who may be adversely affected by his testimony. Nor should he be subjected to insult merely to lower his esteem in the eyes of the jury. This principle is old and well established. *People v. Hatfield*, 18 P.2d 366, 129 C.A. 162 (1933). The principle applies to both direct and cross-examination. *People v. Fong Chung*, 91 P. 105, 5 C.A. 587 (1907).

California acknowledges the close association between argumentative questions and those that might be deemed repetitive. In an automobile negligence action, for example, an objection to a question that had previously been asked and answered both on cross-examination and redirect examination, was properly sustained on the grounds that it was argumentative the next time around. *Thomas v. Laguna*, 248 P.2d 929, 113 C.A. 2d 657 (1952).

Unlike the applicable federal rules, California takes particular care when it comes to protecting young minors. Consider CEC 765(b):

> With a witness under the age of 14, the court shall take *special care* to protect him or her from *undue harassment or embarrassment*, and to restrict the unnecessary repetition of questions. The court shall also take special care to insure that questions are stated in a form which is appropriate to the age of the witness. The court may in the interests of justice, on objection by a party, forbid the asking of a question which is in a form that is not reasonably likely to be understood by a person of the age of the witness.

It would be fair to conclude from the above language that California courts accord greater protection to minors (than adults), in general, even though they may be above 14 years of age.

People v. Chatman, 38 Cal.4th 344, 133 P.3d 534, 42 Cal.Rptr.3d 621 (2006). The prosecutor's cross-examination question about whether the safe at the crime scene was "lying," in response to a capital murder defendant's testimony denying opening the safe, was argumentative, since an inanimate object cannot lie. Moreover, an "argumentative question" is a speech to the jury masquerading as a question; the questioner is not seeking to elicit relevant testimony, and often it is apparent that the questioner does not even expect an answer.

People v. Guerra, 37 Cal. 4th 1067, 129 P.3d 321. An "argumentative question" is designed to engage a witness in argument rather than elicit facts within the witness' knowledge.

COLORADO:

The Colorado Rules of Evidence (Title 13 of the Colorado Revised Statutes) follow the federal rules virtually verbatim. Significant variations, if any, are noted in the following chapters.

CONNECTICUT:

In a fashion similar to several of the less populous states, Connecticut follows the federal rules essentially verbatim. Significant variations, if any, are noted in the following chapters.

DISTRICT OF COLUMBIA:

After sufficient cross-examination has been allowed to satisfy constitutional confrontation requirements, the trial court retains broad discretion to determine the scope and extent of cross-examination. The court may restrict cross-examination within reasonable limits to avoid such problems as harassment, prejudice, confusion of issues, witness safety, or repetitive interrogation that is only marginally relevant. *Elliott v. U.S.*, 633 A.2d 27 (D.C. App. 1993).

FLORIDA:

Section 90.612(1)(c) of the Florida Evidence Code requires judges *to protect the witness from undue harassment or embarrassment*. The provision reflects language similar to that contained in the California Evidence Code, as do most of Florida's rules.

The sponsors of the rule intended it to maintain the dignity of the courtroom and protect the witnesses under examination. *Baisden v. State*, 203 So.2d 194 (Fla. 4th Dist. 1967); *Loftin v. Morgenstern*, 60 So.2d 732 (Fla. 1952).

GEORGIA:

The cross-examination of a witness is a matter of right, and one of the permissible purposes of cross-examination is to attempt to elicit facts demonstrating that a witness's testimony is either unbelievable, biased, or partial. *Hodo v. State*, 528 S.E.2d 250, 272 Ga. 272 (2000).

Shaw v. State, 411 S.E.2d 537, 201 Ga. App. 456 (1991). A defendant in a criminal proceeding does not have an unqualified Sixth Amendment right to cross-examine the state's witnesses as to potential bias; rather, the trial judge has wide latitude to restrict cross-examination to avoid, among other things, harassment, prejudice, and confusion.

The trial court was held to have properly sustained an objection made during cross-examination to a question as to why a motorist failed to mention (in a prior deposition) that he believed the other driver had been drinking. The question was both argumentative and redundant since the other driver's attorney had earlier asked the motorist why he hadn't mentioned his suspicions at the deposition. The motorist responded that he was never asked. *Pitts v. Bode*, 403 S.E.2d 66, 198 Ga. App. 787 (Ga. App.1991).

The trial court may curtail inquiries on cross-examination which are unduly repetitive or harassing and may exercise reasonable judgment in determining when a given subject has been exhausted. *Kier v. State*, 543 S.E.2d 801 247 Ga.App. 431 (2000).

ILLINOIS:

With respect to its state courts in general, Illinois' Rule 611(a) is identical to Fed. R. Evid. 611(a). See also *People v. Triplett*, 485 N.E.2d 9 (Ill. 1985) pertaining to the court's broad discretion to curtail repetitive or harassing questions.

With respect to aggressive cross-examination, the right of the cross-examiner to show bias or motive should remain unfettered, but the questioning cannot be repetitive or unduly harassing. *People v. Schnurr,* 151 Ill. Dec. 674, 564 N.E.2d 1336 (Ill. Ct. App. 2 Dist. 1990). Thus, the trial court did not abuse its discretion in curtailing the cross-examination of a prosecution witness which was unnecessarily repetitive and unduly harassing. *People v. Matthews,* 150 Ill. Dec. 310, 562 N.E.2d 1113. (Ill. App. 1 Dist. 1990). See also *People v. Prevo,* 235 Ill. Dec. 950, 706 N.E.2d 505, 302 Ill.App.3d 1038 (1999); the trial court properly uses its discretion when it restricts the scope of cross-examination in order to preclude repetitive or unduly harassing testimony.

LOUISIANA:

Even though the right of cross-examination is secured by state and federal constitutions, the court has broad discretion to preclude repetitive and unduly harassing interrogation. *State v. Hawkins*, 572 So.2d 108 (La. App. 1 Cir. 1990).

MASSACHUSETTS:

With respect to its state courts in general, Massachusetts has not specifically adopted the

Federal Rules of Evidence, but Massachusetts' courts frequently look to the Federal Rules for guidance; see *Commonwealth v. Weichell*, 390 Mass. 62, 453 N.E.2d 1038 (1983), *cert. denied*, 104 S. Ct. 1298 (1984).

MICHIGAN:

The trial courts have discretion to place limits on cross-examination where questions are intended merely to harass, annoy or humiliate a witness. *People v. Sammons,* 91 Mich. App. 351, 478 N.W.2d 901 (1991). With respect to its state courts in general, Michigan's Rule 611(a) is very similar in content to Fed. R. Evid. 611(a).

NEVADA:

Nevada is consistent with the majority view. Its trial courts retain wide discretion to limit cross-examination based on considerations such as harassment, prejudice, confusion of the issues, and relevancy. *Kaczmarek v. State*, 91 P.3d 16 (Nev., 2004).

NEW JERSEY:

With respect to its state courts in general, New Jersey's Rule 611(a) is identical in content to Fed. R. Evid. 611(a).

NEW YORK:

Even though New York has no uniform set of evidence rules, no one doubts that its state courts would pay the same lip service to interrogation civility that is expressed by the other 99 jurisdictions (50 federal and 49 state). Nevertheless, New York has traditionally placed a high value on the benefits of uninhibited impeachment in the truth-gathering process. See *People v. Malkin*, 250 N.Y. 185, 164 N.E. 900 (1928), and *People v. Lustig*, 206 N.Y. 162, 99 N.E. 183 (1912).

Nevertheless, see *People v. Johnson,* 683 N.Y.S.2d 681 (1998); the county court did not abuse its discretion by limiting questioning that was argumentative or cumulative during defendants cross-examination of a prosecution witnesses.

NORTH CAROLINA:

Cross-examination of an opposing witness for the purpose of showing his bias or interest is a substantial legal right which the trial judge can neither abrogate nor abridge. *Allen v. K-Mart*, 528 S.E.2d 60 (N.C.App. 2000).

The trial judge has discretion during cross-examination to ban unreasonable, repetitious and argumentative questions and matters of tenuous relevance. *State v. Hatcher*, 524 S.E.2d 815 (N.C.App. 2000).

The trial court sustained an objection by the prosecutor, when defense counsel asked an eyewitness (on recross-examination) whether he was changing his testimony. This constituted an appropriate limit on the scope of cross-examination because it protected the witness from harassment or undue embarrassment. *State v. Pharr*, 430 S.E.2d 267 (N.C. App. 1993).

OHIO:

With respect to the state courts in general, Ohio's Rule 611(A) is identical in content to Fed. R. Evid. 611(a).

When a party calling a witness (1) can demonstrate that the testimony of that witness was materially inconsistent with his or her prior statements and (2) counsel did not have reason to expect that the witness would pull a "surprise," and (3) material damage resulted from the about-face, then the credibility of the witness may be attacked by prior inconsistent statements. *State v. Warren*, 588 N.E.2d 905, 67 Ohio App. 3d 789 (1990); Ohio Ev. R. 607. See also Chapter 5.

OREGON:

Oregon has adopted most of the rules and principles set forth in the Federal Rules of Evidence. The Oregon Evidence Code (Oregon Revised Statutes, Chapter 40 et seq.), however, assigns its own rule numbers. Significant variations in substantive text are noted in pertinent chapters.

PENNSYLVANIA:

On May 8, 1998, the Pennsylvania Supreme Court adopted a new and comprehensive set of evidence rules, with an effective date of October 1, 1998. The new rules are patterned after the Federal Rules of Evidence, both by content and number. Prior to the revision, Pennsylvania's courts frequently looked to the Federal Rules of Evidence for direction (*see, e.g., Commonwealth v. Henderson*, No. 823-82, (Pa. Super. Jan 27, 1984).

Pennsylvania's new Rule 611, titled: "Mode and Order of Interrogation and Presentation" is patterned after Fed. R. Evid. 611 (discussed *supra*).

RHODE ISLAND:

State v. Bettencourt, 723 A.2d 1101 (RI. 1999), held that questions which harass, annoy or humiliate a witness are improper and may be excluded.

TENNESSEE:

The defendant's cross-examination of witnesses was not improperly limited when the trial court restricted questions that were repetitious and argumentative; the limitation did not prohibit defendant from cross-examining witnesses regarding relevant matters. *State v. Harris*, 839 S.W.2d 54 (Tenn. 1992).

TEXAS:

The trial court may impose reasonable limits on cross-examination based upon concerns about harassment, prejudice, confusion of the issues, witness safety, or interrogation that is repetitive or only marginally relevant. *Matchett v. State*, 941 S.W.2d 922 (Tex. Crim. App. 1996); See also *Recer v. State*, 821 S.W.2d 715 (Tex. App. 1991).

VERMONT:

Vermont mimics the Federal Rules of Evidence in much the same fashion as several aforementioned states. The rule numbers for the Vermont Rules of Evidence match the federal rules. Significant variations are noted in pertinent chapters.

WEST VIRGINIA:

The West Virginia Rules of Evidence reflect the federal rules virtually word for word. The rule numbers match those of the federal rules. Significant variations are noted in pertinent chapters.

Chapter 2

Best Evidence Rule

§2.100 Introduction

The best evidence rule stands for the proposition that a witness should not be allowed to testify about the contents of a writing, unless the original of that writing is produced in court.

§2.200 Quick Explanation

Generally, the rule states that "secondary" evidence in the form of oral testimony or copies should not be used to establish or prove the contents of a written document when the original document is available.[1] The reason for the rule is somewhat self-explanatory: The "best evidence" would be the written document itself. To paraphrase the rule: Show me the writing, don't tell me about it.

The rule is intended to protect against fraud, perjury and the inaccuracies of a faulty memory, by requiring the production of an original document whenever its contents are in dispute or are sought to be proven.[2] The rule applies only to secondary evidence about a writing.[3] It does not apply to demonstrative or real evidence.

EXAMPLES OF QUESTIONS THAT VIOLATE THE BEST EVIDENCE RULE:

1. What is the date on Sandra Stiff's death certificate?
2. What was written in the official accident report?
3. What did the label on the medicine bottle say?[4]

WHAT TO LOOK FOR:

Reference to anything written, copied, printed or signed. The question "What did it say?" should provide an excellent warning.

OBJECT AND RESPOND

OBJECTION:

"Objection! Best evidence."

(California state courts only) "Objection! A dispute exists over the material terms of the writing, and/or it would be unfair to permit this testimony under the circumstance."

POTENTIAL RESPONSES TO OBJECTION:

A. "The information, your Honor, exists separate and apart from the document and therefore has independent significance."

B. "I served a notice for production of the document upon opposing counsel; no response. I must, therefore, be allowed to use secondary evidence."

---

1 *Amin v. Loyola University of Chicago*, 423 F.Supp.2d 914 (2006). In an action by a former research associate against Loyola University alleging that it had breached a fiduciary duty to him by failing to adequately record benefits and to disclose documents relevant to his retirement plan, a witness' testimony regarding the contents of the retirement plan was inadmissible and would not be considered where no copy of the plan had been submitted, and where there was no claim that the original document was lost, destroyed, unobtainable, or in the possession of an opponent. See Rule 1002 of the Federal Rules of Evidence (discussed herein). See also *Telecom Technical Services, Inc. v. Rolm Co.*, 388 F.3d 820 (11th Cir. Ga., 2004); *Tobias v. Korman*, 141 S.W.3d 468 (Mo. App., 2004); *Lipschitz v. Stein*, 781 N.Y.S.2d 773 (N.Y. 2 Dep't 2004); *Ganske v. Spence*, 129 S.W.3d 701 (Tex. App. Waco 2004).

2 *Matter of the Estate of Saxton*, 673 N.Y.S.2d 625 (1998).

3 The term "secondary evidence," as used above, denotes the dual nature of the Best Evidence Rule. In particular, a testimonial "Best Evidence" violation can occur where a witness attempts to testify as to the contents of a writing. On the other hand, seeking to admit the copy of a writing might also violate the rule, though it is certainly less likely to do so. For both types of potential violations, there are several exceptions. See §20.200.

4 The simple question "What was in the medicine bottle?" might draw a best evidence objection if the witness was a layperson! This might seem like a stretch to some; however, unless the witness was a pharmacist, chemist, or physician, how could he or she know the contents of any drug if not by reading its markings or the label on the bottle?

C. "We have conducted a very thorough, but unsuccessful search for the original document."

D. (California state courts only) "This testimony is specifically allowed under the Secondary Evidence Rule."

§2.300 General Legal Analysis

This rule applies to all forms of writings, whether they be documents,[5] flight logs,[6] books,[7] or even prior convictions.[8] It does not apply to tape recordings.[9] Nor does it bar or prohibit personal observations just because some document may contain the same information.[10]

Unless the absence or destruction of the document is properly established, testimony about "what is in the document" should not be allowed. The proponent should produce the actual writing as evidence. Fed. R. Evid. 1002 describes the best evidence rule as follows:

> To prove the content of a writing, recording, or photograph, the original writing, recording, or photograph is required, except as otherwise provided in these rules or by act of Congress.

Attention should be directed to the word "content" to emphasize that the rule does not apply to testimony that merely identifies a writing or that describes the existence or location of a document. Nor is the best evidence rule intended to interfere with questions intended to prove an event by non-documentary means even though relevant writings are available.[11]

The discharge of a debt, for example, can be established by the witnesses' testimony; "I paid the dude." A receipt is not needed as either a foundation or supplement for such an offering. But if evidence of the contents of the receipt is to be offered, then the best evidence rule applies to that writing.[12]

---

5 *Hedgecock Builders Supply Co. of Greensboro v. White,* 375 S.E.2d 164 (N.C. App. 1989).

6 *Mason Coal Co. v. Insurance Co.*, 210 S.E.2d 747 (W. Va. 1974).

7 *Shreve v. United States,* 77 F.2d 2 (9th Cir. 1935).

8 *O'Toole v. State,* 373 S.E.2d 12 (Ga. 1988).

9 *United States v. Rose,* 590 F.2d 232 (7th Cir. 1978).

10 *DeSoto Wildwood Development v. City of Lewisville*, 184 S.W.3d 814 (Tex.App., 2006). In a developer's lawsuit to recover impact fees from the defending city of Lewisville, for purposes of deciding the city's plea with respect to jurisdiction, a portion of an affidavit stating that the developer had not transferred all of its ownership interests in a residential subdivision did not violate the best evidence rule and was not to be considered as hearsay; the city had already submitted into evidence the plats upon which the affiant's statements were based and neither party was attempting to prove the contents of the deeds. Moreover, the best evidence rule did not apply because no one was seeking to prove the contents of a document. *In re J.C.K.*, 143 S.W.3d 131 (Tex. App. Waco 2004); *Aluminum Products Enterprises, Inc. v. Fuhrmann Tooling and Mfg. Co.*, 758 S.W.2d 119 (Mo. App. 1988); *Matter of United Tractors, Inc.*, 13 Bankr. 239 (D. Mo. 1981). A witness with personal knowledge may testify as to expenses incurred without providing documentation to substantiate that testimony.

11 *Waterloo Furniture Components, Ltd. v. Haworth, Inc.*, 467 F.3d 641, 80 U.S.P.Q.2d 1675 (7th Cir.Ill., 2006). If a witness' testimony is based on his first-hand knowledge of an event as opposed to his knowledge of the contents of a document, the best evidence rule does not apply. *Gutierrez v. Albertsons, Inc.*, 824 P.2d 1058 (N.M. App. 1991). The best evidence rule does not require the introduction of an insurance policy where the insured sought only to establish the fact that she had lost coverage when she lost her employment; she did not seek to establish the contents of the policies.

12 See *In re Marriage of Fahy,* 153 Ill. Dec. 594, 567 N.E.2d 552 (Ill. App. 1 Dist. 1991); see also *O'Sullivan v. DelPonte*, 606 A.2d 43, 27 Conn. App. 377 (1992).

The term "writing" is intended to be quite broad; it includes drawings,[13] X-rays,[14] and further, according to Fed. R. Evid. 1001(1):

> "Writings" and "recordings" consist of letters, words, or numbers, or their equivalent, set down by handwriting, typewriting, printing, photostating, photographing, magnetic impulse, mechanical or electronic recording, or other forms of data compilation.

Rule 1001(2) expands the definition further by attempting to cover all of the latest visual media:

> "Photographs" include still photographs, X-ray films, video tapes, and motion pictures.

Despite its "apparent" clear language to the contrary, the best evidence rule is not intended to encompass demonstrative exhibits. Imagine rummaging around in the basement of some local Fotomat store in an attempt to dig up a negative for some simple photograph. Thus, the apparent simplicity of the federal rule is quite deceiving; it does not make an effort to distinguish documentary evidence from demonstrative presentations.

As suggested, there are exceptions to the rule. If the original is not available, for example, a copy can be used as an adequate substitute.[15] But this allowance is not automatic. "I scrounged around, Judge, but couldn't dig up the original" won't do. A good faith showing is required. More particularly, anyone offering a non-original had better show that he didn't have the original in his possession,[16] or that he used all reasonable means to try to find it.[17] Fed. R. Evid. 1003 provides a relatively liberal standard for the introduction of "duplicates":

> A duplicate is admissible to the same extent as an original unless (1) a genuine question is raised as to the authenticity of the original or (2) in the circumstances it would be unfair to admit the duplicate in lieu of the original.

The term "unfair" leaves quite a bit to the imagination and begs the question, "Why have a 'rule' at all?" Perhaps the answer suggests an attempt by the drafters to set some safeguard against forgery, however small, while at the same time permitting the court to exercise broad discretion with respect to the admissibility of copies.[18]

The judge also has wide discretion when it comes to chattels. To prove the contents of the writings on the side of a battleship, for example, or on a stick of dynamite,[19] the production of the actual object in court should not be required.

---

13 *Seiler v. Lucasfilm, Ltd.*, 797 F.2d 1504 (9th Cir. 1986).

14 *United States v. Leight*, 818 F.2d 1297 (7th Cir. 1987).

15 *Sylvania Elec. Products, Inc. v. Flanagan*, 352 F.2d 1005 (1st Cir. 1965); see also, *United States v. Driscoll*, 449 F.2d 894 (1st Cir. 1971). NOTE: So as to distinguish oral testimony from a copy, the latter has sometimes been referred to as "second best evidence." *Christian Health Care of Springfield W. Park v. Little,* 145 S.W.3d 44 (Mo. Ct. App., 2004). In accordance with the Best Evidence Rule, secondary evidence, such as a photographic copy, may be admitted if the offering party demonstrates that the primary evidence has been lost or destroyed, is outside the jurisdiction, is in the possession or control of an adversary, or is otherwise inaccessible.

§2.400 Parol Evidence Rule.

16 *United States v. Driscoll*, 449 F.2d 894 (1st Cir. 1971).

17 *Sylvania Elec. Products, Inc. v. Flanagan,* 352 F.2d 1005 (1st Cir. 1965); but the party offering secondary evidence is not required to prove unavailability of the original beyond a possibility of any mistake. *Walsh v. St. Louis Nat. Baseball Club, Inc.*, 822 S.W.2d 559 (Mo. App. 1992).

18 See *Dole v. Service Employees Union, AFL-CIO, Local* 280, 950 F.2d 1456 (9th Cir. 1991); a copy of some minutes for a union meeting that were made under a court order would be admissible as evidence in light of the rule admitting duplicates.

19 *Mattson v. Minneapolis*, 98 Minn. 296, 108 N.W. 517 (1906).

There are many exceptions and variations with respect to the above themes. And there is no shortage of material if you wish to study the subject further.[20]

For better or for worse, the federal rules (i.e., Fed. R. Evid. 1001 et seq.) have provided a model for many states to follow. The poorly structured provisions have caused needless confusion (meaning lots of wasted time spent on interpretive decisions) and have produced unwarranted ambiguities for rules pertaining to other forms of evidence (particularly demonstrative and real evidence). Now that the federal rules are spreading among the states, the problems are also proliferating, similar to a disease or computer virus.

At the very least, the federal rule drafters should have understood that it is the origin (and perhaps the purpose for seeking admissibility) that determines whether the offering is documentary, and not its form. At a trial of Lee Harvey Oswald, for example, a photograph of Kennedy's body, taken by FBI agents following his assassination, would certainly constitute documentary evidence, entitling it to best evidence rule considerations. But a photograph of the Texas School Book Depository taken the day before trial to be used for demonstrative or "background" purposes has no relation whatsoever to that rule. The criterion for this latter offering is "clarification for the trier of fact"; and it wouldn't matter whether the photo was original or a 16th generation copy, as long as it fairly and accurately represented what it purported to represent.

It might be best to abolish those confusing and lazily drafted provisions in favor of a simpler directive. A revised rule might provide that originals should be made available to opposing parties during discovery or pre-trial proceedings, and copies should then be freely permitted at trial, unless the non-possessing party has called an item's authenticity into question. Where such authenticity is challenged, the original would be required unless the possessor had a valid excuse for not having it. This rule would apply to any tangible embodiment that we might refer to as a "document," without attempting to enumerate the available media. In truth, when all is said and done, the cases, in their own disconnected manner, universally follow those general precepts.

REFERENCES

Admissibility of lost or destroyed evidence. 83 A.L.R. Fed 554.

Best evidence rule. 14 Am. Jur. 2d Proof of Facts 173.

§2.400 Parol Evidence Rule

The parol evidence rule is akin to the best evidence rule, but the former applies only to contracts. The parol evidence rule quite simply provides that parol (meaning "verbal" or "oral") testimony should not be allowed to contradict or supplement the terms of a written agreement. In other words, the writing counts, not the conversations or discussions surrounding it.[21] Specifically, the parol evidence rule prohibits the introduction of prior or contemporaneous extrinsic evidence to vary the terms of a final written

20 Lipson, *Documentary Evidence* §9.04 (Matthew Bender, 1988); 5 *Weinstein on Evidence* §1002 (Matthew Bender, 1983); *Wigmore on Evidence* §1177 et seq. (Little Brown 3rd Ed., 1940).

21 *Commissioners of State Insurance Fund v. Munkacs Car Service Ltd.*, 809 N.Y.S.2d 868 (N.Y. City Civil Ct., 2006). Once an agreement has been reduced to writing, that writing must be produced, or in the alternative, there must be a sufficient explanation presented together with a showing that the proposed secondary evidence is reliable. *In re Boelson Trust*, 830 N.E.2d 37 (Ind.App., 2005). The parol evidence rules are designed to give certainty to transactions which have been reduced to writing by protecting the parties against the doubtful veracity of interested witnesses and the uncertain memory of disinterested witnesses. See also *Glazer v. Lehman Bros., Inc.*, 394 F.3d 444 (6th Cir., Ohio, 2005), and *Louisiana Workers' Compensation Corp. v. Pro Source Roofing, Inc.*, 907 So.2d 113 (La.App., 2005). *In re Zenith Labs,* 119 Bankr. 51 (D.N.J. 1990); *Federal Land Bank v. Emberton*, 460 N.W.2d 488 (Iowa App. 1990); *Fr. Winkler KG v. Stoller,* 839 F.2d 1002 (3rd Cir. 1988).

agreement, because a written agreement supersedes prior or contemporaneous negotiations;[22] however, the rule has no power to preclude future negotiations.[23]

The concept of "integration" is significant. Whereas parol evidence is inadmissible to extend, vary, or explain a written instrument, prior oral statements can add to the written agreement if that agreement is not completely integrated.[24] An "integrated" contract is one that contains the final and complete expression of the parties with respect to any term of their agreement.[25]

Today, many contracts contain a merger clause (i.e., a paragraph reciting that the written instrument represents the "complete agreement of the parties and may not be amended in the absence of a writing signed by the party to be charged"). The presence of a merger clause is evidence, though not conclusive, that the contract was completely integrated.[26]

---

22 *Holmes v. Jefferson Pilot Financial Insurance Company*, 907 So.2d 185 (La.App., 2005). The testimony of a life insurance policy beneficiary and agent concerning their understanding of whether the insured was covered by the conditional receipt of payment of the premium was inadmissible parol evidence that varied the express terms of the contract. Moreover, parol evidence is not admissible to vary the express terms of a contract. See also *Alstom Power, Inc. v. Balcke-Durr, Inc.*, 849 A.2d 804, 269 Conn. 599 (2004); *Shaw v. City of Sacramento*, 250 F.3d 1289 (9th Cir., Cal., 2001); *Kassebaum v. Kassebaum*, 42 S.W.3d 685 (Mo.App. 2001); *Jordan v. Tri County AG, Inc.*, 546 S.E.2d 528, 248 Ga.App. 661 (2001). The parol evidence rule is based upon the idea that when the parties have deliberately put their engagements into writing, in such terms as import a legal obligation, without any uncertainty as to the object or extent of such engagement, it is conclusively presumed that the whole engagement of the parties, and the extent and manner of their understanding, were reduced to writing.

See also *American Home Assurance Co. v. Merck & Co., Inc.*, 329 F.Supp.2d 436 (S.D.N.Y., 2004); *Carlsten v. Oscar Gruss & Son, Inc.*, 853 A.2d 1191 (R.I., 2004).

23 *Kayne v. First Charter Bank*, 16 Cal.Rptr.2d 450, 12 Cal. App. 4th 1568 (Cal. App. 1993).

24 *Oreck Corp. v. Thomson Consumer Electronics, Inc.*, 796 F. Supp. 1152 (S.D. Ind. 1992).

25 *Travelers Indemnification Co. of Illinois v. CDL Hotels USA, Inc.*, 322 F.Supp.2d 482 (S.D.N.Y., 2004); *General Elec. Capital Corp. v. Ford Motor Credit Co.*, 149 B.R. 229 (D. Me. 1992); *Esbensen v. Userware Internat,* 14 Cal.Rptr.2d 93, 11 Cal. App. 4th 631 (Cal. App. 4 Dist. 1992). Under New York law, a contract which appears complete on its face is an integrated agreement as a matter of law. A party relying on the parol evidence rule to bar the admission of such oral evidence must, nevertheless, show that the writing completely and accurately embodies all mutual rights and obligations of the parties.

W.W. Vincent and Co. v. First Colony Life Ins., Co., 286 Ill. Dec. 734, 814 N.E.2d 960 (Ill. App. Ct., 2004). A court will not consider parol evidence of prior negotiations to create an extrinsic ambiguity, where the parties to a contract have included an integration clause.

26 *First Allmerica Financial Life Insurance Co. v. Minnesota Life Insurance Co,* 188 F.Supp.2d 101 (D.Mass., 2002). A merger clause in a contract is evidence that a writing is integrated and that it represents the final and complete agreement between the parties. According to the Parol Evidence Rule, the admission of antecedent and contemporaneous statements to prove the terms of the writing is prohibited; however, the Parol Evidence Rule does not bar a consideration of statements made after the integration of the agreement.

G.E Life and Annuity Assurance Co. v. Donaldson, 189 F.Supp.2d 1348 (M.D.Ga., 2002). Generally, a contract containing a merger clause indicates a complete agreement between its parties and such a contract may not be contradicted by extraneous material.

See also *Weldon v. Great White North Distribution Services, L.L.C.*, 197 F.Supp.2d 893 (E.D.Mich., 2002).

Where the written agreement is confusing, ambiguous or unclear, however, verbal testimony may be permitted to clarify it.[27] By the same token, if the contract is unambiguous, parol evidence may not be used.[28] Likewise, where a contract has been procured by fraud, mistake or duress, parol evidence may also be permitted.[29] The parol evidence rule is, thus, both a rule of evidence and a rule governing how the law of contracts operates (with respect to writings versus conversations).

The parol evidence rule does not exclude evidence of alleged oral modifications that occur subsequent to the execution of a written agreement.[30]

§2.500 Interaction With Hearsay Rule

Any out of court statement offered to prove the truth of the matters asserted in that statement would constitute hearsay.[31] Hearsay can be oral or it can be written. Often, where the best evidence rule is involved, the hearsay rule will likewise come into play. The interplay between the two rules can be very confusing. Consider the following sample testimony carefully:

[Counsel is in the midst of her direct examination of her witness, a plaintiff injured in an automobile collision.]

---

27 *Indiana Department of Correction v. Swanson Services Corp.*, 820 N.E.2d 733 (Ind.App., 2005). If a contract is ambiguous, the court should resolve the ambiguity and determine its meaning by extrinsic sources. *Bowlby v. Carter Mfg. Corp.*, 138 F.Supp.2d 182 (D.Mass., 2001); *Coscan Florida, Inc. v. Equiventure Florida,* 567 So.2d 17 (Fla. Dist. App., 1990); *Western World, Inc. v. Dansby*, 566 So. 2d 866 (Fla. Dist. Ct. App., 1990). Parol evidence rule bars consideration of prior (or contemporaneous) oral or written agreements which contradict or supplement a completely integrated writing, subject only to a few exceptions; one such exception is ambiguity. *Jacobs v. CNG Transmission Corp.,* 332 F.Supp.2d 759 (W.D. Pa., 2004). Where an ambiguity exists in a written contract, the court may resort to extrinsic or collateral circumstances to resolve that ambiguity, regardless of whether the ambiguity was created by language contained in the instrument or by extrinsic or collateral circumstances.

See also *Alstom Power, Inc. v. Balcke-Durr, Inc.*, 849 A.2d 804, 269 Conn. 599 (2004); *Alberto-Culver Co. v. Aon Corp.*, 812 N.E.2d 369, 285 Ill. App. 549 (2004); *West Point Marine, Inc. v. Prange,* 812 N.E.2d 1016, 286 Ill. Dec 1, 349 Ill. App.3d 1010 (2004); *AG Acceptance Corp. v. Glinz*, 684 N.W.2d 632, 2004 N.D. 154 (2004); *Pittman v. Pittman,* 139 S.W.3d 134, 84 Ark. App. 293 (2003).

28 *Tarulli v. Circuit City Stores, Inc.*, 333 F.Supp.2d 151 (S.D.N.Y., 2004); *Consolidated Edison, Inc. v. Northeast Utilities,* 332 F.Supp.2d 639 (S.D.N.Y., 2004); *Buchman v. BASF Corp.*, 107 Fed.Appx. 378 (5th Cir. Miss., 2004); *Delsack v. Cumella,* 593 N.Y.S.2d 2 (N.Y.A.D. 1 Dept. 1993); *F.D.I.C. v. Rusconi,* 796 F. Supp. 581 (D. Me. 1992); *Haymaker v. General Tire, Inc.,* 420 S.E.2d 292 (W.Va. 1992).

29 For a good shopping list, see *Weldon v. Great White North Distribution Services, L.L.C.*, 197 F.Supp.2d 893 (E.D.Mich., 2002), which enumerated the following exceptions for which the Parol Evidence Rule does not preclude the admission of extrinsic evidence:

[1] to show that the writing was a sham;

[2] to show that the writing was not intended to create a legal relationship;

[3] to show that the contract should have no effect because of fraud, illegality, or mistake;

[4] to show that the parties did not integrate their agreement or assent to it as a final embodiment of their understanding; or

[5] to showthat the agreement was only partially integrated because essential elements were not reduced to writing.

SMR Technologies, Inc. v. Aircraft Parts International Combs, Inc., 141 F.Supp.2d 923 (W.D.Tenn., 2001). Under Delaware law, parol evidence rule bars party from introducing extrinsic evidence to alter, modify, or contradict terms of writing; nevertheless, there are limited exceptions to rule, such as when terms of contract are ambiguous or to show that agreement should be declared invalid, void, or voidable because of fraud. *Alstom Power, Inc. v. Balcke-Durr, Inc.*, 849 A.2d 804, 269 Conn. 599 (2004).

30 *Kayne v. First Charter Bank,* 16 Cal. Rptr. 2d 450, 12 Cal. App. 4th 1568 (Cal. App. 2 Dist. 1993).

31 See Chapter 5.

Q1. Were you involved in an automobile accident during the month of August, 1993?
A. Yes.
Q2. What specifically happened on the date in question as you were driving.
A. The defendant ran a red light and smacked me broadside.
Q3. Did the police show up?
A. Yes; they asked a whole mess of questions.
Q4. Did they make out an accident report?
A. They sure did; I looked at it and read it over.
Q5. Did you get a copy of it?
A. Yup; I got me a copy over yonder in my purse.
Q6. Did you read the report carefully?
A. Yes.
Q7. What did the report say?
Opposing Counsel: Objection!
Q8. Let me rephrase. Is this the copy of the police report that you previously referred to—the one that I just snatched from your purse?
A. Yes.
Q9. What does it say?
Opposing Counsel: Objection!
Q10. All right then, I'll move for its admission, Your Honor?

As an exercise, you might, for each of the nine questions, list all of the objections that you believe are appropriate (based upon common law), then compare your list to this footnote.[32]

§2.600 Selected State Rules and Cases

Reading about the best evidence rule always leaves the distinct impression that too much has been written about too little. State rules on the subject seem to confirm that general notion. The best evidence rule pre-dates computers, faxes, photocopiers, and even photos. But the rule-makers continue to build their foundations for new technologies on the crumbling ruins of a bygone era.

CALIFORNIA:

In 1999, California "abolished" the Best Evidence Rule and asserted in its place a "Secondary Evidence Rule." Aside from the "name change" the new rule is primarily designed to reword the language so that the numerous exceptions become the rule. In particular, California's new Secondary Evidence Rule begins with the proposition that secondary evidence is admissible, and then provides exceptions. Recall that the Best Evidence Rule, unlike this new rule, assumes that secondary evidence is inadmissible. Section 1521(a) of the California Evidence Code states:

The content of a writing may be proved by otherwise admissible secondary evidence. The court shall exclude secondary evidence of the content of [the] writing if the court determines either of the following:

(1) A genuine dispute exists concerning material terms of the writing and justice requires the exclusion.

(2) Admission of the secondary evidence would be unfair.

32 Q1 through Q5 are proper; Q6 might be considered as irrelevant; Q7 is objectionable as hearsay (just because the report is an official document and a business record does not mean that the hearsay contained in it is automatically admissible). Q7 also violates the best evidence rule; Q8 is proper; Q9 is as defective a question as Q7. Q10 fails to lay a proper foundation; an original is required unless a statute permits a copy to be used (many state statutes specifically permit the admission of duplicate official records); but even if the copy were admitted, the only parts of the report that may be used are those based upon the officer's personal knowledge, unless there is another independent hearsay exception covering the statement. See also *Larez v. City of Los Angeles*, 946 F.2d 630 (9th Cir. 1991).

COLORADO:

The Colorado Rules of Evidence (Title 13 of the Colorado Revised Statutes) follow the federal rules virtually word for word, and section number for section number.

CONNECTICUT:

In a fashion similar to many of the less populous states, Connecticut follows the federal rules, essentially word for word and section number for section number.

Whenever the specific terms of a writing are material and must be proved, the best evidence rule requires the offering party to produce the original writing, if it is available; *O'Sullivan v. DelPonte,* 606 A.2d 43, 27 Conn. App. 377 (1992).

FLORIDA:

Section 90.952 of Florida's Evidence Code, together with an accompanying Sponsor's Note, takes steps toward clarifying the distinctions between standard writings and those embodied in recordings or photographs. That section states:

> Except as otherwise provided by statute, an original writing, recording, or photograph is required in order to prove the contents of the writing, recording, or photograph.

The Sponsor's Note, however, makes it clear that the best evidence rule does not pertain to all photos and recordings. For use as demonstrative evidence, an original would not normally be required. It is assumed that Florida would follow the majority rule, however, with respect to X-rays, by requiring originals.

Concerning the admissibility of duplicates, Florida appears to follow the general precepts provided by the federal rules and the California Evidence Code. But Section 90.953(1) of Florida's code restricts the use of duplicates for negotiable instruments, security agreements, or other instruments evidencing a right to the receipt of money.

GEORGIA:

The photocopy of an original contract, which had been lost, was admissible in an action by an employer against an independent contractor for breach of a restrictive covenant. Also, the independent contractor was entitled to introduce evidence to show that the document had been altered. *White v. Lance H. Herndon, Inc.*, 417 S.E.2d 383, 203 Ga. App. 580, cert. denied (Ga. App. 1992).

ILLINOIS:

With respect to the state courts in general, Illinois' Rule 1002 is identical to Fed. R. Evid. 1002.

MASSACHUSETTES:

With respect to its state courts in general, Massachusetts has not specifically adopted the Federal Rules of Evidence, but its courts frequently look to the Federal Rules for direction. For example, see *Commonwealth v. Wiechell, 390 Mass.* 62, 453 N.E.2d 1038 (1983), cert. den. 104 S. Ct. 1298 (1984).

MICHIGAN:

With respect to the state courts in general, Michigan's Rule 1002 is identical in content to 1974 Uniform Rule 1002.

MISSOURI:

The Best Evidence Rule does not exclude evidence based upon personal knowledge even if documents would provide some or the same information. Where the fact to be proved exists independently of a writing (and there is also evidence of such a fact in that writing), then both sources, oral and written, become primary evidence and the best evidence rule is inapplicable. *Elliot v. Director of Revenue, State of Missouri,* 882 S.W.2d 745 (Mo. App. E.D. 1994).

The testimony of an assistant for stadium operations of a baseball club did not violate the best evidence rule by stating that the 1983 tickets contained a revokable license to enter the stadium. The assistant laid a sufficient foundation when he stated that he was not familiar with the current existence of any baseball game tickets from 1983. *Walsh v. St. Louis National Baseball Club, Inc.*, 822 S.W.2d 559 (Mo. App. 1992).

NEW JERSEY:

With respect to its state courts in general, New Jersey's Rule 1002 is similar in content to Fed. R. Evid. 1002, with "Act of Congress" changed to "statute."

NEW YORK:

Many of the procedures and ground rules pertaining to the use of documents for New York's endless maze of trial courts are compiled in its Civil Practice Laws and Rules (see CPLR 4539 et seq.).

The "best evidence" of what the parties to a written agreement intended is what they said in their writing. *Slamow v. Del Col,* 584 N.Y.S.2d 424, 79 N.Y.2d 1016, 594 N.E.2d 918 (1992).

OHIO:

With respect to the state courts in general, Ohio's Rule 1002 is similar in content to Rule Fed. R. Evid. 1002.

OREGON:

Oregon has adopted most of the rules and principles set forth in the Federal Rules of Evidence. The Oregon Evidence Code (Oregon Revised Statutes, Chapter 40 et seq.), however, assigns its own rule numbers.

PENNSYLVANIA:

On May 8, 1998, the Pennsylvania Supreme Court adopted a new and comprehensive set of evidence rules, with an effective date of October 1, 1998. The new rules are patterned after the Federal Rules of Evidence, both by content and number.

Pennsylvania's new Rule 1001 (Definitions), Rule 1002 (Requirement of Original), and Rule 1003 (Admissibility of Duplicates) are all patterned after their respective federal counterparts (discussed supra).

TEXAS:

With respect to the state courts in general, Texas' Rules 1002 (Civil and Criminal) are similar to Fed. R. Evid. 1002. Both the Civil and Criminal Rules change "Act of Congress" to "statute."

VERMONT:

Vermont mimics the Federal Rules of Evidence in much the same fashion as several aforementioned states. The rule numbers for the Vermont Rules of Evidence match the federal rules.

Chapter 3

Questions Calling for a Conclusion

§3.100 Introduction

A question that asks a witness to give his or her *own* personal conclusion, opinion, decision, bias, or judgment is inadmissible unless a proper foundation has been established. Whether or not a question violates this rule may, therefore, depend heavily upon the testimony that precedes it.

§3.200 Quick Explanation

Generally, a witness is expected to present facts, not conclusions, opinions, personal reactions, or feelings. Conclusions should be determined by the court or jury, and not by the witnesses.

There are exceptions, however, particularly where experts are concerned. A "professional" (in some field relating to the trial), or expert may state a conclusion in the form of a professional opinion, after a foundation for his or her expertise has been established (see Overview). A lay person may, in limited circumstances, also give an opinion or determination, as long as it is based upon facts derived from personal experiences, or "rationally based" on that person's perception.

EXAMPLES OF QUESTIONS CALLING FOR A CONCLUSION:

1. Was the defendant lying with respect to his whereabouts?
2. Based upon your investigation, officer, is the defendant guilty of murder?
3. What was the victim's official cause of death?

The first question requires the witness to *conclude* whether or not a party was lying. This is improper, even though the witness may correctly be called upon to *present facts* to show that someone lied or made inconsistent statements (see §3.600).

The second question calls for the ultimate conclusion of a capital case—guilt or innocence. That is precisely what the *jury* is supposed to decide, not the witnesses. The purpose of a murder trial is to prove whether or not the defendant committed murder; the final determination of guilt cannot, therefore, occur until the jury renders a verdict. Such questions, it is said, "invade the province of the jury."[1] Lately, however, there is a tendency by judges to disallow such questions based upon Fed. R. Evid. 403 rather than a claim that they call for a conclusion.

A plumber or carpenter cannot properly answer the third question. A coroner, however, being an expert, *can*, but *only* after his professional status has been established and after he has been asked whether or not he autopsied (or performed tests on) the victim's body. Logic dictates that a lead-in question (i.e., "Did you perform tests on the body of the decedent?") should be asked as a foundation *before* seeking results. Asking for an opinion *before* the coroner lays a proper foundation would give rise to the objection that the questioner was calling for a conclusion. Jumping the gun might also warrant an objection that unestablished facts were assumed by the question (see Chapter 4).

WHAT TO LOOK FOR:

Questions that use words like "conclusion," "opinion," "judgment," or "probably." Also, watch for words or phrases that contain **general** adjectives and adverbs that may be material to the issues of the case. The following words may also mask attempts by the **witness** to provide personal conclusions: drunk, proper, improper, guilty, vulgar, careless, negligent, and unreasonable.

Often, conclusions do not materialize until the question-answer process has been completed; and, by then it's too late to stop them. The world's best trial lawyer cannot object to answers before they are spoken; but he or she can move to strike the answer if it is improper.

1 For a general discussion concerning an attempted distinction between a legal and factual conclusion, see *Terrell v. Reinecker*, 482 N.W.2d 428 (Iowa 1992); for matters involving an expert's attempt to invade the court's province by tendering statutory interpretations, see *Sohaey v. Van Cura*, 180 Ill. Dec. 359, 607 N.E.2d 253 (Ill. App. 2 Dist. 1992). In *U.S. v. Espino*, 32 F.3d 253 (7th Cir. 1994), the defendant was convicted of conspiracy to distribute cocaine along with an assortment of other offenses.During cross-examination, he was required to answer the question: "Are you admitting the conspiracy" (referring to prior drug deals). The question should have been excluded on the grounds that it called for a legal conclusion.

§3.300 Legal Analysis for Non-Expert Witnesses

The Federal Rules of Evidence are slightly more liberal than the traditional state court rules with respect to non-expert testimony. Rule 701 provides:

> If the witness is *not* testifying as an expert, the witness' testimony in the form of opinions or inferences is limited to those opinions or inferences which are (a) rationally based on the perception of the witness and (b) helpful to a clear understanding of the witness'testimony or the determination of a fact in issue.

A significant amendment to Rule 701, effective as of December 1, 2000, makes it clear that lay persons are supposed to stay clear of areas requiring special expertise, and therefore, outside the scope of our next-discussed Rule 702 (pertaining to experts). The new rule retains the above language but adds the limitation that the layperson's testimony be:

> (c) not based on scientific, technical, or other specialized knowledge within the scope of Federal Rule of Evidence 702.

Despite its lean toward admissibility, the rule reinforces the important point that a lay witness should present facts, not judgments or conclusions, particularly not those of other people.[2] The non-expert witness is thus limited with respect to opinions and inferences, which must be rationally based upon his own perceptions.[3]

The conclusion objection can be a very subjective one. Often facts and opinions are mixed together. Sometimes, it is not so easy to pull apart the facts "embraced" by a conclusion. It has been held, therefore, that the purpose of Rule 701 is to allow non-expert witnesses to give opinion testimony when, as a matter of **practical necessity**, events which they have personally observed cannot otherwise be fully presented to the court or jury.[4]

Common examples where such testimony is allowed often involve the emotional state of another person,[5] such as a look of pain,[6] or surprise.[7] These descriptions, it is said, are matters of "common experience" even though they are conclusions.[8]

2 *United States v. Ragano*, 476 F.2d 410 (5th Cir. 1973); see also In re Paternity of K.G., 536 N.E.2d 1033, *reh'g denied* (Ind. App. 4 Dist. 1989).

3 *Kindred v. Human Rights Com'n*., 129 Ill. Dec. 607, 536 N.E. 2d 447, 180 Ill.App.3d 766 (3 Dist. 1989), *First Bank of Billings v. Clark*, 771 P. 2d 84 (Mont. 1989), *Altszyler v. Horizon*, 529 N.E.2d 704, 124 Ill. Dec. 723, 175 Ill.App.3d 93 (1988). See also *U.S. v. Rivera*, 22 F.3d 430 (2d Cir. 1994), and *Keller v United States*, 38 F.3d 16 (1st Cir. 1994).

4 *Randolf v. Collectramatic*, Inc., 590 F.2d 844 (10th Cir. 1979).

5 *Cole v. United States*, 327 F.2d 360 (9th Cir. 1964).

6 *Nichols v. Marshall*, 486 F.2d 791 (10th Cir. 1973).

7 *New York Life Insurance Co. v. Harrington*, 299 F.2d 803 (9th Cir. 1962).

8 *Burchill v. Kearney-National Corp*., 468 F.2d 384 (3d Cir. 1972); *United States v. Wheeler*, 444 F.2d 385 (10th Cir. 1971).

Other matters of common experience, as to which the lay person should be allowed to testify, include the speed of a car[9] and a person's identity in a photo.[10] It has also been held that the question of whether or not a driver's seat pin could slip out due to wear and tear was within the knowledge of a bus driver in a case involving personal injury.[11]

In a trespass action, it was proper for a non-expert witness to testify as to the fair rental value of property in issue.[12] However, a homeowner was *not* allowed to give testimony as to what caused a wall in his home to fall, absent some indication that he possessed special skill or knowledge with respect to the construction of that wall.[13]

Whether or not someone is an expert is not always obvious, even to the person whose skills are being examined. Police officers, perhaps, provide the best example of professionals that straddle the lay/expert fence. Normally, they do not possess the training of rocket scientists; but neither are they on the same playing field as lay persons when it comes to matters within their scope.

With respect to automobile accidents, those investigating police officers who arrive at a collision scene and examine the evidence first hand should be permitted to provide fact-based opinions. As with any witnesses, expert or otherwise, the depth of their opinions should, of course, be related the amount of education, training, skill, and experience that they possess.[14] Those elements should also apply to traffic offenses.[15]

OBJECT AND RESPOND OBJECTION:

A. [Generic] "Objection! The question calls for a conclusion on the part of the witness."

B. [Lay Witness] "Objection! Calls for a conclusion. This witness is not (or has not been qualified as) an expert in matters of ______."

C. [Expert Witness] "Objection! Calls for a conclusion. This question clearly exceeds the scope of the witness' expertise," or "There is no foundation or basis for this question."

POTENTIAL RESPONSES TO OBJECTION:

A. [Lay Witness] "The witness' opinions are clearly based upon his/her rational perceptions."

B. [Expert Witness] "Experts are permitted to draw conclusions; that's why we use them."

9 *Gianfala v. State Farm Mut. Auto. Ins. Co.*, 615 So.2d 558 (La. App. 3 Cir. 1993); *Ho v. United States*, 331 F.2d 144 (9th Cir. 1964). In *Vonch v. American Standard Insurance Company*, 442 N.W.2d 598 (Wisc. App. 1989), a non-expert police officer was permitted to testify about whether a driver braked before impact since his statements were based upon his training, experience, and personal observations. Compare that to *Solomon v. Baum*, 560 A.2d 878 (Pa. Cmnwlth. 1989), wherein the court properly refused to allow lay witness testimony concerning the speed of two vehicles, prior to a collision.

10 *United States v. Jackson*, 688 F.2d 1121 (7th Cir. 1982).

11 *Stewart v. Alvarez*, 131 Ill. Dec. 271, 538 N.E.2d 646, 182 Ill. App. 3d 698 (Ill. App. 1 Dist. 1989).

12 *Zagaroli v. Pollock*, 379 S.E.2d 653 (N.C. App. 1989); see also *Prince v. Franklin County*, 769 S.W.2d 833 (Mo. App. 1989).

13 *Biggerstaff v. Nance*, 769 S.W.2d 470 (Mo. App. 1989).

14 Consider *Stumpf v. Reiss*, 502 N.W.2d 620 (Iowa App. 1993), where a police officer's own determination that he was "not" an expert was held to be "not" determinative; in particular, the officer in that case was permitted to express his opinions relating to a motor vehicle accident which he investigated, even though he stated in his testimony that he was not an expert. See also *Whetstone v. Dixon*, 616 So.2d 764 (La. App. 1 Cir. 1993), where it was held that a police trooper could give opinion testimony concerning the point of impact of a collision, even though the trooper was not an accident reconstruction expert, because the opinion was rationally based on the trooper's perception of the accident scene and the physical evidence that he observed.

15 An experienced police officer, with proper drug-recognition training, should be able to provide opinion testimony in a prosecution for driving under the influence of a controlled substance. *State of Minnesota v. Klawitter*, 518 N.W.2d 577 (Minn. 1994).

§3.400 Legal Analysis for Expert Witnesses[16]

An "expert" has been defined as a person who possesses special skills or knowledge beyond that of the average layman.[17] Fed. R. Evid. 702 speaks of expert testimony:

> If scientific, technical, or other specialized knowledge will assist the trier of fact to understand the evidence or to determine a fact in issue, a witness qualified as an expert by knowledge, skill, experience, training, or education, may testify thereto in the form of an opinion or otherwise.

An extremely important amendment to Rule 702, effective as of December 1, 2000, takes a powerful stab at killing 80 years of confusion and ambiguity concerning the knowledge required by an expert in a given field and legitimacy of the field itself. A line of cases stretching back to 1923 has kept these important issues in a state of turmoil. The amended rule, which is effective as of December 1, 2000, states:

> If scientific, technical, or other specialized knowledge will assist the trier of fact to understand the evidence or to determine a fact in issue, a witness qualified as an expert by knowledge, skill, experience, training, or education, may testify thereto in the form of an opinion or otherwise, *if (1) the testimony is based upon sufficient facts or data, (2) the testimony is the product of reliable principles and methods, and (3) the witness has applied the principles and methods reliably to the fats of the case.*

To qualify as an expert, a person is required to show a minimum level of competency on the subject to which he is about to testify.[18] Opinions of an expert witness must be based upon facts in evidence. Assuming that a proper foundation has been laid, it could be deemed an error for the court to refuse to permit an expert to offer an opinion.[19]

Toward the beginning of our discussion about "proper evidence" (Overview), we mentioned Fed. R. Evid. 703, which echoes the accepted principle that an expert may give opinions and inferences if they are based upon facts

16 Often, questions that call for an improper "conclusion" also involve speculation, particularly with respect to expert testimony; therefore, see Chapter 11. Also note that, while this chapter touches upon Federal Rule 702 pertaining to expert testimony, more detailed discussions of the Rule's "*Daubert*" and "*gatekeeping*" functions are contained in §11.500 and §11.600.

17 *Byrne v. SCM Corp.*, 131 Ill. Dec. 421, 538 N.E.2d 796, 182 Ill.App.3d 523 (Ill. App. 4 Dist. 1989). The weight to be accorded an expert's testimony should be viewed in light of his credibility, which is a matter for the trier of fact to determine. A ruling on the expert's qualifications, however, rests with the discretion of the trial court and will not be overturned absent an abuse of discretion. *Hulman v. Evanston Hosp. Corp.*, 631 N.E.2d 322 (Ill. App. 1 Dist. 1994); and *Lockett v. Bd. of Ed. for School D.* 189, 555 N.E.2d 1055 (Ill. App. 5 Dist 1990); *Brown v. Raymond Corp.*, 318 F.Supp.2d 591 (W.D. Tenn., 2004). A witness is not an expert just because he claims to be.

18 *Potomac Elec. Power Co. v. Smith*, 558 A.2d 768, 79 Md. App. 591 (Md. App. 1989). See also *Owens v. Concrete Pipe & Products Co.*, 125 F.R.D. 113 (E.D. Pa. 1989), where it was held that although the trial court has broad discretion in determining the competency of an expert witness, the modern trend is to allow experts in subjects such as biochemistry and toxicology to offer opinions on causes of illness, even though they are not doctors.

19 *Mayes v. City of Hammond*, 442 F.Supp.2d 587 (N.D.Ind. 2006). A hypnosis expert's testimony was admissible in that the expert was qualified to testify as to the rules governing the use of hypnosis in criminal investigations and whether or not such rules were followed based on the evidence in the record; he was not giving a legal opinion.

Eubanks v. Hale, 752 So.2d 1113 (Ala. 1999); *Dixon v. International Harvester Co.*, 754 F.2d 573 (5th Cir. 1985). Witness should have been allowed to testify as expert with respect to handwriting analysis even though witness did not use microscope in his examination of handwriting samples. Witness, who had been a document examiner for 16 years, was chief document examiner for state Department of Forensic Sciences, and had testified as expert in handwriting cases in Alabama, Georgia, Florida, and Virginia; witness also made presentations at scientific conferences and was member of numerous professional associations.

or data made known to that expert. From that rule, it follows that a witness who has been qualified as an expert may give an opinion based upon his or her own knowledge of the facts after stating them. The witness may also give an opinion based upon a hypothetical question as to the facts already in evidence.

Where personal observation is lacking, however, an expert witness cannot be permitted to give an expert opinion until the underlying facts have been properly hypothesized or established.[20] Various courts may use different terminologies to describe these principles, but their holdings are basically consistent.[21]

Do not assume that experts are free to "shoot from the hip" while giving their conclusions. If the data underlying an expert's opinion is so lacking in reliability that no *reasonable* expert could base his opinions on that data, the opinion must be excluded.[22]

Although certain **hearsay testimony** by experts is permitted (see Chapter 5 with respect to hearsay in general), that testimony must be based upon the type of evidence reasonably relied upon by experts in the particular field of expertise in forming opinions or inferences.[23] It is within the trial court's discretion to decide whether the **information** relied upon by an expert in forming his opinion is of the type reasonably relied upon by experts in the field.[24]

Once we have accepted the fact that experts may form and give opinions, our next problem involves determining when that opinion has reached the stage of being an objectionable conclusion. The "How much is **too** much?" problem will never be resolved by any simple rule of thumb. Fed. R. Evid. 704(a)[25] addresses the problem, but does little to resolve it:

> Except as provided in subdivision (b),[26] testimony in the form of an opinion or inference otherwise admissible is not objectionable because it embraces an ultimate issue to be decided by the trier of fact.

---

20 *Scully v. Fitzgerald*, 843 A.2d 1110, 179 N.J. 114 (2004), *Globe v. Sterling*, 556 A.2d 731, 79 Md. App. 303 (1989); *Yantos v. W.C.A.B.*, 563 A.2d 232, (Pa. Cmnwlth., 1989), *Crawford v. Hall,* 531 So.2d 874 (Ala. 1988). An expert's bare conclusion, unsupported by factual evidence, is inadmissible.

21 *United States v. Hill*, 655 F.2d 512 (4th Cir. 1981); see also *Nanda v. Ford Motor Co.*, 509 F.2d 213 (7th Cir. 1974).

22 *Viterbo v. Dow Chemical Co.*, 646 F. Supp. 1420 (E.D. Tx., 1986); see also *Emigh v. Consolidated Rail Corp.*, 710 F. Supp. 608 (W.D. Pa., 1989), holding that the Federal Rules of Evidence permit an expert to form opinions based upon facts or data that are not admissible in evidence; but when the underlying source is so unreliable as to render the facts and data more prejudicial than probative, the rule cannot be used as a back door to get evidence before a jury.

23 *United States v. Cox*, 696 F.2d 1294 (11th Cir., 1983), *cert. denied*, 104 S. Ct. 99; *Hurst v. U.S.*, 882 F.2d 306 (S.D., 1989).

24 *Plourde v. Gladstone,* 190 E.Supp.2d 708 (D.Vt., 2002). An expert is not permitted to offer an opinion or conclusion with respect to a *different field* or discipline other than the one for which he or she has been qualified.

During March, 1999, a Proposed Amendment to Rule 703 (156 F.3d p.Ct.R-136) was submitted for public comment by the Advisory Committee, directed to the admissibility of the data underlying the opinion; it provides: "If the facts or data are otherwise inadmissible, they shall not be disclosed to the jury by the proponent of the opinion or inference unless their probative value substantially outweighs their prejudicial effect." Subject to Supreme Court and congressional approval, the change takes effect December 1, 2000. See also *Zenith Radio Corp. v. Matsushita Elec. Indust. Co*, 505 F. Supp. 1190 (E.D. Pa. 1980).

25 NOTE: This rule also applies to non-experts.

26 With respect to insanity pleas, Rule 704(b) makes clear its **total distrust** of shrinks: "(b) No expert witness testifying with respect to the mental state or condition of a defendant in a criminal case may state an opinion or inference as to whether the defendant did or did not have the mental state or condition constituting an element of the crime charged or of a defense thereto. Such ultimate issues are matters for the trier of fact alone."

Conclusions will *always* "embrace" the facts upon which they are based.[27] It is often difficult to separate conclusions from their underlying facts.[28] And despite the mandate and spirit of *Rule* 704(a), there are lines that even experts may not cross with respect to their conclusions, regardless of the magnitude of their underlying facts.[29]

A policeman in court will rarely testify that a soused driver was "drunk." Instead he will more likely repeat a rehearsed speech such as, "His eyes were red, his speech was slurred, his walk was staggered, he stunk of gin, and when I asked him for the alphabet, he started counting, backwards." The term "drunk" is certainly embraced by the officer's litany of facts. But "drunk" is a conclusion nevertheless; it should therefore be left to the judge or jury to decide its presence.

REFERENCES

Admissibility of expert testimony. 89 A.L.R. 4th 456.

§3.500 Foundations

Evidence that is to be presented in any trial requires a foundation. Simply stated, a foundation is a basis or "lead-in" for testimony that follows. There are no simple "hard and fast" rules for determining whether an adequate foundation exists for a particular question; common sense is perhaps the best guide.

After a psychiatrist, for example, has testified that he has examined, tested, and analyzed a person, that shrink may *then*, as an expert, conclude that the person is schizophrenic. But to reach that "conclusion" before mentioning those underlying examinations would be objectionable. Thus, for some questions, the "conclusion" objection might be warranted if the questions come too soon or jump the gun. But those very same questions would *not* be objectionable if asked *after* a proper foundation has been presented.[30]

Additional support for an objection directed toward an unsubstantiated opinion or conclusion might come from Fed. R. Evid. 602, a basic foundation guideline, which provides that:

> A witness may not testify to a matter unless evidence is introduced sufficient to support a finding that the witness has personal knowledge of the matter.

The above rule contains a specific exclusion for experts.[31] An expert's underlying foundation need not be personal knowledge; instead it should consist of scientific principles. In particular, expert witnesses should confine their opinions to those matters in issue which are certain or probable and not mere possibilities.[32] An expert's opinion must have a sufficient verifiable scientific basis.[33]

27 *Pierce v. Central Maine Power Co.*, 622 A.2d 80 (Me. 1993), a personal injury case, held that the trial court did not abuse its discretion by allowing the plaintiffs' expert witness to testify that contact between a crane and a high voltage wire (at the accident site) was foreseeable, even though that opinion "embraced" the ultimate issue of negligence to be decided by the trier of fact; the question of foreseeability proposed to the witness was not subject to misunderstanding by the witness or the jury.

28 *Texas Dept. of Human Services v. Green*, 855 S.W.2d 136 (Tex. App. 1993) held that it was not an error for the trial court to permit an expert witness to testify as to mixed questions of law and fact.

29 *Good Shepherd Manor Foundation, Inc. v. City of Momence,* 323 F.3d 557 (7th Cir., Ill., 2003). Expert testimony as to legal conclusions that will determine the outcome of the case is inadmissible; *Thompson v. Sacramento City Unified School District,* 132 Cal.Rptr.2d 748, 107 Cal.App.4th 1352 (2003). A party is not entitled to rely on an expert's opinion to establish a duty that is a matter of law for the court; *Portelli v. Garcia,* 756 N.Y.S.2d 415 (2003). Generally, the opinions of experts are not permited to intrude upon the province of the judge or jury.

30 See *Dine v. Williams*, 830 S.W.2d 453, *rehearing denied* (Mo. App. 1992). Questions calling for conclusions such as "Who was at fault?" or "Who failed...?," are objectionable, because they are improper in form, and are not phrased in such a way as to make it clear that the "opinions" would be based upon well-recognized standards.

31 See §11.300.

32 *Zywicki v. U.S.*, 809 F. Supp. 823 (D.Kan. 1992).

33 *O'Conner v. Commonwealth Edison Co.*, 807 F.Supp. 1376 (C.D.Ill. 1992).

§3.600 Calling Another Witness a Liar

During cross-examination, it is tempting, indeed, to box an opposing witness into a corner by revealing a conflict in factual testimony with a prior witness. And, it often happens that a person will lie about an incident, yet be unable to brand a prior truthful witness as a "liar" (i.e., be unable to conclude that the other witness is lying). It is an effective technique. Unfortunately, this cross-examination device is frowned upon.[34] Consider an example:

Q. At the time that you approached the intersection of Woodward and Six Mile Road, what color was the traffic signal?
A. Green as grass.
Q. Now moments ago, in this court, while she was under oath, you heard Sissy Simpson say that it was as red as hot blood. Isn't that so?
A. I got ears.
Q. Was Sissy Simpson correct?
A. No.
Q. Was Sissy Simpson telling a lie?
Defense Counsel: Objection! The question calls for a conclusion on the part of the witness. She is being asked to conclude that Sissy is a liar.
The Court: Sustained.

Technically speaking, to ask whether or not Sissy was "correct" likewise calls for a conclusion, but that question is more tolerable and less likely to be excluded. It is also notable that the last question directed to the witness is argumentative (see Chapter 1).

§3.700 Selected State Rules and Cases

ARKANSAS:

Generally, accident reconstruction experts are frowned upon, and viewed with disfavor by the Supreme Court; however, an exception to this rule exists where it appears that a particular situation is beyond the jurors' ability to understand the facts and draw their own conclusions. Therefore, an accident reconstruction expert could provide his opinion as to how an automobile-bicycle collision occurred where the motorist, the bicyclist, and an eyewitness offered sharply conflicting testimony as to whether the automobile struck the bicycle from behind or whether the bicycle struck the automobile from the side; it is notable that there were also significant areas of dispute concerning the nature of the damage sustained by the automobile and bicycle, the relative speeds of each, and the impacts. *Banks v. Jackson*, 848 S.W.2d 408, 312 Ark. 232 (Ark. 1993).

CALIFORNIA:

California follows the general rule suggesting that witnesses should testify about facts, not opinions or conclusions. *Evigenger v. MacDougall*, 52 P.2d 194, 28 C.A.2d 175 (1938). A non-expert, however, may provide an opinion if it is rationally based on his or her own perceptions. *People v. Ogg*, 66 Cal. Rptr. 289, 258 C.A.2d 841 (1968); *Alexander v. Central L.&W. Co.*, 38 P. 410, 104 C. 532 (1894). This relaxation of the general prohibition against lay opinions has been embodied in Rule 800 of the California Evidence Code (which is similar to Fed. R. Evid. 701):

> If a witness is not testifying as an expert, his testimony in the form of an opinion is limit-

34 *Duarte v. State*, 598 So.2d 270 (Fla. App. 1992); *Terrell v. Reinecker*, 482 N.W.2d 428 (Iowa 1992); *James v. Texas Dept. of Human Services*, 836 S.W.2d 236 (Tex. App. 1992). But see *U.S. v. Fulford*, 980 F.2d 1110 (7th Cir. 1992); in a drug distribution prosecution, the trial court did not abuse its discretion by permitting a deputy to respond to the prosecutor's request that he consider all of the prior recorded statements of defendant's accomplice and provide a conclusion as to whether or not those statements were consistent.

> ed to such an opinion as permitted by law, including but not limited to an opinion that is
> (a) rationally based on the perception of the witness; and
> (b) helpful to a clear understanding of his testimony.

The need for the "rational perception" exception is no different in California than in any other jurisdiction because, as previously indicated, it is sometimes very difficult to separate facts from conclusions. For example, in a case involving an issue of gross negligence, testimony by the host to the effect that the driver must have been asleep at the time of the accident was admissible, notwithstanding that it was in the form of a conclusion. *Cooper v. Kellogg*, 42 P.2d 59, 2 C.2d 504 (1935). "Drunkenness" is another conclusion of sorts that may be stated, assuming that the witness establishes the underlying factors. *In re Joseph G.*, 87 Cal. Rptr. 25, 7 C.A.3d 695 (1970). Laypersons are also permitted to testify about their own physical condition, within limits. *Waite v. Godfrey*, 163 Cal. Rptr. 881, 106 C.A.3d 760 (1980).

As expected, California lays down its own laws with respect to expert witness testimony. By its very nature, such evidence must encompass conclusions and opinions. Rule 801 of the California Evidence Code states as follows:

> If a witness is testifying as an expert, his testimony in the form of an opinion is limited to such an opinion as is:
> (a) related to a subject that is sufficiently beyond common experience that the opinion of an expert would assist the trier of fact; and
> (b) based on matter (including his special knowledge, skill, experience, training, and education) perceived by or personally known to the witness or made known to him at or before the hearing, whether or not admissible, that is of a type that reasonably may be relied upon by an expert in forming an opinion upon the subject to which his testimony relates, unless an expert is precluded by law from using such matter as a basis for his opinion.

As distinguished from the Federal Rules of Evidence, notice that CEC 801(a) requires that the expert's testimony be "sufficiently beyond common experience"; i.e., California requires that an expert's testimony be necessary, not merely supplementary. The rule seems to echo the common sense proposition that experts should not be permitted to testify as to matters that non-experts are capable of understanding or deducing. As singer-poet Bob Dylan would say, "You don't need a weather man to know which way the wind blows."

An expert's conclusions or assumptions must be supported by the record on matters reasonably relied upon by other experts, and not on factors that are remote, speculative, or conjectural. *Wanland v. Los Gatos Lodge, Inc.*, 281 Cal. Rptr. 890, *rehearing denied and opinion modified* (Cal. App. 6 Dist. 1991).

COLORADO:

The Colorado Rules of Evidence (Title 13 of the Colorado Revised Statutes) follow the federal rules virtually word for word and section number for section number. Colorado Rules 701 and 702 follow the federal rules of the same number, while CRS 704 is similar to Fed. R. Evid. 704(a).

CONNECTICUT:

In accordance with many of the less populous states, Connecticut follows the federal rules essentially verbatim. The Connecticut rules regarding expert and non-expert witness testimony are similar to the federal rules, with the exception of Fed. R. Evid. 704(a). Under Connecticut law, a non-expert witness may not give an opinion on the ultimate issue to be decided by the trier of fact. *Kowalewski v. Mutual Loan Co.*, 159 Conn. 76, 266 A.2d 379 (1970); *State v. Donahue*, 141 Conn. 656, 109 A.2d 364, *cert. denied*, 349 U.S. 926, 75 S. Ct. 775, 99 L. Ed. 1257 (1954).

Fed. R. Evid. 704(a) should be limited to expert witness testimony. Expert opinion on the ultimate issue in a malpractice case may be required, however. *Pisel v. Stamford Hospital*, 180 Conn. 314, 430 A.2d 1 (1980).

FLORIDA:

For non-expert witnesses, Florida does not seem to jump on the "rational perception" bandwagon, as led by the Federal Rules of Evidence and the California Evidence Code. Section 90.701 of Florida's Evidence Code, on the other hand, suggests a more permissive standard:

> If a witness is not testifying as an expert, his testimony about what he perceived may be in the form of inference and opinion when:
> (1) The witness cannot readily, and with equal accuracy and adequacy, communicate what he has perceived to the trier of fact without testifying in terms of inferences or opinions and his use of inferences or opinions will not mislead the trier of fact to the prejudice of the objecting party; and
> (2) The opinions and inferences do not require a special knowledge, skill, experience, or training.

For expert witnesses, Section 90.703 of the Florida Evidence Code provides this foundation: "Testimony in the form of an opinion or inference otherwise admissible is not objectionable because it includes an ultimate issue to be decided by the trier of fact." Section 90.704 follows the majority rule that the underlying facts upon which an expert's opinion is based may be predicated upon extra-judicial knowledge (i.e., hearsay):

> The facts or data upon which an expert bases an opinion or inference may be those perceived by, or made known to, him at or before the trial. If the facts or data are of a type reasonably relied upon by experts in the subject to support the opinion expressed, the facts or data need not be admissible in evidence.

Section 90.705 of the Florida Evidence Code then provides the following:

> (1) Unless otherwise required by the court, an expert may testify in terms of opinion or inferences and give his reasons without prior disclosure of the underlying facts or data. On cross-examination he shall be required to specify the facts or data.
> (2) Prior to the witness giving his opinion, a party against whom the opinion or inference is offered may conduct a *voir dire* examination of the witness directed to the underlying facts or data for his opinion. If the party establishes *prima facie* evidence that the expert does not have a sufficient basis for his opinion, the opinions and inferences of the expert are inadmissible unless the party offering the testimony establishes the underlying facts or data.

There are four requirements for determining the admissibility of expert testimony: (1) that the opinion evidence be helpful to the trier of fact; (2) that the witness be qualified as an expert; (3) that the opinion evidence can be applied to the evidence offered at trial; and (4) that the evidence does not present a substantial danger that unfair prejudice will outweigh its probative value. *Holiday Inns, Inc. v. Shelburne*, 576 So.2d 322 (Fla. App. 4 Dist. 1991).

It should be noted that even if opinion evidence is permitted, the jury may nevertheless discount it if it is determined that the opinion is based upon incorrect data. Consider *Easkold v. Rhodes*, Fla. SC No. 79, 138 (March 1993), involving a medical expert's opinions that may have been predicated upon a false history.

Regardless of whether the witness happens to be an expert or layperson, it is improper, during cross-examination in a criminal prosecution, to ask if another witness had previously lied. See *Duarte v. State*, 598 So.2d 270 (Fla. App. 1992).

GEORGIA:

An expert was forbidden from giving an opinion based entirely on a report which had been prepared by others and which was not admitted into evidence. Moreover, a testifying expert may not serve as a conduit for the opinions of others. *Webb v. Thomas Trucking, Inc.*, 566 S.E.2d 390, 255 Ga.App. 637 (2002).

ILLINOIS:

With respect to the opinions of a non-expert, Illinois' Rule 701 is identical to Fed. R. Evid. 701.

An expert witness is not competent to give testimony regarding statutory interpretations of the law. Moreover, an expert may not testify with respect to legal conclusions which the jury could make without such testimony. It is the province of the court to determine what law applies to a particular case, not the witnesses. It may be prejudicial error to permit an expert to testify concerning the results of legal research. *Sohaey v. Van Cura*, 180 Ill. Dec. 359, 607 N.E.2d 253 (Ill. App. 2 Dist. 1992).

Expert opinions may not be admitted on matters of common knowledge, but opinions on such matters may be admitted if the subject matter is difficult to comprehend. *Martin v. McDonald's Corp.*, 157 Ill. Dec. 609, 572 N.E.2d 1073 (Ill. App. 1 Dist. 1991).

An expert witness may present opinions based upon assumptions if those assumptions are supported by facts or reasonable inferences. *National Sur. Corp. v. Fast Motor Service, Inc.*, 157 Ill. Dec. 619, 572 N.E.2d 1083 (Ill. App. 1 Dist. 1991).

An expert's opinion cannot be based on conjecture or guess; and a medical expert's opinion must be based on a reasonable degree of medical certainty. *Marshall v. Osborn*, 156 Ill. Dec. 708, 571 N.E.2d 492, 213 Ill. App.3d 134 (Ill. App. 3 Dist. 1991); *Wehmeier v. UNR Industries, Inc.*, 157 Ill. Dec. 251, 572 N.E.2d 320, 213 Ill. App.3d 6 (Ill. App. 4 Dist. 1991). The term "reasonable degree of medical certainty" should be memorized by every attorney who plans to try cases involving personal injury or medical malpractice. That standard applies throughout the country.

LOUISIANA:

The opinion of a lay witness as to the speed that a motorist was traveling before an accident was properly admitted into evidence; the witness, a passenger in a second vehicle involved in the collision, saw the motorist's automobile approaching just before the collision, and her perception of speed was relevant to the issue of causation. *Gianfala v. State Farm Mut. Auto. Ins. Co.*, 615 So.2d 558 (La. App. 3 Cir. 1993).

MASSACHUSETTS:

With respect to its state courts in general, Massachusetts has not specifically adopted the Federal Rules of Evidence, but its courts frequently look to the Federal Rules for direction. For example, see *Commonwealth v. Weichell*, 390 Mass. 62, 453 N.E.2d 1038 (1983), *cert. denied*, 104 S. Ct. 1298 (1984).

MICHIGAN:

Michigan's Rule 701 is identical in content to Fed. R. Evid. 701. Rule 702 of the Michigan Rules of Evidence differs, however; Michigan added the portion that appears in bold:

> If the **court determines that** scientific, technical, or other specialized knowledge will assist the trier of fact to understand the evidence or to determine a fact in issue, a witness qualified as an expert by knowledge, skill, experience, training, or education, may testify thereto in the form of an opinion or otherwise.

With respect to Rule 703, the last portion of Michigan's Rule 703 is inconsistent with Fed. R. Evid. 703 (concerning "underlying facts or data"). Compare the two:

> Michigan Rule 703: The facts or data in the particular case upon which an expert bases an opinion or inference may be those perceived by or made known to the expert at or before the hearing. **The court may require that underlying facts or data essential to an opinion or inference be in evidence.**

Fed. R. Evid. 703: The facts or data in the particular case upon which an expert bases an opinion or inference may be those perceived by or made known to the expert at or before the hearing. **If of a type reasonably relied upon by experts in the particular field in forming opinions or inferences upon the subject, the facts or data need not be admissible into evidence.**

MINNESOTA:

Given a proper foundation, an experienced police officer, with "Drug Recognition Protocol" training, should be able to provide opinion testimony in a prosecution for driving under the influence of a controlled substance. The officer performed a twelve step procedure involving a breathalyzer, interviews, and eye exams. *State of Minnesota v. Klawitter*, 518 N.W.2d 577 (Minn. 1994).

MISSOURI:

In a case of *"Physician, heal thy legal problems,"* a doctor, who brought a malpractice action in connection with the death of his mother was allowed to testify as an expert, despite his lack of impartiality; the defendants had an adequate opportunity to bring the physician's obvious bias to the jury's attention. The doctor's qualifications, however, were not attacked. Bias, therefore, is not a basis for excluding an expert witness. *Douglas v. University Hospital*, 150 F.R.D. 165 (E.D. Mo. 1993).

NEW JERSEY:

With respect to the state courts in general, New Jersey's *Rule* 701 is similar in content to Fed. R. Evid. 701, with "Act of Congress" changed to "statute."

NEW YORK:

Consider CPLR 4515:

Unless the court orders otherwise, questions calling for the opinion of an expert witness need not be hypothetical in form, and the witness may state his opinion and reasons without first specifying the data upon which it is based. Upon cross-examination, he may be required to specify the data and other criteria supporting the opinion.

Compare the language of CPLR 4515 to Section 90.705 of the Florida Evidence Code (*supra*). The differences appear to be subtle, but they are not. Under CPLR 4515, an expert witness can deliver a bald, unsupported conclusion without even the benefit of a hypothetical question. It would, according to the rule's Practice Commentaries, be a "bizarre direct examination that did not mention at least some of the facts underlying the expert's conclusion."

CPLR 4515 seems to place greater faith in the ability of the opposing attorney to cross-examine witnesses than to object to the elements of an improper foundation. Ultimately, the Appellate Division and the Court of Appeals (New York's highest court) will face dilemmas in the form of conclusory opinions that lack support in underlying facts. What then? Do the high courts reverse and remand verdicts lacking factual support, or do they honor the court rule?

NORTH CAROLINA:

It was improper to ask an investigating policeman his conclusion as to the cause of an accident. *Mickens v. Robinson*, 404 S.E.2d 359, 103 N.C. App. 52 (N.C. App. 1991).

OHIO:

Ohio has adopted most of the rules and principles set forth in the Federal Rules of Evidence, except under Ohio Ev. R. 703, what the expert relies on may only be "those [things] perceived by him or admitted in evidence at the hearing" that is, an expert's opinion may not be based on inadmissible material.

OREGON:

Oregon has adopted most of the rules in the Federal Rules of Evidence. The Oregon Evidence Code (Oregon Revised Statutes, Chapter 40 et seq.), however, assigns its own rule numbers. ORS 40.405 corresponds to Fed. R. Evid. 701, ORS 40.410 corresponds to Fed. R. Evid. 702, and ORS 40.420 corresponds to Fed. R. Evid. 704(a).

PENNSYLVANIA:

On May 8, 1998, the Pennsylvania Supreme Court adopted a new and comprehensive set of evidence rules, with an effective date of October 1, 1998. The new rules are patterned after the Federal Rules of Evidence, both by content and number.

Pennsylvania's new Rule 701 (Opinion Testimony by Lay Witnesses), Rule 702 (Testimony by Experts), Rule 704 (Opinion on Ultimate Issue), and Rule 602 (Lack of Personal Knowledge), are all patterned after their respective federal counterparts (discussed *supra*).

In a motorcycle accident, a lay witness was properly permitted to **estimate** the speed of the motorcycle, where that motorcycle passed the witness shortly before the accident. The witness saw the entire chain of events, and had an excellent opportunity for observation. *Wicks v. Dept. of Transportation*, 590 A.2d 832 (Pa. Cmwlth. 1991).

TEXAS:

An expert witness may testify on mixed questions of fact and law. *Texas Dept. of Human Services v. Green*, 855 S.W.2d 136 (Tex. App. 1993).

An opinion by one witness as to the truthfulness of another witness is generally inadmissible. *James v. Texas Dept. of Human Services*, 836 S.W.2d 236 (Tex. App. 1992).

VERMONT:

Vermont mimics the Federal Rules of Evidence in much the same fashion as several aforementioned states. The rule numbers for the Vermont Rules of Evidence match the federal rules, including VRE 701-705, with respect to expert opinions.

(This page intentionally left blank.)

Chapter 4

Questions That Assume Unproven Facts

§4.100 Introduction

A question may not assume facts unless they have been established by prior questions or evidentiary presentations. A proper question should seek to discover actual facts, not present unproven ones. This principle applies to direct examination and cross-examination; it also applies to lay persons and experts alike.

§4.200 Quick Explanation

Questions may contain facts that have *already* been established; those are permissible. And within limits, hypothetical questions may also contain unproven facts. But generally, a question is improper if it assumes some fact that has *not* already been proven.

EXAMPLES OF QUESTIONS ASSUMING FACTS:

1. When did you stop beating your wife?
2. Did the defendant murder the victim in the living room or in the cellar?
3. Would you be surprised to learn that the police officer discovered liquor in your boss' desk?

The first example is a perennial classic. No matter how the question is answered, the guilt of the husband has been presumed. The question itself pre-judges him.

The second question assumes that the defendant has committed murder, a determination that *only* the jury is entitled to make. And the third example is a statement that pretends to be a question. All are improper, assuming that the witness (in the first example) had *not* been shown to be a wife beater by prior questioning.

WHAT TO LOOK FOR:

Questions that contain too much information, make assumptions, or deliver messages before an answer is provided.

OBJECT AND RESPOND

OBJECTION:

"Objection! Assumes facts not in evidence."

POTENTIAL RESPONSES TO OBJECTION:

A. "The question, your Honor, fairly and accurately summarizes the evidence, so far."

B. "The question is a fair one; opposing counsel can always cross-examine on the point."

C. "Counsel must have forgotten _____'s testimony (or evidence) in this regard."

§4.300 General Legal Analysis

Witnesses testify for the purpose of *presenting* facts; it is not their function, either during direct or cross-examination, to merely parrot back unsupported assumptions[1] or unestablished facts[2] spoken by lawyers. Lawyers violating this rule will sometimes do so to "sneak in" facts or opinions that have not yet been presented. But regardless of the motive, questions that assume matters that have not yet been established are improper and objectionable.[3]

1 *Phillips v. State*, 728 So.2d 681 (Ala. Crim. App. 1998); *Cheesman v. State*, 230 Ga.App. 525, 497 S.E.2d 40 (1998); *Calley v. Boston and Marine R.R.*, 42 A.2d 329 (N.H. 1945); see also *Berger v. United States*, 295 U.S. 78, 55 S.Ct. 629, 79 L.Ed. 1314 (1935).

2 *Coscino v. Wolfley*, 696 So.2d 257 (La. App. 1997); *Anderson v. Wittmeyer*, 895 S.W.2d 595 (Mo. App. 1995); *Johnson v. Hoffman*, 80 A.2d 624 (N.J. 1951).

3 *Cherry v. Hill*, 283 Ala. 74, 214 So.2d 427 (1968); *Haithcock v. State*, 23 Ala. App. 460, 126 So. 890 (1930); *Price v. Rosenberg*, 200 Mass. 36, 85 N.E. 887 (1908); see also 3 Wigmore on Evidence §771 et. seq; *Simpson v. State*, 708 A.2d 1126, 121 Md.App. 263 (1998). Questions that assume facts not in evidence are objectionable.

While there is no federal rule exclusively devoted to this particular objection, it is, nevertheless, clear that Fed. R. Evid. 403 may be used as its underlying authority. Rule 403 permits the court to exclude otherwise relevant evidence if there is danger of "unfair prejudice, *confusion of the issues*, or *misleading* the jury." By permitting the interrogator to assume unproven facts, it may be convincingly argued that the jury might be misled into accepting their truth or, at the very least, be confused in its attempt to separate established from unestablished facts.

The questioner can, of course, *properly* assume the truth of a fact that has already been established. If this were not the case, it would be difficult, if not impossible, to elicit details about a specific object, event, or relationship. And, it certainly follows that a questioner may always properly assume the truth of a fact previously established by the witness who is currently testifying,[4] even if that fact is disputed by other testimony.

Hypothetical questions may sometimes include facts that have not yet been established, particularly when the interrogator specifically labels the question "hypothetical." Such a question is particularly helpful during cross-examination.[5] But the decision to allow it seems to be related to the likelihood that the missing facts will later be established. An attempt, however, to use a hypothetical question as a substitute for solid evidence on an issue should be opposed.[6]

Absent the use of a hypothetical format, it is improper to assume unestablished facts, even during cross-examination. Consider, for example, *State v. Simpson*,[7] a murder case where the defense cross-examined a detective about "other suspects." The interrogating attorney specifically asked the detective whether or not another person was "still" a suspect. The court found the question to be improper since it assumed that the other person had been a suspect from the beginning.[8]

Wilson v. State[9] involved the cross-examination of a character witness, where the prosecutor was permitted to ask the typical reputation-related questions: "Do you know?" and "Have you heard?" about the defendant's specific acts of misconduct. Nevertheless, the questions must not be framed so as to imply that the subject act or acts have actually been committed. That would, for all practical purposes, assert the truth of matters yet to be established.

§4.400 Timeliness

The critical importance of speed in making objections was demonstrated in *People v. Moore*,[10] a sodomy case where the prosecutor

4 *State v. Marshall*, 105 Iowa 38, 74 N.W. 763 (1898); *Graham v. McReynolds*, 90 Tenn. 673, 18 S.W. 272 (1891).

5 In *U.S. v. Siers*, 873 F.2d 747 (4th Cir. 1989), character witnesses were cross-examined by asking whether their opinion of defendant's good reputation in the community for peacefulness would be changed if defendant had engaged in specifically described acts of wife-beating and asking witnesses who hedged their answer to assume that defendant had engaged in such conduct. This was improper cross-examination; cross-examination of a character witness is limited to whether the witness has heard of a fact that is likely to have caused a negative community impression. If the witness has not heard of the fact, the inquiry should end.

6 In *Combs v. Hartford Ins. Co.*, 544 So.2d 583 (La. App. 1989), a hypothetical question relative to the plaintiff's medical symptoms on the day of trial was improper where the doctor had not recently treated the plaintiff; the question called for an assumption of unproven facts.

7 393 S.E.2d 771, 327 N.C. 178 (1990).

8 With respect to cross-examination, see also *People v. Stack,* 184 Ill. Dec. 583, 613 N.E.2d 1175, 244 Ill. App.3d 166 (Ill. App. 1 Dist. 1993); *State v. Creason,* 847 S.W.2d 482 (Mo. App. W.D. 1993); *Tirado v. State*, 622 A.2d 187, 95 Md. App. 536 (1993).

9 819 S.W.2d 662 (Tex. App. 1991); see also *State v. Creason,* 847 S.W.2d 482 (Mo. App. W.D. 1993), involving questions concerning child molestation and abuse.

10 260 Cal. Rptr. 134, 211 Cal. App. 3d 1400 (Cal. App. 1989).

asked the following improper question of the victim: "About how many times did he try that?" (which assumed that the defendant had already been convicted of one incident of sodomy). The appellate court found that the victim's response ("three") was "regrettable," but it nevertheless found that the testimony provided a reasonable basis from which the jury could have concluded that there were three separate acts of sodomy. Thus, even though the question was improper, the error was not grounds for reversal.

§4.500 Differential Diagnosis

There are many different types or species of unproven facts. It might help to consider some of the most significant:

§4.501 Examiner Suspects Truth of Assumed Facts

First, we might address those questions wherein the examiner suspects that the assumed facts are true (but doesn't have the evidence to prove them) and will therefore anticipate that they will be overlooked as the witness focuses more upon the answer than the unestablished portion of the question. Let's develop our first example (i.e., "When did you stop beating your wife?"). If the witness answers the question by reciting a date before the opponent interrupts, an objection to the question will come too late. And it is highly unlikely that a reversal upon appeal will follow. After all, by the time an appeal takes place, the fact (i.e., beating) will have been established, and the prejudice caused by the question's improper form will be ruled "harmless."

§4.502 Assumed Facts Totally Lacking

By contrast to the preceding section, consider the case where the questioner simply cannot establish the "assumed" portion of the question by another's testimony. If the witness has knowledge of the missing information, then the examiner need only back up and ask the appropriate foundation question, i.e., "Did you ever beat your wife?" On the other hand, if the witness lacked the underlying information (for a different inquiry, of course), the question might draw the additional objection that the witness "lacked personal knowledge."[11]

§4.503 Hypothetical Questions for Expert Witnesses

A failure to establish certain "underlying" facts can be particularly significant with respect to experts. Moreover, expert witnesses frequently provide opinions in response to hypothetical questions. While such methods of interrogation are within the discretion of the court, hypothetical questions are normally allowed as long as the underlying facts have already been established. The opposing practitioner must, therefore, pay particular attention to those facts that may be cleverly worked into a hypothetical question, but have yet to be established by way of other competent evidence. An expert may not reach a conclusion by assuming material facts that are not supported by the evidence.[12]

When posing a hypothetical question to an expert, the underlying facts upon which that question is based may be presented in the form of circumstantial evidence; however, the circumstantial evidence must reasonably support the assumptions contained in the hypothetical.[13]

11 See Fed. R. Evid. (cited and discussed in Chapter 3).

12 *Lee v. Shields,* 591 N.Y.S.2d 522 (N.Y.A.D. 2 Dept. 1992); *Coppedge v. Missouri Highway and Transp. Com'n.,* 809 S.W.2d 164 (Mo. App. 1991); see also Rule 703 of the *Federal Rules of Evidence* and *Chapter 11 (Experts for Existing Forms of Evidence).*

13 *Saylor v. State,* 765 N.E.2d 535 (Ind. 2002). Counsel should be precluded from posing hypothetical questions based on facts that are not in the record.

Gathers By and Through Hutchinson v. South Carolina Elec. and Gas Co., 427 S.E.2d 687 (S.C. App. 1993).

REFERENCES

Admissibility of expert testimony. 89 A.L.R. 4th 456.

§4.600 Selected State Rules and Cases

There is nothing particularly controversial about the basic proposition that underlies this particular objection. Questions that improperly assume the existence of unestablished facts tend to be misleading and confusing. If an unproven fact is asserted in a question, and it passes without challenge, the jury may presume it to be true. All states acknowledge the impropriety of such questions.

ALABAMA:

Where the key issues were whether the defendant participated in crimes of rape, sodomy, and kidnapping, the prosecutor's questions regarding the defendant's use of marijuana was permitted, where there was no evidence of drug use, even though the question assumed facts not in evidence. Although, during cross-examination, questions that assume facts not in evidence are objectionable, such questions are only improper if they assume facts in controversy. *Phillips v. State*, 728 So.2d 681 (Ala. Crim. App. 1998).

Questions assuming facts not in evidence are objectionable. Therefore, the trial court properly sustained a prosecutor's objections to a defense counsel's question which assumed that the state's Alcohol Beverage Control Board had a standard operating procedure to identify the suspect (an unestablished fact). *McIntyre v. State*, 571 So.2d 364 (Ala. Cr. App. 1990).

CALIFORNIA:

In California, there are no special exceptions or exemptions with respect to the general rule involving this objection. Questions that assume the truth of facts that have yet to be proven are improper and objectionable. *Fortner v. Bruhn*, 217 Cal. App.2d 184, 31 Cal. Rptr. 503 (1963); *Department of Public Works v. Lilliard*, 219 Cal. App.2d 368, 33 Cal. Rptr. 189 (1963); *McDonald v. Price*, 80 Cal. App.2d 150, 181 p.2d 115 (1947); *Ray v. Borgfeldt*, 146 P. 679, 169 C. 253 (1915).

Note that §352(b) of the *California Evidence Code* similarly provides that the court in its discretion "may exclude evidence if its probative value is substantially outweighed by the probability that its admission will create substantial danger of undue prejudice, of confusing issues, or of misleading the jury."

CONNECTICUT:

During cross-examination, the examiner may not couch a question in such a manner as to assume as true matters that are in dispute between the parties, to which the witness has not testified. *State v. Rogers*, 674 A.2d 1364, 41 Conn. App. 204 (1996).

FLORIDA:

With respect to Fed. R. Evid. 403, §90.403 of the Florida Evidence Code presents similar provisions.

GEORGIA:

Defense counsel is not entitled to cross-examine a narcotics agent using hypothetical questions about what would have happened if the defendant had tried to back out of a drug deal involving the sale of 15 pounds of marijuana, where there was no evidence that defendant had, in fact, tried to back out. *Cheesman v. State*, 230 Ga. App. 525, 497 S.E.2d 40 (1998).

ILLINOIS:

It is improper, and therefore an error when a prosecutor, during cross-examination, asks a defense witness questions that presume facts not in evidence as a precursor to the impeachment of that witness (in the absence of rebuttal evidence to substantiate the inquiry). *People v. Stack*, 184 Ill. Dec. 583, 613 N.E.2d 1175, 244 Ill. App.3d 166 (Ill. App. 1 Dist. 1993).

It is notable that Illinois' Rule 403 is identical to Fed. R. Evid. 403.

LOUISIANA:

In an informed consent action, the trial court properly refused to allow the plaintiff-patient to be cross-examined with hypothetical questions as to whether she would have had surgery had she known of the risks involved, where the hypothesis did not conform to the facts of case. *Coscino v. Wolfley*, 696 So.2d 257 (La. Ct. App. 1997).

The trial court properly sustained an objection to a tenant's question directed to a landlord's real estate agent as to whether the co-tenant's assignor ever objected to a particular clause in that assignor's agreement with the landlord; the tenant failed to lay a foundation showing that the agent actually had communications with the co-tenant's assignor. *Super Fresh/Sav-A-Center, Inc. v. Ashy-Bickham Baker*, 655 So.2d 531 (La.App. 1 Cir.,1995).

MARYLAND:

During cross-examination, the trial court did not abuse its discretion when it restricted defense counselor's questions, because they required the witness to assume a fact that was not otherwise in evidence (in addition, the question posed by defense counsel was based on hearsay). *Tirado v. State*, 622 A.2d 187, 95 Md. App. 536 (1993).

Assuming that it was intended as a question, defense counsel's statement during the cross-examination of an accomplice: "And so, you claim that defendant pulled the trigger that night?" was properly stricken as argumentative, since it incorporated, by assumption, a fact not otherwise in evidence as to the accomplice's motivation for making statement. A "yes" answer could have been interpreted as either agreeing only that defendant pulled trigger or agreeing with counsel's prior suggestion that accomplice made that claim to save himself. *Clermont v. State,* 704 A.2d 880, 348 Md. 419 (1998). [*Author's note*: "Objection! The question is vague, ambiguous and subject to multiple meanings," would have been more appropriate.]

MASSACHUSETTS:

With respect to Massachusetts' state courts in general, while that state has not specifically adopted the Federal Rules of Evidence, its state courts frequently look to the Federal Rules for guidance. For example, see *Commonwealth v. Wiechell*, 390 Mass. 62, 453 N.E.2d 1038 (1983), *cert. den.* 104 S. Ct. 1298 (1984). Also, see *Price v. Rosenberg*, 200 Mass. 36, 85 N.E. 887 (1908).

MICHIGAN:

With respect to its state courts in general, Michigan's Rule 403 is identical in content to Fed. R. Evid. 403.

MISSOURI:

Cross-examination should not be used to covertly raise suspicions and prejudice among jurors by reciting as fact matters not properly entered as evidence, such as speculative hypothetical situations. *Anderson v. Wittmeyer*, 895 S.W.2d 595 (Mo. Ct. App. 1995).

It was reversible error for the prosecutor to cross-examine the defendant's character witness as to whether that witness was aware of child molestation charges and physical abuse allegations by defendant's children some 20 to 25 years earlier; the questions transcended the limits of cross-examination; moreover, the questions were phrased in a manner designed to elicit personal knowledge in order to imply that the subject matter of the question was a fact (without a hearing to determine a reasonable basis for the allegations). *State v. Creason*, 847 S.W.2d 482 (Mo. App.W.D. 1993).

Expert testimony based on an assumption that is not proven by presented evidence is inadmissible. *Coppedge v. Missouri Highway and Transp. Com'n.*, 809 S.W.2d 164 (Mo. App. 1991).

NEW JERSEY:

With respect to its state courts in general, New Jersey's Rule 403 is very similar in content to Fed. R. Evid. 403. Also, see *Johnson v. Hoffman*, 80 A.2d 624 (N.J. 1951).

NEW YORK:

New York's state courts follow the general rule of disallowing questions that assume unestablished facts. In particular, a question that assumes a fact which is not proven is improper. See *People v. Sifford*, 429 N.Y.S.2d 270, 76 A.D.2d 937 (1980); *People v. Slover*, 232 N.Y. 264, 133 N.E. 633 (1921); *Gray v. Brooklyn Heights R. Co.*, 175 N.Y. 448, 67 N.E. 899 (1903); *People v. Mather, 4 Wend.* 229 (1830); see also *Bender's New York Evidence*, §2.05(2)(a)(iii), Matthew Bender Inc.

With respect to experts, see *Lee v. Shields*, 591 N.Y.S.2d 522 (N.Y.A.D. 2 Dept. 1992), which held that an expert may not reach a conclusion by assuming material facts that are not supported by the evidence; nor may that witness guess or speculate in drawing a conclusion.

OHIO:

With respect to its state courts in general, Ohio's Rule 403 is similar in content to Fed. R. Evid. 403.

PENNSYLVANIA:

On May 8, 1998, the Pennsylvania Supreme Court adopted a new and comprehensive set of evidence rules, with an effective date of October 1, 1998. The new rules are patterned after the Federal Rules of Evidence, both by content and number.

Pennsylvania's new Rule 403 (Exclusion of Relevant Evidence on Grounds of Prejudice, Confusion, or Waste of Time) could be used to support this particular objection. Questions that assume unproven facts are certainly confusing, if not prejudicial.

SOUTH CAROLINA:

Counsel posing a hypothetical question to an expert may rely upon circumstantial evidence to prove the essential fact in framing the question. *Gathers By and Through Hutchinson v. South Carolina Elec. and Gas Co.,* 427 S.E.2d 687 (S.C. App. 1993).

TEXAS:

With respect to its state courts in general, Rule 403 (both Civil and Criminal) presents a slightly modified version of Fed. R. Evid. 403, e.g., the "waste of time" provision is omitted. The remainder of the Texas rules, however, are the same as their federal counterpart:

> Although relevant, evidence may be excluded if its probative value is substantially outweighed by the danger of unfair prejudice, confusion of the issues, or misleading the jury, or by considerations of undue delay, or needless presentation of cumulative evidence.

See also *Wilson v. State*, 819 S.W.2d 662 (Tex. App. 1991).

(This page intentionally left blank.)

Chapter 5

Hearsay Rule

§5.100 Introduction

As the word suggests, "hearsay" refers to statements that the witness has "heard" from someone else. When he or she then attempts to "say" them in court in order to prove their truth, hearsay occurs. "Lloyd Price told me that Staggerlee shot Billy," would be hearsay if I were to make the statement at Staggerlee's murder trial.

A critical element in determining whether or not something is hearsay is whether the statement is being used to prove the truth of the actual facts contained in the statement. The above question would *not*, for example, be hearsay at a copyright infringement trial if, as a witness, I were explaining the subject of Lloyd Price's rock-and-roll hit record of the 50's (Staggerlee); in that case, Billy's murder would not at all be relevant. He is probably a fictitious character, in any event. For these reasons, and the rule's numerous exceptions, hearsay is one of the most complex and misunderstood objections in the entire body of evidence. As a matter of fact, almost half of the law of evidence deals with **just** the exceptions.

§5.200 Quick Explanation

To provide a "quick explanation" of the hearsay rule is almost a contradiction in terms. Basically, hearsay occurs when a witness attempts to prove the truth of some assertion by repeating what someone else said, because he (the witness) didn't happen to observe the event firsthand.

For each of the examples listed below (and for any "hearsay" determination), it is critical to know the *purpose* or reason for asking the question. For our examples, let's assume that a murder trial is involved, and that the statements are being offered to *prove* the facts contained in them. Remember—if the statements are being offered for some other reason, they would not be considered to be hearsay.[1] Such non-hearsay statements are sometimes referred to as "non-assertive."

EXAMPLES OF HEARSAY QUESTIONS:

1. Did Joe tell you that he saw the defendant murder Sandra?
2. What did the police reports say about the murder weapon?
3. After the murder, did you see anyone point the finger at the defendant?

Consider the first question. Assuming that the defendant is on trial for the murder of Sandra, the attempt to "say" what Joe said is hearsay and should not be admitted into evidence. For, it would be clear that the statement by Joe is being offered to prove the truth of the matters asserted in that statement.

If Joe claimed that he saw the defendant murder Sandra, then it would be quite proper for *Joe* to take the stand to tell the court and jury exactly what he saw. That way Joe would be subject to cross-examination. If he were lying, presumably the truth would come out. But when a witness says that somebody else said something, it is impossible to cross-examine that witness for the truth of the statement, since that witness would only be repeating what he or she had heard.

Now assume, for the moment, that we were *not* dealing with a murder trial, but instead, we are observing a sanity hearing for Joe, who had been running around town naked, claiming that he saw people being murdered who in fact were not. Assume further that Sandra is alive and well, and in court. The issue might then turn to whether or not Joe made such a statement, as opposed to whether or not the statement were true or false. In such a case, the statement by Joe would *not* be hearsay, because the truth of the matter asserted in that statement (i.e., the murder of Sandra) would *not* be an issue.

1 *Kemp v. Kemp,* 831 N.E.2d 1038, 161 Ohio App.3d 671 (2005); *Farrell v. Bass*, 879 A.2d 516, 90 Conn.App. 804 (2005); *Lexington Insurance Company v. Western Pennsylvania Hospital*, 423 F.3d 318 (3rd Cir., Penn., 2005); *Rodriguez v. Boehringer Ingelheim Pharmaceuticals, Inc.*, 425 F.3d 67 (1st Cir., Puerto Rico, 2005); *Taylor v. Abernethy*, 620 S.E.2d 242 (N.C.App., 2005); *Floyd v. Floyd*, 615 S.E.2d 465, 365 S.C. 56 (2005); *Miller v. Hometown Propane Gas, Inc.*, 167 S.W.3d 172, 86 Ark.App. 189 (2004).

The second sample question is used to show that written statements are the same as verbal ones with respect to the application of the hearsay rule. In other words, a statement in writing that is offered to prove the truth of the matters contained therein is just as much hearsay as a verbal statement. It just so happens that certain portions of police reports may be considered as "official records," and, therefore, they come within an exception to the hearsay rule, assuming that a proper foundation is laid. We will cover the hearsay exceptions shortly.

The third example requires a little bit of thought. The "statement" made by the outside witness consists of a hand motion or "assertive" gesture. But it is nevertheless a statement. Think about that for a moment; the term "pointing the finger" is really equivalent to saying "that person committed the crime." Therefore, it is hearsay, in any event.

WHAT TO LOOK FOR:

Questions that ask the witness to talk about something that he or she did not personally observe.

OBJECT AND RESPOND

OBJECTION:

"Objection! Hearsay."

POTENTIAL RESPONSES TO OBJECTION:

A. (Non-Hearsay/State of Mind):
"Your Honor, I'm not offering this statement to prove its truth; rather, I'm offering it to show the state of mind of the declarant."

B. (Non-Hearsay/Notice):
"Your Honor, I'm not offering this statement to prove its truth; rather, I'm offering it to show notice (or knowledge) on the part of the recipient."

C. (Non-Hearsay/Admission):
"Your Honor, this is an admission." Admissions can always be used against the parties that make them; they are not even considered to be hearsay under the rules.

D. (Non-Hearsay/Inconsistency) :
"Your Honor, the offered prior-statement contradicts the statement just made by this witness. Prior inconsistent statements are not hearsay."

E. (Recognized Hearsay Exception) :
"Your Honor, the offered statement falls within the ________ hearsay exception (See §5.401 through §5.410.)

F. (*Song and a Prayer* Exception (i.e., Residual Exception)):
"The offered statement is trustworthy and more probative than any other obtainable evidence on the subject; opposing counsel was told about the intended use of this testimony."

REPLIES TO RESPONSES:

A. (Universal Reply for any attempt to use hearsay):
"The statement is not trustworthy."

B. (Reply to *Response E*):
"Opposing counsel has not presented a proper foundation for the exception that he or she claims."

§5.300 General Legal Analysis

Perhaps a good place to start the legal analysis would be with Rule 801(c) of the Federal Rules of Evidence. That rule defines hearsay in this manner:[2]

2 See *Rogers v. Board of Educ. of City of New Haven,* 749 A.2d 1173, 252 Conn. 753 (2000); *In re A.N.*, 995 P.2d 427 (Mont., 2000); *Weaver v. Tech Data Corp.*, 66 F.Supp.2d 1258 (M.D.Fla.,1999). See also *Kempt v. Qualls*, 326 Pa. Super. 319, 473 A.2d 1369 (1984); *Whitman v. Riddell,* 324 Pa. Super. 177, 471 A.2d 521 (1984); *Ours v. West Virginia Dept. of Motor Vehicles,* 315 S.E.2d 634 (W.Va. 1984); *Worcester Textile Co. v. Morales*, 468 A.2d 279 (R.I. 1973).

> Hearsay. "Hearsay" is a statement, other than one made by the declarant while testifying at the trial or hearing, offered in evidence to prove the truth of the matter asserted.

As a follow up, Fed. R. Evid. 802 states that hearsay is not admissible except as provided by the Federal Rules or other rules prescribed by the Supreme Court.[3] Regardless of whether the jurisdiction is state or federal, hearsay evidence is inadmissible unless it falls within an exception.[4]

With respect to evidence in general, perhaps the biggest mistake that lawyers make involves a failure to properly determine whether or not the material contained within the statement is actually being offered to prove the truth of the statement. If not, the statement is not inadmissible hearsay.[5]

Consider *Wal-Mart Stores, Inc. v. Dolph*,[6] a case involving an alleged slander by a Wal-Mart employee. The plaintiff testified that her relative was told by the employee that she (the plaintiff) had been caught shoplifting. The statement was admissible to prove publication of the slander; it was not offered to prove that plaintiff was or was not a shoplifter and, therefore, was not hearsay.

First and foremost, there must be some statement of "fact" involved. If the statement does not assert a fact, then it cannot be hearsay. A threat, for example, is not a statement of fact; rather, it is a future promise to do injury. The contents of a threatening telephone call would, therefore, not constitute inadmissible hearsay,[7] nor would tape-recorded telephone conversations that were only offered to show a pattern of verbal behavior on the telephone.[8] Both items of evidence would, therefore, be admissible.

It is important to remember that even if the statement includes a fact reported to the witness by someone else, that statement will not constitute hearsay unless it is offered (by the witness) to prove the truth of that included fact.[9] Often, facts relayed by others will be used as a foundation for action taken by the person who heard those facts. Assume, for example, that a witness were to testify that he ran home because his wife had telephoned to tell him that his house was burning. If the witness were to testify as to the substance of the call **to show** why he ran home, such testimony would not be hearsay; but if he were to use it **to**

---

3 The basic rule pertaining to the general inadmissibility of hearsay applies in all of the states. See §5.401. See also *Claypool v. City of New York*, 699 N.Y.S.2d 363 (N.Y.A.D. 1 Dept., 1999), and *K-Mart Corp. V. Lovett*, 525 S.E.2d 751, 241 Ga. App. 26, 99 FCDR 4449 (1999). To read more about the hearsay rule, see generally, Lipson, *Documentary Evidence*, §9.05 et seq. (Matthew Bender, 1988).

4 *Alberswerth v. Alberswerth*, 184 S.W.3d 81 (Mo.App., 2006). Hearsay is an out-of-court statement offered to prove the truth of the matters asserted. It is not admissible without an exception.

Brown v. Bright Clouds Ministries, Inc., 891 A.2d 999, 94 Conn.App. 181 (2006). Hearsay is inadmissible in the absence of an exception. Decisions pertaining to the admissibility of evidence fall within the court's discretion and will not be reversed absent an abuse of that discretion.

5 *E.E.O.C. v. International House of Pancakes*, 411 F.Supp.2d 709 (2006). In an age discrimination case brought by a waitress applicant seeking a job at an IHOP restaurant, statements by the restaurant's manager indicating that hiring an older waitress would disrupt the "harmony" among the younger waitresses was admissible. The statement was used to show the state of mind of the declarant; it was not used to prove the truth of the matters asserted.

If a statement is not offered to prove the truth of the matter asserted, it cannot be hearsay. *Puma v. Sullivan*, 746 A.2d 871 (D.C., 2000). Extrajudicial statements that are not offered to prove the truth of the statement, but merely to prove that the statement was made, are not inadmissible hearsay. *Prairie State Bank v. Hoefgen*, 777 P.2d 811, 245 Kan. 236 (1989).

6 25 S.W.2d 810, 308 Ark. 439 (1992).

7 *United States v. Herrera*, 600 F.2d 502 (5th Cir. 1979).

8 *United States v. Abascal*, 564 F.2d 821 (9th Cir. 1977); see also *United States v. Parry*, 649 F.2d 292 (5th Cir. 1981); *United States v. Rubin*, 591 F.2d 278 (5th Cir. 1979).

9 *Patrick v. McGowan*, 104 S.W.3d 219 (Tex.App., 2003); *Gelpi v. 37th Ave. Avenue Realty Corp.*, 721 N.Y.S.2d 380 (N.Y.A.D., 2001). Statement which is not offered to establish truth of facts asserted therein cannot be "hearsay."

show that the house had, in fact, burned, then the testimony would be hearsay.[10]

We also indicated in our examples that written hearsay is just as "bad" as verbal hearsay.[11] Consider a case involving tax evasion, where an IRS agent testified that out of a certain number of returns that she audited, more than 90% contained substantially overstated deductions; according to the court, this constituted inadmissible hearsay, since the testimony of the witness relied upon statements (written) made by taxpayers in their tax returns.[12]

REFERENCES

Hearsay rule, generally, 14 Am. Jur. 2d Proof of Facts 173.

§5.400 Hearsay Exceptions

As if the hearsay rule were not complicated enough, it is laced by several complex exceptions. As previously indicated, almost half of the entire body of the law of evidence is directed toward these hearsay rule exceptions. They might be listed as follows:[13] business records, official records, former testimony, past recollections recorded, learned treatises, market reports, ancient writings, declarations against interest, prior inconsistent statements, statements of physical or mental condition, family history, reputation, spontaneous declarations, and the federal catch-all (Rule 803(24) of the Federal Rules of Evidence);[14] this last item is rarely applicable.

MULTIPLE HEARSAY

It should be noted that hearsay within hearsay (sometimes referred to as "multiple hearsay") is not improper as long as all statements fall within some hearsay exception (not necessarily the same one).[15] Such a situation is most likely to arise when documents are involved. A police report (a **business record**), for example, might contain a statement by a

---

10 In *Vargas v. Retail Clerk's Union Local 1428*, 260 Cal.Rptr. 650, 212 C.A.3d 319 (1989), a police officer testified that customers of a store told him about physical assaults on store employees. The testimony was held not to be hearsay since the statements served as a foundation for the officer's subsequent action.

11 *Flores v. United States*, 551 F.2d 1169 (9th Cir. 1977); see also *United States v. Brown*, 548 F.2d 1194 (5th Cir. 1977).

12 *United States v. Brown*, 548 F.2d 1194 (5th Cir. 1977).

13 Lipson, *Demonstrative Evidence*, Chapter 9 (Matthew Bender, 1989); see also generally, 3 *Weinstein on Evidence*, §802 (Matthew Bender, 1984).

14 Rules 803(24) and 804(5) provide for admissibility where the subject statement is offered (1) to prove a material fact, (2) when it is more probative on that point than any other evidence which can be produced through efforts, and (3) the interests of justice and the purpose of the rules will best be served. The so called "catch-all" was designed to handle extreme situations. It should not be relied upon by the practitioner as a viable tool, since the courts rarely apply it.

15 *The Upper Desk Company, LLC v. Breakey Intern., BV*, 390 Fed.Supp.2d 355 (S.D.N.Y., 2005). In a battle over royalties, the report of a toy manufacturer's managing director of what a third party "informed" him was inadmissible double hearsay. *Burns v. Board of County Commissioners of Jackson County*, 330 F.3d 1275 (10th Cir., Kansas, 2003); *Alvarez v. Jacmar Pacific Pizza Corp.*, 122 Cal.Rptr.2d 890, 100 Cal. App.4th 1190 (2002). In a survivor's negligence action against Jacmar Pizza, records of "911" calls placed from a restaurant to the city police department during the 18 months preceding the murder of a customer at that restaurant constituted "multiple hearsay," when offered by the customers' survivors. A hearsay exception would, therefore, be required at each level.

Fed. R. Evid. 805. See also *Ross Dress for Less, Inc. v. Radcliff*, 751 So.2d 126 (Fla.App. 2000); *NationsBanc Mortgage Corp. v. Eisenhauer*, 733 N.E2d 557, 49 Mass.App. 727(2000); *Canterbury v. West Virginia Human Rights Commission*, 382 S.E. 2d 338 (W.Va. 1989). *Munley v. Carlson*, 125 F.Supp.2d 1117 (N.D., 2000). When statement contains multiple levels of hearsay, entire statement is inadmissible unless exception or exclusion applies at each level. Hearsay within hearsay is inadmissible unless both levels of hearsay fall within an exception to the hearsay rule. *Reynolds v. Green*, 184 F.3d 589 (C.A.6 (Mich., 1999).

motorist who rear-ended another vehicle and described the accident (**admission**) to the officer. Since each statement falls within a hearsay exception, the portion of the report containing the statement would be admissible.

CONDENSED LIST

To get a better grip on the subject (and provide a rapidly readable trial reference), we can efficiently condense the preceding items into the following ten pigeonholes:

1. Former Testimony
2. Past Recollection Recorded
3. Declaration Against Interest
4. Admission
5. Prior Inconsistent Statement
6. Statement of Mental or Physical Condition
7. Dying Declaration
8. Spontaneous Declaration
9. Statement of Reputation
10. Business Records and Other Documents

The Federal Rules of Evidence provide a more numerous list, scattered about three sections: Fed. R. Evid. 801(d) for "non-hearsay," Fed. R. Evid. 803 for exceptions that apply without regard to the presence of the declarant, and Fed. R. Evid. 804 for those exceptions that can be used only when the declarant is absent.

Here is a chart "in a nutshell" that provides a summary for all of the traditional exceptions:

HEARSAY EXCEPTIONS

Italics: Exception is sometimes treated as non-hearsay.

Boldface: Exception only applies where declarant is unavailable.

1. **Former Testimony - 804(1)**
2. Past Recollection Recorded - 803(5)
3. **Declaration Against Interest - 804(3)**
4. Admission - 801(d)(2)
5. Prior Inconsistent Statement - 801(d)(1)
6. Statement of Mental or Physical Condition - 803(3), 803(4)
7. **Dying Declaration - 804(2)**
8. Spontaneous Declaration - 803(2), 803(1)
9. Statement of Reputation - 803(19), 803(20), 803(21)
10. Business Records -803(6), 803(7)
    Public Records - 803(8), 803(10)
    Vital Statistics - 803(9)
    Ancient Documents - 803(16)
    Records of Family History - 804(6), 804(11), 804(12), 804(13)
    Market Reports - 803(17)
    Learned Treatises - 803(18)
    Records Affecting Property Rights - 803(14), 803(15), 803(20), 803(23)
    Judgments - 803(14), 803(22)

In addition to the exceptions listed above, Fed. R. Evid. 807 presents a set of requirements for the "Residual Exception." This "catch-all" permits the admission of those rare instances of hearsay that are so trustworthy that the court should make a special exception, where a standard one does not exist.[16] This new provision took effect as of December 1, 1997.

Each of the above exceptions was developed over the years to reflect a policy or belief that some statements tend to be very reliable, and should, therefore, be admitted *even though* they constitute hearsay. The reason for the reliability is contained in the discussions (below) of each hearsay exception.

Historically, some exceptions weren't even hearsay to begin with.[17] However, because judges and lawyers couldn't always be sure, it

16 For information concerning the residual exception, see §5.411.

17 Consider, for example, the statement, "I am Madonna," made by a mental patient, offered to show the "state of mind" of the declarant. Since the statement is not offered for its truth, it would not be hearsay to begin with. Therefore, it might be argued that no exception is necessary.

was decided that they be listed as exceptions, just to play it safe. We will consider each one separately, after examining briefly the manner in which the majority of states seem to be falling in line with the basic federal structure.

HOW THE STATES APPLY THE EXCEPTIONS

The hearsay rule's basic definition and application are fairly standard from state to state, including those states that have not adopted the Federal Rules of Evidence word for word. All seem to recognize and follow the federal position that hearsay should generally be excluded.

The exceptions vary slightly from state to state, following a general "federal" pattern. Our "list of ten" forms a solid set of pigeonholes that should cover well over 95% of all such matters. That list is not absolute, but it does provide a consistent framework for comparison. A grasp of the federal exceptions (*supra*) and California's slight variations, should enable an attorney to competently handle most problems likely to arise, regardless of jurisdiction. Section 1200 of the California Evidence Code, titled "The Hearsay Rule" provides:

(a) "Hearsay evidence" is evidence of a statement that was made other than by a witness while testifying at the hearing and that is offered to prove the truth of the matter stated.
(b) Except as provided by law, hearsay evidence is inadmissible.
(c) This section shall be known and may be cited as the hearsay rule.

California's use of the word "stated" [Section 1200(a), last word] instead of the word "asserted" [as used in Federal Rule 801(c)] might be construed as eliminating assertive non-verbal statements (see Example 3, *supra*, §5.200)]. Perhaps this was a drafting oversight. CEC 1201 follows the federal rule with respect to multiple hearsay, i.e. hearsay within hearsay is admissible as long as each level of hearsay falls within a recognized exception.

Here is a list of California's hearsay exceptions, as codified by the California Evidence Code:

1. Former Testimony [CEC 1290]
2. Past Recollection Recorded [CEC 1237]
3. Declaration Against Interest [CEC 1230]
4. Admission or Confession [CEC 1220]
5. Prior Inconsistent Statement [CEC 1235]
6. Mental or Physical Condition [CEC 1250]
7. Dying Declaration [CEC 1240]
8. Spontaneous Declaration [CEC 1240]
9. Statement of Reputation [CEC 1320]
10. Business [CEC 1271] or Official Records [CEC 1280], Market Reports [CEC 1340], Family Pedigrees [CEC 1310]

A few additional exceptions recognized by California pertain solely to written evidence. Statements pertaining to wills and claims against estates are admissible according to CEC 1260, judgments may be admitted pursuant to CEC 1300, along with dispositive instruments and ancient writings, both pursuant to CEC 1330.

Section 90.805 of the Florida Rules of Court (in particular, The Florida Evidence Code) conforms to the federal (and California) rule with respect to multiple hearsay; i.e., hearsay within hearsay is admissible as long as each level of hearsay falls within a recognized exception. Florida's exceptions, likewise, closely mirror those of the California Evidence Code. Here is a list derived from the Florida Evidence Code:

1. Former Testimony [FEC 90.904(2)(a)]
2. Past Recollection Recorded [FEC 90.803(5)]
3. Declaration Against Interest [FEC 90.904(2)(c)]
4. Admission or Confession [FEC 90.803(18)]
5. Prior Inconsistent Statement [FEC 90.801(2)(a)]
6. Mental or Physical Condition [FEC 90.803(3) and (4)]
7. Dying Declaration [FEC 90.904(2)(b)]
8. Spontaneous Declaration [FEC 90.803(1) and (2)]
9. Statement of Reputation [FEC 90.803(21)]
10. Business [FEC 90.803(6)] or Official Record [FEC 90.803(8) and (9)], Market Reports [FEC 90.803(17)], Family Pedigrees [FEC 90.904(2)(d) and FEC 90.803(13)]

In a fashion similar to many of the less populous states, Connecticut, West Virginia, and Vermont follow the Federal Rules essentially word for word and section number for section number.

Oregon is not atypical of those several states that provide a slight addition or subtraction here and there. That state, which has adopted most of the rules and principles set forth in the Federal Rules of Evidence, assigns its own rule numbers (see Oregon Revised Statutes, Chapter 40 et seq.). Oregon does not recognize Federal Rule 803(18), with respect to learned treatises. It has also added a new exception [ORS 40.460(18a)]:

> A complaint of sexual misconduct made by the prosecuting witness after the commission of the alleged offense. Such evidence must be confined to the fact that the complaint was made.

On May 8, 1998, the Pennsylvania Supreme Court adopted a new and comprehensive set of evidence rules, with an effective date of October 1, 1998. The new rules are patterned after the Federal Rules of Evidence, both by content and number. With respect to its hearsay exceptions, see Pennsylvania's new Rule 803 (Hearsay Exceptions; Testimony of Declarant Immaterial), Rule 803.1 (Hearsay Exceptions; Testimony of Declarant Necessary), and Rule 804 (Hearsay Exceptions; Declarant Unavailable).

To seasoned lawyers, the recognized hearsay exceptions are as much a part of our justice system as the Constitution. But occasionally, bright students of the law must question a rule that is so laced with exceptions that the rule itself is overshadowed. And where no exception exists, we have a federal catch-all (i.e., Rule 803(24) of the Federal Rules of Evidence) to make certain no part of the rule is immune from attack. Why not just allow hearsay testimony subject to certain well-defined restrictions? That is precisely the approach taken by the United Kingdom. Section 2(1) of the Civil Evidence Act of 1968 provides:

> In any civil proceedings a statement made, whether orally or in a document or otherwise, by any person, whether called as a witness in those proceedings or not, shall, subject to this section and to rules of court, be admissible as evidence of any fact stated therein of which direct oral evidence by him would be admissible.

There are, of course, restrictions in the applicable court rules, including among other things, a notice requirement. The general hearsay exclusion is also abolished for criminal matters (see §23(1) of the Criminal Justice Act of 1988); but as might be expected, the restrictions are more rigorous.

§5.401 Former Testimony

Testimony that has been recorded by an official court reporter for preservation has been deemed to be somewhat reliable, particularly if the witness who gave it had been subjected to cross-examination.[18] This includes depositions.[19]

With or without an official transcript, anyone who was present at a prior court proceeding can testify about what occurred.[20] But dispensing with the need to produce a transcript is not universal. The best evidence rule (see Chapter 2) may be used as a basis for requiring its production.[21]

Rule Fed. R. Evid. 804(b)(1) defines admissible former testimony as follows:

18 *Briones v. Solomon*, 769 S.W. 2d 312 (Tex. App. San Antonio 1989).

19 See Fed. R. Evid. 804(b)(1) of the Federal Rules of Evidence; see also Lipson, *Documentary Evidence*, §9.08 (Matthew Bender, 1988); 4 *Weinstein on Evidence*, §804(b)(1) (Matthew Bender, 1985); *United States v. King*, 713 F.2d 626 (11th Cir. 1983), 543 F. Supp. 1142 (N.D. Cal. 1982).

20 *U.S. v. Rumisel*, 716 F.2d 1404 (9th Cir. 1986).

21 *U.S. v. Fernandez-Roque*, 703 F.2d 808 (5th Cir. 1983).

> Testimony given by a witness at another hearing of the same or different proceeding, or in a deposition taken in compliance with law in the course of the same or another proceeding, if the party against whom the testimony is now offered, or, in a civil action or proceeding, the predecessor in interest, had an opportunity and similar motive to develop the testimony by direct, cross, or redirect examination.

Notice the Rule's final requirement that the person against whom the former testimony is used must have had an opportunity to examine the witness, and a motive to do so as well.[22]

REFERENCES

Exception where declarant unavailable. 75 A.L.R. 4th 199.

§5.401.1 State Application

At common law, the admissibility of prior testimony required an identity of issues to insure that the subject matter of the litigation was handled in an equivalent manner. The recent trend, however, is to employ a more liberal "substantial identity" test.

In California, the former testimony exception encompasses prior inconsistent statements, per the California Evidence Code (CEC); to consider requirements for the use of prior *consistent* statements when given as testimony, see CEC 791. Even though a witness' testimony may have been influenced by several different motives to fabricate it, the prior statement is admissible if it was made before the existence of any one (or more) of the alleged motives to fabricate.

It is not required that the statement be made before the existence of all such biases and motives. *People v. Hayes*, Cal. 802 P.2d 376, 276 Cal. Rptr. 874, 52 Cal. 3d 577 (1990). CEC 1291 sets forth the requirements for using former testimony against a party to the prior proceeding, while CEC 1292 pertains to use against a nonparty. Both rules require that the declarant be unavailable. Special rules apply to former testimony by a complainant minor child (CEC 1293).

The following states have a provision that is either identical or substantially similar to Rule 804(b)(1) of the Federal Rules of Evidence pertaining to former testimony:

FORMER TESTIMONY

Alaska	Rule 804(b)(1)
Alabama	Rule 804(b)(1)
Arizona	Rule 804(b)(1)
Colorado	Rule 804(b)(1)
Delaware	Rule 804(b)(1)
Florida	§90.804(2)(a) & §90.803(22)
Hawaii	Rule 804(b)(1)
Idaho	Rule 804(b)(1)
Illinois	Rule 804(b)(1)
Iowa	Rule 804(b)(1)
Kentucky	Rule 804(b)(1)
Louisiana	Rule 804(B)(1)
Maine	Rule 804(b)(1)
Michigan	Rule 804(b)(1)
Montana	Rule 804(b)(1)
Nebraska	Rule 804(b)(1)
Nevada	§51.325
New Hampshire	Rule 804(b)(1)
New Mexico	Rule 804(b)(1) & 804(b)(2)
North Carolina	Rule 804(b)(1)
North Dakota	Rule 804(b)(1)
Ohio	Rule 804(b)(1)
Oklahoma	Rule 804(b)(1)
Oregon	Rule 804(b)(1)
Pennsylvania	Rule 804(b)(1)
Puerto Rico	Rule 804(b)(1)
Rhode Island	Rule 804(b)(1)
South Dakota	§19-16-30
Tennessee	Rule 804(b)(1)
Texas (Civil & Criminal)	Rule 804(b)(1)
Utah	Rule 804(b)(1)
Vermont	Rule 804(b)(1)

22 *Ohio v. Roberts*, 448 U.S. 561 (1980).

Washington	Rule 804(b)(1)
West Virginia	Rule 804(b)(1)
Wisconsin	§908.045(1)
Wyoming	Rule 804(b)(1)

§5.402 Past Recollection Recorded

Before considering this exception (which the Federal Rules refer to as "Recorded Recollection"), a closely related circumstance should be examined in an attempt to avoid almost-certain confusion. Consider two witnesses, both with "memory problems." Each needs "something" to assist his or her description of some material event. For witness one, some object, writing (or even a smell) would refresh enough of a recollection to permit that witness to provide adequate testimony. Witness Two, however, who also has an "insufficient recollection" of the event, will continue to have it; but unlike Witness One, this witness (i.e., Witness Two) made some notes at the time of the material event. To solve the memory-lapse problem for Witness One, we can use anything we wish to jog his memory; and it does not have to be admissible evidence. Witness Two's memory can't be helped; so his notes may be admitted as an exception to the Hearsay Rule, which we will consider momentarily.

For the Witness One scenario, virtually anything may be used to refresh the recollection of a forgetful witness.[23] This includes the witness' own notes, even though they may be considered as hearsay. Behind the reason for carving out the exception and admitting this type of testimony is the belief that there is a genuine interest in refreshing the recollection of a forgetful witness; a failure to do so might result in the complete loss of material information. Even though hearsay is involved, it should be pointed out that the forgetful witness would be on the stand and, therefore, subject to cross-examination,[24] even if the actual author of the notes were not available.[25]

The skilled practitioner should recognize a distinction between formally admitted evidence, and other evidence that is used for a limited purpose, such as the type that we now consider. Formal evidence may be used for all purposes, including the erection of foundations for other evidence and for closing arguments. Limited-use evidence may not.

In an Ohio murder case, the court held that a police officer could properly use a defendant's own statement to refresh his (i.e., the officer's) recollection as to what the defendant had told him after being arrested.[26] We may therefore conclude that when a writing is used strictly for the purpose of refreshing someone's memory, the witness testifying does not necessarily have to be the actual author of the writing.[27]

The use of a writing for the limited purpose of refreshing a foggy memory does not, by any

23 *Farewell v. State,* 822 A.2d 513 (Md.App., 2003). Almost anything can be used to refresh the recollection of a forgetful witness, including objects and writings. The purpose of this rule is to permit a witness to testify from a present recollection that has been revived or refreshed. But unless it is otherwise admissible, the object, writing or device cannot be admitted into evidence.

24 See generally, Lipson, *Documentary Evidence*, §9.09 (Matthew Bender, 1988); and 4 *Weinstein on Evidence*, §803(5) (Matthew Bender, 1984); see also Fed. R. Evid. 803(5); *U.S. v. Riccardi*, 174 F.2d 883 (3rd Cir. 1949).

25 What happens when counsel begins laying the foundation for a *past recollection recorded*, and then, all of a sudden, that witness' memory is refreshed in the process? Answer—The document can not be admitted into evidence because a key foundation element has disappeared (i.e., lack of memory). *Horace Mann Ins. Co. v. Brown*, 177 Ill. Dec 690, 603 N.E.2d 760, 236 Ill.App.3d 456 (1992).

26 *State v. Bedford*, 529 N.W.2d 913, 39 Ohio St.3d 122 (1988).

27 But see *Cahill v. Gagnon,* 794 A.2d 451 (R.I., 2002). In a truck driver's personal injury action against a bus driver and the Public Transit Authority that hired the driver, a report by a police officer issued at the accident scene was not admissible as a past recollection recorded, where the report was not based upon the officer's personal recollections, but instead upon the statements of others. The report did not, therefore, qualify as a hearsay exception.

People v. Ramos, 535 N.Y.S.2d 663 (N.Y.Sup. 1988).

means, endow that writing with a status of formal admissibility;[28] it cannot be used for all purposes. It has thus been held that a witness could refer to, and look at, his memo while testifying, where that memo was used to refresh his recollection, and was not read to the jury.[29] This particular use does not fall within the scope of the "Past Recollection Recorded" exception to the Hearsay Rule. It is, however, given its force by Rule 612 of the Federal Rules of Evidence.

In contrast to the "refreshed recollection" is the "recorded recollection."[30] The recorded recollection is embodied in Fed. R. Evid. 803(5):

> A memorandum or record concerning a matter about which a witness once had knowledge but now has insufficient recollection to enable the witness to testify fully and accurately, shown to have been made or adopted by the witness when the matter was fresh in the witness' memory and to reflect that knowledge correctly. If admitted, the memorandum or record may be read into evidence but may not itself be received as an exhibit unless offered by an adverse party.

According to the last sentence of the rule, the notes (i.e., "recorded recollection") may be read but not formally *admitted* by the proponent.[31] Those who are often confused about the need to distinguish between a hearsay exception and non-hearsay might obtain some relief from this Rule 803(5) *exception*. In particular, if the "recorded recollection" were non-hearsay, it would not be subject to *any* restrictions on admissibility (See Rule 801 of the Federal Rules of Evidence).

REFERENCES

Use of writing to refresh witness' memory under Rule 612. 73 A.L.R. Fed 423.

Recorded recollection exception. 35 A.L.R. Fed 605.

§5.402.1 State Application

For California, the details of this particular exception are covered by Rule 1237 of the California Evidence Code, which provides that:

(a) Evidence of a statement previously made by a witness is not made inadmissible by the hearsay rule if the

28 *Morse v. Colombo*, 31 A.D.3d 916, 819 N.Y.S.2d 162 (N.Y.A.D., 3 Dept., 2006). In a dog bite case, a physician's affidavit stating that she observed a dog bite on the plaintiff's hand and that she had heard that the dog had bitten someone else prior to that incident was not admissible as a past recollection recorded; the affidavit was signed almost two years after the fact, the physician did not identify the plaintiff or the defendants as the source of information regarding the prior bite, and the physician testified that the document did not accurately represent her recollection when she signed it. Moreover, the criteria for admission of a document as a past recollection recorded are: That the document relates to matters that the witness observed; the matters were fairly fresh when recorded or adopted; the witness testified that the document accurately represented his or her recollection and knowledge when it was made; and the witness is presently unable to recall the facts of the matter.

29 *Branch v. Greene County Bd. of Educ.*, 533 So.2d 248 (Ala. Div. App. 1988).

30 *Overton v. City of Harvey,* 29 F.Supp.2d 894 (N.D.Ill. 1998) provides a concise summary of the foundation elements needed to establish the Past Recollection Recorded exception. Under it, the party seeking to admit such a writing must show that: (1) The record concerns matters about which the witness once had knowledge but now has insufficient recollection to testify fully and accurately, (2) The witness made or adopted the record when the matter was fresh in that witnesss memory, and (3) The record reflects that knowledge correctly. *Pieszak v. Glendale Adventist Medical Center*, 112 F.Supp.2d 970 (C.D.Cal. 2000). In slander action by resident against medical center's director of her residency program, nurse's declaration that director made defamatory statements about resident was admissible under recorded recollection exception to hearsay rule.

31 This practice is not particularly unique to federal rules. See *Rudy s. Bossard*, 997 P.2d 480 (Wyo. 2000), an automobile negligence case, wherein victim was permitted to read into evidence diary that she kept, which described her symptoms during year following her accident. Victim testified that diary was kept on a daily basis and that, while she could generally remember her physical condition, she did not remember day-to-day symptoms.

> statement would have been admissible if made by him while testifying, the statement concerns a matter as to which the witness has insufficient present recollection to enable him to testify fully and accurately, and the statement is included in a writing which:
>
> (1) Was made at a time when the fact recorded in the writing actually occurred or was fresh in the witness' memory;
>
> (2) Was made (i) by the witness himself or under his direction or (ii) by some other person for the purpose of recording the witness' statement at the time it was made;
>
> (3) Is offered after the witness testifies that the statement he made was a true statement of such fact; and
>
> (4) Is offered after the writing is authenticated as an accurate record of the statement.

CEC 1237(b), like its federal counterpart, Fed. R. Evid. 803(5), provides that the writing may be read into evidence, but the physical writing itself may not be received in evidence unless offered by an adverse party.

The following states have a provision that is either identical or substantially similar to Rule 803(5) of the Federal Rules of Evidence pertaining to recorded recollections:

RECORDED RECOLLECTIONS

Alaska	Rule 803(5)
Alabama	Rule 803(5)
Arizona	Rule 803(5)
Colorado	Rule 803(5)
Delaware	Rule 803(5)
Florida	§90.803(5)
Hawaii	Rule 802.1(4)
Idaho	Rule 803(5)
Illinois	Rule 803(5)
Iowa	Rule 803(5)
Kentucky	Rule 803(5)
Louisiana	Rule 803(5)
Maine	Rule 803(5)
Michigan	Rule 803(5)
Montana	Rule 803(5)
Nebraska	Rule 803(5)
Nevada	§51.125
New Hampshire	Rule 803(5)
New Jersey	Rule 803(5)
New Mexico	Rule 803(5)
North Carolina	Rule 803(5)
North Dakota	Rule 803(5)
Ohio	Rule 803(5)
Oklahoma	Rule 803(5)
Oregon	Rule 803(5)
Pennsylvania	Rule 803(5)
Puerto Rico	Rule 803(5)
Rhode Island	Rule 803(5)
South Dakota	§19-16-9
Tennessee	Rule 803(5)
Texas (Civil & Criminal)	Rule 803(5)
Utah	Rule 803(5)
Vermont	Rule 803(5)
Washington	Rule 803(5)
West Virginia	Rule 803(5)
Wisconsin	§908.045(1)
Wyoming	Rule 803(5)

§5.403 Declarations Against Interest

The basis for this particular exception is the idea that a person will *not* normally say something against his or her own personal "interest" unless it is true. One would not, for example, make the statement that "I owe Barfly Betty ten thousand dollars" unless it were true. The statement would be against my pecuniary (monetary) interest. The rationale is that a person is unlikely to fabricate a statement that was against his interest at the time that it was made.[32] Similarly, it is highly unlikely that anyone would admit to criminal responsibility, unless that declaration were true. Such admissions are deemed to be declarations against interest.[33]

32 *Chambers v. Mississippi,* 410 U.S. 284 (1973); see also Lipson, *Documentary Evidence,* §9.13 (Matthew Bender, 1988); and see generally, 4 *Weinstein on Evidence*, §804(b)(3) (Matthew Bender, 1985).

33 *United States v. Thomas*, 571 F.2d 285 (5th Cir. 1978); and *United States v. Scopo*, 861 F.2d 339 (2nd Cir. 1988).

Statements against mere social interest, however, are generally not admissible.[34] For example the statement: "George admitted that he was a wimp, a bum, a slob, and a misfit" would not be considered as an admission against interest.

Fed. R. Evid. 804(b)(3) defines the hearsay exception as follows:

> A statement which was at the time of its making so far contrary to the declarant's pecuniary or proprietary interest, or so far tended to subject the declarant to civil or criminal liability, or to render invalid a claim by the declarant against another, that a reasonable person in the declarant's position would not have made the statement unless believing it to be true. A statement tending to expose the declarant to criminal liability and offered to exculpate the accused is not admissible unless corroborating circumstances clearly indicate the trustworthiness of the statement.

Notice that the last portion of the rule indicates that a statement concerning criminal liability needs to be corroborated where that statement tends to "exculpate" the defendant. This is designed to avoid a situation where one person might falsely admit to a crime, just to get someone else off the hook. This is technically referred to as "taking the fall" or "buying the rap." The corroboration required by the rule could come from any of a number of different sources.[35] But, some corroboration is required where such a declaration is offered, in order to prevent a wrong person from paying for a crime.

The "corroboration" element would have also prevented the "phony plea" maneuver that Cody Jarrett (a James Cagney character) perfected in the classic film *White Heat*; i.e., after committing one of his normal murder-and-mayhem sprees, Cody "copped out" to a relatively minor unrelated bank job (that he didn't commit) which occurred in an unrelated state at the very same time as the said "normal spree." Cody reasoned that the guilty plea would bar prosecution for the more serious offenses.

What happens when a single narrative combines exculpatory and inculpatory statements within the same narrative? Or, in non-legalese: "when good stuff and bad stuff are all mixed together"? A matter involving such a confession was addressed by the High Court. In particular, the United States Supreme Court held that the term "statement," as it appears in Rule 803(b)(3), refers to each single declaration and not the entire narrative (i.e., the "entire confession"); and, therefore, the Rule excludes non- self-inculpatory statements even if they are made within a broader narrative that is generally inculpatory.[36]

Note that, like the other hearsay exceptions listed under Rule 804, the unavailability of the declarant is a pre-condition for its use. For, if the declarant were present, he or she could merely be called to the stand to testify. "But," one might ask, "What if the declarant is a defendant in a criminal case? What about the Fifth Amendment?" In such a case, the declarant would be considered a party to the litigation, and therefore, regardless of whether he or she took the stand, the statement would fall under the scope of Rule 801(d)(2), meaning that it would not even be considered as hearsay.

REFERENCES

Statement against interest, admissibility.
34 A.L.R. Fed 412.

34 *United States v. Dovico*, 380 F.2d 325 (2d Cir. 1967).

35 A guilty plea, for example, might be considered as a statement against interest. *United States v. Scopo*, 861 F.2d 339 (2nd Cir. 1988).

36 *Williamson v. United States,* 114 S. Ct. 2431 (1994); the case involved a prosecution for cocaine possession and distribution, where the trial court permitted a narcotics agent to recount two custodial interviews with the declarant; during the testimony, the court did not take the time to single out for exclusion those statements that were not self-inculpatory.

§5.403.1 State Application

Compared to Fed. R. Evid. 804(b)(3), Rule 1230 of the California Evidence Code appears to be a bit broader (as evidenced by the italicized portions):

> Evidence of a statement by a declarant having sufficient knowledge of the subject is not made inadmissible by the hearsay rule if the declarant is unavailable as a witness and the statement, when made, was so far contrary to the declarant's pecuniary or proprietary interest, or so far subjected him to the risk of civil or criminal liability, or so far tended to render invalid a claim by him against another, *or created such a risk of making him an object of hatred, ridicule, or social disgrace in the community*, that a reasonable man in his position would not have made the statement unless he believed it to be true (emphasis added).

The principle is relatively straightforward even though the types of statements qualifying under this exception provide an endless variety. For example, declarations of a person now deceased (i.e., unavailable) are admissible as evidence for the purpose of establishing a relevant fact, where it appears that the declarant knew the fact stated and had no interest to misrepresent it, and it was opposed to his pecuniary or proprietary interest. *Cale v. Napier*, 412 S.E.2d 242 (W.Va. 1991).

Having a daughter would not seem to constitute a disgraceful event; but admitting that one had a daughter could be deemed a declaration against that person's pecuniary interest (daughters are expensive). Such was the case in *Youmans v. Ormandy*, 424 S.E.2d 828, 206 Ga. App. 255, *cert. denied* (1992), where the court found that a decedent's assertions that the plaintiff was his daughter were admissible in a legitimation action as declarations against his pecuniary interest.

These states have a provision that is either identical or substantially similar to Fed. R. Evid. 804(b)(3) pertaining to declarations against interest:

DECLARATIONS AGAINST INTEREST

Alaska	Rule 804(b)(3)
Alabama	Rule 804(b)(3)
Arizona	Rule 804(b)(3)
Colorado	Rule 804(b)(3)
Delaware	Rule 804(b)(3)
Florida	§90.804(b)(3)
Hawaii	Rule 802.1(4)
Idaho	Rule 804(b)(3)
Illinois	Rule 804(b)(3)
Iowa	Rule 804(b)(3)
Kentucky	Rule 804(b)(3)
Louisiana	Rule 804(b)(3)
Maine	Rule 804(b)(3)
Michigan	Rule 804(b)(3)
Montana	Rule 804(b)(3)
Nebraska	Rule 804(b)(3)
Nevada	§51.345
New Hampshire	Rule 804(b)(3)
New Jersey	Rule 804(b)(3)
New Mexico	Rule 804(b)(3)
North Carolina	Rule 804(b)(3)
North Dakota	Rule 804(b)(3)
Ohio	Rule 804(b)(3)
Oklahoma	Rule 804(b)(3)
Oregon	Rule 804(b)(3)
Pennsylvania	Rule 803(b)(3)
Puerto Rico	Rule 804(b)(3)
Rhode Island	Rule 804(b)(3)
South Dakota	§19-16-32
Tennessee	Rule 804(b)(3)
Texas	(Civil) 803(24) (Criminal) 803(26)
Utah	Rule 804(b)(3)
Vermont	Rule 804(b)(3)
Washington	Rule 804(b)(3)
West Virginia	Rule 804(b)(3)
Wisconsin	Rule 804(b)(5)
Wyoming	Rule 804(b)(3)

REFERENCES

Exception where declarant unavailable.
75 A.L.R.4th 199.

§5.404 Admissions

An admission or confession is a form of "declaration against interest." But there is a difference. A declaration against interest is testimony that is offered when the person who made it is not available to testify in court. Thus, it is necessary to get the declaration in (by way of hearsay) through a witness who heard it being said. An admission, or confession, however, must have been made by someone who is an actual party to the litigation.[37] It should also be noted that an admission must be offered **against** the party who made it, and not **by** that party.

The distinction between an "admission" and a "confession" is not always easy to determine, nor is it critical in most cases. Think of an admission as spilling some of the beans ("I admit being at the scene of the heist"), and a confession as spilling the entire can ("I pulled the heist").

The policy for permitting an admission or confession is somewhat obvious. In a criminal case, for example, it is presumed that a person would not confess to the police, or make an admission of guilt to anyone for that matter, unless he were in fact guilty. This presumes, of course, that the confessor was not beaten senseless with rubber hoses.[38]

In a civil case, it is likewise presumed that a person would not admit that he or she owed money unless it were true. Nor, it is reasoned, would a person make a statement that was contrary to his or her property interests.[39]

It is interesting to note, that an admission or confession might lawfully be obtained from someone's lawyer[40] or accountant.[41]

This makes sense when you consider that the most common statement made when things hit the fan is "talk to my lawyer (or accountant)."[42]

It is quite possible for an admission to be construed and established where a person does nothing but remains silent. In particular, where a statement is made in a person's presence that adversely concerns that person's rights, then such an individual would be expected to speak up. If not, then his or her silence could be construed as an admission that the adverse statement was correct.[43]

The Federal Rules of Evidence, which abhor simplicity, treat an admission as non-hearsay, instead of an exception to the hearsay rule. In

---

37 A statement need not be against the declarant's interest at the time he makes it for it to be an admission in a criminal case. *United States v. Barletta*, 652 F.2d 218 (1st Cir. 1981). Representations made by debt collectors on their Internet website were admissible as admissions of a party-opponent in an action by purported debtors. *Van Westrienen v. Americontinental Collection Corp.,* 94 F.Supp.2d 1087 (D.Or., 2000). See also *Vojas v. K mart Corp.*, 727 N.E.2d 397, 312 Ill.App.3d 544, 245 Ill.Dec.144 (2000), and *Barnes v. Owens-Corning Fiberglas Corp.,* 201 F.3d 815 (C.A.6, Ky., 2000), and *In re Brittany L.,* 737 A.2d 670 (N.H., 1999).

38 Confessions or admissions obtained by duress or torture are not admissible under any circumstances. U. S. Const., 5th and 14th Amendments.

39 *Commonwealth v. Bartos,* 785 N.E.2d 1279, 57 Mass.App.Ct. 751 (2003). An admission of facts or a guilty plea in a criminal prosecution may be offered as a litigant's admission in a subsequent civil action. *Idleman v. Raymer,* 539 N.E.2d 828, 183 Ill. App. 3d 938, 132 Ill. Dec. 265, (Ill.App.4 Dist. 1989). The testimony of witnesses describing how a grantor told them, in various ways, that he had or would make arrangements concerning his property to favor the grantees, was admissible under the exception to the hearsay rule for an admission against economic interest.

40 *Abatti v. Commissioner*, 744 F.2d 1385 (9th Cir. 1981).

41 *United States v. Diez*, 515 F.2d 892 (5th Cir. 1975).

42 *State v. Marr,* 536 A.2d 1108 (Me. 1988). See also Lawyer-Client Privilege, Chapter 9.1.1.

43 *State v. Smith*, 824 S.W.2d 127 (Mo. App. 1992); *State v. Hill*, 823 S.W.2d 98 (Mo. App. 1991); *State v. Garcia*, 83 N.J. Super 345, 199 A.2d 860 (1964); *Casey v. Burns*, 7 Ill. App. 2d 316, 129 N.E.2d 440, 54 ALR 2d 1060 (1955); *Tillman v. Commonwealth*, 185 Va. 46, 37 S.E.2d 768 (1946); *Beck v. Dye*, 200 Wash. 1, 92 P.2d 1113, 127 ALR 1022 (1939); *Donker v. Powers*, 230 Mich. 237, 202 N.W. 989 (1925); *State v. Guffey*, 39 S.D. 84, 163 N.W. 679 (1917).

particular, Fed. R. Evid. 801(d)(2) provides that a statement is not hearsay if:

> The statement is offered against a party and is (A) the party's own statement in either an individual or a representative capacity or (B) a statement of which the party has manifested an adoption or belief in its truth, or (C) a statement by a person authorized by the party to make a statement concerning the subject, or (D) a statement by the party's agent or servant concerning a matter within the scope of the agency or employment, made during the existence of the relationship, or (E) a statement by a coconspirator of a party during the course and in furtherance of the conspiracy.

Whether it is characterized as an exception or as non-hearsay, the admission is perhaps the most clearly recognized and "definitely-admissible" hearsay-related item.[44] Consider, however, a situation where an admission, confession (or any other statement) is made under the influence of so-called "truth serum." The holdings seem to uniformly indicate that such statements may not be used to prove the truth of the matters asserted in those "drugged" statements.[45]

REFERENCES

Admissibility of statement by party's attorney under Fed. R. Evid. 801(d)(2)(C) or 801(d)(2)(D). 117 A.L.R. Fed 599.

§5.404.1 State Application

Rule 1220 of the California Evidence Code applies much more intelligent language than its federal counterpart, recognizing the foolishness and potential confusion inherent when one "deems" something "*not*" when it clearly "*is*." Instead of deeming an admission to be "non-hearsay," Rule 1220 merely says that an "admission" should not be inadmissible:

> Evidence of a statement is not made inadmissible by the hearsay rule when offered against the declarant in an action to which he is a party in either his individual or representative capacity, regardless of whether the statement was made in his individual or representative capacity.

While many states add their own minor embellishments to the "admission" exception, all uphold its spirit and intent. It is, therefore, safe to say that an admission is universally as admissible (i.e., in all fifty states) against the *party* that made it.

Missouri applies a three part test to determine the admissibility of an admission. First, the party opponent must consciously or voluntarily acknowledge the existence of certain facts; second, the matter acknowledged must be relevant to the cause of a party offering the admission; and third, the matter acknowledged must be unfavorable to, or inconsistent with, a position now taken by the party opponent. *Copeland v. Mr. B's Pool Centers, Inc.*, 850 S.W.2d 380 (Mo. App. 1993). With respect to the first test element, an admission against interest is admissible into evidence unless it is shown that the person giving it was under such a mental state that he was unable to narrate facts of the events in a manner that could be relied upon. *McElhiney v. Mossman*, 850 S.W.2d 369 (Mo. App. 1993).

In Florida, an out of court admission of a party opponent is admissible in evidence; more-

---

44 An admission of a party opponent is such a powerful and reliable piece of hearsay that it needs no separate indicia of trustworthiness in order to be admitted. See *Grace United Methodist Church v. City of Cheyenne,* 427 F.3d 775 (10th Cir., Wyo. 2005).

45 *Ramona v. Superior Court,* 57 Cal.App.4th 107, 66 Cal.Rptr.2d 766 (1997) held that there was no general acceptance for the reliability of the drug Sodium Amytal and its alleged ability to retrieve repressed childhood memories; see also *Archie v. Commonwealth*, 14 Va. App. 684, 420 S.E.2d 718 (1992). With respect to the general unreliability of "Truth Serum," see *United States v. Solomon*, 753 F.2d 1522 (9th Cir. 1985) and *People v. Stiles*, 692 P.2d 1124 (Colo. App. 1984).

over, any party is necessarily bound by any relevant admission which either he or his agent makes. *Metropolitan Dade County v. Yearby*, 580 So.2d 186 (Fla. App.3 Dist. 1991).

Generally, any statement made by a party, or on his behalf, that is relevant to a trial issue may be admitted into evidence as an admission by a party opponent. *Vojas v. K mart Corp.*, 727 N.E.2d 397, 312 Ill.App.3d 544, 245 Ill.Dec.144 (2000).

A judicial admission is a clear and unequivocal statement which is made without a reasonable chance of a mistake about a matter within the speaker's personal knowledge. *Burns v. Michelotti*, 178 Ill. Dec. 621, 604 N.E.2d 1144 (Ill. App. 2 Dist. 1992). Wisconsin agrees with this position. *Humphrey v. Elk Creek Lake Protection and Rehabilitation Dist.*, 493 N.W.2d 241, 172 Wis.2d 397 (Wis. App. 1992). In a professional malpractice action against an attorney's estate, a client's daughter (the client also died) was permitted to use the attorney's discovery deposition in evidence against his estate at trial. The attorney's statements, when he made them, constituted admissions by a party which are admissible under an exception to the hearsay rule and are also admissible against that person's estate after his death. The fact that the statements were contained in a discovery deposition doesn't change this result, even though the applicable supreme court rule does not state that nonparty discovery depositions are generally admissible after the deponent dies. *In re Estate of Rennick*, No. 82872, 286 Ill. App. 3d 318 (1997).

A store manager's statement to a clerk (to the effect that a rack, which had fallen on a customer, was not safe) was admissible as an admission. *Rush v. Troutman Inv. Co.*, 854 P.2d 968, 121 Or. App. 355 (Oregon 1993).

In Texas, the failure to mention a fact could be construed as an admission. Consider *Waldon v. City of Longview*, 855 S.W.2d 875 (Tex. App. 1993), where the court found that if an event is of such salient importance that the declarant would ordinarily have been expected to mention it, the failure of that party to mention the event in a prior statement could constitute an admission that the event did not occur.

A party's testimonial declarations that are contrary to that party's contentions in a lawsuit are generally considered as "quasi-admissions" or "judicial admissions." They equate to formal waivers of proof. *Pako Corp. v. Thomas*, 855 S.W.2d 215 (Tex. App. 1993).

In Georgia, as in most states, an admission against interest by a party is "original" evidence and is, therefore, admissible as evidence with respect to the issue of liability. *Crosby v. Cooper Tire & Rubber Co.,* 524 S.E.2d 313, 240 Ga.App. 857 (1999). And, in New Hampshire, admissions of a party-opponent are generally admissible for both substantive and impeachment purposes. *In re Brittany L.,* 737 A.2d 670 (N.H. 1999).

§5.405 Prior Inconsistent Statements

Courts are extremely generous when it comes to admitting evidence to show that someone lied, testified inconsistently, or made statements that contradicted any testimony being presented in court.[46] This reflects the important principle of

46 *State v. Jackson*, 655 N.W.2d 828 (Minn.App. 2003). In theory, the "prior inconsistent statement" exception is predicated upon a notion that the witness has made two contradictory declarations, which raises doubt, not only as to the veracity of one statement over the other, but as to the witness's personal credibility as well.

But see *Richardson v. State*, 581 S.E.2d 528 (Ga., 2003). A prior inconsistent statement is admissible for impeachment purposes only if it meets three criteria: (1) The prior statement must contradict, or be inconsistent with the witness's in-court testimony, (2) the prior statement must be relevant to the case, and (3) the examining attorney must lay a proper foundation with the witness.

Fed. R. Evid. 613 distinguishes between intrinsic impeachment [Rule 613(a)] and extrinsic impeachment [Rule 613(b)]. When examining a witness about a prior statement that he or she made (intrinsic), it is not necessary to show the witness the prior statement or a transcript of it. But if extrinsic evidence is to be used, the witness must be given an opportunity to examine it and explain the inconsistency. See also Fed. R. Evid. 801(d)(1).

justice that anyone who sings two different songs had better watch out. For it is rare indeed, that a court will keep out *any* evidence showing that a witness told a story other than the one currently being delivered from the witness stand.

This is one of those exceptions, referred to earlier, that may, in some instances, not even be hearsay to begin with. In particular, a witness' prior inconsistent statement will *not* be considered as hearsay if its only purpose is to impeach that witness, as long as the statement is not offered for the truth of the matters asserted therein.[47] Where substantive facts are alleged in the question involving the prior inconsistent statement, it has also been held that the statement would be admissible both for purposes of impeachment and also as substantive evidence of the matter asserted.[48] This latter use would be inadmissible hearsay, were it not for the exception.

Prior inconsistent statements may also be admissible for their truth where the declarant is a "turn-coat witness."[49] It has even been held that a prosecutor may impeach his own witness with prior inconsistent statements about the same matter being testified to at trial.[50] The federal position, as reflected by Rule 801(d)(1) and titled "Prior Statement by Witness," begins by indicating that, "A statement is not hearsay" if:

> The declarant testifies at the trial or hearing and is subject to cross-examination concerning the statement, and the statement is (A) inconsistent with the declarant's testimony, and was given under oath subject to the penalty of perjury at trial, hearing or other proceeding, or in a deposition, or (B) consistent with the declarant's testimony and is offered to rebut an express or implied charge against the declarant of recent fabrication or improper influence or motive, or (C) one of identification of a person made after perceiving the person.

To make totally inconsistent statements would be quite foolish. Politicians prove that regularly. Smarter fools will prefer to suffer a loss of memory. In other words, a person who makes an unfortunate statement and then is later called upon to recite it during trial, will sometimes experience a sudden loss of memory. Or, in the alternative, a person who had previously denied seeing or remembering an event may,

---

47 But see *U.S. v. LaVallee*, 439 F.3d 670 (10th Cir.Colo. 2006). If, during the course of her testimony, a witness admits to a prior inconsistent statement, this exception to the hearsay rule will not apply.

State v. McClaugherty, 64 P.3d 486 (N.M. 2003). A prior inconsistent statement made by a testifying witness may be introduced to impeach the in-court testimony of that same witness. Moreover, a prior inconsistent statement used to impeach the in-court testimony of that same witness does not constitute hearsay because, presumably, it is not being offered for the truth of the matter asserted, but rather to call into question the credibility of the in-court testimony of the testifying witness.

State v. Marr, 536 A.2d 1108 (Me. 1988); see also *Eversole v. Consolidated Rail Corp.,* 551 N.E.2d 846 (Ind. App. 1990), reh'g denied. But see *Nucci ex rel. Nucci v. Proper,* 705 N.Y.S.2d 144 (N.Y.A.D. 4 Dept., 2000), a medical malpractice action against an anesthesiologist and hospital, wherein a prior out-of-court statement at a hospital by an anesthesia intern (who happened to be 17 years old) that "nobody was paying any attention" to the patient when he stopped breathing, was not made in a writing subscribed by that intern, or under oath, and thus, was not admissible under an exception to the hearsay rule as a prior inconsistent statement after that intern testified during the patient's case-in-chief.

48 *State v. Kellner,* 103 SW.3d 363. (Mo.App., 2003). Prior inconsistent statements are admissible both to impeach and to be used as substantive evidence. *Belcher v. State,* 372 S.E.2d 650, 188 Ga. App. 244 (Ga. App. 1988); *People v. Jenkins,* 768 P.2d 727 (Colo. App. 1988). Prior contradictory statements may be used as substantive evidence when the witness is present at trial and subject to cross-examination. *Barone v. Law,* 527 S.E.2d 898, 242 Ga.App. 102, 00 FCDR 519 (2000).

49 *United States v. Rivera*, 513 F.2d 519 (2d Cir. 1975).

50 *State v. Duran*, 762 P.2d 890 (N.M. 1988).

depending upon the circumstances, experience a sudden *revitalization* of memory at trial. In either case, where a witness provides evasive answers, claims an inability to recall an event, or claims a lack of memory, the rule of the prior inconsistent statement applies. Either brand of "lack of memory" may, therefore, be testified to as constituting a prior inconsistent statement.[51]

The admission of a prior inconsistent statement in a criminal prosecution does not violate the right of confrontation that is guaranteed by the Sixth Amendment to the United States Constitution, even though it is hearsay.[52]

When an accused in a criminal case takes the witness stand, he is subject to all of the rules that apply to other witnesses, including those which allow impeachment by proof of prior inconsistent statements.[53] As a rule, prosecutorial questions and remarks concerning a defendant's post-arrest silence are generally improper, but once again, with an exception being made for impeaching a defendant's testimony with respect to prior inconsistent statements.[54]

As you can see, the courts are quite permissive with respect to their application of this particular exception. The business of trapping liars is important. After all, a trial without liars is like a hunt without game.

REFERENCES

Admissibility of party's own statement. 48 A.L.R. Fed 922.

Admissibility of witness' prior inconsistent statement. 47 A.L.R. Fed 639.

§5.405.1 State Application

One way or another, the prior inconsistent statement of a witness should always be admissible, since it has a direct impact upon the witness' credibility. Rule 1235 of the California Evidence Code provides as follows:

> Evidence of a statement made by a witness is not made inadmissible by the hearsay rule if the statement is inconsistent with his testimony at the hearing and is offered in compliance with CEC 770.

The "CEC 770" qualifier is similar in structure to the federal distinction between intrinsic and extrinsic evidence. In particular, CEC 770 provides for the exclusion of extrinsic statements unless the witness is provided with an opportunity to explain the inconsistency.

To "set up" an inconsistency, a foundation may be required. Without sufficient specificity, the witness may not have an adequate opportunity to explain or deny the ostensible inconsistency. In that situation, the trial court would properly refuse to allow such evidence. *People v. Garcia*, 273 Cal. Rptr. 666, 224 C.A.3d 297 (Cal. App. 4 Dist. 1990).

In New York, a prior statement made by a defendant during police questioning may be admissible to impeach that defendant's testimony, even where the statement was obtained in violation of the defendant's right to counsel. *People v. Palmer*, 596 N.Y.S.2d 522 (N.Y.A.D. 3 Dept. 1993). With respect to inconsistent statements by practitioners in medical malpractice cases, see *Nucci ex rel. Nucci v. Proper,* 705 N.Y.S.2d 144 (N.Y.A.D. 4 Dept., 2000).

In Georgia, the prior inconsistent statement of a witness who takes the stand and is subject to cross-examination is admissible as substantive evidence; the statement, therefore, is not limited in any way to impeachment purposes. *Barone v. Law,* 527 S.E.2d 898, 242 Ga.App. 102, 00 FCDR 519 (2000); *Bogan v. State*, 426 S.E.2d

51 *United States v. Dennis*, 625 F.2d 782 (8th Cir. 1980); *United States v. Insana*, 423 F.2d 1165 (2d Cir. 1970).

52 *California v. Green*, 399 U.S. 149 (1970).

53 *Boyd v. State*, 774 S.W.2d 37 (Tex. App. 1989); *State v. Poullard*, 532 So.2d 327 (La. App. 3 Cir. 1988); see also *State v. Babich*, 842 P.2d 1053 (Wash. App. 1993).

54 *People v. Pegram*, 124 Ill. Dec. 525, 529 N.E.2d 506, 124 Ill.2d 166 (Ill. 1988).

392, 206 Ga. App. 696, *cert. denied* (1992). Note that inconsistency is the key element of this hearsay exception; "surprise," therefore, is not a required element, even when one wants to impeach his own witness. *McGee v. State*, 423 S.E.2d 666, 205 Ga. App. 722 (1992). A witness may thus be impeached by evidence of contradictory statements that he previously made as to matters relevant to his testimony in the case. *Olivaria v. State*, 428 S.E.2d 624 (Ga. App. 1993). Accordingly, a defendant's confession may be admissible at his trial as a prior inconsistent statement, where that defendant admitted that statement was made after he was given his *Miranda* warnings. *Mack v. State*, 432 S.E.2d 680 (Ga. App. 1993).

In Florida, to be a *prior inconsistent statement*, the statement must either directly contradict or materially differ from expected testimony at trial; and, moreover, the inconsistency must involve a material fact rather than mere details. *State v. Smith*, 573 So.2d 306 (Fla. 1990). A witness may not be impeached by statements of irrelevant or immaterial matters. *Mathews v. State*, 574 So.2d 1174 (Fla. App.5 Dist. 1991). Where prior inconsistent statements are permitted, they should be used to impeach, not for substantive proof. *Anderson v. State*, 574 So.2d 87 (Fla. 1991).

In Illinois, impeachment of a witness by means of a prior inconsistent statement is permissible only where the statement has a reasonable tendency to discredit testimony on a material matter; the inconsistency must be substantial and not merely trivial or collateral. *Burke v. 12 Rothschild's Liquor Mart, Inc.*, 154 Ill.Dec. 80, 568 N.E.2d 80, 209 Ill. App.3d 192 (Ill. App. 1 Dist. 1991).

In the Louisiana case, *State v. Smith*, 594 So.2d 467, *rehearing denied* (La. App. 1991), the defendant (at his second trial) was held to have been denied his constitutional right to fully cross-examine and impeach a police officer's testimony from the first trial, because he wasn't permitted to introduce inconsistent statements made by an officer in a police report.

The Missouri case of *State v. Thomas*, 820 S.W.2d 538 (Mo. App. 1991) presents an interesting dilemma. A witness stated to the police that the defendant admitted having killed someone. At trial, however, the witness specifically denied hearing the defendant make such a statement. So the initial statement given by the witness to the police was admissible, not just for purposes of impeachment, but as substantive evidence. The witness must be a liar; but was he lying when he said that the defendant made the statement? Or was he lying on the stand? By admitting the statement as substantive evidence, isn't the court guessing that the liar's first position was correct?

In Nevada, extrinsic proof of a prior inconsistent statement is inadmissible, unless the statement is material to the case at hand. *Lobato v. State*, 96 P.3d 765 (2004).

If, during cross-examination, a witness admits unequivocally to having made a prior statement, then impeachment is complete and the prior statement is, therefore, not admissible. *Downen v. Texas Gulf Shrimp Co.*, 846 S.W.2d 506 (Tex. App. 1993).

If a witness gives testimony that is inconsistent with a prior statement or testifies that he or she does not recall making the prior statement, sufficient foundation for impeachment has been laid, and the opposing counsel may cross-examine the witness as to the inconsistency. *Smith v. Com.*, 425 S.E.2d 95 (Va. App. 1992).

With respect to the states that we have yet to mention, the reader might note that every jurisdiction (i.e., all fifty states) recognizes the admissibility of prior inconsistent statements. Some may permit the statements as substantive evidence, but all will permit such evidence to be used for purposes of impeachment.

§5.406 Statements of Mental or Physical Condition

Moans, groans, coughs, and exclamations of physical or mental disturbances are admissible as exceptions to the hearsay rule.[55] A lay witness may, therefore, testify about observing pain in another person.[56] Also, an injured party is always competent to testify as to his or her own pain and suffering, and to describe the physical injuries even though that witness may not be competent to testify with respect to his or her own prognosis and treatment.[57] The concept behind this exception is the notion that physical or mental conditions are spontaneous reactions that are not "faked" and must, therefore, be trustworthy. I, however, disagree, as would any kid who ever feigned illness to skip school on report card day.

Fed. R. Evid. 803(3) carves out the following hearsay exception:

> A statement of the declarant's then existing state of mind, emotion, sensation, or physical condition (such as intent, plan, motive, design, mental feeling, pain, and bodily health), but not including a statement of memory or belief to prove the fact remembered or believed unless it relates to the execution, revocation, identification, or terms of declarant's will.

Notice that physical manifestations are not the only items that fit into the exception. Here is a statement that has probably been made by more than one president: "I've got to drop my vice president before the next election because he is a moron." That statement would be admissible to show the motive or reason why the vice president was dropped. But it would not be admissible to prove the actual intelligence of the vice president.

REFERENCES

Mental, emotional, or physical condition exception to hearsay rule. 75 A.L.R. Fed 170.

§5.406.1 State Application

Rule 1250 of the California Evidence Code is similar in content to Fed. R. Evid. 803(3) (see §5.406). CEC 1251 liberalizes admissibility by permitting statements made about pre-existing conditions where the declarant is unavailable, but only if the statement is not being used to prove a fact other than state of mind, emotion, or physical sensation and only if such statement is material.

CEC 1252 imposes an additional condition. The evidence will be inadmissible if it is untrustworthy. That standard provides the court with very broad discretion.

Illinois stays on the main road with respect to this exception. A statement is admissible under a hearsay exception if that statement expresses the declarant's then existing state of mind, emotion, sensation, or physical condition, such as an intent, plan, motive or design, mental feeling, pain or bodily health; but the exception does not extend to a declaration of having performed a past act. *In re Estate of Holmgren*, 178 Ill. Dec. 569, 604 N.E.2d 1092 (Ill. App. 1992), *Horace Mann Ins. Co. v. Brown*, 177 Ill. Dec. 690, 603 N.E.2d 760, 236 Ill. App.3d 456 (Ill. App. 1992). Accordingly, statements made by children as to

---

55 Statements to doctors and therapists are among the most common. See *Willingham v. Crooke*, 412 F.3d 553, 67 Fed. R. Evid. Serv. 6776 (4th Cir. Va. 2005), a §1983 action by an arrestee against a policeman alleging an arrest without probable cause. The arrestee's statements to a treating physician about the officer's pointing a firearm at her during the course of the arrest were pertinent to her diagnosis and treatment for emotional trauma and, thus, were admissible under the hearsay exception for statements made for purposes of a medical diagnosis or treatment. Admissibility is governed by a two-part test: (1) the declarant's motive in making the statement must be consistent with the purposes of promoting treatment, and (2) the content of the statement must be such that it would be reasonably relied on for treatment or diagnosis by a physician.

56 *Nichols v. Marshall*, 486 F.2d 791 (10th Cir. 1973).

57 *Graves v. Graves*, 531 So.2d 817 (Miss. 1988).

whom they prefer as their custodian, or where they desire to live, are admissible as state-of-mind exceptions to the hearsay rule. *In re Marriage of Deckard*, 186 Ill. Dec. 270, 615 N.E.2d 1327 (Ill. App. 1993).

Consider an automobile negligence action; statements made to a physician for the purposes of treatment fall within the exception because it will be presumed that an injured person will not prevaricate at the instant of his injury or while stating a physical condition to a physician from whom he expects aid. Therefore, the testimony of an automobile accident victim as to statements made to him during his emergency treatment by unidentified medical personnel and his responses thereto, are not hearsay; the statements may be admitted, not for the truth of matters asserted, but rather for the limited purpose of demonstrating the effect of the statements on the victim's state of mind relative to his claim for pain and suffering. *Caponi v. Larry's 66*, 176 Ill. Dec. 649, 601 N.E.2d 1347 (Ill. App. 1992).

Consider an Oregon case involving a driver's statement to a treating physician (shortly after being transported from an accident scene) that he had suddenly lost consciousness without warning; that statement was held to be admissible as having been made for purposes of medical diagnosis and treatment, even though the driver's statement was exculpatory. *Hansen v. Heath*, 852 P.2d 977 (Utah 1993).

Poems and a tombstone epitaph written by parents of a motorcycle passenger were admissible under the state-of-mind exception to the hearsay rule in a wrongful death action to establish mental anguish. *Warhurst v. White*, 838 S.W.2d 350, 310 Ark. 546 (1992).

A child sex abuse victim's statements to her therapist regarding the identity of her abusers were admissible in a domestic relations proceeding as statements describing the "general character of the cause" of her injuries and as statements "reasonably pertinent" to the therapist's diagnosis or treatment; therefore, the requirements of the hearsay exception were met. The "medical diagnosis or treatment" exception to the hearsay rule is a firmly rooted exception, such that reliability of statements falling under such an exception may be inferred. *State ex rel. Juvenile Dept. of Multnomah County v. Cornett,* 855 P.2d 171, 121 Or. App. 264 (1993).

These states have a provision that is either identical or substantially similar to Fed. R. Evid 803(3) pertaining to statements of mental or physical conditions:

STATEMENTS OF MENTAL OR PHYSICAL CONDITIONS

Alaska	Rule 803(3)
Alabama	Rule 803(3)
Arizona	Rule 803(3)
Colorado	Rule 803(3)
Delaware	Rule 803(3)
Florida	§90.803(3)
Hawaii	Rule 803(b)(3)
Idaho	Rule 803(3)
Illinois	Rule 803(3)
Iowa	Rule 803(3)
Kentucky	Rule 803(3)
Louisiana	Rule 803(3)
Maine	Rule 803(3)
Michigan	Rule 803(3)
Montana	Rule 803(3)
Nebraska	Rule 803(3)
Nevada	§51.105
New Hampshire	Rule 803(3)
New Jersey	Rule 803(3)
New Mexico	Rule 803(3)
North Carolina	Rule 803(3)
North Dakota	Rule 803(3)
Ohio	Rule 803(3)
Oklahoma	Rule 803(3)
Oregon	Rule 803(3)
Pennsylvania	Rule 803(3)
Puerto Rico	Rule 803(3)
Rhode Island	Rule 803(3)
South Dakota	§19-16-7
Tennessee	Rule 803(3)
Texas (Civil & Criminal)	803(3)
Utah	Rule 803(3)
Vermont	Rule 803(3)
Washington	Rule 803(3)
West Virginia	Rule 803(3)
Wisconsin	Rule 804(b)(5)
Wyoming	Rule 803(3)

§5.407 Dying Declarations

People preparing to meet their maker don't tell lies. Those who are preparing to die, and know it, will only speak truth; at least, that's what the creators of this exception believed.[58]

This is a very narrow exception to the hearsay rule. Normally it will only apply in extreme cases where the speaker is so close to death that there is no hope, whatsoever, of recovery.[59] Then, so as not to disappoint the audience, the speaker is normally required to die (under earlier common law).

In the case of *People v. Mackey*,[60] the victim provided an answer to that most common dying declaration question: "Who shot you?" The answer was held to be admissible.

A typical case involved Edward Conner, who in 1959 used an atypical murder weapon to erase his ex-wife; he ran her over with the family automobile. Before she died, a police officer asked her: "Did your husband do this to you?" She answered "Yes."

The officer then asked a question that was *both* leading and speculative: "Was this an accident or was it deliberate?" She answered: "It was no accident." Judge Horney held on appeal (from a conviction resulting from a trial where the statements were used) that when a dying declaration is involved, leading questions and even "urgent" solicitation may be used.[61]

Fed. R. Evid. 804(b)(2) recognizes this exception by providing that hearsay should not be excluded where:

> In a prosecution for homicide or in a civil action or proceeding, a statement made by a declarant while believing that the declarant's death was imminent, concerning the cause or circumstances of what the declarant believed to be impending death.

For this exception to be applicable, the declarant must be unavailable, but not necessarily dead.[62]

REFERENCES

Exception where declarant unavailable.
75 A.L.R.4th 199.

§5.407.1 State Application

Rule 1242 of the California Evidence Code is similar to Fed. R. Evid. 804(b)(2). The federal rule, however, limits the application to civil actions and prosecutions for homicide; CEC 1242 makes no such limitation. CEC 1242 provides that:

> Evidence of a statement made by a dying person respecting the cause and circumstances of his death is not made inadmissible by the hearsay rule if the statement was made upon his personal knowledge and under a sense of immediately impending death.

Presumably, under CEC 1242, a dying declaration can be used in any type of criminal prosecution; not so under Fed. R. Evid. 804(b)(2) (see §5.407).

58 *People v. Bazaure,* 44 Cal. Rptr. 831, 235 C.A.2d 21, *cert. denied,* 86 S. Ct. 1951, 384 U.S. 1026, 16 L.Ed.2d 1032, *reh'g denied*, 87 S.Ct. 21, 385 U.S. 892, 17 L.Ed.2d 125 (1965); *Connor v. State*, 171 A.2d 699, 225 Md. 543, 86 A.L.R.2d 892, *cert. denied*, 82 S.Ct. 186, 368 U.S. 906, 7 L.Ed.2d 100 (1961); *Burton v. State*, 101 So.2d 564, 39 Ala. App. 332, *cert. denied*, 101 So.2d 572, 267 Ala. 354 (1958); *Helton v. State*, 255 S.W.2d 694, 195 Tenn. 36, *cert. denied*, 74 S.Ct. 28, 346 U.S. 816, 98 L.Ed. 343 (1953); *Missouri Pac. R. Co. v. Haigler*, 158 S.W.2d 703, 230 Ark. 840 (1942).

59 *Shepard v. United States,* 290 U.S. 96 (1933). A statement by a driver, for example, who subsequently died of injuries from his automobile accident, was not admissible as a statement made under belief of impending death, (for the purpose of casting doubt as to who hit whom), because the proponent failed to show that the driver believed that his death was in fact imminent. *Vazquez v. National Car Rental, System, Inc.,* 24 F.Supp.2d 197 (D.Puerto Rico, 1998).

60 185 Colo 24, 521 P.2d 910 (1974).

61 *Conner v. State*, 225 Md. 543, 171 A.2d 699, 86 A.L.R.2d 892 (1961).

62 *Johnson v. People*, 152 Colo. 586, 384 P.2d 454 (1963); *People v. Pickett*, 339 Mich. 294, 63 N.W.2d 681 (1954).

The state of Colorado does not recognize the dying declaration as a valid exception to the hearsay rule.

In North Carolina, to fall within the hearsay exception for dying declarations, the subject declaration must deal with the cause and circumstances of the declarant's anticipated death. *Ferguson v. Williams*, 399 S.E.2d 389, 101 N.C.App. 265 (1991). This state's rule is, by no means, universally accepted.

The following states have a provision that is either identical or substantially similar to Fed. R. Evid. 804(b)(2) pertaining to dying declarations:

DYING DECLARATIONS

Alaska	Rule 804(b)(2)
Alabama	Rule 804(b)(2)
Arizona	Rule 804(b)(2)
Delaware	Rule 804(b)(2)
Florida	§90.804(2)(b)
Hawaii	Rule 803(b)(3)
Idaho	Rule 804(b)(2)
Illinois	Rule 804(b)(2)
Iowa	Rule 804(b)(2)
Kentucky	Rule 804(b)(2)
Louisiana	Rule 804(B)(2)
Maine	Rule 804(b)(2)
Michigan	Rule 804(b)(2)
Montana	Rule 804(b)(2)
Nebraska	Rule 804(2)(b)
Nevada	§51.335
New Hampshire	Rule 804(b)(2)
New Jersey	Rule 804(b)(2)
New Mexico	Rule 804(b)(2)
North Carolina	Rule 804(b)(2)
North Dakota	Rule 804(b)(2)
Ohio	Rule 804(b)(2)
Oklahoma	Rule 804(b)(2)
Oregon	Rule 804(3)(b)
Pennsylvania	Rule 804(b)(2)
Puerto Rico	Rule 804(B)(2)
Rhode Island	Rule 804(b)(2)
South Dakota	§19-16-31
Tennessee	Rule 804(b)(2)
Texas (Civil & Criminal)	804(b)(2)
Utah	Rule 804(b)(2)
Vermont	Rule 804(b)(2)
Washington	Rule 804(b)(2)
West Virginia	Rule 804(b)(2)
Wisconsin	Rule 804(3)
Wyoming	Rule 804(b)(2)

§5.408 Spontaneous and Contemporaneous Declarations

A lay witness may testify as to a look of sudden surprise on the face of another individual.[63] He or she may also testify, in general, as to an emotional state observed in another person.[64]

Sudden reactions or exclamations (sometimes called "excited utterances"), even confessions, are often made without thought; and therefore, it is reasoned that the exclaimer would not have had time to fabricate any false statements. This particular hearsay exception has several facets.[65]

"Excited utterances" are not confined to statements describing or explaining the startling event itself. They may describe incidents remote in time from that event, as long as the statement is made while the declarant is still in a state of excitement.[66]

An excited utterance has been defined as a spontaneous declaration by a person whose mind has been suddenly made subject to an overpowering emotion caused by some unexpected and shocking occurrence.[67] To establish the exception, the circumstances must show that it was the

63 *New York Life Insurance Co. v. Harrington*, 299 F.2d 803 (9th Cir. 1962).

64 *Cole v. United States*, 327 F.2d 360 (9th Cir. 1964).

65 See *McCormick on Evidence*, 2d Ed., Chapter 29 (West Publishing Co., 1972).

66 *City of Dallas v. Donovan*, 768 S.W.2d 905 (Tex. App.-Dallas 1989).

67 *Lira v. Albert Einstein Medical Center*, 559 A.2d 550 (Pa. Super. 1989).

event speaking through a person and not a person speaking about the event.[68] But a statement otherwise admissible under the excited utterance exception to the hearsay rule is admissible even though it was made in response to an inquiry.[69]

Fed. R. Evid. 803(2) provides the following definition:

> A statement relating to a startling event or condition made while the declarant was under the stress of excitement caused by the event or condition.

A statement was once made by a motorist on first happening upon a serious intersection accident. The statement was to the effect that she had notified the city of a missing stop sign days prior to the collision. This was held to be sufficiently "related" to the startling event for evidence of the statement to be admissible under the "excited utterance" exception to the hearsay rule.[70]

Closely related to this exception is the "present sense impression" exception, which is defined by Fed. R. Evid. 803(1) as:

> A statement describing or explaining an event or condition made while the declarant was perceiving the event or condition, or immediately thereafter.

As the notes of The Advisory Committee indicate: "In considerable measure these two examples overlap, though based on somewhat different theories. The most significant practical difference will lie in the time lapse allowable between event and statement."[71]

REFERENCES

When is hearsay statement admissible as excited utterance? 48 A.L.R. Fed 451.

Admissibility of the present sense impression. 60 A.L.R. Fed 524.

§5.408.1 State Application

With respect to spontaneous declarations, Rule 1240 of the California Evidence Code appears to be broader than its federal counterpart, Rule 803(2), by *not* requiring the subject event to be "startling" (see §5.408, *supra*). CEC 1240 provides that:

> Evidence of a statement is not made inadmissible by the hearsay rule if the statement:
> (a) Purports to narrate, describe, or explain an act, condition, or event perceived by the declarant; and
> (b) Was made spontaneously while the declarant was under the stress of excitement caused by such perception.

---

68 *Harris v. Toys "R" Us-Penn, Inc.*, 880 A.2d 1270 (Pa. Super., 2005). In a personal injury suit brought against the store by a patron who suffered a head injury when struck by a toy that allegedly fell from shelf, an unidentified declarant's hearsay statement that he had just placed the unit in question back on the store shelf after showing it to a customer and had not placed it correctly was not admissible under the excited utterance exception to the hearsay rule. There was no evidence that the declarant showed or expressed any emotion at all, let alone an overpowering emotion, and there was no evidence that the declarant participated in, or closely witnessed, the patron's accident. An "excited utterance," for purposes of the exception to the hearsay rule, is a spontaneous declaration: (1) by a person whose mind is affected by an overpowering emotion caused by some unexpected occurrence, (2) which that person had just participated in or closely witnessed, and (3) is made so near the occurrence both in time and place as to exclude the likelihood of it being a product, in whole or in part, of his reflective faculties. *First Southwest Lloyds Ins. Co. v. MacDowell,* 769 S.W.2d 954 (Tex. App.-Texarkana 1989).

69 *In re Jean Marie W.*, 559 A.2d 625 (R.I. 1989).

70 *City of Dallas v. Donovan,* 768 S.W.2d 905 (Tex. App.- Dallas 1989).

71 The present sense impression hearsay exception allows testimony concerning events observed by the declarant regardless of whether or not the declarant was excited. Under this exception, the statement must be made at the time of the event or so shortly thereafter so that the declarant would be unlikely to have the opportunity to decide to make a false statement.

California Evidence Code Section 1241, referring to "contemporaneous statements," provides additional breadth to this hearsay exception:

> Evidence of a statement is not made inadmissible by the hearsay rule if the statement:
> (a) Is offered to explain, qualify, or make understandable conduct of the declarant; and
> (b) Was made while the declarant was engaged in such conduct.

The fact that a statement may have been made in response to questioning does not render it non-spontaneous, if the questioning was simple and non-suggestive. *In re Daniel Z.*, 13 Cal. Rptr.2d 139, 10 C.A.4th 1009 (Cal. App. 1992).

Michigan, unlike California, does require a "startling occasion." In *Berryman v. K Mart Corp.*, 483 N.W.2d 642, 193 Mich. App. 88 (1992), the Michigan Court of Appeals held that for a statement to come within the excited utterance exception of the hearsay rule, it must arise out of an occasion "sufficiently startling" to produce a nervous excitement so as to render the statement spontaneous and unreflecting. It must be made while the declarant is still under the influence of that nervous excitement, before there is any time to contrive or misrepresent, and it must relate to the circumstances of the startling occasion that the declarant observed.

In New York, a bus driver's out-of-court statement to the effect that an unidentified driver had "cut him off," and caused the subject collision, was not admissible under the excited utterance exception to the hearsay rule, because there was no showing with respect to the driver's demeanor or emotional state at the time the statement was made. *Lieb v. County of Westchester*, 575 N.Y.S.2d 87 (1991).

In another case, a woman slipped between two subway cars, and was dragged down the track. An excited bystander gestured wildly as if in a state of shock; he told a platform conductor that a woman was hanging on a subway train as it left the station. The statement was admissible; an excited utterance or spontaneous declaration is admissible as an exception to the hearsay rule. The statement was made under the immediate and uncontrolled domination of the senses during a brief period when considerations of self-interest were not brought to bear. *Taft v. New York City Transit Authority*, 597 N.Y.S.2d.2d 374 (N.Y.A.D. 1 Dept. 1993).

A New York court took the trouble to distinguish between an excited utterance and a present sense impression. In *Berger v. City of New York*, 597 N.Y.S.2d 555 (N.Y. Sup. 1993), the court noted that the rationale for admitting a "present sense impression" is that the statement is reliable because it is contemporaneous in time with the subject event or occurrence, allowing no time for reflection, recollection or deliberate misrepresentation. An "excited utterance" (or "res gestae") exception requires a shocking experience or the excitement of the incident or event that triggered the outburst. See also *Tyrrell v. Wal-Mart Stores Inc.,* 719 N.Y.S.2d 163 (N.Y.A.D., 2000) holding that spontaneous declarations, made contemporaneously with, or immediately after startling event are also generally admissible as part of res gestae exception to hearsay rule.

In Ohio, a child walked into her house accompanying her crying brother, whose eye had just been injured by a snapping branch. Her statement, contradicting her sister's assertion about responsibility for the accident, was admissible as an excited utterance. The statement was spontaneous and made immediately after she walked into the house. The evidence indicated that the child and her brother were both in the woods at the time of the accident. *Williams v. Williams*, 589 N.E.2d 89, 68 Ohio App.3d 529 (1990).

In Texas, a statement relating to a startling event or condition, made while the declarant is under the stress of the excitement caused by that event, is not excluded by the hearsay rule. In *Texas Utilities Electric Co. v. Gold Kist, Inc.*, 817 S.W.2d 749 (Tex. App. 1991), some electrical lines broke and started a fire at a nearby warehouse. Within 15 minutes, a trucking company's traffic manager, who was at the scene of the fire, said that he had told a utility company representative to move a utility pole guy wire "a dozen times." The statement fell within the excited utterance exception to hearsay rule.

In *Almaraz v. Burke*, 827 S.W.2d 80, *error denied* (Tex. App. 1992), the hearsay testimony of an investigating officer as to a van's license plate was admissible as a statement made while under stress caused by an event or condition; the number was obtained from motorists who had either been involved in the accident, or had witnessed it. This is the first time I ever heard of anyone shrieking out a license plate number during a heated moment; perhaps this was the best hearsay exception pigeonhole for a very reliable piece of unadulterated hearsay.

A statement, made within one minute of a serious accident, was admissible as a hearsay exception; the declarant appeared extremely nervous, shaken and upset at the time of the statement. *Behm v. Northwestern Bell Telephone Co.*, 491 N.W.2d 334, 241 Neb. 838 (1992).

Illinois dealt with a statement made shortly after a fatal automobile collision, in the case of *Caponi v. Larry's 66*, 176 Ill. Dec. 649, 601 N.E.2d 1347 (Ill. App. 1992). The statements were made to an accident victim during his emergency treatment by unidentified medical personnel; the statements were admissible under the excited utterance exception because they were made under circumstances that did not permit reflection or rationalization.[72]

There are, according to *In re Estate of Peters*, 765 A.2d 468 (Vt. 2000), two essential requirements for asserting the excited utterance exception to the hearsay rule:

1. A startling event or condition, and
2. A spontaneous utterance in reaction to that event or condition, made under stress of excitement and not as result of reflective thought.

The following states have a provision that is either identical or substantially similar to Fed. R. Evid. 803(1) pertaining to present sense impressions:

PRESENT SENSE IMPRESSIONS

Alaska	Rule 803(1)
Alabama	Rule 803(1)
Arizona	Rule 803(1)
Colorado	Rule 803(1)
Delaware	Rule 803(1)
Florida	§90.803(1)
Hawaii	Rule 803(1)
Idaho	Rule 803(1)
Illinois	Rule 803(1)
Iowa	Rule 803(1)
Kentucky	Rule 803(1)
Louisiana	Rule 803(1)
Maine	Rule 803(1)
Michigan	Rule 803(1)
Montana	Rule 803(1)
Nebraska	Rule 803(1)
Nevada	§51.075
New Hampshire	Rule 803(1)
New Jersey	Rule 803(c)(1)
New Mexico	Rule 803(1)
North Carolina	Rule 803(1)
North Dakota	Rule 803(1)
Ohio	Rule 803(1)
Oklahoma	Rule 803(1)
Oregon	Rule 803(1)
Pennsylvania	Rule 803(1)
Puerto Rico	Rule 803(1)
Rhode Island	Rule 803(1)
South Dakota	§19-16-5
Tennessee	Rule 803(1)
Texas (Civil & Criminal)	Rule 803(1)
Utah	Rule 803(1)
Vermont	Rule 803(1)
Washington	Rule 803(1)
West Virginia	Rule 803(1)

72 With respect to a child's "outcry statement," see *People v. Bowen*, Illinois Supreme Court Opinion No. 83687, 289 Ill. App. 3d 378 (1997). Even though the child's accusatory statements came a month (and then again, three years) after an alleged sexual assault by a baby-sitter, the "outcry," which was used as corroborating evidence to convict, occurred as soon as the child came into contact with the baby-sitter following the incident. The mother noticed that the child, who was only three years old at the time, became hysterical and cried at the sight of the defendant.

Wisconsin	Rule 803(1)
Wyoming	Rule 803(1)

The following states have a provision that is either identical or substantially similar to Fed. R. Evid. 803(2) pertaining to spontaneous declarations:

SPONTANEOUS DECLARATIONS

Alaska	Rule 803(2)
Alabama	Rule 803(2)
Arizona	Rule 803(2)
Colorado	Rule 803(2)
Delaware	Rule 803(2)
Florida	§90.803(2)
Hawaii	Rule 803(2)
Idaho	Rule 803(2)
Iowa	Rule 803(2)
Kentucky	Rule 803(2)
Louisiana	Rule 803(2)
Maine	Rule 803(2)
Michigan	Rule 803(2)
Montana	Rule 803(2)
Nebraska	Rule 803(2)
Nevada	§51.085
New Hampshire	Rule 803(2)
New Mexico	Rule 803(2)
North Carolina	Rule 803(2)
North Dakota	Rule 803(2)
Ohio	Rule 803(2)
Oklahoma	Rule 803(2)
Oregon	Rule 803(2)
Puerto Rico	Rule 803(2)
Rhode Island	Rule 803(2)
South Dakota	§19-16-6
Tennessee	Rule 803(2)
Texas (Civil & Criminal)	Rule 803(2)
Utah	Rule 803(2)
Vermont	Rule 803(2)
Washington	Rule 803(2)
West Virginia	Rule 803(2)
Wisconsin	Rule 803(2)
Wyoming	Rule 803(2)

§5.409 Statements of Reputation

Statements involving "reputation" constitute what is, perhaps, the worst kind of hearsay. As everyone knows, reputation is usually based upon multiple hearsay, rumors, and colored comments from angry in-laws and ex-spouses. It would indeed, therefore, be intelligent to ask the question, "Why would such a statement be considered an exception to the hearsay rule?" For this, we can only speculate that as a matter of common law, perhaps hundreds of years ago when the exception was born, villages were smaller and reputation hearsay was more reliable. But I doubt it.

In any event, it is a recognized common law exception to the hearsay rule, and it is recognized by the Federal Rules of Evidence.[73] It has been held, for example, that evidence that a witness was a resident of a community and had known a person for more than two years, established a proper foundation for that witness testifying that the person in question had a reputation as a car thief.[74]

Cross-examining a witness who offers testimony about a party's reputation could be very difficult. The witness may not be able to recall specific statements as being attributed to specific people.[75] Where the witness **is** able to provide some recollection, his or her memory may still be based on further hearsay.

There are three separate provisions in the Federal Rules that purport to deal with "reputation" evidence. Fed. R. Evid. 803(19) deals specifically with testimony involving relationships such as adoption, marriage, legitimacy, birth, death, and other matters involving family history. Rule 803(20), titled, "Reputation concerning boundaries or general history," describes that exception as follows:

> Reputation in a community, arising before the controversy, as to the boundaries of or

73 See FRE 803(20) and 803(21).

74 *Brown v. State*, 762 P.2d 959 (Okla.Crim. App. 1988).

75 For discussions about cross-examining character witnesses by using hypothetical questions, see *U.S. v. Siers,* 873 F.2d 747 (4th Cir. 1989).

> customs affecting lands in the community or state or nation in which located.

Rule 803(21), concerning reputation as to character, is the juicy provision. It merely describes the defines the exception as:

> Reputation of a person's character among associates or in the community.

REFERENCES

Attacking or supporting credibility of witness by evidence in form of opinion or reputation. 52 A.L.R. Fed 440.

§5.409.1 State Application

Rule 1320 of the California Evidence Code provides as follows:

> Evidence of reputation in a community is not made inadmissible by the hearsay rule if the reputation concerns an event of general history of the community or of the state or nation of which the community is a part and the event was of importance to the community.

This would appear to restrict the common law notion that seemed to permit community gossip and rumors. The "event of general history" requirement would limit admissibility to items of more ubiquitous repute.

A complaining witness in a sex offense case may be impeached by evidence that her general reputation for truth and veracity is bad but not by acts of specific conduct. *State v. Foster*, 854 S.W.2d 1 (Mo. App. 1993).

Although the reputation of a witness for veracity in the community is relevant in assessing credibility, questions about whether that person ever lied or exaggerated provide no helpful information in assessing credibility in the absence of a foundation that would tie the characterization to a "general reputation" in the community. *State v. Morgan*, 608 N.E.2d 1114, 80 Ohio App.3d 150 (Ohio App. 1992).

The following states have a provision that is either identical or substantially similar to Fed. R. Evid. 803(21) pertaining to character reputation:

CHARACTER REPUTATION

Alaska	Rule 803(21)
Alabama	Rule 803(21)
Arizona	Rule 803(21)
Colorado	Rule 803(21)
Delaware	Rule 803(21)
Florida	§90.803(21)
Hawaii	Rule 803(b)(21)
Idaho	Rule 803(21)
Illinois	Rule 803(21)
Iowa	Rule 803(21)
Kentucky	Rule 803(21)
Louisiana	Rule 803(21)
Maine	Rule 803(21)
Michigan	Rule 803(21)
Montana	Rule 803(21)
Nebraska	Rule 803(21)
Nevada	§51.285
New Hampshire	Rule 803(21)
New Jersey	Rule 803(c)(21)
New Mexico	Rule 803(21)
North Carolina	Rule 803(21)
North Dakota	Rule 803(21)
Ohio	Rule 803(21)
Oklahoma	Rule 803(21)
Oregon	Rule 803(21)
Pennsylvania	Rule 803(21)
Puerto Rico	Rule 803(21)
Rhode Island	Rule 803(21)
South Dakota	§19-16-25
Tennessee	Rule 803(21)
Texas (Civil & Criminal)	Rule 803(21)
Utah	Rule 803(21)
Vermont	Rule 803(21)
Washington	Rule 803(21)
West Virginia	Rule 803(21)
Wisconsin	Rule 803(21)
Wyoming	Rule 803(21)

§5.410 Business Records and Other Documents

As we considered earlier, written hearsay is no less "hearsay" than verbal hearsay. Most people can write lies as well as they can speak them. There is, therefore, little difference. However, there are certain documents that have, over the years, achieved status as important exceptions to the hearsay rule. For without those documents, people could not establish important things in court, such as unpaid bills, medical records, information contained in treatises, recognized books, or market reports.

When offering verbal testimony about the substance of documents, a lawyer faces two problems. First, there is the best evidence rule to contend with (see Chapter 2), then comes the more immediate problem involving hearsay. Once the documents are presented in court, assuming that they are originals, or acceptable "duplicates," the best evidence rule will be satisfied. That is important to keep in mind.

The hearsay problem is another matter, however. But as the title of this section indicates, there are several exceptions.

The most important single exception to the hearsay rule is usually referred to as the "business records" exception. There are a lot of different names for it. Sometimes it is referred to as the "regularly conducted activity rule." Both merely state that business records (or records of a regularly conducted activity) form an exception to the hearsay rule and may be admitted into evidence, upon the laying of a proper foundation.[76]

The business records rule is a very powerful one, particularly since the records may be admitted even though the person laying the foundation did not *personally* prepare them or display any knowledge of their contents.[77] Thus, business records utilized for the purpose of showing the amount of cargo loaded onto a ship were admissible even though no one with first-hand knowledge was present to testify.[78] Also, hotel telephone logs are admissible as records of a regularly conducted activity.[79] The key element is that the records must be kept in the normal or regular course of the activity or business.[80]

Very closely associated with the business records exception is the "official records" exception to the hearsay rule. As a matter of fact, it may be said that all official records are, by their nature, *also* records kept pursuant to some regularly conducted activity. Consider, for example, the case of a police officer and chemist, both of whom established official police reports indicating that the substances found on the ground outside of an apartment building, subject to summary eviction proceedings, tested positive for heroin. This evidence was admissible under the business records exception to the hearsay rule.[81]

A death certificate is another example of a document that is both an official record and a business record. A certificate of death is, therefore, admissible to prove a decedent's cause of death as an exception under the hearsay rule; it also constitutes a vital statistics exception to the hearsay rule.[82]

A common point of confusion with respect to admissibility involves official accident reports. Often, a police report, or the report of an official government agency licensed to investigate accidents, will base its conclusions and opinions upon information that was not obtained first-hand. In other words, we would have a matter

76 See Fed. R. Evid. 803(6); see also Lipson, *Documentary Evidence*, §9.06 (Matthew Bender, 1988).

77 *Dorsey v. City of Detroit,* 858 F.2d 338 (6th Cir. 1988); *United States v. Moore*, 791 F.2d 566 (7th Cir. 1986).

78 *Saks Int'l., Inc. v. M/V "Export Champion,"* 817 F.2d 1011 (2d Cir. 1987).

79 *United States v. Chang An-Lo*, 851 F.2d 547 (2d Cir. 1988).

80 *United States v. Catabran*, 836 F.2d 453 (9th Cir. 1988).

81 *New York County Dist. Attorney's Office v. Rodriguez*, 536 N.Y.S.2d 933 (N.Y. City Civ. Ct. 1988).

82 *Corlett v. Smith,* 763 P.2d 1172 (N.M. App. 1988).

involving multiple hearsay. Therefore, with respect to official accident reports, normally opinions and conclusions do not qualify unless they are directly based upon personal knowledge. A police report, for example, regarding an accident would not qualify if the source of the information were unknown.[83] Also, even the fact that a document has been authenticated as an official record does not automatically make all of its contents admissible under the public records exception to the hearsay rule.[84] Specific facts should be admissible; the other contents may be of questionable admissibility.

There is a variety of other types of reports, books, and treatises that are admissible as exceptions to the hearsay rule. As a matter of fact, Fed. R. Evid. 803(18) lists some of them:

> To the extent called to the attention of an expert witness upon cross-examination or relied upon by the expert witness in direct examination, *statements contained in published treatises, periodicals, or pamphlets on a subject of history, medicine, or other science or art*, established as a reliable authority by the testimony or admission of the witness or by other expert testimony or by judicial notice. If admitted, the statements may be read into evidence but may not be received as exhibits.

Market reports[85] and ancient writings[86] are also exceptions to the hearsay rule. In fact, there are enough exceptions to provide some pigeonholes for most reliable documents. If not, there is a federal catch-all.[87]

REFERENCES

Treatises, periodicals, or pamphlets as exception to hearsay rule under Rule 803(18). 64 A.L.R. Fed 971.

Cross-examination of authenticating witness. 14 Am. Jur. 2d Proof of Facts 173.

§5.410.1 State Application

As with the federal sphere, when in California state courts, practitioners should always be aware that there are two potential objections confronting every document: the hearsay rule and the best evidence rule. Some of the documents commonly excepted from the hearsay rule by the California Evidence Code include business records (CEC 1271), public or official records (CEC 1280), and family records such as bibles or other family books, charts, engravings on rings, family portraits, engravings on urns, crypts, or tombstones, etc. (CEC 1312).

CEC 1310 permits certain statements concerning a declarant's own family history. CEC 1311 provides for the admissibility of statements about other families, subject to certain conditions assuring personal knowledge and the trustworthiness of those statements.

The states of Ohio and Oregon do not recognize Federal Rule 803(18), with respect to learned treatises. A statement by an air traffic controller to a pilot (who died in an air crash), that there was "heavy ice all over the area" was admissible as a business record in a personal injury and wrongful death suit arising from the crash; the fact that the statement was "double hearsay" as based on information received from an "unnamed pilot" only affected weight, not admissibility. *Van Steemburg v. General Aviation, Inc.*, 183 Ill. Dec. 496, 611 N.E.2d 1144, 243 Ill. App. 3d 299 (Ill. App. 1993).

83 *Meder v. Everest & Jennings, Inc.*, 617 F.2d 1182 (8th Cir. 1981).

84 *In re D.M.C.*, 503 A.2d 1280 (D.C. 1986).

85 *Commonwealth of Virginia v. State of West Virginia*, 238 U.S. 202 (1915); *First National Bank of Chicago v. Jefferson Mortgage Co.*, 576 F.2d 479 (3rd Cir. 1978).

86 See 7 *Wigmore on Evidence*, §2145(a) (Little Brown, 1978).

87 See Fed. R. Evid. 803(24).

The following states have a provision that is either identical or substantially similar to Fed. R. Evid. 803(18) pertaining to business records:

BUSINESS RECORDS

Alaska	Rule 803(18)
Alabama	Rule 803(18)
Arizona	Rule 803(18)
Colorado	Rule 803(18)
Delaware	Rule 803(18)
Florida	§90.706
Hawaii	Rule 803(b)(21)
Idaho	Rule 803(18)
Iowa	Rule 803(18)
Kentucky	Rule 803(19)
Louisiana	Rule 803(18)
Maine	Rule 803(18)
Michigan	Rule 803(18)
Montana	Rule 803(18)
Nebraska	Rule 803(18)
Nevada	§51.255
New Hampshire	Rule 803(18)
New Mexico	Rule 803(18)
North Carolina	Rule 803(18)
North Dakota	Rule 803(18)
Ohio	Rule 803(18)
Oklahoma	Rule 803(18)
Oregon	Rule 803(18)
Rhode Island	Rule 803(18)
South Dakota	§19-16-22
Tennessee	Rule 803(18)
Texas (Civil & Criminal)	Rule 803(18)
Utah	ule 803(18)
Vermont	Rule 803(18)
Washington	Rule 803(18)
West Virginia	Rule 803(18)
Wisconsin	Rule 803(18)
Wyoming	Rule 803(18)

§5.411 Residual Exception

Known as the "residual" or "catch-all" exception, Fed. R. Evid. 807, which became effective December 1, 1997, provides the following exception for those unique circumstances that warrant a suspension of the hearsay rule even though no recognized exception exists:

> A statement not specifically covered by any of the foregoing exceptions but having equivalent circumstantial guarantees of trustworthiness, is not excluded by the hearsay rule, if the court determines that (A) the statement is offered as evidence of a material fact; (B) the statement is more probative on the point for which it is offered than any other evidence which the proponent can procure through reasonable efforts; and (C) the general purposes of these rules and the interests of justice will best be served by admission of the statement into evidence. However, a statement may not be admitted under this exception unless the proponent of it makes known to the adverse party sufficiently in advance of the trial or hearing to provide the adverse party with a fair opportunity to prepare to meet it, the proponent's intention to offer the statement and the particulars of it, including the name and address of the declarant.

A word of caution: anyone relying on this rule as a means to introduce some worthy form of hearsay had better think twice. The stringent requirements are difficult to meet.

REFERENCES

Residual hearsay exception.
51 A.L.R.4th 999.

§5.411.1 State Application

The following states have a catch-all provision that is either identical or substantially similar to Fed. R. Evid. 803(24):

CATCH-ALL PROVISION

Alaska	Rule 803(24)
Alabama	Rule 803(24)
Arizona	Rule 803(24)
Colorado	Rule 803(24)
Delaware	Rule 803(24)

Florida	90.706
Hawaii	Rule 803(b)(24)
Idaho	Rule 803(24)
Iowa	Rule 803(24)
Kentucky	Rule 803(19)
Montana	Rule 803(24)
Nebraska	Rule 803(22)
New Hampshire	Rule 803(24)
New Mexico	Rule 803(24)
North Carolina	Rule 803(24)
North Dakota	Rule 803(24)
Oklahoma	Rule 803(24)
Oregon	Rule 803(25)
Rhode Island	Rule 803(24)
South Dakota	§19-16-28
Tennessee	Rule 803(24)
Utah	Rule 803(24)
Washington	Rule 803(24)
West Virginia	Rule 803(24)
Wisconsin	Rule 803(24)
Wyoming	Rule 803(24)

The homicide and armed robbery conviction in the case of *People v. Manning*, 182 Ill.2d 193, 695 N.E.2d 423, 230 Ill. Dec. 933 (1998), provides a good example of declarations that do not fall within any hearsay exception, recognized or residual. The victim and the defendant were gun-packing drug dealers, who were set to meet one another to resolve some differences. At trial, the victim's wife testified that her husband said he was going to meet the defendant and that if he were killed, she should contact the FBI and say that the defendant killed him. In its decision, the court held that the wife's testimony as to the victim's statement (naming the defendant as his murderer) was hearsay which should not have been admitted.

Note that even though Fed. R. Evid. 807 has an effective date of October 1, 1997, the concept is not new. Other provisions of the Federal Rules encompassed similar language. Nevertheless, the jury is still out as to whether the remaining states are going to embrace the rule, modify it, or reject it outright.

Pennsylvania, which adopted most of the Federal Rules of Evidence, has not adopted Rule 807.

Michigan retains its Rule 803(24), which has conditions similar to Rule 807, but less strength, as suggested by its preliminary language:

> (24) Other Exceptions. A statement not specifically covered by any of the foregoing exceptions but having equivalent circumstantial guarantees of trustworthiness, if the court determines that... [Remainder of rule is identical to Fed. R. Evid. 807 *(supra)*]. [Notice the missing words: "is not excluded by the hearsay rule."]

North Carolina expresses its application well in the case of *Gibbs v. Mayo*, 591 S.E.2d 905 (N.C. App., 2004): When weighing the circumstantial guarantees of the trustworthiness of a hearsay statement, as an element for admissibility under the catch-all hearsay exception for statements made by an unavailable declarant, the trial judge must consider, among other factors the following: (1) Assurances of the declarants personal knowledge of the underlying events, (2) the declarant's motivation to speak the truth or otherwise, (3) whether the declarant has ever recanted the statement and (4) the practical availability of the declarant at trial for meaningful cross-examination.

(This page intentionally left blank.)

Chapter 6

Irrelevant or Immaterial Questions

§6.100 Introduction

To be admissible, a question must be *both* relevant and material. A question is irrelevant if it has no relationship to the issues of the case. But being "relevant" is only half the battle; a question must also be "material." For, even though a question may be relevant, it might still be immaterial (and, therefore, objectionable) if the information sought is not determinative of the main issues in the case.

§6.200 Quick Explanation

A question is irrelevant if it has no bearing whatsoever on the case. The test of relevance is a very easy one to satisfy. A question will be considered relevant as long as it infers or suggests something about a disputed fact. "Materiality" is a term that is often used synonymously with relevance, but it is, in fact, a stricter standard. To be material, the evidence must tend to prove or disprove a fact that is critical to the outcome of the case.

EXAMPLES:

1. What is the defendant's race, religion, or national origin?
2. Was the defendant ever arrested before for the same crime of which he is charged today?
3. How safely did Maniac Morrey drive one year after the subject accident?

Every part of the first question is *both* irrelevant and immaterial as a matter of law in every jurisdiction of this country, unless, of course, the case happens to involve discrimination or deportation. As a general proposition, a person's racial background should never be used to imply guilt, innocence, or liability.

The second question is immaterial because an "arrest" by itself does not establish guilt. As a matter of fact, a person is presumed to be innocent of a crime until proven guilty beyond a reasonable doubt.

The third question is relevant, but immaterial. In an auto negligence case, an answer to the question might tend to show that Morrey is an "all around" bad (or good) driver; that would be relevant. But, as a general proposition, events that occur *after* the fact (i.e., after the event which is the subject of the trial) are immaterial. Caution in applying this proposition is urged; sometimes subsequent events may be used to show prior occurrences. Here is a subtle example—If a suspect, days after a murder occurred, frantically erases fingerprints on the murder weapon, stuffs the victim into a suitcase, and then attempts to fly to Rio, those *subsequent* acts might very well be deemed relevant and material.

WHAT TO LOOK FOR:

Questions that do *not* lead to a solution or answer to the key issues of the case.

OBJECT AND RESPOND

OBJECTION:

"Objection. The question is irrelevant and immaterial."

POTENTIAL RESPONSES TO OBJECTION:

A. "The question is directly related to ____________."

B. (*Oldest Trick-in-the-Book* Response) "I will link this up later."

§6.300 General Legal Analysis

Fed. R. Evid. 402 starts with the very broad proposition that:

> All relevant evidence is admissible, *except* as otherwise provided by the Constitution of the United States, by Act of Congress, by these rules, or by other rules prescribed by the Supreme Court pursuant to statutory authority. Evidence which is not relevant is *not* admissible.

The rule simply states that relevant evidence, not otherwise objectionable, is admissible. The Federal Rules, in general, provide a very "liberal standard" which favors the admission of evidence if it has any "probative value" for the proof of a material fact.[1] Rule 402, in particular, is intended to set forth a "broad definition" of relevant evidence.[2] Evidence that is not relevant is not admissible.[3] Such evidence is simply referred to as "irrelevant" or "collateral."[4] Irrelevant matters are also excluded from cross-examination.[5] Of course, as a practical matter, issues and facts demonstrating bias or false testimony on the part of a witness are rarely, if ever, deemed irrelevant.

As we indicated early in this book (see Overview), courts and cases often confuse relevant evidence with *material* evidence. While relevant evidence is a very broad concept, as above defined, material evidence is a bit narrower. In particular, while evidence may be relevant if it satisfies the above broad definitions, it is not *material* unless it is specifically needed to prove (or disprove) a critical or important issue in the case. So, as a practical matter, evidence, to be admissible, must be both relevant and material.

Materiality, unlike relevance, will always have a potential for affecting the outcome of the inquiry or case.[6] Evidence is material where it is

1 *Hayes v. Caspers, LTD,* 881 A.2d 428, 90 Conn.App. 781 (2005). Evidence is relevant if it tends to support the conclusion for which it was offered, even if only to a slight degree. The subject evidence need not exclude all other possibilities to be relevant. *In re Estate of Love*, 618 S.E.2d 97 (Ga.App., 2005). Generally, the law favors admissibility; even evidence of doubtful relevance should be admitted with its weight being left for the jury to determine. *Haffey v. Generac Portable Products, LLC,* 171 S.W.3d 805 (Mo.App., 2005). To be admissible in any trial, evidence must be relevant. The evidence is relevant if it tends to support the conclusion for which it was offered, even if only to a slight degree. *Texas Electrical Co-op v. Dillard,* 171 S.W.3d 201 (Tex.App., 2005). To be relevant, the proposed evidence must be sufficiently tied to the facts of the case in such a manner that it will aid the jury in resolving a factual dispute.

United Technologies v. Town of East Windsor, 807 A.2d 955, 262 Conn. 11 (2002). In order to be relevant and admissible, it is not necessary that evidence be conclusive; on the contrary, it is only necessary that the evidence tends to support a relevant fact.

Bettius & Sanderson, P.C. v. National Union Fire Ins. Co., 839 F.2d 1009 (4th Cir. 1988). See also *United States v. Polasek,* 162 F.3d 878 (5th Cir. 1998) holding that relevance should be determined by the relationship between the evidence and the matter to be proved.

In re Johnson, 85 P.3d 1252 (Kan. App., 2004). For evidence to be relevant, it must have some tendency in reason to prove a material fact; in other words, there must be some material or logical connection between the asserted facts and the inference or result that is sought.

Department of Transportation v. Elm Land Co., 593 S.E.2d 131 (N.C. App., 2004). Evidence is relevant if it has any logical tendency to prove or disprove any fact that is of consequence in the case being litigated.

2 *United States v. Shrock,* 855 F.2d 327 (6th Cir. 1988). But see *United States v. Holt,* 170 F.3d 698, 702 (7th Cir. 1999) which involved a prosecution for conspiracy to knowingly and intentionally transfer an automatic weapon. Books and pamphlets that were for sale at defendants gun shop were irrelevant and inadmissible to counter evidence of defendants "law abiding" character, since their sale was not unlawful; the materials were also inadmissible to demonstrate defendants knowledge of weaponry, since there was no evidence that defendant had read the materials. Nevertheless, the admission of the evidence was harmless error.

3 *Eltiste v. Ford Motor Company*, 167 S.W.3d 742 (Mo.App., 2005). Relevance is the principal criterion for the admissibility of evidence. *Hooker v. State Farm Fire and Casualty Company*, 880 A.2d 70 (Pa.Commonwealth, 2005). Relevance is the fundamental consideration in determining the admissibility of evidence. This applies to both direct and cross examination. *Richardson v. State,* 581 S.E.2d 528 (Ga., 2003); see Federal Rules of Evidence, Rule 402.

4 Evidence is "collateral," and thus inadmissible, if it is neither relevant to prove independent fact in issue, nor would it impeach or discredit witness. *Strasser v. Yalamanchi,* 783 So.2d 1087 (Fla.App., 2001).

5 *State v. Williams,* 838 A.2d 214, 81 Conn. App. 1 (2004). Only relevant evidence may be elicited during the course of a trial, and the right to cross-examine is subject to the duty of the court to exclude irrelevant evidence.

6 *United States v. Fiorillo*, 376 F.2d 180 (2d Cir. 1967).

not only relevant, but where it also goes to the substantial matters in the dispute, or has a legitimate or effective bearing on the final decision.[7]

Perhaps the best way to visualize the distinction between relevance and materiality is to consider a situation where the opposition has conceded an important element of the case. That particular element is certainly *relevant* just by virtue of the fact that we have defined it as an element. But it is not material, since the party against whom it would have been used has already conceded the element to be true.[8] Logic suggests that it is not necessary to prove something that is already true. Thus, we have an example of evidence that may be relevant, but yet immaterial.

Since the irrelevant and immaterial objections are so closely related, and so totally confused with one another, many courts treat them synonymously. Fed. R. Evid. 401 provides a nice attempt to "tidy up" the problem by combining relevance and materiality once and for all, and then referring to the combination simply as "relevant evidence":[9]

> "Relevant evidence" means evidence having any tendency to make the existence of any fact that is of consequence to the determination of the action more probable or less probable than it would be without the evidence.

The Federal Circuit Courts can be expected to provide further definitions consistent with Rule 401. The Fifth Circuit Court of Appeals, for example, defines relevant evidence as being probative of the proposition that is of a consequence to the determination of the action. So it is reasonable to assume that this simplified approach will continue.[10]

Another definition suggests that relevancy is the "logical relationship" between an offered item of evidence and a proposition that is provable in a given case. For that test, the relevancy or irrelevancy of the particular evidence turns upon the facts of the given case. In other words, "evidence is relevant if it tends to persuade one that a fact in controversy did or did not exist."[11]

Rule 403 of the Federal Rules of Evidence (discussed in the Overview) provides a list of objections that are available for the opponent of evidence that may otherwise be considered relevant in accordance with the definitions and principles set forth above in this chapter.

---

7 *United States v. DeLucia*, 256 F.2d 487 (7th Cir. 1958).

8 *United States v. Edwards*, 631 F.2d 1049 (2d Cir. 1980).

9 *United States v. Hall*, 653 F.2d 1002 (5th Cir. 1981).

10 See also *Telum, Inc. v. E.F. Hutton Credit Corp.*, 859 F.2d 835 (10th Cir. 1988). Such "continuation" should occur at state as well as federal level. See *Shea v. Esensten,* 622 N.W.2d 130 (Minn. 2001); *In re Interest of Andrew M., Jr.,* 622 N.W.2d 697, 9 Neb.App. 947 (2001); *Peters-Riemers v. Riemers,* 624 N.W.2d 83 (N.D. 2001). See also *State Farm Mutual Insurance Companies v. AMCO Insurance Company,* 621 N.W.2d 553, 9 Neb.App. 872 (2001).

11 *Anderson v. Kohler Co.*, 170 S.W.3d 19 (Mo.App., 2005). The test for relevancy depends upon whether or not the offered fact tends to prove, disprove or corroborate other relevant evidence. *Peterson v. National R.R. Passenger Corp.*, 618 S.E.2d 903, 365 S.C. 391 (2005). Evidence is relevant if it tends to or makes more or less probable some matter at issue in the case. *Anderson v. Buonforte*, 617 S.E.2d 750, 365 S.C. 482 (2005). When determining a dispute involving the relevancy of evidence, the question to be resolved is whether or not there is a logical or rational connection between the fact that is sought to be presented and a fact that is an issue in the case. Stated yet another way, "relevancy" is that quality of evidence which renders it properly applicable in determining the truth and falsity of matters in issue between the parties to a suit. *Wark v. McClellan,* 68 P.3d 574 (Colo.App., 2003). Generally, relevant evidence logically tends to prove or disprove facts in contention or "sheds light" upon contested matters. See also *Dumbakly v. Patire,* 754 N.Y.S.2d 308 (N.Y.A.D. 2nd Dept., 2003); *Greenwood v. Greenwood,* 596 N.W.2d 317 (N.D. 1999); *United States v. Allison*, 474 F.2d 286 (5th Cir. 1973). See also *Turney Media Fuel, Inc. v. Toll Bros., Inc.*, 725 A.2d 836 (Pa.Super. 1999).

§6.400 Problems Pertaining to Criminal Cases

Normally, the rules of evidence that apply to civil cases are no different than those that apply to criminal cases, *except* it is generally understood that in applying rules to criminal cases, they should be *more* strictly construed. This means that objections are more likely to be sustained in criminal cases because when guilt or innocence is involved, constitutional protection is at stake.

In that regard, it has been held that evidence introduced in a criminal trial should relate *only* to the elements of the specific offense charged in the indictment.[12] Evidence of prior crimes, wrongs, or acts are not admissible to prove the character of a party or to show that he acted in conformity on a particular occasion.[13] Nor is it proper to inquire into a witness' arrest history, even upon cross-examination.[14] In a case involving a claim of self- defense, for example, the court ruled that it was irrelevant that the victim had been seen carrying a gun within the year preceding the shooting. It was held that such evidence was not relevant to show that the defendant was the aggressor at the time of the killing because carrying a gun is not a violent or aggressive act.[15]

Notwithstanding the preceding limitations with respect to prior crimes, when the defendant takes the stand, the prosecutor may attack his credibility by asking whether he had ever been convicted of a felony, or a crime that specifically involved dishonesty or false statements.[16] But that principle does not provide a carte blanche for the prosecutor just because the defendant took the stand.

Plea bargaining in criminal cases (like settlement negotiations in civil matters) encourages speedy resolutions and therefore evidence of plea bargains and *nolo contendere* pleas should not be used in evidence against a defendant[17], unless that defendant specifically waives his right to exclude such evidence.[18]

§6.500 Problems Pertaining to Civil Cases

In a civil case, the character of a party is irrelevant and cannot be inquired into unless it is put in issue where damage to character or reputation is specifically involved (such as libel, slander, malicious prosecution, etc.).[19] Nor is it ever proper to ask questions about a person's national origin to show character or credibility.[20] Also, it is generally held that evidence of a person's conduct occurring after an act giving rise to the subject claim should be excluded as irrelevant.[21] However, the habits of a person or organization may be admitted to prove conduct in conformity with those habits.[22]

Certain "post-accident" activities that should be encouraged, would otherwise be discouraged without some special exclusionary rules. Subsequent remedial repairs, for example, would never

12 *United States v. Audsley*, 486 F.2d 289 (5th Cir. 1973).

13 See §6.701; see also *U.S. v. Hedgcorth*, 873 F.2d 1307 (9th Cir. 1989); *Hinnant v. Holland*, 374 S.E.2d 152 (N.C. App. 1988).

14 *McDonald v. State*, 764 P.2d 202 (Okl. Cr. 1988).

15 At least it's not aggressive in *Texas, Gutierrez v. State, 764 S.W.2d 796 (Tex. Cr. App. 1989).*

16 *Gavins v. State,* 587 So.2d 487 (Fla. App. 1991); see also *People v. Trottie,* 582 N.Y.S.2d 31 (1992).

17 See Rule 410 of the Federal Rules of Evidence and and Rule 11(e)(6) of the Federal Rules of Criminal Procedure; see also §6.706.

18 See *United States v. Krilich*, 159 F.3d 1020 (1998), *cert. denied*, 119 S. Ct. 1155 (1999).

19 See §6.701; see also *Williams v. Bailey*, 759 S.W.2d 394 (Mo. App. 1988).

20 Fed. R. Evid. 610 specifically forbids the use of religious beliefs to test credibility.

21 *Holmes v. Drucker*, 411 S.E.2d 728, 201 Ga. App. 687 (1991).

22 See §6.702 infra; see also *Vining v. Enterprise Fin. Group, Inc.*, 148 F.3d 1206 (10th Cir. 1998).

admitted to show ownership or control,[33] to impeach,[34] or to demonstrate the feasibility of precautionary measures.[35]

§6.704 Evidence of Offer of Compromise

Rule 408 echoes the long-standing rule that offers of settlement or compromise should not be admitted to prove the validity of a claim.[36] Were this not so, cases would never be settled.

§6.705 Payment of Medical Bills

Rule 409, which, may involve unilateral gestures, differs from Rule 407 which concerns "offers" in the contractual sense. In particular, Rule 409 provides that the act of offering to pay or the actual payment of someone's medical bills or expenses will not be admissible against the provider to prove liability for the injury.

§6.706 Evidence of Pleas

Rule 410 of the Federal Rules of Evidence basically excludes withdrawn guilty pleas and pleas of *nolo contendere* from subsequent civil and criminal trials.

§6.707 Liability Insurance Exclusion

Rule 411, the insurance carrier's friend, prohibits the mention of insurance in order to prove negligence. The exclusion does not apply where an insurance policy is used to prove agency, ownership, control, bias or prejudice of a witness.

§6.708 Sex Crimes

Rules 411- 415, in keeping with the mood of the times, set forth detailed rules designed to protect victims of sexual assaults in both civil and criminal proceedings.

---

33 *Specialty Products International, Ltd. v. Con-Way Transportation Services, Inc.*, 410 F.Supp.2d 423; *Hughes v. Cold Spring Construction Co.*, 809 N.Y.S.2d 751, N.Y.A.D. 4 Dept. (2006); *Webb v. CSX Transportation, Inc.*, 364 S.C. 639, 615 S.E.2d 440 (2005). See also Rule 407 of the *Federal Rules of Evidence.*

34 *McCarthy v. 390 Tower Associates, LLC.*, 800 N.Y.S.2d 875, 9 Misc.3d 219 (2005). In a manufacturing defect case, evidence of the defendant's remedial measures, such as a recall (or a redesign) of the product, was not admissible to establish defendant's negligence, but it was admissible to impeach the testimony of the president of the manufacturer who claimed that the machine had been manufactured with a required safeguard.

35 *Specialty Products International, Ltd. v. Con-Way Transportation Services, Inc.*, 410 F.Supp.2d 423; *Richardson v. State*, 130 P.3d 634 (Montana, 2006); *Webb v. CSX Transportation, Inc.*, 364 S.C. 639, 615 S.E.2d 440 (2005). See also Rule 407 of the *Federal Rules of Evidence.*

36 *U.S. v. Bailey,* 327 F.3d 1131 (10th Cir., Kansas, 2003). The rules of evidence that forbid the admission of settlement negotiations apply both in civil and criminal proceedings. But see *Basha v. Mitsubishi Motor Credit of America, Inc.,* 336 F.3d 451 (5th Cir., La., 2003) holding that settlement-related letters between the parties are admissible if they are used to interpret their settlement agreement, as opposed to establishing liability.

Arnold v. County of Cook, 220 F.Supp.2d 893 (Ill, 2002) involved an action under the Rehabilitation Act of 1973, 29 U.S.C.A. §§701 et seq., that provided an important distinction involving the purpose of an "offer." A letter sent by the defending county employer to an injured employee offered employment for a position that would have reasonably accommodated the employee's disability; this letter was deemed an offer to settle the employee's claim under the Act and was, therefore, inadmissible. At the time it was sent, the employee was represented by an attorney who had threatened litigation. However, a separate letter whereby the county made an unconditional offer of employment to the employee was *not* considered an offer of compromise and was, therefore, admissible.

§6.800 Selected State Rules and Cases

ALABAMA:

The key issues were whether the defendant participated in crimes of rape, sodomy, and kidnapping; nevertheless, the prosecutor's questions about defendant's use of marijuana was permitted, even though there was no evidence of drug use, and even though the question assumed facts not in evidence. *Phillips v. State*, 728 So.2d 681 (Ala. Crim. App. 1998).

CALIFORNIA:

Rule 350 of the California Evidence Code (the counterpart of Federal Rule 402) provides that: "No evidence is admissible except relevant evidence." CEC Rule 351 further states that: "Except as otherwise provided by statute, all relevant evidence is admissible." Simply speaking, the two rules seem to equate relevance with admissibility, subject only to statutory exclusions. This logical result is not entirely correct, since it implies that every potential objection is embodied in some statute. The rule simply places too much on the shoulders of the relevance objection. CEC Rule 210 provides the following:

> "Relevant evidence" means evidence, including evidence relevant to the credibility of a witness or hearsay declarant, having any tendency in reason to prove or disprove any disputed fact that is of consequence to the determination of the action.

In determining admissibility, the trial court starts with the proposition that all relevant evidence is admissible. *DePalma v. Westland Software House*, 276 Cal. Rptr. 214 (Cal. App. 2 Dist. 1990).

As with the Federal Rules of Evidence, the CEC likewise confuses and obscures the lines between relevance and materiality. The hottest problems in that regard appear in criminal cases and center around prior crimes. Are they relevant in the academic sense? Of course. A crook is a crook. And a crook is more likely to commit a crime than a non-crook. Is such evidence material? No. Just because someone is a past crook does not prove that he or she committed the present offense. So in keeping with the manner in which the Federal Rules combine the concepts of materiality and relevance, evidence of prior crimes is deemed irrelevant when introduced as part of the prosecutor's case in chief.

But introduction of prior misdeeds for purposes of impeachment may be permitted, particularly where moral turpitude is involved. *People v. Lee*, 281 Cal. Rptr. 9 (Cal. App. 5 Dist.1991); *People v. Wheeler*, 281 Cal. Rptr. 758, 230 C.A.3d 1406 (Cal. App. 2 Dist. 1991). Consider *People v. Daniels*, 802 P.2d 906, 277 Cal. Rptr. 122, 52 Cal.3d 815 (1991), where the trial court properly permitted (for impeachment purposes) evidence that the defendant committed many crimes, lied a lot, was sexually promiscuous, and even went so far into the depths of degradation as to be late for work on more than one occasion.

COLORADO:

The Colorado Rules of Evidence (Title 13 of the Colorado Revised Statutes) follow the Federal Rules virtually verbatim. CRS 401 is identical to Federal Rule 401, while CRS 402 is the substantially equivalent to Federal Rule 402 (*supra*).

CONNECTICUT:

Relevance of evidence must be determined according to reason, judicial experience, and the court's discretion. *Baystate Moving Systems, Inc. v. Bowman*, 590 A.2d 462, 24 Conn. App.3d 531 (1991). Moreover, the trial court has broad discretion to exclude evidence when its logical nexus to a material issue has not been established. *Beinhorn v. Saraceno*, 582 A.2d 208, 23 Conn. App. 487 (Conn. App. 1990).

State of Connecticut v. Irizarry, 95 Conn.App. 224, 896 A.2d 828 (2006). Evidence is "relevant evidence" if it has a logical tendency to aid the trier in the determination of an issue; all that is required is that the evidence tends to support a fact, even to a slight degree. When reviewing a trial court's determinations as to the relevancy of evidence and the scope of cross-examination, every reasonable presumption should be made in favor of the correctness of the trial court's ruling in determining whether there has been an abuse of discretion.

FLORIDA:

Section 90.401 of the Florida Evidence Code is similar to California's simple definition. The committee notes reflect this simple majority rule:

> The Florida courts have said that "relevancy describes evidence that has a legitimate tendency to prove or disprove a given proposition that is material as shown by the pleadings. [It is] a tendency to establish a fact in controversy or to render a proposition more or less probable." *Zabner v. Howard Johnson's Inc. of Fla.*, 227 So.2d 543, 545 (Fla. 4th Dist. 1969). Uniform Rule 1(2) [1953] defines relevant evidence as "evidence having any tendency in reason to prove any material fact."

Section 90.402 of the Florida Evidence Code is substantially the same as Rule 351 of the California Evidence Code, i.e., all relevant evidence is admissible unless otherwise provided. The implication is that irrelevant evidence may not be admitted. As a matter of fact, a witness may not even be impeached by statements that involve irrelevant or immaterial matters. *Mathews v. State*, 574 So.2d 1174 (Fla. App.5 Dist. 1991).

In *Sims v. Brown*, 574 So.2d 131 (Fla. 1991), the Florida court defines "legal relevance" by presenting a four-part test. To be legally relevant, evidence must (1) have a bearing on a fact to be proved (materiality), (2) be testified to by one in a position to know (competency), (3) have a tendency to make the fact more or less probable (classic relevancy), and (4) must not be excluded for other countervailing reasons (i.e., constitutional or public-policy reasons).

A very hot issue in recent years centers around the manner in which sexual assault victims are cross-examined about their sexual history, especially where "consent" is a defense. The "relevant" inquiry into the victim's sexual history has become an abusive device for shifting the focus of blame from the defendant to the victim. Thus, *Lewis v. State*, 570 So.2d 412 (Fla. App. 1 Dist. 1990) generally held that evidence of a sex victim's prior sexual activity with one other than the accused is simply irrelevant for determining the guilt of the accused. Virtually every state has followed suit, in this regard, except Utah.

Generally, it is improper, during a trial, to refer to the wealth, poverty, or financial status of one party as contrasted with another. *Batlemento v. Dove Fountain, Inc.*, 593 So.2d 234 (Fla. App. 1991).

GEORGIA:

A defendant's right of cross-examination is not abridged just because that examination is limited to relevant matters. *Stephens v. State*, 428 S.E.2d 661 (Ga. App. 1993). On the other hand, Georgia's Rules of Evidence favor the admissibility of any relevant evidence, no matter how slight its probative value; even evidence of doubtful relevancy or competency should be admitted with its weight left to the jury. *Platt v. National General Ins. Co.*, 423 S.E.2d 387, 205 Ga. App. 705, *cert. den.* (1992).

Briglevich v. Liberty House Restaurant Corp., 277 Ga.App. 433, 626 S.E.2d 625 (Ga. App., 2006) presents an interesting "flip-side" of the rule prohibiting testimony about subsequent remedial repairs. In a slip and fall action against a restaurant, the plaintiff claimed that the trial court erred when it allowed the restaurant employees to testify that no subsequent remedial measures were taken after the subject incident (plaintiff made no objection after the above question was asked). In particular, an employee was asked, "Is that section of the floor in the same condition now as it was in June of 2001?" The employee responded affirmatively. Plaintiff alleged that this statement could have given the jury the impression that the restaurant was claiming that no subsequent remedial measures were needed. She further claimed that this argument was the "flip-side" of the rule prohibiting testimony of subsequent remedial measures. Unfortunately for the plaintiff, there was no authority for excluding the evidence.

HAWAII:

Hawaii's Rules 401, 402, and 403 are substantially identical to their federal counterparts (i.e., Rules 401, 402, and 403 of the Federal Rules of Evidence). Hawaii's Rule 402 has been adapted to state practice.

IDAHO:

Idaho's Rules 401, 402, and 403 are substantially identical to their federal counterparts (i.e., Rules 401, 402, and 403 of the Federal Rules of Evidence). Idaho's Rule 402 has been adapted to state practice.

ILLINOIS:

Illinois case law echoes the "federal" definition of relevancy. Moreover, evidence is relevant if it has a tendency to make the existence of any fact that is of consequence to the determination of an event more probable or less probable than it would be without that evidence. *Lundquist v. Nickels*, 179 Ill.Dec. 150, 605 N.E.2d 1373 (Ill. App. 1 Dist. 1992); *Kniceley v. Migala*, 177 Ill.Dec. 773, 603 N.E.2d 843, 237 Ill. App.3d 72 (Ill. App. 2 Dist. 1992).

In order for evidence to be relevant, it must establish a fact that is of consequence to the determination of the pending action; it must be both material and have probative value. The decision whether or not to admit evidence is "largely within the discretion of the trial court." *Demos v. Ferris-Shell Oil Co.,* 251 Ill.Dec. 179, 740 N.E.2d 9, 317 Ill.App.3d 41 (2000).

INDIANA:

"Relevant evidence" is evidence which logically tends to prove a material fact. *Barnes v. Barnes*, 603 N.E.2d 1337 (Ind. 1992). See also *Ford Motor Co. v. Ammerman,* 705 N.E.2d 539 (Ind.App. 1999).

In *Cahoon v. Cummings,* 715 N.E.2d 1 (Ind.App. 1999), a medical malpractice case, the defending physician made insertions into the patient's medical records after the litigation had commenced. If the issue of breach of duty had not been conceded, the evidence of those insertions and the negative presumptions resulting therefrom would have been relevant and admissible with respect to that issue; the physician's credibility would also have been called into question. Moreover, the spoliation rule permits an adverse inference to be drawn against a party who destroys or suppresses evidence that is in his exclusive possession; however, for that inference to be employed, it must, nevertheless, be relevant.

LOUISIANA:

The defense should be allowed substantial freedom when cross-examining a witness, particularly in a criminal case; but that freedom may be restricted by the trial court when the questions are irrelevant or immaterial to the case. *State v. Bourg*, 615 So.2d 957 (La. App. 1 Cir. 1993).

Even though evidence may be relevant, its probative value might be outweighed by the amount of unfair prejudice that it carries (See Fed. R. Evid. 403, noting that Louisiana's Rules 401, 402, and 403 are similar to each of their federal counterparts); and such evidence may, therefore, be excluded, though otherwise relevant. Consider *Gonzalez v. Allstate Ins. Co*., 615 So.2d 446 (La. App. 4 Cir. 1993), where questions directed to a personal injury plaintiff, concerning whether she had filed income tax returns for each of several years, should have been precluded based on a balancing of probative value versus prejudice. There was no probative value because the plaintiff was not seeking lost wages as part of her damage claim.

A prosecutor claimed that a Spanish-speaking defendant asked for "dos onzas de cocaina," which translates into "two ounces of cocaine." The defendant, however, allegedly requested "dos cosas," meaning "two things." The trial court was held not to have erred by limiting cross-examination of the police officer as to the differences in pronunciation of Spanish among the various countries of South America; the evidence was not relevant to the central issue. *State v. Valenzuela*, 590 So.2d 89 (La. App. 1991).

During the cross-examination of the mother (then unmarried) of a child rape victim, an objection to a question concerning whether she was living with a man was properly sustained as being irrelevant. The defendant was found to be on a fishing expedition to see if someone other than the defendant could have committed the offense. *State v. Bennett*, 591 So.2d 1193 (La. App. 1991).

MICHIGAN:

Rules 401 and 403 of the Michigan Court Rules are substantially identical to their federal counterparts (i.e., Rules 401 and 403 of the Federal Rules of Evidence). Michigan's Rule 402 states as follows:

> All relevant evidence is admissible, except as otherwise provided by the Constitution of the United States, the Constitution of the State of Michigan, these rules, or other rules adopted by the Supreme Court. Evidence which is not relevant is not admissible.

MINNESOTA:

Minnesota's Rules 401, 402, and 403 are substantially identical to their federal counterparts (i.e., Rules 401, 402, and 403 of the Federal Rules of Evidence). Minnesota's Rule 402 has been adapted to state practice.

Evidence is relevant if it logically tends to prove or disprove a material fact in issue. *Shea v. Esensten,* 622 N.W.2d 130 (Minn. 2001).

MISSOURI:

Generally, evidence of a settlement agreement is not admissible absent a clear and cogent reason. It would be deemed irrelevant. *Conley v. Treasurer of Missouri,* 999 S.W. 269 (1999).

Generally, settlement offers cannot be admitted against the offeree to show liability or an admission of liability. To permit such evidence would discourage settlement negotiations. *Banks v. Village Enterprises Inc.,* 32 S.W.3d 780 (Mo.App. W.D. 2000).

NEBRASKA:

Nebraska's Rules 27-401, 27-402, and 27-403 are substantially similar to their federal counterparts (i.e., Rules 401, 402, and 403 of the Federal Rules of Evidence). Nebraska's Rule 27-402 has been adapted to state practice.

For evidence to be "relevant," it must be established that there is a rational, probative connection, however slight, between the offered evidence and a fact that is of consequence to the determination of the action. *State Farm Mutual Insurance Companies v. AMCO Insurance Company,* 621 N.W.2d 553, 9 Neb.App. 872 (2001). Stated in a more ubiquitous manner, relevant evidence is evidence having any tendency to make the existence of any fact that is of consequence to the determination of the action more probable or less probable than it would be without the evidence. *In re Interest of Andrew M., Jr.,* 622 N.W.2d 697, 9 Neb.App. 947 (2001).

NEW JERSEY:

Rules 401 and 403 of the *New Jersey Court Rules* are similar to their federal counterparts (i.e., Rules 401 and 403 of the Federal Rules of Evidence). New Jersey's 402, however, omits the last sentence, and states:

> All relevant evidence is admissible, *except* as otherwise provided by the Constitution of the United States, by Act of Congress, by these rules, or by other rules prescribed by the Supreme Court pursuant to statutory authority.

Evidence of criminal charges that were dismissed as part of a plea agreement are not admissible, even if the dismissed charges appear on a judgment of an admissible conviction; only actual convictions of crimes may be used to address a defendant's credibility. *State v. Burgos*, 619 A.2d 1013, 262 N.J. Super 1 (N.J.Super.A.D. 1992).

NEW YORK:

The trial court did not abuse its discretion in controlling the cross-examination of a robbery complainant over a two-day period by curtailing examination when the questions became confusing, redundant or irrelevant. *People v. Harris*, 706 N.Y.S.2d 392 (N.Y.A.D. 2000).

Reliability and perhaps even sanity are not to be ignored, despite their absence from most definitions pertaining to relevance. In an assault-and-battery suit, for example, evidence of an analysis of the defendant's writings revealed, it is claimed, that the defendant possessed personality traits including sadism and was, therefore, capable of committing assault. The evidence was held inadmissible. *O'Connell v. Jacobs*, 583 N.Y.S.2d 61 (N.Y.A.D. 4 Dept. 1992).

In a criminal case, a defendant may be cross-examined as to his prior criminal acts where the nature of such conduct bears logically and reasonably on the issue of his credibility. *People v. Trottie*, 582 N.Y.S.2d 31 (1992).

NEVADA:

Nevada's §48.015 is identical to Federal Rule 401; §48.025 is similar to Federal Rule 402 with the addition of a new subsection; and §48.035 is similar to Federal Rule 403, also with the addition of a new subsection.

NORTH DAKOTA:

In classic fashion, *Greenwood v. Greenwood*, 596 N.W.2d 317 (N.D. 1999) states that "relevant evidence" is any evidence that reasonably and actually tends to prove or disprove any fact that is of consequence to the determination of an action; relevant evidence is generally admissible, if not excluded for other reasons.

OHIO:

In *State v. Boggs*, 588 N.E.2d 813 (Ohio 1992), an alleged rape victim had made prior false accusations of a sexual assault on a previous occasion. Yet the court held that the attorney defending a charge of rape by this same individual should not be permitted to introduce "extrinsic evidence" of those prior false charges, because they involved a collateral matter. The rationale—the mere fact that the alleged rape victim made prior false accusations did not automatically mean that she was fabricating the present charge. Even the most sympathetic victim's rights advocate should have difficulty accepting this decision. Generally, as stated in *Lewis v. Alfa Laval Separation, Inc.*, 714 N.E.2d 426, 128 Ohio App.3rd 200 (1998), the admission or exclusion of relevant evidence is within the sound discretion of the trial court.

OKLAHOMA:

Oklahoma's §2401 is identical to Federal Rule 401; §2402 is similar to Federal Rule 402; and §2403 is basically similar to Federal Rule 403, except that §2403 omits the "waste of time" provision, and adds an "unfair and harmful surprise" ground.

OREGON:

Oregon has adopted most of the rules and principles set forth in the Federal Rules of Evidence. The Oregon Evidence Code (Oregon Revised Statutes, Chapter 40 et seq.), however, assigns its own rule numbers. ORS 40.155 corresponds to Federal Rule 402.

PENNSYLVANIA:

On May 8, 1998, the Pennsylvania Supreme Court adopted a new and comprehensive set of evidence rules, with an effective date of October 1, 1998. The new rules are patterned after the Federal Rules of Evidence, both by content and number.

See Pennsylvania's new Rule 401 (Definition of "Relevant Evidence" and Rule 402 (Relevant Evidence Generally Admissible; Irrelevant Evidence Inadmissible).

To be admissible, evidence must be both competent and relevant. Evidence is relevant, and therefore admissible, if it logically or reasonably tends to prove or disprove a material fact in issue, or tends to make a fact more or less probable, or affords a basis for a reasonable inference or presumption regarding the existence of a material fact. *Taliferro v. Johns-Manville Corp.*, 617 A.2d 796 (Pa. Super 1992). (The first sentence of Taliferro is correct; the explanation that follows, however, seems to omit the "competence" portion of the equation; see Foundation Chapter). See also *Turney Media Fuel, Inc. v. Toll Bros., Inc.*, 725 A.2d 836 (Pa.Super. 1999), declaring that the basic requirement for the admission of any evidence is that it be both competent and relevant; evidence is relevant if it tends to prove or disprove a material fact in issue.

Evidence is relevant if it has any tendency to make the existence of any fact that is of consequence to the determination of the action more or less probable than it would have been without such evidence. *In re N.C.,* 763 A.2d 913 (Pa. Superior Court, 2000).

SOUTH DAKOTA:

The rule generally prohibiting the admission of compromise or settlement evidence is designed to encourage the out-of-court resolution of disputes. However, evidence of compromises or settlements may be admissible to prove the bias or prejudice of a witness or to negate a contention of undue delay. *First Premier Bank v. Kolcraft Enters. (In re Boone)*, 686 N.W.2d 430, 2004 S.D. 92 (2004).

VERMONT:

Vermont mimics the Federal Rules of Evidence in much the same fashion as several aforementioned states. The rule numbers for the Vermont Rules of Evidence match the Federal Rules, including VRE 402, with respect to relevance.

WISCONSIN:

In *State v. Tee & Bee, Inc.,* 600 N.W.2d 230 (Wis.App. 1999), a civil forfeiture action commenced pursuant to an obscenity statute, the exclusion of a telephone survey purporting to indicate state-wide community standards and expert testimony to complementing the survey, was not an erroneous exercise of discretion; failing to sufficiently apprize survey respondents of nature of charged materials rendered the survey results irrelevant.

Chapter 7

Leading Questions

§7.100 Introduction

A question is a leading question if it is intentionally phrased so that the answer is suggested. A leading question tells the witness how to answer it.

§7.200 Quick Explanation

An obvious violation of the rule prohibiting leading questions would be virtually any question that starts with the phrase—"Isn't it true..."

Note, that unlike most of the other rules of evidence, this rule *may* be relaxed during cross-examination. If counsel is questioning an opposing party or opposing witness, counsel may ask leading questions. However, as a rule, counsel may not lead his or her own witness during direct examination.

EXAMPLES OF LEADING QUESTIONS:

1. Isn't it true that you found the murder weapon under the table?
2. You found the murder weapon under the table, didn't you?
3. You found the murder weapon under the table?

"Where did you find the murder weapon?" would have been the correct way to ask each of the above questions (assuming that the witness had already established that he or she found the weapon). In those examples, however, the questioner is not passively seeking information. He or she is obviously groping for a "yes" answer. A proper question should not suggest the answer; it should, at least theoretically, be objective and "neutral."

Notice that the last of the three leading questions isn't really a question at all. It is more of a statement with which the questioner wants the witness to agree.

WHAT TO LOOK FOR:

Questions that sound like they don't really need a question mark at the end, and questions that have a contraction (i.e., "didn't," "isn't," "don't," "shouldn't," etc.). Any question that starts out "Isn't it true," must be leading.

OBJECT AND RESPOND

OBJECTION:

"Objection. Leading."

POTENTIAL RESPONSE TO OBJECTION:

Simply restate the question properly; the witness will have been adequately cued by your lead.

---

§7.300 General Legal Analysis

Leading questions are designed to suggest the answer to the witness.[1] One might compare this to "coaching" the witness, so that, instead of hearing what the person on the stand has to say, the witness becomes a mere parrot for the statements and opinions of the lawyer asking the questions. This is obviously improper, and for that reason, it has been held that no one has an absolute right to ask a leading question.[2]

This rule may even apply to cross-examination.[3]

1 *U.S. v. Hansen,* 256 F.Supp.2d 65 (D.Mass., 2003). The test of whether or not a question is leading depends upon whether it suggests the answer desired by the examiner. *State v. Boillard,* 789 A.2d 881 (R.I. 2002); *State v. Wiggins*, 526 S.E.2d 207 (N.C.App. 2000); *State v. Smith,* 522 S.E.2d 321, 135 N.C.App. 649 (1999); *State v. Hotoph,* 750 So.2d 1036, (La.App.5.Cir.,1999); *State v. Freeman*, 378 S.E.2d 545 (N.C.App. 1989). A leading question is one which suggests the desired response and often may be answered "yes" or "no."

2 *Oberlin v. Marlin American Corp.*, 596 F.2d 1322 (7th Cir. 1979); *People v. Cobb*, 134 Ill.Dec. 664, 542 N.E. 2d 1171, 186 Ill.App. 3d 898 (1989).

3 *Imperiale v. City of San Diego*, 137 Fed.Appx. 13 (9th Cir., CA, 2005); *Morvant v. Construction Aggregates Corp.*, 570 F.2d 626 (6th Cir. 1978); see also *GAB Business Services, Inc. v. Moore*, 829 S.W.2d 345 (Tex.App. 1992), where the court recognized that, ordinarily, leading questions should be permitted on cross-examination; but the right to lead may be denied when the cross-examination is of a "friendly" witness, as in the case where a party is "cross-examined" by his own attorney after that party was called by an opponent.

As a general definition, a leading question is one which suggests the answer to the witness.[4] Ordinarily, such questions are prohibited when they are posed to one's own witness, unless that witness is hostile or unwilling; but, in any event, the matter is largely within the discretion of the court.[5]

All leading questions are not *per se* evil or improper. In some cases, they serve a beneficial and even welcome purpose.

First, as we stated, it is *generally* recognized that questions of a leading nature may be asked during cross-examination.[6] Also, a prosecutor should be permitted to ask leading questions of any witness who is reluctant,[7] scared,[8] very

---

4 *State v. Gomes*, 764 A.2d 125. (R.I. 2001); *State v. Wiggins*, 526 S.E.2d 207 (N.C.App., 2000); *Powell v. State*, 995 P.2d 510 (Okla. Crim. App., 2000); *State v. Allison*, 845 S.W.2d 642 (Mo.App., 1992). See also *People v. Miles*, 286 Ill. Dec 827, 815 N.E.2d 37 (2004); *State v. Moore,* 877 So.2d 1027, 38 (La. App., 2004).

5 In *U.S. v. Berg,* 178 F.3d 976 (8th Cir. Mo. 1999), a defendant charged with conspiracy to manufacture methamphetamine was not entitled to examine a co-conspirator (who was a defense witness) with leading questions as a hostile witness, even though defendant had difficulty seeking some of the information that he wanted from that co-conspirator. In *U.S. V. Hernandez-Albino,* 177 F.3d 33 (1st Cir., Puerto Rico, 1999), a criminal co-defendant (who testified under a "cooperation" agreement) was unresponsive and showed a lack of understanding; the court was well within the bounds of its discretion by permitting the government to clarify his testimony through the use of leading question and, when appropriate, impeachment. *Craft v. State*, 764 So.2d 1253 (Miss.App. 2000). Decision to allow leading questions rests within discretion of trial court and will only be reversed upon showing abuse of that discretion.See also *Powell v. State,* 995 P.2d 510 (Okla. Crim. App., 2000); *State v. Brown*, 546 So.2d 1265 (La. App. 1989); *State v. Dalton*, 384 S.E.2d 573 (1989); *State v. Odom*, 878 So.2d 582 (La. App., 2004). Generally, leading questions should not be used in the examination of a witness. The trial judge did not, however, abuse his discretion in overruling the defendant's "leading" objection to the prosecutor's direct examination question asking a battery victim if the photographs taken at the police station depicted how she looked the night of the incident and whether her injuries looked worse in the next few days; any objection to the question posed was cured when the prosecutor rephrased the question to ask the victim what the injuries looked like the next few days.

See also *U.S. v. Smith,* 378 F.3d 754 (8th Cir. Minn., 2004).

6 *In re Leonard*, 122 F.Supp. 214 (D.Cal. 1954); *U.S. v. Smith,* 378 F.3d 754 (8th Cir. Minn., 2004). Leading questions should not be used during the direct examination of a witness except as may be necessary to develop the witness's testimony. An unanswered leading question provides no information and is not evidence. The general rule is that leading questions are best reserved for cross-examination; nevertheless, leading questions may properly be used on direct examination with certain witnesses, such as an adverse party or a potentially hostile witness.

7 *Butler v. State,* 541 S.E.2d 653 (Ga. 2001); *State v. Wiggins,* 526 S.E.2d 207 (N.C.App., 2000) provides an excellent comprehensive checklist of exceptions to the general rule that an examining attorney should not ask his own witness leading questions upon direct examination. *Bussey v. State*, 536 N.E.2d 1027 (Ind. 1989) held that a prosecutor could ask a rape victim leading questions regarding whether she was sure that each man had intercourse with her. The victim was emotional while on the stand and, in any event, the question did not harm the defendant. *U.S. v. Perez*, 106 Fed.Appx. 597 (2004). The district court did not abuse its discretion by allowing government to lead a witness (the defendant's mother) who was reluctant to testify and was suffering from a lapse of memory.

8 In *Commonwealth v. Chambers*, 599 A.2d 630 (Pa. 1991), the trial court permitted the prosecutor to ask leading questions on direct examination of a 14-year-old boy who witnessed a robbery and murder; see also *U.S. v. Grey Bear*, 883 F.2d 1382 (N.D. 1989).

young,[9] hostile,[10] or mentally impaired[11] in order to obtain testimony or information.[12]

Second, with respect to non-crucial or non-controversial matters, leading questions can be used to move the trial along more quickly for the benefit of everyone.[13] The practitioner should keep in mind that the principle "evil" to be found in leading questions is their tendency to suggest an answer that the witness would not otherwise provide in the absence of coaching. If the question and answer are not material to the outcome of the proceeding, then the fact that the witness was "led" will be insignificant.

Leading questions are particularly common with respect to introductory matters that are non-controversial. In other words, in order to lay a preliminary foundation so that the witness can be "taken to" the controversial events, leading questions may be asked. This is particularly true where the questions are to be used for settings (times and places) or other such introductory matters.[14]

The court has a great deal of discretion with respect to whether or not it permits leading ques-

---

9 *State v. Bates*, 616 S.E.2d 280 (N.C., 2005). In a trial for multiple counts of statutory sex offenses and other crimes, an order allowing a prosecutor to ask the victim leading questions during direct examination was not reversible error; the victim was 11 years old at the time of trial. *State v. Wiggins,* 526 S.E.2d 207 (N.C.App., 2000); *State v. Lozia*, 829 S.W.2d 558 (Mo.App. 1992); *State v. Murphy*, 394 S.E.2d 300 (N.C.App. 1990); *People v. Kosters*, 438 N.W.2d 651, 175 Mich.App. 748 (Mich.App. 1989); *State v. Rouselle*, 559 A.2d 779 (Me. 1989); *U.S. v. Demarrias,* 876 F.2d 674 (8th Cir. 1989); see also *People v. Calusinski*, 247 Ill.Dec. 956, 733 N.E.2d 420, 314 Ill.App.3d 955 (2000); *State v. Ireland*, 773 P.2d 1375 (Utah 1989); *State v. Dalton*, 384 S.E.2d 573, (N.C.App. 1989); *Strickland v. State*, 550 So.2d 1054 (Ala.App. 1989).

10 *Ostrander v. Ostrander,* 720 N.Y.S.2d 635 (N.Y.A.D., 2001). While it is generally true that adverse party may be viewed as hostile witness, nevertheless, decision whether or not to permit examination through leading questions rests with discretion of trial court. *Ostrander v. Ostrander,* 720 N.Y.S.2d 635 (N.Y.A.D., 2001). While it is generally true that adverse party may be viewed as hostile witness, nevertheless, decision whether or not to permit examination through leading questions rests with discretion of trial court. *State v. Wiggins,* 526 S.E.2d 207 (N.C.App., 2000); *U.S. v. Duncan*, 712 F.Supp. 124 (S.D. Ohio 1988). There is the basic rule which allows the use of leading questions on direct examination of a "witness identified with an adverse party" without any requirement of a showing of hostility. Under that rule, a law enforcement official may qualify as a "witness identified with an adverse party" in an action brought by the government against criminal defendants (absent a positive showing by the government that the witness is not hostile, biased, or so identified with the government that the presumption of hostility should not be applied).

11 *United States v. Nambo-Barajas,* 338 F.3d 956 (8th Cir., Minn., 2003). In a drug conspiracy trial, the prosecutor's use of leading questions during the direct examination of a witness with mental disabilities was proper where the questioning did not result in false or inaccurate testimony.

12 *People v. Marshall*, 534 N.Y.S.2d 623 (N.Y.A.D. 4 Dept. 1988).

13 *Government of Virgin Islands v. Dowling*, 633 F.2d 660 (3rd Cir. 1980); and *McClard v. United States*, 386 F.2d 495 (8th Cir. 1967); *In re Leonard*, 122 F.Supp. 214 (D.Cal. 1954).

14 *U.S. v. Londondio*, 420 F.3d 777 (8th Cir., Minn., 2005); *State v. Wiggins,* 526 S.E.2d 207 (N.C.App., 2000); *Southern Railway Co. v. Hall,* 96 So. 73 (Ala. 1923).

tions during direct examinations and cross-examinations.[15] Fed. R. Evid. 611(c) sums it up by providing:

> Leading questions should not be used on the direct examination of a witness except as may be necessary to develop the witness' testimony. Ordinarily, leading questions should be permitted on cross-examination. When a party calls a hostile witness, an adverse party, or a witness identified with an adverse party, interrogation may be by leading questions.

The federal rule continues an established tradition in this country of *generally* permitting leading questions to be asked during cross-examination, but prohibiting them for direct examination. Of course, where the matter is non-controversial or introductory, then leading questions might be permitted, regardless of whether such matters are presented upon direct or cross-examination.[16]

§7.400 Selected State Rules and Cases

The majority of states have either codified or otherwise issued decisions reflecting the basic rule that you can lead during cross-examination and during undisputed preliminary material, but not upon direct examination of a friendly witness.

If a state is not specifically mentioned in the following list, you should assume that it has a rule that is substantially the same as Fed. R. Evid. 611(c). See §7.300.

ALASKA:

Alaska's Rule 611 is similar to Fed. R. Evid. 611 in some respects. Subdivisions (a) and (b) are identical to Fed. R. Evid. 611(a) and 611(b). Alaska's 611(c), however, has added several specific additional exceptions to those in the federal rule.

ARIZONA:

Arizona's Rule 611 has modified Fed. R. Evid. 611 in some respects. The last two sentences are modified.

---

15 *U.S. v. Anderson*, 446 F.3d 870 (2006). The control of leading questions is a matter generally left to the discretion of the trial judge.

Williams v. CSX Transportation, Inc., 626 S.E.2d 716 (N.C. App., 2006). While it is generally true that a party cannot lead its own witness, it is within the sound discretion of the trial judge to determine whether counsel shall be permitted to ask leading questions, and in the absence of abuse, the exercise of such discretion will not be disturbed on appeal.

Saurini v. Adams County School District No. 12, 191 Fed.Appx. 628 (10th Cir., Colo., 2006). Generally, the district court has discretion in permitting counsel to ask the witnesses leading questions.

Katz v. St. Mary Hospital, 816 A.2d 1125 (Pa.Super, 2003); *State v. Rodriguez,* 839 So.2d 106 (La.App., 2003); *U.S. v. Collins,* 321 F.3d 691 (8th Cir., Minn., 2003). See also *Neal v. State*, 805 So.2d 520 (Miss. 2002); *Dorrough v. State*, 812 So.2d 1077 (Miss.App. 2001); *State v. Humphrey*, 36 P.3d 844 (Kan.App. 2001); *Shelton v. State,* 728 So.2d 105 (Miss.App. 1998); *State v. Hydock,* 725 A.2d 37 Conn.App. 1999; *Commonwealth v. Caldwell,* 634 N.E.2d 124 (Mass.App.Ct. 1994); *State v. McCoy,* 414 S.E.2d 392 (N.C.App. 1992); *Hagood v. State,* 588 So.2d 526 (Ala.App. 1991); *People v. Hirschmann*, 124 Ill.Dec. 779, 529 N.E.2d 760, 175 Ill.App.3d 150 (Ill.App. 1 Dist. 1988); *United States v. O'Brien,* 618 F.2d 1234 (7th Cir. 1980); *Government of Virgin Islands v. Dowling,* 633 F.2d 660 (3rd Cir. 1980); and *McClard v. United States,* 386 F.2d 495 (8th Cir. 1967).

16 For additional discussions, see 3 *Wigmore on Evidence* §770; and for an excellent article on the subject of Leading Questions, see Leading Questions, James W. McElhaney, *The Journal of The American Bar Association*, Vol. 75, Pg. 104 (October, 1989).

ARKANSAS:

It is always within the sound discretion of the trial judge to permit a witness to be asked leading questions on direct examination. D.D. v. State, 842 S.W.2d 62, 40 Ark. App. 75 (1992). Arkansas' Rule 611 is identical to Fed. R. Evid. 611.

CALIFORNIA:

With respect to leading questions, California follows and codifies the basic majority rule by drawing a distinction between direct and cross-examination. CEC Rule 767 provides as follows:

(a) Except under special circumstances where the interests of justice otherwise require:

(1) A leading question may not be asked of a witness on direct or redirect examination.

(2) A leading question may be asked of a witness on cross-examination or recross-examination.

California is also consistent with the majority by placing greater emphasis on the "friendliness" or alignment of the particular witness, than upon the formal distinction between direct and cross-examination.

In applying an "alignment" standard, a trial court would not abuse its discretion in restricting a defendant's use of leading questions during the cross-examination of a defendant's mother (who had been called as a witness by the prosecution), even though the prosecution had been permitted to lead Mom as a hostile witness. *People v. Spain*, 201 Cal. Rptr. 555, 154 C.A.3d 845 (App. 3 Dist. 1984). Also, it might be noted that in at least one case, California applied a subjective test for determining hostility; in *People v. Visciotti*, 825 P.2d 388, 5 Cal. Rptr.2d 495 (1992), leading questions were held not to be improper when they were asked in a "good faith" belief of presumptive hostility on the part of the witness on cross-examination.

Where a witness for the prosecution was the defendant's fiancee and her demeanor on the stand indicated that she was inclined to favor the defense as much as possible, though she had sought and received a formal grant of immunity as the price for her testimony, the trial court did not abuse its discretion in ordering the defense counsel to refrain from the use of leading questions during his cross-examination. *People v. Grey,* 100 Cal. Rptr. 245, 23 C.A.3d 456 (1972).

COLORADO:

The Colorado Rules of Evidence (Title 13 of the Colorado Revised Statutes) follow the Federal Rules virtually word for word and section number for section number. CRS 611(c) mimics the Federal Rule of the same number [see Fed. R. Evid. 611(c), *supra*].

In an employment discrimination action, it was proper for the defendant to use leading questions to cross-examine a former employee of that defendant who was called by the plaintiff as an adverse witness. And likewise, it was appropriate to permit the plaintiff to use leading questions during the direct examination of a former employee of the defendant who remained clearly identified with defendant (and was also carrying on an affair with a key witness for the defendant). *Stahl v. Sun Microsystems, Inc.*, 775 F. Supp. 1397 (D. Colo. 1991).

CONNECTICUT:

In a prosecution for promoting a minor in an obscene performance, the prosecutor may ask leading questions of minor witnesses who were eleven and twelve years old at the time the matter came to trial; the minors were victims of the crimes charged, and had indicated a fear and hesitancy to testify. *State v. Parsons,* 612 A.2d 73, 28 Conn. App. 91 (1992).

In a fashion similar to many of the less populous states, Connecticut follows the Federal Rules essentially word for word and section number for section number. Connecticut's rules regarding leading questions are, therefore, in accord with Fed. R. Evid. 611(c).

FLORIDA:

Section 90.612(3) of the Florida Evidence Code is substantially equivalent to Rule 767 of the California Evidence Code, which seems to reflect an ubiquitous standard:

Except as provided by rule of court or when the interests of justice otherwise require:

(a) A party may not ask a witness a leading question on direct or redirect examination.

(b) A party may ask a witness a leading question on cross-examination or re-cross-examination.

Contrary to the general prohibition against leading, an attorney is authorized to lead and impeach a witness during cross-examination. *Shere v. State*, 579 So.2d 86 (Fla. 1991). Also, it should be noted that as an exception to subparagraph (a), Florida's courts have long permitted the use of leading questions for one's own witness when that witness was persistently unwilling or biased. *Coker v. Hayes*, 16 Fla. 368, 373 (1878); *Caldwell v. State*, 243 So.2d 422 (Fla. 1st Dist. 1971).

Permission to use leading questions has always been within the discretion of the trial judge. *Anderson v. State,* 88 Fla. 93, 101 So. 202 (1924). The courts have upheld the use of leading questions for one's own witness when the witness was young and "very ignorant." *Ellis v. State*, 25 Fla. 702, 6 So. 768 (1889).

GEORGIA:

The state was properly permitted to ask leading questions during direct examination of an accomplice after that accomplice invoked his Fifth Amendment privilege, where the defendant was subsequently permitted to cross-examine the accomplice. *Thomas v. State*, 422 S.E.2d 54, 205 Ga. App. 329 (1992).

There is no question about a prosecutor's right to be an adversary; if a defendant elects to take the stand and testify, he becomes an issue and the prosecutor is entitled to engage in a thorough and sifting cross-examination by means of leading questions. *Fugate v. State*, 431 S.E.2d 104 (Ga. 1993). Also, a prosecutor should be permitted to ask leading questions to impeach his own witness by way of a prior inconsistent statement. *Miller v. State*, 410 S.E.2d 101 (Ga. 1991).

In a murder prosecution, it was improper for the state to ask questions containing their own answers, after a state witness (who had been in jail with defendant), refused to answer those questions about statements allegedly made by the defendant. *Fincher v. State,* 578 S.E.2d 102 (Ga., 2003).

ILLINOIS:

Leading questions are, by definition, suggestive. A leading question is one that suggests the answer to the person being interrogated, especially a question that may be answered by a mere yes or no. *People v. Miles*, 286 Ill. Dec. 827, 815 N.E.2d 37 (Ill. App. Ct., 2004).

The trial court has the discretion to permit the use of leading questions where the witness is a young child. *People v. Calusinski*, 247 Ill. Dec. 956, 733 N.E.2d 420, 314 Ill.App.3d 955 (2000).

With respect to its state courts in general, Illinois' Rule 611(c) is identical to Fed. R. Evid. 611(c). A leading question is one that suggests the answer by putting words or thoughts into the witness' mind. *People v. Cobb*, 134 Ill. Dec. 664, 542 N.E.2d 1171 (Ill. App. 1989).

A lengthy question asked an employee of an asbestos manufacturer (regarding whether the manufacturer operated its plants on the assumption that dust released in any part of the building was likely to become a part of the atmosphere in the rest of the building when there were no partitions or walls and nothing to inhibit movement of the particles) was a bit leading. *Betts v. Manville Personal Injury Settlement Trust*, 167 Ill. Dec. 1063, 588 N.E.2d 1193 (Ill. App. 1992).

INDIANA:

The prosecutor's question to a state witness in a murder prosecution: "The man you saw is this man right here in this purple shirt, isn't it?" constituted impermissible leading of the witness. Moreover, use of leading questions on direct examination generally rests within the trial court's discretion. *Williams v. State*, 733 N.E.2d 919 (Ind. 2000).

A trial court has the discretion to permit leading questions, and will only be reversed for an abuse of that discretion. *Garrison v. State*, 589 N.E.2d 1156 (Ind. 1992).

Not all leading questions result in "yes" or "no" answers. Lengthy questions that suggest that an expert give an opinion may qualify. *Sierp v. Vogel*, 592 N.E.2d 1253 (Ind. App. 1992).

KENTUCKY:

Kentucky's Rule 611 modifies Fed. R. Evid. 611, and broadens the scope of cross-examination.

LOUISIANA:

A "leading question" is generally not appropriate on direct examination. Questions calling for yes or no answers do not constitute impermissible leading questions where the questions do not suggest the answers expected by the witness. The trial court, therefore, did not abuse its discretion by allowing the State to ask leading questions to the defendant's companion (who was involved in a murder). Even though the majority of the questions at issue resulted in yes or no answers, those questions did not constitute impermissible leading questions because they did not suggest the answer that the witness was expected to give. *State v. Moore*, 877 So.2d 1027, 38 (La. App. 2 Cir. June 23, 2004).

A "leading question" is one suggesting the answer that the witness is expected to give; however, a question requiring a "yes" or "no" response is not leading unless the question further suggests the answer to the witness. *State v. Ross*, 604 So.2d 1036 (La. App. 1 Cir. 1992).

The use of leading questions is largely within the discretion of the trial court, and only a clear abuse of that discretion (which prejudices the defendant's rights) will justify the reversal of a conviction. *State v. Young*, 576 So.2d 1048 (La. App. 1 Cir. 1991); see also *State v. Jones*, 593 So.2d 1301 (La. App. 1991).

Generally, a leading question is forgiven if it was meant to relieve a confused or nervous witness, or to clarify or substantiate the prior response of a witness. *State v. Moore*, 575 So.2d 928 (La. App. 2 Cir. 1991).

Louisiana's Rule 611 modifies Fed. R. Evid. 611.

MAINE:

Maine's Rule 611 modifies Fed. R. Evid. 611.

MASSACHUSETTS:

The trial court did not abuse its discretion when it permitted a prosecutor to ask leading questions of his own witness where that witness gave inconsistent, evasive, and ambiguous testimony. *Commonwealth v. Peloquin*, 572 N.E.2d 568, 30 Mass. App. Ct. 960 (1991). Nor did the court abuse its discretion by allowing a prosecutor to ask leading questions of the Commonwealth's own witness (the defendant's girlfriend), in an attempt to impeach her by showing bias. *Commonwealth v. Caldwell*, 634 N.E.2d 124 (Mass. App. Ct. 1994).

MICHIGAN:

Michigan's Rule 611 provides the same general guidelines with respect to leading questions as its federal counterpart; in particular, in Michigan, one may lead during cross-examination but not during direct examination, unless the witness is adverse. Note, however, that Michigan modifies its federal counterpart with respect to 611(b) and 611(c)(3). Moreover, Rule 611 of the Michigan Rules of Evidence, states as follows (The differences with respect to Fed. R. Evid. 611 appear in bold):

(a) Control by Court. The court shall exercise reasonable control over the mode and order of interrogating witnesses and presenting evidence so as to (1) make the interrogation and presentation effective for the ascertainment of the truth, (2) avoid needless consumption of time, and (3) protect witnesses from harassment or undue embarrassment.

(b) Scope of Cross-examination. **A witness may be cross-examined on any matter relevant to any issue in the case, including credibility. The judge may limit cross-examination with respect to matters not testified to on direct examination.**

(c) Leading Questions.

(1) Leading questions should not be used on the direct examination of a witness except as may be necessary to develop the witness' testimony.
(2) Ordinarily, leading questions should be permitted on cross-examination.
(3) When a party calls a hostile witness, an adverse party, or a witness identified with an adverse party, interrogation may be by leading questions. **It is not necessary to declare the intent to ask leading questions before the questioning moves beyond preliminary inquiries.**

MISSISSIPPI:

The decision to allow leading questions rests within the discretion of the trial court and will only be reversed upon a showing of an abuse of that discretion. *Craft v. State*, 764 So.2d 1253 (Miss.App. 2000).

Allowing a prosecutor to repeatedly ask leading questions of his witness can result in reversible error. This particular case involved a narcotics prosecution, and the leading questions dealt with key issues. *McDavid v. State*, 594 So.2d 12 (Miss. 1992). The general rule, however, is that the trial court, in its discretion, may allow leading questions, and unless there has been an abuse of discretion to the prejudice of a complaining party, such permission will not constitute reversible error. *Jones v. State*, 606 So.2d 1051 (Miss. 1992). See also *Shelton v. State,* 728 So.2d 105 (Miss.App. 1999), which held that the use of leading questions is a matter largely left to the discretion of the trial judge.

Mississippi's Rule 611(c) is identical to Fed. R. Evid. 611(c); other portions of Rule 611 are modified.

MISSOURI:

A "leading question" is one which suggests the answer to the witness. *State v. Allison,* 845 S.W.2d 642 (Mo. App.W.D. 1992). It is the discretion of the trial court that controls the use of leading questions; error will not be found unless that discretion is abused. Moreover, such an objection is so within the trial court's discretion to control prejudice that an abuse of discretion will not be readily found; that is particularly the case in circumstances where a witness is informed on the subject matter (and, therefore, not readily led), where the responses are manifestly given in the witness' own terms, and where there is no jury to influence. *McClelland v. Ozenberger*, 841 S.W.2d 227, *reh'g denied* (Mo. App.W.D. 1992).

In a sodomy case, the trial court was held not to have abused its discretion by allowing counsel to lead an 11-year-old witness, who had been lying in bed next to the victim when the alleged acts occurred. She (i.e., the witness) had been touched by the defendant during a strip "spin the bottle" game that he had inaugurated earlier in the evening. *State v. Loazia*, 829 S.W.2d 558 (Mo. App. 1992).

NEBRASKA:

Nebraska's §27-611 is similar to Fed. R. Evid. 611; the term "judge" is substituted for "court."

NEVADA:

Nevada's §50.105 is similar to Fed. R. Evid. 611; the term "judge" is substituted for "court." *Leonard v. State*, 17 P.3d 397 (Nev., 2001). The trial court acted within its discretion by granting prosecutor some latitude in asking questions of state witnesses in order to avoid improper references to defendant's prior murder conviction. Trial court cautioned prosecutor that critical information must come from witnesses and not prosecuting attorney; also, defendant failed to object to particular instances of inappropriate leading questions.

NEW HAMPSHIRE:

Subdivision (c) of New Hampshire's Rule 611 is identical to Fed. R. Evid. 611(c); other portions of Rule 611 have been modified.

NEW JERSEY:

With respect to its state courts in general, New Jersey's Rule 611(c) is very similar in content to Fed. R. Evid. 611(c); that rule does, however, add "unresponsiveness" item to the list of exceptions. Thus, in New Jersey, you may lead your own witness if he or she is "unresponsive."

NEW MEXICO:

New Mexico's Rule 611 is similar to Fed. R. Evid. Rule 611.

NEW YORK:

Even though New York has no uniform set of evidence rules, it is clear that its case law provides a similar result to that required by Fed. R. Evid. 611(c). See Bender's New York Evidence, §2.04(1), (Matthew Bender, Inc.) See also *People v. Hamilton*, 30 N.Y.S.2d 155 (1941), and *Rehm v. Weiss*, 28 N.Y.S. 772 (1894).

NORTH CAROLINA:

Generally, the rules of evidence prohibit the use of leading questions on direct examination; however, leading questions are permissible in certain situations, one of which is if the examiner seeks to aid the witness's recollection or otherwise refresh her memory. *State v. Lesane*, 528 S.E.2d 37 (N.C.App. 2000).

State v. Wiggins, 526 S.E.2d 207 (N.C.App., 2000) provides a checklist of exceptions to the general rule prohibiting leading questions upon direct examination. According to that list, counsel should be permitted to ask leading questions on direct examination when: (1) The witness is hostile or unwilling to testify, (2) the witness has difficulty understanding the question because of immaturity, age, infirmity or ignorance or where (3) the inquiry involves delicate subjects such as sexual matters, or (4) the witness is called to contradict the testimony of a prior witnesses, (5) the examiner seeks to aid the witness's recollection or refresh his memory when the witness has exhausted his memory without answering the stating the particular matters required, (6) the questions are asked for purposes of securing preliminary or introductory testimony, (7) the examiner directs attention to the subject matter at hand without suggesting answers or (8) the mode of questioning is best calculated to elicit the truth.

A "leading question" is one which, by its form or substance, suggests the answer.

State v. Smith, 522 S.E.2d 321, 135 N.C.App. 649 (1999).

In a prosecution for first-degree murder, the prosecution may have engaged in leading questions when it asked a state's witness whether he heard the defendant say anything about that witness "needing to keep his mouth shut"; however, defendant failed to establish that the trial court abused its discretion by allowing such a question. *State v. Marlow*, 432 S.E.2d 275 (N.C. 1993). In a different prosecution for first-degree murder, a prosecutor asked a state's witness about the defendant's emotional state and demeanor (i.e., "What was defendant's emotional state at the time?" and, "What, if anything, did you notice about defendant's emotional state at that time?"); the questions did not suggest any desired response and were, therefore, not leading. *State v. Shoemaker*, 432 S.E.2d 314, (N.C. 1993).

North Carolina's Rule 611 is similar to Fed. R. Evid. 611.

OHIO:

In a capital murder case, a prosecutor did not ask improper leading questions when he directed a witnesses' attention toward the events that occurred on a particular date; moreover, the prosecution was permitted to ask the witness on direct examination about whether the subject killing occurred on Friday morning or Saturday morning since the witness had already testified that the murder occurred on Saturday morning. *State v. D'Ambrosio*, 616 N.E.2d 909, 67 Ohio St.3d 185 (1993).

The trial court has a great deal of latitude with respect to the amount of "leading" that it permits. And, it is within the sound discretion of the trial court to permit the state to ask leading questions of its own witness, and the decision to permit such questions will not be reversed absent a showing of abuse of discretion. *State v. Moore*, 598 N.E.2d 1224, 74 Ohio App.3d 334, *dismissed, jurisdic-*

tional motion overruled, 580 N.E.2d 1099, 62 Ohio St.3d 1469 (Ohio App. 10 Dist. 1991).

In a medical malpractice action against an osteopath, counsel for the patient's widow posed leading questions to an expert witness on direct examination; these were held not to constitute reversible prejudice, because the physician's answers clearly communicated his own thoughts about the osteopath's actions. *Lambert v. Shearer*, 616 N.E.2d 965, 84 Ohio App.3d 266 (1992).

Generally, a party should not be allowed to ask leading questions for the purpose of impeaching his or her own witness with prior inconsistent statements, absent a showing of surprise and affirmative damage. A party may, however, ask leading questions of a witness who is hostile or is, in some manner, identified with an adverse party. *State v. Warren*, 588 N.E.2d 905, 67 Ohio App.3d 789 (1990); see Ohio Ev. R. 611.

OKLAHOMA:

Leading questions which suggest the answer to the witness should not be asked by the party placing that witness on the stand; however, the decision whether or not to permit leading questions is largely a matter of discretion on the part of the trial judge. *Powell v. State,* 995 P.2d 510 (Okla.Crim.App., 2000).

Oklahoma's §2611 modifies and renumbers Rule 611, particularly in regards to subdivision (c).

OREGON:

Oregon has adopted most of the rules and principles set forth in the Federal Rules of Evidence. The Oregon Evidence Code (Oregon Revised Statutes, Chapter 40 et seq.), however, assigns its own rule numbers. ORS 40.370(3) corresponds to Fed. R. Evid. 611(c).

PENNSYLVANIA:

On May 8, 1998, the Pennsylvania Supreme Court adopted a new and comprehensive set of evidence rules, with an effective date of October 1, 1998. The new rules are patterned after the Federal Rules of Evidence, both by content and number.

See Pennsylvania's new Rule 611(c) (Mode and Order of Interrogation and Presentation), which is patterned after its respective federal counterpart (discussed *supra*).

The trial judge has wide discretion in controlling the use of leading questions at trial. *Com. v. Polston*, 616 A.2d 669 (Pa. Super. 1992).

The trial court did not err by permitting a prosecutor to ask leading questions of a 14-year-old who witnessed a murder and robbery, particularly where that prosecutor was exercising care so as to avoid having the witness refer to the defendant's involvement in a different robbery. *Commonwealth v. Chambers*, 599 A.2d 630 (Pa. 1991).

PUERTO RICO:

Puerto Rico's Rule 43 is different from Fed. R. Evid. 611.

SOUTH DAKOTA:

South Dakota's §19-14-18 and §19-14-20 are identical to Fed. R. Evid. 611.

TENNESSEE:

It is within the sound discretion of the trial court whether to allow a party to examine a witness by using leading questions. *Wilkerson v. Altizer*, 845 S.W.2d 744 (Tenn. App. 1992).

The trial court may in its discretion allow counsel to use leading questions on direct examination where an adverse or hostile witness is involved. *State v. Woods*, 806 S.W.2d 205 (Tenn. Crim. App. 1990).

Tennessee's Rule 611(c) modifies its federal counterpart by omitting reference to an "adverse" party.

TEXAS:

It was not an abuse of discretion for the prosecutor to ask leading questions during his direct examination of a rape victim, with respect to the details of the rape, particularly where the elicited testimony had already been presented to the jury without the use of leading questions. *Newsome v. State*, 829 S.W.2d 260 (Tex. App. 1992).

Ordinarily, leading questions should be permitted on cross-examination; however, the use of leading questions may be inappropriate when the cross-examination is of a friendly witness, such as an attorney's own party, who had been called by the opposition. *GAB Business Services, Inc. v. Moore*, 829 S.W.2d 345 (Tex. App. 1992).

Texas' rules of evidence (both civil and criminal) have provisions similar to Fed. R. Evid. 611. With respect to leading questions, Rule 611(c) of the Texas Rules (Civil) provide as follows:

> Leading questions should not be used on the direct examination of a witness. Ordinarily, leading questions should be permitted on cross-examination. When a party calls a hostile witness, an adverse party, or a witness identified with an adverse party, interrogation may be by leading questions.

VERMONT:

Vermont mimics the Federal Rules of Evidence in much the same fashion as several aforementioned states. The rule numbers for the Vermont Rules of Evidence match the Federal Rules, including VRE 611(c), with respect to leading questions; Vermont's Rule 611(c) is similar, but not identical to its federal counterpart.

WEST VIRGINIA:

When a party calls a hostile or adverse witness, the interrogation may include leading questions. *State v. Perolis*, 398 S.E.2d 512 (W.Va. 1990). Any witness who is adverse to the party calling the witness may be examined by leading questions, even if the witness is not "hostile." *Id.*

West Virginia's Rule 611 is similar to Fed. R. Evid. 611; notably (and very curiously), however, 611(c) permits leading questions during the direct examination of expert witnesses. While the exception is strange, it does avoid the pretense that an expert is objectively presenting his own opinions.

WISCONSIN:

Wisconsin's §906.11 is identical to Fed. R. Evid. 611.

WYOMING:

Wyoming apparently takes a more liberal attitude with respect to leading, as evidenced by *Duke v. State,* 99 P.3d 928, 2004 WY. 120 (Wyo., 2004), holding that leading questions during direct examination are not, *per se*, impermissible.

Chapter 8

Multiple Questions

§8.100 Introduction

Attorneys should ask one question at a time. Questions that call for more than one answer may be considered as multiple or compound. Such questions may be objectionable because they are often confusing. They may also interfere with the opposing attorney's ability to interpose an objection after "each" question. Another problem arises if the witness answers with a simple "yes" or "no," since it would be impossible to tell which question the witness had answered.

§8.200 Quick Explanation

A multiple or compound question is one that, in essence, asks two or more questions in the same sentence.

EXAMPLES OF MULTIPLE QUESTIONS:

1. Did you attend the party, and if so, when did you go and why?
2. Did you see the driver of the car, and where was he positioned?
3. What did each of the people do next?

The first two questions can be identified as compound by the conjunction "and," but the third question is trickier. On its face, question number three is not objectionable as long as the witness is able to provide an answer based on personal observations. If, however, the term "people" encompassed a large number, such would not be the case. For example, one person could not simultaneously observe the individual movements of *fifty* people. Hearsay could insidiously work its way into a response that called for such an observation.

WHAT TO LOOK FOR:

Questions that contain the conjunction "and," or request information about more than a single transaction.

OBJECT AND RESPOND

OBJECTION:

"Objection. The question is compound.

"Objection. The question calls for a narrative."

POTENTIAL RESPONSES TO OBJECTION:

A. (Compound) Merely break down the compound question into separate questions, asking them one at a time (As you do, be sure to perform a shoulder-shrug to show your disgust at opposing counsel's time-wasting objections).

B. (Narrative) "Your Honor, I would much prefer the witness to give her own candid report, as opposed to me guiding her through the process."

§8.300 General Legal Analysis

Multiple or compound questions, as they are sometimes called, are generally objectionable, particularly when they combine admissible and inadmissible matters.[1] For example, consider this question which mixes personal observations with hearsay: "What did you see and what was told to you with respect to the defendant's actions?"

Even though each part of a compound sentence may be properby itself, the combination is, nevertheless, improper. For example, in a civil action against a surgeon for alleged negligence in performing an eye operation, a cross-examination question was put to an expert as to whether he would recommend surgery on a distorted lens for a nearsighted condition where the patient's

1 *Board of Trustees v. Schuyten*, 326 P.2d 223 (Cal.App. 1958).

vision was 20/50 and 20/60; this was held to be objectionable as compound.[2] Also held to be objectionable are questions that combine past and present tenses.[3]

Unlike some improper questions, one that is compound interferes, per se, with the lawyer's ability to object. Where several questions are fired off at once, there is no time to even consider each one separately. So this rule involving multiplicity allows the lawyer to object to the entire litany, even though one or more proper inquiries may be contained within the question. Nevertheless, this objection is not one that ordinarily involves reversible error even if the judge should happen to make a clearly wrong ruling.[4]

§8.400 Questions Calling for a Narrative

Closely related to the multiple or compound question is one that calls for a narrative or lengthy discourse on the part of the witness. In fact, such a query might be thought of as an extreme form of compound question, since it seeks an unpredictable number of factual responses, as opposed to merely two or three. *Black's Law Dictionary* defines "narrative evidence" as follows:[5]

> Testimony from a witness which he is permitted to give without the customary questions and answers; e.g., when witness explains in detail what happened without interruption.

Don't be misled by the "permitted" portion of the definition; questions that call for narrative testimony are generally subject to disapproval. They deprive the opposing attorney of an opportunity to object to the witness' answers before they are heard by the court and jury. Moreover, the responses to such questions could cover the entire spectrum of objectionable testimony.

Questions calling for a narrative will normally ask the witness to describe events that transpired over an extended period of time. Often the interrogation will not even be in proper "question" form, but will be more akin to a "request." This invites a vast range of potential responses, some of which may contain hearsay, irrelevant matters, and several other brands of potentially objectionable answers.

After an objectionable piece of dialogue has been spoken, the opposing attorney may attempt to have the material stricken. But that is often like trying to unring a bell. And there is no guarantee that the court will grant the request in any event. For, it is quite possible that an unsympathetic judge may take the position that objections to the **answer** are waived by the attorney's failure to object to the **question.**[6]

Particular caution should be exercised to avoid being "sandbagged" by witnesses who would provide improper non-responsive answers to perfectly proper questions. The only way to combat such a tactic is by making a motion to strike the answer. If the judge denies the motion, a request should be made to have the question and answer read back; then the motion should be renewed.

EXAMPLES OF QUESTIONS THAT CALL FOR A NARRATIVE:

1. Tell us everything that you remember.
2. Tell the court what happened that day.
3. Give us the events in your own words.

Notice that the questions tend to be ambiguous, and may therefore be subject to a vagueness objection.[7] This may be a better objection

2 *Scarano v. Schnoor*, 323 P.2d 178 (Cal.App. 1958).

3 *Wiese v. Rainville,* 343 P.2d 643 (Cal.App. 1959).

4 *Association of Independent Taxi Operators v. Kern*, 13 A.2d 374 (Md. 1940).

5 Sixth Edition, West Publishing, St. Paul, Minn. (1990).

6 *Reagan v. Brock*, 628 F.2d 721 (1st Cir. 1980); see also Overview.

7 See Chapter 12.

choice, since it would have the likely effect of forcing the opposition to rephrase the question. Moreover, a vagueness objection would have a better chance (than a "narrative" objection) of being sustained.[8]

As with leading questions (see Chapter 7), narratives tend to speed up the trial process. Monologues, in general, are far quicker than typical question-answer scenarios. For that reason, courts tend to be quite liberal in permitting narratives during the introductory, non-material portions of witness testimony.

In the federal sphere, Fed. R. Evid. 611(a) permits the court to "exercise reasonable control over the mode and order of interrogating witnesses." *The Notes of the Advisory Committee on Proposed Rules* interpret that rule as granting to the judge some leeway with respect to whether testimony should be "in the form of a free narrative or responses to specific questions."

From the committee notes and applicable cases, it is fair to conclude that a narrative objection has less chance of being sustained in federal court than in a state court lacking a directive similar to Rule 611(a). As a rule of thumb, however, for both federal and state trials, the practitioner should object to narrative testimony that was not limited to background or non-material matters.

§8.500 Selected State Rules and Cases

CALIFORNIA:

California's recognition of the impropriety of the multiple or compound question can be inferred from the cases considered above, i.e., *Board of Trustees v. Schuyten*, 326 P.2d 223 (Cal. App. 1958); *Scarano v. Schnoor*, 323 P.2d 178 (Cal. App. 1958).

With respect to narrative questions, California straddles the fence of discretion as much as most other jurisdictions. In particular, whether or not to allow witnesses to testify in narrative form is addressed to the trial court's sound discretion, and unless prejudice is shown, it cannot be held that the trial court's action amounted to an abuse of that discretion. *Silva v. Dias*, 116 P.2d 496, 46 C.A.2d 662 (1941).

There is even latitude in criminal cases. For example, in a prosecution for assault with intent to rape, the court did not err in directing a minor prosecutrix to tell the story in her own way. *People v. Davis*, 91 P. 810, 6 C.A. 229 (1907).

Wiese v. Rainville, 343 P.2d 643 (Cal. App. 1959) provided an interesting set of specific questions that were ruled objectionable. Notice the manner in which the questions combine both the past and present tense into each single question:

> Does Pearce Plastics or did Pearce Plastics at the time of this accident, produce items that your company would be likely to purchase?
>
> Is your company in any business, or were they in any business relationship to the Pearce Plastics Company in relation to purchase or vendee or vendor relationship?
>
> Did the Pearce Plastic Company, at the time the loss occurred, at the time you went over to the Pearce Plastic Company, produce any item that your company would be interested in purchasing?
>
> Are you and were you, on that date [date of accident] familiar with the mechanisms of the machine?

FLORIDA:

§90.611 of the *Florida Evidence Code* is similar to Fed. R. Evid. 611 with respect to the court's authority to control the witness questioning process.

NEW YORK:

See *Bender's New York Evidence*, §2.01(2).

WASHINGTON:

It was not an error for a judge to permit a witness to provide narrative testimony where the judge was the trier of fact. *Teufel v. Wienir,* 411 P.2d 151 (1966).

8 Wherever narratives tend to move the case along more rapidly, the court is less likely to prohibit such testimony. See *In re Air Crash at Stapleton International Airport,* 720 F.Supp. 1493 (D.Colo. 1989); see also *Goings v. United States,* 377 F.2d 753 (8th Cir. 1967).

Chapter 9

Privilege

§9.100 Introduction

Throughout the years, legal scholars and judges have formed the notion that thieves, muggers, rapists, hit-and-run drivers, squealers, unfaithful spouses, and wrongdoers in general, should all have somewhere safe to go and talk of their afflictions. At least, that's what the creators and perpetuators of the law of privilege believe. More particularly, the theory suggests that it is beneficial if certain people can be "trusted" to keep quiet. Were this not the case, people would be reluctant to seek professional help. And this would, of course, create a national crisis—shrinks, doctors, and we lawyers might be out of business.

In a courtroom setting, the term "privilege" means that the witness has a legal right to refuse to answer a question because of some special relationship, law, or constitutional guarantee. Questions that violate an established privilege may be objected to. If no objection is made, however, the privilege will be waived.

The law of privilege presents a unique set of problems because of its lack of uniformity throughout the fifty states. Some states recognize privileges that others do not. Even the Federal Rules of Evidence, which have created nearly-complete uniformity for 85 out of 100 jurisdictions (i.e., 50 federal plus 35 states) avoids the *privilege* issue by referring the reader back to the laws of the respective states. But despite the diversity, the reader should detect some consistency with respect to certain basic principles that transcend state lines.

§9.200 Quick Explanation

The following is a list of eleven classic groups involving privileged communications. *Certain* conversations between the people listed in each duet are privileged, meaning that those questions are objectionable, and need not be answered. We place some emphasis upon the word "certain," because there are exceptions. Here is the list of the duos:

1. Lawyer - Client
2. Doctor - Patient
3. Therapist - Patient
4. Accountant - Client
5. Clergyman - Penitent
6. Husband - Wife
7. Parent - Child
8. Informant - Police
9. Journalist - News Source
10. Confidential Institutional Communications
11. Self-Incrimination (i.e., Person - Self)

EXAMPLES OF PRIVILEGED QUESTIONS:

1. What did your lawyer tell you to say at this hearing?
2. Did you confess any crimes to your priest?
3. What did you tell your psychiatrist?

WHAT TO LOOK FOR:

Questions that involve conversations or exchanges of information between professionals, clergymen, and close family members. Any "confidential communication" might be a candidate for some type of privilege.

OBJECT AND RESPOND

OBJECTION:

"Objection. Privileged."

POTENTIAL RESPONSES TO OBJECTION:

A. "The privilege has been waived."

B. "Opposing counsel has not established the foundation elements required for the assertion of this privilege." (See §9.501 through §9.512.)

§9.300 General Legal Analysis

The laws pertaining to privilege are complex, at times inconsistent, and may vary from state to state. So determining whether or not a question seeks privileged information is not always a simple task. The Federal Rules of Evidence, which normally provide a model for the states to follow, offer very little help. Fed. R. Evid. 501 directs the reader to other sources with the following wordy instructions:

> Except as otherwise required by the Constitution of the United States or provided by Act of Congress or in rules prescribed by the Supreme Court pursuant to statutory authority, *the privilege of a witness*, person, government, State, or political subdivision thereof *shall be governed by the principles of the common law as they may be interpreted by the courts of the United States in the light of reason and experience*. However, in civil actions and proceedings, with respect to an element of a claim or defense as to which State law supplies the rule of decision, the privilege of a witness, person, government, State, or political subdivision thereof shall be determined in accordance with State law (*emphasis supplied*).

The rule says that the principles pertaining to privilege come primarily from case law,[1] even though they may be modified by statutes and the U.S. Constitution. Perhaps we can shed some light on this complex situation by providing some general principles for each of the eleven duos.

REFERENCES

Scholar's privilege under Rule 501 of Fed. R. Evid. 81 A.L.R. Fed. 904.

§9.400 State Rules

The law of privilege among the several states provides a bit of diversity, untainted by the influence of the Federal Rules of Evidence. Whereas, the other rules of the states seem to look to the feds for guidance, when it comes to privilege, the Federal Rules look to the states (Fed. R. Evid. 501).

Even without obvious space limitations, it would not be practical to spell out all of the privilege rules and laws for all fifty states; nor is that necessary to gain a firm understanding of the topic. Moreover, the majority of states follow California's basic model in most matters. The fastest way to get a grip on the subject would be to refer to our list of eleven,[2] and use it as a starting point. The list includes all of the majors. It can be used to gather some general principles.

All states, for example, recognize the first item, the lawyer-client privilege. The doctor-patient privilege is very weak, but it is recognized in most states. All states recognize a privilege for some form of therapist (i.e., psychiatrist, psychologist, counselor, etc.). The remaining items are fairly common, but vary in strength, excepting the parent-child privilege, which is rare (only four states, most notably New York, recognize it). The last item, the self-incrimination privilege, is the most ubiquitous and the strongest of the set since it enjoys constitutional protection at the state and federal levels.

There are, in addition to our list, an endless number of *de minimis* privileges that exist due to public policy or a respect for the internal processes of a variety of entities, ranging from police conduct review boards to college committees.

In addition to creating some relatively innovative privileges, our model state, California, leaves the door open still farther by acknowledging that any "confidential communications" stand a chance of gaining privilege status even if they are not entitled to the presumptions that accompany some of the majors.

In order to better compare our prior docket of privileges (§9.200) to those specifically recognized by the state of California, consider the following list. One might also consider the protection granted to trade secrets as a form of privilege (CEC 1060), although problems pertaining to it are more likely to arise in a discovery setting than during trial.

1 *United States v. Talley*, 790 F.2d 1468 (9th Cir. 1986).

2 See §9.200.

CALIFORNIA PRIVILEGES

1. ***+Lawyer - Client (CEC 954)**
2. ***+Doctor - Patient (CEC 994)**
3. ***+Therapist - Patient (CEC 1014); *Sexual Assault Counselor - Victim (CEC 1035.8)**
4. Accountant - Client
5. ***Clergyman - Penitent (CEC 1033 & 1034)**
6. ***Husband - Wife (CEC 970 & 980)**
7. Parent - Child
8. Informant - Police (CEC 1040)
9. Journalist - News Source (CEC 1070)
10. Confidential Institutional Communications
11. Self-Incrimination (CEC 940)

KEY

(BOLD) Confidential: Those relationships that appear in bold type are presumed by the California Evidence Code (Rule 917) to have been made in confidence.

(*) **Potential Waiver if Disclosed:** These privileged communications may be waived if any holder of the privilege, without coercion, discloses a significant part of the communication. CEC 912(a). Specifically, CEC 912 refers to the following privileges falling within that group: lawyer-client privilege (CEC 954), confidential marital communications (CEC 980), physician-patient privilege (CEC 994), psychotherapist-patient privilege (CEC 1014), privilege of a penitent (CEC 1033), privilege of a clergyman (CEC 1034), and sexual assault victim-counselor privilege (CEC 1035.8). Rule 912(b) refers to jointly held privileges, holding that a waiver by one does not affect the other. And Rule 912(c) provides that where a disclosure itself is privileged, that disclosure does not constitute a waiver.

(+) **Limited Disclosures Protected:** Rule 912(d) protects limited disclosures for those privileges marked with a plus (+) sign. In particular, when a disclosure is reasonably necessary for the accomplishment of the purpose for which the lawyer, physician, psychotherapist, or sexual assault counselor was consulted, such disclosure is not a waiver of the privilege.

(no cite) **Limited Recognition:** Privileges lacking a specific reference to the CEC enjoy limited recognition, if any.

Section 1060 of the CEC provides a privilege for trade secrets:

> If he or his agent or employee claims the privilege, the owner of a trade secret has a privilege to refuse to disclose the secret, and to prevent another from disclosing it, if the allowance of the privilege will not tend to conceal fraud or otherwise work injustice.

In Arizona, to enjoy an evidentiary privilege, the subject communication must meet four criteria:

(1) it must originate in a confidence that it will not be disclosed;
(2) the confidentiality must be essential to the full maintenance of the relationship between the parties;
(3) the relationship must be one that the community believes should be fostered; and,
(4) the injury to the relationship that would occur from disclosure must be greater than the benefit gained in aid of the litigation.[3]

In furtherance of the standard privileges that Colorado recognizes, Section 13-90-107 of the Colorado Revised Statutes provides an additional prohibition against "examination." Subsection (b), for example, provides:

> An attorney shall not be examined without the consent of his client as to any communication made by the client to him or his advice given thereon in the course of professional employment; nor shall an attorney's secretary, paralegal, legal assistant,

3 *City of Tucson v. Superior Court In and For County of Pima*, 809 P.2d 428 (Ariz. 1991).

> stenographer, or clerk be examined without the consent of his employer concerning any fact, the knowledge of which he has acquired in such capacity.

Similar language contained in other portions of Section 13-90-107 pertains to physicians, surgeons, and licensed psychologists. The statute also provides coverage for certain public officers, certified public accountants and qualified interpreters during the course of their work. Under Section 13-90-119, Colorado recognizes a limited privilege for journalists.

Testimonial privileges based on confidential communications are waived when a communication is made in the presence of a third party or when the party asserting a privilege has voluntarily revealed that confidential information to another.[4]

Connecticut's privilege laws can be found in the form of Court Rule 501 and its subsections. In addition to the classic privileges (i.e., Rule 501(j) provides for the attorney-client privilege and Rule 501(c) pertains to doctor-patient privilege), Rule 501 provides a myriad of other "professions" whose clientele might also enjoy a shopping list of privileges:

> Clergyman-penitent; juvenile judge-child; teacher or school nurse-student (limited to communications regarding alcohol or drug abuse); informer-state; state mediator, agent and assistant agents of board of labor relations; victim service counselor-victim; reports of commissioner of labor-employee; bail commissioner; interpreter (for the hearing impaired); state ethics commission; state banking commissioner; drug test results; employee assistance counselor-judicial employee; and corporate self-evaluation.

For Florida, Section 90 of the Florida Evidence Code assembles and defines some of the common privileges, in California Evidence Code fashion. The lawyer-client privilege is covered in FEC 90.502, the psychotherapist-patient privilege in FEC 90.503, the accountant-client privilege in FEC 90.5055, the clergyman-penitent privilege in FEC 90.505, and the husband-wife privilege in FEC 90.504.

Section 90.506 covers trade secrets. Section 90.5035 covers the sexual assault counselor-victim privilege (similar to California). And Section 90.507 codifies the once common law methods by which privilege can be waived:

> A person who has a privilege against disclosure of a confidential matter or communication waives the privilege if he, or his predecessor while holder of the privilege, voluntarily discloses or makes the communication when he does not have a reasonable expectation of privacy, or consents to disclosure of, any significant part of the matter or communication. This section is not applicable when the disclosure is itself a privileged communication.

For New York, with respect to civil actions in particular, that state's lengthy privilege provisions extend into its CPLR (Civil Practice Laws and Rules). Instead of subdividing its rules into easily readable definitions and sub-parts, the CPLR tends to cram the entire text into lengthy paragraphs.

New York's close neighbor, New Jersey, provides for a strict and narrow construction when it comes to the application of any privilege. The purpose is to favor the admissibility of evidence.[5]

Oregon's privilege laws consist of well-defined terms and readable subparagraphs (compare to New York). Oregon also recognizes the following limited privileges: Rule 40.245, "school employee-student privilege"; Rule 40.265, "stenographer-employer privilege"; Rule 40.270, "public officer privilege"; and Rule 40.275, "identity of informer."

---

4 *People v. Lindsey*, 805 P.2d 1134 (Colo.App. 1990).

5 *State v. Ciba-Geigy Corp.*, 589 A.2d 180, 247 N.J.Super. 314 (N.J.Super.A.D. 1991).

In an excellent law review article written by Franklin D. Cleckley, professor of law at West Virginia University College of Law, the history and description of all of the state's recognized privileges are considered and discussed.[6]

§9.500 The Privileges Individually Considered

§9.501 Lawyer - Client Privilege

Communications that pass back and forth between lawyers and clients form one of the most important "privileges" recognized by law. It has a powerful policy base designed to encourage the free flow of words between lawyers and clients. In particular, the policy suggests that if it were *not* for privilege, clients would withhold the truth from their lawyers. And this, it was decided, would be a "bad thing," particularly since lawyers *already* have enough trouble trying to pry the truth out of clients.

Where legal advice of any kind is sought from a professional legal advisor in his capacity as such, communications relating to that purpose, made in confidence by the client, are at the client's insistence permanently protected from disclosure by himself or by his legal advisor, unless the protection is waived.[7] Generally, an attorney cannot disclose advice given to a client about the matters for which he was consulted professionally, nor can the client be required to divulge advice given to him by his attorney.[8]

The attorney-client privilege does not protect *all* communications between lawyers and their

6 *A Modest Proposal: A Psychotherapist-Patient Privilege for West Virginia*, 93 W.Va. L.Rev. 1 (1990).

7 The elements of the attorney-client privilege are as follows: (1) Where legal advice of any kind is sought (2) from a professional legal advisor in his capacity as such, (3) the communications relating to that purpose, (4) which were made in confidence (5) by the client, (6) are at his instance permanently protected from disclosure by himself or by the legal adviser, (7) except that the protection may be waived. See *Smithkline Beecham Corp. v. Apotex Corp.,* 193 F.R.D. 530 (N.D.Ill.E.Div., 2000). The attorney-client privilege exists to protect not only the giving of professional advice to those who can act on it, but also the giving of information to the lawyer to enable him to give sound and informed advice. See *Transonic Systems, Inc. v. Non-Invasive Medical Tech.,* 192 F.R.D. 710 (D.Utah, 2000) , *VLT Corp. v. Unitrode Corp.,* 194 F.R.D. 8 (D.Mass., 2000) and *Caremark, Inc. v. Affiliated Computer Services, Inc.,* 192 F.R.D. 263 (N.D.Ill.E.Div., 2000).

The attorney-client privilege applies when: (1) the asserted holder of the privilege is or sought to become a client; (2) the person to whom the communication was made (a) is a member of the bar of a court or his subordinate and (b) in connection with this communication is acting as a lawyer; (3) the communication relates to a fact of which the attorney was informed by his client without the presence of strangers for the purpose of securing primarily either (a) an opinion of law or (b) legal services or (c) assistance in some legal proceeding, and not for the purpose of committing a crime or tort; and (4) the privilege has been (a) claimed and (b) not waived by the client. See *Alexander v. F.B.I.,* 193 F.R.D. 1 (D.D.C., 2000); *Polycast Technology Corp. v. Uniroyal, Inc.*, 125 F.R.D. 47 (S.D.N.Y. 1989).

8 Courts have a duty to safeguard the privacy of the attorney-client relationship, so as to maintain public confidence in the legal profession and protect the integrity of judicial proceedings. *Securities Investor Protection Corp. v. R.D. Kushnir & Co.,* 246 B.R. 582 (Bankr.N.D.Ill.E.Div., 2000). Under the doctrine of "attorney-client privilege," confidential communications between a client and an attorney for the purpose of obtaining legal advice are privileged, and a court cannot compel revelation of these communications through discovery or testimony in civil or criminal matters. *Denius v. Dunlap,* 209 F.3d 944, 143 Ed. Law Rep. 736 (C.A.7, Ill., 2000). See also *Lazar v. Mauney,* 192 F.R.D. 324 (N.D., 2000). See also *Ex Parte Great American Surplus Lines Ins. Co.*, 540 So.2d 1357 (Ala. 1989); *Triple A Machine Shop, Inc. v. State*, 261 Cal.Rptr. 493 (Cal.App. 1989).

clients. Rather, it hinges upon the client's belief that he is consulting a lawyer in order to seek confidential legal advice.[9]

The privilege *only* protects those disclosures that are necessary to obtain informed legal advice that might not be given in the absence of such privilege.[10] Communications made by a defendant to his attorney for the purpose of being transmitted to third persons were *not* included within the confidential communications privilege.[11] Nor can a client or potential client create a shield for unprotected materials merely by turning them over to an attorney. In other words, unprivileged materials do not suddenly become privileged just because they are turned over to an attorney. [12]

The attorney-client privilege is predicated on the assumption that lawyers can act effectively only if they are fully advised of the facts by the parties whom they represent and that such disclosure will be promoted if the client knows that his communications cannot be extorted from the lawyer. That privilege recognizes that sound legal advice and services for the public rest on the need to encourage full and frank communication between attorneys and their clients.[13] The purpose of that privilege is to promote the public's interest in the observance of law and the administration of justice.[14]

However, since the privilege works to suppress otherwise relevant evidence and forestall a

---

9 *In re Qwest Communications International Inc., Securities Litigation*, 450 F.3d 1179, 70 Fed. R. Evid. Serv. 492 (10th Cir., Colo., 2006). A critical component of attorney-client privilege under common law is whether the communication between the client and the attorney was made in confidence and under circumstances from which it could reasonably be assumed that the communication would remain in confidence. The attorney-client privilege is lost if the client discloses the substance of otherwise privileged communication to any third party.

In re Sulfuric Acid Antitrust Litigation, 235 F.R.D. 407 (N.D. Ill., 2006). The protection of the attorney-client privilege extends to confidential communications made by a client to his lawyer where legal advice of any kind is sought from a professional legal advisor in his capacity as such. Protection of the attorney-client privilege is limited to situations in which the attorney is acting as a legal advisor.

The attorney-client privilege protects confidential communications made by a client to his or her lawyer where legal advice of any kind is sought from a professional legal advisor in his or her capacity as such. *Rehling v. City of Chicago,* 207 F.3d 1009, 10 A.D. Cases 589 (C.A.7, Ill., 2000). See also *City of Springfield v. Rexnord Corp.*, 196 F.R.D. 7 (D.Mass. 2000); *Colonial Gas Co. v. Aetna Cas. & Sur. Co.*, 144 F.R.D. 600 (D.Mass. 1992); *United States v. Keplinger,* 776 F.2d 678 (7th Cir. 1985). In order for attorney-client privilege to apply to a writing, document must have been intended to be confidential and made for purpose of giving or obtaining legal advice.

10 A party asserting the attorney-client privilege has the burden of demonstrating: (1) a communication between client and counsel, which (2) was intended to be and was in fact kept confidential, and (3) made for the purpose of obtaining or providing legal advice. *National Congress for Puerto Rican Rights v. City of New York,* 194 F.R.D. 105 (S.D.N.Y., 2000). See also *United States v. Upjohn Co.*, 600 F.2d 1223 (6th Cir. 1979); see also *Kai USA Ltd. v. Camillus Cutlery Co. (In re Kroll),* 224 F.R.D. 326 (E.D.N.Y., 2004); *Grossman v. Schwarz*, 125 F.R.D. 376 (S.D.N.Y. 1989). The attorney-client privilege only protects confidential communications between a client and his or her attorney that are made for the purpose of obtaining or providing legal advice; it does not extend to the very framework of the relationship, such as the identity of the client or the fact that a given individual has become a client. Specifically, the substance of a meeting between an attorney and a client may be privileged, but the fact of the meeting itself is not because it does not reveal any confidential communications.

11 *Lahr v. State,* 731 N.E.2d 479 (Ind.App. 2000); *Stirum v. Whalen*, 811 F.Supp. 78 (N.D.N.Y. 1993); *Shelton v. State*, 426 S.E.2d 69, 206 Ga.App. 579 (1992). Attorney-client privilege did not protect information concerning two forged letters that defendant provided to his attorney for purpose of bolstering his self-defense argument in aggravated battery prosecution; defendant clearly had no expectation of privacy in letters because he had intended to make them public.

12 *Blanchard v. EdgeMark Financial Corp.*, 192 F.R.D. 233 (N.D.Ill. 2000). Documents which are not privileged do not become privileged simply because an attorney requests them.

13 *State v. Sanders*, 616 A.2d 1345, 260 N.J.Super 491 (N.J.Super.A.D. 1992).

14 *U.S. Fidelity & Guar. Co. v. Barron Industries, Inc.*, 809 F.Supp. 355 (M.D.Pa. 1992).

search for truth, the limitations which restrict its operation must be assiduously heeded. Put another way, the privilege must be strictly limited to the purpose for which it exists.[15]

When it applies, the attorney-client privilege is a strong one. It extends to the substance of the client's communication to the lawyer as well as the lawyer's advice to the client.[16] It covers confidential disclosures to an attorney by employees of a client.[17] The privilege covers scientific and technical information as well as personal communications.[18] It has even been held that the attorney-client privilege exists even though the client may be dead.[19] A client's mental or emotional problems may also cause special problems and concerns.[20]

To constitute attorney-client privilege, it must be established that the subject communication was to an attorney or his agent, that an attorney-client relationship existed, that the communication was in fact confidential, and that the information sought was derived from that communication.[21] However, attorney-client privilege is not self-executing. When the issue arises in the courtroom, an objection is *required* or else the privilege may be waived.[22]

The privilege can also be waived through disclosure,[23] and it can be waived for limited purposes.[24] The most common cause of privilege waiver is voluntary disclosure. The attorney-client privilege exists to protect confidential communications, and it is waived through any voluntary disclosure by the privilege holder to a third person.[25] A voluntary waiver of the privilege may be effected through a disclosure by the client, the client's express consent to disclose, or an implication gleaned from the client's actions.[26]

Lawyers and clients may assert the attorney-client privilege. However, neither lawyers nor clients are free to abuse that privilege by selectively disclosing privileged communications for their own benefit and then invoking the privilege as to other related communications to the detriment of other litigants.[27]

Like humans, corporations are entitled to the benefits of the attorney-client privilege. For solvent corporations, the authority to assert and

---

15 *Misek-Falkoff v. International Business Machines Corp.*, 144 F.R.D. 48 (S.D.N.Y. 1992); *DiCenzo v. Izawa*, 723 P.2d 171, 68 Haw. 528 (Hawaii 1986).

16 *Arkla, Inc. v. Harris*, 846 S.W.2d 623 (Tex.App. 1993); *Branch v. Greene County Bd. of Educ.*, 533 So.2d 248 (Ala.Civ.App. 1988).

17 *Hubka v. Pennfield Tp.*, 494 N.W.2d 800, 197 Mich.App. 117 (1992).

18 *Hydraflow, Inc. v. Enidine Inc.*, 145 F.R.D. 626 (W.D.N.Y. 1993). *Smithkline Beecham Corp. v. Apotex Corp.*, 193 F.R.D. 530, (N.D.Ill. 2000). In patent infringement suit, technical documents prepared to allow attorneys to assess patentability and prepare applications are immune from discovery under attorney-client privilege. However, documents described as "agendas for meetings," many of which were authored by attorneys, were not protected by attorney-client privilege because of unlikelihood that legal advice was implicated.

19 *Dixson v. Quarles*, 627 F.Supp. 50 (E.D. Mich. 1985).

20 See Cohen, *"The Attorney-Client Privilege, Ethical Rules and the Impaired Criminal Defendant,"* 52 U. Miami L. Rev. 529 (1998).

21 *Grand Jury, County of San Diego v. Superior Court* (Harrison), 259 Cal.Rptr. 404 (Cal.App. 4 Dist. 1989).

22 *Abney v. Patten*, 696 F.Supp. 570 (W.D. Okl. 1987).

23 *People v. Krawitz*, 542 N.Y.S.2d 824 (N.Y.A.D. 3 Dept. 1989). Long ago when there were only mouths and quill pens, disclosure was easier to guard against. Today, our technologies have given us great new tools, but have also presented some serious dangers that didn't previously exist. See Stephens, *"Convenience vs. Confidentiality: An Evaluation of the Effects of Computer Technology on the Attorney-Client Privilege,"* 35 Duq. L. Rev. 1011 (1997).

24 *Century 21 Deep South Properties, Ltd. v. Corson*, 612 So.2d 359 (Miss. 1992).

25 *People in Interest of O.J.S.*, 844 P.2d 1230 (Colo.App. 1992).

26 *Stirum v. Whalen*, 811 F.Supp. 78 (N.D.N.Y. 1993).

27 *In re Shell Oil Refinery*, 812 F.Supp. 658 (E.D.La. 1993); see also *Regan v. Garfield Ridge Trust and Savings Bank*, 163 Ill.Dec. 605, 581 N.E.2d 759, 220 Ill. App.3d 1078 (1991).

waive the corporation's attorney-client privilege rests with management.[28]

§9.501.1 State Application

LAWYER - CLIENT PRIVILEGE IN ARIZONA:

The attorney-client privilege is not absolute; it is, rather, a personal privilege for the client and may be waived. Moreover, a client waives the privilege when he claims that his attorney rendered ineffective assistance. Under such a claim, the accused attorney should be allowed to defend himself; at least with regard to the particular contentions asserted, the privilege will therefore be waived. *State v. Cuffle*, 828 P.2d 773 (Ariz. 1992).

LAWYER - CLIENT PRIVILEGE IN ARKANSAS:

Watch out for boothless telephones in Arkansas, particularly if they happen to be inside of a police station. A defendant made a statement to his attorney by telephone while at the police station, while he was handcuffed and in custody. The conversation was not protected by the attorney-client privilege, despite his contention that since he was handcuffed and in custody, the conversation should not be stripped of its confidentiality. As it turned out, the defendant knew that he was being videotaped during the entire time that he was at the police station and was also aware that third parties were present when he made the statement. *Shankle v. State*, 827 S.W.2d 642, 309 Ark. 40 (1992).

In a medical malpractice case, hospital employees and doctors were considered as "clients" of the attorney who represented the hospital's insurance company; therefore, statements made to that attorney were covered by the attorney-client privilege. *Courteau v. St. Paul Fire & Marine Ins. Co.*, 821 S.W.2d 45, 307 Ark. 513 (1991).

LAWYER - CLIENT PRIVILEGE IN CALIFORNIA:

The attorney-client privilege, while not constitutionally based, is the oldest recognized confidential communication privilege. It is based on grounds of public policy and is deemed to further the proper and orderly functioning of our judicial system, which necessarily depends on confidential relationships between attorneys and clients. The privilege applies not only to communications made in anticipation of litigation, but also to legal advice when no litigation is threatened. However, a communication which was not privileged to begin with may not be made so by subsequent delivery to an attorney. *Magill v. Superior Court*, 103 Cal.Rptr.2d 355, 86 Cal.App.4th 61 (2001).

Rule 952 of the California Evidence Code provides a rather standard definition for the relationship necessary as a prerequisite to the privilege:

> As used in this article, "confidential communication between client and lawyer" means information transmitted between a client and his lawyer in the course of that relationship and in confidence by a means which, so far as the client is aware, discloses the information to no third persons other than those who are present to further the interest of the client in the consultation or those to whom disclosure is reasonably necessary for the transmission of the information or the accomplishment of the purpose for which the lawyer is consulted, and includes a legal opinion formed and the advice given by the lawyer in the course of that relationship.

The element of "confidentiality" is not "presumed present" in California. On the contrary, it constitutes a key aspect of privilege, in general. No attorney-client privilege can attach to a communication unless it was intended to be confidential. *GTE Directories Service Corp. v. Pacific Bell Directory*, 135 F.R.D. 187 (N.D. Cal. 1991).

---

28 *Milroy v. Hanson*, 875 F.Supp 646 (1995).

Moreover, information possessed by a witness does not become privileged merely because it is communicated to an attorney. *County of Los Angeles v. Superior Court* (Martinez), 274 Cal. Rptr. 712, 224 C.A.3d 1446 (Cal. App. 2 Dist. 1990).

Section 954 of the California Evidence Code spells out the elements required to properly establish the privilege:

> Subject to section 912 and except as otherwise provided in this article, the client, whether or not a party, has a privilege to refuse to disclose, and to prevent another from disclosing, a confidential communication between client and lawyer if the privilege is claimed by:
>
> (a) the holder of the privilege;
>
> (b) a person who is authorized to claim the privilege by the holder of the privilege; or
>
> (c) the person who was the lawyer at the time of the confidential communication, but such person may not claim the privilege if there is no holder of the privilege in existence or if he is otherwise instructed by a person authorized to permit disclosure.

The relationship of attorney and client shall exist between a law corporation as defined in Article 10 (commencing with Section 6160) of Chapter 4 of Division 3 of the Business and Professions Code and the persons to whom it renders professional services, as well as between such persons and members of the State Bar employed by such corporation to render services to such persons. The word "persons" as used in this subdivision includes partnerships, corporations, associations and other groups and entities.

The voluntary disclosure of an attorney-client communication constitutes a waiver of that privilege as to all communications on the same subject matter. *McCormick-Morgan, Inc. v. Teledyne Industries, Inc.*, 134 F.R.D. 275 (N.D. Cal. 1991). But permitting a review of allegedly privileged matters "in camera" does not terminate the attorney-client privilege and, on the contrary, is an appropriate way in which to consider matters that may involve privilege. *Ainsworth v. Vasquez*, 759 F. Supp. 1467 (E.D. Cal. 1991).

In a litigation or prosecution setting, the attorney-client privilege normally concerns matters between lawyers and parties (or potential parties). But in *People v. Mincey*, 827 P.2d 388, 6 Cal. Rptr.2d 822, 2 Cal.4th 408, *rehearing denied and opinion modified* (1992), it was made clear that the privilege can also apply to discussions between a witness and that witness' attorney where the subject matter of the conversation relates to possible plea bargains.

Defendant made statements to a psychologist at the request of defense counsel for the purpose of obtaining a psychological evaluation to assist that counsel in the preparation of a defense; the statements were protected by attorney-client privilege. *Rodriguez v. Superior Court*, 18 Cal. Rptr.2d 120 (Cal. App. 5 Dist. 1993).

In the corporate world, a director on the board of a league merchandising corporation could not use his position as a director to request corporate documents (otherwise protected by the attorney-client privilege) for use in litigation as a shareholder against the merchandising corporation; the director's fiduciary duty to the corporation precluded him from passing on the information or delegating his right of inspection. *National Football League Properties Inc. v. Superior Court*, 75 Cal. Rptr.2d 893 (Cal. App. 1998).

LAWYER - CLIENT PRIVILEGE IN COLORADO:

In order to claim the benefit of the attorney-client privilege, the claimant must satisfy five elements by showing that: (1) the asserted holder of the privilege is or has sought to become a client; (2) the person to whom the communication was made is an attorney, or an attorney's subordinate; (3) the communication is made in connection with the person's role as a lawyer; (4) the communication relates to a fact of which the attorney was informed by the client, without the presence of strangers, for the purpose of securing legal advice, services or assistance, and not for the purpose of committing a crime or tort; and, (5) no waiver has occurred. *In re Grand Jury 90-1*, 758 F. Supp. 1411 (D. Colo. 1991).

By merely listing a psychiatrist as a potential witness, that psychiatrist was thus rendered available for a pretrial interview by the prosecution; the defendant, therefore, impliedly waived his attorney-client privilege with respect to the information obtained by the prosecution during the course of that interview. *Lanari v. People*, 827 P.2d 495 (Colo. 1992).

At a hearing to terminate parental rights, the attorney-client privilege did *not* bar the admission of testimony nor the report of a court-appointed psychologist (appointed at the mother's request); the mother knew from the outset that her communications to the psychologist would be disclosed to the children's guardian and to the children (who were present with the mother for part of the psychologist's evaluation). *People in Interest of O.J.S.*, 844 P.2d 1230 (Colo. App. 1992).

Although the attorney-client privilege is not itself a constitutional doctrine, in a criminal context, preservation of the privilege may implicate a defendant's Sixth-Amendment right to counsel. *People v. Johnson,* 999 P.2d 825 (Colo., 2000).

LAWYER - CLIENT PRIVILEGE IN CONNECTICUT:

The client alone holds the attorney-client privilege; that privilege is reserved solely for those whose interest it was designed to protect and not adverse parties or the general population. *In re Sean H.*, 586 A.2d 1171, 24 Conn. App.135 (Conn. App. 1991).

Attorney-client privilege protects communications between a client and an attorney when made in confidence for the purpose of seeking or giving legal advice. *State v. Turner*, 751 A.2d 372, 252 Conn. 714 (2000).

LAWYER - CLIENT PRIVILEGE IN DELAWARE:

An attorney negotiated a settlement agreement which later failed in performance; that lawyer could testify (over the objection of the former client who claimed that the settlement agreement was not authorized) regarding relevant oral statements that he had with opposing counsel and the family court; thus, the contents of correspondence between the attorney, opposing counsel, and the family court were also not privileged, and the attorney could testify as to those communications, as well as other communications with her client, if it was clear that the client did not intend confidentiality with respect to those communications. But testimony that goes beyond the preceding elements and into the advice given the client for not signing the agreement, exceeds the scope of the exception to the privilege. *Moyer v. Moyer*, 602 A.2d 68 (Del. 1992).

LAWYER - CLIENT PRIVILEGE IN FLORIDA:

Section 90.502 of the Florida Evidence Code (lawyer-client privilege) lays out a basic structure for Florida's privileges in general. Subsection (1) provides the necessary definitions:

(a) A "lawyer" is a person authorized, or reasonably believed by the client to be authorized, to practice law in any state or nation.

(b) A "client" is any person, public officer, corporation, association, or other organization or entity, either public or private, who consults a lawyer with the purpose of obtaining legal services or who is rendered legal services by a lawyer.

Section 90.502(1)(c) requires that the communication must have been intended as "confidential." But disclosure "in furtherance of the rendition of legal services to the client" or disclosure that is "reasonably necessary for the transmission of the communication" does not breach confidentiality.

Sections 90.502(2) and (3) make it clear that the privilege is intended for the benefit of the client by providing that it is the client who "has the privilege to refuse to disclose, and to prevent any other person from disclosing, the contents of confidential communications."

Section 90.502(3) provides that the privilege may be claimed by (a) the client; (b) a guardian or conservator of the client; (c) the personal representative of a deceased client; (d) a successor, assignee, trustee in dissolution, or any similar representative of an organization, corporation, or association or other entity, either public or private, whether or not in existence; and (e) the lawyer, but only on behalf of the client. The lawyer's authority to claim the privilege is presumed in the absence of contrary evidence.

Section 90.502(4) provides an important list of notable exceptions to the attorney-client privilege. Moreover, even where a confidential communication satisfies the basic prerequisites, the protection afforded by the privilege will be denied where:

(a) The services of the lawyer were sought or obtained to enable or aid anyone to commit or plan to commit what the client knew was a crime or fraud.

(b) A communication is relevant to an issue between parties who claim through the same deceased client.

(c) A communication is relevant to an issue of breach of duty by the lawyer to his client or by the client to his lawyer, arising from the lawyer-client relationship.

(d) A communication is relevant to an issue concerning the intention or competence of a client executing an attested document to which the lawyer is an attesting witness, or concerning the execution or attestation of the document.

(e) A communication is relevant to a matter of common interest between two or more clients, or their successors in interest, if the communication was made by any of them to a lawyer retained or consulted in common when offered in a civil action between the clients or their successors in interest.

Do not be surprised to see the preceding checklist of exceptions pop up in other states, with substantially identical language.

LAWYER-CLIENT PRIVILEGE IN GEORGIA:

Under Georgia law, the attorney-client privilege bars revelation, discovery, and testimony of attorney-client privileged materials by a lawyer except when waived by the client or in very limited circumstances. The attorney-client privilege protects admissions and communications between the attorney (in his or her representative capacity) and the client, made for the purpose of securing legal advice or assistance. *Lazar v. Mauney*, 192 F.R.D. 324 (N.D., 2000).

LAWYER-CLIENT PRIVILEGE IN HAWAII:

For matters involving communications among counsel for the Internal Revenue Service (IRS) and separate taxpayers involved in a single tax shelter, see *Kersting v. U.S.*, 206 F.3d 817 (C.A.9, Hawaii, 2000).

LAWYER - CLIENT PRIVILEGE IN ILLINOIS:

An insanity defense results in a waiver of the attorney-client privilege, but only with respect to the testimony and reports of experts who are identified by the defense as witnesses who will be called to testify on behalf of the defendant at trial, or whose notes and reports are used by other defense experts who will testify. *People v Knuckles*, 165 Ill.2d 125, 650 N.E.2d 973 (1995).

The attempted selective disclosure of confidential communications by a client will normally result in a waiver of the attorney-client privilege; however, if the client calls a former attorney to testify about non-privileged communications during direct examination, no waiver of privilege will have occurred from that testimony alone. *Regan v. Garfield Ridge Trust and Sav. Bank*, 163 Ill. Dec. 605, 581 N.E.2d 759, 220 Ill. App.3d 1078 (1991).

In order to establish attorney-client privilege, under Illinois law, the proponent must show that the statement sought to be protected originated in the confidence that it would not be disclosed, was made to an attorney acting in his legal capacity for the purpose of securing legal advice or services, and remained confidential. *Caremark, Inc. v. Affiliated Computer Services, Inc.*, 192 F.R.D. 263 (N.D.Ill.E.Div., 2000).

The traditional attorney-client evidentiary privilege protects confidential communications made by an individual to an attorney during a preliminary legal consultation. *Popp v. O'Neil,* 730 N.E.2d 506 (Ill.App.2.Dist., 2000).

To be entitled to the protection of the attorney-client privilege, a claimant must show that: (1) A statement originated in confidence that it would not be disclosed; (2) it was made to an attorney acting in his legal capacity for the purpose of securing legal advice or services; and (3) it remained confidential. *John Cangelosi v. Capasso, Rockford Radiology Associates*, 851 N.E.2d 954, 366 Ill.App.3d 225, 303 Ill.Dec. 767 (2006).

LAWYER - CLIENT PRIVILEGE IN INDIANA:

Taylor v. State, 587 N.E.2d 1293 (Ind. 1992) states the general proposition that communications made by a client to an attorney are confidential, and neither the attorney nor the client should be compelled to reveal the contents of those communications.

A party asserting the attorney-client privilege must show that: (1) the asserted holder of the privilege is a client or has sought to become one; (2) the person to whom the subject communication was made, was a member of the bar, court, or a subordinate of such member; (3) such person was acting as a lawyer in connection with the subject communication; (4) the subject communication relates to a fact of which the attorney was informed by his client without the presence of strangers, for the primary purpose of securing an opinion of law (or legal services or assistance); (5) the communication was not for the purpose of committing a crime or tort; and (6) the privilege has been claimed and not waived by the client. *Harper v. Auto-Owners Ins. Co.*, 138 F.R.D. 655 (S.D. lnd. 1991).

Where a policy of insurance requires the insurer to defend claims against the insured, statements from the insured to the insurer concerning the subject occurrence, which may become the basis of a claim by a third party, are protected from disclosure. *Richey v. Chappell,* 594 N.E.2d 443 (Ind. 1992).

The attorney-client privilege protects communications between the State Attorney General and the Public Employees' Retirement Fund (PERF), the agency that he counsels pursuant to state statute. *Board of Trustees of Public Employees' Retirement Fund of Indiana v. Morley*, 580 N.E.2d 371 (Ind. App. 1991).

The attorney-client privilege protects against judicially compelled disclosure of confidential information; the harm to be prevented is not the manner in which the confidence is revealed, but the revelation itself. *Lahr v. State,* 731 N.E.2d 479 (Ind.App., 2000).

The attorney-client privilege protects against the judicially compelled disclosure of confidential information regardless of whether that information is to be disclosed by way of testimony, or by court-ordered compliance with a discovery request which a party has attempted to resist. *P.T. Buntin, M.D., P.C. v. Becker,* 727 N.E.2d 734 (Ind.App., 2000).

LAWYER - CLIENT PRIVILEGE IN IOWA:

Although communications between a workers' compensation carrier and its attorneys were absolutely privileged, the carrier, nevertheless, waived the privilege as to one of its attorneys by designating him as an expert witness. *Squealer Feeds v. Pickering*, 530 N.W.2d 678 (Iowa 1995).

LAWYER - CLIENT PRIVILEGE IN KANSAS:

If the court can determine that sufficient evidence exists (aside from the subject communication) to warrant a finding that the legal advice was obtained in order to aid the commission or planning of a crime or tort, then the attorney-client privilege does not apply to such communications. *Wallace, Saunders, Austin, Brown &*

Enochs, Chartered v. Louisburg Grain Co., Inc., 824 P.2d 933, 250 Kan. 54 (1992).

Under federal common law governing attorney-client privilege, (1) when legal advice of any kind is sought (2) from a professional legal advisor in his capacity as such, (3) the communications relating to that purpose, (4) made in confidence (5) by the client, (6) are at his instance permanently protected (7) from disclosure by himself or by the legal advisor, (8) except when that protection is waived. *McCoo v. Denny's Inc.*, 192 F.R.D. 675 (D.Kan., 2000).

LAWYER - CLIENT PRIVILEGE IN KENTUCKY:

Using an attorney as a shield to conceal transactions involving malpractice or criminal matters won't work. Those items go beyond the lawyer's intended purpose and beyond the attorney-client privilege. *Futrell v. Shadoan*, 828 S.W.2d 649 (Ky. 1992).

LAWYER - CLIENT PRIVILEGE IN MARYLAND:

The attorney-client privilege is waived by a client in any proceeding where he or she asserts the claim of "ineffective assistance" against the attorney; none of the communications or opinions relevant to the quality of counsel's performance are protected by the privilege. *State v. Thomas*, 599 A.2d 1171, 325 Md. 160 (1992).

The attorney-client privilege is not absolute; it does not prohibit the disclosure of every event that occurs between an attorney and his or her client. *In re Criminal Investigation No. 1/242Q*, 602 A.2d 1220, 325 Md. 740, 326 Md. 1 (1992).

The "attorney-client privilege" is a rule of evidence which prohibits the disclosure of the substance of a communication made in confidence by a client to his attorney for the purpose of obtaining legal advice. *Blair v. State,* 747 A.2d 702, 130 Md.App. 571 (2000).

LAWYER - CLIENT PRIVILEGE IN MASSACHUSETTS:

If an accountant also happens to be an attorney, the attorney-client privilege applies to communications pertaining to legal advice sought from the accountant if the advice was sought in reliance upon the professional acting in the capacity of an attorney. The privilege may also apply to confidential communications made to an accountant if the client is under the mistaken, but reasonable, belief that the professional from whom legal advice is sought is in fact an attorney. *U.S. v. Mullen & Co.*, 776 F. Supp. 620 (D. Mass. 1991).

The "attorney-client privilege" protects the confidential communications between a client and an attorney for the purpose of obtaining legal advice. *Open Software Foundation, Inc. v. U.S. Fidelity & Guar. Co.,* 191 F.R.D. 325 (D.Mass., 2000).

LAWYER - CLIENT PRIVILEGE IN MICHIGAN:

The attorney-client privilege attaches to communications made by a client to an attorney for the purpose of obtaining legal advice. *Ravary v. Reed,* 163 Mich. App. 447, 415 N.W.2d 240 (1987).

LAWYER - CLIENT PRIVILEGE IN MINNESOTA:

When an attorney acts for two different clients who each have a common interest, the communications of either party with the attorney are not necessarily privileged with respect to subsequent litigation between the two clients. *Bituminous Cas. Corp. v. Tonka Corp.*, 140 F.R.D. 381 (D. Minn. 1992).

LAWYER - CLIENT PRIVILEGE IN MISSOURI:

The client claimed that a settlement agreement was "concocted" by the attorneys without her consent or authorization; the attempt to assert the statute of frauds caused the client to waive her attorney-client privilege by creating an issue over the attorney's authority to sign the agreement. *Sappington v. Miller*, 821 S.W.2d 901 (Mo. App. 1992).

Testimony whereby an attorney merely stated his observations of his client's mental condition (as distinguished from private communications), does not violate attorney-client privilege. *State v. Shire*, 850 S.W.2d 923. (Mo. App. S.D. 1993).

LAWYER - CLIENT PRIVILEGE IN NEW YORK:

Section 4503 of the New York CPLR states:

(a) Unless the client waives the privilege, an attorney or his employee, or any person who obtains without the knowledge of the client evidence of a confidential communication made between the attorney or his employee and the client in the course of professional employment, shall not disclose, or be allowed to disclose such communication, nor shall the client be compelled to disclose such communication, in any action, disciplinary trial or hearing, or administrative action, proceeding or hearing conducted by or on behalf of any state, municipal or local governmental agency or by the legislature or any committee or body thereof. Evidence of any such communication obtained by any such person, and evidence resulting therefrom, shall not be disclosed by any state, municipal or local governmental agency or by the legislature or any committee or body thereof. The relationship of an attorney and client shall exist between a professional service corporation organized under article fifteen of the business corporation law to practice as an attorney and counselor-at-law and the clients to whom it renders legal services.

(b) In any action involving the probate, validity or construction of a will, an attorney or his employee shall be required to disclose information as to the preparation, execution or revocation of any will or other relevant instrument, but he shall not be allowed to disclose any communication privileged under subdivision (a) which would tend to disgrace the memory of the decedent.

New York's common law defines the scope of the privilege, although statute provides that the privilege exists for confidential communications made between an attorney and client during the course of professional employment. *Spectrum Systems Intern. Corp. v. Chemical Bank*, 575 N.Y.S.2d 809, 78 N.Y.2d 371, 581 N.E.2d 1055 (1991).

A lawyer, as is the case with many professionals, can wear more than one hat. And if a lawyer acts as a business consultant or economic advisor, there is no special relationship that would give rise to a privilege to protect his advice from disclosure. *Department of Economic Development v. Arthur Andersen & Co.*, 139 F.R.D. 295 (S.D.N.Y. 1991). The holder of the attorney-client privilege must show that the subject communications were made in confidence to an attorney primarily for the purpose of obtaining legal services (and not for the purpose of committing a crime or tort). *Resolution Trust Corp. v. Diamond*, 773 F. Supp. 597 (S.D.N.Y. 1991). But a social worker employed by a law guardian, in a Family Court custody proceeding, is a "representative" of the infant for purposes of providing immunity from the disclosure of mental impressions, conclusions, opinions, or legal theories concerning litigation. *Matter of Lenny McN.*, 584 N.Y.S.2d 17 (N.Y.A.D. 1 Dept. 1992). This case, of course, addresses itself more in the direction of the Work Product Doctrine than attorney-client privilege, although the privilege did apply.

As is the case with every other state, the attorney-client privilege may be waived in New York. Consider *Orco Bank, N.V. v. Proteinas Del Pacifico*, S.A., 577 N.Y.S.2d 841 (N.Y.A.D. 1 Dept. 1992), involving a case where a bank sued a company which had issued a false letter of safekeeping, upon which the bank allegedly relied in making certain loans. The bank was held to have waived its attorney-client privilege when it responded to a discovery request by saying that it had relied upon the advice of counsel during its pre-loan investigation; by making such a disclosure, the bank had placed the subject matter of counsel's advice in issue and had made selective disclosure of that advice.

Although it normally arises in the context of a client's communications to an attorney, the attorney-client privilege likewise extends to communications from the attorney to the client; moreover, the attorney-client privilege is designed to encourage the open dialogue between an attorney and client that is deemed essential to effective representation. *Spectrum Systems Intern. Corp. v. Chemical Bank*, 575 N.Y.S.2d 809, 78 N.Y.2d 371, 581 N.E.2d 1055 (1991).

The attorney-client privilege is, of course, closely related to the work product doctrine. Draft pleadings, along with communication and advice rendered in connection with those pleadings (which were the subject of litigation, and work product), fit within the attorney-related privilege by their nature and were therefore protected from discovery. *John Blair Communications, Inc. v. Reliance Capital Group*, 582 N.Y.S.2d 720 (N.Y.A.D. 1 Dept. 1992). But although the prospect of litigation may be relevant to the subject communications, the protection from disclosure of an attorney's work product and trial-preparation materials is not necessarily tied to the contemplation of litigation; so the attorney-client privilege applies to such materials. *Spectrum Systems Intern. Corp. v. Chemical Bank*, 575 N.Y.S.2d 809, 78 N.Y.2d 371, 581 N.E.2d 1055 (1991).

LAWYER - CLIENT PRIVILEGE IN NORTH CAROLINA:

An attorney's observations concerning a former client's demeanor, dress, and behavior did not fall within the protection of the attorney-client privilege. It is the substance of the communications between the attorney and client that is protected, rather than the fact that there had been such communications. *Scott v. Scott*, 417 S.E.2d 818 (N.C. App. 1992).

LAWYER-CLIENT PRIVILEGE IN OHIO:

The right of a party to assert the attorney-client privilege is not absolute. *In re Miller,* 247 B.R. 704 (Bankr.N.D.Ohio., 2000).

LAWYER - CLIENT PRIVILEGE IN OREGON:

Rule 40.225(1) of the Oregon Evidence Code provides the following definitions:

(a) "Client" means a person, public officer, corporation, association or other organization or entity, either public or private, who is rendered professional legal services by a lawyer, or who consults a lawyer with a view to obtaining professional legal services from the lawyer.

(b) "Confidential communication" means a communication not intended to be disclosed to third persons other than those to whom disclosure is in furtherance of the rendition of professional legal services to the client or those reasonably necessary for the transmission of the communication.

(c) "Lawyer" means a person authorized, or reasonably believed by the client to be authorized, to practice law in any state or nation.

(d) "Representative of the client" means a principal, an employee, an officer or a director of the client:

(A) Who provides the client's lawyer with information that was acquired during the course of, or as a result of, such person's relationship with the client as principal, employee, officer or director, and is provided to the lawyer for the purpose of obtaining for the client the legal advice or other legal services of the lawyer; or

(B) Who, as part of such person's relationship with the client as principal, employee, officer or director, seeks, receives or applies legal advice from the client's lawyer.

(e) "Representative of the lawyer" means one employed to assist the lawyer in the rendition of professional legal services, but does not include a physician making a physical or mental examination under ORCP 44.

Rule 40.225(2) of the Oregon Evidence Code states that a client has a privilege to refuse to disclose and to prevent any other person from disclosing confidential communications made for the purpose of facilitating the rendition of professional legal services to the client:

(a) Between the client or the client's representative and the client's lawyer or a representative of the lawyer;
(b) Between the client's lawyer and the lawyer's representative;
(c) By the client or the client's lawyer to a lawyer representing another in a matter of common interest;
(d) Between representatives of the client or between the client and a representative of the client; or
(e) Between lawyers representing the client.

Rule 40.225(3) of the Oregon Evidence Code states that the privilege created by this section may be claimed by the client, a guardian or conservator of the client, the personal representative of a deceased client, or the successor, trustee, or similar representative of a corporation, association, or other organization, whether or not in existence. The person who was the lawyer or the lawyer's representative at the time of the communication is presumed to have authority to claim the privilege, but only on behalf of the client.

Rule 40.225(4)(a) eliminates the privilege for anyone using the services of a lawyer to further a crime or fraud. The remaining sub-parts of the rule eliminate the privilege for certain matters pertaining to estates, attorney malpractice, attestation of documents, and multiple clients.

LAWYER - CLIENT PRIVILEGE IN PENNSYLVANIA:

The attorney-client privilege did not prevent a defendant's former attorneys from testifying at a homicide trial, where they stated that the defendant had delivered to them clothing worn by that defendant on the date of the homicide (as part of a chain of custody foundation); non-privileged evidence does not become attorney-client protected merely by delivering it to an attorney. Moreover, the defense could have eliminated the need to call the attorneys to testify by stipulating to the authenticity of the physical evidence. *Commonwealth v. Ferri,* 599 A.2d 208 (Pa. Super. 1991).

The attorney-client privilege performs a vital function in our legal system by fostering a confidence between clients and their advocates that will lead to a trusting and open attorney-client dialogue. *Gould v. City of Aliquippa,* 750 A.2d 934 (Pa.Cmwlth.App., 2000).

LAWYER-CLIENT PRIVILEGE IN SOUTH CAROLINA

The attorney-client privilege excludes professional confidential communications between an attorney and his or her client, unless the client, for whose benefit the rule is established, waives the privilege. To assert the privilege, it must appear that the attorney was acting, at the time, as a legal advisor. Only confidential communications are protected by that privilege. *Floyd v. Floyd*, 615 S.E.2d 465, 365 S.C. 56 (2005).

LAWYER-CLIENT PRIVILEGE IN TENNESSEE:

The attorney-client privilege is narrowly construed. *In re Columbia/HCA Healthcare Corp.,* 192 F.R.D. 575 (M.D.Tenn.Nashville.Div., 2000).

LAWYER - CLIENT PRIVILEGE IN TEXAS:

The attorney-client privilege does not protect communications that a law firm has with third parties, such as hospitals or social workers, even if the information is then forwarded to the client. *Methodist Home v. Marshall*, 830 S.W.2d 220 (Tex. App. 1992).

LAWYER - CLIENT PRIVILEGE IN WEST VIRGINIA:

The West Virginia courts recognize a common law lawyer-client privilege. There are no court rules or statutory privileges. The privilege applies when: (1) the relation of lawyer and client is contemplated by both parties or actually exists, (2) the client seeks advice from the lawyer in his or her capacity as a legal adviser, and (3) the lawyer and client intend for their communication to remain confidential. All three elements must be established to claim the privilege.

Under West Virginia law, in order to assert an attorney-client privilege, three main elements must be present: (1) both parties must contemplate that the attorney-client relationship does or will exist; (2) the advice must be sought by the client from the attorney in his capacity as a legal adviser; and (3) the communication between the attorney and client must be intended to be confidential. *Kidwiler v. Progressive Paloverde Ins. Co.,* 192 F.R.D. 536 (N.D.W.Va., 2000).

LAWYER - CLIENT PRIVILEGE IN WISCONSIN:

Where a person retains a lawyer to set up a corporation and that lawyer's involvement with the person is directly related to incorporation, communications between the person and the corporation are privileged; the corporate entity, and not the person holds that privilege. *Jesse by Reinecke v. Danforth*, 485 N.W.2d 63 (Wis. 1992).

§9.501(a) Paralegal Privilege

Licensing requirements for paralegals vary from state to state. Separate and apart from their own ethical requirements, however, are those derivative obligations predicated upon the access to lawyer-client information by virtue of the paralegal's employment relationship. As a matter of agency or privity, it is fair to assume that the lawyer-client privilege should apply to paralegals who are acting under the auspices of an attorney or law firm.[29]

§9.502 The Work Product Doctrine

The "work product doctrine" is a concept that is very closely related to attorney-client privilege; it is possible for both objections to apply to the same problem.[30] The doctrine has been defined as covering "documents and tangible things prepared in anticipation of litigation or for trial, by, or for another party (or that party's representative)."[31] In

29 *Owens v. First Family Financial Services*, 379 Fed.Supp.2d 840 (S.D., Miss., 2005). For purposes of a defendant's motion to disqualify plaintiffs' counsel in a consumer fraud action (based on the employment by plaintiffs' counsel of a paralegal who had assisted in the representation of the defendants while employed by a different law firm), it was held that work performed by the paralegal during her prior employment with the defendant's former counsel fell within realm of the actual attorney-client relationship. Generally, when a paralegal works on behalf of a lawyer who is representing a client, the attorney-client privilege applies with equal force to the paralegal.

30 *Smith v. MCI Telecommunications Corp*., 124 F.R.D. 665 (D.Kan. 1989).

31 *John Cangelosi v. Capasso, Rockford Radiology Associates*, 851 N.E.2d 954, 366 Ill.App.3d 225, 303 Ill.Dec. 767 (2006). The work product doctrine provides a broader protection than the attorney-client privilege and is designed to protect the right of an attorney to thoroughly prepare his case and to preclude a less diligent adversary attorney from taking undue advantage of the former's efforts.

Huet v. Tromp, 912 So.2d 336 (Fla.App., 2005). In an auto negligence action, documents, reports, and videotapes generated by investigators hired by one driver to investigate and provide surveillance of the party injured are protected from discovery by the work product privilege unless the injured party had need of the materials and was unable without due hardship to obtain them. Moreover, information relating to a matter that is the subject of litigation (which is received by a party's attorneys from investigators and adjusters in anticipation of or in connection with litigation) is protected by the work product privilege. An investigator employed by a party may not be required to produce the work-product of his or her investigations, except in unusual circumstances constituting a compelling necessity for the discovery in order to reach the merits of the cause. See *Rule* 26(b) of the *Federal Rules of Civil Procedure*. See also *Kristoff v. Glasson,* 778 N.E.2d 465 (Ind.App. 2002).

See Fed. R. Civ. P. 26(b)(3); see also *Special Project, The Work Product Doctrine*, 68 Cornell L.Rev. 760 (1983), and Lipson, *Documentary Evidence* §6.10 (Matthew Bender, 1988).

essence, work product involves the impressions, conclusions, opinions, or legal theories of a lawyer that are prepared or formulated while representing a client.[32] An attorney can neither discover nor demand information about the personal investigations or legal research conducted by another party's attorney, or any other items that are covered by the work product doctrine.

§9.503 Doctor - Patient Privilege

The privilege that applies to communications between doctors and patients is not nearly as strong as the attorney-client privilege. Matters involving "public interest" may outweigh the application of the privilege.[33] In order for the physician-patient privilege to attach, the communication must be a necessary incident to rendering professional services, must be confidential in nature, and the patient must contemplate that it will be kept confidential.[34]

There are some policy reasons for the weakness of this privilege. First, although truthful communication is important, it is not always crucial. A broken leg, for example, needs little explanation or patient discussions concerning what has occurred. The doctor can pretty much do what is required based upon X-rays, as opposed to symptoms provided by the patient. Also, there has been, in recent years, some concern about the confidentiality of communications concerning highly contagious diseases.

In any event, the privilege does exist, although it is not very well defined. The policy reason behind the privilege is obvious—it promotes privacy,[35] which, in turn, promotes full disclosure. As with the attorney-client privilege, the doctor-patient privilege continues after the death of the client (i.e., patient).[36]

Hospital records are also privileged and their disclosure is not permitted except by the personal consent of the patient, unless his or her treatment in the hospital was by appointment of the court and not the selection of the patient.[37] Those assisting the doctor, including interns, are also included within the scope of the privilege.[38]

A litigant will be deemed to have waived the privilege when, in bringing or defending a personal injury action, that litigant affirmatively places his or her mental or physical condition in issue. However, a party does not waive doctor-patient privilege whenever forced to defend an action in which his or her mental or physical condition is in controversy.[39] In *Slagle v. Superior Court*,[40] it was held that a patient "tenders" the issue of his phys-

32 *EEOC v. Jewel Food Stores, Inc.*, 231 F.R.D. 343 (N.D.Ill., 2005); *Stauffer Chemical Co. v. Monsanto Co.*, No. 84-1660-C(4) (E.D. Mo. dec'd. July 18, 1985); *National Steel Products Co. v. Superior Court*, 164 Cal.App.3d 476, 210 Cal.Rptr. 535 (1985); *Klinzmann v. Beale*, 9 Kan.App.2d 20, 670 P.2d 67, 72 (1983); *Upjohn Co. v. United States*, 101 S.Ct. 677 (1981).

33 *In re Brink*, 536 N.E.2d 1201, 42 Ohio Misc.2d 5 (Ohio Com.Pl. 1989); see also *Estate of Green v. St. Clair County Road Com'n.*, 438 N.W.2d 630, 175 Mich.App. 478 (Mich.App. 1989).

34 *Desai v. Blue Shield of Northeastern New York, Inc.*, 540 N.Y.S.2d 569, 146 A.D.2d 264 (N.Y.A.D. 3 Dept. 1989).

35 *Britt v. Superior Court*, 20 Cal.3d 844, 143 Cal.Rptr. 695 (1978); see also *Leritz v. Koehr,* 844 S.W.2d 583 (Mo.App.E.D. 1993).

36 *Mass. Mut. Life Ins. Co. v. Brei*, 311 F.2d 463 (2nd Cir. 1962).

37 *State v. Eishtadt*, 531 So.2d 1133 (La. App. 4 Cir. 1988).

38 *Franklin Life Ins. Co. v. William J. Champion & Co.*, 353 F.2d 919 (6th Cir. 1965).

39 Nor should a non-party be deemed to have waived the privilege just because his or her information may be relevant to another patient's litigation. See *Tomczak v. Ingalls Memorial Hospital*, 834 N.E.2d 549, 295 Ill.Dec. 968 (2005), declaring that the medical records of non-parties are protected by the physician-patient privilege, as is any information gathered by a nurse for the purpose of enabling a physician's treatment of a patient. The physician-patient privilege exists to both encourage disclosure between a physician and a patient and to protect the patient from an invasion of privacy. *Dillenbeck v. Hess*, 539 N.Y.S.2d 707, 73 N.Y.2d 278, 536 N.E.2d 1126 (N.Y. 1989).

40 260 Cal.Rptr. 122, 211 C.A.3d 1309 (Cal.App. 1 Dist. 1989).

ical health if he files an action for personal injuries, but only as to that information which relates to the claimed injuries. And as to those "claimed injuries" only, the patient will be held to have waived his physician-patient privilege.

Here is a strange note—it has been held that the doctor-patient privilege does not always apply to criminal proceedings.[41] I would not, however, treat that principle as controlling.

§9.503.1 State Application

DOCTOR - PATIENT PRIVILEGE IN ALABAMA:

Alabama law does not recognize a general physician-patient privilege of confidentiality. *Ex parte Smitherman Bros. Trucking, Inc.,* 751 So.2d 1232 (Ala., 1999).

DOCTOR - PATIENT PRIVILEGE IN ARIZONA:

A patient in a medical malpractice action against her treating physicians and others alleged that she had been negligently diagnosed as suffering from multiple personality disorder and that she had been falsely led to believe that she was the victim of satanic or ritual abuse. The patient was not entitled to discovery of non-party patient mental health records, since production of those records could lead to identification of non-party patients. *C.B. v. Sabalos*, 7 P.3d 124, (Ariz.App. 2000).

DOCTOR - PATIENT PRIVILEGE IN ARKANSAS:

Defendant was charged with felonious negligent homicide following an automobile collision; he apparently smelled like a brewery. This driver's defense was to be that he smelled of alcohol because beer cans in the car ruptured and spilled over him at the time of the collision. As a result, he was deemed to have waived any physician-patient privilege regarding his statements to an emergency room nurse pertaining to alcohol consumption. *McVay v. State*, 847 S.W.2d 28, 312 Ark. 73 (1993). Note that in general, however, Arkansas would recognize a privilege for confidential communications made to a nurse (i.e.,a "health provider privilege"). *Cavin v. State*, 855 S.W.2d 285, 313 Ark. 238 (1993).

DOCTOR - PATIENT PRIVILEGE IN CALIFORNIA:

The qualifications for a "confidential communication between patient and physician" are spelled out in Section 992 of the California Evidence Code:

> As used in this article, "confidential communication between patient and physician" means information, including information obtained by an examination of the patient, transmitted between a patient and his physician in the course of that relationship and in confidence by a means which, so far as the patient is aware, discloses the information to no third persons other than those who are present to further the interest of the patient in the consultation or those to whom disclosure is reasonably necessary for the transmission of the information or the accomplishment of the purpose for which the physician is consulted, and includes a diagnosis made and the advice given by the physician in the course of that relationship.

Section 994 of the CEC makes it quite clear that the privilege belongs to the patient, who has the sole right to give or withhold a waiver:

> Subject to Section 912 and except as otherwise provided in this article, the patient, whether or not a party, has a privilege to refuse to disclose, and to prevent another from disclosing, a confidential communication between patient and physician if the privilege is claimed by:
>
> (a) The holder of the privilege;

41 *Com v. Moore*, 458 A.2d 1250 (Pa.Super. 1988), but see *Daymude v. State*, 540 N.E.2d 1263 (Ind. 1989), holding to the contrary.

(b) A person who is authorized to claim the privilege by the holder of the privilege; or

(c) The person who was the physician at the time of the confidential communication, but such person may not claim the privilege if there is no holder of the privilege in existence or if he is otherwise instructed by a person authorized to permit disclosure.

The relationship of a physician and patient shall exist between a medical or podiatry corporation as defined in the Medical Practice Act and the patient to whom it renders professional services, as well as between such patients and licensed physicians and surgeons employed by such corporation to render services to such patients. The word "persons" as used in this subdivision includes partnerships, corporations, associations and other groups and entities.

Both the physician-patient and psychotherapist-patient privileges survive the death of the patient; the personal representative of the decedent has the same right to claim or waive the privileges as would any other. *Rittenhouse v. Superior Court*, 1 Cal. Rptr.2d 595 (Cal. App. 1991).

DOCTOR - PATIENT PRIVILEGE IN FLORIDA:

There is no "general" doctor-patient privilege in Florida. *Arias v. State*, 593 So.2d 260 (Fla. App. 1992).

DOCTOR - PATIENT PRIVILEGE IN ILLINOIS:

Communications between a litigant's doctor and an opposing attorney violated the patient-physician privilege, in part because they involved the revelation of confidences without the prior consent of the patient. *Jones v. Industrial Commission*, 169 Ill. Dec. 153, 591 N.E.2d 33 (1992).

The source of the physician-patient privilege is statutory and the scope of that privilege is generally a matter for the state legislature. *People v. Ernst,* 725 N.E.2d 59, 311 Ill.App.3d 672, 244 Ill.Dec. 264 (2000).

DOCTOR - PATIENT PRIVILEGE IN INDIANA:

In Indiana, the physician-patient privilege is unavailable in proceedings to terminate parental rights. *Shaw v. Shelby County Dept. of Public Welfare*, 612 N.E.2d 557 (Ind. 1993).

DOCTOR - PATIENT PRIVILEGE IN LOUISIANA:

Louisiana, much like New York, takes its physician-patient privilege quite seriously, as evidenced by *Sarphie v. Rowe*, 618 So.2d 905, (La. App. 1 Cir. 1993), which declared that when a person walks into doctor's office and opens his mouth, everything spilling out of it, whether it be his identity or his false teeth, is presumptively privileged and beyond the reach of discovery.

Even in the criminal arena, the privilege remains strong. Consider *State v. Taylor*, 621 So.2d 141 (La. App. 2 Cir. 1993), where a defendant in custody voluntarily consulted a doctor for the examination and treatment of his wound, after he was driven to the emergency room by police. That defendant, who repeatedly asked the doctor to extend the examination to other areas of his body, was eager to receive both the examination and treatment of that doctor (with whom the defendant had already established a physician/patient relationship several years before). The defendant's statements to the physician were protected by the privilege.

DOCTOR - PATIENT PRIVILEGE IN MICHIGAN:

In Michigan, there was no common law physician-patient privilege; statute (MCL 600.2157, MSA 27A.2157) controls. *People v. Johnson*, 111 Mich. App. 383, 314 N.W.2d 631 (1981). The purpose of the statute is to protect the confidential nature of the physician-patient relationship. *Scott v. Henry Ford Hospital*, 501 N.W.2d 259, 199 Mich. App. 241 (1993).

The purpose of the patient-physician privilege is to protect the doctor-patient relationship and ensure that communications between the two are kept confidential. *Baker v. Oakwood Hosp. Corp.*, 608 N.W.2d 823, 239 Mich.App. 461 (2000).

DOCTOR - PATIENT PRIVILEGE IN MISSOURI:

The physician-patient privilege belongs only to the patient, and he alone may waive it. But that privilege is waived once he places his physical condition in issue in the pleadings. *McClelland v. Ozenberger*, 805 S.W.2d 264 (Mo. App. 1991). This case reflects an almost unanimous rule (derived from Fed. R. Civ. P. 35) that once a person's physical condition becomes at issue, his or her privilege is waived.

In a proceeding to terminate parental rights, the doctor-patient privilege was not a ground for excluding the testimony of therapists, counselors, psychiatrists, and other witnesses who evaluated children and parents to determine information about repeated acts of sexual, physical, and emotional abuse. *In Interest of S.J.*, 849 S.W.2d 608 (Mo. App. W.D. 1993).

DOCTOR - PATIENT PRIVILEGE IN NEW YORK:

New York recognizes the doctor-patient privilege as evidenced by Section 4504(a) of the New York CPLR, which states, in part:

> (a) Unless the patient waives the privilege, a person authorized to practice medicine, registered professional nursing, licensed practical nursing, dentist, podiatry or chiropractic shall not be allowed to disclose any information which he acquired in attending a patient in a professional capacity, and which was necessary to enable him to act in that capacity. The relationship of a physician and patient shall exist between a medical corporation, as defined in article forty-four of the public health law, a professional service corporation organized under article fifteen of the business corporation law to practice medicine, and the patients to whom they respectively render professional medical services. A patient who, for the purpose of obtaining insurance benefits, authorizes the disclosure of any such privileged communication to any person shall not be deemed to have waived the privilege created by this subdivision.

New York takes its physician-patient privilege more seriously than most states as evidenced by *Rubin v. Alamo Rent-A-Car*, 593 N.Y.S.2d 284 (N.Y.A.D. 2 Dept. 1993), which declared that the privilege is absolute in the sense that, even in matters involving public justice, the court may not compel the disclosure of confidential information.

The testimony of an emergency medical technician who arrived at the scene of an automobile accident to render first aid to a drunk defendant was not subject to the physician-patient privilege; the technician was not acting as an agent for a doctor. *People v. Ackerson*, 566 N.Y.S.2d 833 (N.Y.Co. Ct. 1991).

People v. Figueroa, 568 N.Y.S.2d 957 (N.Y.A.D. 1 Dept. 1991) involved a defendant who decided to swallow some condoms containing illegal drugs, as a rather innovative method for smuggling the contraband into the jurisdiction. The substances were recovered during surgery. The physician-patient privilege did not apply, since it conflicted with the state's Public Health Law Section 3373 (which permitted the use of such evidence).

DOCTOR - PATIENT PRIVILEGE IN NORTH CAROLINA:

Information that is ordinarily protected by the doctor-patient privilege may be disclosed by order of the court if, in the opinion of the trial judge, disclosure is necessary to insure justice. *State v. Drdak*, 411 S.E.2d 604 (N.C. 1992).

DOCTOR - PATIENT PRIVILEGE IN OHIO:

In a hearing involving a challenge to a will, the trial court erred when it ordered the decedent's physician to proceed with a deposition and answer questions relating to the decedent's mental condition; those questions were improper since they followed an assertion of the physician-patient privilege by the decedent's beneficiaries. *Hollis v. Finger*, 590 N.E.2d 784, 69 Ohio App.3d 286. (1990).

A treating physician may give expert testimony in response to a proper hypothetical question, without violating the physician-patient privilege, as long as he disregards the information that he observed while treating the patient. *Berlinger v. Mt. Sinai Medical Center*, 589 N.E.2d 1378, 68 Ohio App.3d 830, *dismissed, jurisdictional motion overruled*, 569 N.E.2d 505, 58 Ohio St.3d 707, *rehearing denied*, 571 N.E.2d 136, 59 Ohio St.3d 709 (1990).

PHYSICIAN - PATIENT PRIVILEGE IN OREGON:

Not all states recognize this privilege. Oregon does, in the form of Rule 40.235 of the Oregon Evidence Code. Subsection (1) provides definitions:

(a) "Confidential communication" means a communication not intended to be disclosed to third persons except:
   (A) Persons present to further the interest of the patient in the consultation, examination or interview;
   (B) Persons reasonably necessary for the transmission of the communication; or
   (C) Persons who are participating in the diagnosis and treatment under the direction of the physician, including members of the patient's family.

(b) "Patient" means a person who consults or is examined or interviewed by a physician.

(c) "Physician" means a person authorized and licensed or certified to practice medicine in any state or nation, or reasonably believed by the patient so to be, while engaged in the diagnosis or treatment of a physical condition. "Physician" includes licensed or certified naturopathic and chiropractic physicians.

Subsection (2) provides:

> A patient has a privilege to refuse to disclose and to prevent any other person from disclosing confidential communications in a civil action, suit or proceeding, made for the purposes of diagnosis or treatment of the patient's physical condition, among the patient, the patient's physician or persons who are participating in the diagnosis or treatment under the direction of the physician, including members of the patient's family.

Rule 40.240 of the Oregon Evidence Code entitled, "nurse-patient privilege," states:

> A licensed professional nurse shall not, without the consent of a patient who was cared for by such nurse, be examined in a civil action or proceeding, as to any information acquired in caring for the patient, which was necessary to enable the nurse to care for the patient.

DOCTOR-PATIENT PRIVILEGE IN PENNSYLVANIA:

The physician-patient statutory privilege is designed to create a confidential atmosphere in which a patient will feel free to disclose all possible information which may be useful in rendering appropriate treatment. *Kuney v. Benjamin Franklin Clinic,* 751 A.2d 662, 2000 PA Super 129 (2000).

DOCTOR - PATIENT PRIVILEGE IN WASHINGTON:

The doctor-patient privilege did not apply to information pertaining to a blood donor's identity; the donor was not attended by a physician while seeking medical treatment, nor was the information required for the care of the "patient."

Doe v. Puget Sound Blood Center, 819 P.2d 370, 117 Wash.2d 772 (1991).

The purpose of the physician-patient privilege, preventing a physician from testifying in a civil action about information acquired when treating the patient unless the patient consents, is to (1) promote proper treatment by facilitating the full disclosure of information, and (2) to protect the patient from embarrassment or scandal that might result if the intimate details of medical treatment were revealed. *Berger v. Sonneland,* 101 Wash.App. 141, 1 P.3d 1187 (Wash.App. Div. 3, 2000).

DOCTOR-PATIENT PRIVILEGE IN WISCONSIN:

The statutory physician-patient privilege applies to confidential communications made by a patient to a health-care provider, or confidential information relating to the patient which is obtained by or disseminated to a health-care provider, under circumstances where the communication or information (1) is made or disseminated for the purpose of diagnosing or treating the patient's physical or mental condition, and (2) the patient intends that the communication not be disclosed to anyone other than participating health-care providers for any purpose other than to further the patient's interest in the consultation, examination, or interview at which the communication is made. *Crawford ex rel. Goodyear v. Care Concepts, Inc.,* 608 N.W.2d 694, 233 Wis.2d 609, 2000 Wi. App 59 (2000).

§9.504 Therapist - Patient Privilege

Psychiatrists, psychologists, psychotherapists, shrinks, or whatever name they go by,[42] must rely *heavily* upon facts received from their patients. More often than not, these professionals must speak to a patient about personal matters before providing an official technical diagnosis.

In some respects, the therapist-patient privilege is similar to the doctor-patient privilege. Indeed, a psychiatrist is, in fact, a doctor, in addition to being a therapist.[43] As with the previously discussed privileges, the therapist-patient privilege derives its authority from common law, rather than from any constitution.[44] It is, however, stronger than the doctor- patient privilege.

Psychotherapy is another matter. What constitutes a legitimate psychotherapist? That's a pretty broad question. There are limits.[45]

With respect to criminal matters, there are certain instances where a patient is referred to a psychiatrist in order to determine whether or not that person is competent to stand trial. For example, the testimony of a psychiatrist who examined a defendant in order to determine his competency to stand trial and his mental state (at the time of the alleged offense) was admissible in a kidnapping prosecution, and was not subject to

42 Even social workers jump into the mix. See *State v. Orwick,* 790 N.E.2d 1238, 153 Ohio.App.3d 65 (2003).

43 In Arizona, for example, a state statute governing doctor-patient privilege treats the psychiatrist just as a doctor. *State v. Beaty*, 762 P.2d 519 (1988).

44 *United States v. Talley*, 790 F.2d 1468 (9th Cir. 1986).

45 *Cunningham v. Southlake Center for Mental Health, Inc.*, 125 F.R.D. 474 (N.D.Ind. 1989). The Federal psychotherapist-patient privilege did not extend to a crisis intervention specialist who had a master's degree in social work but who was neither a medical doctor nor a licensed psychologist; see also *Thompson v. State*, 615 So.2d 737 (Fla.App. 1 Dist. 1993), where defendant's conversation with a mental health counselor who was "simply" a crisis intervention specialist (and not a psychologist or physician), did not enjoy the protection of the psychotherapist-patient privilege. See Imwinkelried, *"The Supreme Court's Decision to Recognize a Psychotherapist Privilege in* Jaffe v. Redmond: *The Meaning of 'Experience' and the Role of 'Reason' under Federal Rule of Evidence 501*," 65 U. Cin. L. Rev. 1019 (1997). See also Archer, *"All Aboard the Bandwagon!: The Uncertain Scope of the Federal Psychotherapist-Client Privilege in the Aftermath of* Jaffee v. Redmond," 52 Wash. U. J. Urb. 7 Contemp. L. 355 (1997).

the privilege, even though the psychiatrist believed that the privilege existed at the time of the examination.[46]

Privilege often gives way in child abuse cases. For example, in *Cronier v. Cronier*[47] "good cause" existed for requiring a social worker and clinical psychologist to disclose the results of their investigation of a father's possible child abuse in a mother's action for separation from bed and board. The evidence was essential to the determination of custody and visitation.

REFERENCES

Psychotherapist-patient privilege under federal common law. 72 A.L.R. Fed. 395.

§9.504.1 State Application

PSYCHOTHERAPIST - PATIENT PRIVILEGE IN ARKANSAS:

The psychotherapist-patient privilege does not protect the counselor's testimony about what he observed upon entering the defendant's apartment. *Davasher v. State*, 823 S.W.2d 863, 308 Ark. 154 (1992).

THERAPIST - PATIENT PRIVILEGE IN CALIFORNIA:

Section 1010 of the California Evidence Code broadly defines the term "*psychotherapist*," to include social workers, school psychologists, marriage counselors, and even "trainees" [CEC 1010 (a) through (j)]. Nevertheless, it might be fair to mention that each "professional" on the list is required to possess some type of license or credential. Section 1014 then effectuates the privilege for therapy patients by using language similar to that contained in Section 994:

> Subject to Section 912 and except as otherwise provided in this article, the patient, whether or not a party, has a privilege to refuse to disclose, and to prevent another from disclosing, a confidential communication between patient and psychotherapist if the privilege is claimed by:
>
> (a) The holder of the privilege;
> (b) A person who is authorized to claim the privilege by the holder of the privilege; or
> (c) The person who was the psychotherapist at the time of the confidential communication, but such person may not claim the privilege if there is no holder of the privilege in existence or if he is otherwise instructed by a person authorized to permit disclosure.

The relationship of a psychotherapist and patient shall exist between a psychological corporation as defined in Article 9 (commencing with Section 2995) of Chapter 6.6 of Division 2 of the Business and Professions Code, a marriage, family and child counseling corporation as defined in Article 6 (commencing with Section 4987.5) of Chapter 13 of Division 2 of the Business and Professions Code, or a licensed clinical social workers corporation as defined in Article 5 (commencing with Section 4998) of Chapter 14 of Division 2 of the Business and Professions Code, and the patient to whom it renders professional services, as well as between those patients and psychotherapists employed by those corporations to render services to those patients. The word "persons" as used in this subdivision includes partnerships, corporations, associations and other groups and entities.

Section 1035.2 of the California Evidence Code broke some new ground by creating a "sexual assault victim—counselor" privilege. CEC 1035.2 defines the "sexual assault victim counselor" as any person engaged in any office, hospital, institution or rape crisis center, whose primary purpose is the rendering of advice or assistance to victims of a sexual assault. There are many alternative methods by which a person may so qualify, depending upon experience, edu-

46 *State v. Tryon*, 431 N.W.2d 11 (Iowa App. 1988).

47 540 So.2d 1160 (La.App. 1 Cir. 1989); see also *State v. Knight*, 378 S.E.2d 424 (N.C.App. 1989).

cation, and certification. CEC Section 1037.1 grants a similar privilege with respect to "domestic violence counselors."

Even though the therapist privilege is recognized by California as a strong one, there is an important exception where so-called "dangerous patients" are concerned. These include patients who threaten the safety of themselves or others. Where a therapist becomes aware of such a problem, all bets are off when it comes to restricting the ability of that therapist to issue warnings. *Menendez v. Superior Court (People),* 279 Cal. Rptr. 521, *rehearing denied* (Cal. App. 2nd Dist. 1991). The principle has been extended to child abuse cases. *Roe v. Superior Court* (Roe), 280 Cal. Rptr. 380, 229 C.A.3d 832, (Cal. App. 2nd Dist. 1991).

Both the physician-patient and psychotherapist-patient privileges survive the death of the patient; the personal representative of the decedent has same right to claim or waive the privileges as would any other. *Rittenhouse v. Superior Court*, 1 Cal. Rptr.2d 595 (Cal. App. 1991).

THERAPIST - PATIENT PRIVILEGE IN CONNECTICUT:

The fact that a psychiatrist had treated the defendant at a correctional facility was sufficient to establish a psychiatrist-patient privilege. *State v. Brelsford*, 587 A.2d 1062, 24 Conn. App. 287 (Conn. App. 1991).

THERAPIST - PATIENT PRIVILEGE IN FLORIDA:

The psychotherapist-patient privilege applies to discovery, and therefore protects (in a child custody proceeding) all communications (or records) of a physician made for the purpose of diagnosis or treatment of the petitioner's mental or emotional condition; but the privilege does not protect relevant medical records made for the purpose of diagnosis or treatment of a condition that was not mental or emotional. *Oswald v. Diamond*, 576 So.2d 909 (Fla. App. 1 Dist. 1991). This particular case seems to highlight the superiority of the psychotherapist-patient privilege over the doctor-patient privilege.

Picking up California's lead, Florida has adopted the sexual assault counselor-victim privilege in the form of Section 90.5035. Subsection (2) provides that:

> A victim has a privilege to refuse to disclose, and to prevent any other person from disclosing, a confidential communication made by the victim to a sexual assault counselor or any record made in the course of advising, counseling, or assisting the victim. Such confidential communication or record may be disclosed only with the prior written consent of the victim. This privilege includes any advice given by the sexual assault counselor in the course of that relationship.

A child brought suit against her church for sexual molestation and abuse; by doing so, she placed her mental state at issue and thereby waived her rights to confidentiality concerning her mental condition as it related to litigation. Nevertheless, the church was not entitled to videotape the ongoing therapy sessions between the child and her treating psychologist. *F.M. v. Old Cutler Presbyterian Church, Inc.*, 595 So.2d 201 (Fla. App. 1992). But in a negligence action, a minor's psychotherapist-patient privilege was not waived when the minor's parents denied allegations that they knew or should have known that their son would injure someone if left unsupervised; the privilege belongs to the patient, not that of a third party. *Arias v. Urban*, 595 So.2d 230 (Fla. App. 1992).

In a custody case, the mental health of a parent is relevant, but mere allegations that a parent is mentally unstable are not sufficient to place that parent's mental health at issue and overcome psychotherapist-patient privilege. *Schouw v. Schouw*, 593 So.2d 1200 (Fla. App. 1992).

The defendant's conversation with a mental health counselor who was simply a crisis intervention specialist, and not a psychologist or physician, was not protected by the psychotherapist-patient privilege. The only time a patient is authorized to invoke the psychotherapist-patient privilege (based upon reasonable belief that a person is a psychotherapist) is when the psychotherapist is a physician. *Thompson v. State*, 615 So.2d 737 (Fla. App. 1 Dist. 1993).

THERAPIST - PATIENT PRIVILEGE IN GEORGIA:

The privilege concerning communications between a psychiatrist (or a licensed psychologist) and a patient is inapplicable when the psychiatrist is appointed by the court for the purposes of conducting a preliminary examination of the defendant and the psychiatrist is a witness for the court. *Christenson v. State*, 402 S.E.2d 41 (Ga. 1991).

THERAPIST - PATIENT PRIVILEGE IN KENTUCKY:

Psychiatrist-patient privilege survives the death of the patient. *Williams v. Commonwealth,* 829 S.W.2d 942, *review denied*, (Ky. App. 1992).

THERAPIST - PATIENT PRIVILEGE IN LOUISIANA:

The testimony of defendant's therapist was not privileged in defendant's prosecution for sexually abusing his children; the evidentiary privilege did not apply in cases involving child abuse. *State v. Rupp*, 614 So.2d 1323 (La. App.3 Cir. 1993).

THERAPIST - PATIENT PRIVILEGE IN MICHIGAN:

Prior inconsistent statements were made to a mental health therapist by the daughter of a father accused of having sexual intercourse with her; those statements were properly admitted for impeachment purposes, despite the statutory psychologist-patient privilege. That privilege had to yield to the father's constitutional right of confrontation. *People v. Adamski*, 497 N.W.2d 546 (Mich. App. 1993).

PSYCHOTHERAPIST - PATIENT PRIVILEGE IN NEW MEXICO:

Communications between a patient and psychotherapist are not per se confidential; rather, in order for the communication to be considered confidential, the patient must have intended that they be undisclosed. Words or conduct by the patient must have been of the type that would lead a psychotherapist to understand or believe that the information was intended to be confidential. *State ex rel. Human Services Dept., In Matter of Termination of Parental Rights of Sherry C. and John M.*, 824 P.2d 341 (N.M. App. 1991).

THERAPIST - PATIENT PRIVILEGE IN NEW YORK:

The psychiatrist-patient privilege is covered by Section 4507 of the New York CPLR. It makes a direct reference to the attorney-client privilege provision. CPLR 4508(a) extends the coverage to social workers.

PSYCHOTHERAPIST - PATIENT PRIVILEGE IN OREGON:

Rule 40.230 of the Oregon Evidence Code is virtually identical to Rule 40.235. It merely substitutes the word "psychotherapist" for "physician." Rule 40.230 defines psychotherapist as a person who is:

- (A) Licensed, registered, certified or otherwise authorized under the laws of any state to engage in the diagnosis or treatment of a mental or emotional condition; or
- (B) Reasonably believed by the patient so to be, while so engaged.

Rule 40.230 includes the following section not contained in 40.235:

(b) There is no privilege under this rule as to communications relevant to an issue of the mental or emotional condition of the patient:

- (A) In any proceeding in which the patient relies upon the condition as an element of the patient's claim or defense; or
- (B) After the patient's death, in any proceeding in which any party relies upon the condition as an element of the party's claim or defense.

Rule 40.250 entitled, "clinical social worker-client privilege," states:

> A clinical social worker registered by the State Board of Clinical Social Workers shall not be examined in a civil or criminal court proceeding as to any communication given the clinical social worker by a client in the course of non-investigatory professional activity when such communication was given to enable the registered clinical social worker to aid the client, except:
>
> (1) When the client or those persons legally responsible for the client's affairs give consent to the disclosure;
> (2) When the client initiates legal action or makes a complaint against the registered clinical social worker to the board;
> (3) When the communication reveals the intent to commit a crime or harmful act;
> (4) When the information reveals that a minor was the victim of a crime, abuse or neglect; or
> (5) When the registered clinical social worker is a public employee and the public employer has determined that examination in a civil or criminal court proceeding is necessary in the performance of the duty of the social worker as a public employee.

Where the purpose of the consultation is to provide a diagnosis or treatment for drug dependency, the psychotherapist-patient privilege does not apply to related communications. *State v. Ashley*, 818 P.2d 1270, 312 Or. 169 (1991).

THERAPIST - PATIENT PRIVILEGE IN PENNSYLVANIA:

In Pennsylvania, the privilege between a sexual assault counselor and a victim is absolute; it applies to the production of documents as well as the testimony of the counselors. *Commonwealth v. Wilson*, 602 A.2d 1290 (Pa. 1992); see also *Commonwealth. v. Eck*, 605 A.2d 1248 (Pa. Super. 1992). For purposes of applying the privilege, the sexual assault victim remains a "victim" even if it is ultimately determined that no assault occurred. *Commonwealth v. Kunkle*, 623 A.2d 336 (Pa. Super. 1993).

PSYCHOTHERAPIST - PATIENT PRIVILEGE IN WEST VIRGINIA:

Section 27-3-1 of the West Virginia Code, which deals with mental health professionals, states in part: "Communications and information obtained in the course of treatment or evaluation of any client or patient shall be deemed to be 'confidential information'... But the West Virginia Supreme Court of Appeals ruled that this section does not create a psychotherapist-patient privilege." *State v. Simmons*, 309 S.E.2d 89 (W. Va. 1983).

PSYCHOTHERAPIST - PATIENT PRIVILEGE IN WISCONSIN:

The patient's objectively reasonable perceptions and expectations with respect to a medical provider are the proper gauge in applying the physician/psychologist-patient privilege; the patient's intent to disclose confidential information is crucial in determining whether or not a valid privilege exists. *State v. Locke*, 502 N.W.2d 891 (Wis. App. 1993).

§9.505 Accountant - Client Privilege

Accountant-client privilege must have been founded, in part, upon the belief that overstated deductions, padded expense accounts, and hidden cash income are indispensable components of American economics. It is by no means a strong privilege. As a matter of fact, it is a pretty vague one, but it does exist.[48] Therefore, where there is a relationship involved with respect to

48 See 46 N.C.L.Rev. 19 (1967), 32 Texas L.Rev. 453 (1954), and *Lehnhard v. Moore,* 401 S.W.2d 232 (Texas 1966).

giving tax advice and preparing returns, communications between accountants and clients are "generally," though weakly, privileged.[49]

§9.505.1 State Application

ACCOUNTANT - CLIENT PRIVILEGE IN CALIFORNIA:

California does **not** recognize the Accountant-Client Privilege.

ACCOUNTANT - CLIENT PRIVILEGE IN FLORIDA:

Section 90.5055(1) defines an accountant as a "certified public accountant" or just an "accountant." Per Section 90.5055(1)(b), a "client" can be a person, a corporation, or an organization. FEC 90.5055(2) then provides:

> A client has a privilege to refuse to disclose, and to prevent any other person from disclosing, the contents of confidential communications with an accountant when such other person learned of the communications because they were made in the rendition of accounting services to the client. This privilege includes other confidential information obtained by the accountant from the client for the purpose of rendering accounting advice.

The accountant-client privilege does not apply to communications made in the preparation of audit inquiry letters which the client had intended to make available to the public. *In re Hillsborough Holdings Corp.*, 132 B.R. 478 (Bkrtcy. M.D. Fla. 1991).

ACCOUNTANT - CLIENT PRIVILEGE IN ILLINOIS:

Illinois **does** recognize the Accountant-Client Privilege.

ACCOUNTANT - CLIENT PRIVILEGE IN INDIANA:

An accountant, who was an incorporator and officer of a business for which securities were sold, had access to both privileged and non-privileged information. In a prosecution for dealing in unregistered securities, the defendant failed to show that the testimony of his accountant was excludable because it, particularly, divulged privileged communications between the accountant and the client. *Miller v. State*, 593 N.E.2d 1247, *rehearing denied* (Ind. App. 1992).

ACCOUNTANT - CLIENT PRIVILEGE IN MISSOURI (AS APPLIED IN OHIO):

An accountant, called as both a fact and expert witness by a buyer, could not testify about certain internal working papers which the seller was prohibited from discovering before trial, due to the buyer's invocation of the Missouri accountant-client privilege. The accountant could, however, testify about the buyer's accounting records and the treatment of certain expenses in its report to the seller, provided that the accountant did not rely upon privileged information. *Armco, Inc. v. Burns & McDonnell, Inc.*, 809 F. Supp. 43 (S.D. Ohio 1992).

ACCOUNTANT - CLIENT PRIVILEGE IN PENNSYLVANIA:

Pennsylvania **does** recognize the Accountant-Client Privilege.

ACCOUNTANT - CLIENT PRIVILEGE IN TEXAS:

Texas **does** recognize the Accountant-Client Privilege.

§9.506 Clergyman - Penitent Privilege

It is claimed by many that if you confess your sins you will go to heaven. If you do not, you will

49 *United States v. Schmidt,* 360 F.Supp. 339 (M.D. Pa. 1973). Note, there is, of course, no accountant-client privilege under federal law. *In re Hunt*, 153 B.R. 445 (Bkrtcy. N.D.Tex. 1992).

go to hell; that is strong stuff. Thus, people should be encouraged to freely and willingly confess their sins to their priests or ministers. Therefore, we have the clergyman-penitent privilege.[50]

There is a word of caution with respect to this privilege. If you confess your sins, make sure that there is somebody behind the booth to listen to them, and not a machine, or an "institution" in general. For, it has been held that the priest *must* be a natural person and not an "institution" if the privilege is to be properly invoked.[51]

Those who saw the movie *The Exorcist* are probably asking the burning question: "Does the privilege apply to exorcisms in addition to confessions?" I don't know the answer. But I would note that the priest in the film, Father Damien, had **three** bases of privilege covered when the police questioned him about his possessed client: He was a *psychiatrist, doctor,* and a *priest*. Question—Who can investigate a crime, get evidence, and then be barred from using it? A Detective-Minister, who else?[52] Or try this question—Can a repentant priest take advantage of the privilege for his own confessed sins?[53]

Perhaps the furthest extension of the privilege involved a case which held that even non-penitential communications to a clergyman might be protected if those communications were made in search of guidance and advice.[54]

REFERENCES

Communications to clergyman as privilege in federal proceedings. 118 A.L.R. Fed. 449.

§9.506.1 State Application

CLERGYMAN - PENITENT PRIVILEGE IN ARKANSAS:

A minister accused the defendant of molesting boys and the defendant confessed. These communications were not protected by privilege even though the minister had counseled the defendant on previous occasions. The minister did not consider the confrontation to equate to counseling and did not tell the defendant that the conversation was confidential. *Magar v. State*, 826 S.W.2d 221, 308 Ark. 380 (1992).

In a different case, the defendant's employer was a minister. However, that did not make the defendant's statement to the employer regarding sexual abuse subject to the clergyman-penitent privilege, even though the employer had ministered to the defendant once in the past. *Bonds v. State*, 837 S.W.2d 881, 310 Ark. 541 (Ark. 1992).

CLERGYMAN - PENITENT PRIVILEGE IN CALIFORNIA:

Section 1032 of the California Evidence Code defines "penitential communication" to mean:

> ... a communication made in confidence, in the presence of no third person so far as the penitent is aware, to a clergyman who, in the course of the discipline or practice of his church, denomination, or organization, is authorized or accustomed to hear such communications and, under the discipline or tenets of his church, denomination, or

50 See Reese, *Confidential Communications to the Clergy*, 25 Ohio St.L.J. 55 (1963).

51 *United States v. Luther,* 481 F.2d 429 (9th Cir. 1973).

52 *Lewis v. New York City Housing Authority*, 542 N.Y.S.2d 165 (1989). This case involved the surrender of a packaged gun to an off-duty city housing police department detective. The detective just happened to be an ordained minster who was presiding over a church function. These circumstances provided reason to believe that the identity of the person who had surrendered the firearm was confidential, so that the detective-minister could assert clergy privilege in disciplinary proceedings.

53 The answer is "Yes," but his assertions of the privilege would be subject to the same limitations and waivers that normal, less holy sinners are subject to. See *Roman Catholic Diocese of Jackson v. Morrison*, 905 So.2d 1213 (Miss., 2005).

54 *Scott v. Hammock*, 870 P.2d 947 (Utah 1994); but see *State v Buss*, 76 Wash.App. 780 P.2d 920 (1995), which held that the priest-penitent privilege did not extend to a non-ordained church counselor, nor did it extend to activities other than confessions.

organization, has a duty to keep such communications secret.

CEC Section 1033 then states, "Subject to Section 912, a penitent, whether or not a party, has a privilege to refuse to disclose, and to prevent another from disclosing, a penitential communication if he claims the privilege."

CLERGYMAN - PENITENT PRIVILEGE IN FLORIDA:

Section 90.505(1)(a) of the Florida Evidence Code defines "clergyman" as a priest, rabbi, practitioner of Christian Science, or minister of any religious organization or denomination usually referred to as a church, or an individual reasonably believed so to be by the person consulting him. Section 90.505(1)(b) then states:

> A communication between a clergyman and a person is "confidential" if made privately for the purpose of seeking spiritual counsel and advice from the clergyman in the usual course of his practice or discipline and not intended for further disclosure except to other persons present in furtherance of the communication.

Section 90.505(2) then provides that "a person has a privilege to refuse to disclose, and to prevent another from disclosing, a confidential communication by the person to a clergyman in his capacity as spiritual adviser."

CLERGYMAN - PENITENT PRIVILEGE IN ILLINOIS:

The defendant had sexual relations with his stepdaughter, then told his minister. In a sexual assault prosecution, statements to the minister about the frequency of the sexual contacts were not protected by the minister-penitent privilege, even though the defendant claimed that he believed the statements were made in confidence. The minister had told the defendant prior to the conversation that he could not be the defendant's counselor. *People v. Bole,* 165 Ill. Dec. 739, 585 N.E.2d 135, 223 Ill. App.3d 247 (1991).

CLERGYMAN - PENITENT PRIVILEGE IN INDIANA:

That privilege which protects certain communications with a clergyman is derived from statute, and thus must be strictly construed. An example is the Catholic sacrament of reconciliation, which involves confessions made to a clergyman in the course of discipline, and thus falls within the strictures of the statute establishing a privilege for communications directed to a clergyman. *Mullins v. State,* 721 N.E.2d 335 (Ind.App., 1999).

CLERGYMAN - PENITENT PRIVILEGE IN IOWA:

In order to determine whether a communication to a member of the clergy falls within the statutory priest-penitent privilege, the communication must be: (1) confidential, (2) entrusted to a person in his or her professional capacity, and (3) necessary and proper for the discharge of the function of that person's office. *State v. Richmond,* 590 N.W.2d 33 (Iowa, 1999).

CLERGYMAN - PENITENT PRIVILEGE IN LOUISIANA:

The ministerial privilege did not apply to a defendant's statements to ministers to the effect that the defendant committed murder; the minister did not consider the statements to be confidential or for the purpose of gaining religious guidance. Also, the defendant denied the statements altogether. *State v. Mayer*, 589 So.2d 1145 (La. App. 1991)

An aggravated assault defendant's statements to a minister were privileged, despite the presence of the victim (and the wives of the defendant and victim), where the minister was acting in a spiritual capacity; he was the pastor of a church attended by both the defendant and the victim, a private meeting with the minister took place at the church, and the minister was attempting to counsel the couples in order to help them reconcile their differences. *State v. Ellis,* 756 So.2d 418 99-0425 (La.App., 1999).

CLERGYMAN - PENITENT PRIVILEGE IN MONTANA:

Statements made by a defendant to the wife of a non-ordained deacon of his church did not fall within the clergy-penitent privilege because the wife did not qualify as a member of the clergy. *State v. Gooding,* 989 P.2d 304, 296 Mont. 234, 1999 MT 249 (1999).

CLERGYMAN - PENITENT PRIVILEGE IN NEW JERSEY:

Be careful in New Jersey: the clergyperson is not required to obtain the penitent's consent in order to waive the privilege. The clergyperson is the holder of the privilege, not the penitent. State v. Szemple, 622 A.2d 248, 263 N.J.Super 98 (N.J.Super A.D. 1993).

For the cleric-penitent privilege to apply, a person's communication must be made: (1) in confidence; (2) to a cleric, (3) in his or her professional character or role as a spiritual advisor. *State v. Cary,* 751 A.2d 620, 331 N.J.Super. 236 (2000).

Should priests who commit sexual abuse be entitled to assert the privilege? If you happen to be such a priest, New Jersey is definitely the place for you. Consider *Corsie v. Campanalonga,* 721 A.2d 733, 317 N.J.Super. 177 (1998), which involved a lawsuit brought against a priest (and other church officials) by victims who alleged that they had been sexually molested and assaulted by that priest. Communications in a vicar's files made by the priest in confidence to the vicar were protected by the cleric-penitent privilege for purposes of the suit. The vicar was acting in his professional character when the priest confided in him about the alleged sexual assaults; and, therefore, as long as the priest's communications to the vicar were confessions, they were protected from disclosure.

CLERGYMAN - PENITENT PRIVILEGE IN NEW YORK:

Section 4505 of the New York CPLR states:

Unless the person confessing waives the privilege, a clergyman, or other minister of any religion, shall not be allowed to disclose a confession made to him in his professional character as spiritual advisor.

Where the clergy-penitent privilege applies, the penitent is entitled to confidentiality, whether it be in a sealed matrimonial proceeding or in a public or private forum; the privilege belongs to, and may only be waived, by her. *Lightman v. Flaum,* 687 N.Y.S.2d 562, 179 Misc.2d 1007 (1999).

CLERGYMAN - PENITENT PRIVILEGE IN NORTH CAROLINA:

There are two requirements for the clergyman privilege to apply: (1) The defendant must be seeking the counsel and advice of his minister; and (2) The information must be entrusted to the minister as a confidential communication. *State v. Andrews,* 507 S.E.2d 305, 131 N.C.App. 371 (1998).

CLERGYMAN - PENITENT PRIVILEGE IN OREGON:

Rule 40.260 entitled, "clergyman-penitent privilege," states:

(1) As used in this section, unless the context requires otherwise:

(a) "Confidential communication" means a communication made privately and not intended for further disclosure except to other persons present in furtherance of the purpose of the communication.

(b) "Member of the clergy" means a minister of any church, religious denomination or organization or accredited Christian Science practitioner who in the course of the discipline or practice of that church, denomination or organization is authorized or accustomed to hearing confidential communications and, under the discipline or tenets of that church, denomination or organization, has a duty to keep such communications secret.

(2) A member of the clergy shall not, without the consent of the person making the communication, be examined as to any confidential communication made to the member of the clergy in the member's professional character.

CLERGYMAN - PENITENT PRIVILEGE IN PENNSYLVANIA:

Pennsylvania recognizes the Clergyman-Penitent Privilege. *In re Grand Jury Investigation*, 918 F.2d 374 (Pa. 1990).

CLERGYMAN - PENITENT PRIVILEGE IN TENNESSEE:

A clergyman testified that the defendant (parishioner) admitted vandalizing his girlfriend's washing machine; this was held to be a violation of the clergyman-penitent privilege, even though the state claimed that the defendant's statement was made to the preacher in his capacity as a close personal friend. Apparently, the clergyman had taken the defendant to a motel with the intention of giving "comfort to him" since the defendant was "really burdened down." The preacher had asked the defendant, "Are you having problems?" This indicated that the clergyman was ministering to the defendant in his professional capacity. *State v. Boling*, 806 S.W.2d 202 (Tenn. Cr. App. 1990).

CLERGYMAN - PENITENT PRIVILEGE IN TEXAS:

Under Rule 505 of the Texas Civil Evidence Rules, clergymen may refuse to disclose confidential communications made to them in their professional capacity as spiritual advisors. The test to be applied (Wigmore's criteria): (1) The communications originated in the belief that they would not be disclosed, (2) The element of confidentiality is essential to the relationship, (3) The relationship is valuable to the community and worth preserving, and (4) The injury caused by the disclosure would outweigh the benefits to the litigants.

In *Simpson v. Tennant*, 871 S.W.2d 301 (Tex. Ct. App. 1994), a personal injury action against a church, a Texas appellate court found that the identity of a communicant could not be revealed by a pastor, even though the communications were relevant to the litigation.

The protection afforded by the privilege extended to communications with a clergyman is not unlimited; that privilege only extends to communications addressed to a clergyman in his professional capacity as a spiritual advisor, and not to every private communication made to a clergy member. *Kos v. State,* 15 S.W.3d 633 (Tex.App. Dallas, 2000).

CLERGYMAN - PENITENT PRIVILEGE IN UTAH:

Utah Code Ann. §78-24-8(3) presents a three-part test for its clergy-penitent privilege: (1) The communication must be a confession, (2) made to a clergyperson or priest in his or her professional character, and (3) must have been made in the course of discipline imposed by the church to which the clergyman or priest belongs.

Before literally accepting the three-part test set forth in Utah Code Ann. §78-24-8(3), see *Scott v. Hammock,* 870 P.2d 947 (Utah 1994), which held that certain nonpenitential communications to a clergyman were protected because they were made in search of guidance and advice. The case involved a daughter, who while in the process of suing her father for an alleged sexual abuse, subpoenaed certain nonpenitential communications between the father and a bishop. The court rejected the daughter's claim that the term "confession" should be restricted penitential admissions of wrongdoing, and found that a clergy's advice and moral guidance should be included within the privilege. *(Two elements of Utah's three-part test were apparently ignored, perhaps due to the ill-favored nature of the litigation.)*

CLERGYMAN - PENITENT PRIVILEGE IN WASHINGTON:

Washington takes a restrictive view of the clergyman's privilege. Consider *State v Buss*, 76

Wash. App. 780, 887 P.2d 920, (1995), where the defendant was convicted of raping a child. Defendant appealed her conviction, partly because of the priest-penitent privilege. However, the defendant had confessed to a non-ordained church counselor. The court found the priest-penitent privilege did not extend to non-ordained church counselors or to counseling activities not amounting to a confession.

For communications between a member of the clergy and a penitent to be protected by the statutory privilege, the clergy member must be ordained, and the statements must be made as a confession in the course of discipline enjoined by the church to which the member of the clergy belongs; no requirement exists that the penitent must be constrained by a religious obligation to make the confession. *State v. Martin,* 975 P.2d 1020, 137 Wash.2d 774 (1999).

CLERGYMAN - PENITENT PRIVILEGE IN WEST VIRGINIA:

Section 57-3-9 entitled, "communications to priests, nuns, clergymen, rabbis or other religious counselors not subject to being compelled as testimony," states as follows:

> No priest, nun, rabbi or member of the clergy authorized to celebrate the rites of marriage in this state pursuant to the provisions of article one [Section 48-1-1 et seq.], chapter forty-eight of this code shall be compelled to testify in any criminal or grand jury proceedings or in any domestic relations action in any court of this state:
>
> (1) With respect to any confession or communication, made to such person, in his or her professional capacity in the course of discipline enjoined by the church or other religious body to which he or she belongs, without the consent of the person making such confession or communication; or
>
> (2) With respect to any communication made to such person, in his or her professional capacity, by either spouse, in connection with any effort to reconcile estranged spouses, without the consent of the spouse making the communication. This subsection is in addition to the protection and privilege afforded pursuant to section ten-a [Section 48-2-10a], article two, chapter forty-eight of this code.

§9.507 Husband - Wife Privilege

The husband-wife privilege exists so that a family will not be "torn apart" by its members testifying against one another in court.[55]

With respect to this privilege, a word of caution is urged. A valid marriage under state law is normally an absolute prerequisite for the assertion of the marital privilege;[56] therefore, if you must spill your confessions to a lover, make sure that the spillee is your lawfully wedded spouse. In that regard, it has been held that the privilege applies to communications made during the marital relationship, even though at the time of trial, the parties may not be married.[57]

A prevailing view has it that the privilege applies *only* to confidential communications.[58] In *United States v. Byrd,*[59] the United States Court of Appeals for the Seventh Circuit declared that

55 *U.S. v. White*, 974 F.2d 1135 (9th Cir. 1992) summarized by holding that the public policy interests in protecting the integrity of marriages and ensuring that spouses freely communicate with one another underlie the marital communications privilege.

56 *U.S. v. Roberson,* 859 F.2d 1376 (9th Cir. 1988); *People v. Mulgrave*, 558 N.Y.S.2d 607 (1990).

57 *People v. DeWitt*, 433 N.W.2d 325 (Mich.App. 1988); but see *People v. Hamacher,* 438 N.W.2d 43, 432 Mich. 157 (1989).

58 *Sexton v. Sexton,* 129 Iowa 487, 105 N.W. 314 (1905); see also *McCormick, Evidence* (3rd Ed.), #80, p.193.

59 750 F.2d 585, 593 (7th Cir. 1984).

"only communications" that take place during a valid marriage between couples still cohabiting pursuant to that marriage are protected by the privilege. A large cardboard message, left at home, from husband to wife, was held to be *non*-confidential.[60]

In general, the extent to which the husband-wife privilege applies may involve a balancing of society's interest in preserving the confidentiality of marital partners against the strong interest of uncovering the truth, particularly where *criminal* trials are involved.[61]

Consider *People v. Vermeulen*,[62] where the defendant Vermeulen was charged with murdering his second wife, Urime, after he had filed for divorce from his first wife, Sharon, but before that divorce had become final. One week before Urime's death, Vermeulen (a bigamist) felt compelled to tell Sharon that he would kill Urime if she left him. When Urime turned up dead, Vermeulen claimed that it was suicide. Using his statement to Sharon, the prosecutor argued that there was no longer any confidential relationship that existed between Sharon and the defendant; the trial court agreed. However, the Court of Appeals reversed, and the Supreme Court of Michigan affirmed that reversal, holding that a Michigan Statute[63] must govern; it clearly provided that a spouse may not "during the marriage or afterwards" be examined as to any communication made during the marriage. The majority opinion was accompanied by a strong dissent which emphasized the importance of the word "confidential." In *Leonard v. State*,[64] the trial court permitted the state to force an inmate's wife to testify as to the wife's and inmate's jail escape plan. This was held to be a reversible error, despite the State's contention that the plan was not confidential because a second inmate was supposed to receive hidden hacksaw blades (however, the state did not establish that the second inmate knew of the escape plan).

Keeping in line with the confidentiality requirement, as a rule, the spousal communications privilege applies only to husband and wife communications where no other person is present.[65] However, a wife's refusal to testify concerning the involvement of a third person in drug activities was a proper invoking of the husband-wife privilege, *where* the wife's answers might have been used by the prosecutor to obtain an indictment against her husband.[66]

A clarification may be in order with respect to the distinction between "spousal immunity" and "spousal privilege" (i.e., husband-wife privilege). Consider a simple scenario where Husband, in confidence, tells Wife "I shot the Sheriff." Wife is then compelled to testify against Husband. Under the principle of spousal immunity, Faithful Wife may refuse to testify. Later, however, Wife catches Husband in bed with Lisa, and now **wants** to testify against him. At this juncture, even though Unforgiving Wife is willing to testify, Husband may bar the testimony by asserting spousal privilege (not spousal immunity).

---

60 *U.S. v. Davis*, 714 F.Supp. 853 (S.D. Ohio, 1988); *Yoder v. U.S.*, 80 F.2d 665 (10th Cir. 1935).

61 In *Brown v. Commonwealth*, 292 S.E.2d 319, 223 Va. 601 (1982), a husband shot his wife and her grandmother (actions non-conducive to a happy-family environment); the wife could testify against her husband in both of his trials. Generally, a wife may testify against her defendant-husband regardless of whether the offense was committed against the spouse's person or her property. *U.S. v. Roberson*, 859 F.2d 1376 (9th Cir. 1988); *Hudson v. Commonwealth,* 292 S.E.2d 317, 223 Va. 595 (1982); nor should any spousal privilege apply when a spouse commits a crime against a child of either spouse. United States v. Allery, 526 F.2d 1362 (8th Cir. 1975).

62 438 N.W.2d 36, 432 Mich. 32 (1989).

63 M.C.L.A. §8600.2162.

64 537 N.E.2d 480 (Ind. 1989).

65 *United States v. Koehler*, 790 F.2d 1256 (5th Cir. 1986); see also *People v. Gorman*, 542 N.Y.S.2d 225 (N.Y.A.D. 2 Dept. 1989), and *Kindred v. State*, 540 N.E.2d 1161 (Ind. 1988).

66 I*n re Grand Jury Matter, The United States of America*, 673 F.2d 688 (3rd Cir. 1982).

REFERENCES

Marital privilege under Rule 501. 46 A.L.R. Fed. 735.

§9.507.1 State Application

HUSBAND - WIFE PRIVILEGE IN ALABAMA:

During the course of an investigation by drug agents, the defendant's "common law wife" made certain disclosures. The information was not protected by spousal privilege because providing the information to the officers in the course of the investigation was not "testimony" and the so-called "wife" was a joint participant in the criminal activity with the defendant. *Montanez v. State*, 592 So.2d 650 (Ala. App. 1991). For spousal privilege to take effect, the defendant must be married to the witness, either ceremonially or at common law, at the time that the testimony of the witness is sought. *Corbitt v. State*, 596 So.2d 426, *certiorari denied, Ex parte Corbitt*, 596 So.2d 430 (Ala. App. 1992).

Brown v. State, 588 So.2d 551 (Ala. App. 1991) presents the case of a family with problems. The husband (and defendant) abused his step-daughter in the presence of his wife. He waited until she went to sleep and then attempted to smother the step-daughter. The actions of the husband were not intended to be privileged communications, and thus, did not fall within the scope of marital privilege.

HUSBAND - WIFE PRIVILEGE IN CALIFORNIA:

California follows the prevailing view by establishing that only confidential marital communications may be subject to privilege. And California Evidence Code Section 980 so provides:

> Subject to Section 912 (*which pertains to waivers*) and except as otherwise provided in this article, a spouse (or his guardian or conservator when he has a guardian or conservator), whether or not a party, has a privilege during the marital relationship and afterwards to refuse to disclose, and to prevent another from disclosing, a communication if he claims the privilege and the communication was made in confidence between him and the other spouse while they were husband and wife.

In accordance with the spirit of Section 980, CEC 970 provides: "Except as otherwise provided by statute, a married person has a privilege not to testify against his spouse in any proceeding." But in keeping with the general rule, you had better make certain that you're **legally** married to the person to whom you spill the beans.

Consider *People v. Gallego*, 802 P.2d 169, 276 Cal. Rptr. 679, 52 C.3d 115 (1990) where the defendant tried unsuccessfully to have his "wife's" testimony excluded. Unfortunately, his marriage license was invalid because he had never dissolved a prior marriage; so the assertion of marital privilege failed the test.

With respect to immunity as opposed to privilege, consider a case where the defendant's wife testified against him at a preliminary hearing, thereby effectively losing her privilege not to testify (or be called upon to testify) against him during his subsequent trial. The wife was not entitled to be advised of her testimonial privileges before testifying at the preliminary hearing. *People v. Resendez*, 15 Cal. Rptr.2d 575, 12 C.A.4th 98 (Cal. App. 4 Dist. 1993).

HUSBAND - WIFE PRIVILEGE IN COLORADO:

In a personal injury case, information concerning conversations that the plaintiff had with her husband was protected by the marital privilege. *Voight v. Colorado Mountain Club*, 819 P.2d 1088 (Colo. App. 1991).

The Marital Communications Privilege protects from disclosure those private communications between the spouses made in the confidence of the marital relationship. *U.S. v. Cooper,* 85 F.Supp.2d 1 (D.D.C.,2000).

HUSBAND - WIFE PRIVILEGE IN FLORIDA:

Section 90.504 of the Florida Evidence Code provides:

> (1) A spouse has a privilege during and after the marital relationship to refuse to disclose, and to prevent another

from disclosing, communications which were intended to be made in confidence between the spouses while they were husband and wife.

(2) The privilege may be claimed by either spouse or by the guardian or conservator of a spouse. The authority of a spouse, or guardian or conservator of a spouse to claim the privilege is presumed in the absence of contrary evidence.

Section 90.504(3) specifically excludes the application of any privilege in an action (1) brought by or on behalf of one spouse against the other spouse; (2) in a criminal proceeding in which one spouse is charged with a crime committed at any time against the person or property of the other spouse, or the person or property of a child of either; and, (3) in a criminal proceeding in which the communication is offered in evidence by a defendant spouse who is one of the spouses between whom the communication was made.

HUSBAND - WIFE PRIVILEGE IN GEORGIA:

A statute providing that a wife is competent but not compellable as a witness against her husband creates a privilege which belongs to the testifying wife; and the burden is on the defendant asserting the marital privilege to prove that such privilege applies to the testimony at issue. *Brown v. State*, 404 S.E.2d 469, 199 Ga. App. 188, *certiorari denied*, (Ga. App. 1991).

HUSBAND - WIFE PRIVILEGE IN ILLINOIS:

Illinois recognizes the Spousal Privilege. Il. Rev. Stat. Ch. 110 8-801.

HUSBAND - WIFE PRIVILEGE IN INDIANA:

Parties must have a legally recognized marriage in order to claim the benefit of the marital privilege with respect to their communications. Thus, a defendant's statements to his fiancee one month before they were married were not protected by the marital communications privilege. *Hazelwood v. State*, 609 N.E.2d 10 (Ind. App. 1 Dist. 1993).

The state's questioning of a defendant's wife regarding the ownership and disappearance of a gun (used in the charged shootings) did not violate the marital privilege because the wife did not allude to any communication between her husband and herself, but instead, merely recited the fact of ownership of the gun and its disappearance from her purse on the evening in question. *Gordon v. State*, 609 N.E.2d 1085 (Ind. 1993).

The statutory spousal privilege is restricted to those confidential communications and information gained by reason of the marital relationship. *Rubalcada v. State,* 731 N.E.2d 1015 (Ind., 2000).

HUSBAND - WIFE PRIVILEGE IN KENTUCKY:

Marital privilege applies to confidential communications between husband and wife, not to words that are shouted between the two of them in the presence of others. Therefore, a witness could testify about instructions that the defendant shouted to his wife (i.e., not to answer any questions) as the police closed in. *Bills v. Com.*, 851 S.W.2d 466 (Ky. 1993).

The statute precluding the disclosure of confidential marital communications does not render a spouse "incompetent" in any manner, but simply provides a privilege (that is exercisable and waivable by the person who made the confidential communication) to preclude that spouse from disclosing the communication through testimony. *Brown v. State,* 753 A.2d 84, 359 Md. 180 (2000).

HUSBAND - WIFE PRIVILEGE IN MICHIGAN:

The defendant broke into the marital home (in violation of a restraining order), damaged property and removed personal and joint property, then in his wife's possession. The Court ruled that the destruction of the personal property could constitute a personal wrong, an exception to the spousal testimonial privilege statute (under which one spouse may testify for or against the other without the other's consent in actions growing out of a "personal wrong or injury done by one to the other"). *People v. Pohl*, 507

N.W.2d 819, 202 Mich. App. 203 (1993). In another "personal wrong" case, defendant's wife was permitted to testify against her husband at his trial for publishing and uttering, which stemmed from defendant's taking of the wife's Aid to Families with Dependent Children check from a postal worker and cashing it. The personal wrong occurred when the defendant forged an endorsement on the check, thereby depriving his wife and children of a legally entitled benefit. *People v. Eberhardt*, 518 N.W.2d 511, 205 Mich. App. 587 (1993).

The defendant made a statement to his estranged wife that she should tell the police that the victim had fallen on a knife; this was a confidential communication to the wife and was, therefore, privileged even after their divorce. *People v. Fisher*, 476 N.W.2d 762, 190 Mich. App. 598 (1991).

In *People v. Hamacher*, 402 N.W.2d 484, 428 Mich. 844 (1987), the husband and wife were still legally married at the time a communication took place and therefore the Michigan Supreme Court vacated the judgment of the Court of Appeals, stating that "MCL 600.2162 contains no exception to the privilege regarding communications between husband an wife where the husband and wife are separated or are in the process of obtaining a divorce. The defendant and his wife remained husband and wife at the time the communication in question was allegedly made." (M.C.L. 600.2162, M.S.A. 27A.2162 states: "a husband shall not be examined as a witness for or against his wife without her consent; nor a wife for or against her husband without his consent...")

For those readers having difficulty distinguishing spousal *immunity* from *privilege*, the *dicta* of *People v. Zak*, 457 N.W.2d 59, 184 Mich. App. 1 (1990), might help. The Court stated that M.C.L. 600.2162, M.S.A. 27A.2162 (*supra*) contains two distinct privileges (parenthetical expressions added):

> The first privilege, the spousal privilege (i.e.,*spousal immunity*), bars one spouse from testifying for or against the other spouse without the other spouse's consent where the witness and the spouse are married at the time of trial. *People v. Hamacher*, 432 Mich. 157, 438 N.W.2d 43 (1989).
>
> The second privilege, the confidential communication privilege (i.e., spousal privilege), bars one spouse from testifying as to any communications made by one to the other during a marriage without the consent of the spouse. Id. The communication privilege applies whether the testimony is sought during the marriage or afterwards, as long as the communication occurred during the course of the marriage. *Id.*

HUSBAND - WIFE PRIVILEGE IN MISSOURI:

The prosecutor was entitled, during cross-examination, to question the defendant about whether or not he married his wife so that they would not have to testify against one another at their respective trials. *State v. Phegley*, 826 S.W.2d 348. (Mo. App. 1992).

HUSBAND - WIFE PRIVILEGE IN NEW YORK:

Section 4502 of the New York CPLR states:

(a) A husband or wife is not competent to testify against the other in an action founded upon adultery, except to prove the marriage, disprove the adultery, or disprove a defense after evidence has been introduced tending to prove such defense.

(b) A husband or wife shall not be required, or, without the consent of the other if living, allowed, to disclose a confidential communication made by one to the other during marriage.

Singer Billy Joel's former manager claimed that Joel's wife, Christie Brinkley, tortiously interfered with that manager's contract with him. Although privilege would not ordinarily apply to conversations relating to business, in this case, the manager's responsibilities in managing the income and assets of the marital partnership did require that the discussions between Joel and Brinkley about that subject be confidential and subject to statutory privilege. *Joel v. Weber*, 581 N.Y.S.2d 579 (N.Y. Sup. 1992).

The defendant's wife could testify as to the time that the defendant arrived home and as to the discovery of a duffel bag and its contents; those observations were not "communications" protected by marital privilege. *People v. LaPlanche*, 598 N.Y.S.2d 877 (N.Y.A.D. 4 Dept. 1993).

Defendant made inculpatory statements to his estranged wife (normally, a bad idea) concerning a murder. The statements were subject to the marital privilege so that their admission was reversible error which was not cured by trial court's instruction that the jury should disregard the testimony. *People v. Knapper*, 594 N.Y.S.2d 210 (N.Y.A.D. 1 Dept. 1993).

New York does not recognize a tort claim for the violation of attorney-client privilege by the client against an intruder who made an unauthorized inspection of that client's documents in a lawyer's office; existing remedies are adequate to deter third-party invasions, including possible criminal penalties, revocation of a private investigator's license, and a common-law privacy right. *Madden v. Creative Services, Inc.*, 646 N.E.2d 780 (N.Y. 1995).

When criminal activity is aimed at the spouse, the spousal privilege (which normally precludes the disclosure of confidential communications made by the other spouse during the marriage without that spouse's consent) is extinguished with respect to that activity. *People v. Govan,* 701 N.Y.S.2d 474, 268 A.D.2d 689 (2000).

HUSBAND - WIFE PRIVILEGE IN OHIO:

Under Ohio law, the marital communications privilege does not apply where communications are made in the presence of third parties. *In re Carmean*, 153 B.R. 985 (Bkrtcy. S.D. Ohio 1993).

HUSBAND - WIFE PRIVILEGE IN OREGON:

Rule 40.255 entitled, "husband-wife privilege," states:

(1) As used in this section, unless the context requires otherwise:
   (a) "Confidential communication" means a communication by a spouse to the other spouse and not intended to be disclosed to any other person.
   (b) "Marriage" means a marital relationship between husband and wife, legally recognized under the laws of this state.

(2) In any civil or criminal action, a spouse has a privilege to refuse to disclose and to prevent the other spouse from disclosing any confidential communication made by one spouse to the other during the marriage. The privilege created by this subsection may be claimed by either spouse. The authority of the spouse to claim the privilege and the claiming of the privilege is presumed in the absence of evidence to the contrary.

(3) In any criminal proceeding, neither spouse, during the marriage, shall be examined adversely against the other as to any other matter occurring during the marriage unless the spouse called as a witness consents to testify.

(4) There is no privilege under this section:
   (a) In all criminal actions in which one spouse is charged with bigamy or with an offense or attempted offense against the person or property of the other spouse or of a child of either, or with an offense against the person or property of a third person committed in the course of committing or attempting to commit an offense against the other spouse;
   (b) As to matters occurring prior to the marriage; or
   (c) In any civil action where the spouses are adverse parties.

Requiring a defendant's wife to testify against him violated the husband-wife privilege. *State v. Quintero*, 823 P.2d 981, 110 Or. App. 247 (1991).

HUSBAND - WIFE PRIVILEGE IN TEXAS:

The marital communication privilege applies to utterances and not to acts. *Weaver v. State*, 855 S.W.2d 116 (Tex. App. Hous. 1993).

The defendant could not claim spousal privilege after calling his common law wife to testify on his behalf. *Blackwell v. State*, 818 S.W.2d 134 (Tex. App. 1991).

The spousal-communications privilege protects information privately disclosed between a husband and wife in the confidence of the marital relationship. *U.S. v. Martinez,* 44 F.Supp.2d 835 (W.D.Tex., 1999).

HUSBAND - WIFE PRIVILEGE IN VIRGINIA:

She threatened to leave him. He threatened to "torch" the wife's property after she told him about the contemplated departure. The wife's property was destroyed in a fire; and by the way, the whole house, which was owned by the defendant, went up in smoke during this torrid affair. During a prosecution for arson, the statutory exception to the spousal immunity (where one spouse commits an offense against the other) was held to be inapplicable because the defendant was indicted and tried solely for the arson of his house. *Creech v. Commonwealth*, 410 S.E.2d 650 (Va. 1991).

HUSBAND - WIFE PRIVILEGE IN WEST VIRGINIA:

Section 57-3-4, entitled "Confidential communications between husband and wife," states:

Neither husband nor wife shall, without the consent of the other, be examined in any case as to any confidential communication made by one to the other while married, nor shall either be permitted, without such consent, to reveal in testimony after the marriage relation ceases any such communication made while the marriage existed.

The marital privilege is not recognized for cases involving adult neglect or abuse. Similarly, the husband-wife privilege did not apply to the testimony of the defendant's ex-wife concerning alleged sexual assaults committed by the defendant against their child and against the wife's two younger sisters. *State v. Delaney*, 417 S.E.2d 903 (W.Va. 1992). Nor did it bar a wife from testifying at her husband's trials after he shot her (and her grandmother). *Brown v. Commonwealth*, 292 S.E.2d 319, 223 Va. 601 (1982).

§9.508 Parent - Child Privilege

This particular privilege is both rare and vague. It would seem to flow from the same principles that were used to establish the husband-wife privilege. In particular, the idea that family members should not testify against one another forms the basis for this rule of privilege. For incestuous child abuse cases, the privilege should never apply.

§9.508.1 State Application

The privilege is recognized in Nevada[67] and, less extensively, in New York.[68] Two other states recognize a form of the privilege via statute.[69] Most states, however, reject the privilege.[70]

---

67 *In re Agosto*, 553 F.Supp 1298, 1325 (D. Nev. 1983).

68 *People v. Fitzgerald,* 101 Misc.2d 712, 422 N.Y.S.2d 309 (1979); *In re A & M*, 61 A.D.2d 426, 403 N.Y.S.2d 375 (1978).

69 See Idaho Code §9-203(7) and Minnesota Statutes §595.02(1)(i).

70 See, e.g., *People v. Amos*, 414 N.W.2d 147, 163 Mich.App. 50 (1987); *United States v. Davies*, 768 F.2d 893 (7th Cir. 1985) *cert. den.* 474 U.S. 1008, 106 S. Ct. 533, 88 L.Ed.2d 464 (1985); *In re Terry W*, 59 Cal.App.3d 745, 130 Cal.Rptr. 913 (1976).

§9.509 Informant - Police Privilege

A significant percentage of all information pertaining to crimes is provided by informants. Some of them are individuals who are themselves criminals, and desire to maintain a good "working" relationship with the police. In the trade they are affectionately referred to as "slime." Other informers may include conscientious citizens. In any event, informants, regardless of their type or species, would have a very short life expectancy if their identities were made known. There is, therefore, a very rational public policy for protecting the *identity* of informants.

The rule of privilege holds that persons engaged in crime detection are not bound to disclose the sources of the information which lead to the apprehension of suspects. The reason for the rule is that such a disclosure can be of no importance to the defense, and *may* be highly prejudicial to the public in the administration of justice by deterring persons from making similar disclosures.[71] Therefore, as a matter of public policy, it has been held that the courts will not, in criminal proceedings, compel a witness to disclose the source or identity of persons who furnished information which led to the detection of a crime, or the prosecution of a person at trial.[72] But the privilege should not apply where the informer is an active participant in the subject crime, or where the defense of entrapment seems plausible.[73] The rule might also apply to civil proceedings.[74] That makes sense; for the issue here is really one of protection from physical harm.

§9.509.1 State Application

INFORMANT - POLICE PRIVILEGE IN CALIFORNIA:

There will always be a potential clash between the need to preserve secrecy for the identity of informers and the right of a defendant to confront his accusers. CEC 1041 doesn't resolve it, but it does provide a rational standard:

(a) Except as provided in this section, a public entity has a privilege to refuse to disclose the identity of a person who has furnished information as provided in subdivision (b) purporting to disclose a violation of a law of the United States or of this state or of a public entity in this state, and to prevent another from disclosing such identity, if the privilege is claimed by a person authorized by the public entity to do so and;

(1) Disclosure is forbidden by an act of the Congress of the United States or a statute of this state; or

(2) Disclosure of the identity of the informer is against the public interest because there is a necessity for preserving the confidentiality of his identity that outweighs the necessity for disclosure in the interest of justice; but no privilege may be claimed under this paragraph if any person authorized to do so has consented that the identity of the informer be disclosed at the proceeding. In determining whether disclosure of the identity of the informer is against the public interest, the interest of the public entity as a party in the outcome of the proceeding may not be considered.

Section (b) of the rule makes it clear that the privilege applies only to information given to law enforcement officials. And Section 1041(c)

71 *People v. Asta*, 337 Mich. 590, 60 N.W.2d 472 (1953); see also *People v. Ward*, 226 Mich. 45, 196 N.W. 971 (1924).

72 *U.S. v. Conforti*, 200 F.2d 365 (C.A. Ill.) *cert. denied* 73 S.Ct. 782, 345 U.S. 925, 97 L.Ed. 1356 (1953); *Scher v. U.S.*, 59 S.Ct. 174, 305 U.S. 251, 83 L.Ed. 151 (1938).

73 *State v. Florez*, 617 A.2d 670, 261 N.J.Super 12 (1992).

74 *Holman v. Cayce*, 873 F.2d 944 (6th Cir. 1989).

provides that this privilege does not prevent an informer from disclosing his own identity.

INFORMANT - POLICE PRIVILEGE IN OREGON:

The common law "informers privilege" is a qualified privilege; it is limited solely to communications that would reveal the identity of an informer whose cover has not otherwise been disclosed, and only where the informer's identity is not relevant or helpful to the defense of the accused. *Commonwealth v. Kauffman*, 605 A.2d 1243 (Pa. Super. 1992).

§9.510 Journalist - News Source Privilege

The journalist-news source privilege is closely related to the informant-police privilege; both often pertain to revealing the identity of informants with respect to criminal activities. However, it is important to note that the journalist's privilege is not the same; it is weaker. In some instances, the "privilege" is more a rule of journalistic ethics than of law. It has therefore been held that the rule of privilege, in the absence of a specific statute, does not apply to communications to a newspaper editor or reporter.[75] For, although there is a canon of journalistic ethics forbidding the disclosure of a newspaper's source of information, that rule of conduct is subject to qualification and must yield when it comes into conflict with the interests of justice.[76]

We don't want to give the impression that there is no privilege whatsoever protecting journalists, for that is not the case. Rather, journalists enjoy a "qualified" privilege. This means that the privilege exists, but it *may* not be complete and the court may in fact overrule it.[77] Likewise, the privilege is limited to the protection of the identity of confidential sources.[78] Where this so-called "Shield Law" applies, however, it prohibits a court from punishing a nonparty reporter for refusing to disclose a confidential news source, *and* for refusing to state who is **not** the source.[79]

Thus, *reporters*, as indicated, enjoy a non-absolute, qualified privilege. It has been held that reporters of general news are usually protected against the compelled disclosure of confidential sources;[80] however, this qualified privilege, under certain circumstances, may have to yield to another party's need for information.[81]

It has thus been held that journalists possess a limited privilege not to divulge confidential sources and not to disclose unpublished information which is in their possession as a result of the news gathering process; however, as previously indicated, there may be a countervailing interest that will require the privilege to yield in a particular case.[82]

---

75 97 CJS Witnesses, §256 - 259; see also *State v. Donovan*, 30 A.2d 421 (1943) 129 N.J.Law Journal 478.

76 *In re Wayne,* 4 Hawaii Fed. 475.

77 *Wright v. FBI*, 381 F.Supp.2d 1114 (D.C.Cal., 2005). A qualified privilege exists for journalists that protects them against the compelled disclosure of information gathered in the course of their work.

78 *Liggett v. Superior Court* (Gregerson), 260 Cal.Rptr. 161 (Cal.App. 5 Dist. 1989).

79 *Friedman v. Superior Court*, 261 Cal.Rptr. 87, 212 C.A. 3d 464 (Cal.App. 1989).

80 *U.S. v. Cuthbertson*, 630 F.2d 139 (3rd Cir. 1980); *Riley v. City of Chester,* 612 F.2d 708 (3rd Cir. 1979); *Branzburg v. Hayes*, 408 U.S. 665, 92 S.Ct. 2646, 33 L.Ed.2d 626 (1972).

81 The Supreme Court decided that reporters had no First Amendment privilege to resist testifying before a grand jury with respect to a source. However, the court did find that the news-gathering process, itself, does enjoy some First Amendment protection. Nevertheless, journalists have the same duty as other citizens to participate in the criminal justice system where a grand jury is involved. This translates into a qualified privilege under the First Amendment, which is subject to a good faith balancing test. *Branzburg v. Hayes*, 408 U.S. 665 (1972).

82 *May v. Collins*, 122 F.R.D. 535 (S.D.Ind. 1988); see also Fed. R. Evid. 501, and U.S.C.A. Const. Amend. 1.

Criminal cases present the toughest challenge to whatever privilege might otherwise be enjoyed by journalists. Fifth Amendment, Sixth Amendment, and due process arguments provide heavy weights to counterbalance the often-tenuous First Amendment claims of the journalists. Thus, a journalist's privilege not to divulge her sources (and unpublished research notes) is not absolute; that privilege must be balanced against a criminal defendant's right to produce evidence at trial under the compulsory process and confrontation clauses of the Sixth Amendment, and the due process clause of the Fifth Amendment.[83] Even the so-called reporter's privilege statutes must bend under the force of constitutional rights for defendants.[84] It is notable that the electronic media are treated as something "less" with respect to privilege. And it has been held in a Michigan case that television news reporters do not obtain the same degree of protection and privilege as do reporters of newspapers and other print media.[85] But it should be noted that Michigan's ruling in *that* case is based upon a specific statute which is limited to print reporters. Therefore, in order to determine how the law will apply in any other specific state, the Michigan Rule is far from the last word.[86]

§9.510.1 State Application

JOURNALIST - NEWS SOURCE PRIVILEGE IN CALIFORNIA:

Recall from our earlier discussions that, generally, this is a weak privilege in the absence of a specific statute or rule. California does, in fact, have such a rule in the form of CEC 1070, making the state a most aggressive protector of news sources:

(a) A publisher, editor, reporter, or other person connected with or employed upon a newspaper, magazine, or other periodical publication, or by a press association or wire service, or any person who has been so connected or employed, cannot be adjudged in contempt by a judicial, legislative, administrative body, or any other body having the power to issue subpoenas, for refusing to disclose, in any proceeding as defined in Section 901, the source of any information procured while so connected or employed for publication in a newspaper, magazine or other periodical publication, or for refusing to disclose any unpublished information obtained or prepared in gathering, receiving or processing of information for communication to the public.

(b) Nor can a radio or television news reporter or other person connected with or employed by a radio or television station, or any person who has been so connected or employed, be so adjudged in contempt for refusing to disclose the source of any information procured while so connected or employed for news or news commentary purposes on radio or television, or for refusing to disclose any unpublished information obtained or prepared in gathering, receiving or processing of information for communication to the public.

The "Section 901," referred to above, delivers a broad definition for "proceeding." Under CEC 901, the term includes any "action, hearing, investigation, inquest, or inquiry."

An automobile manufacturer sought discovery from a non-party newspaper with respect to

83 *U.S. v. McGoldrick*, 796 F.Supp. 178 (E.D.Pa. 1992); *U.S. v. Hendron*, 820 F. Supp. 715 (E.D.N.Y. 1993).

84 *People v. Palacio*, 180 Ill.Dec. 862, 607 N.E.2d 1375 (Ill.App. 4 Dist. 1993); *People v. Von Villas*, 13 Cal.Rptr.2d 62, 10 C.A.4th 201 (Cal.App. 2 Dist. 1992).

85 *In re Contempt of Stone*, 154 Mich. App. 121, 397 N.W.2d 244 (1986).

86 See Humphrey, *Shield Statutes: A Changing Problem in Light of Branzburg*, 25 Wayne L.Rev. 1381 (1979). Also note that in 1986 Michigan amended its statute (M.C.L.A. §764.5a), so that the privilege would be extended to the "news for broadcast" media.

certain unpublished photographs of an accident which showed the liability of a product. The Superior Court demanded an in camera viewing of the photos in question. The newspaper filed a petition for an extraordinary writ. The Supreme Court found in favor of the Superior Court, holding that the "newspersons" shield law did not preclude statutory sanctions *other* than contempt. Therefore, the newspaper disobeying the subpoena for production could be assessed monetary sanctions pursuant to statute, even though the shield law provided immunity from contempt. the bottom line—the shield law did not create a privilege. *The New York Times v. The Superior Court of Santa Barbara*, 51 Cal.3d 453, 769 P.2d 811 (1990).

JOURNALIST - NEWS SOURCE PRIVILEGE IN FLORIDA:

The mere inconvenience to the media of having to respond to discovery requests for videotapes of a criminal defendant's arrest does not unduly interfere with freedom of the press, nor does it trigger the application of a journalist's qualified privilege. *CBS, Inc. v. Jackson*, 578 So.2d 698 (Fla. 1991).

JOURNALIST - NEWS SOURCE PRIVILEGE IN ILLINOIS:

In Illinois, the prosecutor is required to exhaust attempts to obtain the sought-after materials by other means before divesting a reporter of his privilege. The state must satisfy the trial court that its investigation has been sufficiently thorough and comprehensive, and that further efforts to obtain the sought-after information would not likely be successful; but, it is not sufficient for the state merely to assert that its investigation has not revealed the information. Divestiture of a reporter's statutory privilege should be the last resort by which the state seeks information. *In re Arya*, 168 Ill. Dec. 432, 589 N.E.2d 832, 226 Ill. App.3d 848 (1992).

JOURNALIST - NEWS SOURCE PRIVILEGE IN MICHIGAN:

Michigan provides an example of a state that accords next to nothing in the way of protection for non-confidential materials. In *Marketos v. American Employers Ins. Co.*, 460 N.W.2d 272, 185 Mich. App. 179 (1990), an insurer served a disputed subpoena duces tecum on a newspaper, seeking the production of documents. The unsympathetic court held that:

(1) A qualified privilege does not exist under the First Amendment or under the Michigan Constitution protecting a newspaper from producing in civil litigation unpublished nonconfidential materials gathered in the course of news reporting activities, and
(2) The Michigan press shield law affords no protection from a discovery request in a civil case for nonconfidential materials.

After being issued a subpoena, a reporter refused to submit the required materials in his possession, and was incarcerated as a result. The Court held that the First Amendment does not give a reporter a privilege to refuse to reveal relevant information to a jury unless that jury proceeding is not being conducted in good faith, or there is not a legitimate need of law enforcement for the information, or the information bears only a remote relationship to the investigation at hand. *In re Contempt of Stone*, 397 N.W.2d 244, 154 Mich. App. 121 (1986).

JOURNALIST - NEWS SOURCE PRIVILEGE IN NEW JERSEY:

The editor of a newspaper, which published an anonymous letter-to-the-editor, was entitled to invoke the shield law privilege against disclosing the identity of the letter's author; the fact that the editor was not actually engaged in news gathering, in the investigative sense, was irrelevant. The shield law accords confidentiality to the source of the news, regardless of whether the information was requested or voluntarily given. *Gastman v. North Jersey Newspapers Co.*, 603 A.2d 111, 254 N.J. Super. 140 (1992).

JOURNALIST - NEWS SOURCE PRIVILEGE IN NEW YORK:

The value of a murder defendant's admissions to a newspaper reporter outweighed the reporter's constitutionally based privilege against disclosure and thus the reporter's testimony could be compelled at the defendant's trial, even though the defendant had also given a similar statement to the police and others. *People v. Craver*, 569 N.Y.S.2d 859 (N.Y. 1990).

JOURNALIST - NEWS SOURCE PRIVILEGE IN RHODE ISLAND:

A television interview was conducted by newspersons on a public sidewalk at the request of someone who was wanted by authorities in connection with an ongoing grand jury investigation; unpublished portions of the interviews were held to be "not secret" and thus were not protected by Rhode Island's Newsman's Privilege Act. *Outlet Communications, Inc. v. State*, 588 A.2d 1050 (R.I. 1991).

JOURNALIST - NEWS SOURCE PRIVILEGE IN TEXAS:

A county sheriff brought a libel action as a result of a newspaper article that accused him of being involved in drug trafficking and other illegal activities. He failed to meet the burden of producing substantial evidence of the falsity of the statements, attributed to confidential sources, so as to overcome the journalists' qualified privilege. In applying the journalists' qualified privilege, the courts will look to the facts on a case-by-case basis as they balance the need for the testimony against the claims of the news gatherer that the public's right to know would be impaired. Also, once a journalist has asserted the privilege, the burden of producing substantial evidence sufficient to overcome that privilege shifts to the party seeking discovery. *Dallas Morning News Co. v. Garcia*, 822 S.W.2d 675 (Tex. App. 1991).

§9.511 Confidential Institutional Communications

Matters involving national secrets are, of course, subject to privilege.[87] Once successfully invoked, the effect of the State Secrets Privilege is to completely remove the evidence from the case.[88] As strong as this privilege may be, not unlike the other privileges, there is always room for exceptions. Even executive privilege is sometimes overridden by stronger concerns. After all, if this privilege were absolute, no one would have caught Nixon (or his tapes). And thus, it has been held that a private or "in camera" inspection of documents may be appropriate in certain cases[89] to determine the application of the privilege.

A closely related item is sometimes referred to as "The Deliberative Process Privilege." This privilege, which belongs to the government,[90] is designed to protect parts of its decision-making processes. In part, the philosophy behind the privilege is the notion that if the public knew what went on, the behind-the-scenes discussions would be chilled. Putting our representatives in a fishbowl, so to speak, would interfere with the free exchange of pork barrels.

§9.511.1 State Application

CONFIDENTIAL INSTITUTIONAL COMMUNICATION IN CALIFORNIA:

It has been held that a police officer's surveillance location is privileged. See CEC 1040; *People v. Walker*, 282 Cal. Rptr. 12, 230 C.A.3d 230, *opinion modified* (Cal. 2nd Dist. 1991).

---

87 *Fitzgerald v. Penthouse International, Ltd.*, 776 F.2d 1236 (4th Cir. 1985); and *United States v. Reynolds*, 345 U.S. 1 (1953).

88 *In re U.S.*, 872 F.2d 472 (D.C. Cir. 1989).

89 *American Civil Liberties Union v. Brown*, 619 F.2d 1170 (7th Cir. 1980).

90 *Matter of Nelson*, 131 F.R.D. 161 (Neb. 1989).

§9.512 Privilege Against Self-Incrimination

People talk to themselves all the time; but there is a strong constitutional prohibition against forcing an individual to *testify* against, or incriminate, himself. The Fifth Amendment to the United States Constitution contains a specific right against self-incrimination. This is a jealously guarded privilege; and it has been held that the privilege against self-incrimination must be accorded liberal construction in favor of the right that it was intended to secure.[91] It has even been held that it is extortion to force an individual to disclose the contents of his own mind.[92]

The privilege against self-incrimination can be invoked in any proceeding where the judge concludes that a witnesses' testimony could conceivably be used against him or her in a criminal prosecution or could lead to other evidence that might be so used.[93]

A witness may refuse to testify unless it is perfectly clear (from a careful consideration of all circumstances in the case) that he is mistaken and that his answers cannot possibly have such a tendency to incriminate.[94] The privilege against self-incrimination, however, is not absolute. A witness who invokes the Fifth Amendment may not do so without some logical basis. Rather, the witness must demonstrate a real danger of self-incrimination.[95] And although a criminal defendant has an absolute right not to testify, a witness may invoke the privilege against self-incrimination **only** as to those specific questions to which his answers would be incriminating.[96]

The privilege can be waived by providing testimony voluntarily.[97] If a defendant has previously waived the privilege against self-incrimination by voluntarily testifying at trial, that waiver continues into sentencing with respect to testimony voluntarily given at the trial.[98]

No discussion of self-incrimination would be complete without mentioning the classic *Miranda v. Arizona*.[99] The landmark provided the perennial litany for police who are about to commence a custodial interrogation; suspects must be warned that:

1. they have a right to remain silent,
2. any statement they make may be used as evidence against them, and
3. they have the right to the presence of an attorney, either retained or appointed.

§9.512.1 State Application

PRIVILEGE AGAINST SELF-INCRIMINATION IN ALABAMA:

A witness, other than the defendant himself, cannot refuse to take the stand and testify by "taking the fifth"; a witness may only invoke his

91 *Sachs v. U.S.*, 281 F.2d 189 (9th Cir.) *cert. den.* 81 S.Ct. 272, 364 U.S. 909, 5 L.Ed.2d 224; *Wilson v. U.S.*, 558 A.2d 1135 (D.C.App. 1989). With respect to "reiteration" of prior testimony, see *State v. Girouard*, 561 A.2d 882 (R.I. 1989), where the appellate court held that it was not an abuse of discretion on the part of the trial court to overrule an objection to a leading question which consisted of a reiteration of prior testimony.

92 St. *George v. State*, 564 So.2d 152 (Fla.App. 1990).

93 *Andover Data Services, a Div. of Players Computer, Inc. v. Statistical Tabulating Corp.*, 876 F.2d 1080 (2nd Cir. 1989).

94 *Commonwealth v. Sasu,* 536 N.E. 2d 603, 404 Mass. 596 (Mass. 1989); see also *In re Growers Packing Co., Inc.*, 150 B.R. 82 (Bkrtcy.S.D.Fla. 1993).

95 *In re Braun,* 502 N.W.2d 219 (Minn.App. 1993); *In re J.M.V.*, 90 B.R. 737 (Bkrtcy. PA. 1988); see also *Adkins v. State*, 557 A.2d 203 (Md. 1989).

96 *Wilson v. U.S.*, 558 A.2d 1135 (D.C.App. 1989).

97 *State v. Patino*, 502 N.W.2d 601 (Wis. App. 1993).

98 *State v. Lankford*, 775 P.2d 593 (Idaho 1989); *State v. Hennum*, 441 N.W.2d 793 (Minn. 1989).

99 384 U.S. 436 (1964).

Fifth Amendment privilege against self-incrimination after he has been sworn and asked a question which would elicit incriminating evidence if answered by such witness. *J.D.S. v. State*, 587 So.2d 1249 (Ala. App. 1991).

PRIVILEGE AGAINST SELF-INCRIMINATION IN ALASKA:

A state's constitutional prohibition against compelling a person to be a witness against himself does not prohibit forcing that person to testify in criminal case against another person, even though the testimony may show that the witness was guilty of the crime. *State v. Gonzalez*, 853 P.2d 526 (Alaska 1993).

PRIVILEGE AGAINST SELF-INCRIMINATION IN ARKANSAS:

The widow of a victim is entitled to invoke her constitutional right against self-incrimination by refusing to testify as a witness for the defendant, where she is under suspicion for her husband's murder. *Sutton v. State*, 844 S.W.2d 350, 311 Ark. 435 (1993).

PRIVILEGE AGAINST SELF-INCRIMINATION IN CALIFORNIA:

The privilege against self-incrimination is universally recognized by all of the states because of its constitutional mandates. CEC Section 940:

> To the extent that such privilege exists under the Constitution of the United States or the State of California, a person has a privilege to refuse to disclose any matter that may tend to incriminate him.

While the privilege against self-incrimination is generally recognized as a strong one, it can be lost whenever a defendant voluntarily testifies. *People v. Cooper*, 809 P.2d 865, 281 Cal. Rptr. 90, 53 C.3d 771 (1991). As a general proposition, a witness is free to waive the privilege against self-incrimination. *People v. St.Joseph*, 276 Cal. Rptr. 498, 226 Cal. App.3d 289 (1 Dist. 1990).

PRIVILEGE AGAINST SELF-INCRIMINATION IN COLORADO:

For impeachment purposes, the prosecution used statements made by the defendant to his psychiatrist; the prosecution learned of those statements during discovery. The use of the statements did not violate the defendant's privilege against self-incrimination, because his ability to assert the privilege remained available to him, right up until the time that he elected to present testimony to the jury which contradicted the statements he had voluntarily made to the psychiatrist. *Lanari v. People*, 827 P.2d 495 (Colo. 1992).

PRIVILEGE AGAINST SELF-INCRIMINATION IN FLORIDA:

Although separate questions may each address a different discrete aspect of a crime and its surrounding circumstances, that, in and of itself, does not limit a person's ability to exercise the Fifth Amendment privilege as to the entire subject. *Lundy v. State*, 596 So.2d 1167 (Fla. App. 1992).

Even though Section 90.501 wipes out the effect of all common law privileges and, moreover, all privileges not specifically spelled out in the FEC, and even though the privilege against self-incrimination is not specifically provided for in the FEC, nevertheless, that privilege remains unaffected, since it is constitutionally based. *Boynton v. State,* 75 So.2d 211 (1954).

PRIVILEGE AGAINST SELF-INCRIMINATION IN ILLINOIS:

A defendant who waives the privilege against self-incrimination may reassert it and refuse to testify at a subsequent proceeding concerning the same matter; but the defendant's reassertion of the privilege does not render his testimony in the prior proceeding inadmissible in the later hearing. *People v. Lamb*, 167 Ill. Dec. 179, 587 N.E.2d 61, 224 Ill. App.3d 950 (1992).

PRIVILEGE AGAINST SELF-INCRIMINATION IN LOUISIANA:

The court did not err in finding that questions to be propounded to an alleged co-conspirator would require inculpatory answers so that he was entitled to assert his privilege against self-incrimination. *State v. Jones*, 587 So.2d 787 (La. App. 1991).

PRIVILEGE AGAINST SELF-INCRIMINATION IN MINNESOTA:

If reasonable grounds exist to fear incrimination or criminal prosecution by giving testimony in a civil action, then the privilege against self-incrimination may be invoked. *Engelby v. Engelby*, 479 N.W.2d 424 (Minn. App. 1992).

PRIVILEGE AGAINST SELF-INCRIMINATION IN MISSOURI:

The constitution guarantees a criminal defendant the right to offer testimony of witnesses in his favor; that right, however, does not supersede the right of the reluctant witness to invoke his Fifth Amendment privilege. *State v. Grays*, 856 S.W.2d 87 (Mo. App. E.D. 1993).

PRIVILEGE AGAINST SELF-INCRIMINATION IN NEBRASKA:

A person's right against self-incrimination normally emanates from three distinct sources: The United States Constitution, A State Constitution, and State Statutes. See U.S.C.A. Const.Amend. 5; Nebraska Const. Art. 1, § 12; Neb.Rev.St. § 25-1210. See *In re Interest of Clifford M.*, 577 N.W.2d 547, 6 Neb.App. 754 (1998).

PRIVILEGE AGAINST SELF-INCRIMINATION IN NEW JERSEY:

Physicians who do not specifically assert their privilege against self-incrimination before answering questions asked by the Board of Medical Examiners (regarding drug or alcohol abuse or mental illness) are deemed to have waived the privilege. Per statute, the immunity is not self-executing. *Hirsch v. New Jersey State Bd. of Medical Examiners*, 600 A.2d 493, 252 N.J. Super. 596 (1991).

PRIVILEGE AGAINST SELF-INCRIMINATION IN NEW YORK:

With respect to civil actions, the district court cannot compel a witness to give incriminating testimony without first granting immunity, where that witness asserts a Fifth Amendment privilege. *U.S. v. District Council of New York City*, 782 F. Supp 920 (S.D.N.Y. 1992). But by the same token, the court sitting in a civil case may draw adverse inferences from a defendant's invocation of the Fifth Amendment privilege. *In re Lederman*, 140 B.R. 49 (Bkrtcy. E.D.N.Y. 1992).

PRIVILEGE AGAINST SELF-INCRIMINATION IN NORTH CAROLINA:

A wife can invoke the privilege against self-incrimination during a deposition in a divorce proceeding where the wife is questioned as to her alleged adulterous behavior; adultery constitutes a misdemeanor under North Carolina law. *Cantwell v. Cantwell*, 427 S.E.2d 129 (N.C. App. 1993).

PRIVILEGE AGAINST SELF-INCRIMINATION IN OHIO:

The privilege against self-incrimination is personal; therefore, an individual may not claim the privilege on behalf of a collective entity or organization of which that individual happens to be a member. *Cincinnati v. Bawtenheimer*, 586 N.E.2d 1065, 63 Ohio St.3d 260 (1992). Moreover, a corporation has no right to privacy and no Fifth Amendment privilege against self-incrimination. *State v. CECOS International, Inc.*, 583 N.E.2d 1118, 66 Ohio App.3d 262 (1990).

The protection of the Fifth Amendment privilege against selfincrimination extends only to witnesses who have reasonable cause to apprehend a danger that might arise from a direct answer. An inquiry into as to whether or not a witness has reasonable cause to apprehend danger, justifying assertion of the privilege, is for the court. A witness's naked assertion does not, by itself, establish the risk of incrimination. *Ohio v. Reiner,* 121 S.Ct. 1252 (Ohio 2001).

PRIVILEGE AGAINST SELF-INCRIMINATION IN RHODE ISLAND:

The privilege against self-incrimination may be invoked in a civil proceeding, regardless of whether there is a pending criminal matter arising out of the same set of facts; but the right to utilize the privilege does not extend to blanket invocation. *Tona, Inc. v. Evans*, 590 A.2d 873 (R.I. 1991).

PRIVILEGE AGAINST SELF-INCRIMINATION IN TEXAS:

The Fifth Amendment privilege can only be asserted with respect to compelled testimonial disclosure, which is incriminating. *In re Piperi*, 137 B.R. 644 (S.D. Tex. 1991).

PRIVILEGE AGAINST SELF-INCRIMINATION IN WISCONSIN:

A defendant waived his right to remain silent as to all relevant facts by voluntarily taking the stand to testify on his own behalf; the prosecution was, therefore, permitted to cross-examine him. *State v. Patino*, 502 N.W.2d 601 (Wis. App. 1993).

§9.513 Self-Critical Analysis Privilege

Closely related to the privilege against self-incrimination is a relatively new privilege for those naive enough to require its assistance. Known as the "self-critical analysis privilege," this newcomer to the "I promise not to tell" scene is designed for those unsophisticated persons innocent enough to believe in "Your secret is safe with me." Its basic purpose is provide an incentive to fill out self-assessment surveys that employers, with nothing better to do, provide to their employees. Of course, anyone with knowledge of the power of an admission would either check "Excellent" responses across the board or refuse to answer outright. For, "secrets" will always be subject to a balancing act with someone's "need to know" on the other side of the scale.

For example, see *Tice v. American Airlines, Inc.*, 192 F.R.D. 270 (N.D.Ill. 2000). In an age discrimination lawsuit brought by retired airline pilots; the court purported to engage a "balancing act" to determine whether or not airline safety reports containing self-criticism should be admitted into evidence. The case held not, stating that a privilege for self-critical analysis is important and is grounded on the premise that the disclosure of documents reflecting candid self-examination will deter socially useful investigations and analysis. In determining whether or not to apply the privilege, the court found that it must balance the public interest in protecting candid corporate self-assessments against the private interest of the litigant in obtaining all relevant documents through discovery. The court provided the following test for the application of the privilege:

(1) The materials were prepared for mandatory government reports,

(2) The privilege is being asserted only to protect subjective, evaluative materials,

(3) The privilege is not being asserted to protect objective data in the same reports, and (4) The policy favoring exclusion clearly outweighs the plaintiff's need for the information.

See also *Roman Catholic Diocese of Jackson v. Morrison*, 905 So.2d 1213 (Miss., 2005), which rejected the "self-critical analysis" privilege altogether.

Chapter 10

Repetitive Questions

§10.100 Introduction

Sometimes, when lawyers don't get the answer that they want from a particular witness, they follow the old rule of try, try again. Other times, lawyers will repeat the same question, hoping to get inconsistent information from a witness. Both tactics tend to be argumentative and, of course, "repetitive."

§10.200 Quick Explanation

A lawyer should be allowed to ask a question only once, assuming that he or she gets a proper answer.

WHAT TO LOOK FOR:

Questions that are too similar to prior questions.

OBJECT AND RESPOND

OBJECTION:

"Objection. Asked and answered."

POTENTIAL RESPONSES TO OBJECTION:

A. "On the contrary. He refuses to answer."

B. "On the contrary. I'm only repeating myself because the witness refuses to answer the question."

C. "If the witness would merely answer the question, there would be no need to repeat it."

D. (Most Common Strategy) Keep re-phrasing the question until everyone gets sick of hearing the objections.

§10.300 General Legal Analysis

The identical repetition of a prior question is an easy matter on which to rule. The court reporter can merely parrot back the question to see if it has already been asked and answered; if so, the repeated question would be objectionable and excludable,[1] even during cross-examination.[2] In most cases, a lawyer will not be quite so obvious. Instead, he or she will repeat the question, but with an "ever so slight" variation, so that the question does not appear to be identical. Whether or not the question is, in fact, repetitive, may therefore be left to the discretion of the trial judge, even where the constitutional right to confrontation (6th Amendment) is involved.[3]

A lawyer may repeat a question if the witness' answer is evasive.[4] If an objection to a

---

1 *U.S. v. Saunders,* 166 F.3d 907 (7th Cir. Ill 1999); *Fettson v. James,* 298 Ill. App.3d 77, 232 Ill. Dec. 201, 697 N.E.2d 1131 (Ill.App.1.Dist. 1997); the trial judge has broad discretion to preclude repetitive and unduly harassing interrogation.

2 The trial court does not abuse its discretion in limiting the right to a thorough cross-examination by disallowing the repetition of a question. *Jackson v. State,* 270 Ga. 494, 512 S.E.2d 241 (1999); *U.S. v. Saunders*, 166 F.3d 907 (7th Cir. 1999); *People v. Prevo,* 235 Ill.Dec. 950, 706 N.E.2d 505, 302 Ill.App.3d 1038 (1999); *U.S. v. Cordova*, 157 F.3d 587 (8th Cir. 1998); *U.S. v. Laboy-Delgado*, 84 F.3d 22 (1st Cir. 1996). The trial court properly uses its discretion when it restricts the scope of cross-examination on order to preclude repetitive or unduly harassing testimony. See also *City of Champaign v. Sides,* 284 Ill. Dec. 634, 810 N.E.2d 287 (Ill. App. Ct., 2004); *People v. Harris*, 706 N.Y.S.2d 392 (N.Y.A.D. 2000).

3 *People v. Riel*, 998 P.20 969, 96 Cal.Rptr.2d 1, 22 Cal.4th 1153 (2000); *U.S. v. Baptista-Rodriguez*, 17 F.3d 1354 (11th Cir. 1994); *State v. Lindesy*, 543 So.2d 886, *reh. denied* (La. 1989); *Sachs v. U.S.*, 281 F.2d 189 (9th. Cir.) *cert. denied*, 81 S. Ct. 272, 364 U.S. 909, 5 L.Ed.2d 224 (1960).

4 *People v. Garwood*, 106 P. 113, 11 C.A. 665 (1909).

question is sustained on the ground that it is improper in form, a lawyer may rephrase the question.[5] But to engage in continuous repetition is not only time consuming and irritating, it is also potentially argumentative.

Even cross-examination has its limits. Consider the following excerpt of questions that were taken to task by the United States Supreme Court in reviewing the conduct of the United States Attorney who secured a conviction (which the high court reversed) in a conspiracy case:[6]

[The defendant is on the stand; cross-examination is conducted by the United States Attorney.]

Q. The man who didn't have his pants on and was running around the apartment, he wasn't there?

A. No, Mr. Singer. Mr. Godby told me about this, he told me, as long as you ask me about it, if you want it, I will tell you, he told me 'If you give this man's name out, I will give you the works.'

Q. *Give me the works?*

A. No, Mr. Godby told me that.

Q. *You are going to give me the works?*

A. Mr. Singer, you are a gentleman, I have got nothing against you. You are doing your duty.
Mr. Wegman (Defense Counsel): You are not going to give Mr. Singer the works.
Court: Apparently Mr. Singer misunderstood you. Who made that statement?
The Witness: Mr. Godby says that.

Q. Wait a minute. *Are you going to give me the works?*

A. Mr. Singer, you are absolutely a gentleman, in my opinion, you are doing your duty here.

Q. Thank you very much. But I am only asking you *are you going to give me the works?*

A. I do not give anybody such things, I never said it.

Q. All right. Then do not make the statement.
Mr. Wegman: The witness said that Mr. Godby said that.

Consider another matter, *State v. Wise*,[7] where the prosecutor just didn't know when to give up. In *Wise*, that prosecutor continued to a badger a twelve-year-old rape victim concerning her prior inconsistent statement.[8] The question, "So what you were saying earlier wasn't true?" was held to be repetitive and argumentative.[9] The two objections "Argumentative" and "Repetitive" often coincide.[10] Consider Fed. R. Evid.611(a):

> The court shall exercise reasonable control over the mode and order of interrogating witnesses and presenting evidence so as to (1) make the interrogation and presentation effective for the ascertainment of the truth, (2) avoid needless consumption of time, and (3) protect witnesses from harassment or undue embarrassment.

The standards listed in Rule 611(a) are vague at best. For that reason, the trial judge

5 *Viens v. Lanctot*, 144 A.2d 711, 120 Vt. 443 (1958).

6 *Berger v. United States*, 295 U.S. 78, 55 S. Ct. 629, 79 L. Ed. 1314 (1935). With respect to limiting cross-examination repetition, in general, see *Sullivan v. State*, 222 Ga. 691, 152 S.E.2d 382 (1966).

7 390 S.E.2d 142, 326 N.C. 421 (1990).

8 For discussion of prior inconsistent statements, see §5.405.

9 See also *Rock v. State*, 558 So.2d 967 (Ala. 1989); *People v. Wright*, 552 N.Y.S.2d 285 (1990); and *Stewart v. State*, 558 So.2d 416 (1990).

10 See Chapter 1.

must be accorded wide discretion with respect to its application.[11]

The principle granting the trial court broad discretion to exclude relevant evidence that is repetitive must be exercised with caution when used against a defendant in a criminal case, since due process and "right of confrontation" considerations may come into play.[12] Citing the trial court's "wide latitude," however, more recent cases may pay lip service to this Sixth Amendment right, but they have, nevertheless, clearly tilted the scale in favor of the trial court's ability to curtail repetitive questioning.[13]

§10.400 Questions That Are Cumulative or Waste Time

Closely related to "repetitive questions" are those which are considered "cumulative." The key distinction would seem to rest in the lapse of time between the introduction and re-introduction of the duplicate evidence. In particular, repetitive questions are normally those which immediately follow one another with little or no intermission. Cumulative offerings, on the other hand, are likely to be separated by time or circumstances.

Cumulative questions sometimes involve different forms of evidence. If, for example, detailed documents or demonstrative exhibits

11 *United States v. Wood*, 171 Fed.Appx. 534 (8th Cir., Ark., 2006). The federal district court could limit the defense's cross-examination of a government witness as repetitive where the defense questioned the witness about eight different government grants after the court already had sustained the government's objection to the continued questioning.

State v. Tran, 712 N.W.2d 540 (Minn., 2006). The trial court has wide latitude to impose reasonable limits on cross-examination, particularly where those limits are directed toward questions that are repetitive or are only marginally relevant.

Jensen v. State of Wyoming, 116 P.3d 1088 (Wyoming, 2005); *Adams v. U.S.*, 883 A.2d 76 (D.C., 2005); *State v. Oliveira,* 882 A.2d 1097 (R.I., 2005); *Wright v. State*, 836 N.E.2d 283 (Ind.App., 2005); *State v. Smith,* 65 P.3d 648, 2003 Ut.App. 52 (2003); *Vance v. Vance,* 784 N.E.2d 172, 151 Ohio.App.3d 391(2003); *Commonwealth v. Conde,* 822 A.2d 45 (Pa.Super. 2003); *ARB Construction, LLC v. Pinney Construction Corp.,* 815 A.2d 705, 75 Conn.App. 151 (2003). *U.S. v. Saunders,* 166 F.3d 907, (C.A.7, Ill.,1999); *State v. Durham*, 673 So.2d 1103 (La.App. 5 Cir. 1996); *U.S. v. Baptista-Rodriguez*, 17 F.3d 1354 (11th Cir. 1994); *People v. Tenner*, 157 Ill.2d 341, 193 Ill. Dec. 105, 626 N.E.2d 138 (1993); *State v. Rapp*, 67 Ohio App.3d 33, 585 N.E.2d 965 (1990); *Hunter v. Allis-Chalmers Corp*., Engine Div., 797 F.2d 1417 (7th Cir. 1986); see also *U.S. v. Falcon*, 766 F.2d 1469 (10th Cir. 1985). *State v. Hatcher*, 524 S.E.2d 815 (N.C.App. 2000). The trial judge has discretion during cross-examination to ban unreasonable, repetitious and argumentative questions and matters of tenuous relevance.

12 *Adams v. U.S.*, 883 A.2d 76 (D.C., 2005). Although the Sixth Amendment guarantees a defendant in a criminal prosecution the right to be confronted with the witnesses against him, which includes the opportunity to cross-examine government witnesses, this right is not without reasonable limitation. The extent of cross-examination of a witness with respect to an appropriate subject of inquiry is within the sound discretion of the trial court, and that court may always limit cross so as to preclude repetitive and unduly harassing interrogations or to prevent inquiry into matters having little relevance or probative value to the issues raised at trial. However, for a Confrontation Clause error caused by a trial court's restriction of a defendant's cross-examination to be considered harmless, it must be clear beyond a reasonable doubt either (1) that the defendant would have been convicted without the witness' testimony or (2) that the restricted line of inquiry would not have weakened the impact of the witness' testimony. *Matchett v. State*, 941 S.W.2d 922 (Tex. Crim. App.,1996); *People v. Frieberg*, 168 Ill. Dec. 108, 589 N.E.2d 508, 147 Ill.2d 326 (1992); *State v. Harris*, 839 S.W.2d 54 (Tenn. 1992); *U.S. v. Falcon*, 766 F.2d 1469 (10th Cir. 1985); *U.S. v. Sellers*, 566 F.2d 884 (4th Cir. 1977); *Payne v. U.S.*, 451 U.S. 972, 68 L.Ed.2d 351.

13 *Myers v. State,* 133 P.3d 312, 2006 OK CR 12 (2006). During cross-examination, a criminal defendant is not entitled to ask questions that are speculative, argumentative, or previously asked and answered. *U.S. v. Cordova*, 157 F.3d 587, (8th Cir. 1998); *U.S. v. Laboy-Delgado*, 84 F.3d 22 (1st Cir. 1996); see also *Delaware v. Fensterer*, 474 U.S. 15, 20, 106 S.Ct. 292, 295, 88 L.Ed.2d 15 (1985).

were offered to prove a particular point, then the subsequent (and separate) introduction of testimonial evidence to establish that same point could constitute cumulative, and therefore objectionable, evidence.

Both cumulative and repetitive questions waste the time of the court.[14] To deal with them, Fed. R. Evid. 403 [in addition to Rule 611(a), *supra*] empowers the court to exclude such evidence by providing:

> Although relevant, evidence may be excluded if its probative value is substantially outweighed by the danger of unfair prejudice, confusion of the issues, or misleading the jury, or *by considerations of undue delay, waste of time, or needless presentation of cumulative evidence* (emphasis supplied).

Because Rule 403 permits the exclusion of otherwise relevant and proper evidence, it should be used sparingly.[15]

§10.500 Selected State Rules and Cases

ALABAMA:

It is within discretion of trial court to refuse to permit questions which call for the mere repetition of a witness' testimony that is already in the possession of the jury. *Houston v. State,* 565 So.2d 277 (Ala.Cr.App.,1990).

CALIFORNIA:

Rule 765(a) of the California Evidence Code requires the court to exercise reasonable control, "To make the interrogation of a witness as rapid, as distinct, and as effective for the ascertainment of the truth, as may be, and to protect witnesses from undue harassment or embarrassment." Repetitive questioning is not "rapid" nor is it "distinct." Also, repetitive questions can become argumentative. By implication, therefore, CEC 765(a) grants to the court the power to limit repetition. It is interesting to note that CEC 765(b) specifically directs the court to take special care to "restrict the unnecessary repetition of questions" for witnesses under 14 years of age. *Thomas v. Laguna*, 248 P.2d 929, 113 C.A.2d 657 (1952); see also Chapter 1.

Often, some amount of repetition is required for effective cross-examination. However, a court should not, over objection, permit an attorney to subject witnesses to ceaseless reiteration about endless matters about which they testified they knew nothing. *People v. Riel*, 998 P.20 969, 96 Cal.Rptr.2d 1, 22 Cal.4th 1153 (2000).

Cross-examination is also subject to restriction if it is cumulative or if it constitutes impeachment on collateral issues. *People v. Greenberger*, 58 Cal. App.4th 298, 68 Cal. Rptr.2d 61 (Cal. App. 2.Dist. 1997).

COLORADO:

The Colorado Rules of Evidence (Title 13 of the Colorado Revised Statutes) follow the Federal Rules virtually word for word and section number for section number.

CONNECTICUT:

In a fashion similar to many of the less populous states, Connecticut follows the Federal Rules essentially verbatim.

As is near universal rule, the interrogation of a witness must not be repetitive or unduly harassing. *State v. Johnson*, 573 A.2d 1218, 21 Conn.App. 291 (1990).

14 Cumulative evidence often involves a mix and match of different types of evidence. But, regardless of the form or forms (i.e. Testimonial, Documentary, Real or Demonstrative), such evidence is subject to limitation, *Huckaby v. A.G. Perry & Son, Inc.,* 20 S.W.3d 194 (Tex.App., 2000), or complete exclusion. *Kirkham v. Will,* 724 N.E.2d 1062, 311 Ill.App.3d 787, 244 Ill.Dec. 174 (2000); *Hyatt v. Raggio,* 757 So.2d 773, 99-887 (La.App., 2000).

15 *Nelson v. Waxman,* 9 S.W.3d 601 (Mo., 2000); *U.S. v. Cole*, 755 F.2d 748 (11 Cir. 1985); *Hendrix v. Raybestos - Manhattan, Inc.*, 776 F.2d 1492 (11th Cir. 1985).

DISTRICT OF COLUMBIA:

After sufficient cross-examination has been allowed to satisfy constitutional confrontation requirements, the trial court retains broad discretion to determine the scope and extent of cross-examination. The court may restrict cross-examination within reasonable limits to avoid such problems as harassment, prejudice, confusion of issues, witness' safety, or repetitive interrogation that is only marginally relevant. *Elliott v. U.S.*, 633 A.2d 27 (D.C. App.,1993).

FLORIDA:

Section 90.612(1) of the Florida Evidence Code requires the trial judge to exercise reasonable control over the mode and order of interrogation of witnesses and the presentation of evidence, so as to "... (b) Avoid needless consumption of time." The Sponsor's Note states that its purpose is to exclude repetitious or wasteful questions. *Eatman v. State*, 48 Fla. 21, 37 So. 576 (Fla.1904).

GEORGIA:

The trial court does not abuse its discretion when limiting the right to a thorough cross-examination is caused by disallowing the repetition of a question. *Jackson v. State,* 70 Ga. 494, 512 S.E.2d 241 (1999). Likewise, the trial court may curtail any cross-examination which is unduly repetitive or harassing and may exercise reasonable judgment in determining when a subject is exhausted. *Daniels v. State*, 235 Ga. App. 296, 509 S.E.2d 368 (1998).

A trial judge may restrain the useless and unnecessary repetition of questions that have been asked and fully answered. *Sullivan v. State*, 222 Ga. 691, 152 S.E.2d 382 (1966).

The trial court does not abuse its discretion by allowing the prosecution to ask a14- year-old child molestation victim a single repetitive question. *Roberts v. State,* 503 S.E.2d 614, 232 Ga.App. 745 (1998).

ILLINOIS:

The trial court properly uses its discretion to restrict the scope of cross-examination to preclude repetitive or unduly harassing testimony, or to exclude evidence of bias that is too remote or uncertain. *People v. Prevo*, 302 Ill. App.3d 1038, 235 Ill. Dec. 950, 706 N.E.2d 505 (Ill. App.4.Dist., 1999).

The trial judge enjoys wide latitude in imposing reasonable limits on cross-examination to prevent repetitive interrogation. *People v. Tenner*, 157 Ill.2d 341, 193 Ill. Dec. 105, 626 N.E.2d 138 (1993).

In a medical malpractice case, it was held that questioning four different witnesses about the same matters, did not necessarily constitute repetitive or unduly harassing interrogation; each witness provided a different perspective. *Uhr v. Lutheran General Hosp.*, 168 Ill. Dec. 323, 589 N.E.2d 723, 226 Ill. App.3d 236 (1992).

The right of cross-examination to show bias or motive should remain unfettered, but the questioning cannot be repetitive or unduly harassing. *People v. Schnurr*, 151 Ill. Dec. 674, 564 N.E.2d 1336 (Ill. App. 2 Dist. 1990). Thus, the trial court did not abuse its discretion in curtailing the cross-examination of a prosecution witness which was unnecessarily repetitive and unduly harassing. *People v. Matthews*, 150 Ill. Dec. 310, 562 N.E.2d 1113. (Ill. App. 1 Dist. 1990). Moreover, the circuit court has broad discretion to disallow repetitive and unduly harassing questions, notwithstanding its inability to deny a defendant his Sixth Amendment right to cross-examination. *People v. Frieberg*, 168 Ill. Dec. 108, 589 N.E.2d 508, 147 Ill.2d 326 (1992).

In a personal injury action, the defendants were not prejudiced when the trial court sustained objections to a question as to whether plaintiff was paid in cash for his engagements as a performing artist and what he did with the cash. The court did not prohibit that line of questioning, but sustained the objection on the basis that the particular question had been asked and answered; defendants were allowed in closing argument to argue that plaintiff had exaggerated his wage loss claim. *Fettson v. James*, 298 Ill. App.3d 77, 232 Ill. Dec. 201, 697 N.E.2d 1131 (Ill. App.1.Dist. 1997).

In a dog bite case, the trial court acted within its discretion by excluding testimony concerning the demeanor and disposition of a dog, and the appearance of puncture wounds on a victim's leg; nothing indicated that the witness had adequate experience in observing dog bites to give him an objective basis for determining that the puncture wounds on the victim's leg were consistent with a dog bite, and such testimony would have been cumulative of evidence regarding patient's medical history, in any event. *Kirkham v. Will,* 724 N.E.2d 1062, 311 Ill.App.3d 787, 244 Ill.Dec. 174 (2000).

KANSAS:

It is not an abuse of discretion to exclude repetitious questions during cross-examination. *State v. Vargas*, 260 Kan. 791, 926 P.2d 223 (1996).

LOUISIANA:

The trial court is afforded wide discretion in limiting repetitive, harassing, and irrelevant questioning on cross-examination. *State v. Durham*, 673 So.2d 1103 (La. Ct. App. 5 Cir. 1996).

For a matter where the trial court was held to have properly sustained the state's objection to defense counsel's questioning of a police officer (as being increasingly repetitive), see *State v. McNeil*, 613 So.2d 752 (La. Ct. App. 4 Cir. 1993).

In a medical malpractice action, the trial court did not err by limiting, as repetitious, a patient's re-direct examination of his expert witness, during which he attempted to restate hypothetical fact situations. *Sinha v. Dabezies,* 590 So.2d 795 (La. Ct. App. 1991).

The trial court did not err by limiting the cross-examination of a police officer with respect to whether the defendant had told him, "I'm here to pick up two ounces of cocaine," or whether he had said, "Where is the cocaine?" The entire line of questioning was marginally probative and had become redundant and unduly time-consuming. Moreover, it was actually an attempt to describe the officer's testimony to the jury. *State v. Valenzuela*, 590 So.2d 89 (La. Ct. App. 1991).

The trial court did not abuse its discretion in excluding expert witness testimony offered by a patient in a medical malpractice case, where that expert would have offered essentially the same type of testimony as the patient's other witnesses. *Hyatt v. Raggio,* 757 So.2d 773, 99-887 (La.App., 2000).

MINNESOTA:

The scope of cross-examination is always subject to the broad discretion of the trial judge to preclude repetitive and unduly harassing interrogation. *State v. Lanz-Terry*, 535 N.W.2d 635 (Minn. 1995).

MICHIGAN:

With respect to its state courts in general, Michigan's Rule 403 is identical in content to Fed. R. Evid. 403. See *People v. Lloyd*, 5 Mich. App. 717, 147 N.W.2d 740 (1967).

MISSOURI:

Even if evidence is cumulative, that alone is not sufficient to exclude its admission. *Nelson v. Waxman,* 9 S.W.3d 601 (Mo., 2000).

In general, evidence should not be rejected as cumulative where it goes to the very root of the matter in controversy or otherwise impacts upon the main issue in the case. *Smith v. Kansas City Southern Ry. Co.,* 87 S.W.3d 266 (Mo.App. W.D. 2002).

NEW JERSEY:

With respect to its state courts in general, New Jersey's Rule 403 is very similar in content to Fed. R. Evid. 403.

NEW YORK:

Although the trial court has discretion to prevent repetitious questions on cross-examination, that authority should be exercised sparingly and only when the questions are truly shown to be repetitious. The court should refrain from anticipatory or preemptive preclusion, particularly in criminal cases. *People v. Gerace*, 568 N.Y.S.2d 833 (N.Y.A.D. 2 Dept. 1991). But when the duplication goes far beyond the scope of the hearing and becomes repetitive, precluding such questions is not an abuse of discretion. See *People v. Sul*, 652 N.Y.S.2d 57 (N.Y.A.D. 2 Dept.

1996) and *People v. Johnson*, 568 N.Y.S.2d 611 (N.Y.A.D. 1 Dept. 1991).

The trial court did not abuse its discretion in controlling the nature or extent of the cross-examination of a robbery complainant over a 2-day period by curtailing the examination when the questions became confusing, redundant or irrelevant. *People v. Harris*, 706 N.Y.S.2d 392 (N.Y.A.D. 2000).

The same principles concerning repetitive questions apply to hearings other than trials. Consider, for example, a suppression hearing wherein it was held that the limitations placed on defense counsel's cross-examination of a detective were proper exercises of discretion in light of the repetitive and irrelevant nature of the questions posed. *People v. Goodridge*, 674 N.Y.S.2d 24 (N.Y.A.D. 1 Dept. 1998).

NORTH CAROLINA:

During a murder trial, the court did not err by stopping the defense attorney from asking the witness how many people were in the parking lot after victim had been shot; the question had been asked in different forms several times and was properly excluded as repetitious. *State v. Taylor*, 344 N.C. 31, 473 S.E.2d 596 (1996). In another murder trial, the court was proper in limiting the scope of defense counsel's cross-examination of a murder victim's son, since the son had already presented the very same evidence that defendant sought to elicit. *State v. Murillo*, 349 N.C. 573, 509 S.E.2d 752 (1998). See also *State v. Walls*, 463 S.E.2d 738, 342 N.C. 1 (1995).

For repetitious questions in a criminal case concerning the motives of co-conspirators, see *State v. Jaynes,* 464 S.E.2d 448, 342 N.C. 249 (1995).

OHIO:

The trial court has wide latitude to impose reasonable limits on cross-examination to restrict harassment, prejudice, confusion of issues, or interrogation about matters that are repetitive or only marginally relevant. *State v. Rapp*, 585 N.E.2d 965, 67 Ohio App.3d 33 (1990).

The trial court was entitled to exercise reasonable control over an attorney's examination of witnesses, and therefore properly sustained the defendant's objections to previously asked and answered questions. *Baker v. Cuyahoga Cty. Court of Common Pleas*, 572 N.E.2d 155, 61 Ohio App.3d 59, dismissed, 539 N.E.2d 164, 43 Ohio St.3d 702 (Ohio Ct. App. 1989), citing Rule 611(a) of the Ohio Rules of Evidence.

The trial judge has broad discretion to preclude repetitive and unduly harassing interrogation. *State v. Green,* 609 N.E.2d 1253, 66 Ohio St.3d 141 (1993).

OREGON:

Oregon has adopted most of the rules and principles set forth in the Federal Rules of Evidence. The Oregon Evidence Code (Oregon Revised Statutes, Chapter 40 et. seq.), however, assigns its own rule numbers.

PENNSYLVANIA:

On May 8, 1998, the Pennsylvania Supreme Court adopted a new and comprehensive set of evidence rules, with an effective date of October 1, 1998. The new rules are patterned after the Federal Rules of Evidence, both by content and number. In particular, see Pennsylvania's new Rule 611 (Mode and Order of Interrogation and Presentation), which is fashioned after its respective federal counterpart (discussed *supra*).

The trial court properly limited the scope of defendant's cross-examination of a witness, where that question had been repeatedly asked and answered. *Comm. v. Williams*, 554 Pa. 1, 720 A.2d 679 (1998).

The trial court may exclude evidence that is irrelevant, confusing, misleading, cumulative or prejudicial. *First Steps Internal Adoptions, Inc. v. Department of Public Welfare*, 880 A.2d 24 (Pa.Commonwealth, 2005).

TENNESSEE:

The defendant's cross-examination of witnesses was not improperly limited when the trial court restricted questions that were repetitious and argumentative; the limitation did not prohibit defendant from cross-examining witnesses regarding relevant matters. *State v. Harris*, 839 S.W.2d 54 (Tenn. 1992).

TEXAS:

A trial court may impose reasonable limits on cross-examination with respect to concerns about harassment, prejudice, confusion of the issues, the witness' safety, or interrogation that is repetitive, or only marginally relevant. *Matchett v. State*, 941 S.W.2d 922 (Tex. Crim. App. 1996); see also *Recer v. State,* 821 S.W.2d 715 (Tex. App. 1991).

In a wrongful death automobile negligence action by parents of a passenger, the admission of only one (of 16) photographs of the deceased passenger taken at the accident site was warranted. Even if all of the other photographs were relevant to the issue of damages, the parents did not establish that the other photographs would prove any element not already shown by the photograph admitted into evidence. *Huckaby v. A.G. Perry & Son, Inc.,* 20 S.W.3d 194 (Tex.App., 2000).

VERMONT:

Vermont mimics the Federal Rules of Evidence in much the same fashion as several aforementioned states. The rule numbers for the Vermont Rules of Evidence match the Federal Rules.

WEST VIRGINIA:

The West Virginia Rules of Evidence reflect the Federal Rules virtually word for word. The rule numbers match those of the Federal Rules.

WASHINGTON:

During the course of limiting counsel's questions directed toward an expert witness, to prevent repetitive questioning (among other things), comments on the evidence by the trial judge were not improper. *Jones v. Halvorson-Berg*, 847 P.2d 945, 69 Wash. App. 117 (Wash. App. Div. 3 1993).

(This page intentionally left blank.)

Chapter 11

Speculative Questions

§11.100 Introduction

A question that requires the witness to guess, conjecture, or present information that he or she does not actually possess is objectionable. Testimony should be based upon knowledge, not guesswork or speculation.

§11.200 Quick Explanation

A question is speculative if, by its very nature, it asks the witness to provide information that he or she does not possess. A question is likewise objectionable if it specifically requires the witness to speculate. Questions that employ terms such as "guess," "conjecture," or "speculate," are likely candidates for a valid objection. However, a question calling for an estimate or approximation may be proper as long as it has been demonstrated that the witness has some factual basis for presenting it. The answer might be thought of as an "educated guess," even though a question that specifically used that term would probably fall on the objectionable side of the dividing line between speculation and approximation.

As a rule, any question that asks the witness to state what was, or is, in the mind of another individual is automatically improper and speculative. Mind-reading has never been established as being scientifically acceptable.

EXAMPLES OF SPECULATIVE QUESTIONS:

1. Why do you suppose O.J Simpson took off in the White Bronco?
2. What were Frank's real feelings about firing Jim?[1]
3. Could you venture a guess as to the weight of the subject Ford Van?

The first question is speculative by its very nature. No one knows what a person's inner motives are other than the person who actually formulated them.

The second question asks about another person's "feelings." Such a question is speculative because of its form. The witness could have *properly* been asked questions such as: "What was Frank's stated purpose for firing Jim?" or "What was the reason given for Frank's firing of Jim?" But no one can know Frank's feelings, except Frank.

It is the *form* of the third question that creates the problems. Someone with relevant experience or knowledge, such as an automotive engineer, might be permitted to "approximate" the weight of a Ford Van. But any question that specifically calls for a "guess" or "speculation" is objectionable.

WHAT TO LOOK FOR:

Questions that ask witnesses to guess about information that they do not personally possess. Ask yourself, "How could this witness know the answer to the question"? If not from personal knowledge or hearsay, then speculation must be involved.

OBJECT AND RESPOND

OBJECTION:

"Objection. The question calls for speculation."

POTENTIAL RESPONSES TO OBJECTION:

A. "On the contrary, the question calls for an estimate, which is admissible."

B. "The witness has demonstrated knowledge with respect to this particular subject matter."

1 No one, expert or otherwise, can know what another person is thinking. See *S.E.C. v. Lipson*, F.Supp.2d 758 (N.D. Ill. 1998).

§11.300 General Legal Analysis

This objection is very closely related to the *Conclusion* objection discussed in Chapter 3; the two overlap and may be tricky to distinguish. For, it often happens that a witness' conclusions are based upon speculation or guesswork. There is, however, a difference between the two objections.

The *speculation* objection generally applies to facts and events at the threshold of their introduction. *Conclusions*, on the other hand, most often involve the opinions (right or wrong) that one might be tempted to derive from those facts and events, after they have already been properly established (see Chapter 3). For example, if blood stains were found on the person of an accused murderer, one might, in the absence of test results, guess or "speculate" about whether or not they actually linked the accused to the victim. However, after tests reveal that the stains do in fact match the victim's blood type, then one might improperly "conclude" that the accused is a cold-blooded murderer. Perhaps the following dialogue will help clarify the distinction:

Q. (By the Prosecutor) Now, detective, did you examine the defendant while he was in your custody, at the police station, on the night that Mickey was killed?

A. Yes, I did.

Q. What, if anything did you find?

A. Blood stains on the shirt of the defendant.

Q. Whose were they?

Defense Counsel: Objection! The question calls for **speculation** on the part of the witness. Without being tested, the blood could have come from anywhere or anyone.

The Trial Court: Sustained.

Q. Perhaps I should lay a better foundation. Were tests performed on the blood stains?

A. Yes. A serologist performed tests on the sample (which were properly introduced at the preliminary examination).

Q. What was the result?

A. The blood matched that of the victim.

Q. Is the defendant the one who murdered Mickey?

Defense Counsel: Objection! The question calls for a **conclusion** on the part of the witness.

The Trial Court: Sustained.

Notice from the preceding example that the *speculative* objection dealt with the threshold issue involving an identification of the evidence. After the evidence was properly identified as belonging to the defendant, the status of the blood stain was no longer a matter of conjecture or guess; and, certain inferences could rationally be drawn. How far, then, might one go toward implicating the defendant? The witness might properly conclude that the defendant experienced some contact with the victim. But to jump to the premise that the defendant committed murder, would not be permitted. Such a "jump" in logic would clearly call for *conclusion* (see Chapter 3).

The distinction between a question that calls for speculation and one that seeks a conclusion may not be as easy to discern. For practitioners, there is a simple rule—If in doubt, state both objections as grounds for excluding the testimony. Indeed, both grounds are supported by Fed. R. Evid. 602, which indirectly prohibits speculation and guesswork by stating:

> A witness may *not* testify to a matter unless evidence is introduced sufficient to support a finding that the witness has personal knowledge of the matter. Evidence to prove *personal knowledge* may, but need not, consist of the witness' own testimony. This rule is subject to the provisions of rule 703, relating to opinion testimony by expert witnesses (emphasis supplied).

As Rule 602 implies, a witness should testify based upon matters that he or she *knows about*. Guessing and speculating should not be permitted.[2] Nor should the interrogator be permitted to require a witness to answer questions based upon speculative hypotheticals.[3]

Generally, the rule stands for the proposition that a lay witness may not testify as to a given matter unless there is evidence to support a finding that he or she has personal knowledge of that matter; such a rule, therefore, excludes testimony concerning matters that the witness did not have an opportunity to observe.[4]

The Federal Rules, in general, tend to be quite liberal when it comes to permitting testimony that some might consider objectionable. As a corollary, principles that tend to exclude testimony are often strictly and narrowly construed by the federal courts. For Rule 602, the construction is extremely narrow, so much so that it has been held that a witness will be deemed competent to testify unless it is nearly impossible that he had first-hand knowledge of the matter.[5] Likewise, it has been held that a judge may exclude evidence only when no reasonable juror could conclude that the witness possessed personal knowledge to support the substance of the testimony.[6]

Looking at the broader picture, when analyzing testimony to determine whether it is reliable as opposed to speculative, we must invariably consider the skill-level of the inquiry, the education of the witness, and the reliability of the principles upon which that witness bases his or her testimony. For example, a lay witness might properly testify as to the cause of Sonny's death after personally observing machine guns pump two hundred rounds into the previously-healthy Sonny. However, in the absence of such first-hand knowledge, the only competent person to testify as to the cause of death would be a coroner or medical examiner. Others might only speculate. But even an experienced medical examiner must use scientifically acceptable techniques for his examination and conclusions, or else the testimony of this medical professional might be deemed speculative.

At the risk of oversimplification, we might summarily state that lay persons should be concerned about describing simple day-to-day events, while experts should be employed to provide "simple explanations" for more complicated matters requiring some brand of "science." But the analysis goes further, as we must distinguish between "established" scientific principles and "new" or "untested" science. We are thus led to three different (though related) lines of case law.

§11.400 Lay Witnesses

As the preceding discussion indicates, Fed. R. Evid. 602 (*supra*) and Fed. R. Evid. 701 work in conjunction with one another to define the limits of lay testimony. Rule 701, which is also considered in Chapter 3, provides:

If the witness is *not* testifying as an expert, the witness' testimony in the form of opinions or inferences is limited to those opinions or inferences which are (a) rationally based on the perception of the witness and (b) helpful to a clear understanding of the witness' testimony or the determination of a fact in issue.

---

2 *Moore v. Chesapeake & Ohio Railway Company*, 340 U.S. 573, 95 L. Ed. 547, 71 S. Ct. 428 (1951); and *Coal Resources, Inc. v. Gulf & Western Industries, Inc.*, 865 F.2d 761 (6th Cir. 1989); *Prudential Insurance Company of America v. Gutowski*, 49 Del. 233, 113 A.2d 579, 52 A.L.R. 2d 1073 (1955); see also *Personal Knowledge Under the Federal Rules of Evidence: A Three-Legged Stool,* Ronald Raitt, 18 Rutgers L.J. 591 (1987).

3 *Cheesman v. State*, 230 Ga. App. 525, 497 S.E.2d 40 (1998); *State v. Knowles,* 946 S.W.2d 791, (Mo.App., 1997); *Anderson v. Wittmeyer*, 895 S.W.2d 595 (Mo. App. 1995).

4 *U.S. v. Lyon*, 567 F.2d 777 (8th Cir. 1977) *cert. denied*, 98 S. Ct. 1476, 435 U.S. 918, 55 L. Ed.2d 510; see also *C. Itoh & Co., Inc. v. M/V Hans Leonardt*, 719 F. Supp. 514 (E.D. La. 1989) where it was held that the "opinion" testimony of a lay witness as to the cause of a crack in a barge's hopper was not admissible because that witness did not personally view the crack.

5 *Adkins v. Dirickson*, 523 F. Supp. 1281 (E.D. Pa. 1981).

6 *State v. Bennett*, 617 So.2d 550 (La. App 3 Cir. 1993); *U.S. v. Owens*, 699 F. Supp. 815 (D.C. Cal. 1988).

Upon encountering terms such as "opinions" and "inferences," the practitioner is correct by reacting "Objection! The question calls for a conclusion on the part of the witness." But a speculation objection should also be appraised. Consider a wrongful discharge case against a company that terminated the plaintiff for sleeping on the job; the sample testimony is that of a defense witness:

Q. (Attorney for Defendant) State your name and occupation.

A. Sam Sprinklemeyer... I'm a supervisor at the Darn Dandy Delivery Company.

Q. Did you have occasion to observe the plaintiff during the working day of January 4, 1995?

A. Yes; I did.

Q. Tell us what you saw, if anything?

A. I saw Peter Plaintiff sleeping in his truck when he should have been working.

Plaintiff's Counsel: Objection! The question and answer should be stricken; they call for **speculation** the part of the witness and they call for a **conclusion**. Moreover, there has not been any foundation to establish the location of the witness with respect to the plaintiff.

The Court: At this point, the Court is unable to determine whether the witness is guessing or whether he observed the facts and circumstances that may have properly led to such a conclusion. The objection is Sustained. Can you lay a better foundation, Counselor?

Q. Where were you standing at the time of the alleged observation?

A. I was standing next to the Plaintiff's truck.

Q. What specifically did you see?

A. Plaintiff was sitting up in the truck... His eyes were closed... he was making snoring sounds. And I had to nudge him several times in the shoulder before he finally responded.

Q. Was the plaintiff asleep?

Plaintiff's Counsel: Same objections as before.

The Court: Overruled. From the foundation that was just established, it is clear that the question is not, by any means, speculative. Clearly, the witness based his response on something other than mere guesswork. Was the witness' last answer in the form of a conclusion? Perhaps. But I find that it was rationally based on the perception of the witness; according to Federal Rule 701, the question should be allowed.

As suggested by the Court's ruling, a lay witness should be granted some leeway when providing opinions that are based upon "rational perceptions." The dividing line between a speculation and "valid conclusion" may be thin at best. The key factor in determining admissibility will often hinge on the quality of the underlying foundation, as it did in the preceding example. Consider the issue of accident reconstruction. Even though we don't normally think of a lay person as an "accident reconstruction expert," one may, nevertheless, present testimony relevant to a reconstruction.[7]

The actual subject matter or "area" under consideration (as opposed to mere "labels") will always be relevant in determining whether or not a lay person is competent to testify. As indicated above, labeling an issue "traffic reconstruction" does diminish a layperson's ability to testify about everyday "traffic" matters. Never-

7 But see *Strickland v. Doe,* 577 S.E.2d 124 (N.C.App., 2003) holding that a lay witness may not testify as to the speed of a vehicle involved in an accident where that witness did not actually see the accident. *Pomella v. Regency Coach Lines, Ltd.*, 899 F. Supp. 335 (E.D. Mich. 1995), permitted a lay person to testify about perceived time and distance, but refused to allow him to testify about whether or not a vehicle could stop. See also *Lievrouw v. Roth*, 157 Wis.2d 332, 459 N.W.2d 850 (1990). See also *Lucas v. Love*, 519 SE.2d 253, 238 Ga.App. 463 (1999), an automobile negligence action, wherein it was held that a motorist who rear-ended another motorist was qualified to render a lay opinion, during direct examination, as to whether she felt that she was a safe enough distance away from the rear-ended vehicle to come to a complete stop on a wet road. Moreover, a lay witness may express opinions regarding the speed and stopping distance of her vehicle, based upon personal observations.

theless, where special experience or expertise is, in fact, required, lay persons will not be permitted to testify.[8]

§11.500 Experts and Existing Forms of Evidence

Fed. R. Evid. 602, which limits witness testimony to matters of personal knowledge, does not apply to expert witnesses. As a matter of fact, experts are specifically excluded from that limitation by Rule 602's cross-reference to Fed. R. Evid. 703. Rule 703 provides as follows:

> The facts or data in a particular case upon which an expert bases an opinion or inference may be those perceived by or made known to the expert at or before the hearing. If of a type reasonably relied upon by experts in the particular field in forming opinions or inferences upon the subject, the facts or data need not be admissible in evidence.

While Rules 602 and 703 carve out a special exemption (with respect to personal knowledge) for expert witnesses, there are, nevertheless, limits to the type of testimony that experts can give before even "their speculation lines" are crossed. According to the *Notes of the Advisory Committee*, the facts upon which experts may base their opinions can be derived from three possible sources:

1. Firsthand observation of witnesses
2. Presentations at trial
3. Presentations of data outside of the courtroom

The Committee Notes provide the examination of a treating physician as an example of the first item on the list. This, of course, is the least controversial form of expert testimony.

The second item often results in the hypothetical question that is posed to the expert, who will have attended the trial and may, therefore, use the underlying facts as a basis for his or her conclusions. While hypothetical questions are common, the court, in its discretion, may exclude them as speculative. That decision will, of course, depend on the quality of the underlying foundations. Moreover, there is no absolute right to ask a hypothetical question, even during cross-examination.[9]

The third item on the list suggests that the expert may examine objects and scenes outside the courtroom prior to trial and then base his opinions on those observations; it goes much farther, however, by permitting hearsay as an additional method by which the expert may become aware of material underlying facts. That is where the "need not be admissible" part of Rule 703 comes into play.[10] This luxury is, of course, not available to lay persons.

The *special treatment* that is accorded to experts is based on the underlying notion that these professionals, unlike their lay counterparts, come armed with scientific knowledge and methods. They cannot use crystal balls, nor can they provide testimony that is based upon matters which are not scientifically accepted. For example, it was held that a party could *not* use evidence of a psychological stress evaluation test for the purpose of showing malice, since it was not generally accepted as scientifically reliable; the court found that the results would, therefore,

8 *Jones v. Jitney Jungle Stores of America, Inc.,* 730 So.2d 555 (Miss. 1998).

9 *Trademark Research Corp. v. Maxwell Online, Inc.*, 995 F.2d 326 (C.A.2 N.Y. 1993). A hypothetical question is one that is framed in such manner as to call for opinion from expert based on series of assumptions claimed to have been established by evidence in case. *Portis v. Greenhaw*, 38 S.W.3d 436 (Mo.App., 2001).

10 Nearly all of the states have closely worded, if not identical, provisions; Michigan's similarly numbered rule, however, provides that the court "may" require the underlying evidence to be admitted. Note that Fed. R. Evid. 705 states that the expert may testify in terms of opinion or inference and give reasons therefore without "prior disclosure" of the underlying facts or data. The expert may, in any event (per Rule 705), be required to disclose those underlying facts upon cross-examination.

be speculative.[11] Likewise, in a case where a sports fan may have fallen over an arena railing, the court found that it was an error to permit a so-called expert on "crowd psychology and control" to present evidence with respect to the method by which the arena was constructed.[12] But expert testimony about an IQ loss in children exposed to lead-based paint was not too speculative.[13]

While experts are entitled to give opinions about matters not personally experienced, they are by no means permitted to speculate or guess.[14] Just as the testimony of a lay person should be based on personal observations, the opinion of an expert should be grounded on reliable data rather than speculation.[15] Opinions that are so fundamentally unsupported that they offer no assistance to the jury, should be excluded as mere speculation or guesswork.[16]

Some matters, by their very nature, require the testimony of experts in a related field. One would, for example, normally expect the presence of an expert for a medical, chemical, technical, or ballistic issue. Without such expertise, the unsupported testimony of a lay witness might be deemed "speculative," even though that witness confined his or her offerings to factual observations. The fingerprint provides an excellent example of evidence requiring expert testimony, because it is beyond the understanding of lay jurors.[17]

Often, depending upon the type of case, the testimony of an expert will be required to keep

11 *Sabag v. Continental of South Dakota*, 374 N.W.2d 349 (S.D. 1985).

12 *Edwards v. California Sports, Inc.*, 254 Cal. Rptr. 170, 206 C.A.3d 1284 (Cal. App. 2 Dist. 1988).

13 *Richwind Joint Venture 4 v. Brunson*, 625 A.2d 326, 96 Md. App. 330 (1993).

14 *Falconer v. Penn Maritime, Inc.*, 380 F.Supp.2d 2 (D.Me., 2005). An expert may not give an opinion based on speculation or conjecture. *Carroll County Water Authority v. L.J.S. Grease & Tallow, Inc.*, 617 S.E.2d 612, 274 Ga.App. 353 (2005). An expert's opinion may not be based on speculative reasoning or conjectural reasoning.

Lippe v. Bairnco Corp., 288 B.R. 678 (S.D.N.Y. 2003). In a discrimination case, statistical expert testimony based on assumptions that are so unrealistic and contradictory as to suggest bad faith or where the testimony is speculative or conjectural should be excluded. In this particular case, there were no efforts made to account for major variables or to account for varying explanations for statistical disparities. *Modelski v. Navistar Intern. Transp. Corp.*, 236 Ill.Dec. 394, 707 N.E2d 239, 302 Ill.App.3d 879 (1999). Expert opinions based upon the witness guess, speculation, or conjecture as to what he believed might have happened, are inadmissible. See also *O'Conner v. Commonwealth Edison Co.*, 807 F.Supp. 1376 (C.D.Ill. 1992). *Card v. State*, 747 A.2d 32, 57 Conn.App. 134 (2000). Expert opinions must be based on reasonable probabilities rather than mere speculation or conjecture if they are to be admissible. *In re TMI Litigation*, 193 F.3d 613 (3rd Cir. Pa. 1999). For expert testimony to be reliable, and thus admissible, it must be based on methods and procedures of science rather than subjective belief or speculation. *In re Silicone Gel Breast Implants Products Liability Litigation*, 318 F.Supp.2d 879 (C.D. Cal., 2004). With respect to all proffered expert testimony, the trial judge must find that such testimony is properly grounded, well-reasoned, and not speculative before it can be admitted.

Message Center Management, Inc. v. Shell Oil Products Co., 857 A.2d 936, 85 Conn. App. 401 (2004). The court has the discretion to exclude speculative evidence, expert or otherwise.

15 *Carnival Corp. v. Stowers*, 834 So.2d 386 (Fl.App., 2003); *O Reilly v. General Dynamics Corp., Electric Boat Division*, 728 A.2d 527, 52 Conn.App. 813 (1999). Expert opinions must be based on reasonable probabilities, rather than mere speculation or conjecture, if they are to be admissible. An expert s testimony as to the reasonable probability of an occurrence does not depend on semantics or the use of any particular term or phrase, but rather, is determined by looking at the entire substance of testimony. See also *Ryan v. Beisner*, 844 P.2d 24 (Idaho App. 1992); *American Bearing Co. v. Litton Industries, Inc.*, 540 F.Supp. 1163 (E.D. Pa. 1982); *Murphy Tugboat Company v. Crowley*, 658 F.2d 1256 (9th Cir. 1981); *United States v. 91.9 Acres of Land, Etc.*, 586 F.2d 79 (8th Cir. 1978); *cert. denied*, 441 U.S. 944; 79 S. Ct. 2162, 60 L.Ed.2d 1045 (1979); *Mills v. United States*, 363 F.2d 78 (8th Cir. 1966); *Syracuse Broadcasting Corp. v. Newhouse*, 319 F.2d 683 (8th Cir. 1966).

16 *Johnson v. Piggly Wiggly of Pinetops, Inc.*, 575 S.E.2d 797 (N.C.App., 2003); *McKnight v. Johnson Controls, Inc.*, 36 F.3d 1396 (8th Cir. 1994).

17 *Scott v. Henrich*, 978 F.2d 481 (9th Cir. 1992).

"*prima facie*" offering from being deemed "speculative." Consider *Spivey v. Atteberry*.[18] The plaintiff, after being bitten by the defendant's dog, underwent injections to safeguard against a possible infection, and then became ill. The jury's conclusion that the plaintiff's illness was attributable to the bite or the vaccine was held to be speculative and not sustainable, in the absence of testimony from one possessing special knowledge in the diagnosis and treatment of physical disorders or diseases.

Other types of disputes, however, do not welcome expertise. In particular, when experts testify about automobile accidents, they enter a very controversial arena. When testimony involves braking distances, motion, velocity, impact, and other measurable quantities, there is little dispute about admissibility. But the ability of the "reconstruction experts" to pinpoint the manner in which accidents occurred always seems to raise the specter of speculation.[19] According to the *Notes of the Advisory Committee*, Rule 703 is not intended to permit such speculation:

> If it be feared that enlargement of permissible data may tend to break down the rules of exclusion unduly, notice should be taken that the rule requires that the facts or data "be of a type reasonably relied upon by experts in the particular field." The language would not warrant admitting in evidence the opinion of an "accidentologist" as to the point of impact in an automobile collision based on statements of bystanders since this requirement is not satisfied.

Another controversial area involves psychiatric opinions in criminal cases. As previously indicated, no one can know what another person is thinking. Speculation is the only thing that can result from any attempt to ascertain the inner workings of another person's head. Even a specialist in psychiatry, forensic medicine, and neurology cannot determine another person's state of mind.[20] Facial expressions and physical gestures (which may properly be described by any witness) suggest what a person is thinking, but even the most perceptive judge of human character can never be certain.

REFERENCES

Admissibility of expert testimony. 89 A.L.R. 4th 456.

§11.600 Experts and New Forms of Evidence

Years ago the word "scientific" was synonymous with terms such as "trustworthy," "established," or "tried and true." A single scientific principle might be developed over the course of years, sometimes centuries. If the body of knowledge was old, it was "scientific"[21]; if, on the other hand, it was new, one might assume that it was "untested" or "speculative." Now, things move very fast. Exchanges of information among experts and scientists move electronically; the transfer of learned information is no longer limited to the horse and buggy, or worse yet, the Post Office.

In order to weed out "junk science" and attempts to bestow an air of scientific window

18 205 Okla. 493, 238 P.2d 814, 27 A.L.R. 2d 1259 (1951).

19 See *Lipson, The Art of Advocacy - Demonstrative Evidence*, §18.02[3][b], *Matthew Bender & Co.*, 1988 – 2006.

20 *U.S. v. Pino*, 606 F.2d 908 (C.A.N.M. 1979). In *Pino*, such a "specialist" testified in an involuntary manslaughter case, claiming that because of defendant's personality traits, he would not have driven his vehicle in a wanton or reckless manner; the court held such testimony to be improper. Moreover, see *Fed. R. Evid.* 704(b): "No expert while testifying with respect to the mental state or condition of a defendant in a criminal case may state an opinion or inference as to whether the defendant did or did not have the mental state or condition constituting an element of the crime or a defense thereto."

21 Time as a sole determinant, however, can be misleading. Newton's laws of motion were thought to be irrefutably correct for centuries; they weren't. Also, see *Study Shows Computerized EEG Evidence Often Faulty*, 8 Mich.L.W. 1774 (Michigan Lawyers Weekly October 3, 1994).

dressing upon otherwise speculative and untrustworthy processes, the court must exercise its so called "gatekeeping function" to ensure that speculative procedures stay out of the courtroom.[22] At its threshold, such matters are to be determined by the judge, not weighed by the jury.[23]

How then do the courts treat "new" forms of evidence such as DNA testing, truth-detection devices, psychic phenomena, and other yet-to-be-accepted older "sciences" such as astrology? The answer—It depends on the rule that the court chooses to follow. There are two. We will consider them historically:

§11.601 *Frye* Rule

As learning accelerated in the early Twentieth Century, it became necessary to separate fact from fancy, science from speculation; and thus came about a very difficult-to-satisfy standard in the form of the infamous rule of *People v. Frye*.[24] Ironically, a "truth" machine was actually the subject of the Frye case; it was a device known as The Systolic Blood Pressure Deception Test (the grandfather of our polygraph or lie detector). *Frye* found that the detector's reliability had yet to be established; and thus, more than 70 years ago, the lie detector was deemed to be too speculative.

Ever since *Frye*, polygraph test results and the experts who support them have had a rocky ride when confronting objections based upon speculativeness. The courts have repeatedly found the so-called "lie detector tests" to be unreliable and therefore too speculative.[25]

Outlawing the polygraph for ages to come was by no means a small accomplishment for a single non-Supreme Court level case (i.e., *Frye*). But even more far reaching was the dicta, which would also impact the concept of "speculativeness" for decades to come. As its basis for refusing to admit results from the Systolic Blood Pressure Deception Test, the *Frye* court held:[26]

> Just when a scientific principle or discovery crosses the line between the experimental and demonstrable stages is difficult to define. Somewhere in this twilight zone the evidential force of the principle must be recognized, and while courts will go a long way in admitting expert testimony deduced from a well-recognized scientific principle or discovery, the thing from which the deduction is made must be *sufficiently established to have gained general acceptance in the particular field in which it belongs.*

The *Frye* test (i.e., the italicized portion of the preceding passage) spread throughout the land, much like the ancient Mongol hordes spread across Europe. Many phrases derived from the preceding language, some un-publishable, took the place of the precise dicta used by the court.[27]

---

22 *Vargas v. Lee,* 317 F.3d 498 (5th Cir., La., 2003). Before expert testimony can be admitted, the district court must first conduct a preliminary inquiry to ensure that it is both relevant and reliable. Moreover, the objective of this "gatekeeping requirement" applies regardless of whether the testimony is based upon professional studies or personal experience. Either way, it must employ the same level of intellectual rigor that characterizes the practice of an expert in the relevant field.

23 See§11.603 and §11.604.

24 54 App.D.C. 46, 293 F. 1013 (1923).

25 *Sabag v. Continental South Dakota*, 374 N.W.2d 349 (S.D. 1985); *Caldwell v. State*, 267 Ark. 1053, 594 S.W.2d 24 (1980); *People v. Tarsia*, 67 A.D.2d 210, 415 N.Y.S.2d 120 (1979), affirmed, 50 N.Y.2d 1, 405 N.E.2d 188, 427 N.Y.S.2d 944 (1980); *State v. Makerson,* 52 N.C.App. 149, 277 S.E.2d 869 (1981); *State v. Ochalla*, 285 N.W.2d 683, (Minn. 1979); *State v. Schouest*, 351 So.2d 462 (La. 1977); *Smith v. State*, 31 Md.App. 106, 355 A.2d 527 (1976).

26 *Frye v. United States*, 293 F. 1013, 1014 (D.C. Cir. 1923).

27 A state by state analysis would be unwarranted at this juncture due to the impact of *Daubert v. Merrill Dow Pharmaceuticals, Inc.*, 113 S. Ct. 2786, 125 L. Ed. 2d 469 (1993); see §11.603.

At some point, terms such as "general acceptance in the scientific community" and "relevant community" wormed their way into the law, as the standard took some twists and turns. In any event, the key phrase "general acceptance" survived; and those two words, more than any others, were responsible for creating the high hurdles for new forms of evidence that have plagued litigators for decades.

§11.602 Fed. R. Evid. 702

In 1972 the Federal Rules of Evidence went into effect. Fed. R. Evid. 702, pertaining to expert testimony, in general, stated as follows:

> If scientific, technical, or other specialized knowledge will assist the trier of fact to understand the evidence or to determine a fact in issue, a witness qualified as an expert by knowledge, skill, experience, training, or education, may testify thereto in the form of an opinion or otherwise.

There was no doubt that Rule 702 created a gentler, milder standard, but was it intended to replace or overrule *Frye*? This question was never answered. The Committee Notes made no mention of *Frye*.[28] If the Rule were intended to overrule *Frye*, many argued, the Notes could easily have said as much. But then there were others who claimed with equal force that if the Rule were intended to preserve *Frye*, the Notes could have made mention of that intention.

The issue concerning the intention or (non-intention) to overrule *Frye* was hotly debated for years. Some states adopted *Frye*, some employed the standard suggested by Rule 702, and others utilized a combination of the two.

In any event, as it applied to "new" evidentiary developments, the *Federal Rule v. Frye* debate was finally put to rest in 1993 by the United States Supreme Court. The case of *Daubert v. Merrell Dow Pharmaceuticals, Inc.*[29] sets forth a flexible, logical standard for determining the admissibility of new scientific and technical evidence in the federal courts. It is interesting to note that despite the overwhelming acceptance of the Federal Rules of Evidence, *Daubert* has not become a universal standard. The case is carefully considered in the section that follows.

§11.603 *Daubert v. Dow* - 1993

In 1993 the United States Supreme Court resolved the conflict between Rule 702 and *Frye* by holding that, at least in the federal courts, Rule 702 prevailed.[30] Some analysts incorrectly suggest that *Frye* was thereby completely overruled.[31] In fact, the Supreme Court amalgamated *Frye* and Rule 702 into a new test.

The Supreme Court stated that, "Many factors will bear on the inquiry, and we do **not** presume to set out a definitive checklist or test;" the high court then proceeded to set forth the following definitive checklist or test to determine whether a particular scientific or technical form of evidence should be admissible:

1. Whether or not the subject theory or technique can be and has been tested.
2. Whether the theory or technique has been subjected to peer review and publication.
3. The known or potential rate of error.
4. The "general acceptance" of the theory or technique.

Other factors may be considered. The high court made that clear. Until such time as other

28 The Notes of the Advisory Committee seemed to expand the scope of then-permissible evidence beyond rigorous "scientific" knowledge, by allowing "specialized" knowledge (i.e., a plumber, carpenter, or candlestick maker could offer "specialized" knowledge with respect to their particular area of expertise) to be admitted. But with respect to "new" forms of evidence, the infamous name "Frye" was never considered.

29 113 S. Ct. 2786, 125 L. Ed. 2d 469 (1993).

30 *Daubert v. Merrell Dow Pharmaceuticals, Inc.*, 113 S. Ct. 2786, 125 L. Ed. 2d 469 (1993).

31 See, for example, George J. Annas, *Scientific Evidence in the Courtroom - The Death of the Frye Rule*, The New England Journal of Medicine, at 1018 (April 7, 1994).

factors develop, however, the above list should be thought of as a standard test, and one which is likely to gain wide, if not universal acceptance.

Fans of *Frye* will observe that with respect to the Fourth item, the high court noted that:

> Widespread acceptance of scientific theory or technique can be an important factor in ruling particular evidence admissible, and known technique that has been able to draw only minimal support within the community may properly be viewed with skepticism..."

Enemies of *Frye*, on the other hand may sing this verse of *Daubert*:

> "General acceptance" is not a necessary precondition to the admissibility of scientific evidence under the Federal Rules of Evidence, but the Rules of Evidence - especially Rule 702 - do assign to the trial judge the task of ensuring that an expert's testimony both rests on a reliable foundation and is relevant to the task at hand. Pertinent evidence based on scientifically valid principles will satisfy those demands.

With respect to any new form of evidence introduced in the federal realm, *Daubert* has left no doubt about the test that will be applied in separating the "admissible" from the "speculative." The states, however, many of whom have lived and slept with *Frye* for years, will have to select their own destinies.[32]

Things are rapidly changing because of an increase in new technologies. It once seemed reasonable to predict that because so many states have similar, if not identical counterparts to the Federal Rules of Evidence, all states would adapt the *Daubert* test. The test is, by its own admission, a flexible one, which leaves plenty of room for modification.[33] But in truth, acceptance of *Daubert* has been far from universal. Even in the federal courts where *Daubert* would seem impregnable, jurists are using the *Daubert* "flexibility" to flex themselves away from *Daubert*. [34]

---

32 See Thompson, *"Scientific Testimony after Daubert: Some Early Returns from Lower Courts,"* 8 Trial 23 (August 1994); see also Stewart, *A New Test - Decision Creates Uncertain Future for Admissibility of Expert Testimony*, Journal of The American Bar Association, at 48 (November 1993).

33 *Gallatin Fuels, Inc. v. Westchester Fire Insurance Company*, 410 F.Supp.2d 417 (W.D. Pa., 2006). The factors used to assess reliability of expert opinions under the *Daubert* test include whether: (1) the theory or technique can be tested; (2) the theory or technique has been peer reviewed; (3) there is a high rate of known or potential error; (4) there are standards of control; (5) the theory is "generally accepted"; (6) there is a sufficient relationship between the technique and methods which have been established to be reliable; (7) the expert's qualifications are sufficient; and (8) the method has been put to non-judicial uses.

In re Vioxx Products Liability Litigation, 414 F.Supp.2d 574 (E.D.La., 2006). The non-exclusive list of *Daubert* factors to consider in determining the scientific reliability of expert testimony includes: (1) whether the theory has been tested; (2) whether the theory has been subject to peer review and publication; (3) the known or potential rate of error; (4) whether standards and controls exist and have been maintained with respect to the technique; and (5) the general acceptance of the methodology in the scientific community. Whether some or all of the *Daubert* factors for determining the scientific reliability of expert testimony apply in a particular case depends on the facts, the expert's particular expertise, and the subject of his testimony. In a drug-based products liability action, in addition to the five *Daubert* factors, the trial court may consider factors that include: (1) whether the expert's opinion is based on incomplete or inaccurate dosage or duration data; (2) whether the expert has identified the specific mechanism by which the drug supposedly causes the alleged disease; (3) whether the expert has unjustifiably extrapolated from an accepted premise to an unfounded conclusion; (4) whether the expert has adequately accounted for alternative explanations; and (5) whether the expert proposes to testify about matters growing directly out of research that he or she has conducted independent of the litigation.

34 According to *Heller v. Shaw Industries, Inc.* 167 F.3d 146 (3rd 1999), which upheld the dismissal of a products liability lawsuit, the *Daubert* factors have been downgraded to "simply useful signposts."

§11.604 *Kumho v. Carmichael* - 1999 Landmark

The prior cases seem to suggest an "either/or" solution to the admissibility problem for new forms of evidence; i.e., either the evidence is "scientific" or it is "speculative." This use of the term "speculative" creates no major problem because "speculativeness" is clearly equated to "inadmissibility." "Scientific" is another problem; its use in this context is vague, indeed. For example, might a new form of evidence be admissible even if it doesn't involve test tubes and geeks in white coats? In other words, can it involve geeks in other coats, i.e., "technicians" or technical experts? And should the *Daubert* "gatekeeping" rules be applied to these latter groups? The answer to both questions, according to the high court, is "yes."

The Supreme Court decided in *Kumho v. Carmichael*[35] that the *Daubert* test applies not only to "scientific" evidence, but to all expert testimony. Therefore, the *Daubert* factors apply to engineers, technicians and other experts who are not necessarily "scientists." Moreover, Rule 702, does not distinguish between "scientific," "technical" or other forms of "specialized" knowledge.

§11.605 Amendment to Rule 702

With an effective date of December 1, 2000, amendments to Rule 702 resolve much of the conflict between *Frye* and Rule 702. The amendments do what the imprecise, circular language of *Daubert* could not. The amended rule states:[36] If scientific, technical, or other specialized knowledge will assist the trier of fact to understand the evidence or to determine a fact in issue, a witness qualified as an expert by knowledge, skill, experience, training, or education, may testify thereto in the form of an opinion or otherwise, *if (1) the testimony is based upon sufficient facts or data, (2) the testimony is the product of reliable principles and methods, and (3) the witness has applied the principles and methods reliably to the facts of the case.*

The three additional provisions all boil down to issues of *methodology* and employment of "sufficient" underlying facts or data. Unlike the circular *Daubert* elements, the components of the amendment make sense. The amendment's precise, yet broad language, permits the court to exercise its gate-keeping function in a logical, consistent manner. It certainly presents a formidable attack on the *Frye* standard.

The intentional omission of the word "scientific" was a wise move indeed. Evidence that is technical and reliable (but not quite "scientific") would be permitted without the difficulties presented by *Kumho.*[37]

§11.700 Selected State Rules and Cases

ALABAMA:

It was speculative to ask a police officer to testify in a sodomy prosecution about what the victim thought and why she was upset. *Dyson v. State*, 591 So.2d 559 (Ala. App. 1991). This case follows the "iron clad" rule that no witness can know what was in the mind of another person. See §11.200.

A law enforcement officer who found a box containing drug paraphernalia in the defendant's bedroom, was asked this question on cross-

35 *Kumho Tire Co., Ltd., et al. v. Carmichael et al.*, ____ U.S. ____ , No. 97-1709 (March 23, 1999).

36 See Federal Judiciary Homepage, <http://www.uscourts.gov>, *Proposed Amendments to the Federal Rules of Evidence.*

37 Nevertheless, our faith in the "scientific" will not die easily. See *Bourne ex rel. Bourne v. E.I. DuPont De Nemours and Co., Inc.,* 189 F.Supp.2d 482 (S.D.W.Va., 2002), holding that an expert's testimony should be grounded in scientific knowledge to constitute more than unsupported speculation.

examination: "It would be very logical for the person who did work where this kind of box is kept [to] have this stuff there at home in it, would it not?" The court held that the question called for speculation and conjecture. *Porter v. State*, 570 So.2d 823 (Ala. App. 1990).

The trial court properly precluded a defending attorney in a theft case from asking a police investigator if there was anything he had found in the course of his investigation proving that the defendant took the subject money; such a question could call for speculation, hearsay, or irrelevant conclusions. *Hodges v. State*, 570 So.2d 1252 (Ala. App. 1989).

ALASKA:

With respect to scientific, technical, or other specialized knowledge, Alaska's Rule 702 is similar to Fed. R. Evid. 702; see §11.602 for a discussion of Rule 702 and its application to new scientific and technical forms of evidence.

ARIZONA:

For scientific, technical, or other specialized knowledge, Arizona's Rule 702 is similar to Fed. R. Evid. 702; however, Arizona refuses to follow *Daubert*. See *State v. Bible*, 858 P.2d 1152 (Ariz. 1993). See also §11.602.

ARKANSAS:

With respect to scientific, technical, or other specialized knowledge, Arkansas' Rule 702 is identical to Fed. R. Evid. 702; see §11.602.

CALIFORNIA:

Speculative questions are, by their very nature, improper. Therefore, there is no reason to expect a departure from the general rule prohibiting their use.

Evidence which produces only speculative inferences is irrelevant. *People v. De La Plane*, 151 Cal. Rptr. 843, 88 C.A.3d 223, *cert. denied*, 100 S. Ct. 81, 444 U.S. 841, 62 L.Ed.2d 53 (1979). California also follows the general precept that permits expert testimony only where the underlying area of expertise is scientifically accepted. See *Edwards v. California Sports, Inc.*, *supra*, at n.8. And where an expert bases his or her conclusions on assumptions not reasonably relied on by other experts, or on factors that are remote, speculative, or conjectural, then his or her opinion lacks evidentiary value. See *Wanland v. Los Gatos Lodge, Inc.*, 281 Cal. Rptr. 890, *rehearing denied and opinion modified* (Cal. App. 6 Dist. 1991).

A religious counselor's prediction concerning the likelihood of a defendant (in a capital case) leading a "moral life" in prison was properly excluded where that counselor was not shown to possess academic credentials or the experience necessary to make such an assessment. *People v. Ruiz*, 244 Cal. Rptr. 200, 749 P.2d 854, 44 Cal.3d 589, *cert. denied*, 109 S. Ct. 186, 102 L.Ed.2d 155 (1988).

"What if" questions always seem to be ready candidates for a "speculative" objection. Common sense dictates that "what might have happened" or "could have happened" must involve guesswork. Consider a case where a witness testified about the reputation of someone else. A subsequent question, asking whether the witness' opinion would have changed if certain matters had been known, was held to be incompetent and speculative. *People v. Weber*, 86 P. 671, 149 Cal. 325 (1906).

POLYGRAPH TEST RESULTS IN CALIFORNIA STATE COURTS

California follows the overwhelming majority view with respect to its distrust of the polygraph (i.e., lie detector) test. Accordingly, Rule 351.1(a) of the California Evidence Code states:

Notwithstanding any other provision of law, the results of a polygraph examination, the opinion of a polygraph examiner, or any reference to an offer to take, failure to take, or taking of a polygraph examination, shall not be admitted into evidence in any criminal proceeding, including pretrial and post conviction motions and hearings, or in any trial or hearing of a juvenile for a criminal offense, whether heard in juvenile or adult court, unless all parties stipulate to the admission of such results.

Rule 351.1(b) stands as a warning for anyone who would make admissions or statements during the course of a polygraph examination. According to that subsection, they are not excludable.

With respect to new scientific evidence, it is important to note that California has specifically rejected the so-called "flexible approach" of *Daubert v. Dow* (See *supra*) by electing to maintain the tougher "general acceptance" standard. See *People v. Leahy,* 8 Cal. 4th 587 (1994).

COLORADO:

With respect to scientific, technical, or other specialized knowledge, Colorado's Rule 702 is similar to Fed. R. Evid. 702; see §11.602 with respect to new forms of evidence.

CONNECTICUT:

In a fashion similar to many of the less populous states, Connecticut follows the Federal Rules essentially word for word and section number for section number.

There must be a factual basis for expert opinions; they must be based on reasonable probabilities rather than mere speculation or conjecture if they are to be admissible. *Card v. State*, 747 A.2d 32, 57 Conn.App. 134 (2000).

DELAWARE:

With respect to scientific, technical, or other specialized knowledge, Delaware's Rule 702 is similar to Fed. R. Evid. 702; see §11.602.

FLORIDA:

Section 90.604 of the Florida Evidence Code provides:

> Except as otherwise provided in 90.702, a witness may not testify to a matter unless evidence is introduced which is sufficient to support a finding that he has personal knowledge of the matter. Evidence to prove personal knowledge may be given by the witness himself.

The Sponsor's Note states, "Occasionally the witness has made a personal observation but does not have a definite "impression," e.g., he saw a man and "thought" it was the accused. To this defect in the quality of the impression, the law makes no objection, but receives it for what it is worth." *Herndon v. State*, 73 Fla. 451, 74 So. 511 (1917), and *Kennard v. State*, 42 Fla. 581, 28 So. 858 (1900).

In order to be admissible, an expert's opinion must be predicated upon valid underlying data which, in turn, must have a proper factual basis. *Carnival Corp. v. Stowers,* 834 So.2d 386 (Fl.App., 2003).

HAWAII:

Hawaii Evidence Rule 702, which is similar to its federal counterpart, contains the following provision: "[I]n determining the issue of assistance to the trier of fact, the court may consider the trustworthiness and validity of the scientific technique or mode of analysis employed by the proffered expert." See also §11.602.

IDAHO:

A verdict cannot rest on speculation or conjecture; therefore, an expert opinion is inadmissible if that opinion is speculative, conclusory, or unsubstantiated by the facts in the record. Such an opinion is of no assistance to the jury in rendering its verdict. *Ryan v. Beisner*, 844 P.2d 24 (Idaho App. 1992).

With respect to scientific, technical, or other specialized knowledge, Idaho's Rule 702 is identical to Fed. R. Evid. 702; see §11.602.

ILLINOIS:

An expert witness is not permitted to guess nor base an opinion on surmise or conjecture. *O'Conner v. Commonwealth Edison Co.*, 807 F. Supp. 1376 (C.D. Ill. 1992). Nor may an expert guess, surmise or conjecture as to the possible cause of an injury based on matters which could not be shown to have existed. *Baird v. Adeli*, 157 Ill. Dec. 861, 573 N.E.2d 279 (Ill. App. 4 Dist. 1991). But compare *Aguinaga v. City of Chicago*, 183 Ill. Dec. 648, 611 N.E.2d 1296 (Ill. App. 1 Dist. 1993), which held that an expert may testify as to what might or could have caused a particular injury despite an objection that the testimony is inconclusive or speculative.

An expert's opinion cannot be based on conjecture or guess; and a medical expert's opinion must be based on a reasonable degree of medical certainty. *Marshall v. Osborn*, 156 Ill. Dec. 708,

571 N.E.2d 492, 213 Ill. App.3d 134 (Ill. App.3 Dist.1991); *Wehmeier v. UNR Industries, Inc.*, 157 Ill. Dec. 251, 572 N.E.2d 320, 213 Ill. App.3d 6 (Ill. App. 4 Dist.1991).

INDIANA:

Indiana Evidence Rule 702 (B) provides that "Expert scientific testimony is admissible only if the court is satisfied that the scientific principles upon which the testimony rests are reliable."

IOWA:

Allowing a police officer to express his opinions about a motor vehicle accident which he investigated, was not an abuse of discretion where the officer possessed skill and training that would assist the jury to understand the accident scene and the cause of the accident. *Stumpf v. Reiss*, 502 N.W.2d 620 (Iowa App. 1993). Note that with respect to scientific, technical, or other specialized knowledge, Iowa's Rule 702 is identical to Fed. R. Evid. 702; see §11.602.

KENTUCKY:

With respect to scientific, technical, or other specialized knowledge, Kentucky's Rule 702 is identical to Fed. R. Evid. 702; see §11.602.

LOUISIANA:

Where State Trooper #1 testified that he had no personal knowledge about what happened to a bundle of cash after he turned it over to State Trooper #2, cross-examination questions about a delay in fingerprinting the money (directed at Trooper #2) called for mere speculation. *State v. Bennett*, 617 So.2d 550 (La. App. 3 Cir. 1993).

With respect to scientific, technical, or other specialized knowledge, Louisiana's Rule 702 is identical to Fed. R. Evid. 702; see §11.602.

MAINE:

With respect to scientific, technical, or other specialized knowledge, Maine's Rule 702 is identical to Fed. R. Evid. 702; see §11.602 for a discussion of Rule 702 as applied to new scientific or technical evidence.

MARYLAND:

Expert testimony pertaining to the average IQ loss sustained by children who were exposed to lead-based paint was not mere conjecture or speculation, where a witness testified that the children (for whom the suit was initiated) ingested lead in quantities sufficient to cause brain damage. The expert also opined that children ingested lead-based paint while residing in an apartment building. Moreover, the expert also considered the effect of other factors such as a mother's alcoholism and the children's home environment that might also result in the loss of IQ by children. *Richwind Joint Venture 4 v. Brunson*, 625 A.2d 326, 96 Md. App. 330 (1993).

MASSACHUSETTS:

Expert testimony must be predicated on facts legally sufficient to provide a basis for the expert's opinion and, thus, an expert should not be permitted to give an opinion that is based on conjecture or speculation from an insufficient evidentiary foundation. *Damon v. Sun Co., Inc.*, 87 F. 3d 1467 (Mass. 1996).

In determining whether or not an expert is qualified to testify regarding the proper standard of care of a physician, the crucial issue is whether the witness has sufficient education, training, experience and familiarity with the subject matter of the testimony, which ensures that the expert has sufficient knowledge of the practices of other physicians to assert that the average qualified practitioner would, or would not, take a particular course of action in the relevant circumstances. Under *Daubert*, in assessing the reliability of the expert's opinion for purposes of admissibility, the judge must determine whether the reasoning or methodology underlying the testimony is scientifically valid and whether that reasoning or methodology properly can be applied to the facts in issue. *Palandjian v. Foster*, 842 N.E.2d 916, 446 Mass. 100 (2006).

MICHIGAN:

Michigan's Rule 701 is identical in content to Fed. R. Evid.701. With respect to scientific, technical, or other specialized knowledge, Michigan's Rule 702 differs from Fed. R. Evid. 702 (See "Michigan" heading under Chapter 3); see also §11.602. And Michigan's Rule 703 is inconsistent with its federal counterpart (supra). In particular, Rule 703 of the *Michigan Rules of Evidence* (with its inconsistent portion in bold), states:

> The facts or data in a particular case upon which an expert bases an opinion or inference may be those perceived by or made known to the expert at or before the hearing. **The court may require that underlying facts or data essential to an opinion or inference be in evidence.**

MINNESOTA:

With respect to scientific, technical, or other specialized knowledge, Minnesota's Rule 702 is identical to Fed. R. Evid. 702; see §11.602 for a discussion of Rule 702.

MISSISSIPPI:

With respect to scientific, technical, or other specialized knowledge, Mississippi's Rule 702 is identical to Fed. R. Evid. 702; see §11.602.

MISSOURI:

Asking defendant what he "would" say to the victim about events that occurred on the day of a theft from a store called for a narrative statement that was vague, speculative, and improper. *State v. Knowles,* 946 S.W.2d 791, (Mo.App., 1997).

MONTANA:

With respect to scientific, technical, or other specialized knowledge, Montana's Rule 702 is identical to Fed. R. Evid. 702; see §11.602.

NEBRASKA:

Nebraska's Rule 27-702, pertaining to scientific, technical, and other specialized knowledge, is identical to Rule 702 of the Federal Rules of Evidence. See §11.602.

NEVADA:

The mere fact that an expert used the word "think" did not place his expert opinion into the category of conjecture or unreliability. *Smith v. Cotter*, 810 P.2d 1204 (Nev. 1991).

On the subject of scientific, technical, or other specialized knowledge, Nevada's Rule 50275 is similar to, but modifies, its federal counterpart (Rule 702).

NEW HAMPSHIRE:

With respect to scientific, technical, or other specialized knowledge, New Hampshire's Rule 702 is identical to Fed. R. Evid. 702; see §11.602.

NEW MEXICO:

With respect to scientific, technical, or other specialized knowledge, New Mexico's Rule 702 is identical to Fed. R. Evid. 702; see §11.602.

NEW JERSEY:

New Jersey's state courts do not tolerate guesswork any more than do its federal courts. That position applies to both lay witnesses and experts. According to *Fedorczyk v. Caribbean Cruise Lines, Ltd.*, 82 F.3d 69 (N.J. 1995), if an expert opinion is based on speculation or conjecture, it may be stricken.

NEW YORK:

The district court could properly refuse to allow the defense's "economic expert" to critique certain "wasted expenses" calculations performed by the plaintiff's expert, since the critique required accounting expertise that the defense expert con-ceded he did not possess; such testimony could confuse the jury and invite speculation. *Trademark Research Corp. v. Maxwell Online, Inc.*, 995 F.2d 326 (C.A.2 N.Y. 1993).

An expert may not reach a conclusion by assuming the existence of material facts not supported by the evidence, nor may the expert guess or speculate in drawing a conclusion. *Lee v. Shields*, 591 N.Y.S.2d 522 (N.Y.A.D. 2 Dept. 1992).

Did Defendant rape the victim? Did the two have a prior sexual relationship? Did Defendant "unconsciously" communicate with the victim? In Defendant's prosecution for rape, such questions (asked of the victim's mother) were properly held to be too speculative. *People v. Martinez*, 575 N.Y.S.2d 938 (1991).

NORTH CAROLINA:

With respect to scientific, technical, or other specialized knowledge, North Carolina's Rule 702 is similar to Fed. R. Evid. 702; see §11.602.

With respect to the rules governing the admissibility of expert testimony, baseless speculation can never be used to "assist the jury." *Johnson v. Piggly Wiggly of Pinetops, Inc.*, 575 S.E.2d 797 (N.C.App., 2003).

NORTH DAKOTA:

With respect to scientific, technical, or other specialized knowledge, North Dakota's Rule 702 is identical to Fed. R. Evid. 702; see §11.602.

OHIO:

Ohio Evidence Rule 702 provides that a witness may testify as an expert if: (A) the witness's testimony relates to matters beyond the knowledge or experience is asked by lay or dispels a misconception common among lay persons; (B) the witness is qualified as an expert by specialized knowledge, skill, experience, training, or education regarding the subject matter of the testimony; and (C) the witness' testimony is based on reliable scientific, technical, or other specialized information. To the extent that the testimony reports the result of a procedure, test, or experiment, the testimony is reliable only if (1) the theory upon which the procedure, test or experiment is based is objectively verified or is validly derived from widely accepted knowledge, facts, or principles; (2) the design of the procedure, test or experiment reliably implements the theory; and (3) the particular procedure, test, or experiment was conducted in a way that would yield an accurate result.

OKLAHOMA:

With respect to scientific, technical, or other specialized knowledge, Oklahoma's Rule 702 is identical to Fed. R. Evid. 702; see §11.602.

OREGON:

With respect to scientific, technical, or other specialized knowledge, Oregon's Rule 702 is identical to Fed. R. Evid. 702; see §11.602.

PENNSYLVANIA:

On May 8, 1998, the Pennsylvania Supreme Court adopted a new and comprehensive set of evidence rules, with an effective date of October 1, 1998. The new rules are patterned after the Federal Rules of Evidence, both by content and number.

Pennsylvania's new Rule 701 (Opinion Testimony by Lay Witnesses), Rule 702 (Testimony by Experts), Rule 704 (Opinion on Ultimate Issue), and Rule 602 (Lack of Personal Knowledge), are all patterned after their respective federal counterparts (discussed *supra*).

In an action arising from a single-vehicle motorcycle accident, a lay witness was properly allowed to give an estimate of a motorcycle's speed, where the motorcycle passed the witness shortly before the accident, the witness was an eyewitness to the entire chain of events, and the witness was familiar with the road and had an excellent opportunity for observation. *Wicks v. Com. Dept. of Transp.*, 590 A.2d 832 (Pa. Cmwlth. 1991).

PUERTO RICO:

For scientific, technical, or other specialized knowledge, Puerto's Rico's Rule 52 is identical to Fed. R. Evid. 702; see §11.602 for a discussion of Rule 702 and its application to new scientific and technical forms of evidence.

RHODE ISLAND:

For scientific, technical, or other specialized knowledge, Rhode Island's Rule 702 is similar to Fed. R. Evid. 702; see §11.602 for a discussion of Rule 702 and its application to new scientific and technical forms of evidence.

SOUTH CAROLINA:

The mother of an injured motorist failed to establish that a highway patrol trooper qualified as an expert for an accident reconstruction. The trooper was not a member of the highway patrol's official accident reconstruction team, and he did not use any reconstructive techniques to determine the speeds of the drivers; he basically relied upon what the drivers told him. Moreover, to qualify as an expert, a person must have acquired by study or practical experience a special knowledge of a subject matter about which the jury's good judgment and average knowledge is inadequate. *McDill v. Mark's Auto Sales*, 626 S.E.2d 52, 367 S.C. 486 (2006).

SOUTH DAKOTA:

South Dakota's 19-15-2 (pertaining to scientific, technical, and other specialized knowledge) is identical to Fed. R. Evid. 702; see §11.602 for a discussion of Rule 702 and its application to new scientific and technical forms of evidence.

TENNESSEE:

For scientific, technical, or other specialized knowledge, Tennessee's Rule 702 is similar to Fed. R. Evid. 702; see §11.602 for a discussion of Rule 702 and its application to new scientific and technical forms of evidence.

TEXAS:

A device known as a "penile plethysmograph" was connected to a father's penis in order to test for sexual deviancy. It was held that the ability of that device to accurately reach such a conclusion was too speculative. *In Interest* of A.V., 849 S.W.2d 393 (Texas 1993).

It is universally accepted that no witness can testify as to what another person is thinking or intending. However, one may give inference testimony about another person's "state of mind" if that evidence is rationally based on the witness' perception. *Ethicon, Inc. v. Martinez*, 835 S.W.2d 826 (Tex. App. 1992).

Following an alleged sexual assault, the victim underwent counseling, but discontinued the sessions after several months. The trial court did not abuse its discretion by disallowing, as too speculative, the defendant's cross-examination of the police officer concerning whether the discontinuance of the sessions might be indicative of whether the sexual assaults really occurred. *Jaramillo v. State*, 817 S.W.2d 842 (Tex. App. 1991).

Texas Rule 702 (for both civil and criminal matters) is identical to Fed. R. Evid. 702; see §11.602 for a discussion of Rule 702 and its application to new scientific and technical forms of evidence.

UTAH:

For scientific, technical, or other specialized knowledge, Utah's Rule 702 is similar to Fed. R. Evid. 702; see §11.602 for a discussion of Rule 702 and its application to new scientific and technical forms of evidence.

VERMONT:

For scientific, technical, or other specialized knowledge, Vermont's Rule 702 is similar to Fed. R. Evid. 702; see §11.602 for a discussion of Rule 702 and its application to new scientific and technical forms of evidence.

VIRGINIA:

An expert's opinion which is neither based upon facts within his knowledge nor established by other evidence is speculative and possesses no evidentiary value. *Waynesboro Police v. Coffey,* 544 S.E2d 860, 35 Va.App. 264 (2001).

WASHINGTON:

For scientific, technical, or other specialized knowledge, Washington's Rule 702 is similar to Fed. R. Evid. 702.

WEST VIRGINIA:

For scientific, technical, or other specialized knowledge, West Virginia's Rule 702 is similar to Fed. R. Evid. 702.

WISCONSIN:

For scientific, technical, or other specialized knowledge, Wisconsin's Rule 702 is similar to Fed. R. Evid. 702.

WYOMING:

For scientific, technical, or other specialized knowledge, Wyoming's Rule 702 is similar to Fed. R. Evid. 702.

Chapter 12

Vague Questions

§12.100 Introduction

Questions should be concise and comprehensible, or else they will be objectionable. They don't have to be grammatically perfect; but the question and information requested should be both clear and specific.

§12.200 Quick Explanation

Questions may not be over-broad, ambiguous, or confusing. Questions should be clearly stated, and avoid slang. They should also call for specific answers, not a speech or "story."

EXAMPLES OF VAGUE QUESTIONS:

1. What's the story on the defendant?
2. Was it colder in the factory than it was in the summer?
3. What's with you?

The first question is, by its nature, very vague; it also calls for a narrative.[1] The second question makes no sense whatsoever; and the third could mean anything.

WHAT TO LOOK FOR:

Questions that you don't thoroughly understand, or questions that call for information that is non-specific.

OBJECT AND RESPOND

OBJECTION:

"Objection. The question is vague, ambiguous, and generally makes no sense."

POTENTIAL RESPONSES TO OBJECTION:

A. (Common Option) Restate the question (To be used where objection was warranted).
B. (Aggressive Option) "Which word didn't you understand."

§12.300 General Legal Analysis

Vagueness and "confusion" of issues seem to go hand in hand quite naturally. Fed. R. Evid. 403 states that evidence may be excluded if there is a danger of "confusion of the issues, or misleading the jury."

Often, vague questions lead to vague answers, which, in turn, lead to confusion. Such was the case in *Wright v. Hartford Accident & Indemnity Co.,*[2] where Fed. R. Evid. 403 was applied. In *Wright*, a workman's compensation case, defense counsel for Hartford (the loser), was specifically warned via objection that his offering of medical testimony was too vague and confusing. On appeal, the court summarized its attitude:

> An additional reason to affirm the trial court is the confusing and misleading nature of the testimony. The question was asked in the form of a double negative and after asking counsel to repeat the question, the expert replied, "I would be doubtful."
>
> . . . .
>
> Because of the extremely complicated nature of defendant's question and ambiguous answer, the trial judge may have con-

1 See Chapter 8.

2 580 F.2d 809 (5th Cir. 1978).

cluded that the testimony should be excluded because its probative value was substantially outweighed by its danger of misleading the jury. Fed.R.Evid. 403.

The reference to the "double negative" is worth noting. Such questions all but invalidate a yes/no answer. Consider the following example:

Q. Did you not refuse the offer to purchase?
A. No.

Can you tell whether the witness refused the offer or not? Probably not. Double negatives should be avoided. Most often they will help neither the examining nor the opposing attorney. They serve to confuse everyone, and leave the attorneys guessing about what the witness really intended to say.

There are an infinite number of possible candidates for the vagueness objection. Individual circumstances will, therefore, often play a role in determining whether or not the question is sufficiently precise. For example, the question "What did you do next?" might be perfectly clear and specific, depending upon the question and answer that preceded. But if the question were asked first of a witness, it would make no sense.

Some questions, on the other hand, will never make sense, such as, "Was it warmer in the winter than it was in the country?" or, "What was the result of the conversation?" A person might take some action as the *result* of a conversation. But conversations, *per se*, don't have "results." Nevertheless, more important than dissecting the logical structure of the ambiguity, is the realization that vague questions can elicit the most unpredictable responses.

Consider our prior example ("What was the result of the conversation?"), which provided some interesting points in a matter involving an alleged case of food poisoning.[3] It raised issues of vagueness, hearsay, and the need for a quick objection trigger-finger. Examine the following portion of direct examination testimony by the defendant:

Q. Now, sometime around August 29 or 30 did you receive a telephone call from someone related to the plaintiff?
A. Yes, I did.
Q. And who was that; can you identify the person?
A. Somebody named Allen from the theater.
Q. You don't know his last name?
A. No.
Q. And what did he say to you with reference to this incident?
A. He said that Deborah (referring to plaintiff) had eaten there, the other night and she had gotten ill and he thought it was from the food.
Q. And what did you say?
A. I asked what she had eaten and where she was.
Q. And did you find out where she was?
A. Yes, she was in the Pittsfield Hospital and I....
Q. What did you do?
A. I got the name of the doctor and I called him and spoke to him.
Q. **What was the result of your conversation?**
A. Well, he said that from the tests they had done that there was no reason to believe her problem had anything to do with the food.

Plaintiff's Counsel: I object and move that be stricken.

The Court: I will let it stand. **Could have been objected to before the question was answered.**

Plaintiff's Counsel: Note my exception.

After suffering a distasteful directed verdict of no cause for action, Deborah appealed, claiming that the hearsay response could not have been anticipated from the tenor of the vague question. The higher court admitted that the question was "ambiguous," but took specific note of the manner in which the plaintiff had **failed** to object to the hearsay which preceded it. Consider the dictum:

3 *Reagan v. Brock*, 628 F.2d 721 (1st Cir. 1980).

If defendant's lawyer had asked her, "What did the doctor say to you?" the question would clearly have called for a hearsay response and plaintiff would have waived any objection to the answer if her counsel had not objected to the question. Counsel is not allowed to gamble upon the possibility of a favorable answer, but must object to the admission of evidence as soon as the ground becomes apparent.

In effect, the court provided a stern warning to those who would relax momentarily and permit vague questions to go unchallenged. The case should serve as a handy precedent for those who are admonished by the court for objecting "too soon." Often it is difficult to tell precisely when an examining lawyer has completed a question. In close calls, what should you do? If in doubt, make your OBJECTION!

§12.400 Selected State Rules and Cases

Black's Law Dictionary defines the term "vague" as meaning "Indefinite. Uncertain; not susceptible of being understood." Vague questions are *per se* improper. Therefore, it makes no difference whether such a question is presented in a federal or state court. Nor should there be a material distinction between direct and cross-examination. Vague questions should be excluded.

CALIFORNIA:

A question that is overbroad might also be considered as vague and, therefore, excludable. *Neher v. Kauffman*, 242 P. 713, 197 C. 674 (1925). Or, if a question to a witness is so indefinite that it is not possible to tell whether its answer would be material or relevant, then excluding it is not an error. *Roche v. Baldwin,* 76 P. 956, 143 C. 186 (1904).

Sentences containing disjunctive connectors ("or") are not automatically vague. The following, however, is very vague (and a bit leading): "Now, when you went to the butcher shop or slaughter house for the first time, you didn't go in?" The question was held to be too uncertain and was therefore properly excluded; there was no specific way to determine which of the two places the witness did or didn't go into. *People v. Machado*, 63 P. 66, 6 C.U. 600 (1900). The use of the "negative lead" further confuses the matter. Would a "no" answer mean "No; I didn't go in"? Or would it mean "No; you're wrong—I did go in"?

ILLINOIS:

If the evidence is so vague and conjectural that it is not helpful in proving or disproving a material issue, then the evidence is not probative. *Moore v. Swoboda*, 157 Ill. Dec. 37, 571 N.E.2d 1056, 213 Ill. App.3d 217 (1991).

MISSOURI:

In an action for alienation of affection, the trial court did not abuse its discretion in sustaining the plaintiff's objections to defendant's questioning of the plaintiff's daughter on direct examination in connection with defendant's relationship with plaintiff's wife; the questions were objected to as being "vague and speculative." The questions were very general, the trial court did not prevent defendant's line of questioning as to plaintiff's behavior towards his family, and the trial court did not communicate displeasure with defendant for having called the daughter. *Miller v. Neill,* 867 S.W.2d 523 (Mo.App.,1993).

PENNSYLVANIA:

On May 8, 1998, the Pennsylvania Supreme Court adopted a new and comprehensive set of evidence rules, with an effective date of October 1, 1998. The new rules are patterned after the Federal Rules of Evidence, both by content and number.

Pennsylvania's new Rule 403 (Exclusion of Relevant Evidence on Grounds of Prejudice, Confusion, or Waste of Time) could be used to support this particular objection. Vague questions are certainly confusing, if not prejudicial.

Chapters 13-19

Reserved for Supplementation

Chapters 13 through 19 are reserved for supplementation. Also, to maintain our decimal structure, **Part II - Documentary Evidence** was designed to start at Chapter 20.

(This page intentionally left blank.)

Part II - Documentary Evidence

TABLE OF CONTENTS

Chapter 20
Basics of Documentary Evidence

Chapter 21
Governmental Documents

Chapter 22
Private Sector Business Records

Chapter 23
Personal Documents

Chapter 24
Published Writings

Chapter 25
Legal Documents

Chapters 26-29
Reserved for Supplementation

(This page intentionally left blank.)

Chapter 20

Basics of Documentary Evidence

§20.100 Introduction

Evidence in the form of a writing or document provides one of the oldest and most important methods for establishing or attacking a case in court. In most cases, such evidence is far more reliable than oral testimony, which tends to waver unpredictably, often for truth-tellers as well as liars.

Documents are much easier to establish, assemble, and prepare than witnesses, who are inevitably slaves to their health, emotional well-being, automobiles, and other frail human dependencies. Moreover, documents, unlike live witnesses, don't change their testimony in the middle of a trial.

Once, when stones, ink, papers and typewriters were the only writing implements, it was relatively easy to define what a "document" or "writing" was, and then to formulate the appropriate rules. Today, however, things have changed dramatically. Computers, modems, lasers and photocopiers have played havoc with the once simple notion that a writing meant nothing more complex than pen on paper. Now, a single document can be constructed, simultaneously, by several people in different states and stored invisibly.[1] The finished product can't be read by unassisted human eyes, yet its microscopic embodiments still constitute a "writing."[2]

There are several ubiquitous rules that govern the admissibility and use of documentary evidence.[3] We are going to provide the most important elements for each, and summarize them. Then, before moving on to chapters dealing with specific types of writings, a generic foundation process will be presented.

§20.200 Best Evidence Rule

The best evidence rule requires that anytime the contents of a document or writing are to be established, the original document should be produced.[4] Neither oral evidence nor photocopies should be permitted to prove the contents of the original. There are, of course, many exceptions to this rule. The most notable involve official documents, for which photocopies are preferred, and lost documents, for which any

1 The use of e-mail to rapidly construct electronic documents from afar is becoming ubiquitous. See generally *B.S. ex rel Schneider v. Board of School Trustees, Fort Wayne Community Schools,* 255 F.Supp.2d 891 (N.D.Ind., 2003). And, despite its relative newness, it suffers from all of the ailments and objections that have long been endured by traditional writings. See, for example, *Tuchscher Development Enterprises, Inc. v. San Diego Unified Port District,* 132 Cal.Rptr.2d 57, 106 Cal.App.4th 1219 (2003) [Improper foundation], *Finke v. Walt Disney Co.,* 2 Cal.Rptr.3d 436, 110 Cal.App.4th 1210 (2003) [Inadmissible hearsay]; and *State ex rel. Medical Assurance of West Virginia, Inc. v. Recht,* 583 S.E.2d 80 (W.Va. 2003) [Attorney client privilege].

2 *Black's Law Dictionary* initially defined "Writing" in this limited fashion: "The expression of ideas by letters visible to the eye."

3 For most writings, formal admissibility is a critical process. See, for example *Greenfield v. Lykes Bros.,* S.S., Co., 848 So.2d 30 (2003), holding that neither the trial nor the appellate courts are permitted to consider documents that have never been properly offered, introduced, or admitted into evidence, for until such evidence is formally introduced, the opposing party has no opportunity to legally confront and challenge it. See also *Zannini v. Ameritrade Holding Corp.,* 667 N.W.2d 222, 266 Neb. 492 (2003) finding that unless an exhibit is marked, offered, and accepted, it does not become part of the record and cannot be considered as evidence in the case.

Robin Farms, Inc. v. Bartholome, 989 S.W.2d 238 (Mo.App. 1999) reflects the "multiple personality" of documentary evidence by stating that in order for a document to be received into evidence, it must meet a number of foundational requirements including: relevancy, authentication, exceptions to the Best Evidence Rule and the Hearsay Rule.

4 See Rules 1001 and 1002 of the Federal Rules of Evidence, and *Telecom Technical Services, Inc. v. Rolm Co.,* 388 F.3d 820 (11th Cir. Ga., 2004); *Tobias v. Korman,* 141 S.W.3d 468 (Mo. Ct. App., 2004); *Lipschitz v. Stein,* 781 N.Y.S.2d 773 (N.Y.A.D. 2 Dep't 2004); *Ganske v. Spence*, 129 S.W.3d 701 (Tex. App. Waco 2004).

See also §2.100.

kind of evidence might be permitted, depending upon the circumstances.

As a matter of fact, photocopies, in general, are as admissible as originals unless there is a dispute concerning the original writing.[5] Once a genuine issue concerning the original is raised, the original should be produced.[6] If, however, after a diligent search, it has been determined that the original has either been lost or destroyed, then secondary evidence should be permitted.[7] Where, however, the contents of the writing are not in issue, the Best Evidence Rule should not apply.[8] Documents or writings can assume a variety of forms. They can be carved in stone, written on paper, magnetized as binary bits on a floppy disk, or stored optically. The Federal Rules of Evidence draw no distinction between writings and documents. Classically, the subtle distinction hinged on permanency. Anything intended to "last," however long or short, would comprise a "document." Most writings, excepting perhaps skywriting and letters in the sand, would seem to qualify.

---

5 *Bank of America v. David W. Hubert, P.C.,* 62 P.3d 904, Wash.App. (2003). In an action by a bank to recover sums lost during a check kiting scheme, the trial court did not abuse its discretion by admitting a duplicate of an original card and agreement pertaining to the subject bank account, even though the photocopy was not crystal clear. Moreover, duplicates are admissible under the applicable rules of evidence.

Cadle Co. v. Errato, 802 A.2d 887, 71 Conn.App. 447 (2002). In general, the best evidence rule requires a party to produce an original writing, if available, whenever the terms of that writing are material and must be proved. Where, however, the terms of the document are not in actual dispute, it is both inconvenient and pedantic to insist upon the production of the original instrument itself.

See Rule 1002 of Federal Rules of Evidence, which states: "A duplicate is admissible to the same extent as an original unless (1) a genuine question is raised as to the authenticity of the original or (2) in the circumstances it would be unfair to admit the duplicate in lieu of the original." See also §2.300. *U.S. v. Szehinskyj,* 104 F.Supp.2d 480 (E.D.Pa. 2000). With respect to denaturalization proceedings against purported Nazi camp guard, original official documents were more than fifty years old, in extremely delicate condition, and held in various nation's archives; thus, absent a genuine challenge to their authenticity, the Best Evidence Rule did not preclude admission of copies. See also *Iberia Building Systems, Inc. v. Bank One,* 768 So.2d 106 (La. App., 2000); *Jacobs v. Yates,* 27 S.W.3d 734 (Ark. 2000); *Simons v. Simons,* 11 P.3d 20 (Idaho 2000). *Braut v. Tarabochia,* 17 P.3d 1248, 104 Wash.App. 728 (2001). In mortgage foreclosure action, photocopy of promissory note was admissible under best evidence rule, even though note holder could not remember details surrounding alleged loan. Moreover, decision to admit or exclude photocopies is left to sound discretion of trial court.

6 *Kroh v. Kroh,* 567 S.E.2d 760 (N.C.App., 2002) involved your everyday, run of the mill, marital bestiality charge, which in this case, resulted in a slander lawsuit by the husband against the wife who leveled the charge. Reports containing notes of veterinarians were both hearsay and were irrelevant. They were allegedly offered to show the wife's state of mind after reading them. The wife was required to produce the original veterinary reports and properly authenticate them, after the husband challenged copies of the report.

Bell Atlantic Yellow Pages v. Havana Rio Enterprises, Inc., 710 N.Y.S.2d 751 (2000). Where existence or contents of a document, or any of its signatures are in dispute, the Best Evidence Rule requires production of original document to protect against perjury, fraud, inaccuracies, or mistakes caused by copying.

7 *Smith v. Buckley,* 753 N.Y.S.2d 581, N.Y.A.D. 3 Dept. (2003). A fire at a courthouse resulted in the loss of official documents, which the court clerk had a duty to keep; the use of secondary evidence should, therefore, be allowed. *Hoerner v. ANCO Insulations, Inc.,* 812 So.2d 45 (La.App., 2002); *In re Wallace & Gale Co.*, 275 B.R. 223 (D.Md. 2002); *Wagman v. Bradshaw*, 739 N.Y.S.2d 421 (N.Y.A.D., 2002).

8 *Luebbert v. Simmons,* 98 S.W.3d 72 (Mo.App., 2003). The "Best Evidence Rule" states that where the terms of a writing are material, the original must be produced unless it shown to be unavailable for some reason other than the fault of the proponent; but the rule only applies where the terms of the writing are in dispute. *Forester v. Director of Internal Revenue*, 85 S.W.3d 122 (Mo.App., 2002). The Best Evidence Rule only applies where the terms or contents of the writing itself are in dispute. See also *Cadle Co. v. Errato,* 802 A.2d 887, 71 Conn.App. 447 (2002).

Presumably, for the purposes of applying the best evidence rule, Fed. R. Evid. 1001 includes within its definition of "writing," all forms of photography, recordings, computer storage, X-rays, videotapes and film. The best evidence rule then requires that the contents of a writing be established by presenting the original in court, not by oral testimony.[9]

The federal definition seems to create gross confusion with respect to demonstrative evidence. It might help clarify this apparent overlap by remembering that the federal rule's focus seems to be media that was **not** created for demonstrative purposes. Rule 1001 was not very artfully drafted, and apparently does not mean what it says, as attested by the *Advisory Committee Notes*:

> The assumption should not be made that the rule will come into operation on every occasion when use is made of a photograph in evidence. On the contrary, the rule will seldom apply to ordinary photographs.

Instead of using the term "ordinary," which is undefined, the rule's drafters should have used a few extra words to distinguish and exclude all evidence intended to be used for demonstrative purposes.

§20.300 Parol Evidence Rule

The Parol Evidence Rule is a very close relative of the best evidence rule. It applies only to contracts.[10]

§20.400 Completeness Rule

The so-called Completeness Rule suggests that where any party enters a portion of a document into evidence, any other party should then be permitted to enter any other portion that is relevant, or that may explain or modify the previously offered portion. It is not intended as an exclusionary rule.[11] The principle has also been referred to as "The Rule of Completeness" and "Opening the Door." Its purpose is to avoid misleading the trier of fact by offering bits and pieces of writings that are "taken out of context." Fed. R. Evid. 106 provides as follows:

> When a writing or recorded statement or part thereof is introduced by a party, an adverse party may require the introduction at that time of any other part... which ought in fairness to be considered contemporaneously.

---

9 The best evidence rule is set forth in Fed. R. Evid. 1002 (See Chapter 2). *Baltimore Harbor Charters, Ltd. v. Ayd*, 759 A.2d 1091, 134 Md.App. 188 (2000). In accordance with Best Evidence Rule, if the contents of a writing are at issue, unless original writing is produced, or unless its absence is satisfactorily explained, trial court must exclude any other evidence of its contents.

10 See §2.400.

11 *Taylor Pipeline Construction v. Directional Road Boring, Inc.*, 438 F.Supp.2d 696 (E.D.Texas, 2006). A portion of an e-mail submitted in a plaintiff's exhibit would not be excluded upon the defendant's objection based on the completeness rule, where the defendant did not attempt to introduce any missing pages required for the sake of fairness.

If one party to litigation places a portion of a document or item of correspondence, which is detrimental to the opposing party, in evidence, then the latter should be permitted to introduce the balance of the writing, but only to the extent necessary to rebut or explain the adverse inferences which might arise from the fragmentary or incomplete character of the evidence.[12]

REFERENCES

Requirement under Rule 106 that when writing or recorded statement or part thereof is introduced in evidence, another part or another writing or recorded statement must also be introduced into evidence. 75 ALR Fed 892.

§20.500 Hearsay Rule

Documents are just as much subject to the hearsay rule as oral testimony. Thus, if a document is offered into evidence for the purpose of proving the truth of its contents, it is no less hearsay than if it were orally presented.

As is the case with oral hearsay, statements that are used for some purpose *other* than to prove the truth of the contents are not hearsay.[13] For example, a statement would not be considered as hearsay if it were used to show notice,[14] or a person's state of mind.[15]

The difference lies in the number of exceptions that apply only to writings.[16] It is interesting to note that these so-called exceptions seem to propel certain items well past the hurdle created by the hearsay rule and even past some foundation obstacles that would otherwise trap relevant oral testimony that did not concern hearsay. The power of the exceptions seems to reflect the respect that is generally accorded documentary evidence.

§20.501 Multiple Hearsay

Documents which are offered to prove the truth of matters asserted in them are hearsay and must fall within a recognized exception to the

12 *In re A.W. Lawrence & Co., Inc.,* 289 B.R. 20 (N.D.N.Y., 2003). Under the completeness doctrine, the omitted portion of a writing or recorded statement must be placed in evidence where it is necessary to explain the admitted portion or place it in a proper context; the purpose of the rule is to avoid misleading the jury and to ensure a fair and impartial understanding of the previously admitted portion. *Benson v. Honda Motor Co., Ltd.*, 32 Cal.Rptr.2d 322, 26 C.A.4th 1337 (Cal.App. 2 Dist. 1994); *U.S. v. Corrigan*, 168 F.2d 641 (C.C.N.Y. 1948); see also *Camps v. N.Y. City Transit Authority*, 261 F.2d 320 (2d. Cir. N.Y. 1958).

13 *Taylor v. Abernethy*, 620 S.E.2d 242 (N.C.App., 2005). An out-of-court statement or document is inadmissible hearsay when offered to prove the truth of the matters contained in the document. Statements offered for other purposes are not considered as hearsay.

14 See generally, Chapter 5. *Noah v. GMC*, 882 So.2d 235 (Miss. Ct. App., 2004). In a products liability action against an auto manufacturer and dealership arising from an automotive brake failure, reports of prior incidents of brake failure were not hearsay; the statements contained within the reports were not being offered to prove the truth of matters asserted, but they were offered to show that the auto manufacturer was aware that the reports had been made.

15 *Cary Oil Co., Inc. v. MG Refining & Marketing, Inc.,* 257 F.Supp.2d 751 (S.D.N.Y. 2003). Statements and records offered for their effect on party's state of mind are not considered as hearsay.

16 For an attempt to use a "shopping list" of exceptions, all unsuccessful, see *Current v. Perry*, 178 Fed.Appx. 686 (9th Cir., Cal., 2006). The case involved an employee's action alleging discriminatory retaliation under Title VII; the District Court was held to have been within its discretion in excluding a written declaration as inadmissible hearsay, where the employee failed to demonstrate that the exception for past recollection recorded was applicable in the absence of the declarant's acknowledgment that she either made or adopted the declaration. The residual hearsay exception was also inapplicable because the declaration lacked circumstantial guarantees of trustworthiness. In addition, the statement was not an excited utterance because it lacked the requisite startling event; and lastly, it was not a present sense impression because it did not describe an event occurring at the time that the statement was issued.

For a more comprehensive list and discussion of the hearsay exceptions, see *supra*, §5.400.

Hearsay Rule to be admissible. But often, writings falling within such an exception may themselves contain additional hearsay (from other sources) within their borders. Whenever this happens, in order to be admissible, such multiple hearsay must have an exception at each level.[17]

§20.600 Remaining Chapters in This Part

The following chapters in this part are designed for the practitioner who has a specific document in mind and does not want to consider unrelated general principles. It is intended to provide some fast answers to the three most important questions where Documentary Evidence is concerned, and when **relevance is presumed**: (1) Is it admissible or useable as evidence during trial? (2) If so, how do I get it admitted, or (3) How do I oppose it?

We do not pretend that the list is all-inclusive. However, it should cover the most commonly used documents that surface during the course of litigation. To accelerate access, we have listed the documents alphabetically by their most common names, within each of our five groups:

Governmental Documents (Chapter 21)
Private Sector Business Records (Chapter 22)
Personal Documents (Chapter 23)
Published Writings (Chapter 24)
Legal Documents (Chapter 25)

The groups were constructed with a special mission in mind. In particular, the documents within each group share some very important characteristics that are often obscured or misunderstood as a result of the definitions found in most treatises. Many texts, for example, would lump together all documents kept "in the ordinary course of business," without drawing any finer distinctions.

An "accident report" issued and kept in the ordinary course of business by a police department would not have equal evidentiary status as the report prepared by a Kroger supermarket employee after some lady fell and broke her head in aisle three. Nor would either of those reports be treated in the same fashion as an accident report kept in a regularly maintained personal diary. With our new group structure in mind, here is an outline of the topics to come:

- Chapter 21: **Governmental Documents** coincide with what are commonly referred to as "Official Records." Such documents, by their nature, are often kept in the ordinary course of business.

---

17 *Davis v. Town of Pualsboro*, 421 F.Supp.2d 835 (D.N.J., 2006) involved an excessive force action by the parent of an arrestee, who brought federal civil rights claims against a county, township, and various law enforcement officers, arising from arrestee's death (which occurred after he had been struck in head by a bottle during a fight and then taken into police custody). With respect to the defendants' motion for summary judgment, reports prepared by a county detective stating that the arrestee's girlfriend and another person told him that law enforcement officers punched the arrestee, constituted inadmissible double hearsay.

Birt v. Firstenergy Corp., 891 A.2d 1281 (Pa.Super, 2006). In a construction worker's negligence action against a utility company arising out of a construction accident and resulting electrical burns, an incident report filed by the electric utility's employee was inadmissible under the business records exception to the hearsay rule; the worker made no attempt to acknowledge that the report included a hearsay statement by another worker who indicated that he believed that the power lines were not "live," and the worker made no attempt to provide a basis for admitting that hearsay statement. Merely characterizing a document as a business record is insufficient to justify its admission; moreover, a business record which contains multiple levels of hearsay is admissible only if each level falls within a recognized exception to the hearsay rule.

Nissan Motor Co. Ltd. v. Armstrong, 145 S.W.3d 131 (Tex., 2004) involved a products liability action against an automobile manufacturer that resulted from an accident that allegedly arose from a defective throttle mechanism. Consumer complaints received by the defendant manufacturer alleged that an unintended acceleration of its vehicles had occurred (Level 1 Hearsay); those complaints were then compiled by the government into a database (Level 2 Hearsay). The complaints were inadmissible because the database consisted of double hearsay.

- Chapter 22: **Private Sector Business Records** encompass writings kept in the ordinary course of business, but this chapter's title is broader so as to include those writings generated by a business that might be considered as extraordinary, and narrower, in that governmental and official documents are excluded.
- Chapter 23: **Personal Documents** cover miscellaneous documents not covered by the other groups. Notes, diaries, and letters are the most common examples.
- Chapter 24: **Published Writings** are somewhat self-explanatory; they were designed to be read by the general public, or some significant segment thereof.
- Chapter 25: **Legal Documents** cover those writings most often prepared by lawyers specifically for pending litigation or with a lawsuit in mind; they do not include exhibits or attachments consisting of writings from the other chapters.

§20.700 Generic Foundation for Admissibility of Documents

Whereas "knowledge" provides a one-word foundation requirement for oral testimony, "authenticity" might be considered as the key element for documentary evidence. With the understanding that more definite foundations may be required for certain specific documents, here is a general foundation blueprint:

Q. (By Proponent's Attorney) State your name for the record.

A. (Witness) My name is _______.

Q. (Proponent) [Questions are asked pertaining to the writing for background purposes only, not for proving contents].

(Tendering the writing to the court reporter if it has not already been marked) I'll ask that this writing be marked as ______'s Exhibit (number) ____ .

Q. (Addressing the Witness) Can you identify this exhibit that has just been marked?

A. Yes; it is _________ [Brief but specific description].

Q. (Tendering the writing to opposing counsel, who should be provided with a copy if requested, while facing the judge) I'll ask that ______'s Exhibit ____, which I have just handed to opposing counsel, be entered into evidence.

COURT: Any objections?

OPPOSING COUNSEL: None.

COURT: Very well, I'll receive ______'s Exhibit (number) ___.

Notice the lack of fanfare in the above foundation. The identification process was simple and direct. If there are special problems, they may be raised by the opposition, in which case the proponent will be provided with an opportunity to establish a more thorough foundation. But, as a proponent, there is no point in looking for trouble or red flagging potential problems.

From the opponent's point of view, the qualification process can be used as a method for attacking the document and everything that the proponent would have it stand for, depending upon the skill of the attack. A request by the opponent to "voir dire" the witness can lead to a preemptive strike long before that opponent is otherwise entitled to cross-examine the witness.

(This page intentionally left blank.)

Chapter 21

Governmental Documents

§21.100 Introduction

Our classification scheme for "governmental documents" includes any writing or document created by, or for, some governmental entity, whether federal, state or local. The witness establishing the foundation for this type of evidence will often be a law enforcement officer or other public official.

The writings covered by this chapter are among the easiest to admit.[1] Thus, the biggest danger, from the proponent's perspective, is that of laziness. For, admissibility is by no means automatic.[2] A foundation must be established. And above all, the proponent should remember that admissibility may be limited or qualified as it is granted.

Remember, not every writing created by a governmental agent or agency is admissible. For a document to qualify as an official document so as to be admissible, it must have been generated pursuant to some law or statute requiring that it be maintained, and, also, it must have been generated by a person authorized or required to do so.[3]

There are no general rules governing letters, notes, memos and enclosures that might accompany an official or governmental document. Such writings may, however, serve either to support or cast suspicion upon the primary governmental document.[4]

The general strategy for the proponent will be to "avoid a fuss." Keep the foundation process so simple and "matter of fact" that there is nothing to attack. If a deficiency in the foundation is raised by the enemy, then go back and fill in the missing bricks.

REFERENCES

Admissibility of tape recording or transcript of 911 emergency call. 3 A.L.R. 5th 784.

Police reports, admissibility under Federal Business Records Act (Fed. R. Evid. 803). 31 A.L.R. Fed. 457.

---

1 *Gross v. King David Bistro, Inc.*, 84 F.Supp.2d 675 (D.Md. 2000). Admissibility of government reports under official documents hearsay exception is assumed because of general reliability of public agencies in conducting their investigations and absence of a motive other than informing the public; thus, the party opposing admission bears burden of showing that report is unreliable. *Lorillard Tobacco Co. v. Reilly*, 84 F.Supp.2d 180 (D.Mass. 2000). Generally, government reports are admissible as government documents.

2 *Larsen v. Decker*, 995 P.2d 281 (Ariz.App. 2000). In action seeking damages for injuries sustained in auto accident, trial court did not abuse its discretion by refusing to admit (under hearsay exception for public records and reports) a Social Security Administration report finding that plaintiff was permanently disabled after subject accident; report was not sufficiently reliable. Plaintiff was apparently sole source of information provided to Agency and no medical expert ever appeared or was cross-examined in Agency proceeding. Moreover, even though generally opinions and conclusions are within scope of hearsay exception for public records and reports, whether or not they are sufficiently reliable is for trial court's discretion. *Claussen v. State, Department of Transportation*, 750 So.2d 79 (Fla.App. 1999). Correspondence sent to Department of Transportation was not admissible under public records exception to hearsay rule because it was based upon information supplied by a source outside of that public agency.

3 *Volkswagen of America, Inc. v. Gentry*, 564 S.E.2d 733, 254 Ga.App. 888 (Ga.App., 2002). In a wrongful death action against an automobile manufacturer, a letter written by the director of the National Highway Traffic Safety Administration was inadmissible hearsay; the manufacturer failed to explain how or why the letter fell into any exception covering documents from a legal investigation.

Robinson v. Avis Rent A Car System, Inc., 22 P.3d 818 (Wash.App., 2001). In action charging defendant Avis with unfair and deceptive trade practices, report issued by National Association of Attorneys General was hearsay and thus not admissible to show that specific conduct of defendant was unfair or deceptive.

4 *Riggs National Corporation & Subsidiaries v. C.I.R.*, 295 F.3d 16 (D.C.Cir., 2002). Inaccuracies in documents that accompany official government records do not automatically rebut the presumption of regularity that would normally attach those official records, especially where the accompanying documents do not directly address the matters that are intended to be proved by the official records.

§21.200 Basic Foundation for Governmental Documents

Q. (By Proponent's Attorney) State your name for the record.
A. (Witness) My name is Nick Trickson.
Q. State your title and occupation.
A. I'm a governmental employee; I work for the National Graft Foundation. I'm a records clerk.
Q. (Tendering the writing to the witness) I'll show you plaintiff's Exhibit 1, *which purports to be*[5] an "Annual Graft Report," and ask if you can identify it?
A. Yup. It's one of our annuals all right; from 1990.
Q. As a records clerk, is it part of your normal duties to keep and maintain such records?
A. Yes.
Q. Was plaintiff's Exhibit 1 kept in the ordinary course of business pursuant to the rules and laws of your agency?
A. Yes.
Q. (Tendering the writing to opposing counsel, who should be provided with a copy if requested) I'll ask that plaintiff's Exhibit 1, which I have just handed to opposing counsel, be entered into evidence as an official document.
COURT: Any objections?
OPPOSING COUNSEL: None.
COURT: Very well, I'll receive plaintiff's Exhibit 1.

As suggested by the above testimony, it is normally not required that the actual signer of the document be present. A mere custodian can act as the foundation witness.

In the event that the admissibility of your document is challenged, keep two things in mind: first, "trustworthiness" is generally the key that turns the admissibility lock; second, the burden of establishing a lack of trustworthiness is upon the opponent who seeks to strike public or official documents.[6]

§21.300 Opposition Checklist

Opposing counsel may wish to attack the preceding foundation as being over-simplistic. But even though Nick Trickson was not the creator or signer of the writing, it will nevertheless be admitted unless some specific ground for opposition is stated. That, of course, makes the official records exception to the hearsay rule much more than a mere exception to an exclusionary rule. It paves the way for admissibility by a person who had little or no contact with the events that are addressed in the writing.

Official documents are, indeed, powerful. They are not only "official" but are also kept in the "ordinary course of business," giving them a double punch. But they are by no means impregnable. And above all, remember that merely because an official report is admitted into evidence pursuant to applicable rules, it does not follow that every statement contained therein is also admissible.[7] The greatest likelihood of a successful attack will come from one of the following claims:

---

5 If you are going to name or identify the document for the record, always use the italicized term. This will avert an objection that the witness is being led.

6 *Amtrust, Inc. v. Larson,* 388 F.3d 594 (8th Cir. Minn., 2004). The rule governing the admissibility of public records assumes that the writings are admissible abinitio, but with ample provision for escape if sufficient negative factors are present. The burden of showing that an official report is untrustworthy, therefore, falls upon the party opposing admission.

City of Bangor v. Citizens Communications Co., 339 F.Supp.2d 135 (D.Me., 2004). In a lawsuit seeking to impose liability on a corporation for its alleged river pollution, the defending corporation bore the burden of demonstrating the untrustworthiness of a governmental agency's report setting forth the findings of an investigation conducted pursuant to a state statute.

See also *Barlow v. Connecticut,* 319 F.Supp.2d 250 (D. Conn., 2004).

7 *D'Alessandro v. Pa. State Police,* 878 A.2d 133 (Pa.Super., 2005). See also §21.300 et seq.

OPPOSITION CHECKLIST

1. The document contains unreliable statements by investigators or persons who did not witness the subject event.[8]
2. The report contains unsubstantiated conclusions instead of facts.[9]
3. The report is untrustworthy.[10]
4. The writing is a forgery or it has been altered.
5. The document is inadmissible due to a statutory exclusion.[11]

---

8 *Young v. Time Warner Cable Capital*, 443 F.Supp.2d 1109 (W.D.Mo., 2006). In a technician's discrimination action against his employer, an Equal Employment Opportunity Commission (EEOC) investigator's interview notes do not constitute "factual findings" subject to a hearsay exception for records from an investigation made pursuant to authority granted by law, or "administrative findings" under the public records exception to the hearsay rule. *Reichenberg v. Davis,* 846 So.2d 1233 (Fla.App., 2003). In a custody modification hearing, the reports of the Department of Children and Families, which contained witness interviews wherein allegations were made that the subject child had been the victim of "sexual touching" by the mother's stepdaughter, were not admissible under the business records exception to the hearsay rule, nor were they admissible under the public records exception to the hearsay rule; the authors of the reports simply related the substance of what other witnesses had told the authors. See *infra*, §21.401.

9 See *infra*, §21.401. See *Pilgrim's Pride Corp. v. Smoak,* 134 S.W.3d 880 (Tex. App. Texarkana 2004) holding that an investigating officer's conclusions pertaining to the causation of a motor vehicle accident as contained in the officer's official police report were not admissible under the public records exception to the hearsay rule; the officer's skill and experience in accident reconstruction were insufficient to permit him to render an expert opinion.

10 *Carignan v. Wheeler*, 898 A.2d 1011, 153 N.H. 465 (2006) involved a negligence action by a motorcycle passenger against a motorist, an auto racetrack owner, and a driver of a motorcycle after sustaining injuries from an accident that occurred adjacent to racetrack grounds. A police officer's accident report, which contained a conclusion of fault, lacked trustworthiness and thus was not admissible under the public records exception of the hearsay rule even though the report was timely and was made without any improper motive. The officer had not learned any accident reconstruction skills, aside from using triangulation, which did not determine what or who caused the accident. The conclusion of fault was formed from witness statements. Moreover, although there was no requirement under the hearsay rule's public records exception that a police officer who prepares an accident report be an expert in accident reconstruction, nevertheless, the officer's limited training and experience could be considered as factors when evaluating the trustworthiness of the officer's findings in order to determine whether or not the report should be admitted. Thus, the accident report was excludable because it lacked trustworthiness.

Blake v. Pellegrino, 329 F.3d 43 (1st Cir., Mass., 2003). The term "trustworthiness," as used in the context of a public document takes into account matters such as self-authentication, contemporaneousness, and the skill and experience of the authenticating individual.

Rodriguez v. City of Houston, 250 F.Supp.2d 691 (S.D.Texas, 2003). In a Title VII action by a female police officer against the city of Houston, a report was issued by the police department's Internal Affairs Division regarding an investigation into the plaintiff's complaint that a male superior was sexually harassing her; the report was deemed to contain factual findings resulting from an investigation made pursuant to law, and was thus admissible against the city, under the public records exception to the hearsay rule. There was no evidence that the sources of the information contained in the report lacked trustworthiness. *Coleman v. Home Depot, Inc.*, 306 F.3d 1333 (3rd Cir., N.J., 2002). For purposes of determining whether or not a public record or report is too untrustworthy to qualify as a hearsay exception, the court may consider the political bias of the institution that prepared it, and whether or not the report was consistent with that bias.

See *Frank Shop, Inc. v. Crown Cent. Petroleum Corp,* 540 S.E.2d 897 (Va. 2001). See also *infra*, §21.401.

11 *Department of Transportation v. Taylor*, 841 A.2d 108 (2004). In a prosecution for vehicular homicide, involuntary manslaughter, and driving under the influence of alcohol, a defendant driver's due process rights were not violated by applying the absolute statutory privilege which states that in-depth accident investigations and safety studies (and the information, records, and reports used in their preparation) are not discoverable or admissible as evidence.

6. The writing or report contains disclaimers of its own accuracy.[12]
7. The document is incomplete or unintelligible.[13]

The preceding attacks on the document's authenticity and/or credibility must be backed up by specific facts or evidence.

REFERENCES

Availability of record maker for cross-examination as defeating objection to admission based on untrustworthiness. 34 Am. Jur. Proof of Facts 2d 509.

§21.400 Specific Documents

§21.401 Accident Reports

***ARE THEY ADMISSIBLE? CIVIL CASES:* YES; *CRIMINAL CASES*: NO.**

KEY POINTS FOR PROPONENT:

As with most governmental documents, the two most powerful foundation tools will normally apply. First, the writing will constitute an "**official document**" and secondly, the fact that it was "official" will imply that it was kept "**in the ordinary course of business.**" Both are recognized exceptions to the hearsay rule in every jurisdiction. And both terms may be used for your foundation.

Accident reports are not automatically admissible; there is a foundation to lay for contested matters. In particular, the proponent should be prepared to show that the report was authorized or required by law, and that its contents are trustworthy.[14] Statements of fact con-

---

12 *Miriam Osborn Mem. Home Assn. v. Assessor of City of Rye*, 800 N.Y.S.2d 909 (2005). In tax sale litigation, an electronic print-out of data regarding real estate sales, compiled by the New York State Office of Real Property Services was not admissible under the statutory public records exception to the hearsay rule. The compilation was not in the form of a certificate or affidavit of a public officer, and numerous disclaimers of accuracy precluded the necessary finding that the print-out was reliable.

13 *Figueroa v. U.S. Postal Service*, 422 F.Supp.2d 866 (N.D. Ohio, 2006). In an action by a female U.S. Postal Service employee alleging age discrimination and other tortious workplace misconduct on the part of her supervisors, a document which purported to be a letter from the Equal Employment Opportunity Commission (EEOC) to the Postal Service regarding a notice of intent to file an age discrimination action lacked credibility and authenticity for purposes of showing that the employee exhausted her administrative remedies; the document contained only the first page of a two-page document and no signature, and there was no way to determine if it was a true copy of the original.

14 *Apodaca v. AAA Gas Co.,* 73 P.3d 215, 134 N.M. 77 (2003). In a personal injury action, the trial court did not abuse its discretion when it determined that a report of an Occupational Safety and Health Administration (OSHA) investigator (concerning an interview with one of the plaintiffs) was sufficiently trustworthy for the jury to consider, despite an inability to verify the accuracy of the contents. See also *Coleman v. Home Depot, Inc.*, 306 F.3d 1333 (3rd Cir., N.J., 2002).

McRae v. Echols, 8 S.W.3d 797 (Tex.App. 2000). In personal injury action resulting from collision between automobile and forklift, police officer's conclusions and opinions in his accident report as to cause of accident were based on his factual investigation of accident and, thus, were admissible, along with remainder of report, under public records exception to hearsay rule, absent any evidence showing a lack of trustworthiness of report. In order to make such a showing, an appropriate custodian may be required. See, for example, *Phipps v. Skyview Farms, Inc.*, 610 N.W.2d

723, 259 Neb. 492 (Neb. 2000), a breach of lease action, where owner of truck leasing company, who had no personal knowledge of information contained in OSHA document or police report relating to accident in which truck driver was injured, was not custodian, and, thus, could not establish proper foundation for admitting those

(Footnote 13 continued on page 21-5.)

tained within accident reports may require their own independent hearsay exceptions.[15]

KEY POINTS FOR OPPOSITION:

It is critical to keep in mind that even though the report itself may be admissible, it does not follow that all of the **statements**, **opinions**, and **conclusions** will also be admitted; in most cases, they will not be admitted.[16] This means that the personal observations, measurements, and other so-called "facts" gathered by the investigating officer will be allowed. But hearsay from witnesses will not.[17] Nor should the opinions of the investigating officer be admitted where he or she did not personally observe the accident.[18]

---

14 (Continued from page 21-6.) documents. *Hurd 5. U.S.*, 134 F.Supp.2d 745 (D.S.C. 2001). National Transportation Safety Board report containing testimony of Coast Guard personnel regarding boating accident was trustworthy and fell within public records exception to hearsay rule. See *Hadox v. Martin,* 544 S.E.2d 395 (W.Va. 2001), declaring that under official records exception to hearsay rule, contents of public report, record or document are exception to hearsay rule and are assumed to be trustworthy, unless opponent of report establishes that it was sufficiently untrustworthy. See also *infra*, §21.413.

15 See §5.400. *Newton v. Ryder Transportation Services*, 206 F.3d 772 (8th Cir. Ark. 2000). In negligence action by truck driver against truck lessor, police officer's accident report was admissible under hearsay exception for past recorded recollections notwithstanding fact that source of information in report was unknown; officer was experienced highway patrol officer and routinely prepared such reports, he acknowledged that he prepared and signed report on day of accident, that it was accurate to best of his knowledge, and that information in it could have come only from driver.

16 *Shephard v. Scheeler*, 674 So.2d 1135 (La. App. 4 Cir. 1996); *Luke v. Spicer,* 194 Ga. App. 183, 390 S.E.2d 267 (1990); *Frias v. Valle*, 698 P.2d 875 (Nev. 1985); *Ryan v. Campbell "66" Express, Inc.*, 304 S.W.2d 825 (Mo. 1957). *Smalls v. South Carolina Department of Education*, 528 S.E.2d 682, 339 S.C. 208 (S.C.App. 2000) involved fatal collision between truck and pedestrian that resulted in wrongful death and survival action. Investigating officer's accident scene sketch, showing debris resulting from collision, was properly excluded from evidence, despite claim that it showed that driver crossed center line and struck victim in opposite lane of travel. *Dennis v. Capital Dist. Transportation Authority*, 711 N.Y.S.2d 836 (2000) involved personal injury action brought on behalf of bicyclist to recover for her injuries. In absence of any evidence that investigating officer witnessed accident or was otherwise qualified to render opinion as to its cause, notation on officer's report referring to "bicyclist error" was inadmissible hearsay. *Pilgrim's Pride Corp. v. Smoak,* 134 S.W.3d 880 (Tex. App. Texarkana 2004). In a negligence action brought by an injured motorist against a truck driver and the driver's employer, an investigating officer's conclusions pertaining to the causation of the accident as contained in the officer's official police report were not admissible under the public records exception to the hearsay rule; the officer's skill and experience in accident reconstruction were insufficient to permit him to render an expert opinion with respect to negligence. Moreover, the trial court had an obligation under those circumstances to exclude the report or those portions thereof that the court deemed untrustworthy.

17 *Rivera v. City of New York,* 741 N.Y.S.2d 30 (N.Y.A.D., 2002). In a personal injury action against the city of New York by a child who was injured during a fall on school property, statements in a police report attributed to the father, suggesting that the child was hit with a rock, were inadmissible. The statements were not based on personal knowledge and the father was under no duty to make them.

Conners v. Duck's Cesspool Service, Ltd., 533 N.Y.S.2d 942 (1988); *Peerless Insurance Co., v. Milloul,* 527 N.Y.S.2d 838 (App. Div. 1988); *MacLean v. San Francisco*, 151 Cal. App. 2d 133, 311 P.2d 158 (1957).

18 For a triple hearsay scenario, see *Jones v. Marcum*, 197 F.Supp.2d 991 (S.D. Ohio, 2002). A statement in a police report indicating that an arena security guard participated in the alleged assault of an unauthorized concert attendee did not fall within the hearsay exception for public records and reports; the officer who prepared the report did not observe the guard at the scene of the alleged assault, but rather obtained his information from another officer, who obtained that information from yet other arena employees.

Shephard v. Scheeler, 674 So.2d 1135 (La. App. 4 Cir. 1996); *Hagicostas v. National Freight Sales, Inc.*, 641 N.Y.S.2d 365 (N.Y.A.D. 2 Dept. 1996); *Battista v. Rizzi,* 644 N.Y.S.2d 332 (N.Y.A.D. 2 Dept. 1996). See also *Maiden v. Rozwood,* 597 N.W.2d 817, 461 Mich. 109 (1999). *Figueroa v. Luna,* 721 N.Y.S.2d 635 (N.YA.D., 2001). Police accident report made by police officer, who was not eyewitness, containing hearsay statements regarding ultimate issues of fact may not be admitted into evidence for purpose of establishing cause of subject accident.

Witness statements taken by the officer and recorded in his or her report would become a form of double hearsay.[19] For example, the oral statement by one of the drivers to a police officer ("That idiot in the Edsel ran the red light.") would be hearsay. When the officer records the statement in his or her report, it becomes double hearsay or "hearsay within hearsay." The official report exception will forgive the second occurrence but not the first. So the statement will be excluded even though the report will not. However, as previously suggested, if a separate independent hearsay exception exists for the "first occurrence," the statement may be admissible.

Let's change the facts a little. Assume that the declarant said, "I'm the one who ran the red light, not the idiot in the Edsel." Then **both** occurrences of hearsay would have an exception because **admissions** are also excepted.[20] Thus, both the report and the statement would be admitted into evidence.[21]

Another consideration for the opponent involves the initial question as to whether or not the report truly falls within the scope of an "official document." In that regard, a red flag should go up whenever the subject documents were prepared by non-governmental entities. For example, accident summaries, which were not prepared by the National Highway Traffic Safety Administration (NHTSA), but were rather prepared by an automobile manufacturer regarding accidents involving a specific model and did not come within the public records exception. They were not prepared by a public official who was required to record the information pursuant to a duty imposed by law.[22]

§21.401(a) Aircraft Accident Reports

ARE THEY ADMISSIBLE?
YES (QUALIFIED).

KEY POINTS:

See generally, "Accident Reports" (*supra*). In order to use an official report to establish negligence, the proponent should be prepared to show that it is trustworthy, and that it was issued pursuant to law. The trustworthiness factor is one that overpowers prior distinctions between facts and opinions.[23] But that distinction is not entirely extinct.[24] Be aware of the possible existence of a statute precluding its use as evidence. And, as indicated above, parts of

19 *Jacobs v. City of Neches*, 7 F. Supp. 2d 829 (Tex. 1998); *Flores v. Pharmakitis*, 618 N.Y.S.2d 293 (N.Y.A.D. 1 Dept. 1994); *Kratz v. Exxon Corp.*, 890 S.W.2d 899 (Tex. App.El Paso 1994).

20 See §5.404.

21 Fed. R. Evid. 805 provides that "hearsay included within hearsay is not excluded if each part of the combined statements conforms with an exception..." See also Chapter 5.

22 *Kroeger v. Ford Motor Co.*, 527 N.W.2d 178, 247 Neb. 323 (Neb. 1995).

23 *Beech Aircraft Corp. v. Rainey*, 488 U.S. 153, 109 S. Ct. 439, 102 L. Ed. 2d 444 (1988), *reversing* 784 F.2d 1523 (11th Cir. 1986). Consider also *Van Steemburg v. General Aviation, Inc.*, 183 Ill. Dec. 496, 611 N.E.2d 1144, 243 Ill. App. 3d 299 (Ill. App. 1 Dist. 1993), a wrongful death action, involving a statement by the air traffic controller to a pilot (who died in the air crash), that there was "heavy ice all over the area." The statement was admissible as a business record since the plaintiffs failed to show a lack of trustworthiness; the "double hearsay" aspect of the evidence affected its weight, not admissibility.

24 *Rainey (supra)*, notwithstanding, the trustworthiness factor may, in turn, hinge upon the distinction between "facts," which are considered reliable and "opinions," which are not. See *Daniels v. Tew Mac Aero Services, Inc.*, 675 A.2d 984 (Me. 1996), involving an action arising from an airplane crash, where the "probable cause" portion of the National Transportation Safety Board report of the crash was not admissible; however, the factual portions of that same report was.

the report may be excluded even though, as a whole, the report is admitted.[25]

§21.401(b) Automobile Accident Reports

ARE THEY ADMISSIBLE?
YES (QUALIFIED AS TO CONTENTS).

As we have seen from the preceding discussions and cases pertaining to accident reports in general, the real battles involve the individual components of the report, as opposed to the report itself. Absent a statute prohibiting the admissibility of an automobile accident report, there is little doubt about the admissibility of the report itself.[26] The report prepared by a police officer pursuant to law should be admissible.[27] As to the contents, that's another set of issues.[28] Information obtained by the officer from third parties constitutes multiple hearsay and will not be admitted unless that information falls within its own hearsay exception.[29]

---

25 *Desrosiers v. Flight Inter. of Florida, Inc.* 156 F.3d 952 (9th Cir. 1998). In an action involving a fatal air crash, the District Court did not abuse its discretion by admitting only portions of a Judge Advocate General's report which set forth both findings of fact and opinions regarding the cause of a crash. The report primarily consisted of the opinions of its author, whom the owner of the airplane did not attempt to qualify as an expert witness. In *Walker v. Fairchild Industries*, 554 F. Supp. 650 (D. Nev. 1982), an official United States Air Force Aircraft Accident Investigation Report was admitted in a wrongful death case, but certain "vague statements" by an investigating officer were excluded.

26 *Gaddy v. Hartford Life Insurance Co.*, 218 F.Supp.2d 1123 (E.D.Mo., 2002). A police accident investigation report prepared by an investigating highway patrol officer pursuant to state law is admissible under the public records hearsay exception, absent a sufficient showing that reports were not authentic. *Department of Transportation v. Taylor,* 841 A.2d 108 (2004). In a prosecution for vehicular homicide, involuntary manslaughter, and driving under the influence of alcohol, a defendant driver's due process rights were not violated by applying an absolute statutory privilege which states that in-depth accident investigations and safety studies (and information, records, and reports used in their preparation) are not discoverable or admissible as evidence.

27 This, of course, implies that the officer is identifiable. *Holliday v. Hudson Armored Car & Courier Service, Inc.*, 753 N.Y.S.2d 470, N.Y.A.D. 1st Dept (2003) held that a police accident report is inadmissible under the business records exception to the hearsay rule unless there is adequate evidence to establish the identity of the officer who made the report or the source of the information contained therein.

Bolduc v. U.S., 265 F.Supp.2d 153 (D.Mass., 2003). Police reports, which recorded first-hand observations of the officers, were admissible in a civil trial under the public records exception to the hearsay rule.

28 *Mendez v. Queens Plumbing Supply, Inc.*, 12 Misc.3d 1064, 820 N.Y.S.2d 707 (2006). In an auto negligence action, for purposes of the motion for summary judgment by the vehicle driver and owner with respect to the passenger's personal injury claim, police reports pertaining to the collision underlying the passenger's lawsuit were inadmissible to the extent that they contained statements made by the driver (who was precluded from testifying at trial due to his failure to submit to a scheduled examination before trial) and therefore the reports did not support the driver and vehicle owner's motion for summary judgment. See §20.401. See *Pilgrim's Pride Corp. v. Smoak,* 134 S.W.3d 880 (Tex. App. Texarkana 2004).

29 *DeLuca v. Blanco*, 31 A.D.3d 600, 819 N.Y.S.2d 86 (N.Y.A.D., 2 Dept., 2006). In a negligence action commenced by a pedestrian who was injured when a vehicle swerved to avoid a squad car, a statement in the accident report made by a witness who did not testify at trial was not admissible under any recognized exceptions to hearsay rule. *Brown v. Reece,* 753 N.Y.S.2d 825, 194 Misc.2d 269 (N.Y.City.Civ.Ct., 2003). Generally, in order for the report to be admissible under the public records exception to the hearsay rule, it must be shown that: The entrant of the facts was a witness or was under a business duty to relay those facts to the entrant. See also general discussions in §21.401.

§21.401(c) Consumer Products Accident Reports

ARE THEY ADMISSIBLE?
YES (QUALIFIED).

When consumer products are associated with death or injuries, a number of agencies and experts may be involved. The reports that they generate may provide a key link between the injury and liability. The basic qualifiers discussed throughout this chapter apply. In particular, to be admissible, the report must be trustworthy[30], based upon first hand knowledge[31], and generated pursuant to a duty imposed by law,[32] by one whose duty it was to generate the report.[33]

§21.401(d) Environmental Reports

ARE THEY ADMISSIBLE?
A HIGHLY QUALIFIED YES.

Unlike writings pertaining to discrete, specific accidents and defective objects, reports that purport to establish dangerous environmental conditions seem prone to failure insofar as admissibility is concerned. Theoretically, they should be no different than any other governmental report, to be sure. But they are. Environmental consequences tend to be diffuse and occur imperceptibly over time, thereby requiring scientific explanation, which in turn requires the presence of experts. And with the experts, of course, come the *Daubert* attacks.[34] In any event, if a judge distrusts the report, he or she can find many reasons for its exclusion,[35]

---

30 The same basic standards of trustworthiness also apply to industrial products that cause injury. See *Kennedy v. Joy Technologies, Inc.*, 455 F.Supp.2d 522 (W.D.Va., 2006). A portion of an investigatory report of the United States Mine Safety and Health Administration (MSHA) found that the most likely cause for the malfunction of a remote control unit that led to a miner's being crushed by a continuous miner machine was debris within unit; the report was entirely speculative and thus inadmissible under the public records exception to the hearsay rule.

See §21.300, §21.401. See also *Knotts v. Black & Decker, Inc.*, 204 F.Supp.2d 1029 (N.D.Ohio, 2002), a products liability, wrongful death brought against the manufacturer of a battery charger. Statements made by young children to a fire investigator after a fatal house fire were inadmissible. The circumstances of the statements, made four days after the incident, indicated a lack of trustworthiness. The factual findings of an investigation were likewise inadmissible under the public records exception to the hearsay rule where the sources of the information or other circumstances suggested a lack of trustworthiness.

31 See §21.401. See also *Knotts v. Black & Decker, Inc.*, 204 F.Supp.2d 1029 (N.D.Ohio, 2002). Even if documents by the Consumer Product Safety Commission concerning battery chargers were authenticated, such documents would be inadmissible as untrustworthy; the documents contained witness statements by persons who were not employees of the Commission.

32 *Federico v. Ford Motor Company,* 854 N.E.2d 448, 67 Mass.App.Ct. 454 (Mass.App.Ct., 2006) involved a products liability lawsuit against Ford Motor Company that was commenced by the administratrix of the estate of a pedestrian who was killed when the operator of a Ford-manufactured vehicle accelerated at a high rate of speed, hit a traffic barrier, jumped a curb, and struck the pedestrian. Portions of a 1989 National Highway Traffic Safety Administration study that examined sudden acceleration, together with similar documents prepared by agencies of the Canadian and Japanese governments, were reliable and relevant to the claim by the administratrix that sudden acceleration of the driver's vehicle resulted from a malfunction that allegedly caused the vehicle to accelerate. Portions of the study and documents were admissible as substantive evidence. See §21.401.

33 See generally, §21.100.

34 *Daubert v. Dow*, 113 St.Ct. 2786 (1993), directing the admissibility of scientific, technical and specialized knowledge became a landmark for the Federal District Courts and a guidepost for most states. See §§11.603, 40.600, and 49.300.

35 See §21.300.

even though a single word, "untrustworthy," should otherwise suffice.[36]

§21.402 Automotive and Vehicular Records

ARE THEY ADMISSIBLE? NO.

KEY POINTS:

A person's past driving record should not be admitted as substantive evidence of current conduct. This would be akin to allowing a person's past criminal record to be used to prove a current crime.[37]

§21.403 Autopsy Reports

ARE THEY ADMISSIBLE? YES.

KEY POINTS FOR PROPONENT:

Autopsy reports are **official documents** and they are records kept **in the ordinary course of business**. In addition, Fed. R. Evid. 803(9) specifically excepts "Records of Vital Statistics" from the scope of the hearsay rule as being "public records," regardless of whether the declarant is available or not.[38] Furthermore the conclusions contained in the documents may also be admissible (i.e., conclusions pertaining to birth, death, etc.).[39]

---

36 *Mattoon v. City of Pittsfield*, 775 N.E2d 770, 56 Mass.App.Ct. 124 (2002) involved a lawsuit against the city of Pittsfield by some of its citizens to recover damages allegedly caused from contaminated drinking water. An order issued by the Department of Environmental Quality Engineering that required the city to advise its residents to boil water prior to consuming it was not admissible under the public records exception to the hearsay rule. The order constituted a conclusion or opinion and was, therefore, not admissible. Likewise, a statement of facts contained in the order was not admissible under the public records exception to the hearsay rule because those facts were not based upon first hand knowledge or information.

McCorkle Farms, Inc. v. Thompson, 84 S.W.3d 884 (Ark.App., 2002) involved a farmer's negligence action against the employer of a crop duster for damage sustained to his crops when they were allegedly exposed to a harmful pesticide applied to nearby fields. A report from the Plant Board Pesticide Committee, concluding that there was insufficient evidence presented to the board to indicate that the crop duster was responsible, was hearsay and not excepted under public records exception to hearsay rule. The report involved a special investigation for a special problem, as opposed to involving a regularly conducted activity.

37 *Ogden v. J.M. Steel Erecting, Inc.*, 31 P.3d 806 (Ariz.App., 2001). In auto negligence action against corporation and its owners for injuries arising out of accident involving corporation's intoxicated employee, police report supplement containing history of employee's driving record was offered to prove employee's driving history, and was thus hearsay. There was no evidence that supplement was prepared pursuant to any duty imposed by law and could, thus, not be considered under public records exception. Nor could it gain admission under "catch-all" hearsay exception. Although trial court believed in supplement's reliability and trustworthiness, unauthenticated portion conflicted with official motor vehicle department records.

38 Fed. R. Evid. 803(9) provides that the following are not excluded by the hearsay rule: "Records or data compilations, in any form, of births, fetal deaths, deaths, or marriages, if the report was made to a public office pursuant to requirements of law."

39 *Sosna v. Binnington,* 321 F.3d 742 (8th Cir., Mo., 2003). In a widow's malpractice action against a surgeon resulting from the death of her husband, an autopsy report containing the pathologist's opinions as to the cause of death was admissible as a business record exception to the hearsay rule. *Noseworthy v. Allstate Life Ins. Co.*, 664 N.E.2d 470 (Mass. App. Ct. 1996).

KEY POINTS FOR OPPOSITION:

A departure from recognized pathological techniques (due to negligent performance or bias) used during an autopsy could cause the opinions and conclusions of the report to be impeached.[40] But even those alleged improprieties will likely fail to keep the document from being admitted. Where applicable, however, opposing counsel should always advance the proposition that while factual findings of autopsy report are admissible, conclusions as to cause of death are not.[41]

REFERENCES

Factual findings, admissibility under Rule 803(8)(C). 47 A.L.R. Fed. 321.

§21.404 Birth Certificates

ARE THEY ADMISSIBLE? **YES.**

KEY POINTS:

Birth Certificates are official documents and they are records kept in the ordinary course of business; they are also public records. And if that is not enough, Birth Certificates are also "Vital Statistics" within the meaning of Fed. R. Evid. 803(9).[42]

§21.404(a) Marriage Certificates

ARE THEY ADMISSIBLE?
GENERALLY, YES.

KEY POINTS:

Marriage Certificates are **public records** and are, therefore, presumably kept **in the ordinary course of business.**[43]

§21.405 Booklets

For Governmental Booklets, see Pamphlets (*infra*).

§21.406 Breathalyzer Maintenance Records

ARE THEY ADMISSIBLE? **YES.**

KEY POINTS:

Maintenance records of a breathalyzer machine are admissible under the business records exception to the hearsay rule. But where no custodian or other qualified witness appears for the purpose of establishing a necessary foundation, they will not be admitted.[44]

---

40 *Murray v. Shanks*, 27 Wash. App. 363, 618 P.2d 102 (1980).

41 *Bogdan v. Peekskill Community Hosp.*, 642 N.Y.S.2d 478 (N.Y. Sup. 1996).

42 See the rules pertaining to autopsy reports, *supra*.

43 But see *Alfonso v. Gravois,* 739 So.2d 946 (La.App. 1999). In proceedings seeking to a rescind a property settlement agreement, an alleged marriage certificate was admissible, despite the putative ex-husband s claim that the document had not been authenticated. The putative ex-wife testified that the document in question was the one given to her by her putative ex-husband. Further, she didn't offer it to prove that the parties were married; instead, it was to show her state of mind, and, in particular, why she believed that she had been lawfully married.

44 *Goodloe v. Director of Revenue*, 838 S.W.2d 506 (Mo. App. W.D. 1992).

§21.407 Citations and Traffic Tickets

ARE THEY ADMISSIBLE? **NO.**

KEY POINTS FOR PROPONENT:

Convictions are admissible in certain instances,[45] but charges or tickets are not.[46] This, of course, follows the general principle that nothing short of a conviction should be admissible.

KEY POINTS FOR OPPOSITION:

Many states have enacted statutes prohibiting any evidentiary use of convictions for minor traffic offenses. For charges or citations, opposing such evidence is a simple matter of informing the court that mere charges are inadmissible because everyone is presumed innocent until proven guilty. Moreover, even for convictions and guilty pleas, evidence of prior speeding tickets may be inadmissible under Fed. R. Evid. 404(b) in an automobile negligence action to show negligence or that the driver was speeding.[47]

§21.408 Codes

See Safety Standards (*infra*).

§21.409 Death Certificates

ARE THEY ADMISSIBLE? **YES.**

KEY POINTS FOR PROPONENT:

Death Certificates are **official documents kept in the ordinary course of business**, and they are also public records within the meaning of Fed. R. Evid. 803(9).

Often, the signer need not be a medical pathologist.[48] A Death Certificate is *prima facie* evidence of its contents.[49]

A word of warning is warranted; as indicated hereunder, the Death Certificate may not be used to prove the cause of death.[50] The practitioner must, therefore, determine in advance of trial whether or not there should be a serious challenge to "cause of death" as listed in the Death Certificate. If so, he or she must be prepared to present extrinsic evidence.[51]

---

45 *People v. Miner*, 197 Ill. App.3d 1078, 136 Ill. Dec. 626, 545 N.E.2d 150 (1989).

46 *Hood v. Oakley*, 519 So.2d 1236 (Miss. 1988).

47 *Sparks v. Gilley Trucking Co.*, 992 F.2d 50 (4th Cir. 1993).

48 See Sullivan, *When Death is the Issue: Uses of Pathological Testimony*, 19 Wil. L. Rev. 579 (1983).

49 *Edwards v. W.C.A.B.*, 585 A.2d 56 (Pa. 1990), *allocatur denied*, 598 A.2d 286 (1991).

50 But see *Wible v. Aetna Life Ins.*, 375 F.Supp.2d 956 (C.D. Cal., 2005) wherein a plan beneficiary's death certificate was evidence that the beneficiary died of complications from lupus in an action challenging an ERISA plan's denial of the beneficiary's claim for long-term disability benefits. In a wrongful death case, *Gilmer v. Carney*, 608 N.E.2d 709 (Ind. App. 3 Dist. 1993), the admission into evidence of the decedent's death certificate, for the purpose of proving the cause of death, was an error, but the admission was held to be harmless because the certificate was merely cumulative of other evidence.

51 But see *Noseworthy v. Allstate Life Ins. Co.*, 664 N.E.2d 470 (Mass. App. Ct. 1996) which involved litigation to determine whether an insurer properly denied payment for an insured's death, caused when he jumped over a guardrail while escaping from police. The insurer was properly permitted to introduce an unredacted death certificate, which listed his cause of death as suicide. Other facts in the record that were not consistent with suicide affected the weight to be given to the certificate, not its admissibility.

KEY POINTS FOR OPPOSITION:

The death certificate will always be admissible with respect to the *fact of death*,[52] but the *cause of death* is another matter.[53]

The trustworthiness and correctness of the listed cause of death is always subject to impeachment.[54]

§21.410 DNA Matching Test Results

***ARE THEY ADMISSIBLE?* YES.**

KEY POINTS FOR OPPOSITION:

DNA profiling is rapidly becoming a widely recognized, authoritative tool for identification.[55] Assuming that proper methodology is employed, DNA matching is no longer a novel, suspect science,[56] subject to the *Frye* or *Daubert* standards.[57]

---

52 Elvis sightings notwithstanding.

53 *Blake v. Southcoast Health System, Inc.*, 206 F.Supp.2d 174 (D.Mass., 2002) concerned a medical malpractice lawsuit against a physician and a hospital. Under Massachusetts law, a death certificate is prima facie evidence of the facts recorded therein and it is generally admissible (despite words that may incidentally bear on the question of liability). Nevertheless, such admissibility is limited where the sources of the information or other circumstances indicate a lack of trustworthiness. Here, the court was not persuaded by a fair preponderance of the evidence that choking constituted the cause of death for a disabled patient. Therefore, the patient's entire death certificate suggesting asphyxia was not admissible as a vital statistics exception to the hearsay rule.

The death certificate is admissible with respect to the fact of death, but not the cause of death. See *Combined American Insurance Co. v. McCall*, 497 S.W.2d 350 (Tex. Ct. App. 1973) and *Commonwealth v. Bastarche*, 414 N.E.2d 984 (Mass. 1980). But see *All American Life Insurance Company v. Puckett Bros. Manufacturing Co., Inc.,* 139 F.Supp.2d 1386 (N.D. Ga., 2001). In action to determine coverage under life insurance policy, certified copy of death certificate, which stated that "suicide" was cause of death (from self-inflicted gunshot wounds) was not only admissible, it was prima facie evidence of death by suicide.

54 In *Commonwealth v. Bastarche*, 414 N.E.2d 984 (Mass. 1980), an appellate court found that even though the certificate itself was properly admissible, the jury should not have seen the cause of death, which was listed as "homicide." See also *Combined American Insurance Co. v. McCall*, 497 S.W.2d 350 (Tex. 1973).

55 The most respected DNA testing methods include: Restriction Fragment Length Polymorphism (RFLP) and Polymerase Chain Reaction (PCR). See §18-3, Giannelli and Imwinkelreid, *Scientific Evidence*, The Michie Company. See also *supra*, §21.410.

56 *State v. Forte*, 629 S.E.2d 137, 360 N.C. 427 (2006). In a capital murder trial, reports of a State Bureau of Investigation (SBI) agent that contained information relating to the chain of custody of DNA material and the agent's DNA analysis were records of purely ministerial observations and, thus, were allowable under the public records exception to the hearsay rule. The reports contained routine, nonadversarial matters. Their potential use in court was only one purpose among several served by the creation and compilation of the reports, and the agent's analysis of the evidence also facilitated further examination of evidence within the SBI laboratory.

Folger v. Dugan, 876 A.2d 1049, 2005 PA Super 215 (2005). A trial court need not conduct a *Frye* hearing to determine whether PCR testing is sufficiently reliable prior to admitting PCR test results where the parties do not challenge the methodology employed. Here, they did not challenge the general existence of PCR testing in the medical field, nor did they claim that PCR methodology was novel or junk science. Moreover, the *Frye Rule* requiring scientific evidence to be reliable and generally accepted in the scientific community prior to its admission does not apply every time science enters the courtroom. The results of the PCR test, the veracity of which was sufficiently established, were therefore admissible.

57 The *Frye* and *Daubert* standards provide a test for determining whether new or untested scientific methodologies should be admissible. See §11.603, §40.600, and §49.300.

§21.411 E-Mail

E-mail is now a ubiquitous method of communication for both private businesses and public agencies conducting governmental business.[58] See also the same heading in Chapter 22.

§21.412 Foreign Public Documents

ARE THEY ADMISSIBLE? **YES.**

KEY POINTS FOR PROPONENT:

Foreign public documents, properly presented, may warrant judicial notice, and thus, may not need to be formally admitted into evidence.[59] Even if the foreign document has not been certified, it will be treated as *presumptively authentic* if the parties have been given a reasonable opportunity to investigate its authenticity and accuracy.[60]

§21.413 Investigative Reports

ARE THEY ADMISSIBLE?
YES, FOR FACTUAL FINDINGS.

KEY POINTS FOR PROPONENT:

Hundreds of governmental agencies—state, local and federal—spend a lot of time issuing reports. Their subject matter is broad, ranging from carcinogen identification to air crashes.

The rules governing accident reports are very similar; as a matter of fact, an auto accident report is a form of investigative report, and one which happens to have gained a great deal of acceptability and trustworthiness, as compared to others.

Investigative reports made pursuant to law are **official documents** and are normally **kept in the ordinary course of business.**[61] But while the report itself may be admissible, it's quite possible that its meat may not. Each portion may be subject to challenge.[62] Of those potential pitfalls discussed below, any opponent's attack on "conclusions or opinions" has been dealt a serious blow by the Supreme Court:[63]

> We hold, therefore, that portions of investigatory reports otherwise admissible under

---

58 *Slay v. Spell*, 882 So.2d 254 (Miss. Ct. App., 2004). Weekly kill reports issued by U.S. Department of Agriculture and Commerce field inspectors for each inspected slaughterhouse were used to generate statistical information to track the number and the weight of animals that were slaughtered within the state; the reports, which were prepared on-site, were admissible as government records prepared in the regular course of business. Although the reports were available in e-mail form only (and therefore, unsigned), they were, nevertheless, authenticated by their custodians.

59 Keep in mind that Judicial Notice is a **substitute** for admissibility.

60 *Raphaely Intern., Inc. v. Waterman S.S. Corp.*, 972 F.2d 498 (2nd Cir. 1992).

61 The infamous Warren Report prepared by the President's Commission on the Assassination of President Kennedy (from Executive Order No. 11130, November 29, 1963) would constitute one of those rare official documents not kept in the ordinary course of business. See also, *Dubois v. State Farm Fire & Casualty Co.*, 734 F. Supp. 722 (E.D. La. 1990). *Noble v. Sheahan*, 132 F.Supp.2d 626 (N.D. Ill. 2001). In civil rights action against Sheriff and his office, investigative report covering deputy sheriff was admissible over objection; it was offered not for truth but rather to establish state of mind of investigator at time he recommended deputy be suspended.

62 In *Federal Deposit Insurance Corp. v. Mmahat*, 907 F.2d 546 (5th Cir. 1990), a report of the Federal Home Local Bank Board was properly admitted. The court of appeals ruled that hearsay statements within such reports, however, were not admissible unless they fell within a specific hearsay exception. In this case, statements from the defense attorney constituted admissions and were, therefore, admissible.

63 *Beech Aircraft Corp. v. Rainey*, 488 U.S. 153, 109 S. Ct. 439, 102 L. Ed. 2d 444 (1988), *reversing* 784 F.2d 1523 (11th Cir. 1986).

> Rule 803(8)(C) are not inadmissible merely because they state a conclusion or opinion. As long as the conclusion is based on a factual investigation and satisfies the Rule's trustworthiness requirement, it should be admissible along with other portions of the report.

Fed. R. Evid. 803(8)(C) provides that reports from public agencies are not excluded from evidence by the hearsay rule in civil actions, to the extent that the reports contain:

> Factual findings resulting from an investigation made pursuant to authority granted by law, unless the sources of information or other circumstances indicate lack of trustworthiness.[64]

KEY POINTS FOR OPPOSITION:

The **first three pointers** in our "opposition checklist" above, come heavily into play. In addition, it is quite possible that special rules or laws pertaining to a given agency may expressly prohibit the use of that agency's report in a civil action.[65] Every conclusion or opinion that is harmful to your case should be challenged; no item is an automatic slam-dunk for the proponent.[66] So-called factual findings are admissible. Conclusions and opinions are **generally** inadmissible.[67] Other statements, such as subsequent remedial measures following an accident, may also be inadmissible.[68]

REFERENCES

Factual findings, admissibility under Rule 803(8)(C). 47 A.L.R. Fed. 321.

---

64 *Young v. James Green Management, Inc.*, 327 F.3d 616 (7th Cir., Ill., 2003). In a civil rights lawsuit by employees against their former employer, the court did not abuse its discretion by refusing to admit a determination issued by the Equal Employment Opportunity Commission (EEOC) finding that African-American former employees had been discriminated against by their employer. During trial, the EEOC representative testified incorrectly on a matter of significance, indicating that the report was unreliable. By way of contrast, see *Rodriguez v. City of Houston,* 250 F.Supp.2d 691 (S.D.Texas, 2003), a Title VII action by a female police officer against the city of Houston; here, a report was issued by the police department's Internal Affairs Division regarding an investigation into the plaintiff's complaint that a male superior was sexually harassing her. The report was deemed to contain factual findings resulting from an investigation made pursuant to law, and was thus admissible against the city, under the public records exception to the hearsay rule. There was no evidence that the sources of the information contained in the report lacked trustworthiness. See *Owens v. City of Philadelphia*, 6 F. Supp.2d 373 (Pa. 1998). Statements made in an investigative report by prison nurses, who were eyewitnesses to the scene of a detainee's hanging, were admissible hearsay as "factual findings" by the Prison Internal Affairs Division. That agency was empowered to investigate prison incidents and nothing in the report suggested that the nurses were untrustworthy.

65 With respect to reports concerning aircraft accidents, see Section 701(e) of the Federal Aviation Act, 49 U.S.C. 1441(e).

66 Despite the mountains of facts and scientific evidence linking cigarette smoke to lung cancer, the conclusion that the smoke caused lung cancer in *Surgeon General's Advisory Committee on Smoking and Health* (1964) was denied admissibility; see Lipson, *Art of Advocacy - Documentary Evidence*, §20.07 (Matthew Bender 1991). See also *Brom v. Bozell, Jacobs, Kenyon & Eckhardt, Inc.*, 867 F.Supp. 686 (N.D. Ill. 1994), where the "Conclusion" section of an Illinois Department of Human Rights investigation report, regarding a former employee's age discrimination claim, was excluded because its prejudicial effect substantially outweighed its probative value.

67 *Budden v. U.S.*, 748 F.Supp. 1374 (D. Neb. 1990); *Jet Air, Inc. v. Epps Air Service*, 194 Ga. App. 829, 392 S.E.2d 951 (1988); *Bloomgren v. Fire Insurance Exchange*, 162 Ill. App. 2d 594, 517 N.E.2d 290 (1987). See also *E.E.O.C. v. Manville Sales Corp.*, 27 F.3d 1089 (5th Cir. 1994).

68 *Masemer v. Delmarva Power and Light Co.*, 723 F. Supp. 1019 (D. Del. 1989).

Admissibility of evidence of subsequent remedial measures. 50 A.L.R. Fed. 935.

§21.413(a) Internal Investigative Reports

ARE THEY ADMISSIBLE? GENERALLY, NO.

KEY POINTS:

Internal investigative reports are distinguishable from run-of-the-mill investigative reports (*supra*, §21.413) because internal reports target the very agency or entity that is conducting the investigation. In other words, the agency is investigating itself. This situation creates a trustworthiness problem from the start, since agencies are prone to whitewash such investigations or otherwise exonerate themselves. Self-serving reports are most likely going to be deemed untrustworthy and, therefore, inadmissible.[69] And while fault-finding reports may contain admissions,[70] even they are, by no means guaranteed admissibility.[71]

§21.413 (b) Investigator's Interview Notes

ARE THEY ADMISSIBLE? NO.

KEY POINTS:

An investigator employed by a governmental agency will, of course, have occasion to generate and maintain notes for the purpose of authoring an official report, but the notes themselves do not constitute such a report.[72]

§21.414 Lie Detector Results

See "Polygraph Test Results" (*infra*).

§21.415 Maps

The term "map" has a wide variety of meanings. As used in this chapter, the term refers exclusively to official governmental documents. For maps produced by private businesses, see the heading "Maps" in Chapter 22. And, for maps that are used for clarification (i.e., demonstrative) purposes, see Chapter 42.

---

69 See *supra*, §21.413.

70 See *supra*, §5.404.

71 But see *In re Removal of Kuehnle*, 830 N.E.2d 1173, 161 Ohio App.3d 399 (2005). In an action for the removal of school board members for alleged misconduct, a memorandum written by the Director of Special Education regarding a teacher's alleged sexual misconduct along with notes written by a school counselor were admissible. (Note, however, that there was an issue of waiver of objection present in this case.) See, for example, *Karoon v. New York City Transit Authority,* 730 N.Y.S.2d 331 (N.Y.A.D., 2001). In action to recover damages arising from traffic accident involving city bus, trial court properly excluded municipal defendant's internal investigatory report; even though it labeled city bus driver "at fault" for accident in question, city's internal rules and policies exceeded standard of care applicable for common-law negligence.

72 *Estate of Stolarazyk v. Senator International Freight Forwarding, LLC*, 376 F.Supp.2d 834 (N.D.Ill., 2005). In an action by a deceased former employee against a former employer under the Americans with Disabilities Act (ADA), interview notes made by the EEOC investigator containing the employee's statements were not admissible because they did not constitute "factual findings" that might otherwise be subject to the hearsay exception for records resulting from an official investigation made pursuant to law. Also, the plaintiff offered no hearsay exception for the employee's statements, which were hearsay within hearsay. Moreover, hearsay statements are not exempted from the hearsay bar simply because they were related to a government officer or investigator.

ARE THEY ADMISSIBLE? **YES.**

KEY POINTS:

The Official Agricultural Department Geographical Survey is about as official as you can get. It is also self-authenticating.[73] Official maps created by any political subdivisions should be accorded similar respect.

§21.416 Medical Reports and Findings

An endless variety of state and private medical boards are designed to assure the public that the medical profession is well regulated. The objectivity of their opinions and reports, however, are always open to legitimate concern.

ARE THEY ADMISSIBLE?
NO (VERY QUALIFIED).

KEY POINTS:

Documents issued by the Office of Professional Medical Conduct (OPMC), in connection with proceedings on professional misconduct charges, and by the Public Health Council (PHC), in connection with a doctor's complaint challenging her summary suspension by a hospital, were not admissible; with respect to the OPMC determinations and orders, those documents contained opinions of witnesses who were not public officers.[74]

REFERENCES

Factual findings, admissibility under Rule 803(8)(C). 47 A.L.R. Fed. 321.

§21.417 MRI (Magnetic Resonance Imaging) Test Results

See same heading in Chapter 22.

§21.418 Pamphlets

The United States government prints numerous pamphlets, including many that contain standards or guidelines.

ARE THEY ADMISSIBLE? **YES.**

KEY POINTS:

Generally, official publications issued by the United States Government should be admissible,[75] but admissibility is not automatic. Such is the case for political subdivisions.

With respect to publications that present governmental standards or regulations, it may be important for the practitioner to distinguish between compulsory standards and advisory standards. As to the former, compliance is mandatory; mere advisory regulations, however, are discretionary and carry no criminal sanctions.

As a general rule, compulsory or mandatory regulations carry the full force of law and should be admissible as official documents.[76] But, of

---

73 Fed. R. Evid. 902(5), pertaining to self-authentication, applies to "... publications purporting to be issued by public authority."

74 See also *Limatta v. Vest*, 45 P.3d 310 (Alaska, 2002). In a personal injury action resulting from a bicyclist's collision with a motorist, a letter sent by a doctor to the Social Security Administration Disability Determination Unit indicating that there did not seem to be a great deal of impairment in the bicyclist, was inadmissible. There was no showing that it was the regular practice of the doctor to prepare such letters; therefore, the document did not fall within the business records exception to the hearsay rule.

Bogdan v. Peekskill Community Hosp., 642 N.Y.S.2d 478 (N.Y. Sup. 1996).

75 See *Phillips v. K-Mart Corp.*, 588 So.2d 142 (La. App. 1991), which involved a pamphlet prepared by the United States Department of Treasury, Bureau of Alcohol, Tobacco and Firearms, entitled, "Your Guide to Federal Firearms Regulation 1988-89." The pamphlet, which contained federal regulations of a U.S. administrative agency, was admissible.

76 *Smith v. Ithaca Corp.*, 612 F.2d 215 (5th Cir. 1980); see also *Carleton v. Tortosa*, 17 Cal. Rptr. 2d 734, 14 C.A. 4th 745 (Cal. App. 1993), where it was held that a California Department of Real Estate bulletin containing a revised Code of Ethics for real estate licensees was the proper subject of judicial notice.

course, if the subject code provisions do not happen to apply specifically to your particular case, then they would not be relevant.[77]

Regulations that are purely advisory and do not carry the threat of punishment or fine may not be admissible.[78]

§21.419 Polygraph Test Results

ARE THEY ADMISSIBLE? **NO.**

KEY POINTS:

Despite what many perceive as the overruling of the landmark *Frye v. United States*,[79] the inadmissibility of polygraph test results has never been seriously questioned. They are clearly inadmissible.[80] Note that the landmark case that overruled the so-called "*Frye* Standard" pertaining to new scientific evidence is considered under "Scientific Reports" (*infra*). See also §11.601.[81]

The overruling of the *Frye* standard (in the federal sphere) did not imply that the *Frye* holding, with respect to polygraphs, was also overruled. On the contrary, except under certain special circumstances, polygraph results remain inadmissible.[82] A polygraph should not even admitted for purposes of impeachment.[83] At a sentencing hearing, when the defendant attempted to introduce the results of a polygraph test, the judge (whose ruling of inadmissibility was upheld), eloquently described the evidence as "flat out wrong."[84]

It is worth noting that the beleaguered polygraph has been gaining accuracy and respectability. Where the parties stipulate, polygraph results may be admitted.[85] Before hailing the rebirth of the lie detector, recall that almost anything is possible *where all parties stipulate*. But the majority of federal and state jurisdictions consider the evidence "*per se*" inadmissible; i.e., they won't allow polygraph results to be admitted even if all parties plus the Pope stipulate.[86]

REFERENCES

Admissibility of results of lie detector test in federal criminal case. 140 A.L.R. Fed. 525.

§21.420 Reprimands

ARE THEY ADMISSIBLE? **YES.**

KEY POINTS:

An official letter of reprimand written to a game warden at the close of an agency's internal investigation was admissible hearsay, as a state-

77 See *Schotis v. North Coast Stevedoring Co.*, 163 Wash. 305, 1 P.2d 221 (1931).

78 *Parker v. James A. Granger, Inc.*, 298 U.S. 644 (1935); see also *Hercules Powder Co. v. Di Sabatino*, 188 A.2d 529 (Del. 1963).

79 293 F. 1013 (D.C. Cir. 1923).

80 *East St. Louis School District No. 189 v. Hayes*, 178 Ill. Dec. 301, 604 N.E.2d 557 (Ill. App. 5 Dist. 1992); *Sabag v. Continental South Dakota*, 374 N.W.2d 349 (S.D. 1985); *State v. Makerson*, 52 N.C.App. 149, 277 S.E.2d 869 (1981); *Caldwell v. State*, 267 Ark. 1053, 594 S.W.2d 24 (1980); *People v. Tarsia*, 67 A.D.2d 210, 415 N.Y.S.2d 120 (1979), *affirmed*, 50 N.Y.2d 1, 405 N.E.2d 188, 427 N.Y.S.2d 944 (1980); *State v. Ochalla*, 285 N.W.2d 683, (Minn. 1979); *State v. Schouest*, 351 So.2d 462 (La. 1977); *Smith v. State*, 31 Md. App. 106, 355 A.2d 527 (1976).

81 The subject case, *Daubert v. Dow*, 113 S. Ct. 2786, 125 L. Ed. 2d 469 (1993), overruled the use of the strict *Frye* standard in the federal court system. According to *Daubert*, *Frye's* "general acceptance" standard should be considered as but one of several elements for determining the admissibility of new scientific evidence.

82 *United States v. Scheffer*, 118 U.S. 303, 118 S.Ct. 1261, 140 L.Ed.2d 413, 66 U.S.L.W. 4235, 4237 (1998). The evidence could even be constitutionally excluded by the Military. And, a polygraph should not even admitted for purposes of impeachment, as announced in *United States v. Sanchez*, 118 F.3d 192 (4th Cir. 1997).

83 *United States v. Sanchez*, 118 F.3d 192 (4th Cir. 1997).

84 *United States v. Messina*, 131 F.3d 36 (2nd Cir. 1997).

85 *United States v. Posado*, 57 F.3d 428 (5th Cir. 1995); *Ivey v. State*, 203 Ga. App. 886, 418 S.E.2d 71 (1992).

86 *Boling v. Boling*, 887 S.W.2d 437 (Mo. Ct. App. 1994); *Conti v. Commissioner*, 39 F.3d 658 (1994).

ment of a public office or agency.[87] Keep in mind that a reprimand (or any form of discipline) is an "act," which may or may not contain statements or assertions of fact. For example, the words, "You're fired," constitute a directive, not a statement of fact; they would not be considered as hearsay.

§21.421 Safety Standards and Codes

Legislative and governmental agencies frequently promulgate safety standards and codes. Code violations often give rise to liability and thereby constitute important evidence. There are basically two types of regulations, "compulsory" (or "mandatory") and discretionary (or "advisory").

***ARE THEY ADMISSIBLE IF THEY ARE COMPULSORY?* YES.**

***ARE THEY ADMISSIBLE IF THEY ARE ONLY ADVISORY?* PROBABLY.**

KEY POINTS:

Where some legislative or governmental agency has determined that a safety code or standard is mandatory or compulsory, that standard may be admitted into evidence as an official record.[88] Where, however, the standard or code is merely advisory, it does not carry the same weight, and may be excluded.[89] Nevertheless, evidence of a professional safety standards may be relevant and admissible even though those standards have not been imposed by statute or promulgated by any regulatory body (and, therefore, do not have the force of law).[90]

§21.422 Scientific Reports

***ARE THEY ADMISSIBLE?* IT DEPENDS UPON TRUSTWORTHINESS.**

KEY POINTS FOR PROPONENT:

Regardless of whether the reports originate in the public or private sector,[91] the critical test of admissibility is trustworthiness. Scientific reports contained within public documents are more likely to be considered trustworthy and, therefore, stand a greater chance of gaining admissibility than private studies.[92] But scientific reports made in the regular course of business may also be admissible, under the business records exception to the hearsay rule.

When we speak of science and "scientific reports," in general, we are normally referring to a broad range of reliability and trustworthiness. The advance of knowledge engenders new discoveries and technologies; some provide good science, others provide junk science. Some advances may involve the evidence gathering-process itself.

An examination of the field of the entire field of "scientific evidence" suggests a spectrum or scale for reliability and trustworthiness. We might start at the far left with accepted principles of mathematics and physics that are beyond dispute.[93] At the opposite end of our spectrum would lie the discredited "sciences" such as Graphology

87 *Tveraas v. Coffey*, 818 F. Supp. 75 (D. Vt. 1993).

88 *Blacker v. Oldsmobile Div., General Motors Corp.*, 869 F. Supp. 313 (E.D. Pa. 1994).

89 *Grossheim v. Freightliner Corp.*, 974 F.2d 745 (6th Cir. 1992).

90 *Stone v. United Engineering*, 475 S.E.2d 439 (W. Va. 1996); *Miller v. Solaglas California Inc.*, 870 P.2d 559 (Colo. Ct. App. 1993).

91 See §22.427.

92 *Ellis v. International Playtex, Inc.*, 745 F.2d 292 (4th Cir. 1984). In a wrongful death action against a tampon manufacturer, the trial court committed a reversible error by not admitting toxic shock syndrome studies prepared by the National Center for Disease Control and various state health departments. The appeals court stated that the studies were no different from other findings of fact pursuant to the public records exception to the hearsay rule. See also *Kehm v. Proctor & Gamble Manufacturing Co.*, 724 F.2d 613 (8th Cir. 1983).

93 The more one learns about physics, the more one doubts. Wasn't Newtonian Physics "beyond controversy" before Einstein?

(handwriting analysis) and Astrology. Those in the middle create the most problems. Consider this list as we start "left" and move to the right, before analyzing the individual items:

1. Scientific principles that are "Beyond Reasonable Controversy."
2. Scientific principles that passed the "*Frye* Plus" test.
3. Scientific principles that passed the *Frye* test.
4. Scientific principles that are still in dispute.
5. Discredited principles.

Science is always on the move, creating new evidentiary tools while discrediting older ones. See §§11.500 - 11.601 for discussions of the landmark cases relating to the standards for admitting new forms of scientific evidence. Here is a summary of the standards set forth on our "trustworthiness" scale:

1.
Beyond Reasonable Controversy Standard

Those facts and principles that are considered "beyond reasonable controversy" may be subject to judicial notice. Fed. R. Evid. 201(b) provides:

> A judicially noticed fact must be one not subject to reasonable dispute in that it is either (1) generally known within the territorial jurisdiction of the trial court or (2) capable of accurate and ready determination by resort to sources whose accuracy cannot be reasonably questioned.

The *Advisory Committee Notes* echo the Rules 9(1) and (2) of the *Uniform Rules of Evidence* by limiting judicial notice to facts that are "so universally known that they cannot reasonably be the subject of dispute." Laws of physics involving force, velocity, time, and acceleration would clearly fit within this pigeonhole.

2.
The Frye Plus *Standard*

People v. Frye, 293 F. 1013 (1923) set forth a strict "general acceptance" standard for scientific evidence, one that states followed for decades. A more thorough discussion of *Frye* can be found in §11.510. *Frye* was so strict a standard that it was radically altered (i.e., loosened) by the United States Supreme Court in 1993 (see §11.603).

Because of the power of DNA matching, some courts have gone beyond *Frye* to apply an even stricter criterion. This new measure has been referred to as the *Frye - Plus* standard (See DNA MATCHING TEST RESULTS, *supra*).

3.
The Frye *Standard*

We have mentioned *People v. Frye*, 293 F. 1013 (1923), perhaps more than any other case; as indicated above, its "general acceptance" standard has stood the tests of time, criticism, and even attack by the U.S. Supreme Court; it is a stubborn standard, to be sure.[94] Some of our most cherished forms of evidence live or die by the *Frye* standard.[95]

4.
Disputed Scientific Principles

The newcomers affectionately known as "Fad Science" and "Junk Science" won't survive the *Frye* standard; but they certainly have a shot at admissibility under *Daubert v. Dow*, 113 S. Ct. 2786, 125 L.Ed. 2d 469 (1993). See §11.603.

---

94 See *supra*, §11.603.

95 INCLUDING: Voiceprints, *United States v. Smith*, 869 F.2d 348 (7th Cir. 1989); ballistics residue, *State v. Smith*, 362 N.E.2d 1239 (Ohio 1976); hair analysis, *United States v. Brady*, 595 F.2d 359 (6th Cir.), *cert. denied*, 444 U.S. 862 (1979); hypnosis, *People v. Shirley*, 31 Cal.3d 18 (1982).

5.
Discredited Principles

Palm reading, Astrology, and Graphology don't stand a chance of admissibility under any standard. Technically, however, under Fed. R. Evid. 702, if a "qualified expert" were to lay the appropriate foundation, the literal requirements of that rule would be satisfied. See §11.602.

§21.423 Thermographic Test Results

See same heading in Chapter 22.

§21.424 Traffic Tickets

See "Citations and Traffic Tickets" (*supra*).

§21.425 Weather Reports

***ARE THEY ADMISSIBLE?* YES.**

KEY POINTS FOR PROPONENT:

Official weather reports are maintained by the U.S. Weather Service in the **ordinary course of business**. They are also public records and reports within the meaning of Fed. R. Evid. 803(8).[96]

KEY POINTS FOR OPPOSITION:

Admissibility would be very difficult to attack in the absence of proof of fraud or mistake. But keep in mind that the weather bureau's measurements are taken at specific locations, often at the airport. Not many people live at the airport; the point is that temperature and weather can vary significantly within a given region. No report can accurately reflect the precise weather at every point. Also note that weather records which are not issued by an "official" weather bureau may be inadmissible.[97]

§21.426 Administrative Agency Reports and Orders

***ARE THEY ADMISSIBLE?* YES, IF THEY ARE DEEMED TRUSTWORTHY.**

KEY POINTS FOR PROPONENT:

The key factor used to draw the line between admissible and inadmissible reports (or portions thereof) was the distinction between facts (admissible) and opinions or conclusions (inadmissible hearsay). That factor continues to be important,[98] but it is clearly overshadowed and heavily outweighed by the broader "trustworthiness" test.[99] Always remember that public

96 *Johnson v. District of Columbia,* 728 A.2d 70 (D.C. 1999). See also *Hefele v. National Supermarkets, Inc.*, 748 S.W.2d 800 (Mo. 1988).

97 But see *Maffett v. Bliss*, 264 Ill.Dec. 741, 771 N.E.2d 445, 329 Ill.App.3d 562 (2002). In a personal injury action, weather reports and weather-related observations are generally admissible in evidence, particularly when they tend to refute testimony pertaining to relevant weather conditions on the date of an accident. The fact that the readings and observations did not occur at the exact moment of the accident and were not taken at the exact location of the accident scene should affect the weight, not the admissibility of the evidence.

See *Ghere v. Industrial Commission*, 215 Ill. Dec. 532, 663 N.E.2d 1046 (Ill. App. 4 Dist. 1996).

98 *Guild v. General Motors Corp.,* 53 F. Supp.2d 363. (W.D.N.Y. 1999). In a motorist's products liability action against an automobile manufacturer based on an allegedly defective seat belt buckle, the fact that conclusions as well as factual findings were included within the report of an investigation of the inertial release of side-release seat belt buckles conducted by National Highway Transportation Safety Administration (NHTSA) did not render the report inadmissible as evidence of non-defect, under the hearsay exception for public records, so long as the conclusions were factually based. Moreover, administrative reports and investigations are admissible under public records hearsay exception.

99 See also *Coleman v. Home Depot, Inc.*, 306 F.3d 1333 (3rd Cir., N.J., 2002). For purposes of determining whether or not a public record or report is too untrustworthy to qualify as a hearsay exception, the court may consider the political bias of the institution that prepared it, and whether or not the report was consistent with that bias.

See §22.401 and §22.402.

records are presumably admissible, thereby placing the burden on the opposition to show that the document is other wise excludable.[100]

In addition to reports and findings, Administrative Agencies may issue orders. The name, title or characterization of the writing, however, does not, for admissibility purposes, seem as important as the contents and the reliability (and trustworthiness) of the facts and information upon which the writings are based.[101]

100 *Bhatt v. Department of Health Services*, 35 Cal.Rptr.3d 335, 133 Cal.App.4th 923 (2005). The official records hearsay exception permits the court to admit an official record or report without necessarily requiring a witness to testify as to its identity and mode of preparation, particularly if the court takes judicial notice or if there is sufficient independent evidence to show that the record or report was prepared in such a manner as to assure its trustworthiness. The object of the official records hearsay exception is to eliminate the calling of each witness involved in the preparation of the record. And, the presumption that an official duty has been regularly performed with respect to the document shifts the burden of proving the foundational issue of trustworthiness of the preparation to the party objecting to its admission.

Hyundai Motor Co. v. Alvarado, 989 S.W.2d 32 (Tex.App. 1998). A document prepared by the National Highway Transportation Safety Administration, Office of Defect Investigation, as a product of its investigation, concerning consumer complaints about passive restraint systems for particular models of an automobile, fell within the hearsay exception for public records and reports. See also *Regent Corp., U.S.A. v. Azmat Bangladesh, Ltd.,* 686 N.Y.S.2d 24 (1999), wherein a report by a customs agent (who had refused to admit imported goods into the United States) was admissible as a business record in an importer s action against the seller. *City of Bangor v. Citizens Communications Co.*, 339 F.Supp.2d 135 (D.Me., 2004). In a lawsuit seeking to impose liability on a corporation for its alleged pollution of a river, the defending corporation bore the burden of demonstrating the untrustworthiness of a governmental agency's report setting forth the findings of an investigation conducted pursuant to a state statute. The report by the state's EPA designated the site of the pollution as an "uncontrolled hazardous substance site," naming the corporation as a responsible party. Because the document was the report of a public agency setting forth findings of an investigation conducted pursuant to a state statute, and because it appeared to be one produced by an unbiased agency (that had been genuinely working to fulfill its legal obligations), it satisfied the prima facie elements for admission under the public records exception to the hearsay rule. The corporation, on the other hand, failed to show that the report was untrustworthy.

Slay v. Spell, 882 So.2d 254 (Miss. Ct. App., 2004). Weekly kill reports issued by U.S. Department of Agriculture and Commerce field inspectors for each inspected slaughterhouse were used to generate statistical information to track the number and the weight of animals that were slaughtered within the state; the reports, which were prepared on-site, were admissible as government records prepared in the regular course of business.

Niam v. Ashcroft, 354 F.3d 652 (7th Cir., 2004). State Department asylum reports have the status of official reports, which are admissible in a regular trial even though they are hearsay.

101 *Mattoon v. City of Pittsfield,* 775 N.E2d 770, 56 Mass.App.Ct. 124 (2002), involved a lawsuit against the city of Pittsfield by some of its citizens to recover for damages allegedly caused from the consumption of contaminated drinking water. An order issued by the Department of Environmental Quality Engineering that required the city to advise its residents to boil water prior to consuming it was not admissible under the public records exception to the hearsay rule. The order constituted a conclusion or opinion and was, therefore, not admissible. Likewise, a statement of fact contained in an order issued by the Department that required the city to advise its residents to boil water prior to consuming it was not admissible under the public records exception to the hearsay rule because those facts were not based upon first hand knowledge or information.

KEY POINTS FOR OPPOSITION:

Just because a report may be admissible, doesn't mean that you can't exclude, black-out or simply "cut the guts out of the document." Inadmissible hearsay may always be excluded.[102]

§21.427 Arrest and Incarceration Records

ARE THEY ADMISSIBLE? **A QUALIFIED YES.**

KEY POINTS:

Official records kept by prison officials or jailers should be admissible under the basic principles applicable to official writings (or business records), in general. If they are relevant and used for non-hearsay purposes, they should be admitted.[103] If their contents are to be admitted in order to prove the truth of the matters asserted, then those contents must fall within an applicable hearsay exception or be excluded.[104] These same general principles should apply to records that are generated in conjunction with an arrest or detention.[105]

§21.428 IRS Certificates of Assessment

ARE THEY ADMISSIBLE? **YES.**

Generally, IRS Certificates of Assessment and payments, along with a summary record of

102 See *Gamblin v. Ford Motor Co.,* 513 5.8.20 467 (W.Va. 1998), which concerned a products liability action involving the roll-over of sport utility vehicle. A National Highway Traffic Safety Administration (NHTSA) official wrote a letter to the manufacturer of the vehicle requesting that manufacturer to provide the NHTSA with a written response to allegations by counsel for plaintiff that it withheld information from the NHTSA during the Agency's investigation of alleged defects in the vehicle. The letter was not a "public report" for purposes of determining its admissibility under the public records exception to the hearsay rule. The letter merely repeated counsel s allegations and outlined the inquiries of the NHTSA during a prior investigation, and thus, the letter did not involve matters observed by the agency pursuant to a duty imposed by law; nor did the letter contain any findings of fact. In any event, interim agency reports and preliminary memoranda are not admissible under "public report" exception to the hearsay rule.

103 *Thomas v. Dragovich,* 142 Fed.Appx. 33 (3rd Cir., Pa., 2005). A prison inmate's grievance forms that he wrote to the prison staff were not barred as hearsay or as self-serving. The inmate's contemporaneous grievance forms stated his belief that (1) the prison doctors and medical staff were not treating his hepatitis and related pain, (2) that provided medicines were inappropriate and contraindicated, and (3) that the prison staff knew this but did nothing. Had they not been excluded, the forms would have shown notice to the prison staff, i.e., the staff's state of mind. *Johnson v. Herman,* 132 F.Supp.2d 1130 (N.D. Ill., 2001). Where issue in §1983 lawsuit involved the plaintiff's detention, jailer's record notations that judge had ordered detainee to remain in jail and had later ordered his release were admissible as non-hearsay evidence. Writing was not being offered to prove what judge had actually ordered but rather was being admitted for non-hearsay purpose of proving that jailer did not act with deliberate indifference in retaining custody.

104 For qualifying Inmate Logs, see *White v. Godinez,* 301 F.3d 796 (7th Cir., Ill., 2002). A sheriff testified that it was the jail's practice to record all inmate visits; he indicated that in 20 years, he could not recall a single incident in which an officer had failed to record an attorney's visit. The log was, therefore, admissible under the hearsay exception as records of a regularly conducted activity.

Martino v. Korch, 131 F.Supp.2d 313 (D.Conn., 2000). In inmate's lawsuit against correctional facility, prison disciplinary tickets were hearsay and were not admissible under business records exception to hearsay rule.

105 *Davis v. Town of Pualsboro,* 421 F.Supp.2d 835 (D.N.J., 2006) involved an excessive force action by the parent of an arrestee, who brought federal civil rights claims against a county, township, and various law enforcement officers, arising from arrestee's death (which occurred after he had been struck in head by a bottle during a fight and then taken into police custody). With respect to the defendants' motion for summary judgment, reports prepared by a county detective stating that the arrestee's girlfriend and another person told him that law enforcement officers punched the arrestee, constituted inadmissible double hearsay.

the assessments, are admissible as self-authenticating official records of the United States.[106]

§21.429 Summaries

ARE THEY ADMISSIBLE? **YES.**

KEY POINTS:

Summaries often arise in the context of private sector business records and are normally accepted because they tend to do nothing more than condense and simplify other documents that have either been admitted into evidence or have been provided to the opposition for inspection.[107] There is every reason to believe that public records should equally share this pragmatic attitude.[108]

§21.430 Foreign Official Documents

Foreign documents do not share the same general "ease of admissibility" as those experienced by official writings from federal, state and local agencies, but they are, nevertheless, probative and admissible if properly authenticated.

ARE THEY ADMISSIBLE? **YES.**

If properly authenticated, foreign public documents may be admissible, assuming that they are properly certified.[109] And, as is the case with domestic public records, they will be subject to exclusion if they are confusing or lack trustworthiness.[110]

---

106 *U.S. v. Burdine,* 205 F.Supp.2d 1175 (W.D.Wash., 2002).

107 See §22.428.

108 *Malchose v. Kalfell,* 664 N.W.2d 508, 2003 ND 75 (2003). In an automobile negligence action, a medical bills summary provided by the Workers' Compensation Bureau to the injured motorist fell within the public records exception to the hearsay rule, and, as such, was admissible to show the amounts incurred in medical expenses, despite the fact that the custodian of the records did not testify at trial; the defendants were, however, given an opportunity to cross-examine the motorist about the document. Generally, a record or data compilation does not have to be publicly available to fall within the public records exception; it need only be made by an officer of the government.

109 See Rule 803(8) of the Federal Rules of Evidence. See also *Georgis v. Ashcroft,* 328 F.3d 962 (7th Cir., 2003).

110 *Jones v. Ford Motor Co.*, 320 F.Supp.2d 440 (E.D. Va., 2004), involved a products liability action brought against an auto manufacturer wherein the probative value of reports of Canadian and Japanese government agencies (about sudden acceleration caused by defective cruise control systems) were outweighed by the danger of potentially misleading jurors and a confusion of the issues. The Japanese report focused on another manufacturer's vehicles, while the Canadian report focused on cruise control systems in general that were not functionally similar to those used in the manufacturer's products. Moreover, the public records exception to the hearsay rule is not a rule of exclusion, but rather a rule of admissibility as long as the public record meets the requirements of the rule. The admissibility of a public record specified in the public records exception to the hearsay rule is assumed as a matter of course unless there are sufficient negative factors to indicate a lack of trustworthiness.

(This page intentionally left blank.)

Chapter 22

Private Sector Business Records

§22.100 Introduction

The most-used foundation tool for documents, by far, is the business records exception to the hearsay rule. That exception, during its lengthy journey over years of common law, has acquired a variety of names: the Shopbook Rule, the New York Rule, and the Business Entry Rule, to name a few.

The drafters of the Federal Rules of Evidence, in uncharacteristic fashion, clarified the subject, by expanding the concept to all regularly conducted activities. As a matter of fact, Rule 803(6) is titled "Records of regularly conducted activity." It encompasses:

> A memorandum,[1] report, record, or data compilation, in any form, of acts, events, conditions, opinions, or diagnoses, made at or near the time by, or from information transmitted by, a person with knowledge, if kept in the ordinary course of a regularly conducted business activity, and if it was the regular practice of that business activity to make the memorandum, report, record, or data compilation, all as shown by the testimony of the custodian or other qualified witness, unless the source of information or the method or circumstances of preparation indicate a lack of trustworthiness. The term "business" as used in this paragraph includes business, institution, association, profession, occupation, and calling of every kind, whether or not conducted for profit.

The rule is quite detailed with respect to the foundation requirements for admitting a business record.[2] But it is, nevertheless, recommended

1 The term "memorandum," or just plain "memo," encompasses a very broad range of business related subjects, some admissible, others not. It is interesting, if not ironic, to note that while the memo "form" may be one of the most common business related records, its content is not necessarily generated in the ordinary course of business. It's possible that another hearsay exception may be required. See, for example, *Detroit/Wayne County Stadium Authority v. Drinkwater, Taylor & Merrill, Inc.,* 705 N.W.2d 549, 267 Mich.App. 625 (2005).

See also §22.408.

2 *Birt v. Firstenergy Corp.*, 891 A.2d 1281 (Pa.Super, 2006). The trial court properly admits a business record if the evidence shows that the record was made in the ordinary course of business, was not opinion testimony, and was properly identified by the person who made it or was conversant with the necessity for its preparation and custody. Moreover, for evidence to be admissible as a business record, a foundation must be laid through the testimony of a witness indicating that he or she is familiar with the method of keeping the records.

City of Chicago v. Old Colony Partners, 364 Ill.App.3d 806, 847 N.E.2d 565, 301 Ill.Dec. 555 (2006). For purposes of establishing a proper foundation for admission of business records, anyone familiar with the business and its procedures may testify as to the manner in which records are prepared and the general procedures for maintaining such records in the ordinary course of business. A document is not inadmissible as outside the business records exception to the hearsay rule simply because it was prepared by a third party authorized to act for the business.

Emigrant Mortgage Company, Inc. v. D'Agostino, 896 A.2d 814, 94 Conn.App. 793 (2006). Generally, authentication is a necessary preliminary procedure for the introduction of evidence for most writings. A proponent may authenticate a document by demonstrating proof of authorship of such writings. A writing may be authenticated by a number of methods, including direct testimony, circumstantial evidence or proof of custody. The requirements for authenticating a business record are identical to those for laying a foundation for its admissibility under the business records hearsay exception. To qualify a document as a business record, the party offering the evidence must present a witness who testifies that the record was made in the regular course of business, that it was in the regular course of such business to make such a record, and that it was made at the time of the act described in the report, or within a reasonable time thereafter.

Farmers Alliance Mutual Insurance Company v. Naylor, 452 F.Supp.2d 1167 (D.N.M., 2006). In an insurer's breach of contract action against an insurance investigator, business records, which normally would be admissible at trial under the business records exception to the hearsay rule, may be considered only if authenticated by a person through whom the exhibits could be admitted into evidence. An e-mail purporting to reflect payment by a property insurer to a fire investigator for his services in connection with an investigation of the origin of a fire on the

(Footnote 2 continued on page 22-4.)

that a simple foundation be presented unless and until opposition is voiced.

REFERENCES

Fingerprints, admissibility as business records. 36 Am. Jur. Proof of Facts 2d 285.

Records kept in course of regularly conducted business activity. 34 Am. Jur. Proof of Facts 2d 509.

Bank records. 14 Am. Jur. Proof of Facts 2d 173.

§22.200 Basic Foundation for Business Records

Q. (By Proponent's Attorney) State your name for the record.

A. (Witness) My name is Kip Keeper.

Q. State your title and occupation.

A. I work for Tasteless Choice Coffee Company; I'm in the accounting department.

Q. (Tendering the writing to the witness) I'll show you plaintiff's Exhibit 1, which purports to be an employment record of the plaintiff; and I'll ask if you can identify it.

A. Yes. It's the employee records for Elvis Ramirez.

Q. Is it part of your normal duties to keep and maintain such records?[3]

A. Yes.

Q. Was plaintiff's Exhibit 1 kept in the ordinary course of your company's business?

A. Yes.

Q. (Tendering the writing to opposing counsel, who should be provided with a copy if requested) I'll ask that plaintiff's Exhibit 1, which I have just handed to opposing counsel, be entered into evidence as a business record.

COURT: Any objections?

OPPOSING COUNSEL: None.

COURT: Very well, I'll receive plaintiff's Exhibit 1.

REFERENCES

Foundation for business records. 34 Am. Jur. Proof of Facts 2d 509.

§22.300 Opposition Checklist

Those opposing business records should not be buffaloed by the simplified and quickly set foundation presented above. There is a normal tendency to let one's guard down during such processes, particularly where the foundation is rapidly and smoothly presented.

It is also important to keep in mind that despite the power of the business records exception, there are many avenues of attack, some of which are suggested by Fed. R. Evid. 803(6).

---

2 (Continued from page 22-3.) insured's premises was not admissible under the business records hearsay exception where the insurer failed to provide the testimony of a custodian or other qualified witness to authenticate the e-mail.

Century Indemnity Co. v. Aero-Motive Co., 254 F.Supp.2d 670 (W.D.Mich., 2003). Generally, a document may be admitted as a business record if: (1) it was made in course of a regularly conducted business activity, (2) it was kept in regular course of business, (3) it was the result of a regular practice of the business to create such a document, and (4) it was made by a person with knowledge of the transaction or from information transmitted by a person with knowledge.

3 The "power" and key benefit derived from the business records "rule" is the ability to lay a foundation for such records *without* the presence of those who authored them. See, for example, *State ex rel. Fischer v. Sanders,* 80 S.W.3d 1 (Mo.App., 2002), holding that the fundamental purpose for the business records exception to the hearsay rule is that it allows the introduction of business records without requiring the appearance of those who prepared them; but the court should, nevertheless, be satisfied that the sources of the information and the preparation of those records indicate trustworthiness.

OPPOSITION CHECKLIST

1. The record was not contemporaneous.[4]
2. The record was not kept in the ordinary course of the company's business.[5]
3. It was not the regular practice of the business to keep or maintain the record.[6]
4. It was not demonstrated that the person who made the record possessed sufficient knowledge. (Someone should be prepared to testify that he or she made

4 *Emigrant Mortgage Company, Inc. v. D'Agostino*, 896 A.2d 814, 94 Conn.App. 793 (2006). To admit evidence under the business record exception to the hearsay rule, the court must determine, before concluding that it is admissible, that the record was made in the regular course of business, that it was in the regular course of the business to make such a record, and that it was made at the time of the act described in the report, or within a reasonable time thereafter.

The records must have been made at or near the time that the information is gathered. *United States v. Weinstock,* 153 F.3d 272 (6th Cir. 1998); *New England Savings Bank v. Bedford Realty Corp.*, 717 A.2d 713 (Conn. 1998). Or the records must have been prepared within a reasonable time after the subject event. *Datamatic Services v. United States*, 909 F.2d 1029 (7th Cir. 1990); see also *Trolley Square Associates v. Nielson*, 886 P.2d 61 (Utah App. 1994), and *Amos v. Norfolk Ry.*, 191 Ill. App.3d 637, 138 Ill. Dec. 866, 548 N.E.2d 96 (1989); *Adams v. The New Jersey State Fair,* 71 N.J. Super. 528, 177 A.2d 486 (1961).

5 *Gatto v. Mortgage Specialists of Illinois, Inc.*, 442 F.Supp.2d 529 (N.D.Ill., 2006). In a Fair Labor Standards Act (FLSA) lawsuit, a former employee's handwritten documents containing the hours that she allegedly worked did not fall within the business records exception to the hearsay rule, and thus, they were inadmissible; the employee's maintenance of her own notes pertaining to the time that she worked was not in the course of her employer's regularly conducted business activity.

The primary reason for admitting business records is their trustworthiness, which arises from the fact that the records reflect the day-to-day operations of the business. *Kearney v. City of New York*, 543 N.Y.S.2d 879 (Sup. Ct. 1989). *Weir v. Crown Equipment Corp.*, 217 F.3d 453 (7th Cir. Ind. 2000). In personal injury action, accident reports collected by forklift manufacturer were derived from variety of sources, under different circumstances; injured forklift operator was, thus, unable to show that they fell within hearsay exception for reports of regularly conducted business activity. *Lust v. Sealy, Inc.*, 383 F.3d 580 (7th Cir. Wis., 2004). In a sex discrimination lawsuit, a manager's memos explaining why he hadn't promoted the subject female employee were not records of a regularly conducted activity within the meaning of the hearsay exception. The only purpose of the memos was to create evidence for use in the employee's anticipated sex discrimination lawsuit. A memo is normally hearsay because it is normally offered to prove the truth of statements made out of court.

Andrews v. Dufour, 882 So.2d 15 (La. App. 4th Cir. June 2, 2004). In a products liability lawsuit against an automobile manufacturer, exhibits that consisted of notes that an expert made while reviewing the manufacturer's business records were not themselves business records and were, therefore, inadmissible.

6 *Hertz v. Luzenac Am., Inc.*, 370 F.3d 1014 (10th Cir. Colo., 2004); *United States v. Weinstock*, 153 F.3d 272 (6th Cir. 1998); *New England Savings Bank v. Bedford Realty Corp.*, 717 A.2d 713 (Conn. 1998); *Zundel v. Bommarito,* 778 S.W. 2d 954 (Mo., 1989). The district court did not abuse its discretion in refusing to admit (pursuant to business records exception to the hearsay rule) a meeting memo prepared by a supervisor who thought that he was going to fire an employee; there was no evidence that it was the ordinary course of business for the supervisor to prepare such a memo, and the circumstances under which the memo was created made it untrustworthy.

the entries or knows them to be correct.)[7]

5. The qualifying witness was not a true custodian or was otherwise unqualified.[8]
6. The circumstances surrounding the document generally lack trustworthiness.[9]
7. The document was prepared in anticipation of litigation, or for use during litigation.[10]
8. The document is not original.[11]
9. The document has erasures, deletions, or alterations that cannot adequately be explained.[12]
10. The document's entries are vague, illegible, or otherwise cannot be read.[13]
11. Even if the document itself were to qualify as a business record, the material entries are either irrelevant or they consist of inadmissible hearsay.[14]

---

7 *Birt v. Firstenergy Corp.*, 891 A.2d 1281 (Pa.Super, 2006). In a construction worker's negligence action against a utility company arising out of a construction accident and resulting electrical burns, an incident report filed by the electric utility's employee was inadmissible under the business records exception to the hearsay rule; the worker made no attempt to acknowledge that the report included a hearsay statement by another worker who indicated that he believed that the power lines were not "live," and the worker made no attempt to provide a basis for admitting that hearsay statement. Merely characterizing a document as a business record is insufficient to justify its admission; moreover, a business record which contains multiple levels of hearsay is admissible only if each level falls within a recognized exception to the hearsay rule.

Davis v. First Healthcare Corp., 507 S.E.2d 563, 234 Ga. App. 744 (Ga. App. 1998); *Datamatic Services v. United States*, 909 F.2d 1029 (7th Cir. 1990); *U.S. v. Wyant,* 576 F.2d 1312 (8th Cir.1978); *Mansfield v. Gushee*, 130 Me. 333, 114 A. 296 (1921).

8 See *United States v. Reyes*, 157 F.3d 949 (1st Cir. 1998) and *Belber v. Lipson*, 905 F.2d 549 (1st Cir. 1990).

9 *Bailey v. Edmundson*, 630 S.E.2d 396, 280 Ga. 528 (2006). The business records exception to the hearsay rule was inapplicable in a will contest alleging undue influence; the messages that employees of the testator's oncologist wrote as a result of speaking with the testator by telephone noted the contents of a conversation, not an act, transaction, occurrence, or event. Moreover, evidence admitted under the business records exception should involve routine facts whose accuracy is not affected by bias, judgment, or memory.

See *Southern Co., v. Hamburg*, 503 S.E.2d 383 (Ga. App. 1998); *Belber v. Lipson*, 905 F.2d 549 (1st Cir. 1990); *McElroy v. Perry*, 753 So.2d 121 (Fla.App. 2000). Because trustworthiness is presumed to exist with most business records, trial court may exclude evidence meeting literal requirements of business record exception to hearsay rule, where underlying circumstances tend to indicate lack of trustworthiness. See *Stewart v. CSX Transportation, Inc.*, 602 S.E.2d 665, 268 Ga. App. 434 (2004). Generally, a document otherwise admissible as a business record is not admissible if it contains opinions or conclusions which may or may not be based upon facts.

10 *City of Chicago v. Old Colony Partners*, 364 Ill.App.3d 806, 847 N.E.2d 565, 301 Ill.Dec. 555 (2006). Business records made in anticipation of litigation do not possess the same trustworthiness as other records prepared in the ordinary course of business. For Latin lovers, this was referred to as the "Anti-Litem Motem" exception to the business records rule; roughly translated, it means that documents prepared with an eye toward litigation are per se suspect. *U.S. v. Robertson*, 588 F.2d 578 (8th Cir. 1978); *U.S. v. Johns-Mansville Corp.*, 231 F.Supp. 690 (E.D. Pa. 1963). *Lust v. Sealy, Inc.*, 383 F.3d 580 (7th Cir. Wis., 2004); *Hertz v. Luzenac Am., Inc.*, 370 F.3d 1014 (10th Cir. Colo., 2004).

11 See Chapters 2 and 20 with respect to the best evidence rule.

12 *Bartolucci v. DAL Bianco,* 228 Ill. App. 113 (1923).

13 *In re Huffman's Estate*, 349 Pa. 59, 36 A.2d 640 (1944).

14 *Gil v. Gil*, 892 A.2d 318. Once the criteria of the business records exception to the hearsay rule have been met by the party seeking to introduce the record, it does not necessarily follow that the record itself is generally admissible, nor does it mean that everything in it is required to be admitted into evidence.

12. The information contained in the document came from scattered sources, or the writing otherwise consisted of multiple, non-excepted, hearsay.[15]

The best feature of the business records exception is the manner in which it permits a mere custodian to act as the sole foundation witness; the person who actually prepared or authored the documents need not be present.[16] But that feature can also be a pitfall.[17] A mere custodian would be easy to attack with respect to several of the items on the above hit list, depending upon the custodian's actual knowledge or lack thereof.

As we provide "quick answers" for each of the documents listed below (and those in the remaining chapters of Part II, Documentary Evidence), do not forget that with respect to every "Are they admissible?" question, THRESHOLD RELEVANCE IS ASSUMED.

REFERENCES

Contemporaneous with transaction recorded, necessity for. 34 Am. Jur. Proof of Facts 2d 509.

Cross-examination of authenticating witness. 14 Am. Jur. Proof of Facts 2d 173.

§22.400 Specific Records

§22.401 Accident Reports

ARE THEY ADMISSIBLE?
GENERALLY, NO.

Keep in mind that as used in this particular chapter, the subject "accident reports" are private records, not those of governmental agencies. As such, they were prepared and maintained by private businesses, not an official source, such as a police or governmental agency pursuant to law.[18] While the former are generally admissible, the latter are not.

15 *Reichenberg v. Davis,* 846 So.2d 1233 (Fla.App., 2003). In a custody modification hearing, the reports of investigations conducted by the Department of Children and Families, which contained witness interviews wherein allegations were made that the subject child had been the victim of "sexual touching" by the mother's stepdaughter, were not admissible under the business records exception to the hearsay rule, nor were they admissible under the public records exception to the hearsay rule; the authors of the reports simply related the substance of what other witnesses had told the authors.

Ross Dress for Less, Inc. v. Radcliff, 751 So.2d 126 (Fla.App. 2000). In personal injury action, treating orthopedic surgeon's medical report contained inadmissible hearsay; several passages in report quoted conclusions of other physicians. *Johnson v. Herman,* 132 F.Supp.2d 1130 (N.D.Ind. 2001). Hearsay exception for records of regularly conducted activity does not encompass entries made by third parties. *Chadwell v. Koch Refining Co.,* L.P., 251 F.3d 727 (8th Cir., Minn., 2001). Employee's statements contained in notes that union steward took during meeting in which employer questioned employee concerning alleged whistle blowing activities were properly excluded as double hearsay. They constituted out-of-court statements regarding employee's out-of-court statements. Notes also did not qualify as hearsay exception for records of regularly conducted business activity; even assuming that note-taking qualified as "regularly conducted business activity," there was no evidence that source of information had any guarantees of trustworthiness.

16 *Forester v. Norman Roger Jewell & Brooks Intern., Inc.*, 610 So.2d 1369 (Fla. App. 1 Dist. 1992).

17 *Midstates Resources Corp. v. Dobrindt*, 798 A.2d 494, 70 Conn.App. 420 (2002). Even though a party complies with the basic requirements necessary for admitting a document under the business records exception to the hearsay rule, such a document does not automatically carry a presumption of accuracy; its credibility always remains a question for the trier of fact.

18 The very same heading (i.e. "Accident Reports") delivers a different story in Chapter 21. Note that evidence that is otherwise barred as hearsay is admissible under business records exception if proponent of document shows either (1) that document's author had personal knowledge of matters reported, or (2) that information he reported was transmitted by another person who had personal knowledge acting in course of a regularly conducted activity, or (3) that it was author's regular practice to record information transmitted by persons who had personal knowledge. See *Coyle v. Kristjan Palusalu Maritime Co., Ltd.*, 83 F.Supp.2d 535 (E.D.Pa. 2000).

KEY POINTS FOR PROPONENT:

The news is generally bad. Whenever an accident occurs that affects a business, the report issued by that business must *per se* be untrustworthy and should therefore fail to meet the requirements of the business records exception. The hearsay rule would warrant exclusion. But if the report contains material adverse to the entity that prepared it, then that material may constitute an admission, and might, therefore, be admissible as a hearsay exception.[19]

KEY POINTS FOR OPPOSITION:

Whatever the nature of the business may be, in all probability it does not make a living by engaging in accidents; therefore, the resulting reports are normally not considered to have been prepared "in the ordinary course of business."[20]

Moreover, anyone opposing these reports should claim that they are inadmissible hearsay. Refer to items 2 through 7 on the Opposition Checklist (*Supra*, §22.300).

§22.402 Appraisals

ARE THEY ADMISSIBLE? **NO.**

KEY POINTS:

An appraisal is basically an opinion as to the value of an item of property. As such, it is normally offered to prove the truth value asserted, and is, therefore, hearsay. In a wrongful foreclosure action, for example, which challenged the adequacy of a price obtained at a mortgage foreclosure sale, appraisals performed by a now-deceased appraiser were not

---

19 See also *Lee v. Thomason*, 627 S.E.2d 168, 277 Ga.App. 573 (2006). Accident reports were admissible under the business records exception to the hearsay rule in an automobile accident case; the motorist's supervisor personally made the reports in the regular course of business shortly after the subject collision occurred based on what the motorist had told him, and both the motorist and the supervisor testified at trial and were available for cross-examination.

Ulm v. Ford Motor Co., 750 A.2d 981 (Vt. 2000) products liability action was brought by passenger of vehicle that experienced steering system failure; passenger was paralyzed by resulting accident. Internal documents obtained from Ford that referred to seven incidents of such failure were relevant and admissible as business records; the documents supported passenger's theory that a driver could be unaware of the impact causing an initial crack in a sector shaft of steering system. *Kilgo v. Wal-Mart Stores, Inc.*, 531 S.E.2d 883 (N.C.App. 2000). In personal injury action against Wal-Mart, report prepared by store manager was not objectionable (for use against defending Wal-Mart) as hearsay or improper opinion testimony, even though report contained manager's comments as to how incident occurred. Moreover, manager was agent of store when he entered his comments on report, such entry concerned matters within scope of his employment. *Grayson v. R.B. Ammon and Associates, Inc.*, 778 So.2d 1 (La. App., 2000). In personal injury action brought by plaintiff employee who was injured at job site, portion of accident report prepared by non-testifying, non-party employee of employer was not excluded from definition of hearsay since report was offered against plaintiff employee, not employer.

20 *Hamby v. Crescent Ford Truck Sales, Inc.*, 839 So.2d 138 (La. App., 2003). In an action by a truck driver against a dealership and insurer, alleging negligence after the truck's brakes allegedly failed, an accident report of the driver's employer was improperly admitted under business records exception to the hearsay rule; the proponents of the report failed to prove that someone with knowledge issued the report. Moreover, the report did not constitute the type of record contemplated by the business records exception. *Owens v. Seattle*, 49 Wash. 2d 187, 299 P.2d 560 (1956); *Palmer v. Hoffman*, 318 U.S. 109 (1943). See *Coyle v. Kristjan Palusalu Maritime Co., Ltd.*, 83 F.Supp.2d 535 (E.D.Pa., 2000); *Mullican v. Transamerican Insurance Group,* 773 So.2d 207 (La. App., 2000). In negligence action from resulting from customers' slip and fall in restaurant, handwritten statement concerning accident was not admissible under business records exception to hearsay rule; restaurant's assistant manager, author of statement, was not person whose duty it was to routinely report such information. Statement was, thus, not prepared in ordinary course of manager's business. Thus, it could not be admitted since it was offered to prove truth of matters asserted.

admissible under the business record exception to the hearsay rule; the appraisals were the opinions of the appraiser and, as such, did not come within that exception.[21]

§22.403 Bills and Statements of Account

ARE THEY ADMISSIBLE? YES.

KEY POINTS FOR PROPONENT:

The primary purpose for the business records exception to the hearsay rule,[22] both historically and legally, was to avoid the necessity of shutting down part of the company's business to parade its managers into court every time a deadbeat failed to pay a bill.

KEY POINTS FOR OPPOSITION:

If a bill or statement of account is not timely objected to *before* litigation becomes necessary, the business records will not only be admitted, but, in the absence of fraud or mistake, may be unassailable as a matter of contract law. Thus, improper bills should always be contested in writing, before litigation is commenced. If not, then "non-receipt" of the bill or statement by the defendant may be the only viable avenue of opposition.

Despite their favored acceptance, all bills are not automatically admissible.[23] And estimates generally lack probative value and are not admissible.[24]

§22.403(a) Bills of Lading

ARE THEY ADMISSIBLE? YES.

KEY POINTS FOR PROPONENT:

Bills of Lading are records kept in the ordinary course of business and, therefore, fall within the business records exception to the hearsay rule.[25]

§22.403(b) Charge Slips

ARE THEY ADMISSIBLE? YES.

KEY POINTS:

Documents relating to customer account balances, if kept in the ordinary course of business, are admissible. Charge slips are clearly examples of such records. The classic "Shop Book Rule," which later gave way to the "Business Records Rule," was created so that a shop owner would not be required to testify firsthand to such matters.[26]

---

21 *Dickens v. Calhoun First Nat. Bank,* 448 S.E.2d 237, 214 Ga. App. 490 (Ga. App. 1994).

22 See *supra*, Fed. R. Evid. 803(6). See also *Fawer, Brian, Hardy & Zatzkis v. Howes*, 639 So.2d 329 (La. App. 4 Cir. 1994). Not every document pertaining to bills or billing constitutes hearsay. See, for example, *Anderson v. United States Fid. & Guar. Co.,* 600 S.E.2d 712 (2004). In an action by a surety against indemnitors, billing summaries attached to the surety's attorney's affidavit in support of summary judgment were not hearsay; by signing the indemnity agreement, the indemnitors agreed that vouchers or other evidence of the surety's payments on behalf of a construction company (or an itemized statement sworn to by the surety's officer) would be prima facie evidence of payments made by the surety on behalf of the construction company.

23 *Andreani v. Feygin*, 812 N.Y.S.2d 740, 11 Misc.3d 54 (2006). In an action by a landlord against tenants for damages to an apartment rented pursuant to an oral lease, bills for repairs were not admissible. Most of them were itemized and marked paid, but they nevertheless failed to contain any requisite certification.

24 *Harris v. Hamilton*, 569 So.2d 1 (La.App. 4 Cir., 1990).

25 *State Department of Environmental Regulation v. CTL Distribution, Inc.*, 715 So.2d 562 (Fla. App. 1998).

26 *Trotti v. Estate of Buchanan*, 706 N.Y.S.2d 534 (N.Y.A.D. 2000). In action by grocery store owners and operators to recover customer's account balance and set aside fraudulent conveyances, charge slips and ledger papers representing the account of the deceased customer were admissible as business records.

Broadcast station operators, engineers, ship captains, pilots and truck drivers are required by law to maintain logs. Recently, the truckers' logs have been a focus of attention; they often provide important information about the number of hours that a driver was on the road prior to his involvement in an accident. Federal Regulations require that the entries be "true and correct" and that the forms be signed[34], making them perfect impeachment devices.[35]

§22.404 (b) Suspension Orders

***ARE THEY ADMISSIBLE?* IT DEPENDS UPON THE SOURCE AND PURPOSE.**

KEY POINTS:

Our primary concern is directed toward those suspension orders issued to or by a manufacturer in order to preserve records or data that may be relevant to pending or future litigation. If they were generated as part of the company's ordinary business practices, they might be admissible as business records[36]; on the other hand, if they were issued by an attorney for the manufacturer, they might be subject to attorney-client privilege.[37]

§22.405 Canceled Checks

***ARE THEY ADMISSIBLE?* YES.**

KEY POINTS:

Generally, a check is an order directed to a banking institution, not a statement of fact and, therefore, would not constitute hearsay.[38] Where a check is presented to show or prove the reasonableness of a debt as opposed to payment, a hearsay argument can be advanced. In such a case, the principles pertaining to bills (see above) might apply, depending upon the facts.

REFERENCES

Bank records, admissibility. 14 Am. Jur. Proof of Facts 2d 173.

Checking account, admissibility of record of individuals. 34 Am. Jur. Proof of Facts 2d 509.

§22.406 Computer-Generated Documents

ARE THEY ADMISSIBLE?
YES. TO THE SAME EXTENT AS NON-COMPUTERIZED RECORDS.

KEY POINTS:

It is safe to say that computer-generated business records are no less admissible nor more admissible by virtue of their computer-generated nature. Indeed, most of the business records

34 See C.F.R. §395.

35 See Altman, *Truckers and Their Driving Logs*, 35 Trial, Vol. 3, at 34 (March 1999).

36 See §22.100.

37 See §9.501. See also *Kirk v. Ford Motor Co.,* 116 P.3d 27, 141 Idaho 697 (2005).

38 Most cases involving admissibility of checks center around "copy" or Best Evidence problems, thus taking admissibility of originals for granted. See, *Iberia Building Systems, Inc. v. Bank One*, 768 So.2d 106 (La.App. 2000). In customer's action against bank for negotiating forged checks, photocopies of forged checks were admissible since no contrary evidence established that they did not accurately reflect originals. Moreover, when document offered into evidence is mechanical reproduction of original, that reproduction is admissible unless it can be shown that its contents do not accurately reflect original. See also *Jacobs v. Yates*, 27 S.W.3d 734 (Ark. 2000). In election contest concerning timeliness of payment of filing fee, copies of returned check were admissible where party challenging evidence possessed original. For Best Evidence issues, see Chapter 2 and §20.200.

presently produced are computer-generated.[39] Today, the important admissibility considerations relate more to the manner in which the business records were generated and maintained rather than to whether or not they consisted of computer files, database records, or printouts.

Therefore, computer-generated records kept in the ordinary course of business should be able to maintain the same basic degree of admissibility as non-computerized documents.[40] They are not, however, accorded any special or preferred treatment.[41]

---

39 Today, special distinctions questioning the reliability of computerized record generation is rare. But see *Duplissie v. Devino*, 902 A.2d 30, 96 Conn.App. 673 (2006). In a former employee's breach of contract action to recover unpaid commissions, a computer-generated record of job cost details for the subject construction project was admissible under the business records exception to the hearsay rule even though the record was not a complete statement of all costs for the project; the data entries were accurate, made in the regular course of business, and were contemporaneous with the specific events described in the record. Also, evidence is not inadmissible under the business records exception merely because a business record was created, stored, or produced by means of computer technology. When computer records are offered as evidence, however, the proponent must satisfy a two-part test; in particular, in addition to meeting the three requirements of the business records exception to the hearsay rule, the proponent also must establish that the basic elements of the computer system are reliable. See also *Emigrant Mortgage Company, Inc. v. D'Agostino*, 896 A.2d 814, 94 Conn.App. 793 (2006). Business record evidence is not inadmissible because the business record happens to be created, stored or produced by means of computer technology.

Garden State Bank v. Graef, 775 A.2d 189, 341 N.J. Super. 241 (2001). In bank's action against debtor and guarantors to accelerate loan balance resulting from defendants' default, computer printouts of payment history submitted by bank were routine records which were kept in regular course of business. Thus printouts were admissible under business records exception to hearsay rule; authenticity of demand note contained in record was never disputed, bank's credit manager was sufficiently familiar with record system used to enable him to establish that it was bank's regular practice to make record in regular course of business, prior to commencement of dispute among parties. *Guillermety v. Secretary of Education of U.S.*, 341 F.Supp.2d 682 (E.D. Mich., 2003). In an action by the United States seeking to collect repayment of a student loan, computer printouts that were generated and maintained in the regular course of business at or near the time of the recorded transactions were admissible as business records. Moreover, a computer printout may be admissible as a business record if a proper foundation is established.

40 *Federal Express Corporation v. Federal Jeans, Inc.*, 14 A.D.3d 424, 788 N.Y.S.2d 113, (App.Div., 1st Dept., 2005). In an action based on account-stated, computer-generated invoices and billing records of amounts due were admissible as business records since the plaintiff established that the information contained in them was entered into the subject computer during the regular course of business. *Beal Bank, SSB v. Eurich*, 831 N.E.2d 909, 444 Mass. 813 (2005). In an action to recover a deficiency on a mortgage note after a foreclosure sale, computer printouts generated by a company that serviced loans for the bank were admissible as the bank's records under the business records exception to hearsay rule. The bank's servicing agent had a business duty to accurately report information to the bank, and the bank routinely accessed and relied on that information to determine whether or not there was any new activity on a loan. *Huffy Corp. v. Custom Warehouse, Inc.*, 169 S.W.3d 89 (Mo.App., 2005). In an action by a bicycle manufacturer against a warehouse for property damage sustained to its bicycles, a computer-generated spreadsheet that set forth the number of bikes damaged and the costs of production for each bike was admissible under the business records exception to the hearsay rule. The information reflected in the spreadsheet was generated in the ordinary course of the manufacturer's business, and the spreadsheet was generated near the time of the incident in order to properly manage inventory.

Van Dusen v. Petty, 709 N.Y.S.2d 791 (N.Y.A.D. 2000). In proceedings initiated by County Department of Social Services to obtain reimbursement of medical assistance expenditures from unwed fathers, certified computer-generated records kept in ordinary course of business pertaining to those expenditures were admissible. Those records constituted prima facie evidence of medical assistance expenditures made by Department.

41 *In re Dow Corning Corp.*, 250 BR. 298 (Bankruptcy, E.D.Mich. 2000). As long as proper foundation is laid, computer-generated data may qualify as "report," for purposes of business records exception to hearsay rule. Generally, however, business records are not self-proving; rather, proper foundation must be laid through testimony of witnesses qualified to explain record-keeping process.

§22.407 Consumer Complaints

Such correspondence may be maintained by businesses as part of their normal record-keeping functions, but they still originate from individual sources; see §23.403.

§22.408 Corporate Memos

ARE THEY ADMISSIBLE? YES.

KEY POINTS FOR PROPONENT:

Memos may be admissible if they are kept in the regular course of business.[42] They may even be admissible if they are not classified as ordinary business records.[43]

KEY POINTS FOR OPPOSITION:

The opponent should object to memos not kept in the ordinary course of business.[44] See also, Opposition Checklist items 1, 3, 4, 5, 6, 7, 8, 9.

§22.408(a) Corporate Minutes

ARE THEY ADMISSIBLE? YES.

KEY POINTS:

Corporate minutes are a bit more official than corporate memos, though both documents share some material characteristics. Both are designed to memorialize information and execute corporate directives. Whereas the memo could be either formal or informal, minutes are certainly formal and "official." And, whereas a memo normally represents the expression of a single author, the corporate minutes purport to speak on behalf of the corporation as whole.[45]

§22.409 Customer Lists

ARE THEY ADMISSIBLE?
YES (QUALIFIED).

KEY POINTS:

The customer list is a very common record that is maintained by nearly every business.

---

42 See *supra*, Fed. R. Evid. 803(6). *Tracy v. Cotterell*, 524 S.E.2d 879 (W.Va. 1999) involved products liability action wherein plaintiff alleged that seat belt system was defectively designed. Memorandum prepared by former employee of auto manufacturer during course and scope of his employment (discussing how design of certain of manufacturer's automobiles permitted inadvertent slack in shoulder restraint systems) did fit within hearsay exception for records of regularly conducted business activity.

43 *Detroit/Wayne County Stadium Authority v. Drinkwater, Taylor & Merrill, Inc.*, 705 N.W.2d 549, 267 Mich.App. 625 (2005). A memorandum prepared by the corporate director of gaming development for a casino company (regarding details of his meeting with the mayor to explore the possibility of developing a casino in the city) was sufficiently trustworthy and could be admitted under the catch-all exception to the hearsay rule. In general, evidence admitted under the catch-all exception must satisfy four elements: (1) it must have circumstantial guarantees of trustworthiness equal to the categorical exceptions; (2) it must tend to establish a material fact; (3) it must be the most probative evidence on the fact that the offering party could produce through reasonable efforts; and (4) its admission must serve the interests of justice.

44 *Snyder v. Whittaker Corp.*, 839 F.2d 1085 (5th Cir. 1988). A memo written by employees of another company, which was received and kept by the defendant, was not kept in the regular course of business and was ruled inadmissible.

45 *Higginsville Memorial Post 6270 v. Benton,* 108 S.W.3d 28 (MoApp., 2003). Corporate minutes are prima facie evidence of what transpires at corporate meetings.

Therefore, it is clear that such an item would constitute a record kept in the ordinary course of business, and would be admissible in accordance with Fed. R. Evid. 803(6). Therefore, it is clear that such an item would constitute a record kept in the ordinary course of business, and would be admissible in accordance with Fed.R.Evid. 803(6) or its applicable state counterpart.[46]

What about lists of ex-customers? While they *may* also be considered as records kept in the ordinary course of business, they may not share the same ease of admissibility; the purpose for seeking the admission may be a critical factor. In an action involving an alleged tortious interference with business relations, lists of customers who no longer traded at a particular store were held to be too speculative to be admissible to show a purchaser's actual financial loss.[47]

§22.410 DNA Matching Test Results

DNA tests are normally used in criminal matters; see §21.410.

§22.411 E-Mail

IS IT ADMISSIBLE? **IT DEPENDS.**

KEY POINTS:

E-mail should now be treated as any other common medium of documentary expression. To question a writing merely because it happens to be an *e-mail* makes no more sense than to question a writing just because it is a fax or telegram. In either event, the answer would always depend upon the source and content of the underlying information.[48]

Pay particular attention to the dangers of violating attorney-client privilege. As in the case of the facsimile, special care and attention must given to the nature of the medium.[49]

REFERENCES

E-mail recovery and reconstruction as evidence. 41 POF3d 1.

§22.412 Employment Records

ARE THEY ADMISSIBLE? **YES.**

KEY POINTS:

Employment records are discoverable.[50] They are generally used in personal injury cases to prove lost wages or loss of future earnings.

§22.412(a) Payroll Scales

ARE THEY ADMISSIBLE? **YES.**

KEY POINTS:

Such "scales" are normally kept within the course and scope of a company's business and should, therefore, fall within the business records exception to the hearsay rule.[51]

---

46 See *Tire Shredders, Inc. v. ERM-North Central, Inc.,* 15 S.W.3d 849 (Tenn.Ct.App. 1999).

47 *Cenac v. Murry*, 609 So.2d 1257 (Miss. 1992).

48 See also *Riisna v. American Broadcasting Companies, Inc.,* 219 F.Supp.2d 568 (S.D.N.Y., 2002). See also *Sealand Service, Inc. v. Lozen International, L.L.C.*, 285 F.3d 808 (9th Cir., Cal., 2002).

See Jablon, "*Got Mail: Authentication and Admissibility of Electronic Mail in Federal Courts.*" 34 Am. Crim. L. Rev. 1387 (1997).

49 See Stevenson, "*Making a Wrong Turn on the Information Superhighway: Electronic Mail, the Attorney-Client Privilege and Inadvertent Disclosure,*" 26 Cap. U. L. Rev. 347 (1997).

50 See *Soler v. G and U, Inc.*, 86 F.R.D. 524 (S.D.N.Y. 1980); *Adams v. Dan River Mills, Inc.*, 54 F.R.D. 220 (W.D.Va. 1972); *Banks v. Lockheed-Georgia Co.*, 53 F.R.D. 283 (N.D. Ga. 1971).

51 See *Boudreau v. S/V Shere Khan C,* 27 F.Supp.2d 72 (D.Maine 1998).

§22.412(b) Time Cards

ARE THEY ADMISSIBLE? YES.

KEY POINTS:

Time cards, like time records, are typical employee documents, generated, maintained and kept in the ordinary course of business. There is little doubt about their admissibility.[52]

§22.413 Garbage

See same heading in Chapter 23.

§22.414 Industry or Trade Standards

ARE THEY ADMISSIBLE? YES.

KEY POINTS FOR PROPONENT:

While industry or trade standards and regulations are generally not admissible to prove liability[53] some standards are admissible under the hearsay exception for public records.[54] However, the proponent must request the proper hearsay exception.[55]

KEY POINTS FOR OPPOSITION:

The opponent should pay particular attention to Opposition Checklist items 1-9.

§22.415 Insurance Records

ARE THEY ADMISSIBLE? YES.

KEY POINTS:

The proponent should look to the business records exception to the hearsay rule for those records which are kept in the ordinary course of business.[56] Keep in mind that "relevance," and therefore admissibility, may depend upon the purpose for which the records are being offered. If, for example, the only purpose for offering the records is to show the existence of insurance, the records may be excluded in a case where such existence is deemed irrelevant or improper by the court. Just because an insurance record or log happens to be admissible under the business records exception to the hearsay rule, one should not assume that such a record can become a vehicle for inadmissible information or notes.[57]

§22.416 Letters

ARE THEY ADMISSIBLE? YES.

KEY POINTS:

Letters are a very normal part of doing business. There is no reason to believe that they should be treated as anything other than business records, assuming, of course, that appropriate foundations

---

52 With respect to writings attached to time cards, see *Hoodco of Poplar Bluff, Inc. v. Bosoluke*, 9 S.W.3d 701 (Mo.App. 1999), holding that written note attached to time card was admissible under business records exception to hearsay rule, where that time card had already been ruled admissible.

53 *Hercules Powder Co. v. Di Sabatino*, 188 A.2d 529 (Del. 1963); *Sloan v. Carolina Power and Light Co.*, 248 N.C. 125, 102 S.E.2d 822 (1958); *Parker v. James E. Granger, Inc.*, 298 U.S. 644 (1935).

54 *Lockwood v. Baptist Regional Health Services, Inc.*, 541 So.2d 731 (Fla. 1989); *Garbincius v. Boston Edison Co.*, 621 F.2d 1171 (1st Cir. 1980); *Johnson v. Ellis & Sons Iron Workers, Inc.*, 609 F.2d 820 (5th Cir. 1979); *Gordy v. City of Canton, Mississippi,* 543 F.2d 558 (5th Cir. 1976).

55 *Alexander v. Conveyors and Dumpers, Inc.*, 731 F.2d 221 (5th Cir. 1984).

56 See Fed. R. Evid. 803(6). See also *Sana v. Hawaiian Cruises, Ltd.,* 181 F.3d 1041 (9th Cir. 1999).

57 *Horn v. Gov't Emples. Ins. Co.,* 86 Fed.Appx. 405 (10th Cir. Okla., 2004). In a recording in an insurance company's accident log, a brother-in-law's statement that the plaintiff lived with him at the time that the plaintiff was involved in an automobile accident was inadmissible hearsay.

are laid. But the "normal" condition must not be taken for granted.[58] In many instances, letters written during the course of business may be offered for reasons other than proving the truth of the matters contained within, in which case, the hearsay rule will not apply; thus, assuming the letters are relevant, they should be admitted.[59] For letters written by judges, arbitrators, or mediators, refer to this heading in Chapter 25.

KEY POINTS FOR OPPOSITION:

As used in the above heading, the term "Letters" refers specifically to "business" letters, which, in turn, implies that the subject letters were generated in the ordinary course of business and further that it was a normal business practice that caused the generation of the letters. For evidentiary purposes, however, letters that consist of, or contain, conclusions, impressions or self serving statements are not considered as "ordinary business records."[60]

---

58 In a strict liability case, a handwritten notation on the bottom of a letter, made by an employee of the defendant (as to a telephone conversation with another employee), was not admissible under the hearsay exception for business records because there was no indication that the employee had **regularly** memorialized telephone conversations through written notations, or that such notations were a part of the employer's regular business practices. *Feldman v. Lederle Laboratories*, 625 A.2d 1066, 132 N.J. 339 (1993). *Gilbert v. Ireland*, 758 So.2d 1050 (Miss.App. 2000). Treating physician's letter to plaintiff's counsel, summarizing his treatment and his diagnosis of plaintiff four years before trial was prepared in anticipation of litigation, and thus was not admissible as record of regularly conducted activities; letter was not trustworthy. *Tire Shredders, Inc. v. ERM-North Central, Inc.*, 15 S.W.3d 849 (Tenn.Ct.App. 1999). In negligence action arising from shredding of shredding machine (lots of irony here), documents relating to contract between machine owner and third party were admissible; items included: customer lists, draft agreements, shipping records, and correspondence. These writings were among types of records that machine owner would normally maintain in ordinary course of business.

59 *Lake Superior Center Authority v. Hammel, Green & Abrahamson, Inc.*, 715 N.W.2d 458 Minn.App., 2006). In an architectural malpractice action by public owners of an aquarium against an architect and tank design consultant (as a result of defective concrete poured for the wall of an exhibit tank), a letter from the concrete additive manufacturer to the company that provided the concrete mix design for the aquarium was not admitted to prove the truth of the matter asserted, and thus was not inadmissible hearsay. The letter was relevant to determine whether or not the company knew that the concrete mixture could benefit from the additive and whether the company had notice of the additive's characteristics.

Central States Southeast and Southwest Areas Pension Fund v. Bomar National, Inc., 253 F.3d 1011 (7th Cir., Ill., 2001). In suit to collect interim withdrawal liability payments, letter sent by multi-employer pension plan to employer to confirm that employer had ceased operations was not hearsay but was admissible to demonstrate disagreement as to date of commencement of employers' withdrawal liability. *Kursh v. Iowa Department of Transportation*, 628 N.W.2d 1 (Iowa, 2001). *Tewani Imports, Inc. v. Norwest Bank, N.A.*, 139 F.Supp.2d 805 (S.D.Texas, 2001). Letter from Postal Service manager to director of association of Mexican currency exchange houses was not inadmissible hearsay; letter had independent legal significance of discontinuing Postal Service's practice of sending claims for alleged wrong payments to association prior to paying claims and invoicing presenting banks.

60 *Pendley Quality Trailer Supply, Inc. v. B & F Plastics, Inc.*, 578 S.E.2d 915, 260 Ga.App. 125 (2003). The testimonial of a buyer's customer was not admissible under the business records exception to the hearsay rule, where the buyer attempted to introduce it in order to establish that its purchasing agent had "commended" the quality of the buyer's services and products. Generally, the conclusions, opinions, and impressions of third parties not presented before court are not admissible under the business records exception.

§22.416(a) Service Bulletins, Warnings and Notices to Customers

ARE THEY ADMISSIBLE? YES, BUT NOT TO PROVE NEGLIGENCE.

KEY POINTS:

There are a number of reasons why manufacturers send letters and notices to their customers. If the letters are to be used to show the state of mind of the sender or for some other non-hearsay purpose, they should be allowed.[61] But if they are going to be used against the sender to prove negligence, they may be excludable, either as hearsay, or as evidence of subsequent remedial repairs.[62]

§22.416 (b) Settlement Letters

ARE THEY ADMISSIBLE? NO.

KEY POINTS:

Discussions directed toward the resolution of business related disputes are often reduced to letters, particularly prior to a final resolution. We know that evidence of a compromise or settlement should not be permitted to establish the validity of the subject claim, regardless of the form of that evidence.[63] But where settlement negotiations are being used for another purpose, admissibility may be warranted.[64]

§22.417 Lie Detector Results

See "Polygraph Test Results" (*infra*).

§22.418 Manufacturer Specification Booklets

ARE THEY ADMISSIBLE? YES.

KEY POINTS:

Booklets such as owners' manuals or guides provided to retailers may be admissible.[65] But the booklets must be accurate and non-prejudicial.[66]

---

61 See §5.406. See also Rule 803(3) of the *Federal Rules of Evidence*.

63 *HDM Flugservice Gmblt v. Parker Hannifin Corp.*, 332 F.3d 1025 (6th Cir., Ohio, 2003). A service bulletin was issued by the manufacturer of a helicopter landing gear indicating that additional remedial measures needed to be taken during the inspection of component parts. Because the bulletin was issued voluntarily, it was properly excluded from evidence as remedial measures taken subsequent to an event causing injury or harm.

See also §6.703 and Rule 407 of the *Federal Rules of Evidence*.

63 See §6.704. See also *Douris v. Genuardi's Family Markets, Inc.*, 132 Fed.Appx. 425 (3rd Cir., Pa., 2005).

64 *Zurich American Insurance Company v. Watts Industries, Inc.*, 417F.3d 682 (7th Cir., Ill., 2005). In an insurer's action to compel arbitration with respect to the parties' separate deductible agreements, the admission of a letter written by an insured, in an effort to settle a dispute as to whether the liability policies provided coverage for state court fraud lawsuits against the insured, to a liability insurer was warranted. The letter could have discussed the settlement of the state court action without mentioning the deductible agreements, and it was not offered to prove that the insured was obligated to arbitrate under the agreements.

65 *Link v. Mercedes-Benz of North America, Inc.*, 788 F.2d 918 (3rd Cir. 1986). The plaintiff was allowed to introduce into evidence "time-guides" that provided instructions to dealers.

66 *Haynes v. American Motors Corp.*, 691 F.2d 1268 (8th Cir. 1982). The plaintiff was injured in a rollover of a consumer Jeep CJ. The plaintiff attempted to enter into evidence the operator's manual of an AMC military Jeep to show that a warning contained in the latter manual should have been included in the Jeep CJ's manual. Because the two vehicles are structurally different, the court ruled that the military Jeep's manual was irrelevant.

§22.419 Maps

The term "map" has a many meanings. As used in this chapter, it refers to those maps and surveys that are created by private companies and societies. For maps created by any governmental agency, see §21.415. And, for maps that are used for clarification (i.e., demonstrative) purposes, see §42.200.

***ARE THEY ADMISSIBLE?* YES.**

KEY POINTS:

Maps created by non-governmental agencies do not enjoy self-authentication; but a witness with some personal knowledge of its accuracy may, nevertheless, lay an appropriate foundation.[67]

§22.420 Medical and Hospital Records

***ARE THEY ADMISSIBLE?* YES.**

Medical records are business records within the meaning of the business records exception to the hearsay rule.[68] All of the applicable aspects of that exception apply.

KEY POINTS FOR PROPONENT:

If personal injuries are involved, whenever a patient commences litigation concerning those injuries, he or she is deemed to waive any doctor-patient privilege that may exist with respect to those injuries.

A medical record is admissible under the business records exception to the hearsay rule as long as the information is pathologically germane,[69] and entries in a medical record are

67 *Albig v. Municipal Authority of Westmoreland County*, 348 Pa. Super 505, 502 A.2d 658 (1985); for a map offering that did not purport to establish boundaries, see *Blackburn v. Richardson*, 849 S.W.2d 281 (Mo. App. 1993).

68 *Long v. St. John's Regional Health Center, Inc.,* 98 S.W.3d 601 (Mo.App., 2003); *Lambert v. Shearer*, 616 N.E.2d 965, 84 Ohio App.3d 266 (1992); *Baylis v. Lourdes Hosp.*, 805 S.W.2d 122 (Ky. 1991).

69 *Ruffin v. City of Boston*, 146 Fed.Appx. 501 (1st Cir., Mass., 2005). In a §1983 action by an arrestee against an arresting officer alleging the use of excessive force, an emergency medical technician's own observations as contained in a contemporaneously recorded patient care report of his evaluation of the arrestee's injuries at the police station were admissible under the business records exception to the hearsay rule. *Rodriguez v. Piccone,* 774 N.Y.S.2d 185, 5 A.D.3d 757 (N.Y.A.D. 2 Dep't 2004); *Eitner v. 119 West 71st Street Owners Corporation,* 6774 N.Y.S.2d 555 (1998); *Criski v. Sadler 119 West 71st Street Owners Corporation,* 676 N.Y.S.2d 646 (1998); *Chadderton v. M.A. Bongivonni, Inc.*, 647 A.2d 137, 101 Md. App. 472 (Md. App., 1994). Medical records are admissible as business records to the extent that the entries therein are germane to the diagnosis and treatment of the patient's ailments.

admissible if they are relevant to the patient's diagnosis and treatment.[70] When statements are made to hospital personnel, a two-part test must be satisfied for those statements to be admissible: (1) the statement must be within the scope of the entrant's business duty to record it, and (2) the declarant must be under a business duty to report

70 *Troyan v. Reyes*, 855 N.E.2d 967, 367 Ill.App.3d 729, 305 Ill.Dec. 451 (2006). In a motorist's automobile negligence action to recover for injuries sustained in a traffic accident, diagnoses and opinions contained in the motorist's medical records were admissible under the business records exception to the hearsay rule, even though the medical providers were not available to testify; the diagnoses and opinions were relevant and not too complex for the jury to understand on its own. In general, medical records are admissible as long as a sufficient foundation is laid to establish that they are business records. Moreover, medical diagnoses should be admissible to the same extent as objective facts because a diagnosis is the major premise from which the physician draws his or her conclusions as to the proper treatment to be rendered; normally the progress of the patient depends upon its accuracy. Because diagnoses form an integral part of medical records, the same reliability requirements for business records in general should apply to the opinions underlying those diagnoses. Records containing statements of medical opinions constitute a firmly rooted exception to the hearsay rule, and as such, their reliability is inferred.

Bucci v. Essex Insurance Co., 393 F.3d 285 (1st Cir., Miss., 2005) involved a personal injury action by a nightclub patron following a bar room fight. As to the issue of whether or not the injuries were intentionally caused (and therefore excludable from coverage under the nightclub's liability insurance policy), statements in the patron's medical records describing the specific interactions causing the injuries included a statement that the patron complained of neck pain after being struck by a fist; the evidence was admissible under the hearsay exception pertaining to statements made for the purpose of medical treatment or diagnosis. *Brooks v. Friedman,* 769 N.E.2d 696 (Ind.App., 2002). Hospital records should not be excluded from evidence, as hearsay, merely because they contain opinions and diagnoses. But to be admissible, the opinions and diagnoses must meet the conditions normally required of expert opinions.

Fox v. Mahoney, 22 P.3d 839 (Wash.App., 2001). In auto negligence action, letter from plastic surgeon who examined plaintiff motorist to evaluate scar she received in car accident (while addressing options for scar's removal and cost of producing best possible result) was for purpose of treatment and was not merely a forensic report, thus letter was admissible against other driver, even though it was sent to plaintiff's attorney. There was no indication that surgeon could not have testified about same information contained in his letter had he been available at trial. *McCollum v. McDaniel,* 136 F.Supp.2d 472 (D.Md., 2001). In auto negligence action by injured taxi driver, medical records of physicians who testified at trial were admissible to show driver's medical condition; they were allowable under hearsay exception for business records.

First Premier Bank v. Kolcraft Enterprises, Inc., 686 N.W.2d 430, 2004 S.D. 92 (2004). In a products liability action against a playpen manufacturer, a statement in a hospital record was held to have been made for the purpose of the medical diagnosis and treatment of an infant. Assuming that the mother's statement (that she thought the fire in her infant's playpen had been caused by a blanket catching fire) was hearsay, the statement was, nevertheless, admissible under the medical records exception to the hearsay rule. Moreover, statements made for purposes of diagnosis or treatment relating to someone other than the declarant may be admissible under the medical records exception to the hearsay rule.

Bruneau v. Seabrook, 854 A.2d 818, 84 Conn. App. 667 (2004). In a personal injury action alleging auto negligence, a letter from the plaintiff's treating physician summarizing his impression of the plaintiff's shoulder injury (sustained in the accident) was properly admitted; the letter was signed by the plaintiff's treating physician on his (i.e., the physician's) letterhead. Also, the letter expressed an opinion by the doctor based on treatment that was consistent with his contemporaneous medical reports.

the statement (or the statement must otherwise fall within an exception to the hearsay rule).[71]

KEY POINTS FOR OPPOSITION:

Any notations by a physician must be shown to have been kept in the ordinary course of business or the exception will not apply.[72] Also, some statements contained within medical records, particularly those which were not necessary for the patient's treatment, may not be admissible.[73] Also consider a medical malpractice action, where it was held that the trial court did not abuse its discretion by excluding portions of hospital records in which non-testifying physicians concluded that fractures suffered by the patient were "non-traumatic"; the records involved a complex diagnosis involving a critical issue in dispute. Moreover, medical opinions in hospital records may not be admissible under the business records exception to the hearsay rule where the party against whom the opinions are introduced will be deprived of an opportunity to cross-examine the declarant on a critical issue.[74] In another medical malpractice case, statements contained in unauthenticated hospital records, made by an unidentified third person were hearsay and not admissible against the plaintiff.[75]

Doctors are not necessarily medical experts. Moreover, expertise in a particular field or area of specialization requires special training over and above the basic M.D. Degree.[76]

Opponents may want to keep in mind *Smith v. Victory Memorial Hospital*,[77] which held that the business records exception would not apply unless the proponent called as a witness every person who made entries on the records. The ruling doesn't, however, seem to make a lot of

71 *Commissioner of Social Services of City of New York on Behalf of Alex K. v. Ligia K.*, 615 N.Y.S.2d 923 (N.Y.A.D. 2 Dept. 1994). *Knight Maersk Container Service Co., Inc.*, 728 N.E.2d 968, 49 Mass.App.Ct. 254 (2000). In personal injury action, medical report was prepared by physician who had examined injured plaintiff at request of defendants; physician stated that he had difficulty causally relating plaintiff's symptoms to subject accident. Report was admissible under business records exception to hearsay rule, even though attestation for report did not accompany copy of report that was sent to plaintiff's counsel (attestation was later submitted at trial). *Wright v. New York City Housing Authority*, 709 N.Y.S.2d 600 (N.Y.A.D. 2000). Ordinary business of hospital is to diagnose and treat patients' ailments. A narration of accident causing injury is generally inadmissible as business record if it is not germane to diagnosis or treatment; however, patient's explanation as to how he was hurt may, nevertheless, be helpful for understanding medical aspects of his case.

72 *Beachel v. Long,* 420 N.W.2d 482 (Iowa 1988); *Dunn v. Ove Skou Rederi ALS* 45 F.R.D. 18 (E.D.Pa. 1968). Requirements may also apply to nurse's notes. See *Wisholek v. Douglas,* 722 N.Y.S.2d 316 (N.YA.D., 2001), involving medical malpractice action, where uncertified notes of hospital's nurses were inadmissible as hearsay.

73 *Rock v. Huffco Gas & Oil Co.*, 922 F.2d 272 (5th Cir. 1991); *Visconti v. Hollywood Rental Service*, 580 So.2d 197 (Fla. 1991); *Echeverria v. City of New York*, 166 A.D.2d 409, 560 N.Y.S.2d 473 (1990); *Mercedes v. Amusements of Am.*, 559 N.Y.S.2d 252 (1990); *Stull v. Fuqua Indus.*, 906 F.2d 1271 (8th Cir. 1990).

74 *Nowacki v. Community Medical Center,* 652 A.2d 758, 279 N.J. Super. 276 (N.J. Super. A.D. 1995).

75 *Dellenbach v. Robinson*, 642 N.E.2d 638, 95 Ohio App.3d 358 (Ohio App. 10 Dist. 1993). See also *In re Sullivan*, 710 N.Y.S.2d 853 (2000). It is generally true that physicians' office records and hospital records are admissible, including medical opinions, so long as they are relevant to diagnosis and treatment of patient; nevertheless, where source of information on hospital's or doctor's record is unknown, record is inadmissible. *Adams v. Metropolitan Atlanta Rapid Transit Authority,* 542 S.E.2d 130, 246 Ga.App. 698 (2000). But even though medical records containing diagnostic opinions, conclusions and statements of third parties are not admissible if tendered in their entirety, relevant portions not subject to such defects may be admissible.

76 *Wilkinson v. Swafford,* 811 N.E.2d 374 (Ind. Ct. App., 2004). A physician's report that contained an opinion that an injured motorist did not have a herniated disk and should try to work without restriction was not admissible under the business records exception to the hearsay rule in a personal injury trial. The doctor who wrote the report did not testify, and there was no evidence that he was qualified as a medical expert.

77 167 Ill. App.2d 618, 521 N.E.2d 210 (1988).

sense.[78] Nevertheless, medical records are not self-authenticating; someone should be prepared to lay a foundation, even if that someone is only a mere custodian.[79]

Florida lawyers should be aware of an important distinction. The federal hearsay rule allows for the "universal" admission of diagnostic, opinion evidence even though it is introduced solely through the hospital's own records, without the diagnostician being present; but in Florida, there is an added requirement that the business records evidence be able to stand alone as opinion evidence, thus adding a "trustworthiness" factor.[80]

SPECIAL ALERT:

Medical records are often crucial elements in establishing malpractice claims. Unfortunately, many less than honorable physicians have become painfully aware of this fact, and have managed to see to it that harmful records perform a disappearing act, if not a presto-change-o act. Plaintiffs' attorneys who handle such cases must become skilled investigators as a matter of course.[81]

And for you defense attorneys who represent less than honorable physicians (who got caught), consider a tactical concession for the purpose of eliminating the relevancy of the altered or deleted material.[82]

§22.420(a) Doctors' Notations

ARE THEY ADMISSIBLE?
GENERALLY, NO.

KEY POINTS:

We use the term "notations" to convey a *non-official* tone to these particular writings so as to distinguish them from the regularly maintained business and medical records normally generated by physicians.[83] Such notations will be considered as inadmissible hearsay unless

78 If you have to call every witness, what is the benefit or purpose of the business records exception to the hearsay rule?

79 *Wolde-Giorgis v. Christiansen*, 438 F.Supp.2d 1076 (D.Ariz. 2006). In an employment discrimination action, the employee provided no foundation for his medical documents and records, and thus, they were inadmissible. *Boscia v. Sharples*, 860 A.2d 674 (R.I., 2004). In an automobile negligence action that resulted from a rear-end collision, the rear-ended driver (Plaintiff) had no personal knowledge of the making and keeping of the medical records relating to his treatment and, therefore, he was not a competent witness to authenticate them for purposes of their admission under the business records exception to the hearsay rule.

80 *Love v. Garcia*, 611 So.2d 1270 (Fla. App. 4 Dist. 1992).

81 See Palmer, *Altered and 'Lost' Medical Records,* 35 Trial No.5, at 30 (May 1999).

82 *Cahoon v. Cummings,* 715 N.E.2d 1 (Ind.App. 1999) involved a medical malpractice case wherein the defending physician made insertions into the patient's medical records after the litigation had already commenced. If the issue of breach of duty had not been conceded, the evidence of those insertions and the negative presumptions resulting therefrom would have been relevant and admissible with respect to that issue; the physician's credibility would also have been called into question. Moreover, the spoliation rule permits an adverse inference to be drawn against a party who destroys or suppresses evidence in his possession; however, for that inference to be employed, it must, nevertheless, be relevant.

83 *Lunsford v. Laboratory Corp. of America*, 568 S.E.2d 597, 256 Ga.App. 432 (2002) involved a patient's lawsuit against a medical laboratory resulting from the insertion of a needle that allegedly caused nerve damage. A page from a doctor's notes pertaining to an electromyogram (EMG) study, which indicated that the patient's median nerve was working well, was admissible as original evidence of the EMG. The doctor supporting the evidence was a board certified neurologist who provided opinions with respect to the medical issues presented in the action.

Where entries or notes constitute regularly maintained business records, they may be admissible, assuming that requirements of Business Records Rule are satisfied. See *supra*, §22.420 "Key Points for Opposition."

they were made contemporaneously with regularly kept medical records. [84]

§22.420(b) Nursing Home Records

***ARE THEY ADMISSIBLE?* YES.**

Generally, nursing home records kept in the ordinary course of business would be governed by the business records exception to the hearsay rule.[85]

§22.420 (c) Physicians' Letters

ARE THEY ADMISSIBLE?
GENERALLY, NO.

KEY POINTS:

Sworn or unsworn, letters by a physician or anyone else are hearsay if they are offered to prove the truth of the matters asserted and are therefore excludable,[86] unless they fall within a recognized hearsay exception, such as medical records kept in the ordinary course of business.[87] Of course, if the letters are admitted or used for some purpose other than to prove the truth of the matters asserted, they would not be considered hearsay.[88]

---

84 See *Brown v. Liberty Mutual Insurance Co.*, 774 A.2d 232 Del. Super., 2001). In patient's breach of contract action against insurer, physician's office notation offered by plaintiff insured (to show that defendant insurer refused in bad faith to pre-authorize necessary medical procedure) constituted hearsay and was not admissible under residual hearsay exception; it was made after fact and under circumstances that seriously undermined its reliability. In fact, physician did not make notation until at least three months after his billing clerk told him that insurer had refused to authorize procedure. For case involving notes that *were* contemporaneous, see *Calcano v. Calcano,* 777 A.2d 633, 257 Conn. 230 (2001), where defendant sought introduction of handwritten notes prepared by now-deceased chiropractor concerning plaintiff's treatment under business records exception to hearsay rule; defendant made sufficient showing that notes were made contemporaneously with or within reasonable time after treatment was performed; chiropractor's office manager testified that chiropractor was very orderly, that he wrote down everything he did to patients as he treated them, and that he took these notes while he was meeting with patient or shortly thereafter. Transcription of notes was also admissible under business record exception because notes themselves were admissible, transcription closely tracked notes with respect to dates and terms, and testimony indicated that it was normal practice to make typewritten transcriptions from notes upon request.

85 But see *Rachau v. Cornerstone Village, Inc.*, 839 So.2d 473 (La.App., 2002). In an action against a nursing home by a patient, the nursing home's records, indicating that the patient was dropped in the shower by an aide, were inadmissible for purposes of establishing negligence. The records were not deemed trustworthy. After the plaintiff's attorney requested the records from the nursing home, he hired a nursing consultant to go through them; the consultant took files out of the attorney's office to organize them. Some sheets were inserted and some were removed. The records introduced were copies of copies.

86 *Bronstein-Becher v. Becher*, 809 N.Y.S.2d 140, N.Y.A.D. 2 Dept. (2006). At a Family Court hearing on the issue of whether or not a father failed to make child support payments (as required by a stipulation of settlement), letters from the father's psychiatrist were not admissible as business records, since they simply summarized the psychiatrist's diagnosis and treatment, and provided an opinion concerning the father's ability to return to work; no proper foundation was provided that demonstrated that they were, in fact, business records. See §5.300.

87 See §22.420.

88 *Capobianco v. City of New York*, 422 F.3d 47 (2nd Cir., N.Y., 2005). In a discrimination action brought by a discharged employee pursuant to the Americans with Disabilities Act of 1990, unsworn letters of a physician regarding the employee's medical condition should not have been sua sponte excluded by district court in considering the defendant employer's motion for summary judgment. While unsworn letters from physicians are generally inadmissible hearsay, this particular letter, which was addressed to the department's medical division, was admissible as evidence of the department's state of mind prior to firing the discharged employee.

§22.420(d) Nurses' Notes

ARE THEY ADMISSIBLE? YES.

KEY POINTS:

Customary medical record entries that comprise and form the records themselves are generally admissible. Nurses' notes would often fall within that category. Where, however, a nurse offers opinions or diagnoses outside the scope of his or her authority or expertise, a different result might be warranted.[89]

§22.420(e) Ambulance Call Report

ARE THEY ADMISSIBLE? YES.

KEY POINTS:

Under normal circumstances, a person telephoning for an ambulance will not have time for deliberation or fabrication; some degree of trustworthiness might, therefore, be implied. The information provided by the caller would, nevertheless, constitute double hearsay, thereby requiring an additional hearsay exception.[90]

§22.421 Medical Bills

ARE THEY ADMISSIBLE? YES.

KEY POINTS FOR PROPONENT:

Generally, medical bills receive the same treatment accorded to other medical and business records. For any case involving injuries, the bills will be relevant with respect to the issue of damages; and as a rule, the courts admit the evidence.[91] Where the amount of the bill or the cost of services rendered is in issue, there can be no question about the admissibility of the bill itself.

KEY POINTS FOR OPPOSITION:

In *McMunn v. Tatum*,[92] the court set down a four-part test for admitting medical bills in personal injury cases by requiring that they be:

1. Authentic and accurate,
2. Reasonable in light of the prevailing cost of the service,
3. Medically necessary, and
4. Rendered necessary solely by the defendant's negligence.

---

89 *Evans v. City of Natchitoches*, 927 So.2d 608 (La.App., 2006). In a premises liability action by a mother against a city, after her daughter fell into a partially open manhole and was trapped by the weight of the manhole cover, the medical notes of a nurse who questioned whether Osgood-Slater's disease was related to the fall were properly excluded; although the nurse's notes concerning treatment would have ordinarily been a part of the medical record, the notes did not concern any treatment that the nurse had given to the patient; and, two doctors were of the opinion that Osgood-Slater's disease was related to the child's injury and trauma, and thus the weight which would have been given to the questioned documents would have been so extraordinarily low that its probative value would have been substantially outweighed by the danger of unfair prejudice.

90 *Bayne v. City of New York*, 29 A.D.3d 924, 816 N.Y.S.2d 179 (2 Dept., 2006). A pedestrian's statement in an ambulance call report made to an emergency medical services worker that she had tripped and fallen would have been admissible as a present sense impression, and was relevant to the issue of whether or not the pedestrian had "tripped" or "slipped" on the sidewalk, had the medical services worker been permitted to lay a business records foundation for the document.

91 *Cincinnati Insurance Company v. Raymond Samples*, 192 S.W.3d 311 (Ky., 2006). An automobile accident victim's medical bills were admissible without expert proof that they were necessary for, and related to, the treatment for injuries caused by the accident which was the subject of the lawsuit.

Daspit v. Barber, 786 So.2d 962 (La. App., 2001); *Fowler v. Roberts*, 526 So. 2d 266 (La. 1988); *Rood v. Kansas City Power and Light Co.*, 755 P.2d 502 (Kan. 1988). Generally, plaintiff's medical bills are admissible under hearsay exception, where provider testifies concerning plaintiff's injuries and treatment provided, particularly where plaintiff testifies to having received treatment from physician regarding each bill and to having responsibility for paying each bill.

92 379 S.E. 2d 908 (Va. 1989).

In an automobile negligence action, the plaintiff offered a medical bill that was refused admissibility under the business records exception to the hearsay rule because neither the physician who sent the bill nor anyone from his office testified to lay a foundation or otherwise identify it.[93]

§22.422 Mortgage Applications

ARE THEY ADMISSIBLE? **YES (QUALIFIED).**

KEY POINTS:

The statements of fact contained in response to questions on the application could constitute hearsay if offered to prove the truth of the answers. Absent evidence of untrustworthiness, however, the application should be treated as any application form would.[94]

§22.423 MRI (Magnetic Resonance Imaging) Test Results

ARE THEY ADMISSIBLE? **YES (QUALIFIED).**

KEY POINTS:

MRI is a relatively new non-invasive diagnostic tool. Case law is still scant. As the equipment and technology is refined, the chances of admitting test results should also improve. The preliminary indications favor admissibility.[95]

§22.424 Polygraph Test Results

Private businesses often make use of polygraph tests for job applicants and theft-loss control, despite the judicial disfavor and unreliability of the results.

ARE THEY ADMISSIBLE? **NO.**

KEY POINTS:

A more thorough discussion of this subject can be found in §21.419.

REFERENCES

Admissibility of results of lie detector test in federal criminal case. 140 A.L.R. Fed.525.

§22.425 Reports, In General

ARE THEY ADMISSIBLE? **YES.**

Businesses maintain an endless variety of reports about products, sales, profits, complaints and safety features, along with an endless list of topics that no treatise could begin to cover. So a generic approach may be required where there is no case law directed to the specific report in question. In such a case, the practitioner should look to the general rules pertaining to business records.

KEY POINTS FOR PROPONENT:

As with any business record, a report can be admissible if it is kept in the ordinary course of

93 *Austin v. Pascarelli,* 612 So.2d 201 (La. App. 4 Cir. 1992).

94 *Leech v. Rozbicki*, 552 A.2d 451, 17 Conn. App. 352, (1989). A mortgage application was admissible under the business records exception to the hearsay rule in a broker's action for tortious interference with a contractual relationship with a customer.

95 But this doesn't mean that MRI's are exempt from the Best Evidence Rule. See *Wagman v. Bradshaw,* 739 N.Y.S.2d 421 (N.Y.A.D., 2002). Generally, a MRI report prepared by a non-testifying healthcare provider should not be admitted into evidence, where the proponent does not contend that the original MRI films were lost, destroyed or otherwise unavailable. Usually, the contents of the report should also be barred.

Diamond Fertilizer v. Davis, 567 So.2d 451 (Fla. Dist. Ct. App. 1990).

business. Reports may be admissible if they are relevant, material, non-prejudicial[96] and fall into a recognized hearsay exception.[97] Generally, admissibility can be expected for reports which are used against the company or entity which created them.[98] Some private sector investigatory reports may fall under the public records exception to the hearsay rule, if the reports are created pursuant to governmental regulations.

Be careful about rushing to the assumption that a particular report needs a hearsay exception to be admitted; remember to examine the purpose for which the report is used. Unless the document is offered to prove the truth of the matters asserted, it is not hearsay, and may therefore be admitted without asserting an exception.[99]

KEY POINTS FOR OPPOSITION:

Opponents of private sector reports should consider the case of *Cox v. Oliver Mach. Co.*[100] A report of a saw manufacturer's service representative, with respect to the cause of the saw's malfunction, contained opinions of employees. The report was not admissible under the business records exception to the hearsay rule because the employees did not make their statements in the regular course of their business.

The opponent should pay particular attention to Opposition Checklist items 1, 2, 3, 4, 5, 6 and 7 (*supra*). If the documents were prepared with an eye toward litigation, by an attorney or an agent acting on behalf of that attorney, serious thought should be given to the work product doctrine.

§22.425(a) Personnel Records

ARE THEY ADMISSIBLE?
GENERALLY, YES.

KEY POINTS:

Personnel records are normally relevant in cases involving employee discharge and discipline, work place discrimination, sexual harassment and collective bargaining disputes. They will always contain hearsay but, by the same token, they will often be at the very center of the controversy and, therefore, difficult to exclude. Most often, the introduction of personnel records will involve mixed purposes. In addition (or as an alternative to) the obvious hearsay nature of the statements, they may be offered to show the facts surrounding the transaction (i.e., discharge) or they may be offered to show the state of mind of the author or recipient.[101]

---

96 *Rocky Mountain Helicopters v. Bell Helicopters Textron*, 805 F.2d 907 (10th Cir. 1986). The defendant's post-accident report was admitted into evidence, despite the defendant's objection that the report contained evidence of subsequent remedial measures.

97 *Sabel v. Mead Johnson & Co.*, 737 F. Supp. 135 (D. Mass. 1990). In a product liability case involving a medication, notes kept by a Food and Drug Administration employee, based on telephone conversations that he had with an employee of the defendant pharmaceutical manufacturer, appeared to demonstrate that the FDA asked the manufacturer not to use a packing insert without first making certain labeling changes. The notes did not fall into a recognized hearsay exception and were inadmissible. However, a **letter** from the FDA to the defendant company which suggested that a warning be included in the medication's label was admissible as a public record.

98 In a products liability action, *Ford Motor Co. v. Massey*, 855 S.W.2d 897, 313 Ark. 345 (1993), a report listing warranty repairs to a truck's throttle cable assembly was sufficiently similar to the issue in the litigation to be admissible; it dealt with repairs to equipment that was identical to that at issue in the case, and the repairs were clearly analyzed and described by witnesses.

99 In *Morgan v. Massachusetts General Hospital,* 901 F.2d 186 (1st Cir. 1990), a discrimination lawsuit brought by a former employee against a defending hospital, all of the following reports were admitted for the non-hearsay purpose of establishing the investigative steps taken by the hospital: counseling report, grievance committee reports, and affidavits of hospital employees.

100 41 Ohio App.3d 28, 534 N.E.2d 855 (1987).

101 *Cameron v. Community Aid For Retarded Children, Inc.,* 335 F.3d 60 (2nd Cir., N.Y., 2003).

KEY POINTS FOR OPPOSITION:

Some theoreticians will argue that every good personnel memo or record should be designed, in part, to cover the rear end of the person or entity that will later fire the target matter of the writing. There is, of course, some truth to this. Therefore, it might be argued that most such memos are motivated by litigation and are self-serving and, therefore, should be excluded.[102] If the writing was not clearly within the normal course of the business duties of the author, the memo should definitely be excluded.[103]

§22.425(b) Engineering Reports

ARE THEY ADMISSIBLE?
YES, IF PROPERLY QUALIFIED.

KEY POINTS:

Independent engineering reports from third parties constitute hearsay and should therefore be excluded[104] unless they are offered for some purpose *other* than to prove the truth of the matter asserted (in which case, they would *not* be hearsay), or unless they fall within some hearsay exception.[105] If the report is truly "independent," it might qualify as a learned treatise,[106] or it may be used for impeachment purposes.[107] But unless it is properly authenticated and provided with a hearsay exception, it may be excluded.[108]

REFERENCES

Admissibility of evidence of subsequent remedial measures. 50 A.L.R. Fed. 935.

§22.426 Sales Agreements/ Contracts

ARE THEY ADMISSIBLE? YES.

KEY POINTS FOR PROPONENT:

But for the so-called "recital" provisions that commonly appear to describe the intentions of the parties, contracts normally contain terms of agreement, not statements of fact. Put another way, a contract is form of "verbal act," to which the law attaches duties and liabilities, and which, therefore, is not "hearsay."[109]

---

102 This exclusion is sometimes referred to as the "anti litem motem" exception to an otherwise valid hearsay exception. See Checklist Item 7 of §22.300.

103 *Hertz v. Luzenac Am., Inc.*, 370 F.3d 1014 (10th Cir. Colo., 2004). The district court did not abuse its discretion in refusing to admit (pursuant to the business records exception to the hearsay rule) a meeting memo prepared by a supervisor who thought that he was going to fire an employee; there was no evidence that it was the ordinary course of business for the supervisor to prepare such a memo, and the circumstances under which the memo was created made it untrustworthy.

See also *Lust v. Sealy, Inc.*, 383 F.3d 580 (7th Cir. Wis., 2004). In a sex discrimination lawsuit, a manager's memos explaining why he hadn't promoted a female employee were not records of a regularly conducted activity (within the meaning of the hearsay exception). The only purpose of the memos was to create evidence for use in the employee's anticipated sex discrimination lawsuit.

104 However, as stated in *Coleman v. Fortner,* 579 S.E.2d 792, 260 Ga.App. 373 (2003), an expert, in formulating his opinions, may rely upon the reports of others.

105 See §20.500.

106 See §24.202.

107 See §25.210(a).

108 *McEuin v. Crown Equipment Corporation,* 328 F.3d 1028 (9th Cir., Or., 2003). In a products liability lawsuit, independent engineering reports that were offered to show that the design of a doorless forklift was not defective constituted hearsay and were, therefore, inadmissible; the engineers were not presented as expert witnesses and, therefore, the reports could not be adequately authenticated.

109 *Mueller v. Abdnor,* 972 F.2d 931 (8th Cir. 1992).

§22.427 Scientific Reports

ARE THEY ADMISSIBLE?
YES, IF TRUSTWORTHY.

KEY POINTS FOR PROPONENT:

The crucial test of admissibility for scientific reports is trustworthiness. Scientific reports contained within public documents are more likely to be considered trustworthy and, therefore, stand a greater chance of gaining admissibility than private studies.[110] But scientific reports made in the regular course of business may also be admissible, under the business records exception to the hearsay rule.[111] Where official scientific reports claim to state "factual findings," it is well established that the term should be broadly interpreted.[112] Scientific reports which do not involve the specific subject of the action may still be admissible, if the reports are substantially similar to the facts of the case.[113]

KEY POINTS FOR OPPOSITION:

Scientific reports that involve new or unproven research and testing may be considered untrustworthy.[114] Not too long ago, such reports had to run the gauntlet of the "*Frye*" test, based on the case of *Frye v. United States*.[115] Under *Frye*, scientific data and techniques are admissible only when they are "generally accepted" as accurate by the relevant scientific community. In the federal sphere, the *Frye* test conflicted with the more liberal Rules 702 and 703 of the Federal Rules of Evidence.

We now have a new standard enunciated by the United States Supreme Court in *Daubert v. Merrell Dow Pharmaceuticals, Inc.*[116] In reaching a decision concerning the conflict between the *Frye* Rule and the Federal Rules, and opting in favor of the Federal Rules, the High Court set forth the following test to govern a new form of scientific evidence:[117]

1. Whether it can be (and has been) tested,
2. Whether the theory or technique has been subjected to peer review and publication,
3. The known or potential rate of error, and
4. The "general acceptance" of the theory or technique (ghosts of *Frye*).

The High Court made it clear that the preceding is not all-inclusive. Other unmentioned or yet-

---

110 *Ellis v. International Playtex, Inc.*, 745 F.2d 292 (4th Cir. 1984). In a wrongful death action against a tampon manufacturer, the trial court committed a reversible error by not admitting toxic shock syndrome studies prepared by the National Center for Disease Control and various state health departments. The appeals court stated that the studies were no different from other findings of fact pursuant to the public records exception to the hearsay rule. See also *Kehm v. Proctor & Gamble Manufacturing Co.*, 724 F.2d 613 (8th Cir. 1983). See generally Chapter 21 (Scientific Reports).

111 *Minneapolis Pub. Housing Authority v. Greene,* 463 N.W.2d 558 (Minn. 1990); *LaDuke v. State Farm Ins. Co.*, 158 A.D.2d 137, 557 N.Y.S.2d 221 (1990); *March v. Victoria Lloyds Ins. Co.*, 773 S.W.2d 785 (Tex. 1989); *Rocky Mountain Helicopters, Inc. v. Bell Helicopters Textron*, 805 F.2d 907 (10th Cir. 1986); *U.S. v. Ware,* 247 F.2d 698 (7th Cir. 1957); *Moran v. Pittsburgh-Des Moines Steel Co.*, 86 F.Supp. 255 (D.C.Pa. 1949), *reversed on other grounds*, 183 F.2d 467 (3d Cir. 1949).

112 See *Wetherill v. University of Chicago,* 518 F. Supp. 1387 (N.D. Ill. 1981); *Baker v. Elcona Homes Corp.*, 588 F.2d 551 (6th Cir. 1978), *cert. denied*, 441 U.S. 933, 99 S. Ct. 2054, 60 L.Ed.2d 661 (1979); *Melville v. American Home Assurance Co.*, 584 F.2d 1306 (3d Cir. 1978).

113 *Hahn v. Sterling Drug, Inc.*, 805 F.2d 1480 (11th Cir. 1986).

114 *Alpert v. Slatin*, 305 F.2d 891 (C.C.P.A. 1962).

115 293 F. 1013 (D.C. Cir. 1923).

116 *Daubert v. Merrell Dow Pharmaceuticals, Inc.*, 113 S. Ct. 2786, 125 L. Ed. 2d 469 (1993).

117 See §11.500 and §11.600 et seq for additional discussion concerning the new standards.

to-be considered factors may also weigh in the decision whether or not to accept a given scientific theory or report that might result therefrom.

REFERENCES

Reliability of scientific technique. 105 A.L.R. Fed.299.

§22.427(a) Experts' Reports

***ARE THEY ADMISSIBLE?* QUALIFIED NO.**

KEY POINTS:

Reports of experts, as distinguished from the scientific reports covered above, deal with matters and conclusions that are specific to the issues of a particular case. Bias is to be expected among privately retained experts since they are paid to present the particular views of the attorneys who retain them. While an expert's report may be required (most often for discovery purposes) pursuant to court rules, it does not follow that such a report is admissible as substantive evidence.[118] Where, however, the court through its rules or orders permits it, expert reports may be admitted as to any purpose for which those rule or orders provide. [119]

§22.428 Summaries

***ARE THEY ADMISSIBLE?* YES.**

KEY POINTS FOR PROPONENT:

Summaries do nothing more than condense, abstract, or recapitulate other more lengthy documents. The concept is simple, but powerful; it is based on the notion that it is better to allow the courtroom to look at a single document as opposed to hundreds or even thousands of writings.

Simplification, clarification, and savings of time are powerful enough to overcome some potent rules of evidence that would otherwise exclude such an offering. A key weapon to counter any opposition would consist of a showing that the underlying documents were either in evidence,[120] in court, or were made available to the opposition for inspection.[121]

---

118 See *Law v. National Collegiate Athletic Association,* 185 F.R.D. 324 (D.Kansas 1999).

119 *J.W. ex rel. D.W. v. CM.,* 627 N.W.2d 687 (Minn.App., 2001). Reports made for purposes of court-ordered evaluation of child's best interests are admissible as business records. Moreover, admission of court-ordered report does not constitute abuse of discretion if parties are given opportunity to cross-examine author of report.

120 *Harris Market Research v. Marshall Marketing and Communications, Inc.*, 948 F.2d 1518 (10th Cir. 1991). *Jean Doe v. DeBuono*, 193 F.R.D. 117 (S.D.N.Y. 2000). In lawsuit against county, spreadsheets summarizing county data pertaining to children with autism and developmental disorders may be admissible under rule permitting summaries of voluminous writings or recordings which cannot be conveniently examined in court, but only if underlying documents, upon which spreadsheets were based, were also admissible. *In re Fanaras,* 263 B.R. 655 (Mass., 2001). In order to properly lay foundation for admission of summary, proponent should first establish that (1) underlying documents upon which summary is based are admissible, (2) underlying documents were available to opposing party for inspection, and (3) summarized material is itself admissible and accurate.

121 *Healthcare Services of the Ozarks, Inc. v. Copeland,* 198 S.W.3d 604 (Mo., 2006). A summary of voluminous records is admissible in evidence, under the business records exception to the hearsay rule, provided that the competency of the underlying records is first established and such records are made available to the opposite party for cross-examination purposes.

Reed v. Reed, 44 P.3d 1108, 137 Idaho 53 (2002). In order for a hearsay summary to be admissible, the party offering it must make the source documents reasonably available to the opposing party.

Table Steaks v. First Premier Bank, N.A., 650 N.W.2d 829 (S.D., 2002). In a lawsuit by the Table Steaks Restaurant against a credit card company alleging a breach of contract and tortious interference with a business relationship, the restaurant's exhibits showing a summary and calculation of its lost profits were admissible; even though the exhibits were not produced during trial, they had been provided to the defendants prior to trial.

(Footnote 121 continued on page 22-30.)

Remember—volume counts. It always seems to be a most relevant consideration; but I have yet to come across a rule or case that provides any specific minimum number or standard.[122]

KEY POINTS FOR OPPOSITION:

At the outset, a summary is a derivative document, and one that is often prepared for litigation and, therefore, *not* in the ordinary course of business.[123] It may present hearsay in that it purports to "say" what another document has already said. Without an exception, a summary would violate the best evidence rule since it would not constitute the original writing. Despite these rules, summaries are commonly admitted.

The best opposition would be to cite the hearsay rule and the best evidence rule but then attack the summary because it:

1. is biased,
2. has material information omitted, and
3. is inaccurate.

---

121 (Continued from page 22-29.) *T/F Systems, Inc. v. Malt*, 814 So.2d 511 (Fla.App., 2002). In a patent owner's action for royalties under a licensing agreement, the trial court properly admitted an accounting summary at the request of the licensor; the summary was based on the licensee's own invoices. The licensee had 3½ weeks before the hearing to investigate and analyze the records in order to determine whether or not the summary was accurate.

Brane v. Roth, 590 N.E.2d 587 (Ind. App. 1992). Where corporate books and records are in court or made available to the opposing party, a summary of those records may be admitted notwithstanding a hearsay objection. *In re Marriage of DeLarco*, 245 Ill.Dec. 921, 728 N.E.2d 1278, 313 Ill.App.3d 107 (2000). Where fact may be ascertained only by inspection of large number of documents, summary of those documents may be received into evidence, but mass of underlying documents must be placed in hands of t court or be made accessible to opposing party for inspection. See also *U.S. v. Crisp,* 190 F.R.D. 546 (E.D.Cal. 1999).

Crackel v. Allstate Ins. Co., 92 P.3d 882, 208 Ariz. 252 (Ariz. Ct. App., 2004). The rule allowing witnesses to summarize information contained in voluminous records requires that the parties be given an opportunity to detect and prepare for inaccurate summaries. See also *Peat, Inc. v. Vanguard Research, Inc.*, 378 F.3d 1154 (11th Cir. Ala., 2004).

122 In *Owens-Corning Fiberglas Corp. v. Watson*, 413 S.E.2d 630 (Va. 1992), a summary of 44 workers' compensation claims was admissible in a products liability suit concerning asbestos, to show that the manufacturer had notice that its own workers were at risk of contracting lung diseases. In *American Cast Iron Pipe Co. v. Williams*, 591 So.2d 854 (Ala. 1991), the court applied the voluminous records exception to the best evidence rule because the documents were so numerous that they could not be "conveniently examined" in court. In *F.L. Walz, Inc. v. Hobart Corp.*, 167 Ill. Dec. 42, 586 N.E.2d 1314, 224 Ill.App.3d 727 (1992), a summary exhibit was allowed because it simplified and clarified more than 9,000 invoices.

John C. Lincoln Hosp. and Health Corp. v. Maricopa County, 96 P.3d 530 (Ariz. Ct. App., 2004). In a private hospital's action seeking reimbursement from the county for emergency medical treatment rendered to indigents, the hospital's summary exhibit accurately represented documents which consisted of more than 100,000 writings.

Heaps v. Heaps, 124 Cal.App.4th 286, 21 Cal.Rptr.3d 239 (2004). In an action concerning trust property, a schedule of assets created by the successor trustee was admissible because the schedule constituted a general compilation of documents that could not be examined individually by the court without a great loss of time.

123 *Crawford v. Dammann*, 626 S.E.2d 632, 277 Ga.App. 442 (2006). In a trial involving various homeowners and their claims that assessments (and a levying of fees) were not authorized by subdivision covenants, a lot owner's summaries of business records showing building fees and permit processing fees paid to the homeowners' association were not admissible to show the owner's damages; the owner did not testify that the summaries provided were made in the regular course of his business at the time of the underlying transaction or within a reasonable time thereafter.

Peat, Inc. v. Vanguard Research, Inc., 378 F.3d 1154 (11th Cir. Ala., 2004). In an action involving an alleged misappropriation of trade secrets, an exhibit summarizing the secrets, allegedly misappropriated by the defendant, was prepared by the plaintiff's employees at the request of counsel in response to defendant's discovery request. The summary was, therefore, not an admissible exhibit because it was not compiled in the ordinary course of the plaintiff's business; it was, rather, based on inadmissible hearsay and contained conclusory allegations concerning defendant's conduct and intent. The rule authorizing admission of exhibits summarizing the contents of voluminous writings, records, or photographs is not a back-door vehicle for the introduction of evidence which is otherwise inadmissible.

It might also help to attack the knowledge or credibility of the person who prepared the summary.[124]

REFERENCES

Admissibility of summaries of writings, recordings, or photographs. 50 A.L.R. Fed.319.

Admissibility of evidence summaries. 59 A.L.R. 4th 971.

§22.429 Telephone Bills

See §23.412.

§22.430 Thermographic Test Results

Thermography is both a diagnostic tool and an evaluation device that purports to display "pain" in terms of colored images known as thermograms. The tool is very controversial.

ARE THEY ADMISSIBLE? **AUTHORITIES ARE SIGNIFICANTLY SPLIT.**

KEY POINTS:

Some jurisdictions admit the evidence;[125] some do not.[126] And some can't make up their minds.[127] See "Scientific Reports" (this chapter) for a discussion of the standards used to determine the admissibility of new scientific evidence, in general. A newer, more liberal standard announced by the United States Supreme Court may invite additional and otherwise reluctant states to accept thermographic evidence.[128]

§22.431 Toxicology and Safety Tests

ARE THEY ADMISSIBLE? **YES.**

KEY POINTS:

The admissibility rules for toxicology and safety tests are essentially the same as those for

---

124 *Coman v. Thomas Mfg. Co., Inc.*, 411 S.E.2d 626 (N.C. App. 1992); *American Cast Iron Pipe Co. v. Williams*, 591 So.2d 854 (Ala. 1991). *Nissan Motor Co. v. Armstrong,* 145 S.W.3d 131 (Tex., 2004) involved a products liability action against an automobile manufacturer resulting from an accident that allegedly arose from a defective throttle mechanism. Consumer complaints received by the defendant manufacturer alleged that an unintended acceleration of its vehicles had occurred (those complaints were then compiled by the government into a database). The complaints deemed to be inadmissible because the database basically consisted of double hearsay. None of the other complaints in the database alleged defects in the same throttle mechanism. In addition, the other incidents were reported eight to ten years after the plaintiffs purchased their vehicle. A compilation of consumer complaints by a manufacturer may constitute a business records exception to the hearsay rule if used to show notice; however, such claims could not be used to establish the truth of the claims unless the employee making the record possessed personal knowledge.

125 *Fay v. Mincey,* 454 So.2d 587 (Fla. Dist. Ct. App. 1984) is thought of as a pro-admissibility landmark, even though its jurisdiction (i.e. Florida) has also ruled against the evidence in *Crawford v. Shivashankar*, 474 So.2d 873 (Fla. Dist. Ct. App. 1985); in New Jersey, *Procida v. McLaughlin*, 195 N.J. Super 396, 479 A.2d 447 (1984), allows the evidence but only after a lengthy hearing; other cases permitting the evidence include *Cherico v. National R.R. Passenger Corp.*, 758 F. Supp. 258 (E.D. Pa. 1991); *Destin v. Sears Roebuck & Co.*, 803 S.W.2d 113 (Mo.Ct.App. 1990); *Stoczynski v. Livermore*, 782 P.2d 834 (Colo.Ct.App. 1989); *Tenuta v. Heckler,* 606 F. Supp. 624 (E.D. Wis. 1985); and *Thornton v. United States Department of Agriculture*, 715 F.2d 1508 (11th Cir. 1983).

126 *K-Mart Corp. v. Morrison*, 609 N.E.2d 17 (Ind. Ct. App 1993); *Burkett v. Northern,* 43 Wash. App. 143, 715 P.2d 1159 (1986); *McAdoo v. U.S.*, 607 F.Supp. 788 (E.D. Mich. 1984).

127 *Fay v. Mincey*, 454 So.2d 587 (Fla. Dist. Ct. App. 1984) ruled in favor of admissibility; another Florida court ruled against it in *Crawford v. Shivashankar*, 474 So.2d 873 (Fla. Dist. Ct. App. 1985). In New Jersey, *Procida v. McLaughlin*, 195 N.J. Super 396, 479 A.2d 447 (1984), ruled in favor of the evidence, but another court in that state rejected it in *Ferlise v. Eiler*, 202 N.J. Super. 330, 495 A.2d 129 (1985).

128 *Daubert v. Merrell Dow Pharmaceuticals, Inc.*, 113 S. Ct. 2786, 125 L. Ed. 2d 469 (1993); see also §11.500 and §11.600 *et seq* for additional discussion concerning the new standards.

scientific reports. Tests which are trustworthy and timely are generally admissible.[129]

§22.432 Trade Secrets

ARE THEY ADMISSIBLE? NO.

KEY POINTS FOR PROPONENT:

Trade secrets are not automatically privileged.[130] Such secrets may be discoverable when they are relevant and necessary to properly prepare a case for trial.[131]

KEY POINTS FOR OPPOSITION:

Federal Rule of Civil Procedure 26(c)(7) gives some protection for trade secrets and similar confidential materials.[132] But efforts must have been taken to protect the secret or the court will not protect it.

In *Burlington Northern R. Co. v. Omaha Public Power Dist.*,[133] a railroad's contract to transport coal to an electric generating station was held to be a "trade secret" that was exempt from disclosure; the railroad had gone to considerable lengths to prevent the disclosure of the information, including the negotiation of strict confidentiality requirements and vigorous prosecution of a suit to block disclosure.

§22.433 Vote Buying Account Records

ARE THEY ADMISSIBLE? ONLY IN LOUISIANA.

The jails of Louisiana are regularly occupied by those who keep the state's colorful political arena alive and interesting. There's at least one former governor there now.[134] If vote buying is to be considered as an "ordinary business" in Louisiana, then perhaps the records associated with it should be admissible.[135]

---

129 See *Smith v. Ithaca Corp.*, 612 F.2d 215 (5th Cir. 1980). In a wrongful death action in which benzene exposure allegedly contributed to a seaman's death, a report that discussed benzene's properties, its effects on the human body, and the conditions under which it should be transported was relevant and admissible. Certain opinions and conclusions from the report were excluded, however. See also *Robins v. Whelan*, 653 F.2d 47 (1st Cir. 1981); *Givens v. Lederle*, 556 F.2d 1341 (5th Cir. 1977); *Reyes v. Wyeth Laboratories*, 498 F.2d 1264 (5th Cir. 1974).

130 *Healthcare Services of the Ozarks, Inc. v. Copeland*, 198 S.W.3d 604 (Mo., 2006). The following factors should be considered in determining whether a person's information is a trade secret: (1) The extent to which the information is known outside of his business; (2) the extent to which it is known by employees and others involved in his business; (3) the extent of measures taken by him to guard the secrecy of the information; (4) the value of the information to him and to his competitors; (5) the amount of effort or money expended by him in developing the information; and (6) the ease or difficulty with which the information could be properly acquired or duplicated by others. The burden of proof rests upon an employer to substantiate its asserted interest in its trade secrets.

National Utilities Service, Inc. v. Northwestern Steel & Wire Co., 426 F.2d 222 (7th Cir. 1970); *V.D. Anderson Co. v. Helena Cotton Oil Co.*, 117 F.Supp. 1932 (E.D. Ark. 1953).

131 *Russ Stonier, Inc. v. Droz Wood Co.*, 52 F.R.D. 232 (E.D.Pa. 1971).

132 The Advisory Committee Notes on the 1970 Amendments to Rule 26(c) state in part: "[t]he new reference to trade secrets and other confidential commercial information reflects existing law." The courts have not given trade secrets automatic and complete immunity against disclosure, but have in each case weighed their claim to privacy against the need for disclosure. Frequently, they have been afforded a limited protection.

133 888 F.2d 1228 (8th Cir. 1989).

134 The Honorable Edwin Edwards is presently serving a lengthy term.

135 See *Nugent v. Phelps*, 816 So.2d 349 (La.App., 2002). In a lawsuit challenging a Louisiana election, a copy of a list that documented a "running tab" from a store at which the unsuccessful candidate allegedly set up an account to buy votes, was inadmissible. There was inadequate testimony about the circumstances under which the list was created and maintained. [Author comment: But for the inadequate foundation, we should assume the list might have been admitted.]

Chapter 23

Personal Documents

§23.100 Introduction

People write and maintain a wide variety of documents that are not a part of any regularly conducted activity or business. Letters, diaries and notes are but a few. These writings do not enjoy the easy-to-establish foundations accorded to regularly conducted activities.

§23.200 Foundations

It is important that the proponent not fall into a self-made hearsay trap that does not otherwise exist. In particular, regardless of the stature of the document and its author, unless the writing is being offered to prove the truth of the matters asserted in the writing, it is not hearsay. A letter, for example, might be admitted to show the state of mind of the author, or to prove receipt of notice on the part of the recipient.

Even if the statement contained in the document constitutes hearsay, it may, nevertheless, be admitted if that statement falls within a recognized hearsay exception.[1]

§23.300 Opposition

Without a specific exception, personal memoranda may be the purest form of hearsay and therefore excludable for that reason. Unless some exception applies, attacks upon the writing's authenticity should be waged wherever a writing "pops up" during litigation, particularly when its contents are suspiciously favorable to the possessor.

If a forgery or alteration is suspected, a qualified document examiner should be sought.[2] Using infrared photographic procedures, and other scientific techniques, these experts are capable of detecting improprieties.

§23.400 Specific Documents

§23.401 Ancient Writings

***ARE THEY ADMISSIBLE?* YES, IF THEY ARE AT LEAST 20 YEARS OLD.**

There's no hearsay like old hearsay. The ancient documents rule is quite universal; it is predicated upon the notion that whatever hearsay an old writing contains will have pre-dated the controversy. Of course, since age knows no boundaries, ancient writings can take virtually any form and shape. They can consist of publications, personal writings, legal papers, business records, official documents or a mix and match.[3]

KEY POINTS FOR PROPONENT:

Fed. R. Evid. 803(16) provides that "statements in a document in existence twenty years or more the authenticity of which is established" will not be excluded by the hearsay rule, regard-

1 See Chapter 5 for exceptions.

2 The expert should be a member of the *American Board of Forensic Document Examiners* (ABFDE), and not a so-called "graphologist."

3 *LensCrafters, Inc. v. Wadley,* 248 F.Supp.2d 705 (M.D. Tenn., 2003) involved a case wherein retailers of prescription eyewear challenged the constitutionality of a Tennessee statute that prohibited optometrists from practicing their profession in any retail store where merchandise was displayed or offered for sale. Documents produced by the state optometric association in response to a subpoena, which were more than 20 years old, were admissible as ancient documents.

less of whether or not the declarant is available.[4] The rule even applies to old newspaper stories.[5]

KEY POINTS FOR OPPOSITION:

Notice that Fed. R. Evid. 803(16) still requires that authenticity be established.[6] Note that if the document in question was found under suspicious circumstances instead of in a place where such writings would normally be expected, then authenticity might be attacked for that reason.[7]

§23.402 Bible Entries

***ARE THEY ADMISSIBLE?* YES.**

Fed. R. Evid. 803(13) provides the following exception from the hearsay rule:

> Statements of fact concerning personal or family history contained in family Bibles, genealogies, charts, engravings on rings, inscriptions on family portraits, engravings on urns, crypts, or tombstones, or the like.

---

4 *United States v. Mandycz*, 447 F.3d 951 (6th Cir., Mich., 2006). In a denaturalization proceeding against a former German concentration camp guard, World War II-era Soviet interrogation records were admissible under the ancient documents exception to the hearsay rule, notwithstanding a claim that the documents did not correctly identify the naturalized citizen as a former German concentration camp guard; the documents' contents were relevant to the weight to be accorded them, not the threshold determination of authentication or admissibility. Moreover, the authentication requirement that a document be free of suspicion goes not to the content of the document, but rather to whether the document is what it purports to be.

Sokaogon Chippewa Community v. Exxon Corp., 805 F. Supp. 680 (E.D. Wis. 1992), an action by the Sokaogon Chippewa Community, a Native American tribe, for the right to possess land, held that documents which were at least 100 years old were admissible as an exception to the hearsay rule (and their authenticity could not be impeached); see also *McGuire v. Walker*, 423 S.E.2d 617 (W.Va. 1992), where it was held that ancient school-land sale deeds were admissible hearsay evidence in an action to quiet title to the property; recitals on one of the ancient deeds (relating to persons from whom the title was derived) were also admissible in evidence, but only in connection with other proof of a long continued and undisputed possession, in accordance with the right or title claimed. *Martha Graham Sch. & Dance Found., Inc. v. Martha Graham Ctr. of Contemporary Dance, Inc.*, 380 F.3d 624 (2d Cir. N.Y., 2004). In a copyright ownership dispute, letters written by an executive administrator for a dance center (indicating that the choreographer employed by the center had assigned rights in all of her works to her) were admissible as authenticated ancient documents; the letters were more than 20 years old at the time offered, and there was no reason to suspect problems with respect to their authenticity. The witness, who had relevant personal knowledge, testified that the letters were what they purported to be.

5 *Aon Risk Services, Inc. v. Liebenstein*, 710 N.W.2d 175, 2006 WI App. 4 (2005). Newspaper articles constitute inadmissible hearsay, even for purposes of summary judgment. Generally, they may not be considered for summary judgment unless they are being submitted in conjunction with a libel action against the newspaper, or in the alternative, unless the articles are at least 20 years old.

Gonzales v. North Tp. of Lake County, 800 F. Supp. 676 (N.D. Ind. 1992), held that 20-year-old newspaper articles were both admissible and self-authenticating, as "ancient" writings; thus, the statements contained therein were admissible into evidence; see also *Dallas County v. Commercial Union Assurance Co.*, 286 F.2d 388 (5th Cir. 1961).

6 *Goguen v. Textron, Inc.*, 234 F.R.D. 13, 69 Fed. R. Evid. Serv. 726 (2006). In a products liability case involving wrongful death, annual reports of a publicly-traded company were not sufficiently authenticated as "ancient documents," and thus any exhibit containing those reports could not be considered by the district court when deciding the company's motion for summary judgment. The company submitted no affidavit from any witness that provided the necessary authentication to show that the documents were in fact the company's annual reports from certain years or that they were taken from the company's files.

7 *Bailey v. Descendants of Fowler*, 746 S.2d 130 (La.App. 1999). Ancient documents carry presumption of admissibility, but they are not automatically admitted.

KEY POINTS FOR PROPONENT:

Be prepared to lay a foundation using a witness who has some familiarity with the writing, if not the subject event. But the qualifying witness need not be the person who made the entry.[8]

KEY POINTS FOR OPPOSITION:

If possible, try to determine whether the entry was contemporaneous with the subject event or occurrence. Also, determine whether or not the entry was made independently of the pending litigation. It is possible that there may have been a motive to fabricate the writing.

§23.402(a) Budgets

***ARE THEY ADMISSIBLE?* GENERALLY, NO.**

KEY POINTS:

A monthly or annual budget consists of nothing more than a projection or prediction of expenses that are "likely" to occur at some point in the future. Such a writing would seem to have limited probative value, at best, and would seem to be objectionable as hearsay[9] and as being speculative in nature.[10] If, however, the writing was used to show the state of mind of the author, a different result might be warranted.[11]

§23.403 Complaint Letters

***ARE THEY ADMISSIBLE?* YES, TO SHOW NOTICE OR STATE OF MIND; NO, TO SHOW TRUTH OF CONTENTS.**

Letters of complaint are frequently written by customers of various products; they may be directed to one or more governmental agencies, the seller, or the manufacturer. Where products are not involved, citizens often complain to police, fire, and other agencies about people, animals, places and things. The rules concerning admissibility are fairly consistent. Complaints normally consist of unsworn hearsay, and are clearly inadmissible to prove the truth of their contents.[12]

KEY POINTS FOR PROPONENT:

Ordinarily, complaints may not be used as evidence to prove the truth of the matters contained in them.[13] But they may be used to show that the recipient received notice of the substance of the complaint.[14] The complaints may also be

8 *Ewell v. Ewell,* 163 N.C. 233, 79 S.E. 509 (1913).

9 *Fuentes v. Fuentes,* 97 P.3d 876 (Ariz. Ct. App., 2004). In a marital dissolution proceeding, a wife's exhibit setting forth her budget of anticipated monthly expenses was "hearsay," as it was not a statement made while the declarant was testifying at trial.

10 See generally, Chapter 11.

11 See generally, Chapter 5.

12 *Peters v. Johnson & Johnson Prods.*, 783 S.W.2d 442 (Mo. 1990); *Ford Motor Co. v. Phelps,* 389 S.E.2d 454 (Va. 1990).

13 But see *F.T.C. v. Figgie Intern. Inc.*, 994 F.2d 595 (9th Cir. 1993), where the catch-all exception to the hearsay rule was successfully invoked in a Federal Trade Commission's action for consumer redress regarding the seller's unfair (and deceptive) marketing practices; the letters of complaint (regarding heat detectors) were sent independently to the FTC from unrelated members of the public, and all of them reported similar experiences. Moreover, "reasonable efforts" would not have produced more probative evidence, and the seller had adequate notice of the letters. The purpose of the hearsay was to establish the price of the detectors.

14 *Olson v. Ford Motor Company*, 410 F.Supp.2d 855 (D. N.Dakota, 2006) involved a wrongful death action commenced by a motorist's widow against an automobile manufacturer, alleging products liability, negligence, strict liability, failure to warn, and breach of warranty; the subject one-vehicle accident which resulted in the death of her husband was allegedly caused by a sudden acceleration of his vehicle. Customer complaints regarding other incidents of sudden vehicle acceleration were not admissible as evidence of other crimes, wrongs, or acts, or otherwise admissible character evidence; however, they were admissible through the plaintiff's expert witness to show the basis for the expert's opinion, and to establish that the manufacturer had notice of the complaints.

used to show the state of mind of a recipient who took action based upon the contents.[15]

KEY POINTS FOR OPPOSITION:

Where "notice" is alleged merely as an excuse for placing unfavorable material before the jury, the opponent should argue that the probative value of the complaint is outweighed by its potential prejudice. In certain special cases, the opponent might even consider admitting "notice," and thereby render the evidence immaterial.

§23.404 Diary Entries

ARE THEY ADMISSIBLE?
NO, IF HEARSAY.

Herein lies a very pure and unadulterated form of hearsay where facts are often offered for their truth.

KEY POINTS FOR PROPONENT:

Remember that if the entry is offered to show the state of mind of the author, or for any purpose other than proving the truth of the matters asserted, then it should not be excluded under the hearsay rule.[16] In a medical malpractice action, the decedent's "memory book," which stated her plans to attend technical college and take up computer programming, was admissible because the showed her existing state of mind, and her declaration of intent was admissible to prove that she actually had such intentions.[17]

Those who keep diaries should be forewarned; the "good" stuff that you say about yourself will generally be deemed inadmissible, self serving hearsay. But, as Murphy's law would have it, "bad" stuff could constitute an admission[18], or a declaration against interest[19], or even a prior inconsistent statement[20] if you try to lie about it. And, if you claim that you recorded certain "types" of events, the mere omission of a specific instance of that type may be used to impeach you.[21]

Keep in mind that under Fed. R. Evid. 803(5), personal notes can become "Past Recollections Recorded" (and therefore admissible) if they were written when the author's memory was fresh, and if they are needed to refresh the author's recollection concerning a relevant mat-

15 *Borne v. Haverhill Golf Club, Inc.*, 79 N.E.2d 903, 58 Mass.App.Ct. 306 (2003). In an action involving golf club gender discrimination, letters from two female members regarding discrimination against women at the club were admissible for the purpose of demonstrating the females' state of mind with respect to gender oppression at the club, despite the fact that the letters had a contentious quality about them. *Alexander v. Cit Technology Financing Services, Inc.*, 217 F.Supp.2d 867 (2002). In a former employee's ADEA age and Title VII sex discrimination action, a customer complaint letter, stating that the customer had been subjected to rudeness and profanity should be admissible for purposes other than for the truth of the matter asserted; in particular, the letter showed a basis for the employer's belief that the former female employee was in fact rude and used profanity when speaking to customers. Nevertheless, the letter must be properly verified and authenticated. *Vaughn v. Ems*, 744 S.W.2d 542 (Mo. 1988).

16 See *Kehm v. Proctor and Gamble Manufacturing Co.*, 724 F.2d 613 (8th Cir. 1983); see also *Shoemaker v. Crawford*, 603 N.E.2d 1114, 78 Ohio App.3d 53 (1991).

17 *Mackey v. Irisari*, 445 S.E.2d 742 (W.Va. 1994).

18 See §5.404.

19 See §5.403.

20 See §5.405.

21 *Cairns v. Commonwealth*, 579 S.E.2d 340, 40 Va.App. 271 (2003). In a prosecution for rape, journals kept by the victim detailed her sexual activities. The journal was admissible for purposes of impeachment; the victim testified that the accounts listed in her journals were true even though the journals did not mention any sexual contact with the defendant. In addition, the journals were not consistent with the victim's statements to the police whereby she claimed that she kept a detailed account of the defendant's sexual abuse of her.

ter that has been recorded in those notes. Where permitted, the notes may be read into evidence but may not themselves be admitted unless offered by an adverse party.[22]

In the federal sphere, if all else fails, you might look to the federal catch-all.[23] But don't hold your breath; a diary entry by a saint whose only opposition is a proven telephone solicitor and child molester might stand a slight chance. The rule is rarely applied.

KEY POINTS FOR OPPOSITION:

Unless the foundation for a specific exception is established, entries offered to prove the truth of the matters asserted should be excluded as hearsay.

§23.405 E-Mail

E-mail should now be treated as any other common medium of documentary expression. In particular, for determining admissibility, the practitioner should be more concerned with the content and purpose of the writing rather than its *historical* status as a writing tool.[24]

§23.406 Garbage

***IS IT ADMISSIBLE?* YES.**

KEY POINTS FOR PROPONENT:

Evidence can show up in the strangest places, even in the trash. Just because evidence may have been discarded, however, does not alter its relevance or lack thereof.

Assuming that writings retrieved from garbage cans or other receptacles are relevant, there is no reason why they should not be as admissible as any other document. Even once-privileged material can be retrieved from the rubbish bin and admitted into evidence.[25]

Garbage is considered as abandoned property after it has departed the premises. The prior owner therefore has no reasonable expectation of privacy in it, thereby rendering ineffective claims for Fourth Amendment (Search and Seizure) protection.[26]

KEY POINTS FOR OPPOSITION:

Authenticity, custodianship, and the hearsay rule are all potential weapons. But if the documents are otherwise admissible, they will not be excludable merely because they were discarded by their custodian. Therefore, if documents are to be discarded, they should be shredded or burned

---

22 The exception applies only where the declarant is present in court. *Zenith Radio Corporation v. Matsushita Elec. Indus. Co.*, 505 F. Supp. 1190 (E.D. Pa. 1980).

23 Fed. R. Evid. 803 (24).

24 *McPheeters v. Black & Veatch Corp., Inc.,* 427 F.3d 1095 (8th Cir., Mo., 2005). In a former employee's age discrimination action against a former employer, a group of e-mails written by other dissatisfied employees after the employee's discharge were not relevant, warranting their exclusion. The e-mail authors were not decision-makers or supervisors, so that their views could not demonstrate a pretext for age discrimination arising from employee's discharge, and there was no claim of post-termination discrimination or retaliation. *Riisna v. American Broadcasting Companies, Inc.,* 219 F.Supp.2d 568 (S.D.N.Y., 2002). An e-mail from the executive producer of a television news show directed to a freelance producer (stating the network's refusal to hire her for a program) constituted an admission of a party opponent, and, therefore, was not hearsay. The e-mail was offered to prove that the executive producer communicated its content to the producer; the truth or falsity of the statement itself was not an issue.

See also *Sea Land Service, Inc. v. Lozen International, L.L.C.*, 285 F.3d 808 (9th Cir., Cal., 2002) and §22.411.

25 *Suburban Sew'n Sweep, Inc. v. Swiss-Bernina, Inc.*, 91 F.R.D. 254 (N.D. Ill. 1981).

26 *United States v. Cella*, 568 F.2d 1266 (9th Cir. 1972); *United States v. Mustone*, 469 F.2d 970 (1st Cir. 1972).

beyond recognition; discarded documents, like wounded animals, can return to harm their attackers with a vengeance.

§23.407 Insurance Policies

ARE THEY ADMISSIBLE?
FOR INJURY ACTIONS—NO; FOR CONTRACT ACTIONS—YES.

KEY POINTS:

Evidence of insurance is generally inadmissible, particularly in negligence and products liability actions. If the policy is to be admitted to show dominion or control over a given facility, or property, it may be admissible. Likewise, in an action to collect the benefits, the insurance policy would be admissible as well as any other contract in a suit involving its breach.

§23.408 Letters

***ARE THEY ADMISSIBLE?* ONLY WITHIN A HEARSAY EXCEPTION.**

KEY POINTS:

Generally a personal letter (as opposed to "business" letter) is hearsay and inadmissible if offered to prove the truth of the matters asserted.[27] On the other hand, if the letter is not being used to prove the truth of the matters contained therein, it would not be considered as hearsay, and may be admissible if it is otherwise probative.[28] Thus, if a letter is not being used to refresh

27 *Menne v. Keowee Key Property Owners' Association, Inc.*, 629 S.E.2d 690, 368 S.C. 557 (2006). In a landowner's declaratory judgment action against his property owners' association (seeking a determination regarding the validity of a restrictive covenant that prevented him from building an individual boat dock on his lakefront property), letters regarding evidence of alleged changed conditions were hearsay and irrelevant.

Kashaka v. Baltimore County, Maryland, 450 F.Supp.2d 610 (D.Md., 2006). In a homeowner's §1983 action brought against Baltimore county and some of its police officers for alleged violations of the constitutional rights of the homeowner and his family, letters that the family wrote to public officials detailing alleged harassment by county police officers, and the officials' letters in response, could not be considered by the district court in a summary judgment motion. The letters were unauthenticated and constituted unsworn hearsay.

Pendley Quality Trailer Supply, Inc. v. B & F Plastics, Inc., 578 S.E.2d 915, 260 Ga.App. 125 (2003). The testimonial of a buyer's customer was not admissible under the business records exception to the hearsay rule, where the buyer attempted to introduce it to establish that its purchasing agent had "commended" the quality of the buyer's services and products. Generally, the conclusions, opinions, and impressions of third parties not presented before court are not admissible under the business records exception. *King v. Town of Wallkill*, 302 F.Supp.2d 279 (S.D.N.Y., 2004). On the town's motion for summary judgment on its counterclaim to recoup benefits a police officer improperly collected for an injury sustained during the course of employment, a letter relied upon by the town to prove the amount of damages was inadmissible hearsay; the letter was an out-of-court statement offered to prove the truth of the matter asserted and was not subject to any of the hearsay exceptions.

28 *Holly & Smith Architects, Inc. v. St. Helena Congregate Facility,* 872 So.2d 1147 (La. App., 1 Cir. Feb. 23, 2004) involved a declaratory-judgment action brought against a corporation and its alleged alter ego, wherein the plaintiff sought to pierce the corporate veil. The primary purpose of admitting letters directed to the corporation, from persons unrelated to it, was not to prove the truth of each statement asserted in the letters, but rather to establish the alter ego claim. Under this latter purpose, the letters would not be considered as hearsay.

the recollection of some forgetful witness, and if it is offered to prove the truth of some statement contained in it, the proponent had better have a hearsay exception handy.[29] With or without an exception, however, a letter may always be used to impeach its writer.[30]

In an action for the wrongful death of a seven-year-old child who drowned while on a school field trip, the trial court did not abuse its discretion in admitting a letter written by the child's sister, where the letter dealt with her reaction to her brother's death, and showed her close relationship with her brother (i.e., state of mind).[31]

§23.408(a) Anonymous Letters

ARE THEY ADMISSIBLE? **NO.**

KEY POINTS:

Is it possible to conceive of a piece of evidence that would be less probative than an anonymous letter? Think about it. Hearsay—from someone who won't even provide a name![32]

---

29 *Odegard v. Odegard,* 69 P.3d 917, 2003 Wy. 67 (2003). In a divorce case, a letter from the husband's grandmother, an unavailable declarant, was not admissible under the residual hearsay exception to contradict deeds conveying real property to both the husband and the wife, even though the letter had some marginal utility as evidence of a material fact, since the letter lacked the requisite circumstantial guarantees of trustworthiness. The letter was not dated, the husband wrote the body of the letter, and the grandmother knew the consequences of gifts of property to the husband and wife.

Using residual hearsay exception is not, however, out of the question; see *Freedman v. Value Health, Inc.*, 135 F.Supp.2d 317 (D.Conn., 2001). In securities fraud suit, letter from attorney to state, projecting losses that client would experience on contract to provide drugs to state, was admissible under residual hearsay exception; authenticity of letter was not challenged, and it was more probative regarding amount of estimated loss than any other evidence. For letters that happen to be more than 20 years old, don't forget the "Ancient Writings" exception. See *Martha Graham Sch. & Dance Found, Inc. v. Martha Graham Ctr. of Contemporary Dance, Inc.*, 380 F.3d 624 (2d Cir. N.Y., 2004). See also §23.401.

For a case involving an unsuccessful attempt to use love letters under the "prior inconsistent statement" exception, see *Via v. Commonwealth*, 590 S.E.2d 583, 42 Va. App. 164 (2004). The letters between an alleged sexual assault victim and her boyfriend were not admissible as impeachment evidence in a sexual abuse prosecution of the defendant victim's father, even though the letters allegedly contradicted the victim's testimony that she was never with her boyfriend un-chaperoned. It turned out that the letters were composed after the victim had lodged the complaint against the defendant, and the defendant laid no foundation for the introduction of the letters as prior inconsistent statements.

30 Consider *State v. Guthrie*, 428 S.E.2d 853 (N.C. App. 1993): an "alleged" sexual offense victim had previously written letters to the defendant, inferring that she would have sex with him for money and other favors; they were admitted, as was her testimony regarding a similar letter that she wrote to another person. The trial court, however, refused to permit defense counsel to cross-examine the "victim" about yet another letter that she wrote to a friend, asking that friend to have sex with her; that denial was held to be reversible error.

31 *Johnson v. Washington County*, 518 N.W.2d 594 (Minn. 1994).

32 But that won't stop 'em from trying. See *Bellow v. Charbonnet*, 100 F.Supp.2d 398 (E.D.La. 2000). In political patronage lawsuit, anonymous letter purported to come from supporters of successful candidate for parish office, stating that its authors knew that parish employee who campaigned for unsuccessful incumbent would be out of office; to no one's amazement, letter was held to be inadmissible hearsay.

§23.408(b) Letters of Explanation

ARE THEY ADMISSIBLE? NO, UNLESS USED AGAINST THE AUTHOR.

KEY POINTS:

Letters describing an incident, accident or event constitute hearsay if used to prove the matters contained therein and are, therefore, inadmissible.[33] Moreover, it's not entirely clear why anyone would write such a letter, since the admissions contained in such a letter could always be used against its author.[34]

§23.409 Personal Memos and Notes

Personal notes and memos pertaining to business matters, judicial proceedings or administrative hearings are not necessarily considered as either official records or records kept in the ordinary course of business.[35]

See "Diary Entries" above.

§23.409(a) Personal Tax Returns

ARE THEY ADMISSIBLE? YES.

KEY POINTS:

As indicated in §20.600, all of our documentary examples pre-suppose relevance on the part of the subject evidence. But in the case of tax returns, relevance, itself, is often the key to the answer. In tax litigation, for example, personal returns would certainly be relevant and admissible. But in situations involving *only* economic issues, personal returns would not only be deemed irrelevant, they would also be non-discoverable.[36]

§23.410 Postal Certificates of Mailing

ARE THEY ADMISSIBLE? YES.

KEY POINTS:

A copy of a certificate of mailing endorsed by the postal service and a specimen notice of cancellation were admissible in an action to determine coverage under an automobile insurance policy.[37] Certificates of mailing may also be admissible under the official records exception to the hearsay rule.[38]

---

33 *Madden v. Dake*, 30 A.D.3d 932, 819 N.Y.S.2d 121 (N.Y.A.D., 3 Dept., 2006). In a personal injury action resulting from a collision between a bus and a motorist's vehicle, the exclusion of a letter of explanation written by the driver of the bus that struck the motorist's vehicle (regarding the accident and her plea of guilty to a traffic law violation) was warranted where the bus driver had the ability and opportunity to testify during the course of the trial.

34 See §5.400, §5.404, and §48.201.

35 *SEC v. Treadway*, 438 F.Supp.2d 218 (S.D.N.Y., 2006). In a Securities and Exchange Commission (SEC) enforcement proceeding, two of the mutual funds' portfolio managers had sufficient personal knowledge from their positions to testify as to any disruption or harm that they experienced or perceived in the funds that they managed as the result of the defendants' market timing arrangement with a particular trader. However, notes of a third party regarding what a witness said are not admissible as prior statements of that witness in the absence of the witness' endorsement of those notes as constituting his own statement.

36 See *Gramman v. Stachkunas*, 750 So.2d 688 (Fla.App., 1999). Medical opinion witness in injury action should not be required to produce or disclose contents of his business records or his 1099 tax returns regarding his prior work as expert in other cases.

37 *Bullock v. Hanover Ins. Co.*, 534 N.Y.S. 2d 197 (N.Y.A.D. 2 Dep't. 1988).

38 *Preis v. American Indem. Co.*, 220 Cal.App.3d 752, 269 Cal.Rptr. 617 (1990).

§23.411 Promissory Notes

ARE THEY ADMISSIBLE? YES.

KEY POINTS FOR PROPONENT:

Negotiable instruments are most likely to appear in cases involving their enforcement. They will always be relevant in that context. And since such instruments contain directives as opposed to statements of fact, the hearsay rule will most likely not apply. In particular, in the absence of an offered statement of fact, the note will not constitute hearsay.

KEY POINTS FOR OPPOSITION:

The best evidence rule is more than a mere formality.[39] Historically, the note itself constituted the debt. The destruction of the note, therefore, would both symbolically and legally effectuate a cancellation or discharge. For such formalities, there was no place for copies.

Rules permitting duplicates in most circumstances may contain special restrictions for negotiable instruments.[40]

REFERENCES

Admissibility of duplicates. 72 A.L.R. Fed. 732.

§23.412 Surveys and Questionnaires

The term "survey" has many meanings. It could refer to an official map or geographical chart; or it could refer to a scientific, independent poll. As used in this particular chapter, however, none of those meanings apply. Rather, we are using the term to denote a do-it-yourself poll taken on behalf of a party.

ARE THEY ADMISSIBLE? NO.

KEY POINTS FOR PROPONENT:

If the proponent were to use a written format for the survey, at least its objectivity, or lack thereof, can be scrutinized. But the road to admissibility would still be difficult. At the very least, a poll involves two levels of hearsay (i.e., information passes from the questionee to the poll taker, who then records and compiles the results.[41]

---

39 See Chapter 2.

40 Section 90.953(1) of the Florida Evidence Code, for example, restricts the use of duplicates for negotiable instruments, security agreements, or other documents evidencing a right to the receipt of money.

41 *Jackson v. National Action Financial Services, Inc.*, 441 F.Supp.2d 877 (N.D.Ill., 2006). In a lawsuit by debtors under the Fair Debt Collection Practices Act (FDCPA) against a debt collection company (alleging that the company made false statements in its settlement letters), a consumer survey compiled by an expert was unreliable and irrelevant, and thus would not be considered for purposes of summary judgment. The phrase "limited-time offer," as used in the survey without any definition or explanation, was too ambiguous to provide insight as to whether or not participants were confused as to the meaning of the offer allegedly presented in the letters.

U.S. v. Southern Indiana Gas and Electric Company, 258 F.Supp.2d 884 (2003). A survey sent to companies in the utility industry questioning their usual routine maintenance, with respect to exemptions under the Clean Air Act, was not admissible under the residual hearsay exception, since the risk of insincerity was very high; the survey was based on responses from interested parties who were informed of the purpose of the survey. Moreover, the risk of faulty memory was inherent in questions concerning projects that were over 60 years old; and, the attorney involvement in the design and administration of the survey exceeded what was necessary to assure the legal relevance of the questionnaire. See *Brokerage Concepts, Inc. v. U.S. Healthcare, Inc.*, 140 F.3rd 94 (3rd Cir. 1998).

KEY POINTS FOR OPPOSITION:

The survey would really be nothing more than self-serving do-it-yourself hearsay, and could be excluded on that basis alone.[42] The objectivity of the poll should also be challenged.[43]

Whenever opposing a survey, be sure to consider attacking the poll as unscientific. For there is no such thing as a purely objective and scientific poll.[44] Even a "valid" poll may require an expert to present the conclusions.[45]

§23.413 Telephone Bills

ARE THEY ADMISSIBLE? YES.

KEY POINTS FOR PROPONENT:

If the bills are relevant, there is no reason why they should not be admitted, as long as a proper foundation is set. The proponent may wish to consider qualifying the bills as business records of the telephone company.

---

42 *Olle v. Columbia University*, 136 Fed.Appx. 383. In an employment discrimination lawsuit brought by an employee who was hired to work with the defendants in managing an academic fellowship program, an anonymous survey of prior fellows which allegedly demonstrated an extensive bias constituted inadmissible hearsay. But see *Beacon Mut. Ins. Co. v. Onebeacon Ins. Group,* 376 F.Supp.2d. 251 (2005). In a trademark infringement lawsuit, market surveys may be used as a means of establishing the secondary meaning of a trademark. The issue of confusion in the minds of the public is a relevant consideration. A "Confusion Matrix" in which an insurance company summarized evidence of actual confusion experienced by employers, employees, vendors, doctors, court personnel, and others in the state with respect to the relationship between the company and a competitor was hearsay and was not admissible. *Gacke v. Pork Xtra, L.L.C.*, 684 N.W.2d 168 (Iowa 2004). Questionnaires completed by persons who had been on or around the plaintiffs' property, concerning odors emanating from nearby hog confinement facilities, were hearsay; even though the plaintiffs claimed that they offered the questionnaires for the purpose of showing that the defendant was put on notice of an odor problem, the probative value of the questionnaire statements depended upon the truth of the statements made by questionnaire respondents.

43 In a products liability case involving a forklift injury, *Nye v. Fostoria Distrib. Serv. Co.*, 604 N.E.2d 795, 78 Ohio App.3d 319 (1992), a survey of employer practices regarding warning devices on forklifts was held to be inadmissible hearsay. The qualifying witness conducted the survey by telephoning various businesses which utilized forklifts. That witness had no personal knowledge of the matters about which he questioned the participants in the survey; moreover, the survey was simply a compilation of hearsay and was offered to prove the truth of the matter asserted. See also *Graves v. Atchison-Holt Elec. Co-op.*, 886 S.W.2d 1 (Mo. App. W.D. 1994). See also *State v. Tee & Bee,* Inc.,600 N.W.2d 230 (Wis.App. 1999), a civil forfeiture action commenced pursuant to an obscenity statute, wherein the exclusion of a telephone survey purporting to indicate state-wide community standards was not an erroneous exercise of discretion. Failing to sufficiently apprize survey respondents of nature of charged materials rendered the survey results irrelevant.

44 *Collier v. Bradley University*, 113 F.Supp.2d 1235 (2000). In employment discrimination lawsuit brought by African-American professor against university, survey responses devoted to issues of multiculturalism and need to improve relationships on campus among people with culturally diverse backgrounds were inadmissible; information was unscientific and its probative value was substantially outweighed by danger of unfair prejudice and confusion regarding issues.

45 *Lanphere Enterprises, Inc. v. Jiffy Lube International, Inc.* 138 Fed.Appx. 20 (9th Cir., Oregon, 2005). In a lawsuit brought against the Jiffy Lube oil change business for unlawful trade practices and intentional interference with business relations (based on certain radio advertisements), an automobile dealership's preliminary customer survey and related expert report and testimony were inadmissible since the survey results provided only marginal support for the expert's opinions. Furthermore, the automobile dealership's follow-up customer survey and related expert report and testimony were also inadmissible since the survey failed to establish that the customers would have gone to the dealership for oil changes if it weren't for the allegedly false advertisements. *Simon Property Group, L.P. v. mySimon, Inc.*, 104 F.Supp.2d 1033 (S.D.Ind. 2000). Consumer survey results must be presented through expert witness testimony.

KEY POINTS FOR OPPOSITION:

If the bills are offered to prove the time or place of a call from or to someone, then hearsay may be involved.[46]

§23.414 Tombstone Epitaphs

IS SUCH EVIDENCE ADMISSIBLE? **YES (QUALIFIED).**

KEY POINTS:

Poems along with a tombstone epitaph written by the parents of a motorcycle passenger were admissible under the state-of-mind exception to the hearsay rule in a wrongful death action, for purposes of establishing mental anguish.[47]

§23.415 Spontaneous Written Declarations

ARE THEY ADMISSIBLE? **NO.**

KEY POINTS:

Stupid question? How can something be "spontaneous" if the author has time to take pen in hand and write it?[48]

§23.416 Personal Resume

ARE THEY ADMISSIBLE? **GENERALLY, NO.**

KEY POINTS:

A personal resume is basically a list of biographical traits pertaining to a person's vital statistics, education, experience, skills and publications. It is basically hearsay.[49]

---

46 Consider *Barnes v. Barnes*, 843 S.W.2d 835, 311 Ark. 287 (1992), a paternity proceeding, where the putative father sought to introduce a telephone bill over a hearsay objection; the proponent tried to use the residual hearsay exception (bad choice) in order to show that he was not in the company of the mother during the conception period. The evidence was found to have lacked sufficient circumstantial guarantees of trustworthiness to be admissible.

47 *In re estate of Holmgren*, 178 Ill. Dec. 569, 604 N.E.2d 1092 (Ill. App. 3 Dist. 1992).

48 *Current v. Perry*, 178 Fed.Appx. 686 (9th Cir., Cal., 2006). In an employee's action alleging discriminatory retaliation under Title VII, the District Court was held to have been within its discretion in excluding a written declaration as inadmissible hearsay, where the employee failed to demonstrate that the statement was an excited utterance because it lacked the requisite startling event. But see *People v. Gutierrez*, 78 Cal.App.4th 170, 92 Cal.Rptr. 2d 626 (2000). As a case of first impression and a truly unique case, California Court of Appeal held that note containing license number of vehicle used in crime, written by witness to crime, may qualify as "spontaneous declaration" for purposes of hearsay rule exception.

49 *Helen of Troy, L.P., v. Zotos Corporation*, 235 F.R.D. 634, 64 Fed.R.Serv.3d 998 (W.D.Texas, 2006). An unsworn and uncertified resume and report by the plaintiff's expert were not competent evidence for the limited purpose of demonstrating the magnitude of the damages in opposition to defendant's summary judgment motion.

Chapter 24

Published Writings

§24.100 Introduction

Publications, in general, provide a substantial dilemma for evidence rule-makers. No one would doubt the integrity of *Gray's Anatomy,* or its reliability. But anyone can write a book.

§24.200 Specific Writings

§24.200(a) Advertisements and Brochures

***ARE THEY ADMISSIBLE?* IT DEPENDS UPON THE PURPOSE.**

KEY POINTS:

If the advertisement or brochure is itself the subject of the controversy, it would unquestionably be relevant and admissible. Claims made in false advertisements, for example, would not be considered as inadmissible hearsay; they would presumably be admitted to prove their underlying *untruth*, as opposed to their truth.[1] In other circumstances, admissibility may depend upon the particular purpose for the requested admission. [2]

§24.201 Bibles

ARE THEY ADMISSIBLE?
GENERALLY NO.

KEY POINTS:

Don't confuse the inscriptions with biblical tales. Family inscriptions and notes (i.e., birth dates, marriages, baptisms and divorces) are admissible pursuant to a specific exception (see §23.402). But the stories about the parting of the Red Sea, etc., are not universally accepted truths.

In the case of *Burns v. Burns*,[3] the Bible and the Encyclopedia Judaica were subject to judicial notice; in that matter, it was the procedural, and not the substantive writings, that were material to the case.

§24.201(a) Religious Writings

ARE THEY ADMISSIBLE?
YES (QUALIFIED).

Religious writings that are not offered to prove the truth of the matter contained within them may be admissible if relevance is shown. So too is the testimony pertaining to them.[4] On the other hand, without authority, it is safe to

1 See §20.500.

2 *Massok v. Keller Indus., Inc.*, 147 Fed.Appx. 651 (9th Cir., Cal., 2005). In a product liability personal injury action resulting from a fall from a ladder, a brochure displaying the model of the ladder owned by the plaintiff set up just as the plaintiff had set it up at the time of his fall was relevant evidence of both the foreseeability of the plaintiff's use of the ladder and the manufacturer's anticipation of such use, even though the plaintiff had not seen it prior to his accident. Thus, the exclusion of the brochure from evidence was an abuse of discretion.

3 223 N.J. Super. 219, 538 A.2d 438 (1987). *Caruolo v. John Crane, Inc.*, 226 F.3d 46 (2nd Cir. N.Y. 2000). It was not improper for expert to rely on study relating to dust and asbestos release from certain gasket materials during use, since authoritativeness of study was adequately established, particularly in light of challenge to expert's direct testimony. *Kahanek v. Rogers*, 12 S.W.3d 501 (Tex.App. 1999). Physicians Desk Reference was learned treatise rather than compilation of market material and thus was not itself admissible in medical malpractice action. Moreover, learned treatise is admissible only in conjunction with expert's testimony and may not be taken into jury room. *Miskin v. Baxter Healthcare Corp.,* 107 F.Supp.2d 669 (D. Md. 1999). In products liability action against silicone breast implant manufacturer, unauthenticated medical treatises were inadmissible hearsay and would, thus, not serve to preclude summary judgement absent evidence that they were authentic and qualified as learned treatises.

4 *Williams Island Synagogue v. City of Aventura,* 329 F.Supp.2d 1319 (S.D. Fla., 2004). A Rabbi's statements regarding the requirements of the temple under Orthodox Judaism were properly characterized as the opinion of a potential expert on the subject of Jewish law, rather than as hearsay statements concerning the content of certain treatises, even though the statements were offered for the truth of their description of Jewish law.

state that religious writings offered to prove their truth would be excludable as hearsay.

§24.202 Learned Treatises

ARE THEY ADMISSIBLE?
YES (QUALIFIED).

KEY POINTS FOR PROPONENT:

Learned treatises enjoy a limited protection from the hearsay rule under Fed. R. Evid. 803(18). Learned treatises are admissible if the court takes judicial notice of the work or if an expert testifies that the treatise is a reliable authority.[5] It is within the broad discretion of the trial court to admit learned treatises. Generally, learned treatises are admissible for impeachment purposes, but not as substantive proof.[6] Gaining admission for a treatise as substantive evidence is more difficult, but still possible, if the work is trustworthy.[7]

---

5 *Mayes v. City of Hammond*, 442 F.Supp.2d 587 (N.D.Indiana, 2006). In a former prisoner's §1983 action against police officials, treatises were not admissible under the hearsay exception for learned treatises where the former prisoner failed to identify any expert testimony showing that the proposed treatises were relied upon for expert testimony.

Gant v. Novello, 754 N.Y.S.2d 746 (N.Y.A.D. 3rd Dept., 2003). Learned Treatises, which have been established as authoritative, are admissible into evidence, but only to the extent that they are called to the attention of an expert witness upon cross-examination or otherwise relied upon by the expert witness during the course of his or her direct examination.

Burgess v. Premier Corporation, 727 F.2d 826 (9th Cir. 1984); *Lewandowski v. Preferred Risk Mutual Ins. Co.*, 33 Wis.2d 69, 146 N.W.2d 505 (1966).

6 *Mizell v. Glover* 570 S.E.2d 176, 351 S.C. 392 (2002). In a patient's medical malpractice action against a physician, it was proper for the trial court to deny admission of an article in a medical textbook that was written by the physician's expert; it was also proper to allow the patient to cross examine the physician's expert regarding the article, while publishing portions of it throughout the cross examination.

Freshwater v. Scheidt, 714 N.E.2d 591, 56 Ohio St.3d 260 (1999). The use of learned treatises is limited to impeachment purposes only. See also *Morfesis v. Sobol*, 567 N.Y.S.2d 954 (1991); *Johnson v. Mountainside Hosp.*, 239 N.J.Super. 312, 571 A.2d 318 (1990); *Ellis v. International Playtex Corp.*, 745 F.2d 292 (4th Cir. 1984); *Burgess v. Premier Corp.*, 727 F.2d 826 (9th Cir. 1984); *Connecticut Light & Power Co. v. Federal Power Commission*, 547 F.2d 349 (2d Cir. 1977). But see *DaGraca v. Laing*, 672 A.2d 247, 288 N.J. Super. 292 (N.J. Super.A.D. 1996) which delivered the following summary: "The learned treatise exception allows texts to be established as reliable authority by experts, as well as by judicial notice; it avoids the possibility that an expert may block cross-examination by refusing to concede to its authoritativeness. Moreover, the exception permits learned treatise statements to be admitted as substantive evidence on both direct and cross-examination, but it limits their use as substantive evidence to situations in which the expert is on the stand and available to explain the application of the treatise if desired. Otherwise stated, text will qualify as 'reliable authority' and will be admissible if it represents the type of material reasonably relied on by experts in the field."

7 *Federico v. Ford Motor Company,* 854 N.E.2d 448, 67 Mass.App.Ct. 454 (Mass.App.Ct., 2006). Material from learned treatises is initially admissible on cross-examination only after the judge decides that the treatise is a reliable authority. In determining the admissibility of testimony drawn from a learned treatise, the judge must determine the relevance and materiality of the statement and should consider carefully any claimed unfairness or confusion that the admission of the statement may create. A statement drawn from a learned treatise may be read into evidence, and the witness should be given an opportunity to assess the statement and comment on it during either cross-examination or redirect examination. Once the statement drawn from a learned treatise has been admitted, it is admitted for its substance.

J.R. Simplot Co. v. Rycair, Inc., 67 P.3d 36 (Idaho 2003). Extrinsic evidence, such as an expert's testimony and information from learned treatises, may be helpful for understanding the terms of art in a contract, but such evidence is not controlling and should be received at the discretion of the court.

Taylor, Thon, Thompson & Peterson v. Cannaday, 749 P.2d 63 (Mont. 1988); *Ensor v. Wilson By and Through Wilson*, 519 So.2d 1244 (Ala. 1987). Note, however, that to establish a foundation for the admission of an article under the Learned Treatise Exception to hearsay rule, the status of the publication itself is not sufficient to establish that the writer of the article is reliable. See *Ansani v. Cascade Mountain, Inc.,* 588 N.W.2d 321, 223 Wis.2d 39 (1998).

Can a videotape constitute a learned treatise? Can your heart stand the shock of a "yes" answer? There *is* new authority to support this innovative idea.[8]

KEY POINTS FOR OPPOSITION:

Learned treatises are not automatically excepted from the hearsay rule, where they are offered to prove the truth of the matters asserted.[9] Also, the learned treatise exception to the hearsay rule is apparently limited to documentary evidence.[10] In the last analysis, keep in mind that the learned treatise exception is a weak one; admissibility might very well depend upon the recognized trustworthiness of the subject matter. And, even that standard varies from state to state.[11]

§24.202(a) Dictionaries

***ARE THEY ADMISSIBLE?* YES.**

Assuming that there is a dispute with respect to the definition of a word or term, a dictionary would seem to be the normal, if not obvious place to find a resolution.[12] The same may be said of foreign dictionaries.[13]

§24.202(b) Handbooks

ARE THEY ADMISSIBLE?
YES (QUALIFIED).

There are a variety of handbooks created by businesses and industrial representatives on a wide range of subjects. Safety-related evidence (one such subject) that is non-scientific in nature clearly has an uphill battle with respect to admissibility. It is, however, possible for the publication of a private entity to achieve hearsay exception status as a "treatise" if the publication happens to be reputable.[14]

---

8 See *Costantino v. David M. Herzog, M.D., P.C.*, 203 F.3d 164 (2nd Cir. N.Y. 2000).

9 *Duhon v. Petroleum Helicopters, Inc.*, 554 So.2d 1270 (La. 1989); *Majdic v. Cincinnati Machine Co.*, 537 A.2d 334 (Pa. 1988). See also *Owens-Corning Fiberglas Corp. v. Malone*, 916 S.W.2d 551 (Tex. App. 1 Dist, 1996).

10 *Simmons v. Yurchak*, 28 Mass. App. 371, 551 N.E.2d 539 (1990). A physician's instructional videotape was inadmissible in a medical malpractice action.

11 *Beard v. Meridia Huron Hosp.*, 834 N.E.2d 323, 106 Ohio St.3d 237 (2005). Statements contained in certain professional literature fell within Ohio's definition of hearsay. Ohio has no learned treatise exception. Such works were, therefore, not admissible as independent evidence of the theories and opinions expressed therein.

12 Among others, consider *Webster's Dictionary* and The *Oxford Dictionary* as recognized authority.

13 *Impax Labs., Inc. v. Aventis Pharms., Inc.*, 333 F.Supp.2d 265 (D. Del., 2004). Dictionary and glossary definitions of a French term used in a witness' deposition testimony were admissible, under a commercial publication exception to the hearsay rule, as relevant to the disputed translation of the term.

14 *Paulos v. Covenant Transport, Inc.*, 86 P.3d 752, 2004 UT. App. 35 (2004). In a personal injury action by a motorcyclist against a truck driver (where the trucker struck the motorcyclist while attempting to pass a truck), the *American Trucking Association* (ATA) handbook, which set forth accepted standards of care as to what semi-truck drivers should do when being overtaken, was admissible under the hearsay exception for learned treatises, and thus, could be read into evidence (but not received as exhibit for jury to use during deliberations). Although no state case explicitly extended the hearsay exception for learned treatises to include non-governmental safety codes or non-scientific safety codes, the ATA handbook was of the same nature as other materials explicitly mentioned in the learned treatise exception.

§24.203 Magazine and Newspaper Articles

ARE THEY ADMISSIBLE? GENERALLY NO.

Magazine articles are generally not excepted from the Hearsay Rule.[15] The same is true with respect to newspaper articles.[16]

KEY POINTS FOR PROPONENT:

While generally considered hearsay, magazine and newspaper articles occasionally gain admission.[17] The business records exception to the hearsay rule provided an avenue for the admission of newspaper articles in *U.S. v. Reese*.[18] A hospital regularly dated and recorded articles in which it was mentioned. The articles were admitted to show the hospital's visiting hours during the time when a witness was hospitalized.

---

15 *Goguen v. Textron, Inc.*, 234 F.R.D. 13, 69 Fed. R. Evid. Serv. 726 (2006). In a products liability case involving wrongful death, a serial number reference book for metalworking machinery, which was updated every five years and was in its 11th edition, did not qualify as a self-authenticating "periodical," and thus the company's failure to authenticate a relevant excerpt from the book precluded the district court from considering any exhibit containing that excerpt when deciding the company's motion for summary judgment. Moreover, the term "periodical" cannot be stretched to include any publication published on a regular schedule. See *Pirelli Armstrong Tire Corp. v. Titan Tire Corp.*, 4 F.Supp.2d 794 (Ill. 1998); and *Federal Election Commission v. GOPAC, Inc.*, 917 F.Supp. 851 (D.D.C. 1996).

16 *Aon Risk Services, Inc. v. Liebenstein*, 710 N.W.2d 175, 2006 WI App. 4 (2006). Newspaper articles constitute inadmissible hearsay, even for purposes of summary judgment. Generally, they may not be considered for summary judgment unless they are being submitted in conjunction with a libel action against the newspaper, or in the alternative, unless the articles are at least 20 years old.

Good v. Bd. of County Comm'rs of Shawnee, 331 F.Supp.2d 1315 (D. Kan., 2004). In a 1983 lawsuit by a former deputy sheriff who brought action against the Board of County Commissioners county prosecutors (based on an alleged violation of First Amendment association rights), newspaper articles constituted hearsay because they were offered to prove the truth of the matters asserted therein.

Plowman v. Pratt, 684 N.W.2d 28, 268 Neb. 466 (2004). In a personal injury lawsuit, news articles regarding the dangerousness of pit bull terriers constituted inadmissible hearsay; the articles were offered to prove the matter asserted, in particular, that pit bull terriers were dangerous animals.

Gantt v. Whitaker, 57 Fed.Appx. 141 (4th Cir., N.C., 2003). An arrestee's attempt to admit a newspaper article in his action against police, alleging false arrest and malicious prosecution, was unsuccessful. He failed to establish any prerequisites for the applicability of an exception to the hearsay rule.

Hutira v. Islamic Republic of Iran, 211 Fed.Sup.2d 115 (D.D.C., 2002). In a lawsuit against the Republic of Iran by an Iranian dissident's daughter, newspaper articles that detailed an alleged plot by the Republic to assassinate her were offered to prove the truth of the matters asserted; they were, therefore, hearsay and inadmissible.

State v. Hardy, 651 A.2d 322 (Me. 1994).

17 *Young v. Horton*, 855 P.2d 502 (Mont. 1993); *Deerhake v. DuQuoin State Fair Ass'n*., 185 Ill. App.3d 374, 133 Ill. Dec. 508, 541 N.E.2d 719 (1989). *Chase Manhattan Bank v. Traffic Stream Infrastructure Ltd.*, 86 F.Supp.2d 244 (S.D.N.Y. 2000). In action by trustee for breach of contract, Chinese newspaper article disclosing changes in Chinese policy regarding remittance of guaranteed funds to foreign investors was admissible under residual exception to hearsay rule. Article supported defendant's claim that change in Chinese policy rendered its performance under subject agreement impossible; official notice of policy change was not publicly released, making article the most probative evidence available. Chinese government published newspaper so there was little risk that it would inaccurately reflect that government's official position.

18 568 F.2d 1246 (6th Cir. 1977).

In a products liability action, a doctor's "letter to the editor" of a medical journal was permitted under the learned treatise exception to the hearsay rule; the letter criticized a chlordane mortality study which the defendant manufacturer relied on to show that workers exposed to much higher levels of chlordane suffered no long lasting adverse health effects. The evidence tended to undermine the manufacturer's assertion that epidemiological studies demonstrated that chlordane was not a significant health risk.[19]

A magazine article and reporter's accompanying notes concerning a corporate merger, when offered with the reporter's testimony, possessed the circumstantial guarantees of trustworthiness required by the "residual" or "catch-all" exception to the hearsay rule, and thus were admissible in a Rule 10b-5 action. The notes provided work product to back up the article, which made sense out of the reporter's incomplete notes and memory; also, the article provided a contemporaneous record of the reporter's understanding of the meaning of the subject's answers to her questions.[20]

On the other hand, a journalist's investigative report about the sexual safety of swingers was not deemed trustworthy. In particular, in an action challenging the constitutionality of a city ordinance prohibiting the operation of businesses that provide kinky sexual activities, the report of the investigative journalist was deemed inadmissible.[21] It apparently advocated the proposition that swingers generally engaged in safer sexual practices than sexually active non-swingers. The report, which was predicated upon random interviews with swingers and club owners was lacking reliable statistical methodology and was, therefore, unreliable.

If the newspaper article happens to be 20 years old or older, it may qualify as an "ancient document" and thereby be admissible (See §23.401). Also, some articles may qualify as learned treatises (see §24.202).

In those rare cases where an article is *not* being admitted to prove the truth of the matters contained in it, relevance may be enough to obtain admissibility.[22] A similar result might also be expected with respect to press releases.[23]

---

19 *Conde v. Velsicol Chemical Corp.*, 804 F. Supp. 972 (S.D.Ohio 1992).

20 *In re Columbia Securities Litigation*, 155 F.R.D. 466 (S.D.N.Y. 1994).

21 *Recreational Developments of Phoenix, Inc. v. City of Phoenix*, 220 F.Supp.2d 1054 (Arizona, 2002).

22 *Martin v. Roy,* 767 N.E.2d 603, 54 Mass.App.Ct. 642 (2002). In a professor's defamation action against a student newspaper reporter, two newspaper articles portraying the college professor as an anti-Semite were admissible to show that the professor's reputation could have been damaged from those publications; they were not offered to prove the truth of the matters asserted.

Richardson v. Calderon, 713 N.E.2d 856 (Ind.App. 1999) held that a trial Court errs by excluding newspaper articles on hearsay grounds, where those articles were not offered into evidence to establish the truth of the matter asserted, but rather were properly offered to establish other facts or inferences. See also *Horton v. McCrary,* 620 So.2d 918 (La. App. 1993). An automobile accident victim's scrapbook, containing newspaper articles about his athletic achievements, was not inadmissible hearsay; the scrapbook was not offered to establish the truth of the newspaper articles, but rather to show the victim's desire for athletics, and to help quantify the loss that he suffered because of his inability to continue participation.

23 *Zeigler v. Fisher-Price, Inc.*, 302 F.Supp.2d 999 (N.D. Iowa 2004). A Consumer Product Safety Commission press release announcing a toy vehicle's voluntary recall was not hearsay in a products liability action against the toy manufacturer; the language in the press release was not mandated by the CPSC. The press release was instead issued as part of a voluntary settlement agreement entered into between the CPSC and the manufacturer.

KEY POINTS FOR OPPOSITION:

Newspaper and magazine articles are generally offered in an attempt to prove the truth of the matters asserted therein, and are, therefore, considered hearsay.[24]

§24.204 Market Reports

ARE THEY ADMISSIBLE? YES.

KEY POINTS FOR PROPONENT:

Market reports contained within widely used and recognized publications are generally admissible under Fed. R. Evid. 803(17), because such reports are based on authentic sources.[25] But lesser-known publications may require the proponent to lay a foundation in order to secure admissibility.[26]

KEY POINTS FOR OPPOSITION:

Although most market quotations are admissible, opinions or editorials concerning those quotations are not.[27] Also, where superior evidence of market value is available, market reports may not be admissible.[28]

§24.205 Medical Articles

ARE THEY ADMISSIBLE?
GENERALLY, NO.

KEY POINTS:

Unless the article is being used to cross-examine its author, or a physician who acknowledges the article as authoritative, it, generally, may not be used. For example, in a products liability action against the manufacturers of

24 *U.S. v. Fennell*, 381 Fed.Supp.2d 1312 (D.N.M., 2005). Journal and newspaper articles regarding alleged Mexican settlements in the national forest constituted inadmissible hearsay in the United States' trespass action against the holders of unpatented mining claims within the national forest. The materials contained hearsay within hearsay and were not material to the issue of ownership of the subject area or to the issue of whether or not the subject area was included within the national forest.

Hubbert v. Dell Corp., 835 N.E.2d 113, 296 Ill.Dec. 258 (Ill.App., 2005). A newspaper article suggesting that an arbitration firm selected by a computer manufacturer had a bias in favor of the credit card firms and retailers was hearsay and was not admissible in action by the computer purchasers against the manufacturer.

United States v. Teamsters Local 560, 780 F.2d 267 (3d Cir. 1985). In a RICO (Racketeer Influenced and Corrupt Organizations Act) action, the U.S. sought admission of newspaper and magazine articles which described the defendants' criminal activities, in order to show that the defendants had an established criminal reputation. The government claimed that the defendants' reputation intimidated many union members and kept them from exercising their rights. The court ruled against the government because it could not prove that the members read any of the articles. See also *Chicago Firefighters Local 2 v. City of Chicago,* 249 F.3d 649 (7th Cir., Ill., 2001); *Arkwright v. Taulbee,* 546 S.E.2d 335, 208 Ga.App. 219 (2001); *In re Fischer,* 259 B.R. 23 (E.D.N.Y., 2001). See also *Abruzzi Foods, Inc., v. Pasta & Cheese, Inc.*, 986 F.2d 605 (1st Cir. 1993); *City of Austin v. Houston Lighting & Power Co.*, 844 S.W.2d 773 (Tex. App. 1992); *Conde v. Velsicol Chemical Corp.*, 804 F. Supp. 972 (S.D. Ohio 1992); and *Tanksley v. Alabama Gas Corp.*, 568 So.2d 731 (Ala. 1990).

25 *Daimler-Benz Aktiengesellschaft v. Olson*, 21 S.W.3d 707 (Tex.App. 2000); *In re Byington*, 197 B.R. 130 (Bkrtcy. D.Kan. 1996); *McDonald v. Johnson & Johnson*, 537 F. Supp. 1282 (D.C. Minn. 1982); *First National Bank of Chicago v. Jefferson Mortgage Co.*, 576 F.2d 479 (3d Cir. 1978); *U.S. v. Anderson*, 532 F.2d 1218 (9th Cir. 1976); *Commonwealth of Virginia v. State of West Virginia*, 238 U.S. 202 (1915); *Kibler v. Caplis*, 140 Mich. 28, 103 N.W. 531 (1905). Publications containing market prices or statistical compilations that are proven to be generally recognized as reliable and regularly used in trade or specialized activity are admissible for truth of matter published. *Dugan v. Gotsopoulos,* 22 P.30 205 (Nev. 2001). Market quotations, tabulations, lists and other published compilations, which are generally used and relied upon by public do not constitute inadmissible hearsay.

26 *Johnson v. Nickels*, 66 N.M. 181, 344 P.2d 697 (1959); *Curtis v. Schwartzman Packing Co.*, 61 N.M. 305, 299 P.2d 776 (1956).

27 *First National Bank of Chicago v. Jefferson Mortgage Co.*, 576 F.2d 479, 495 (3d Cir. 1978); *Wann v. Dickson*, 213 Mo. 66, 111 S.W. 817 (1908).

28 *Johnson v. Nickels*, 66 N.M. 181, 344 P.2d 697 (1959); *Nelson Morris & Co. v. Columbian Iron Works & Dry Dock Co.*, 76 Md. 354, 25 A. 417 (1892).

asbestos products, medical articles on asbestos hazards were "hearsay" and, thus, were inadmissible. The plaintiff attempted to offer those articles as substantive evidence;[29] they were not being offered to impeach a witness nor as the basis of an expert's opinion, and plaintiff did not contend that defendants ever received those articles so as to constitute notice.[30]

§24.206 Medical Textbooks

ARE THEY ADMISSIBLE? **YES.**

KEY POINTS FOR PROPONENT:

A medical textbook, treatise or professional article should be admissible to prove the facts contained therein (if the literature is authoritative), when it is called to the attention of an expert witness upon cross-examination, or if it is relied upon by the expert during direct examination.[31] When a physician testifies about the contents of medical literature, the testimony is not hearsay.[32] Admissibility will often depend upon the particular circumstances and the jurisdiction.[33]

Of course, the best way to avoid hearsay problems, and thereby enhance your chances for admissibility, would be to offer the text for some purpose *other* than to prove the truth of the matters contained in it.[34]

KEY POINTS FOR OPPOSITION:

Gaining admission for medical manuals or articles may be more difficult than for larger texts.[35] Also, it has been said that while medical texts may be used for cross-examination or for

29 *Rieker v. Kaiser Foundation Hospitals*, 96 P.3d 833, 194 Ore. App. 708. Medical treatises or articles, like all learned treatises, are considered hearsay and are not admissible as substantive evidence.

30 *Costa v. Dresser Industries, Inc.*, 205 Ill. Dec. 33, 642 N.E.2d 898 (Ill. App. 3 Dist. 1994). But see *Wilson v. Knight,* 982 P.2d 400, 26 Kan.App.2d 226 (Kan.App.1999) which involved a medical malpractice action resulting from a failure to diagnose a post-operative infection following an appendectomy. Medical journal articles dealing with the use of antibiotics in cases involving perforated appendicitis, and with the general diagnosis and treatment of appendicitis were admissible as independent substantive evidence under learned treatise exception to hearsay rule. That exception permits the introduction of relevant medical treatises into evidence as independent substantive evidence provided that a proper foundation is shown to establish admissibility. A trial judge should, however, carefully weigh the probative value of medical treatise evidence against its prejudicial effect before admitting the evidence. Moreover, the application of the learned treatise exception to the hearsay rule must be considered on a case by case basis, weighing the probative value of the evidence against its potential prejudicial impact.

31 *McCarty v. Sisters of Mercy Health Corp.*, 176 Mich. App. 593, 440 N.W.2d 417 (1989); *Davenport By and Through Davenport v. Ephraim McDowell Memorial Hosp., Inc.*, 769 S.W.2d 56 (Ky. 1988); *Tart v. McGann*, 697 F.2d 75 (2d Cir. 1982). See also *Denton v. Critikon, Inc.*, 674 So.2d 1169 (La.App. 1996).

32 *Landrigan v. Celotex Corp.*, 243 N.J.Super.449, 579 A.2d 1268 (1990); *Thomas v. American Cystoscope Makers, Inc.*, 414 F.Supp. 255 (E.D.Pa. 1976).

33 *Young v. Horton*, 855 P.2d 502 (Mont. 1993). Medical journal articles were used in a medical malpractice action in Montana; they weren't formally admitted, but the lower court was correct in permitting them to be referred to as accepted studies.

34 *Gourley v. Nebraska Methodist Health System, Inc.,* 663 N.W.2d 43, 265 Neb. 918 (2003). In a medical malpractice action, a book pertaining to the concerns of expectant mothers was not "hearsay" when offered by the parents who alleged that negligent prenatal care caused brain damage to their child. The book was offered not for the truth of its contents, but rather for the limited purpose of showing what information the clinic (where the mother received prenatal care) would have provided to its patients during the time period in question. Moreover, out-of-court statements are not hearsay unless they are offered to prove the truth of the facts asserted.

35 *Schuchman v. Stackable*, 198 Ill.App.3d 209, 144 Ill.Dec. 493, 555 N.E.2d 1012 (1990); *Forstall v. Daigrepont,* 551 So.2d 653 (La. 1989); *Hickok v. G.D. Searle & Co.*, 496 F.2d 444 (10th Cir. 1974).

foundation purposes, they are, nevertheless, not admissible when used as substantive evidence.[36]

§24.206(a) Mortality Tables

ARE THEY ADMISSIBLE? YES.

KEY POINTS FOR PROPONENT:

A mortality table constitutes evidence of life expectancy, which is to be considered with other evidence, such as to the health, constitution, and habits of the person or decedent in question.[37]

KEY POINTS FOR OPPONENT:

If the subject decedent does not precisely fall within the scope of the statistical data reflected by the tables, it should be argued that the tables are irrelevant and speculative.[38]

§24.206(b) The Physician's Desk Reference

IS IT ADMISSIBLE?
GENERALLY, YES.

KEY POINTS:

If any medical textbook is to be considered as reliable and authoritative, you would think that the *Physician's Desk Reference* would head the list. But it also suffers from the basic limitations imposed upon treatises in general.[39]

§24.207 Newspaper Articles

See "Magazine and Newspaper Articles," *supra.*

§24.208 Weather Reports

ARE THEY ADMISSIBLE? YES.

KEY POINTS:

Under the official records exception to the hearsay rule, weather bureau maps and records are generally admissible.[40] The records of the Department of Commerce Weather Bureau, in particular, are admissible even without proof that they were prepared in the regular course of business.[41]

---

36 *Gant v. Novello,* 754 N.Y.S.2d 746 (N.Y.A.D. 3rd Dept., 2003). Even if the statements contained in medical books are authoritative, they are not necessarily admissible as proof of the facts or the opinions contained therein.

Shane v. Family and Children Services, 720 N.Y.S.2d 219 (N.Y.A.D., 2001); *Freshwater v. Scheidt,* 56 Ohio St.3d 260, 714 N.E.2d 591 (1999); *Hoem v. Zia,* 239 Ill.App.3d 601, 606 N.E.2d 818 (1992).

37 *In re Cain,* 235 B.R. 812 (Bkrtcy.M.D.N.C. 1998).

38 *Estate of Eggleston v. Gorski*, 266 Mich.App. 105, 698 N.W.2d 892 (2005). Where a dispute involves the health of a person whose life expectancy is in issue, mortality tables are admissible, but the trier of fact may or may not permit the use of mortality tables depending on the disposition of the disputed question of fact. *Boudreau v. S/V Shere Khan C,* 27 F.Supp.2d 72 (D.Maine 1998).

39 *Swallow v. Emergency Medicine of Idaho, P.A.,* 67 P.3d 68 (Idaho 2003). In a medical malpractice action, information from the *Physician's Desk Reference* and the Food and Drug Administration's adverse reaction report, was not admissible to support the assertion that an excessive dose of an antibiotic caused a heart attack; the connection between the drug and the heart attack was predicated solely upon a temporal concurrence of events.

40 *Loughnane v. City of Chicago*, 188 Ill.App.3d 1078, 136 Ill. Dec. 626, 545 N.E.2d 150 (1989). Weather reports were admissible in this slip-and-fall action. The distance between the weather station and the location of the accident, as well as the difference between the time the readings were taken and the time of the accident, went to the weight, not the admissibility, of the report. See also *Hefele v. National Super Markets, Inc.*, 748 S.W.2d 800 (Mo. 1988); *Flyth v. U.S.*, 405 F.2d 1324 (D.C. Cir. 1968); *Beauty Shopping Center, Inc. v. Monarch Ins. Co. of Ohio*, 315 F.2d 467 (4th Cir. 1963).

41 *Minnehaha County, S.D. v. Kelly,* 150 F.2d 356 (8th Cir. 1945).

(This page intentionally left blank.)

Chapter 25

Legal Documents

§25.100 Introduction

There are a number of legal documents that attorneys commonly seek to enter into evidence. These include such things as affidavits, answers to interrogatories, briefs, contracts, and deposition transcripts. There is no hard and fast rule concerning admissibility here. While many such documents are generally admissible, the admissibility of others will depend on the purpose for which they are offered. And, several other types of legal documents, such as witness statements and prior expert witness testimony, are generally inadmissible.

§25.200 Specific Documents

§25.201 Affidavits

ARE THEY ADMISSIBLE?
YES, IF PURSUANT TO STATUTE OR TO SUPPORT PLEADINGS.

KEY POINTS FOR PROPONENT:

The courts seem to allow affidavits to be used on an ad hoc basis. So the practitioner should never rest confidently or be assured that an affidavit will take the place of sound evidence during the course of trial. If there is any doubt, it should be resolved during pretrial proceedings, not during trial.

Affidavits which are offered to prove the truth of the statements contained in them are hearsay. Therefore, as a general rule, affidavits are only admissible as substantive evidence when they fall within one of the standard hearsay exceptions.[1] For example, a party's admission, made in an affidavit, may be admissible.[2]

Occasionally, however, affidavits which do not meet the usual criteria are admitted into evidence.[3] And affidavits offered for some purpose other than proving the truth of the statements contained therein, may also be admissible.[4] For example, affidavits may be used as building blocks to develop other evidence.[5]

---

1 *Everett v. State,* 835 So.2d 118 (Miss.App. 2003); *Colonial Mortgage & Loan Corporation v. Sino,* 812 So.2d 817 (La.App. 2002). In an action by creditors to recover a deficiency balance on a promissory note following the release of a mortgage, summary judgment affidavits were not admissible evidence at trial, and the court could not consider them in reaching a judgment.

Converse v. Ameritech Corp., 179 F.R.D. 533 (Mich. 1997); *F.T.C. v. Amy Travel Service, Inc.*, 875 F.2d 564 (7th Cir. 1989).

2 *Ede v. Ede*, 598 N.Y.S.2d 90 (N.Y.A.D. 3 Dept. 1993); *Chanute v. Williams Natural Gas Co.*, 743 F.Supp. 1437 (D. Kan. 1990).

3 *Three Notch Elec. Membership Corp. v. Bush*, 380 S.E.2d 720 (Ga. 1989). An affidavit submitted by an expert was accepted by the court during a motion for summary judgment by the defendant. The expert's analysis was based on personal knowledge and was beyond that which a layperson could provide. See also *Wagner v. Department of Agriculture*, 28 F.3d 279 (3rd Cir. 1994), which stated that affidavits are a form of probative evidence, and though live testimony may generally be favored over them, the interests of cross-examination and credibility-determination would be adequately safeguarded where the affiant appears in court.

4 *Bolen v. Paragon Plastics, Inc.*, 754 F.Supp. 221 (D. Mass. 1990).

5 See *Morgan v. Massachusetts General Hospital*, 901 F.2d 186 (1st Cir. 1990). In a discrimination suit brought by a former employee against the defendant hospital, several documents, including affidavits of various hospital employees, were all admissible to establish the steps taken by the hospital to investigate the plaintiff's assault of a co-worker. See also *Department of Corrections, State of Fla. v. Williams*, 549 So.2d 1071 (Fla. 1989). In a personal injury action, it was proper for an expert, in formulating his opinion, to consider the affidavit of a former inmate who could not be located to testify, even though the affidavit itself was hearsay and inadmissible as evidence. *March v. Victoria Lloyds Ins. Co.*, 773 S.W.2d 785 (Tex. 1989). In a fatal truck accident, the affidavit of a forensic toxicologist, who analyzed a blood sample for alcohol concentration, was sufficient to self-authenticate the resulting blood alcohol report as a business record.

Affidavits intended to be used as evidence should be based upon personal knowledge.[6] Those based upon "information and belief" are generally insufficient unless authorized by statute.[7] Affidavits should also state specific facts as opposed to opinions or conclusions.[8]

KEY POINTS FOR OPPOSITION:

Affidavits which are not specifically authorized by statute will be excludable at the request of the opposition.[9] And even if an affidavit is authorized by statute, the court may still limit its use.[10] Generally, affidavits taken without authority, in the absence of the other party and without notice, have no weight as direct evidence and ought not to be considered as testimony in a case (unless the parties consent to their use, or no timely objection is made, or the affidavit, as used in the case, falls within one of the statutory exceptions to the hearsay rule).[11]

§25.202 Ancient Writings

See §23.401.

§25.203 Answers to Interrogatories

ARE THEY ADMISSIBLE?
AGAINST THE ANSWERING PARTY:
YES. *AGAINST OTHERS:* NO.

KEY POINTS:

Answers to interrogatories, which appeared to be mere unsworn statements made by counsel and not statements made under oath by a proper party, are hearsay and inadmissible at trial unless they fall within some recognized exception to the hearsay rule.[12] Moreover, it is clear that with respect to the answering party, the answers could constitute admissions and would, therefore, be admissible. With respect other individuals referred to in the answers, however, those answers, whether sworn or unsworn, would constitute hearsay.

---

6 *Reuther v. Smith*, 926 So.2d 9 (La.App., 2006). Generally, a sworn affidavit is hearsay and is not competent evidence unless its use is specifically authorized by statute. An affidavit is generally inadmissible as hearsay, but in the rare instances where it is acceptable as a substitute for testimony, it must be based on personal knowledge, must set forth only facts admissible in evidence, and must show that the affiant is competent to testify as to the matters contained therein. *Ackler v. Raymark Industries, Inc.*, 551 A.2d 291 (Pa. 1988).

7 *State ex rel. Simmons v. Moore*, 774 S.W.2d 711 (Tex. 1989); *State Dept. of Human Service for Martin v. Neilson*, 771 S.W.2d 128 (Tenn. 1989).

8 *North Broward Hosp. Dist. v. Royster*, 544 So.2d 1131 (Fla. 1989).

9 *Kulshrestha v. First Union Commercial Corp*, 131 Cal.Rptr.2d 881, 107 Cal.App.4th 415 (2003). A declaration is inadmissible hearsay in the absence of a statute permitting it. *Travelers Cas. & Sur. Co. of Am. v. Wells Fargo Bank N.A.*, 374 F.3d 521 (7th Cir. Ill., 2004); *Home Bank of Guntersville v. Perpetual Federal Savings and Loan Ass'n.*, 547 So.2d 840 (Ala. 1989); *Lee v. Schroeder*, 529 N.E.2d 349 (Ind. 1988). Affidavits that contained the testimony of affiants who were not available for cross-examination constituted inadmissible hearsay.

10 *Agha v. Rational Software Corporation,* 252 F.Supp.2d 1074 (D.Or., 2003). A third party's declaration in an employment discrimination action consisted of a statement of what a terminated Arabian account representative said to the declarant regarding the speaking of Arabic. The declaration was stricken as hearsay.

Reid v. Pyle, 51 P.3d 1064 (Colo.App., 2002). In a lawsuit against a debtor to recover money used to purchase a motor home, a police officer's "affidavit of probable cause" for the arrest of the lender was not admissible under the public records exception to the hearsay rule. The probable cause affidavit arose from an alleged assault on the lender's wife. The affidavit contained statements of the wife to the effect that she told the lender that she had an affair with the purchaser of the motor home.

Schraer v. Berkeley Property Owners' Ass'n., 255 Cal. Rptr. 453 (1989).

11 *Ohlen v. Shively*, 430 S.E.2d 559 (Va.App. 1993).

12 *Taeger Enterprises, Inc. v. Herdlein Technologies, Inc.*, 445 S.E.2d 848, 213 Ga. App. 740 (Ga. App. 1994).

§25.204 Assignment of Interest in Property

***IS IT ADMISSIBLE?* GENERALLY, YES.**

KEY POINTS:

If the document is filed with a governmental office, pursuant to statute, then it is admissible under Fed. R. Evid. 803(14), "Records of documents affecting an interest is property," which states:

> The record of a document purporting to establish or affect an interest in property, as proof of the content of the original recorded document and its execution and delivery by each person by whom it purports to have been executed, if the record is a record of a public office and an applicable statute authorizes the recording of documents of that kind in that office.

§25.205 Briefs

***ARE THEY ADMISSIBLE?* ANSWER CONDITIONED ON PURPOSE.**

KEY POINTS:

As with pleadings in general, briefs, and the assertions contained in them, may constitute admissions and may, therefore, be used against the party making them.[13] But without a specific hearsay exception, statements in briefs (that are not admissions) are not to be considered as evidence.[14]

§25.206 Contracts

***ARE THEY ADMISSIBLE?* YES.**

KEY POINTS:

A contract's chances for admissibility may be enhanced when it is attached to a pleading. In a medical malpractice action, a contract between a health insurance company and a medical group was denied admissibility. The appellate court reversed and ruled that the contract was admissible. The appellate court placed great weight on the fact that the contract was attached to the defendant's answer, "and, hence, was always before the court."[15] Note that contracts, in general, recite agreements, not facts. And unless a document is entered to prove the truth of the matters (i.e., facts) asserted, the hearsay rule does not become an issue.

§25.207 Deposition Transcripts

***ARE THEY ADMISSIBLE?* YES, IF THE DECLARANT IS UNAVAILABLE.**

KEY POINTS FOR PROPONENT:

Deposition transcripts can generally be used for impeachment purposes or to show prior inconsistent statements. Also, under Federal Rule 804(b)(1) prior testimony may be allowed if the declarant is not available, and if there was an adequate opportunity for cross-examination during the deposition.

---

13 *Kansas City v. Keene Corp.*, 855 S.W.2d 360 (Mo. 1993). On remand after an appeal, assertions in an appellate brief were "ordinary admissions" rather than "conclusive judicial admissions," where the statements in the brief were made at a time when discovery was limited to a statute of limitations issue.

14 *Flippen Alliance v. Brannan*, 601 S.E.2d 106, 267 Ga. App. 134 (2004).

15 *McGovern v. Attie*, 30 A.D.2d 559, 291 N.Y.S.2d 167 (1968). See also *F.T.C. v. Hughes*, 710 F.Supp. 1520 (Tex. 1989).

KEY POINTS FOR OPPOSITION:

The term "unavailability" means something more than inconvenience on the part of the proponent. See Fed. R. Evid. 803.

Note that in *Schraer v. Berkeley Property Owner's Ass'n.*,[16] a statute which stated that testimony may be "taken" by affidavit, deposition and oral examination, did not place affidavits or deposition transcripts on the same evidentiary level as oral testimony.

REFERENCES

Admissibility of depositions. 84 A.L.R. Fed 668.

§25.208 Former Testimony

***IS IT ADMISSIBLE?* YES, IF THE DECLARANT IS UNAVAILABLE.**

KEY POINTS:

Fed. R. Evid. 804(b) (pertaining to "hearsay exceptions"), provides that the following are not excluded by the hearsay rule if the declarant is unavailable as a witness:

(1) **Former testimony.** Testimony given as a witness at another hearing of the same or a different proceeding, or in a deposition taken in compliance with law in the course of the same or another proceeding, if the party against whom the testimony is now offered, or, in a civil action or proceeding, a predecessor in interest, had an opportunity and similar motive to develop the testimony by direct, cross-, or redirect examination.

REFERENCES

Admissibility of depositions. 84 A.L.R. Fed. 668.

§25.209 Pleadings, Generally

***ARE THEY ADMISSIBLE?* IT DEPENDS UPON THE PURPOSE.**

KEY POINTS:

Pleadings, as we all know, contain allegations and "alleged" statements of fact. When offered to prove the truth of the matters asserted, they would constitute hearsay. When used against the party who made the allegations or

16 255 Cal.Rptr. 453 (1989).

statements, as one might expect, the chances for admissibility improve.[17] This is also true with respect to discovery responses.[18]

§25.210 Prior Expert Witness Testimony

IS IT ADMISSIBLE?
GENERALLY NO, UNLESS RULE OR STATUTE PERMITS IT.

KEY POINTS:

Court rules or statutes may provide for the admissibility of depositions (including video depositions); this is particularly useful where doctors are needed to provide expert testimony. Absent such a provision, it must be remembered that an expert witness will be a person who, most likely, did not observe any relevant events first-hand.

Expert witness testimony, made at a Coast Guard hearing, was not admissible as prior testimony because the party against whom it was offered did not have a chance to properly cross-examine the witness in the prior hearing.[19]

§25.210(a) Report of Expert

IS IT ADMISSIBLE? **GENERALLY NO, UNLESS USED TO IMPEACH.**

KEY POINTS:

As a general proposition, when an expert prepares and issues a report to be used during the course of litigation, it is expected that the expert

---

17 *Lee v. Puamana Community Association*, 128 P.3d 874, 109 Hawaii 561 (2006). A factual admission contained in a complaint or other pleading constitutes a judicial admission and is binding. Moreover, an admission by a party or his attorney is a formal statement made in the course of a judicial proceeding that removes the admitted fact from the field of controversy.

Enoch Adams v. Teck Cominco Alaska, Inc., 414 F.Supp.2d 925 (2006). A statement in an answer is a "judicial admission," as is the failure to deny an allegation in an answer.

Edmands v. CUNO, Inc., 892 A.2d 938, 277 Conn. 425 (2006). Factual allegations contained in pleadings upon which a case is tried are considered as judicial admissions and hence are irrefutable as long as they remain in effect; moreover, an admission in a pleading is equivalent to proof.

Ryder Integrated Logistics, Inc. v. BellSouth Telecommunications, Inc., 627 S.E.2d 358, 277 Ga.App. 679 (2006). A pleader is bound by the allegations of his own pleadings unless or until they are removed by an amendment; he or she is not permitted to introduce evidence in denial of such an admission. The rule that a pleader is bound by the allegations of his own pleadings, however, applies only to admissions of fact, not to opinions or conclusions of law.

But see *In re Parmalat Securities Litigation*, 412 F.Supp.2d 392 (S.D.N.Y., 2006). While prior inconsistent pleadings are normally admissible against a party, they ordinarily are controvertible, as opposed to conclusive admissions.

City of Gulf Shores v. Harbert Intern., 608 So.2d 348 (Ala. 1992). A party's pleadings in a prior case are admissible against that party in subsequent action as an admission against interest; the prior pleadings must be inconsistent with the party's present position and must be drawn under the party's direction or with his consent. *Lofton v. Kearney,* 257 F.Supp.2d 1372 (S.D.Fla. 2001). Admissions contained in pleadings are deemed judicial admissions and are binding on party who makes them, even if that party offers post-pleading evidence that contradicts those admissions. See also *Norwel Equipment Co. Ltd. Partnership V. Hardy*, 773 So.2d 905 (La.App., 2000), holding that, although admission in answer constitutes judicial confession, in order to be admissible, admission must, nevertheless, be express acknowledgment of adverse fact. *Svege v. Mercedes-Benz Credit Corp.,* 329 F.Supp2d 285 (D. Conn., 2004). A party's pleadings are generally admissible as admissions, both judicial and evidentiary when the statements contained in those pleadings are to be used against the persons submitting those pleadings.

18 *Federico v. Ford Motor Company*, 854 N.E.2d 448, 67 Mass.App.Ct. 454 (Mass.App.Ct., 2006). Answers to interrogatories in the same case constitute evidentiary, not judicial, admissions. The contents of the answers to interrogatories must be relevant to an issue in the case to be admissible. *Primavera Familienstifung v. Askin*, 130 F.Supp.2d 450 (S.D.N.Y., 2001). Answers to interrogatories are judicial admissions; they generally estop answering party from later seeking to assert positions at variance with the responses contained in those answers.

19 *United States v. Paducah Towing Co., Inc.*, 692 F.2d 412 (6th Cir. 1982).

will testify. The report itself, however, is hearsay and not admissible.[20] Nor should an expert's notes, writings or memos be considered as ordinary business records.[21]

§25.211 Witness Statements

ARE THEY ADMISSIBLE? GENERALLY NO, EXCEPT FOR IMPEACHMENT.

KEY POINTS:

Witness statements are generally contained within other documents, such as police or investigative reports. Even where the reports themselves are admissible in part, the witness statements contained within the documents are generally inadmissible.[22]

As with expert witnesses, or any witnesses, written statements that contradict a witness' testimony should always be allowed for purposes of impeachment, assuming, of course, that the witness authored the statement.

§25.212 Promissory Notes

See same heading in Chapter 23.

§25.213 Judgements

ARE THEY ADMISSIBLE? A QUALIFIED YES.

KEY POINTS:

The purpose of the party seeking to admit the judgement will normally be determinative of its admissibility. Generally, where one seeks to use or admit a prior judgement from a state or federal court, the admissibility issue will often turn upon matters involving res judicata or collateral estoppel, or both.[23] For arbitration awards, mediation awards, and rulings by administrative agencies, relevance and potential hearsay problems will govern.[24]

---

20 *Corcoran v. Sears Roebuck and Co.*, 711 A.2d 371 (N.J. Super. 1998).

21 *Andrews v. Dufour,* 882 So.2d 15 (La. App. 4 Cir. June 2, 2004). In a products liability lawsuit against an automobile manufacturer, exhibits that consisted of notes that an expert made while reviewing the manufacturer's business records were not themselves business records and were, therefore, inadmissible.

22 *Parsons v. Honeywell, Inc.*, 929 F.2d 901 (2d Cir. 1991); *Anchor Hocking v. Container Corp. of America*, 756 F.2d 411 (5th Cir. 1985). But see *Silva v. Lucky Stores Inc.*, 76 Cal.Rptr.2d 382 (1998) and *Vaughn v. Ems*, 744 S.W.2d 542 (Mo. 1988), where a city council did not renew a lounge's liquor license, witness statements contained within police reports, with respect to activity in the lounge, were admissible to show the facts upon which the city council acted. *Pickett v. Detella*, 163 F.Supp.2d 999 (N.D.Ill., 2001). In prisoner's lawsuit against prison guards, written statement summarizing witness statement concerning incident in which guards restrained prisoner was inadmissible hearsay.

23 Basically, the principle of *Res Judicata* holds that once an issue between parties has been litigated and a final ruling or judgement reached, that ruling or judgement would bar re-litigating the same issues between the parties. *Collateral Estoppel* works similarly (in a more limited setting), but the parties and issues to the subsequent litigation may be different.

24 *Zeus Enterprises, Inc. v. Alphin Aircraft, Inc.,* 190 F.3d 238 (4th Cir., Va., 1999) involved a breach of contract action by an aircraft owner against a company hired to restore the subject aircraft to "airworthy" condition. A proceeding in which an Administrative Law Judge for The National Transportation Safety Board (NTSB) rendered a decision finding that the restored aircraft was not airworthy, qualified as an "investigation" under the public records exception to the hearsay rule, even though the proceeding was triggered by the aircraft owner's appeal from an FAA (Federal Aviation Administration) order suspending the aircraft's certificate of airworthiness. The NTSB's decision was, therefore, admissible under the public records exception. On the other hand, an order in which the NTSB dismissed the appeal on grounds that the restoration company lacked standing to appeal, was not admissible because the order was strictly a legal ruling which involved no factual determinations.

§25.214 Letters

ARE THEY ADMISSIBLE?
GENERALLY NO.

KEY POINTS:

Letters come in all shapes and types; so be sure to check this heading under the other Document Groups (particularly, Chapters 23). When we speak of "legal letters," we are indeed, dealing with a strange bird. Judicial tribunals and quasi-judicial tribunals normally speak through their orders and rulings as opposed to letters.[25]

§25.215 Inventory (Verified)

ARE THEY ADMISSIBLE?
YES (QUALIFIED).

KEY POINTS:

Asset inventories are typically filed in all types of probate matters. They are also commonly filed in marriage dissolution (divorce) cases. As is the case with any such writing, verified or otherwise, its contents will often involve pure inadmissible hearsay. If, however, the inventory is to be used against the individual who prepared it or made oath as to its accuracy, the document would constitute an admission and would, in that instance, be admissible.[26]

§25.216 Deeds

***ARE THEY ADMISSIBLE?* YES.**

A deed is more than evidence of a conveyance, it is the very means by which real estate *is* conveyed or transferred. Typically, a deed will serve as *evidence* of title or ownership. It is noteworthy that the typical language contained in a deed,[27] constitutes an act (i.e., a conveyance) as opposed to a statement of fact. Theoretically, therefore, information contained in a deed would not be offered to prove the truth of the matters contained therein, and therefore should not be subject to hearsay challenges. This, however, does not foreclose other issues involving interpretation or ambiguities.[28]

25 *Thomsen v. Aqua Massage Intern., Inc.,* 721 A.2d 137 (Conn. 1998) was a proceeding based on the defendant s motion to enforce a settlement agreement, A mediator s letter, which stated that an arbitration between the parties had been "successful," was inadmissible hearsay since it was offered to show that the settlement agreement had in fact been reached between those parties. See also *Stahl v. Wal-Mart Stores, Inc.,* 47 F.Supp.2d 783 (S.D.Miss. 1998), wherein a "confirmation letter" written by the attorney for a slip-and-fall plaintiff, following an ex-parte conversation with an employee of Wal-Mart was inadmissible because it was merely the attorney's version of the conversation.

26 *Dutton v. Dutton,* 18 S.W.3d 849 (Tex.App. 2000). In course of judicial proceedings, husband's sworn inventory and appraisement listing property as community property constituted admission, which prevented him from taking contrary position on appeal.

27 "*The Undersigned does hereby grant, transfer and convey the property described hereunder to ...*"

28 See *Heartz v. City of Concord,* 808 A.2d 76 (N.H., 2002). The courts should not consider extrinsic evidence where the language of a deed is clear and unambiguous.

Chapters 26-29

Reserved for Supplementation

Chapters 26 through 29 are reserved for supplementation. Also, to maintain our decimal structure, **Part II - Documentary Evidence** was specifically designed to start and end in the 20s; **Part III - Real Evidence** was designed to start at Chapter 30.

(This page intentionally left blank.)

Part III - Real Evidence

Table of Contents

Chapter 30
Basics of Real Evidence

Chapter 31
Physical Objects

Chapter 32
Samples

Chapter 33
People

Chapter 34
Animals

Chapter 35
Views

Chapter 36
On-Site Recordings

Chapters 37-39
Reserved for Supplementation

(This page intentionally left blank.)

Chapter 30

Basics of Real Evidence

§30.100 Introduction

Real evidence consists of some physical object or substance that was once a part or component of the controversy itself; it can also encompass geographical locations (most commonly referred to as "views"). The gun that actually shot John F. Kennedy (or Louie the local bank teller, for that matter), would be real evidence. But a replica, photograph, or diagram of a weapon would be demonstrative, not real. A blood-stained "piece" of Billy The Kid's shirt, Swiss-cheesed by Pat Garrett's bullets, would also be real.

The actual intersection where two motorists collided would constitute real evidence. A map or photo would not.

The key distinguishing features of real evidence are (1) its existence at the time of the event which gave rise to the litigation, and (2) its stature as a physical component or "piece" of the controversy itself. As suggested by these features, real evidence is unique and irreplaceable. Therefore, foundation elements relating to "verification," or "chain of possession," are necessary to establish identity.[1] Another component to consider while building a foundation for real evidence is "freedom from material alteration," in order to establish that the one-of-a-kind item has not been tampered with.

It is quite common to confuse real evidence with demonstrative evidence. Generic terms such as "tangible" and "objective" contribute to the confusion. Those terms would best be deleted from our vocabulary. Real and demonstrative evidence should be distinguished; the foundation requirements are different, as are the purposes for admitting them.

Real evidence, as previously indicated, comprises a part or component of the subject controversy. Thus, its physical characteristics may be very telling. A defective altimeter or brake rod may constitute crucial one-of-a-kind evidence used to determine the outcome of a trial.

Demonstrative evidence, on the other hand, is normally prepared after the fact, solely to illustrate or clarify some point. If that evidence is lost, destroyed, or tampered with, it can generally be reconstructed.

§30.200 Admissibility in General

Real evidence will, by its very nature, always be relevant. Since it forms a component of the subject event itself, the offering will, if nothing else, always tend to make it appear more likely that the subject event occurred.

Excepting "views," which are conducted outside of the courtroom, presenting real evidence is akin to bringing a piece of that event right into the courtroom. For this reason, it is most likely that such evidence will either be formally admitted or totally excludable as being cumulative or unduly prejudicial.[2]

Real evidence should be divided into six distinct forms:

(1) physical objects
(2) samples
(3) people
(4) animals
(5) views
(6) on-site recordings

If nothing else, this division helps one examine admissibility requirements in greater depth. The chapters that follow will provide some detail for each form of real evidence.

---

1 But see *Pearl Investments, L.L.C. v. Standard I/0, Inc.*, 257 F.Supp.2d 326 (D.Me., 2003) and *Malchose v. Kalfell,* 664 N.W.2d 508, 2003 N.D. 75 (2003), both holding that with respect to real evidence, any defects in the chain of custody should go to the weight not the admissibility of the evidence.

See also §31.401, Checklist Item 1.

2 Real evidence is unlike demonstrative evidence, which may be denied formal admissibility and yet permitted to be used and displayed for demonstrative purposes.

§30.300 Care and Handling

Real evidence is unique and therefore irreplaceable. If a material piece of such evidence is lost, destroyed, or stolen, a valuable case may go up in smoke. The solution? Sue, what else? That's right—a cause of action separate and apart from the involuntarily abandoned underlying claim. It's called "spoliation" and it started in California.

The new tort began to develop as a plaintiff named Smith was injured when her automobile collided with a van. The dealer who repaired the van agreed to retain the squashed parts until an investigation could determine the reason for the mechanical failure that led to the collision. But the dealer lost the parts, so there could be no investigation and, therefore, no cause of action against the van's maker. So Smith sued the dealer.

The trial court dismissed the action as being a bit too strange, even by California standards; the appellate court, however, reversed,[3] recognizing the possibility that the defendant interfered with a valuable "prospective expectancy." So the new tort was officially christened.[4]

Next, consider the case of *Wilson v. Beloit Corp.*,[5] where plaintiff Wilson suffered a very severe leg injury while working at the International Paper Company, his employer. After Wilson successfully obtained workers' compensation benefits, he and his wife filed a third-party products liability action against Beloit, the manufacturer and supplier of the machine that caused the injury. However, to his dismay, during the period between the injury and the commencement of the litigation, some critical components of the machine were lost.

The Wilsons claimed that because of the loss of the evidence, their products liability action against Beloit was irreparably damaged. And thus, despite the exclusive remedy of the Arkansas Workers' Compensation Act, the plaintiffs maintained an action against the employer for an amount equal to the claim of damages that the plaintiffs would have been entitled to recover against Beloit. The Arkansas federal district court reasoned that to allow the plaintiffs to sue their employer for "spoliation of evidence" would, in effect, enable them to circumvent the exclusivity bar of the state Workers' Compensation Act. Therefore, that court entered a summary judgment of dismissal. Upon appeal, however, the Eighth Circuit reversed and remanded the case, finding that the Arkansas Act did not, in any way, apply to an injury suffered by the plaintiffs from the spoliation of evidence by the International Paper Company. The appellate court reasoned that the Workers' Compensation Act applies only to claims for "injuries and death based upon accidents." And thus, the appellate court found that since those matters were not covered by the Workers' Compensation Act, the independent action for spoliation of evidence could be maintained against the employer.

Consider *Ober v. City of Plantation, Florida*,[6] one of that state's more interesting spoliation cases. While riding on his motorcycle down a Florida highway, Daniel Ober was struck and fatally injured by a drunk driver. The impact caused him to fly into the windshield of the drunk's automobile at the roof-line of the car. Ober then somersaulted over the automobile and landed several feet away. Witnesses to the accident indicated that they saw Ober's helmet fly off at impact. His injuries included skull fractures, brain damage and a complete spinal separation; the victim died on the way to the hospital.

The homicide investigator on the scene happened to be an experienced motorcyclist by

3 *Smith v. Superior Court*, 151 Cal. App. 3d 491, 198 Cal. Rptr. 829 (1984).

4 We should, however, note from the outset that California, which led the charge for this new tort, is presently sounding the loudest retreat. It seems intent on eliminating the tort. See *R.S. Creative, Inc. v. Creative Cotton, Ltd.* 75 Cal.App.4th 486, 89 Cal.Rptr. 2d 353 (1999) and *Cedars-Sinai Medical Center v. Superior Court,* 18 Cal.4th 1, 74 Cal.Rptr. 2d 248 (1998).

5 869 F.2d 1162 (8th Cir. 1989).

6 Broward County Circuit Court No. 86-14476-CP, 31 ATLA L.Rep. 264 (August 1988).

the name of Officer Corey Altenberger. Knowing that the accident might very well have been survivable if Ober's safety helmet had remained on his head, Altenberger retrieved it and carefully examined each portion. He noticed that the chin strap was still fastened, but had apparently torn on one side. Knowing that Florida law requires motorcyclists to wear helmets, Altenberger realized the potential importance of an "uncrashworthy" helmet, particularly in view of Ober's circumstances.

The death might very well have been attributable to a failure to have the helmet fastened securely to his head at the time of the collision, as opposed to the motorists' drunk driving. Altenberger took the helmet into police custody as crucial evidence. Later, when Ober's widow and three daughters went to the police station, two days after the accident, to collect Ober's personal effects, Mrs. Ober was told that the helmet had to remain in police custody pending the outcome of a criminal case against the drunk driver, but that she would be notified when to come and collect it. Counsel for Ober realized that there might be financial problems on the part of the drunk, and he therefore turned an immediate eye toward the motorcycle helmet manufacturer.

Unfortunately, one year after the drunk's criminal case was concluded, plaintiff's attorney called the police department and made repeated efforts, all in vain, to obtain possession of the helmet. Only when he decided to depose Altenberger, did it become apparent that the helmet could not be produced because, contrary to department regulations, it had been destroyed at the end of the criminal drunk driving case. Without the helmet, the plaintiffs were in deep trouble with respect to any products liability action against the manufacturer.

The plaintiffs commenced an action against the city of Plantation, Florida. The spoliation claim against the city asserted that its agents and employees had negligently or intentionally lost Dan Ober's helmet, which they had reason to believe was indispensable to a products liability claim against the manufacturer. The jury awarded a sizeable verdict against the city, apportioning $1 million to the widow, and $400,000 to each of the three children, with $25,000 to the estate.

Not all spoliations have happy endings. *Velasco v. Commercial Bldg. Maintenance Co.*[7] should flash a strong warning to anyone who must handle real evidence involving a defective product. In *Velasco*, an attorney representing the plaintiff in a products liability claim left a defective broken liquor bottle in a paper bag on his desk. You may be less than shocked to learn that the cleaning crew perceived this apparent garbage as "garbage," and disposed of it. A suit against the maintenance crew was tossed out just as fast. The court could hardly blame a garbage crew for cleaning.

As lawyers, we're pretty good at handling, filing, and preserving paper. But when it comes to shattered bottles, chipped hammers, broken heels and defective valves, special and rather extraordinary care is warranted. For firms that handle products liability cases on a regular basis, special lock-and-key cabinets should be strongly considered.[8]

Starting separate lawsuits for spoliation is well and good for litigators who want to add to their dockets, but it does not necessarily provide

---

7 169 Cal.App.3d 874, 215 Cal.Rptr. 504 (1985).

8 See Bell, David A., Margaret M. Koesel and Tracey L. Turnbull, *"Let's Level the Playing Field: A New Proposal for Analysis of Spoliation of Evidence Claims in Pending Litigation,"* 29 ARIZ. ST. L.J. 769 (1997).

the required remedies for the instant litigation.[9] Something more immediate is needed. The most common and universally accepted solution is the "adverse inference." Moreover, the deliberate spoliation of evidence, relevant to a case, should raise a presumption that the evidence would have been unfavorable to the spoilator.[10] This inference may be pointed out to the jury. But the

9 See also *Glotzbach v. Froman*, 854 N.E.2d 337 (Ind., 2006). In a worker-comp-related wrongful death claim involving a workplace accident, a worker was killed by an explosion from an "explosion proof" pump while under the supervision of Midwest Material Services. Midwest's owner collected debris from the pump, but despite an instruction to him from the Indiana Occupational Safety and Health Administration (OSHA) to preserve the debris, he nevertheless later reported that "everything" had been thrown away. The resulting lawsuit filed by the estate of the deceased worker included claims for both negligence and intentional spoliation of evidence. The Illinois appellate court affirmed the trial court's refusal to dismiss the spoliation claims. However, the Indiana Supreme Court reversed, noting that the state does not recognize an independent cause of action for first party spoliation. Third party liability for spoliation was, however, a different matter, but one that would yield the same result. The high court rejected the notion of a special relationship between an employer and employee that created a duty to preserve evidence. It also rejected the estate's claim that the order from the OSHA to preserve the evidence created a duty in its favor.

The spoliation lawsuit, as a separate independent cause of action, has been gradually falling into disfavor. See, for example, *Martino v. Wal-Mart Stores, Inc.*, 908 So.2d 342 (Fla., 2005), wherein the Florida Supreme Court held that the remedy against a defendant for the spoliation of evidence is not an independent cause of action for spoliation, but rather discovery sanctions and a rebuttable presumption of negligence for the underlying tort, thereby disapproving of *Bondu v. Gurvich*, 473 So.2d 1307 (Fla. Dist. Ct. App. 1984).

10 *Southeast Mental Health Center, Inc. v. Pacific Ins. Co., Ltd.*, 439 F.Supp.2d 831, 65 Fed.R.Serv.3d 1070 (W.D.Tenn., 2006). The insured filed a bad faith suit against an insurance carrier to enforce a claim under an "All Risks" business insurance policy. In cross-motions for summary judgment, the insured would not be precluded from introducing evidence regarding damage to a computer (the subject of spoliation allegations) even though one of its employees discarded the computer's damaged drive. Generally, the doctrine of spoliation of evidence permits a negative inference against a party that has intentionally, and for an improper purpose, destroyed, mutilated, lost, altered, or concealed evidence; however, the insured in this case would not be precluded from introducing evidence regarding the subject damage because there was no indication that the insured, who kept the damaged drive for approximately one year, had disposed of it to conceal its contents or cause its failure.

Think Pink, Inc. v. Rim, Inc., 798 N.Y.S.2d 413 (N.Y.A.D ., 1 Dept., 2005); *Clark Construction Group, Inc. v. City of Memphis*, 229 F.R.D. 131 (W.D., Tenn., 2005); *Martino v. Wal-Mart Stores, Inc.*, 908 So.2d 342 (Fla., 2005); *Zubulake v. USB Warburg LLC*, 382 Fed.Supp.2d 536 (S.D.N.Y., 2005); *Clark Construction Group, Inc. v. City of Memphis*, 229 F.R.D. 131 (W.D., Tenn., 2005). *Martino v. Wal-Mart Stores, Inc.*, 835 So.2d 1251 (Fla. App., 2003), involved a personal injury action resulting from a crash between a Wal-Mart customer and a shopping cart; here, the customer was entitled to an adverse inference due to the unexplained disappearance of a store videotape and the errant shopping cart. In general, the "adverse inference" is not based on a strict legal duty to preserve evidence; rather, it may arise in any situation where potentially self-damaging evidence is in the possession of a party who either loses or destroys it.

Swick v. The New York Times Co., 815 A.2d 508 N.J.Super. (2003). There are a number of various civil remedies available when the spoliation of evidence occurs. One such remedy includes an inference in the underlying litigation whereby it would be presumed that the missing evidence, that was destroyed or otherwise concealed, would have been unfavorable to the spoliator. Another remedy might include a separate tort action for intentional or negligent spoliation. *Parkinson v. Guidant* Corp., 315 F.Supp.2d 760 (W.D. Pa., 2004); *Coletti v. Cudd Pressure Control,* 165 F.3d 767 (10th Cir. Wyo., 1999); *Page Intern. Ltd. v. Adam Maritime Corp.*, 53 F.Supp.2d 591 (S.D.N.Y., 1999); *Lamarca v. U.S.*, 31 F.Supp.2d 110 (E.D.N.Y., 1998); *Lucas v. Christiana Skating Center, Ltd.*, 722 A.2d 1247 (Del.Super. 1998); *Wal-Mart Stores, Inc. v. Middleton,* 982 S.W.2d 468 (Tex. App., 1998). Under the Spoliation Doctrine, evidence that one party destroyed evidence relevant to the subject in dispute is admissible and such evidence permits a spoliation inference that the destroyed evidence would have been unfavorable to the position of the offending party. However, for the spoliation inference to arise, it is essential that [1] the evidence in question be within the offending party's control and [2] that there has been an actual suppression or withholding of the evidence. No unfavorable inference arises when the circumstance indicates that the document or article has been lost or accidentally destroyed, or where the failure to produce it is otherwise properly accounted for.

adverse inference should only apply where the destruction of evidence came as a result of bad faith,[11] and likewise, it should only apply where the destructive party had an obligation to preserve the evidence.[12] In addition, the alleged "spoiliated" evidence must be relevant before any type of sanction is warranted.[13]

In addition to the above solutions, another potential remedy for spoliation lies in the ability of the court to exclude evidence in order to create a level playing field for a variety of situations that might arise. For example, a plaintiff, as well as a defendant, might be guilty of the spoliation of unfavorable evidence.[14] And, negligence in addition to intentional destruction may furnish the cause for the missing evidence.[15]

It might be argued that there is a "too-fine" line of distinction between information that is *culpably* destroyed and evidence that is *properly* disposed of. Both instances may be intentional, to be sure. Virtually anything can constitute evidence. But efficiency, nevertheless, dictates the removal and destruction of unnecessary or obsolete objects and information. The drafters of the 2006 amendments to the Federal Rules of Civil Procedure apparently recognized this fact by

11 *Castillo v. Chief Alternative, LLC*, 140 P.3d 234 (Colo.App., 2006). In a premises liability suit arising from injuries suffered by a nightclub patron when a column in the club fell against her, the denial of the patron's motion for sanctions against the nightclub for spoliation of evidence was not an abuse of discretion. Even though the club manager destroyed the entire column apparatus (including the split locknut which had been securing the column before it fell), he kept the entire apparatus until the nightclub closed a year and a half after the incident, during which time the patron failed to inquire about the evidence and, furthermore, had indicated that she wasn't planning to file a lawsuit.

Kirk v. Ford Motor Co., 116 P.3d 27, 141 Idaho 697 (2005); *Bass-Davis v. Davis,* 117 P.3d 207 (Nevada, 2005). *Penalty Kick Management Ltd. v. Coca Cola Co.*, 318 E.3d 1284 (11th Cir., Ga., 2003). In an action involving an alleged misappropriation of trade secrets, an adverse inference was not warranted against the defendant just because it was unable to produce a bottle label that was once provided to a printer, despite other suspicious circumstances. While it is true that an adverse inference should be drawn from a party's failure to preserve evidence, the inference should only apply where the absence of that evidence is predicated upon bad faith.

See also *Vigorito v. Ciulla Builders, Inc.*, 783 N.E.2d 883, 57 Mass.App.Ct. 446 (2003).

Banco Latino, S.A.C.A. v. Gomez Lopez, 53 F. Supp. 2d 1273 (S.D. Fla. 1999); *Wal-Mart Stores, Inc. v. Middleton,* 982 S.W.2d 468 (Tex.App. 1998).

12 *Samsung Electronics Co., Ltd. v. Rambus, Inc.*, 439 F.Supp.2d 524 (E.D.Va., 2006). The duty to preserve material evidence arises not only during litigation but also extends to that period before the litigation when a party reasonably should know that the evidence may be relevant to the anticipated litigation. While a litigant is under no duty to keep or retain every document in its possession, it is under a duty to preserve what it knows, or reasonably should know, is relevant in the action, is reasonably calculated to lead to the discovery of admissible evidence, is reasonably likely to be requested during discovery, or is the subject of a pending discovery request. See *Thornhill v. A.B. Volvo,* 757 N.Y.S.2d 598 (N.Y.A.D., 2nd Dept., 2003); *LaMarca v. U.S.*, 31 F.Supp.2d 110 (E.D.N.Y. 1998).

13 *Rodriguez v. Pelham Plumbing & Heating Corp.*, 20 A.D.3d 314, 799 N.Y.S.2d 27 (N.Y.A.D. 1 Dept., 2005). *Vaughn v. St. Helena Parish Police Jury,* 261 F.Supp.2d 553 (M.D.La., 2002). In a lawsuit by an adult lounge, seeking relief against a parish ordinance prohibiting partial nudity, the lounge's alleged failure to provide evidence concerning the amount spent to build it, along with information concerning the degree to which the lounge's business increased after commencing erotic dancing, did not warrant a dismissal of the action, nor an exclusion of evidence on the basis of spoliation. The requested information was irrelevant because the plaintiffs had already established the injury required for standing and, further, compensatory damages were not at issue.

14 In *Kambylis v. Ford Motor Co.*, 272 Ill.Dec. 697, 788 N.E.2d 1 (2003), a product liability action based on a failed airbag, photographs of a damaged plaintiff's automobile were excluded because the neglectful plaintiff failed to take affirmative steps to preserve the car. Under those circumstances, the court found that the failure to preserve the evidence supported sanctions, including the exclusion of evidence.

15 *Kambylis v. Ford Motor Co.*, 272 Ill.Dec. 697, 788 N.E.2d 1 (2003).

adding the following new provision to Rule 37 ("Failure to make Disclosure or Cooperate in discovery; Sanctions"):

> (f) Absent exceptional circumstances, a court may not impose sanctions under these rules on a party for failing to provide electronically stored information lost as a result of the routine, good-faith operation of an electronic system.

In addition to the so-called "routine" disposal of evidence, problems sometimes arise pertaining to the necessary destruction or alteration of evidence through testing. This problem is particularly prevalent in products liability cases. A key aspect of the discovery process for such cases is to test, analyze, measure and determine the state of the evidence at the time of the subject incident or accident, not to destroy or alter that state. And yet, some tests may require such partial destruction or alteration. This can be problematic since the destruction of evidence is a serious matter and should not be undertaken without the consent of the relevant parties or a very specific court order.[16] Often, a balancing test is employed with the weight tending to favor the tests.

16 *Mirchandani v. Home Depot, U.S.A., Inc.*, 235 F.R.D. 611 (D.Md., 2006). In ruling on motion for destructive testing of evidence, the court should consider whether: (1) the proposed testing is reasonable, necessary, and relevant to proving movant's case; (2) the non-movant's ability to present evidence at trial will be hindered, or non-movant will be prejudiced in some other way; (3) there are any less prejudicial alternative methods of obtaining evidence sought; and (4) there are adequate safeguards to minimize prejudice to non-movant, particularly non-movant's ability to present evidence at trial.

(This page intentionally left blank.)

Chapter 31

Physical Objects

§31.100 Introduction

A gun, chain saw, smashed Buick, defective ladder, steam engine, pill bottle, chipped hammer—you name it and the "object" has probably been offered as evidence somewhere at some time.[1]

Physical objects are basically discrete, inanimate things. Unlike samples, which exemplify a portion or part of real evidence, "objects," as we now employ that term, require extra-special attention, over and above that which should be accorded to samples. When an object is lost or destroyed, there may be nothing to take its place. That is why most spoliation actions seem to center around objects.

§31.200 Admissibility

As suggested above, just about every type of item has been offered as evidence at one time or another. And far more likely than not, if it was offered, it was also admitted. For, as previously indicated, real evidence will always be relevant. So if some external quality or condition is material, then inspection by the tribunal is always proper.[2]

For physical objects, "identification" is a paramount concern for establishing a foundation to admit real evidence in the form of an object. That, of course, conjures up thoughts of some rigorous chain-of-possession testimony requiring the presence of every person who handled the item. The historical roots of that requirement reflect a desire to ensure that the admitted item was the real thing and not a substitute.[3] In truth, such extreme rigorous prerequisites are rare, even in criminal cases.[4] But don't be misled. The

---

1 Even computer diskettes containing written business records might assume the form of real evidence. It is not until after information on diskettes is put before trier of fact that it becomes necessary to authenticate that information under business records rule. See *F.D.I.C. v. Carabetta*, 739 A.2d 301, 55 Conn. App. 369 (1999).

2 *Hudson v. Lansingburgh Central School District*, 812 N.Y.S.2d 678 (N.Y.A.D. 3 Dept., 2006) involved a personal injury action against a school district commenced by the mother of a middle school student who managed to cut off a portion of his finger with an apparatus known as a jointer-planer; the mother claimed that the defendant failed to adequately supervise and instruct the student regarding the proper use of the equipment. The jointer-planer was held to be admissible in the negligence action when the school district offered no evidence to establish that the probative value of the tool (which was the actual machine involved in the accident) was outweighed by undue prejudice or that its admission would otherwise mislead the jury in any manner.

Smith v. Crouse-Hinds Co., 175 Ind. App. 679, 373 N.E.2d 923 (1978); *Helmick v. Rankin*, 166 Pa. Super. 189, 70 A.2d 362 (1950).

3 But see *Arriola v. Orleans Parish School Board,* 809 So.2d 932 (La.App., 2002), holding that gaps or holes in the chain of custody generally go to the weight as opposed to the admissibility of the evidence.

Mendoza v. Mashburn, 747 So.2d 1159 (La.App. 1999) simply and correctly stated that purpose of Chain of Custody Rule is to assure integrity of evidence.

4 *Dachlet v. State,* 40 P.3d 110, 136 Idaho 752 (2002). Ordinarily, the party offering an exhibit must establish its chain of custody to create a presumption that the object has not materially been altered. If, however, the chain of custody has been broken, the proponent can still rely upon other evidence to show a lack of material alteration. Then, the party challenging the chain of custody should carry the burden of establishing that the evidence has been altered or tampered with. The standard of admissibility for evidence subject to a chain-of-custody challenge is whether the district court can determine, in all reasonable probability, that the offered exhibit has been changed in any material respect; mere speculation that the evidence was mishandled or tampered with is insufficient to establish a break in the chain of custody.

establishment of a formal foundation *is* required and important evidence can be excluded because of a simple failure to set one.[5]

A common sense evaluation of the importance of the evidence will often serve as a good indicator of the depth required for an adequate foundation. If in doubt, favor the heavier-than-required route.

An automobile bumper (which suffered the indignity of a rear end hit), that has been observed by the parties, photographed, and inspected by the police, is not what we refer to as "extra hot." Yes, it's irreplaceable. But the case won't rise or fall if it were mishandled.

A single witness who is ready to say, "That's the bumper" might be all that is warranted. But the foundation required for a death-causing defective product might be far more extensive. Consider, for example, a case where the issue turns on aircraft instrument failure versus pilot error.

Showing that an object has been "free from tampering" may be required, particularly where the opposition tosses that concern into the arena. In *Siegal v. American Honda Motor Company, Inc.*,[6] it was held that the trial court properly excluded an otherwise relevant motorcycle because its handlebar had been intentionally altered after the parties' inspection of it; that tampering occurred while the potential evidence was under the plaintiff's exclusive dominion and control. For that reason, the trial court found that the evidence had not been properly authenticated.

Among the most common forms of real-object evidence is the fired bullet. But identifying the target from which the bullet came is only half the battle for that particular type of evidence. The "science" of ballistics, thereafter, is responsible for identifying the gun from which it came. This type of "comparison" evidence based on the underlying real objects (i.e., the gun and the bullet) is commonly admitted.[7]

The computer has provided some new and interesting twists on the ancient subject of "real objects." It is too easy to get carried away with the computer's ability to generate evidence[8] and its fictitious ability to think. We tend to forget that it, too, is merely an object. So when a computer purports to *tell us* about its internal clock or report when someone has downloaded confidential information, it is not generating hearsay. It is merely a machine, a piece of real evidence, similar to a clock. If the clock is broken, it may be able to *tell us* when it was broken. But that does not make it any less of a machine or inanimate object.[9]

---

5 *Danbury v. Jackson County*, 990 S.W.2d 160 (Mo.App. 1999) said it simply and accurately: Generally, a proper foundation for evidence [i.e. an object] is laid when testimony is given that the offered object is the one that was involved in the incident and that the object s condition is substantially unchanged. See also *Ferguson v. Williams*, 399 S.E.2d 389 (N.C. App. 1991). *Van Hattem v. Kmart Corp.*, 241 Ill.Dec. 351, 719 N.E.2d 212, 308 Ill.App.3d 121 (1999). Before real evidence may be admitted at trial, adequate foundation must be laid establishing that item sought to be introduced is actual item that was involved in alleged occurrence and that its condition is substantially unchanged.

6 921 F.2d 15 (1st Cir. 1990).

7 Rule 901(a) and 901(b)(3) of the Federal Rules of Evidence, pertaining to authentication and identification, form the basis for the admissibility of ballistics evidence in the federal sphere. As a matter of fact, the 1972 Advisory Committee Notes (Example 3) specifically mention "ballistics comparison." See also *State v. Mack*, 73 Ohio St. 3d 502, 653 N.E.2d 329 (1996) and *Bently v. Scully*, 41 F.3rd 818 (2nd Cir. 1996).

8 See Chapter 47.

9 *People v. Hawkins*, 121 Cal.Rptr.2d 627, 98 Cal.App.4th 1428 (2002). In a case involving the theft of computerized information, the precise time of a backup or download was material; the appellate correctly observed: "*Now, if the computer is found to be functional, if the computer has been examined and it is found that the clock has not been tampered with, then it's just a question as to whether or not this is reliable evidence that the court can admit. But it's not, in my view, a statement made by anybody. It's a date and time left by a machine.*"

§31.300 Foundation Requirements

Don't go looking for trouble. Establishing a foundation for an object of real evidence can be the simplest task or the most difficult. Unless the evidence is being used for impeachment and there is a desire for drama, keep the process short and sweet:

Q. (By Proponent's Attorney) State your name for the record.
A. (Plaintiff) Elvis O'Mannion.
Q. Are you the plaintiff in this action?
A. Yes.
[Other questions and answers will intervene as the case unravels. Under most circumstances, the evidence should be offered at such time as it fits naturally into the overall presentation.]
Q. Can you identify plaintiff's proposed Exhibit 1? (The exhibit should have been marked and labeled prior to trial.)
A. Yes, it's the rock that was removed from the bowl of soup I had at the Natcho Mamma Restaurant that chipped my tooth.
Q. (Addressing the court, while tendering the object to opposing counsel) I ask that plaintiff's Exhibit 1 be admitted.
COURT: Any objections?
OPPOSING ATTORNEY: None.
COURT: Very well, it will be received.

Even more complex offerings (i.e., defective mechanical parts) should employ a simple foundation unless the opposition speaks up, in which case the proponent should be prepared to present some testimony pertaining to possession of the item during the time that elapsed between the incident and the trial.

§31.400 Opposition

The first line of attack involves questioning the identification processes, something that many attorneys too often neglect. For example, the foundation established by Elvis (*supra*) was very simple, perhaps too simple. Notice that Elvis was never required to mention the how's and why's. In particular—How did Elvis know that plaintiff's Exhibit 1 was the same unyielding rock that chipped his tooth? Did he have it in his possession every moment from the accident until the trial?

In Elvis' case, the rock was relevant (as all real evidence is) but it was probably not material; i.e., it didn't add anything to the proceeding that couldn't be established by oral testimony. Absent some specific basis or educated suspicion for questioning authenticity, it would not be advisable, however, to oppose such evidence. Fishing expeditions should be conducted during discovery, not trial.

At the opposite end of the spectrum (from Elvis' rock) are objects that are not only material, but they may hold the only keys that unlock the secrets pertaining to fault and liability, keys that no human being possesses. In such a case, attacking the foundation may be warranted. And the first step may involve searching for a break in the chain of possession.

It is important to keep in mind that the proponent is required to establish "identity," not mere proximity. This means that the object must be the real thing, not a look-alike or close second. Terms such as "substantial similarity" may carry the day for demonstrative evidence, but not real evidence.[10]

However, establishing identity does not require mathematical certainty.[11]

10 *Mykytiuk v. Stamm*, 143 Ill. Dec. 570, 554 N.E.2d 505, 196 Ill. App. 3d 928 (Ill.App. 1 Dist. 1990); see also *Texpor Traders, Inc. v. Trust Co. Bank*, 720 F. Supp. 1100 (S.D.N.Y. 1989). There was adequate evidence to show that 70 sweatshirts presented as exhibits at a trial were the actual garments that the seller shipped to the buyer, where the buyer's quality audit supervisor identified the sweatshirts at the trial as those she had previously examined.

11 *Brunson v. Com., Unemployment Bd. of Review*, 570 A.2d 1096 (Pa. Cmwlth. 1990); *Hinote v. Oil, Chemical and Atomic Workers International Union, AFL-CIO*, Local 4-23, 777 S.W.2d 134 (Tex. App. 1989).

§31.401 Checklist: Real Object Attack

The second line of attack involves questions concerning tampering. Just because the evidence has not been "switched" does not mean that it wasn't subjected to tampering. Tampering with a defective part in a products liability case can have some serious results; they may include defaults, ethical sanctions, and criminal responsibility. At the very least, intentional tampering with a material aspect of the evidence should preclude its use by the tampering party.[12] Along with the two primary concerns discussed above, here is a checklist of potential attacks:[13]

REAL OBJECT ATTACK CHECKLIST

1. There was a material break in the chain of possession; the object is not authentic; it's not the same one involved in the subject incident.[14]
2. The object has been tampered with, was materially altered, or was not adequately shown to be in the same condition that it was in at the time of the subject incident.[15]
3. The object is irrelevant or immaterial.[16]
4. The evidence is cumulative (particularly if it has been the subject of demonstrative exhibits).
5. Bringing the evidence into court would be inconvenient (if it's large) or dangerous (if it's toxic or explosive).
6. The evidence is unduly prejudicial.

---

12 See Siegal, *supra*, 921 F.2d 15.

13 See Lipson, *Art of Advocacy - Demonstrative Evidence*, §5.04[4] (Matthew Bender, Inc. 1989).

14 *Malchose v. Kalfell,* 664 N.W.2d 508, 2003 N.D. 75 (2003). With respect to real evidence, any defects in the chain of custody should go to the weight, not the admissibility, of the evidence. See also *Pearl Investments, L.L.C. v. Standard I/0, Inc.,* 257 F.Supp.2d 326 (D.Me., 2003).

But see *In re A.C.,* 770 N.E.2d 947 (Ind.App., 2002). To establish a proper foundation for the admission of exhibits (real evidence), absolute proof of authenticity is not necessary; however, there must be a reasonable probability that the exhibit is what it purports to be and that its condition is substantially unchanged as to any material feature.

15 *Krause, Inc. v. Little*, 34 P.3rd 566 (Nevada 2001) involved a products liability action that resulted from the collapse of a ladder. The trial court did not abuse its discretion by permitting the plaintiff to admit the ladder into evidence even though the plaintiff's experts had kicked it repeatedly. The defendant failed to show that the ladder had been altered to the point where its prejudicial effect exceeded its probative value.

Henson By and Through Lincoln v. Board of Educ. of Washington School Dist., 948 S.W.2d 202 (Mo. App. E.D. 1997) involved a situation where time alone caused a material alteration; in particular, it involved a personal injury action against a school district, on behalf of a student who was injured during a fall; the admission of three tree stumps (which were removed from the hillside from which the student fell), was an error in view of the failure of the student's counsel to lay a proper foundation. A four year period had passed between the time of the accident and the removal of the stumps, there was no evidence that the stumps were removed from the location on the hill where the student fell, and no one testified as to the condition or appearance of any stump at time of accident.

16 Because of its character as an actual "piece" or part of the subject incident, it is rare that real evidence, properly identified, would be deemed irrelevant in the classical sense of the term. Nevertheless, with the merger of the concept of "*materiality*" into "*relevance*," it is indeed possible for evidence that is "relevant" in the classical sense (but immaterial) to be excluded on the basis of relevance. Consider *Holley v. Pambianco*, 613 S.E.2d 425 (Va., 2005). In a medical malpractice action against a medical group, a videotape that was shown to a patient several weeks before a colonoscopy (which explained possible complications and symptoms) was deemed not to be relevant in proving whether that patient knew of a burden imposed upon him to take post operative steps for his own protection, and thus the video was not "relevant" to establish whether or not that patient failed to mitigate injuries from a perforated colon by waiting several days to report his symptoms.

(This page intentionally left blank.)

Chapter 32

Samples

§32.100 Introduction

There are two kinds of samples in the world of real evidence. There are those that provide a high degree of resemblance to the subject substance (Type 1), and those that were, at one time, actually a part of it (Type 2). Type 1, if any use were permitted by the court, would be demonstrative. Type 2 is real. Herein lies the finest of distinctions between real and demonstrative evidence. The physical differences are often minimal, but the legal ones are not, for the foundation requirements are very different.

§32.200 Admissibility

Consider the Type 1 case of *Talley v. J & L Oil*,[1] a wrongful death action brought by representatives of the estate of a small boy who drowned in an oil storage tank. The estate sought to introduce a "sample" of oil from a different storage tank (the court refused the evidence). Recall that if the proposed evidence is anything other than the identical substance, it won't be real; and if it isn't real, then it is not "automatically" relevant.

Ferguson v. Williams,[2] another attempt at Type 1, was a medical malpractice action brought against a pharmacist by a decedent's widow. The widow attempted, over the pharmacist's objection, to introduce into evidence some empty bottles of medicine, the labels of which listed various active ingredients. The trial court found, however, that the widow failed to properly lay a foundation because she did not show that they were "sufficiently identical" to the ones used by the decedent at the time he ingested the medication. Later in the trial, when she arguably elicited testimony to show that the exhibits were identical duplicates, no motion was made to have the bottles formally introduced as exhibits. It was, therefore, properly held that the exhibits should be excluded.

Union Camp Corp. v. Daley[3] seems to straddle the real-demonstrative dividing line. A jar of soapy material, which witnesses said was "very similar" to material which accumulated near the plant where a railroad employee was injured when he slipped, was brought into court. The sample was held to be relevant because it showed the nature of the foreign substance and was, therefore, admissible even though the witness did not know exactly where the substance came from. I would place this squarely on the "demonstrative" side of the fence, since something less than "identity" was established.

As opposed to fencing with terms such as "similar" and "sufficiently identical," real samples (i.e., Type 2) involve a mathematically pure form of "identity." In other words, the so-called sample must have been a part of the very substance that it represents, in order to gain admission as real evidence. The case of *Brunson v. Com., Unemployment Bd. of Review*[4] is a good all-around chain-of-possession case for proponents. It involved the chain of custody of a urine sample. The court found that even though the toxicologist, who supervised testing at the lab, did not personally transfer the sample from the employer's medical facility to that lab, and even though the person who actually received the sample at the lab did not testify, the chain was nevertheless established. Any gaps in the chain of custody were applied the weight given the related testimony, and not to its admissibility.

Hinote v. Oil, Chemical and Atomic Workers International Union, AFL-CIO, Local 4-23[5] is a

1 224 Kan. 214, 579 P.2d 706 (1978).

2 399 S.E.2d 389 (N.C. App. 1991).

3 374 S.E.2d 329 (Ga. App. 1988).

4 570 A.2d 1096 (Pa.Cmwlth. 1990). See also *Middlesex County Department of Health v. Importico*, 718 A.2d 727 (N.J. Super. 1998).

5 777 S.W.2d 134 (Tex. App. 1989).

case that straddles the fence between objects and samples. In an action against a union, its members, and officials to recover damages for harassment and personal injury (when plaintiff Hinote was shot by a .22 caliber rifle), it was held that the trial court did not abuse its discretion when it admitted pieces of a rifle found by the police. There was sufficient evidence to connect the rifle to shootings that had occurred during the subject incidences and, moreover, the rifle was of the same type that the investigating officer considered to have been used in the shooting.[6]

Consider *Mykytiuk v. Stamm.*[7] In an automobile negligence case, the court refused to allow the defendant to admit into evidence hair fibers taken from the side of his car at the time of the accident, finding that the defendant failed to lay a sufficient foundation, and failed to have the fibers analyzed to determine whether they belonged to the plaintiff. Moreover, the defendant admitted that he owned a dog, thereby rendering it possible that the subject hairs were not even human.

For our last Type 2 example, consider *Texpor Traders, Inc. v. Trust Co. Bank.*[8] There was adequate evidence to show that 70 sweatshirts presented as exhibits at a trial were the actual garments that the seller shipped to the buyer, where the buyer's Quality Audit Supervisor identified the sweatshirts at the trial as those she had previously examined.

"Handwriting samples" should not keep you up nights worrying about whether they fall into Category Type 1 or Type 2. The use and admissibility of such evidence are more important concerns.[9]

§32.300 Foundation Requirements (Type 1)

Samples that accurately represent a given substance or object may be probative, and constitute a valid display. But if those samples were not a part, portion or component of the actual material that is the subject of the litigation, formal admissibility may not be warranted. In such a case, the proponent should present the following arguments to the court:

1. The sample is, for all practical purposes, identical to the subject object or substance.
2. The sample will help clarify and simplify some material issue for the trier of fact.
3. The sample is offered for demonstrative purposes only; the offering is not intended to mislead the jury by representing that it was a part of the subject object.

6 See also *Lopez v. Wal-Mart Stores, Inc.*, 700 So.2d 215 (La. App. 4 Cir. 1997), a premises liability action which resulted when a box of toys fell from a store shelf and struck a customer. A box containing a toy, of the type which the customer had listed in her pretrial exhibits as one of the kinds of toys which had fallen on her, was admissible, even though the customer later contended that the box was not reflective of the one that struck her.

7 143 Ill. Dec. 570, 554 N.E.2d 505, 196 Ill. App. 3d 928 (Ill. App. 1 Dist. 1990).

8 720 F. Supp. 1100 (S.D.N.Y. 1989).

9 *Commonwealth v. O'Connell,* 783 N.E.2d 417, 438 Mass. 658 (2003) involved a trial on a charge of forgery. Where the signatures of the defendant had been admitted into evidence as genuine and submitted to the jury, they may be used as a standard against which the jury may compare the disputed signatures and decide the question of authorship without the need for expert testimony.

§32.400 Foundation Requirements (Type 2)

The suggestions pertaining to objects (*supra*) should similarly apply to samples. Expect the identification process, however, to be a bit more difficult and laden with pitfalls. So, as with objects, keep it simple, but be prepared for chain-of-possession problems.

Q. (By Proponent's Attorney) State your name for the record.
A. (Plaintiff) Sgt. Barry O'Mally.
Q. What is your relationship, if any, to this litigation?
A. I'm the policeman who investigated the scene of the homicide.
Q. Can you identify plaintiff's proposed Exhibit 1? (The exhibit should have been marked and labeled prior to trial.)
A. Yes; it's a sample of hair that I found on the couch, next to the victim.
Q. How do you know that it's the same?
A. I sealed it up in this bottle; it has my name and my markings on it.
Q. (Addressing the court, while tendering the object to opposing counsel) I ask that people's Exhibit 1 be admitted.
COURT: Any objections?
OPPOSING ATTORNEY: None.
COURT: Very well, it will be received.

§32.500 Checklist: Sample Attack

HOW TO OBJECT

1. The substance has not been shown to be an actual part or component of the subject object or material, due to the lack of a proper foundation or a break in the chain of possession.
2. The substance or object has been tampered with and/or materially altered.
3. The substance, if chemical or perishable, has materially deteriorated with time to the extent that it its once-probative characteristics are now useless.
4. The sample is immaterial.
5. The evidence is cumulative (particularly if it has been the subject of demonstrative exhibits).
6. If toxic, bringing the evidence into court would be inconvenient, and may impose a risk of harm to the jurors and court personnel.

Chapter 33

People

§33.100 Introduction

People and their afflicted parts can be relevant in a wide range of cases. In particular, this type of real evidence has been used to great success in personal injury cases.

§33.200 Admissibility

Real people and their component parts have been permitted as exhibits long before auto negligence and products liability cases came into vogue. The first such use of the human anatomy involved the now-deceased cause of action known as "seduction." More particularly, a child born as the result of a seduction could be exhibited in a seduction action to corroborate evidence of intercourse.[1]

By far, the single greatest use of the human anatomy as real evidence has involved personal injury actions. Not only are proximately caused injuries automatically relevant, they are also material (as long as "damages" remains in issue).

A display of injuries that resulted from a negligent act or product can be very powerful. Defense attorneys make meritorious arguments when they oppose such evidence, exclaiming it "highly prejudicial"; but unless the display is unduly gruesome,[2] the plaintiff will normally prevail.[3]

Every imaginable type of injury and anatomical display has the been the subject of an evidentiary controversy, at one time or another.[4] We will spare you mention of most. Among the common types of displays permitted by the courts are burns,[5] punctures,[6] scars,[7] and injured limbs.[8]

REFERENCES

Burn injuries, exception to hearsay rules. 1 Am. Jur. Proof of Facts 3d 197.

§33.201 Limbs and Other Portions of the Body

Pickled arms, legs, and fingers may be relevant, but what little case law there is on the subject, suggests that such items are both unduly inflammatory and immaterial.[9] This "immateriality" is not always obvious, even though there's no disputing it. For no one can "dispute" a missing limb; nor is such evidence needed to establish damages—what's gone is gone.

The so-called "intimate parts" have been sources of unsettled controversy. Generally, the younger the age, the greater the likelihood that the display will be allowed.[10]

1 *Shadix v. Brown*, 216 Ala. 516, 113 So. 581 (1927).

2 *Russell v. Coffman*, 237 Ark. 778, 376 S.W.2d 269 (1964).

3 Note, however, that the admission of such evidence rests with the sound discretion of the court. See *Parkway Hospital, Inc. v. Lee*, 946 S.W.2d 580, (Tex.App. Houston, 14 Dist. 1997); see also *Brown v. Billy Marlar Chevrolet, Inc.*, 381 So.2d 191 (Ala. 1980). But see *Schou v. Whitely,* 780 N.Y.S.2d 659, 9 A.D.3d 706 (N.Y.A.D. 3 Dep't 2004).

4 *Rubert Torres v. Hospital San Pablo, Inc.*, 205 F.3d 472 (1st Cir. Puerto Rico, 2000) involved medical malpractice action where trial court improperly refused to allow plaintiff, who had cerebral palsy, to be in courtroom for purpose of physical demonstration during an expert's testimony. Despite trial court's determination that viewing plaintiff would be unfairly prejudicial, exclusion was abuse of discretion. Evidence was highly relevant because both parties' experts based their conclusions on plaintiff's physical appearance; thus, evidence was fundamental to central issue of causation. Moreover, less restrictive means than total exclusion was available to minimize prejudicial effect that might have arisen from plaintiff's appearance.

5 *Magnolia Petroleum Co. v. Angelly*, 306 P.2d 309 (Okl. 1955).

6 *Tatreau v. Buecher*, 256 Wis. 252, 40 N.W.2d 509 (1949).

7 *Zeller v. Mayson*, 168 Md. 663, 179 A. 179 (1935).

8 *Stegall v. Carlson*, 6 Ill. App. 2d 388, 128 N.E.2d 352 (1955).

9 *Evans v. Chicago Ry.*, 133 Minn. 293, 158 N.W. 335 (1916).

10 *Yellow Cab Co. v. Henderson*, 183 Md. 546, 39 A.2d 546 (1944).

§33.202 Blood, Hair, Tissue and DNA Samples

There is no contest, whatsoever, about law enforcement's right take blood, hair, semen, and other tissue samples from a defendant in a criminal case. The normal purpose, of course, is to link a given person with a particular crime scene. The evidence runs the normal gauntlet of challenges that relate to the validity of a related search and/or seizure. Such matters are standard fare in criminal cases. More recently, they are also prevalent in civil matters.[11]

Not so standard, however, is the legal community's awareness of just how fragile blood and tissue samples can be as they make their way to and from the laboratories that conduct the relevant tests. Chain of possession becomes a very important factor, since mix-ups are known to occur.[12] Also, contamination and delays may give rise to the validity of the analyses, particularly with respect to DNA testing.[13]

DNA profiling is rapidly becoming a widely recognized, authoritative tool for identification.[14] Assuming that the proper methodology is employed, it is no longer a novel, suspect science.[15] A person's DNA is derived from his or her blood. From that sample, a profile is created. That profile is, in turn, compared to the profile of the specimen that is normally taken from the crime scene. These two pieces of real evidence are then compared. Assuming that both samples are free from contamination, the controversy then turns to the odds or chance that others in the community could have the same match.[16]

---

11 *McGrath v. Nassau Health Care Corporation,* 209 F.R.D. 55 (E.D.N.Y. 2002). In a sex harassment lawsuit, a female employee claimed that she and the defendant never had sexual intercourse; the defendant was entitled to an order requiring her to produce a DNA sample for comparison against the DNA profile on a blanket that was allegedly stained with her menstrual blood. The defendant claimed that the two had consensual intercourse on the blanket and that the defendant, therefore, met the burden of showing a reasonable possibility that the DNA testing was likely to yield a match.

12 *South Carolina Department of Social Services v. Cochran*, 614 S.E.2d 642 (S.C., 2005). In a termination of parental rights hearing, the Department of Social Services established a proper chain of custody for the mother's blood samples that were used for drug testing, even though the courier who transported the sample from the collection site was neither named, nor identified. Every other person who handled the blood samples was identified, and Department presented adequate testimony indicating that the samples were secured at a collection site and arrived at the testing facility sealed and intact and that each person involved in the actual testing procedure testified as to their handling.

13 Tests results involving DNA (deoxyribonucleic acid) matching and profiling, which are generally accepted by the scientific community, are admissible. *United States v. Jakobetz*, 955 F.2d 786 (2nd Cir. 1992); however, even though such tests meet the standard of general acceptance in the scientific community, the test results are subject to challenge on the grounds of relevancy, privilege, contamination, and problems with respect to chain of custody. *State v. Dykes*, 252 Kan. 556, 847 P.2d 1214 (1993).

14 The most respected testing methods include: Restriction Fragment Length Polymorphism (RFLP) and Polymerase Chain Reaction (PCR). See §18-3, Giannelli and Imwinkelreid, *Scientific Evidence*, The Michie Company. See also *supra*, §21.410.

15 *Folger v. Dugan*, 876 A.2d 1049, 2005 PA Super 215 (2005). A trial court need not conduct a *Frye* hearing to determine whether PCR testing is sufficiently reliable prior to admitting the test results where the parties do not challenge the methodology employed. Moreover, the *Frye Rule* requiring scientific evidence to be reliable and generally accepted in the scientific community prior to its admission does not apply every time science enters the courtroom.

16 For an excellent article that delves into the fine points of DNA matching, see Jim Schefter, *DNA Fingerprints on Trial, Popular Science*, p.60 (November 1994).

§33.300 Foundation Requirements

As for foundation requirements for people and their parts, there's nothing complicated here. The wounded party need only testify that the injury, scar, disfigurement, or dismemberment came as a direct and proximate result of the negligent act or defective product.

Q. (By Proponent's Attorney) State your name for the record.
A. (Plaintiff) Jimmy Onearm.
Q. Are you the plaintiff in this action?
A. Yes.
[Other questions and answers pertaining to the accident will intervene.]
Q. Were you injured as a result of the accident?
A. Yes.
Q. Please describe your injuries.
A. My arm and leg got all messed up.
Q. Did you have those injuries prior to the accident?
A. No.
Q. Please stand and show your injuries to the court and jury.

§33.400 Opposition

People and their afflicted parts will normally be relevant in personal injury cases. And the courts will normally grant an injured plaintiff quite a bit of slack in that regard. *Unfair prejudice*, though weak, may be the best defense. Also, where vivid descriptions precede the offering of such evidence, a *cumulativeness* argument may assist the opposition (See Fed. R. Evid. 403 for both grounds).

Depending upon the circumstances and the venue, exposing body parts to the jurors may be inappropriate, and may therefore cause such evidence to be excluded.[17] But whenever sensitive private parts are involved, the opposition should have a fighting chance.[18]

17 What might be considered inappropriate in the Bible Belt (i.e., south of the Mason Dixon Line) might, however, be perfectly proper in West Hollywood, California.

18 *Schou v. Whitely*, 780 N.Y.S.2d 659, 9 A.D.3d 706 (N.Y.A.D. 3 Dep't 2004). In an automobile negligence action, the trial court properly exercised its discretion when it precluded the publication of one of the plaintiff's scars to the jury; the plaintiff would have been required to partially remove his pants to do so. While such a scar was relevant to the issue of disfigurement, no prejudice resulted from the ruling in light of the prior expert testimony describing the size of the scar and its location.

Chapter 34

Animals

§34.100 Introduction

Reiterating the distinction between real and demonstrative evidence, keep in mind that we are now considering the animals themselves, not photographs or videos. The latter would be considered as "demonstrative," not "real."

§34.200 Admissibility

Lots of unexpected things can happen when **live** animals are pranced into court. But as long as there is no danger to the courtroom participants, material evidence, even if alive, should be permitted.[1]

Animals don't ordinarily excuse themselves to go to the rest room, honor the "Silence—Court in Session" sign, use an effective dry deodorant, or concern themselves about threats of contempt. Each of these reasons, not to mention public safety, constitutes a potential point of contention for anyone opposing a live show. But assuming that the safety issue is put to rest by adequate safeguards and assurances, an animal should be permitted, assuming that its presence is relevant.

Do not confuse the animal's relevance with the relevance of the exhibit. Only the latter case justifies an actual appearance by the animal itself. In a dog bite case, for example, where there is no issue as to the fact of the bite or the severity of the injury, the dog itself might be relevant, but its presence would not necessarily resolve any material issue in the trial. If, however, the appearance and demeanor of the dog were an issue, then its presence might be warranted.[2]

§34.300 Foundation Requirements

For animals, both living and deceased, the principles pertaining to real objects should apply. Identity would seem to be a concern with respect to living animals. And freedom from material alteration would be a concern for dead animals.

Do not lose sight of the fact that formal admissibility foundations are not required where impeachment is the sole purpose for the presentation. If, for example, a plaintiff testified that he was attacked by a large vicious dog, common sense would dictate that the defending owner should be permitted to display the animal. That display would not require formal admissibility since the animal was being used for impeachment purposes only.

1 *Arnold v. Laird*, 94 Wash. 2d 867 (1980).

2 Id.

Chapter 35

Views

§35.100 Introduction

A "view" can be thought of as a judicial field trip. The trier of fact, which may include the entire jury plus alternates, leaves the courtroom's sheltered halls to get a glimpse of the real scene of the crime, accident, or incident. This is a special case of "real evidence," and special rules apply.

§35.200 Admissibility

Is such evidence relevant? Of course. Material? Normally, yes. So then it must always be permitted, right? Wrong! This is one form of real evidence where time consumption, inconvenience, cost, and just plain "disruption" permit the court to refuse admission. Therefore, in general, no party has an absolute right to have the jury view the scene of an accident.[1] Permission for a view should always be sought at the earliest opportunity, prior to trial.

The practitioner should keep in mind that many states have specific statutes governing views. They are considered to be very special procedures that occur outside of the court's laboratory environment, and there is no way to predict what entities, welcome or otherwise, will enter the view.

In the celebrated "Twilight Zone" manslaughter trial, producer John Landis found himself defending some allegedly dangerous conditions in an outdoor mock-Vietnam battle-set that resulted in the deaths of Vic Morrow and two other actors.[2] Jurors were taken to view the actual scene of the occurrence. In the middle of the proceeding, a large helicopter made an unexpected fly-by. The defense moved for a mistrial, claiming that the unanticipated presence of the helicopter had a powerful emotional effect on the jurors since the subject deaths were caused by the blades of a crashed helicopter; the motion was, nevertheless, denied.

California's rules governing "views" are representative of those jurisdictions that treat the proceeding as an extension of the courtroom, in which all of the judicial rules, formalities, and courtesies apply. Perhaps the Pacific Coast's mild climate had something to do with the development of this particular approach. Section 651(a) of the California Civil Procedure Code provides:

> On its own motion or on the motion of a party, where the court finds that such a view would be proper and would aid the trier of fact in its determination of the case, the court may order a view of any of the following: (1) the property which is the subject of the litigation, (2) the place where any relevant event occurred, or (3) any object, demonstration, or experiment, a view of which is relevant and admissible in evidence in the case and which cannot with reasonable convenience be viewed in the courtroom.

Section 651(b) of the California Civil Procedure Code defines the scope of the field trip guest list so as to include the judge, jury, the court reporter and any necessary officers. For all practical purposes, the court remains "in session" throughout the view. Testimony is conducted in much the same manner as if the parties were in the court house.

Compare California's procedure to Michigan's "closed mouth" policy, as enunciated by Rule 513 of the Michigan Court Rules Annotated;[3] it states, in part, that:

> ... no person other than the officer designated by the court shall speak to the jury concerning any subject connected with the trial...

---

1 *Rinehart v. Schubel,* 794 A.2d 73, 2002 ME 53 (2002). The decision whether or not to grant a motion for a view is a discretionary decision for the trial court.

Boner v. Peabody Coal Co., 154 Ill.Dec. 662, 568 N.E.2d 883, 142 Ill.2d 523 (1991).

2 *People v. Landis*, No. A391-583 L.A. Sup.Ct. (1987).

3 For similar provisions, see Rule 48(c) of the Alaska Rules of Civil Procedure, and Rule 47(k) of the Colorado Rules of Civil Procedure.

§35.300 Foundation Requirements

Something more than materiality and relevance is required. This, of course, presents another reason why you should not "believe" Federal Rule 402.[4] In actual practice, something much more than relevance is needed. You had better have a very good reason for uprooting the courtroom and moving it out into traffic. As you weigh the decision, be aware of the preferable demonstrative alternatives, such photographs and videotapes; the judge will be. In most circumstances, demonstrative alternatives will be preferable. They permit more control, and fewer unpleasant surprises. If it rains, sleets, becomes too warm or too cold, rest assured that the jurors will blame the proponent. Views should be reserved for those circumstances where second hand evidence simply would not do—a particularly strange intersection, a unique building, or an object, the design of which is different from anything that the jurors had previously experienced. Above all, however, the view must be beneficial to your claim or position. The foundation that you present to the court must, therefore, be equally unique and compelling, and should include the following points:

1. The view is so unique that the trier of fact cannot gain an appreciation of a material aspect of it without seeing it first hand.
2. The probative value of the procedure outweighs the consequential inconvenience to the court and its members.
3. The safety, convenience, and comfort of the jurors can be assured.

In addition to the above arguments, the proponent should not forget to cite the standard required by the applicable court rule. There are but a few, and they are all quite generic. Federally speaking, there is only the minimum requirement of "relevance" per Fed. R. Evid. 402.

Some states have what we refer to as a "next to nothing standard," under which the court is given complete discretion by language to the effect that it "may" order a view.[5] Others permit a view where the court finds that it would be "proper."[6] As indicated above, California applies a two-part requirement—in addition to being "proper," the view must also "aid the trier of fact in the determination of the case."

Another popular standard permits the court to order a view where it is "necessary to a just decision."[7] In truth, it might be argued that all of the standards are equally vague.

The proponent of a view should remember that with or without a cost-imposing rule or statute, the court will most likely charge the expenses of the proceeding to the party requesting it. Consider Pennsylvania's Rule of Civil Procedure 219:

> A party desiring to have the jury view any premises involved in the litigation, may make application therefore either prior to the call of the case for trial, or at the bar during the actual trial of the case. In all such cases, the allowance of the application shall be within the discretion of the court, which may impose upon the applicant such reasonable costs or expenses as may be involved in connection with such a view, or may direct that any costs thereby incurred involved in connection with such view, or may direct that any costs thereby incurred shall follow the judgment entered in such action as in other cases.

4 Relevance, contrary to what it says, does not equate to admissibility.

5 See, for example, Rule 513 of the Michigan Court Rules; Rule 1.520 of the Florida Rules of Civil Procedure; Rule 219 of the Pennsylvania Rules of Civil Procedure; New Hampshire Rev. Stat. Ann., §415-21; and Virgin Islands Code Ann. Tit. 5, §352.

6 See, for example, Indiana Code Ann., §34-1-21-3; Rule 194 of the Iowa Rules of Civil Procedure; Nebraska Rev. Stat., §25-1108; and Ohio Rev. Ann. Code, §2315.02.

7 See the Delaware Code Ann. Tit. 10, §4527; South Carolina Code Ann., §14-7; Virginia Code, §8.01-376; and West Virginia Code, §56-6-17.

§35.400 Checklist: View Opposition

Checklist: View Opposition

1. The view will unduly interrupt and interfere with the judicial proceedings.
2. The probative value of the time-consuming procedure will be outweighed by the inconvenienceof transporting the judge, court reporter, jurors, and associated personnel to an extra-judicial location.
3. Moving the proceedings to a site outside of the protected environment of the courtroom introduces the risk that extraneous scenes and objects will cause the jury to engage in unwarranted prejudicial speculation.
4. The evidence is cumulative since the subject matter of the view has been the subject of testimony and/or demonstrative exhibits.
5. The weather conditions, lighting, and temperature are not as they were on the date of the subjectincident.
6. The scene has materially changed since the subject incident.
7. Older jurors or those with infirmities might be inconvenienced and subjected to hardship during a field trip.
8. It is not possible to predict all of the events and problems that surround such an undertaking.
9. Today, inexpensive video equipment is readily available; a film or videotape of the scene should accomplish the proponent's purpose, but without all of the preceding problems and inconvenience.

CAUTION—Using this last argument may constitute an open invitation for the enemy to admit a video which may be equally, or more, detrimental to your case.

§35.500 Counter-Argument

Proponents of the view should not be unduly deterred by the preceding shopping list. A single argument may be as persuasive as all of them combined:

HOLLYWOOD APPROACH:

Our entire excuse for being here is to determine the truth. If we confine ourselves to this courtroom, the proceedings may be very safe and protected, but at the expense of that truth. If we leave momentarily, the jury can see for themselves the actual scene instead of hearing debates about it. How can we sacrifice this "truth" because of a little bit of temporary inconvenience?

NO-NONSENSE APPROACH:

How much sense does it make to stand outside, as we are now, and argue about what's on the inside? Why not just open the door and let everyone have a look?

MIKE WALLACE APPROACH:

Why is the enemy attorney opposing this view? Is he afraid of the truth? What does his client have to hide?

GUILT APPROACH:

If we don't permit the view, there may be truths and answers that the jury will never see. And we may never know the harm caused by that refusal. (Can you live with yourself?)

In the last analysis, of course, the court will have the final say. And, as previously suggested, its decision will rarely be disturbed on appeal.

Chapter 36

On-Site Recordings

4. **Taped Telephone Conversations:** In the absence of court ordered wiretaps or "surveillance," telephone conversations are often recorded for a variety of reasons. Telephone answering machines and calls to 911 are among the best known.
5. **Transportation Devices:** The little black box that is required by all airlines is the best example of a "transportation device," but it is not the only example. In the future, automobiles will contain such devices.
6. **Recorded Electromagnetic Transmissions:** This category will become prominent in the future as transmissions of all sorts are emitted, decoded, and recorded by a variety of instruments that we have yet to conceive.

For our definition of an "on-site" recording, a word or two should be said about the "on-site" requirement. It is not necessary that the recorder itself be "on-site." Such would be the case for a typical bank surveillance camera, but the presence of any reliable recording device is adequate. Recognizing the status of our technology, it should make little difference whether the camera's images are taped at the scene or whether those same images are transmitted miles away to a recorder. As long as the image is of sufficient quality, the distance between the sensing device and the recorder device should be irrelevant. After all, we have heard transmissions from deep space that rival some local telephone calls. Therefore, by "on-site," we mean that only the sensing device need be "on-site," not the actual recorder. A 911 emergency call that happens to capture the voice of an outraged murder suspect would serve as an excellent example.

§36.300 Admissibility

The nice thing about films or videos that fall within the "on-site recording" pigeonhole is that, substantially, they all share the same foundation requirements. And well they should, even though their physical characteristics may vary significantly.

The images on the film should fairly and accurately represent what they purport to represent, a standard that should bring to mind photographic evidence.[2] Why then is photographic evidence *demonstrative*, while on-site videos are *real*? After all, isn't a movie nothing more than a series of still photos? The answers to those questions is no farther away than our three-part test (*supra*). Photos are normally taken at a point in *time* after the subject event, for the *purpose* of furthering litigation, by some interested person or agent, not an inanimate machine. There is, however, no need to quibble; if a surveillance camera were to take stills instead of videos, in satisfaction of the test, there would be no reason to deny the photographs standing as real evidence. As a matter of fact, depending upon the circumstances, a photograph could wear any one of three hats: Demonstrative, Real, or Documentary evidence.

Back to our foundation requirements. Before we bog down with what seems to be a number of differing judicially-pronounced standards, let's use common sense. Courts may use terms such as "fair," "accurate," and "substantial,"[3] but aren't they really saying that images should be clear and free from human manipulation? Do we really doubt the "accuracy" of the today's cheapest lens? And, have you ever known an unfair camera!

2 See Chapter 44.

3 *Louis Vuitton v. Spencer Handbags Corp.*, 765 F.2d 966 (2d Cir. 1985); *People v. Bowley*, 59 Cal. 2d 855, 382 P.2d 591 (1963).

Similarly, we don't really question the fairness or accuracy of sound recordings, only their clarity. With respect to other less common devices, such as in-flight recorders, we might want to inquire a bit about the inner-workings of the recording device.

As previously considered, on-site recordings can assume a variety of physical forms. As you prepare to examine them on an individual basis (*infra*), do not lose sight of the simple foundation requirements for real evidence in general. Recall that our one-word foundation requirement "Identity" is two-fold. In particular, as used for all forms of real evidence, *identity* implies: (1) that the proposed evidence is the actual item that "came from" the scene of the incident (in this case, a transmission), and (2) that there are no material alterations.

§36.301 Surveillance Cameras

They watch over banks, liquor stores, casinos, and even greasy hamburger outlets. The films from these "surveillance cameras" are not in the same league as demonstrative movies or videos; they are *not* self-serving, *nor* are they lawyer-created, nor are they originated to support some specific piece of existing litigation. Rather, they might be thought of as robotic eye witnesses capable of testifying with sounds and images. Indeed, the camera should be thought of as a component of the subject event, an impartial piece of real evidence.

The images captured by the camera are potent pieces of evidence; as we shall see (*infra*), the foundation requirements for surveillance films should track with those of real evidence, with an emphasis on "chain-of-position" as opposed to "clarification" (the buzzword for demonstrative evidence[4]).

If reasonable steps are taken to safeguard the film or videotape, and if the relevant portions were not edited or altered, there is every reason to expect that the evidence should be admitted.[5]

Surveillance, however, is not without its limits. There are still rights to some semblance of

4 See Chapter 40.

5 *Hubbard v. Gross*, 199 Fed.Appx. 433 (6th Cir., Ky., 2006). In an arrestee's §1983 claim against arresting officers (alleging excessive force, deliberate indifference to serious medical needs, malicious prosecution, §1983 violations and various state claims), the probative value of a videotape of the arrestee at the police station following his arrest was not outweighed by the danger of unfair prejudice, even though the video included mention of the arrestee's prior arrests. Because the videotape showed the arrestee being abusive, drunk, and cursing, it was, therefore, highly probative of the arrestee's demeanor at the time of the arrest, and it was also indicative of his credibility since the arrestee claimed that he was cooperative. Any prejudice was slight, because mention of the prior arrests was brief and barely audible.

Stotler v. State, 834 So.2d 940. (Fla.App. 2003). During a trial involving a charge of burglary, comments that were made by the defendant immediately before and during the alleged burglary captured on a videotape were relevant to his participation in the crime, and thus were within the proper scope of the cross-examination of an alleged accomplice; the subject matter of alleged accomplice's direct examination involved the commission of the alleged burglary as depicted on the videotape. The video showed the defendant's physical conduct during the alleged burglary.

U.S. v. Corona-Chavez, 328 F.3d 974 (8th Cir., Minn., 2003). Silent video surveillance is not regulated nor prohibited by the Electronic Communications Privacy Act, 18 U.S.C.A. 2510 et seq.

Chiasson v. Zapata Gulf Marine Corp., 988 F.2d 513 (5th Cir. 1993); *Rehab Project Inc. v. Sarno*, 80 Ohio App.3d 265, 608 N.E.2d 1188 (1992); *Palmer v. Goudchaux-Maison Blanche, Inc.*, 588 So.2d 737 (La.Ct.App. 1991).

privacy, and entitlements to common decency that should be free from invasion.[6]

Following are examples of cases in which videotape evidence was admitted:

1. *Brokamp v. Mercy Hospital*, 726 N.E.2d 594, 132 Ohio App.3d 850 (1999). In a medical malpractice case, a surveillance videotape showing a patient's participation in golf outings was admissible where the lawsuit arose from the administration of an intramuscular injection prior to those outings; the videotape was relevant to the seriousness of the patient's claimed injuries, and was not unduly prejudicial.
2. *Phelps v. Provident Life and Accident Insurance Co.,* 60 F.Supp.2d 1014 (CD.Cal. 1999). In an insured's suit challenging the insurer's termination of disability payments, surveillance films compiled by the insurer were admissible over relevance and hearsay objections. Transcripts of the surveillance films compiled by that insurer were also admissible over similar objections.
3. *Mier v. Martin,* 755 So.2d 958 (La.App. 1999). The admission of surveillance videotapes into evidence in personal injury cases is largely within the trial court's discretion. *Kelly v. Riles*, 751 So.2d 302 (La.App. 1999) involved an action for personal injuries sustained by a grocery store customer that occurred when the store's manager struck the customer's wrist with a shopping cart. The trial court acted within its discretion when it ruled that surveillance videotapes were admissible which showed the customer performing work which tended to demonstrate that her injuries were exaggerated. Moreover, determining the admissibility into evidence of videotapes must be done on a case-by-case basis, depending on the individual facts and circumstances. In making that determination, the trial court must consider whether the videotape accurately depicts what it purports to represent, whether it tends to establish a fact of the proponent's case, and whether it will aid the jury's understanding. Against those factors, the trial court must consider whether the videotape will unfairly prejudice or mislead the jury, confuse the issues, or cause undue delay.

It should be noted that real evidence is always relevant, regardless of the shape or physical structure that it may decide to assume. Real video evidence is no exception. But the existence of "relevance" pre-supposes that the video camera is pointed at the event which is the subject of the litigation, not some other event, regardless how closely related it may appear to be.[7]

---

6 *National Freight, Inc. v. Snyder*, 191 S.W.3d 416 (Tex.App., 2006). In a motorist's negligence action resulting from injuries sustained when the motorist's vehicle collided with a truck, the probative value of a surveillance video, showing the motorist employing a full range of motion with his injured arm simulating an inappropriate act, was outweighed by its prejudicial effect; the conduct depicted in the video was inflammatory, many jurors likely would have been offended by it, and the challenged footage was only a small portion of a much longer video showing the motorist working in his shop. (One remaining portion of the video showed the plaintiff using both of his arms to pick up a large object.)

Publix Supermarkets, Inc. v. Griffin, 837 So.2d 1139 (Fla.App., 2003). In a personal injury action, a private investigator went far past the bounds of decency and propriety when he captured footage of the plaintiff's seven-year-old son while conducting surveillance in a restroom. To make matters worse, the scene was never included in copies provided to the plaintiff. Nevertheless, the plaintiff was deemed to have waived her right to a mistrial after making a motion for a mistrial and then withdrawing it in favor of a curative instruction to the jury. The videotape evidence was, of course, stricken.

7 *Falgoust v. Richardson Industries*, 552 So.2d 1348 (La.Ct.App. 1989), involved a personal injury action against an above-ground swimming pool manufacturer, resulting from a dive. A videotape of a television news show concerning the potential dangers of such pools was excluded on the basis of hearsay and lack of trustworthiness. Neither grounds would have barred an on-site recording.

Surveillance videos are universally perceived as being objective and accurate; they are, for that reason alone, highly prejudicial. So it should not be assumed that they will always be admitted. Admission of such videotapes into evidence is largely within discretion of trial court, which must consider: (1) Whether tape accurately depicts what it purports to represent, (2) whether it tends to establish fact of proponent's case, and (3) whether it will aid or confuse jury's understanding so as to unfairly prejudice or mislead jury, confuse issues, or cause undue delay.[8]

§36.302 Manual Videotape Cameras

In the hands of a steady, disinterested nonparty, a videotape camera can be just as objective and sound as a stationary camera. The two events that changed the face of video evidence involve such circumstances. On November 22, 1963, Abraham Zapruder captured the assassination of President Kennedy. On March 3, 1991, George Holiday captured the beating of Rodney King. Both motion pictures have had a tremendous impact upon the attention directed toward video evidence in general.

Matters concerning the condition of the equipment (i.e., the camera), in addition to the care and handling of the film or tape might be addressed during the foundation process.[9] However, the single most important concern for this particular form of evidence would involve the editing of the actual event, i.e., the "stops and starts." This crucial element is normally not a concern for the stationary surveillance camera because it is normally a perpetual device.

Regardless of the motives of the cameraperson, if the event is selectively photographed so as to be misleading, the video, though relevant and perhaps very probative, might nevertheless be excluded.[10] For example, the videotape of a police officer beating the tar out of pedestrian might be excluded if it failed to show the events that might have provoked the beating; perhaps the pedestrian took a swing at the officer or threw a stone at him. To provide a visual account of only "one side of the story" might render this

8 See *Read v. Ellenville National Bank*, 20 A.D.3d 408, 799 N.Y.S.2d 78 (N.Y.A.D. 2nd Dept., 2005), wherein a bank customer sued for personal injuries that she allegedly sustained when the lid on a night deposit box suddenly snapped shut on her left hand. In support of its motion for judgment on the ground that the alleged incident did not occur, the bank submitted a videotape from its closed-circuit television surveillance system which showed the plaintiff making a deposit in the night deposit box, apparently without incident. After appeals, the New York Supreme Court denied the defendant's motion, finding that the plaintiff raised issues of fact concerning the authenticity and validity of the videotape and was entitled to full disclosure and an opportunity to test the validity of the tape. *Quinn v. Wal-Mart Stores, Inc.*, 774 So.2d 1093 (La.App., 2000). In damages phase of negligence action against department store, court properly excluded evidence of surveillance videotapes of customer on grounds that it was more prejudicial than probative; tapes were offered without context or explanation and injured customer did not claim that she was completely disabled and could not perform activities portrayed in videos, but rather claimed that her mobility was restricted so that activities on tape produced discomfort or pain.

9 But see *People ex rel Sherman v. Cryns,* 271 Ill.Dec. 881, 786 N.E.2d 139, 203 Ill.2d 264 (2003), an action to enjoin a midwife from the unlicensed practice of midwifery (following a "water delivery" which resulted in the death of a newborn). No adequate foundation was established for the admission of a videotape of the birth. Testimony by a witness that the videotape was an accurate portrayal of the events that occurred during the newborn's birth was inadequate. The videotape was admitted into evidence but not played for the jury because there was no testimony that the videotape that was actually admitted was a true and accurate portrayal of what it purported to show. Generally, a videotape may be admitted as demonstrative evidence when it is properly authenticated and is deemed relevant to a particular issue in the case. A videotape will be considered as relevant only as long as its probative value is not substantially outweighed by the danger of unfair prejudice. The admission of a videotape into evidence is within the sound discretion of the circuit court and will not be disturbed absent an abuse of that discretion.

10 See Fed. R. Evid. 403.

otherwise-admissible evidence, inadmissible because its probative value would be outweighed by its unfair prejudicial effect.

Adding time/date markers and titles can also present some problems; but once again, the magnitude of those problems often depend upon who (or what) is doing the marking. For stationary surveillance cameras, such markings are automatically placed on the film; there is nothing controversial there. But where titles and time/date stamps are imposed by humans, hearsay problems arise, and credibility, if not admissibility may be jeopardized.[11]

There is a popular form of surveillance that does **not** fall within this particular evidence subgroup, and, moreover, should not even be considered as real evidence. I am referring to those private investigators who are often hired to catch people in compromising positions. The practice is quite common in personal injury and workers' compensation cases. A alleged "permanently crippled" plaintiff, for example, may be captured on film while running, jumping, carrying heavy objects, and in general, looking as if he belonged in some form of iron-man competition. Such evidence is often admissible to rebut the plaintiff's claim at trial that he was crippled, or otherwise disabled.[12] But there is also evidence to suggest that some of the tide may be turning against admissibility as courts begin to recognize that surveillance videos are selective in nature, often failing to capture "feelings" of pain that cannot be translated into photographic images, or long periods of incapacitation, where the plaintiff is unable to perform the captured activities.[13]

11 *International Union v. Russell*, 264 Ala. 456, 88 So.2d 175 (1956).

12 For a situation wherein a plaintiff "spies on herself," see *Sgambelluri v. Recinos*, 747 N.Y.S.2d 330, 192 Misc.2d 777 (2002). In an auto negligence action, the plaintiff claimed that she could no longer engage in running or horseback riding because of the permanent injuries suffered during the accident. Her wedding videos, however, were deemed relevant to show that she was able to engage in activities such as dancing.

In *Aibrecht v. Dorsett,* 508 S.E.2d 319 (N.C.App. 1998), some personal injury plaintiffs were unexpectedly caught by a surveillance videotape camera while engaging in various physical activities. Despite its length and repetitive nature, the videotape was relevant to the issues of whether the unwilling film subjects were actually disabled by injuries allegedly sustained in the automobile accident; such evidence was not unfairly prejudicial.

The practitioner should note that while surveillance videotapes are admissible they are not self-authenticating. See *Cirillo v. Davis,* 732 So.2d 387 (Fla.App.1999), wherein the surveillance videotape of a personal injury plaintiff made by a private investigative firm retained by the defense, was held to be not self-authenticating. See also Chapter 44.

13 *Franklin v. HealthSouth*, 940 So.2d 83 (La.App., 2006). In a workers' comp action, a surveillance videotape may form a basis for the forfeiture of workers' compensation benefits for a claimant who willfully makes false statements if that video directly contradicts the statements. However, determining whether certain pictures or videotapes are admissible is largely within the discretion of the trial court, and evidence in the form of motion pictures or videotapes is approached with great caution since these formats show only intervals of the activities of the subject; they do not show rest periods, and they do not reflect whether the subject was suffering pain during or after the activity.

Carroll v. Preston Trucking Co., 285 Ill. Dec. 611, 812 N.E.2d 431, 349 Ill. App.3d 562 (Ill. App. Ct., 2004) involved a personal injury action by an employee against a truck owner and driver that arose when the employee sustained a knee injury when a switch gear fell on top of him while he was riding in the back of the subject's truck. A videotape recording showing the employee performing various tasks around his home was not relevant; while the videotape was probative to show the extent of the employee's incapacitation and to rebut the employee's testimony that he experienced constant pain, there was, nevertheless, danger of unfair prejudice that outweighed the probative value. The videotape recording was edited to show only those short periods of time when the employee was actively participating in yard work, which gave the impression that the employee's activity was constant. See also *Franz v. First Bank Sys.,* 868 So.2d 155 (La. App. 4 Cir. Feb. 11, 2004) which involved a personal injury action that resulted from a runaway elevator that came to an abrupt stop. The trial court did not abuse its discretion by excluding from evidence a surveillance videotape taken of the plaintiff which showed him lifting and moving heavy furniture without any apparent pain. The videotape had nothing to do with the elevator accident (there was sufficient testimony at trial with respect to the plaintiff's credibility). Moreover, the admission or exclusion of videotaped evidence is within the trial court's discretion.

A film that catches an unsuspecting plaintiff off-guard may, with the setting of a proper foundation, present probative, convincing evidence; but such a presentation, is a far cry from "real evidence." It is also outside the scope of the "on-site" recording as defined by our three-part test (*supra*). The *objectivity* and *purpose* requirements are totally lacking. The time element, interestingly, is not lacking. While it is true the camera, in such an instance, did not capture the event giving rise to the injury, nevertheless, the actions and physical movements of the plaintiff following the accident or injury are discrete probative events that factor significantly into the damages equation. Clearly, however, this type of surveillance belongs in the "Demonstrative Evidence" category. After all, a camera, operated by the litigant of a representative, is far from an "objective" device.[14]

§36.303 Audiotaped Sounds and Conversations

There is little need to distinguish audiotapes from videotapes when speaking strictly of surveillance devices. As a matter of fact, today's sophisticated cameras are able to capture both sights and sounds. It would, therefore, make little sense to classify the visual images as real, while labeling the audio portion as something else. Therefore, it should be clear that the sound track for *real* video evidence should also be considered as *real*, assuming, of course, that it was not dubbed.

Where sound alone is captured on tape, our concern must shift to the ease with which words can be edited and transposed. Not so with respect to visual images; they are more difficult to splice without leaving serious tell-tale incongruities. For this reason and others that we will shortly consider, audiotapes, while often admissible, achieve that admissibility as something other than *real* evidence.

As previously mentioned earlier in this chapter, unlike the video recordings, which less frequently intrude upon a person's household, surveillance tape recordings are more likely to invade those private nooks and crannies. Sound travels through walls; light does not. This ability to invade areas where there is a greater expectation of privacy, often raises *Fourth Amendment* issues.

Fortunately or unfortunately, depending upon your bent, when government informers wear a "wire" or "bug," the taped result can be used against you.[15] Keep in mind, however, that if taped conversations are being offered to prove the truth of the matters asserted in the conversation, hearsay problems will arise.[16] Those tapes would, therefore, require an exception to the hearsay rule to be admissible.[17]

Keep in mind that most tape recordings involving criminal cases, will focus upon matters concerning events that already occurred; they would not, therefore, fall within our *on-site recording* category. Conspiracy is an exception. Where a conspiracy is taped, that recording would capture the crime itself; you can't get more **real** than that.

14 A motion picture camera, in the hands of a skilled professional, is much more than a disinterested objective observer. It is no less a paint brush in the hands of a skilled artist, who can use his or her tool to paint a very subjective image. See Lipson, *The Art of Advocacy - Demonstrative Evidence*, §13.04 (Production Techniques), Matthew Bender & Co., 1988-2006.

15 *United States v. Pinalto,* 771 F.2d 457 (10th Cir. 1985); *United States v. Busch,* 758 F.2d 1394 (10th Cir. 1985).

16 See Fed. R. Evid. 801 and 802.

17 The most common exceptions involve admissions and inconsistent statements. See Application to Quash Grand Jury Subpoena 597 N.Y.S.2d 557 (Sup. Ct. 1993); *State v. Williams,* 256 N.W.2d 207 (Iowa 1977) [admissions]; *Stevenson v. State,* 619 A.2d 155 (Md.App. 1993); *Zawistowski v. Kissinger,* 466 N.W.2d 664 (Wis.Ct.App. 1991) [inconsistent statements].

Where a court of competent jurisdiction issues an order permitting a wiretap, it is to be assumed that the party or governmental agency conducting the tap will act in a professional manner, and will produce a result that is similar to those referred to in the preceding discussions. Our concern at this point, however, involves privately initiated audiotapes, such as telephone answering machines or emergency calls to 911. They could constitute on-site recordings if they occur at the time of the material incident.

Keep in mind that classification as *real* evidence is a two-edged sword. On the proponent's side, the evidence can be extremely potent, since real evidence is presented as a peek at the real event which is the subject of the controversy. But, on the other hand, such evidence can often be extremely difficult to admit into evidence for that very reason.[18]

§36.304 Transportation Devices

The in-flight recorder is the most common example of a "little black box" that records data relating to vehicular movement for the purpose of capturing an unanticipated disaster. The little black box that is required by all airlines is the best example of a "transportation device," but it is not the only example. In the future, automobiles will contain such devices.

A competent practitioner must be aware of the difference between the little black box itself (i.e., in-flight recorder) and the man-made (and often self-serving) images that are generated as a result. The black box itself, is perhaps the best example of an accurate professional on-site recorder. It is real evidence, to be sure, and should be admissible for purposes of proving what took place just prior to an air crash. Computer simulations, reconstructions, or animations that are made from the box's data are by no means to be considered as real evidence. They are man-made renderings even though jurors, lawyers, and experts are often confused about where the real evidence ends and the demonstrative renderings start.[19]

Plaintiff and defendant attorneys alike should be aware that computer simulations, based upon data from in-flight recorders, have been admitted.[20] Defendants must be extra cautious in seeing to it that the jury is made aware of the fact that they are viewing demonstrative self-serving evidence, not an objective statement by the little black box.

§36.305 Recorded Electromagnetic Transmissions

This is our catchall category. There is no reason to believe that we can predict every form that recorded evidence may assume in future decades. Nor is there any reason to believe that such evidence will be any less reliable than our current devices. Regardless of the sophistication level of

18 See also *Larocque v. O'Connor*, 876 A.2d 1229, 90 Conn.App. 156 (2005) involving a will contest and a failure to authenticate an audiotape that an attorney for the testator's daughter made of a Probate Court's hearing. See *Phillip Morris Inc. v. Emerson,* 368 S.E.2d 268 (Va. 1988), concerning an emergency telephone call regarding a toxic spill.

19 See Lipson, *The Art of Advocacy - Demonstrative Evidence*, Chapter 24 (Using Demonstrative Evidence in Air Crash Cases), Matthew Bender & Co., 1988-2006.

20 The most notable case involves the crash that occurred at Dallas/Fort Worth International Airport on August 2, 1985. A computerized reconstruction visually recreated the events leading up to that crash in *Connors v. United States*, 720 F.Supp. 1258 (N.D.Tex. 1989); see also *In re Air Crash at Detroit Metro Airport*, 791 F.Supp. 1204 (E.D. Mich.1992).

the instrument, admissibility will always require a proper foundation, one which demonstrates that devices have been used properly and employed in such a manner as to ensure accuracy.[21]

§36.400 Sample Generic Foundation

Q. (By Proponent's Attorney) State your name for the record.
A. (Custodian) Candy Keeper.
Q. Do you maintain a recording device known as a _____________ ?
A. Yes.
Q. Please briefly describe the device and how it operates.
A. Sure.
[The witness will briefly describe the recording equipment, identifying it by name, brand, and perhaps model number, so as to provide a complete record.]
Q. Can you identify plaintiff's proposed Exhibit 1? (The exhibit could consist of a film, tape, or any form of magnetic or optical medium.)
A. Yes; it was a ___________ that was recorded on the date of __________; the device has a self-dating feature... so the time and date are automatically marked on the ________.
Q. Did you personally remove the _______ (tape, film, etc.)?
A. Yes.
[A reasonable chain-of-custody should be demonstrated; it is not necessary that the tape be guarded twenty-four hours a day.]
Q. Did you edit, change or alter the _________ (tape, film, etc.)?
A. No.
Q. Did you permit anyone else to edit, change or alter the _________ (tape, film, etc.)?
A. No.
Q. (Addressing the court, while tendering the object to opposing counsel) I ask that Exhibit 1 be admitted.
COURT: Any objections?
OPPOSING ATTORNEY: None.
COURT: Very well, it will be received.

Notice that the key feature which distinguishes our "on-site" recording from physically similar forms of demonstrative evidence is the "chain of possession" element. In keeping with our one-word foundation element[22] for all forms of real evidence (i.e., "Identity"), the above foundation boils down to a single concern—that the recording which made its way into the courtroom is the identical recording that came out of the camera (or other recording device).

If a given film or recording were to be used for demonstrative purposes only, we shouldn't care less about the chain of possession (i.e., from artist to paralegal, to clerk, etc.). Chain of possession would be irrelevant. If the exhibit helps clarify issues and facts, no one should care where it came from; after all, it must be presumed that the jurors would be well informed that the presentation presented one side and only one side of the story. The jurors would thus be made aware of the self-serving nature of the exhibit; they would take it for what it was worth—a tool of persuasion. That is a far cry from an on-site recording that purports to present the one and only truth.

21 *Hotaling v. CSX Transport,* 773 N.Y.S.2d 755, 5 A.D.3d 964 (N.Y.A.D., 2004). In an action arising from a collision between two trains, speed tapes that recorded speedometer and odometer readings, along with the time from the night of the accident, were properly precluded from admission into evidence to show the relative positions of the trains immediately before the collision; the tapes from each train were not calibrated to one another, and it would not be accurate to compare them side by side. Also, the railroad had no expert to interpret the speed tapes.

22 See Overview.

(This page intentionally left blank.)

Chapters 37-39

Reserved for Supplementation

Chapters 37 through 39 are reserved for supplementation. Also, to maintain our decimal structure, **Part III - Real Evidence** was specifically designed to start and end in the 30s. **Part IV - Demonstrative Evidence** was designed to start at Chapter 40.

(This page intentionally left blank.)

Part IV - Demonstrative Evidence

Table of Contents

Chapter 43
Documents

Chapter 44
Photographs, Slides, Films and Videos

Chapter 45
Audiotapes

Chapter 46
Finger, Foot, and Palm Prints

Chapter 47
Computer-Generated Materials

Chapter 48
Live Demonstrations

Chapter 49
Internal Pictures

Appendix A
Responding to Objections at a Glance

Table of Cases

Index

Chapter 40

Basics of Demonstrative Evidence

§40.100 Introduction

Demonstrative evidence, under most circumstances, is created precisely for litigation, after the material events have already occurred. It is, by definition, self-serving. Contrast that scenario with real evidence which must have formed a physical part of the subject incident at the time that it occurred, and must have come into existence **without** the self-help of the litigants.

The police officer who photographed the bar following a shoot-out created a demonstrative exhibit. Similarly, the charts, graphs, simulations, and models, prepared by attorneys for the estate of the losing combatant could also be considered as demonstrative. The gun itself would be real evidence, and so would the bar and the corpse (though the latter's appearance in court would be unlikely in lieu of the coroner's official testimony and report).

There once lived a claim that demonstrative evidence was not really "evidence" at all; this was due to an inherent foundation requirement that it be predicated upon "other admissible" evidence. However, it has recently come to take on a life of its own, as **evidence**. More precisely, a demonstrative presentation is really a method of presenting, clarifying, or amplifying other "more substantive" items of evidence (such as documentary, real, or testimonial.[1]). The "non-evidence" notion likened the demonstrative presentation to an opening or closing statement, which of course, is more akin to argument than evidence. But after all is said and done, demonstrative evidence would most accurately be described as a form of "derivative" evidence.

The actual purpose for a demonstrative "exhibit" is to clarify, simplify, explain, and illustrate the interrelationship between other previously admitted items of evidence.[2] It is a tool of persuasion, and a very powerful one. Demonstrative presentations have proven their worth. They make more lasting impressions than arguments and testimony alone; their value cannot be overstated.[3]

It seems as if the different forms of "demonstrative evidence," which we consider more thoroughly in the chapters that follow, managed to slowly edge their way into the "admissible evidence" arena. Those forms were aided by the confusion caused as a result of some poorly drafted federal rules. (See, for example, Fed. R. Evid. 1001, which, with the stroke a pen, converts everything imaginable into a "writing.")

The courts universally accept demonstrative evidence as a proper component of the evidentiary process. In the past, they seemed to take a neutral stance with respect to its general value as compared to other forms of evidence. More recently, however, this attitude is changing to suit our era of technological and audio-visual expansion.[4]

Judges have just "assumed" that demonstrative exhibits are evidence. And, right or wrong, when the courts treat the items as evidence, their decisions make it so.[5] Nevertheless, the following analysis sums up the true status of demonstrative presentations:

1 See *Bachman v. General Motors Corp.,* 267 Ill.Dec. 125, 776 N.E.2d 262 (2002), which declared that demonstrative evidence has no probative value in itself; rather, it serves as a visual aid in comprehending the witnesses' verbal testimony. Generally, according to Bachman, courts look favorably upon the use of demonstrative evidence because it helps the jury understand the issues raised during the course of the trial.

2 Assuming that courts apply correct standard, there should be no issue with respect to "relevance" unless formal admissibility is involved. Fact that exhibit "clarifies" a relevant point, should be enough. Courts, however, sometimes continue to use "relevance" as decisive standard. See *Davis v. Traylor,* 530 S.E.2d 385, 340 S.C. 150 (2000).

3 See generally, Lipson, *The Art of Advocacy - Demonstrative Evidence* (Matthew Bender & Co., 1988).

4 *Schuler v. Mid-Central Cardiology,* 246 Ill.Dec. 163, 729 N.E.2d 536, 313 Ill.App.3d 326 (2000) provided positive declaration about demonstrative evidence by finding that courts "look favorably" upon use of demonstrative evidence, because it helps jury understand issues raised during trial.

5 At least one court has elevated demonstrative evidence to a "preferred status." See *Hernandez v. Schittek,* 238 Ill. Dec. 957, 713 N.E.2d 203, 305 Ill.App.3d 925 (1999), wherein it was held that the use of demonstrative evidence with a jury is favored because it presents an aid with respect to testimonial comprehension.

The only purpose of demonstrative evidence is to illustrate or clarify previously admitted other evidence. It has no independent effect on the determination of the existence of a fact of consequence, other than its helpfulness as an illustrative aid to another, independently relevant piece of substantive evidence. That is, a diagram of an apartment that has been burglarized does not, in and of itself, make it any more or less probable that the defendant was the one who committed the crime; it only clarifies previous testimony as to what the apartment looked like. Demonstrative evidence's relevance is thus derivative and different from that of admissible substantive evidence. Hence, when modern courts allow demonstrative exhibits to be used at trial based on traditional relevance tests, they do so illegitimately, without sufficient theoretical support.[6]

Our purpose for pointing out this "illegitimacy" is more than academic. The discussion is designed to arm practitioners (proponents and opponents) with additional weapons.

The illegitimacy of demonstrative evidence provides it with a split personality and a double-barreled benefit for proponents. If demonstrative exhibits are denied formal admissibility, the proponent gets a second bite at the apple. In particular, even if the common foundations for such evidence are lacking and admissibility is denied, the exhibit may then be used "for demonstrative purposes only" upon a showing that it would clarify issues or presentations for the trier of fact. Thus, the overriding foundation elements for demonstrative evidence are **simplification** and **clarification**.[7] Evidence that satisfies those elements and yet fails to qualify as formally admissible evidence is sometimes described as "pedagogical."[8]

By contrast, the opposition's key cries will be that the exhibit "is **misleading** and will tend to **confuse** the jury." And, of course, that opponent may wish to point out the exhibit's lack of relevance.[9]

---

6 *Spyrka v. County of Cook,* 851 N.E.2d 800, 366 Ill.App.3d 156, 303 Ill.Dec. 613 (2006). Citing the landmark case of *Cisarik v. Palos Community Hospital,* 144 Ill.2d 339, 341, 162 Ill.Dec. 59, 579 N.E.2d 873 (1991), "demonstrative evidence" has no probative value in itself; it serves, rather, as a visual aid to the jury in comprehending the verbal testimony of a witness. Before a film can become evidence at trial as demonstrative evidence: (1) a foundation must be laid, by someone having personal knowledge of the filmed subject; (2) that the film is an accurate portrayal of what it purports to show; and (3) that the film's probative value cannot be substantially outweighed by the danger of unfair prejudice.

The Derivative Relevance of Demonstrative Evidence: Charting Its Proper Evidentiary Status, Robert Brain & Daniel Broderick, 25 U.C. Davis Law Review 957, 965 (1992); Robert Brain, Esq. is an Associate Professor of Law at Pepperdine University School of Law. In the treatise, the authors speak of a "derivative relevance" as they point out that demonstrative evidence is, in truth, relevant to clarify or simplify other relevant evidence, but is not directly relevant to the material facts of the case. Id. at 973.

7 *State v. Stewart,* 643 N.W.2d 281 (Minn. 2002). Visual aids are relevant if they assist the jury in understanding a witness's testimony.

8 See *Minebea Co., Ltd. v. Pabst,* 231 F.R.D. 1 (D.D.C., 2005), which considered the distinction between formally admissible evidence and "demonstrative or pedagogical" evidence designed to summarize facts or issues in order to simplify a complex case. *U.S. v. Buck,* 324 F.3d 786 (5th Cir., Miss., 2003). In a prosecution for the misapplication of federal funds and the filing of false documents, a diagram showing the name and title of an organization's chief executive officer, and displaying connections between that officer and various federal grant payments, constituted a pedagogical aid that was properly shown to the jury in order to assist its understanding of the testimony and documents that had already been produced, but it should not have been admitted into evidence, and the jury should have been instructed that it was not to be considered as evidence.

9 *Ford v. Estate of Clinton,* 656 N.W.2d 606, 265 Neb. 285 (2003). Generally, demonstrative exhibits are admissible if they supplement a witness' spoken description of a transpired event, clarify some issue in the case, and are more probative than prejudicial. A demonstrative exhibit is inadmissible when it does not illustrate or make clearer some issue in the case; that is, where it is irrelevant or where the exhibit's character is such that its probative value is substantially outweighed by the danger of unfair prejudice.

Compare the two methods of presentation. Both are based upon the same foundation elements. The testimony is skeletal (more detailed foundations will be considered in the chapters that follow).

§40.200 Skeletal Foundation–Formal Admissibility

Q. (By Proponent's Attorney) State your name for the record.

A. (Plaintiff) Elton Exhibitionist.

Q. I call your attention to Exhibit 1 positioned to your right and ask if you prepared (or directed the preparation of) it.

A. Yes.

Q. Would you briefly describe your preparation of the exhibit?

A. Yes... (Generally, the witness should describe the manner in which the exhibit came into being; its preparation should have been based upon admissible facts established by eyewitnesses or other competent evidence.)

Q. Is it accurate (or substantially similar, or drawn to scale, or does it represent or show what it purports to represent)?[10]

A. Yes, except for... (The witness should point out discrepancies and inaccuracies.)

Q. Will this exhibit **assist** your explanation of the subject event?

A. Yes, it will make it easier for me to explain what happened.

Q. Will this exhibit **clarify** the issues for the jury (or trier of fact)?

A. Yes, it will **simplify** things for the jury (or trier of fact).

Q. (Addressing the court) I ask that plaintiff's Exhibit 1 be admitted.
COURT: Any objections?[11]
OPPOSING ATTORNEY: None.
COURT: Very well, it will be received.

§40.300 Skeletal Foundation–Use for Demonstrative Purposes Only

Briefly consider the boldfaced questions in the preceding foundation. An effective opposition will probably be aimed toward them.

Assuming that the evidence is not unduly cumulative or unduly prejudicial, an escape hatch may exist for the proponent, as above indicated, even if a formal admissibility foundation fails:

Q. (Addressing the court) I ask that plaintiff's Exhibit 1 be admitted.
COURT: Any objections?
OPPOSING ATTORNEY: Yes, the exhibit is inaccurate.

Q. (Addressing the court) Since the exhibit will aid the witness' explanation and will clarify matters for the jury, I ask that the court permit me to use the exhibit for demonstrative purposes only, with the clear understanding that no one is claiming that it is accurate.
COURT: I'll permit such limited use. The jury is instructed that plaintiff's Exhibit 1 is being used solely as a tool to enable the plaintiff to better explain her case. The exhibit, in and of itself, does not constitute evidence.

---

10 The particular standard will vary depending upon the medium; see the chapters that follow for more detailed requirements.

11 The best phrase to guarantee admissibility is: "Your Honor, several months ago I offered to permit opposing counsel to inspect the exhibit and inform me of any objections; we received none."

§40.400 Summary of Key Buzzwords

FOR PROPONENT:

The exhibit will simplify and clarify the issues.
The exhibit will assist a witness'testimony.
The exhibit was offered to the opponent for inspection long ago.

FOR OPPONENT:

The exhibit will confuse and mislead the jury.
The exhibit is cumulative, etc. (See items on Opposition Checklist, below.)

§40.500 Checklist: Opposition

Each form of demonstrative evidence that we consider in the following chapters has its own matrix of vulnerabilities. Here is a brief list of "generic objections" that pertain to various forms of demonstrative evidence:

OBJECTIONS TO DEMONSTRATIVE EVIDENCE

1. The evidence will confuse or mislead the jury.
2. The evidence is unduly prejudicial.
3. The evidence is cumbersome and time consuming.
4. The evidence is cumulative.
5. The evidence is inaccurate.
6. The evidence is unreliable.
7. The evidence is intentionally misleading.
8. The evidence is toxic or dangerous.
9. No proper foundation has been laid for the evidence.
10. The evidence reflects or presents hearsay.
11. The evidence is inflammatory.
12. The evidence incorporates inadmissible hearsay.
13. The evidence is predicated upon unestablished facts.

In conjunction with the above items, always keep in mind the shopping list of objections provided by Rule 403 of the Federal Rules of Evidence. In particular, any evidence, including demonstrative evidence and exhibits may be excluded if the probative value is substantially outweighed by the danger of unfair prejudice, confusion of the issues, or misleading the jury, or by considerations of undue delay, waste of time, or needless presentation of cumulative evidence.[12]

As a general proposition, the court has wide discretion when it comes to admitting or rejecting demonstrative evidence.[13] On appeal, the court's decision in that regard will not be disturbed unless there is a clear showing of abuse.[14]

§40.600 New Forms of Demonstrative Evidence

One of the most fascinating aspects of demonstrative evidence is its ever-increasing

12 See *Tritek Technologies, Inc. v. U.S.*, 67 Fed.Cl. 727 (2005).

13 *Bachman v. General Motors Corp.*, 267 Ill.Dec. 125, 776 N.E.2d 262 (2002).

Rogers v. Raymark Industries, Inc., 922 F.2d 1426 (9th Cir. 1991); *Tripp v. Anderson,* 1 Conn. App. 433, 472 A.2d 804 (1984). *Hernandez v. Schittek,* 305 Ill.App.3d 925, 713 N.E.2d 203, 238 Ill.Dec. 957 (1999); *Constans v. Choctaw Transport,* 712 So.2d 885 (La.Ct.App. 1997).

14 *Piatz v. Austin Mutual Insurance Co.,* 646 N.W.2d 681 (N.D., 2002). The determination of whether or not a particular exhibit should be excluded for lack of foundation is primarily within the sound discretion of the trial court; the exercise of that discretion will not be disturbed on appeal unless it shown that it affected the substantial rights of the parties.

Butz v. Werner, 438 N.W.2d 509 (N.D. 1989); *DeRosa v. Kolb,* 90 Or. App. 548, 752 P.2d 1282 (1988); *Goff v. Continental Oil Co.,* 678 F.2d 593 (5th Cir. 1982).

variety and scope. As soon as a new device satisfies the challenges of the scientific community, it then seems to meet its toughest challenges in the courtroom.

Historically, we might re-examine what once purported to be the ultimate demonstrative device; known as the *Systolic Blood Pressure Deception Test*, it claimed to show a veritable picture of "truths" and "lies." We now call it a "lie detector" or "polygraph," and know that, much to the disappointment of many, it was deemed to be quite unreliable and speculative. The case that pulled the plug on the device became known and feared throughout the land for the stringent rule that it laid down for all new scientific evidence. *People v. Frye*,[15] was the author of the so-called "general acceptance" standard, a difficult foundation requirement, to say the least.[16]

In any event, the Frye standard has been significantly expanded in the federal sphere, and can be expected to do as much among the states. This is due to the new landmark—*Daubert v. Merrell Dow Pharmaceuticals, Inc.* set down by the United States Supreme Court.[17] In accordance with *Daubert*, whether the "new science" involves voice prints, MRI, DNA matching, or thermography, or anything else that mankind can devise, the test used to determine its admissibility involves the following elements:

1. Whether or not the subject theory or technique can be and has been tested
2. Whether the theory or technique has been subjected to peer review and publication
3. The known or potential rate of error, and
4. The "general acceptance" of the theory or technique[18]

Those who consider computer generated evidence (in any form) as some new "form of evidence" requiring the application of one of the above tests, are egregiously wrong. Judges frequently err in that regard because they fail to thoroughly understand the nature of the software involved.[19]

15 54 App.D.C. 46, 293 F. 1013 (1923).

16 See §11.601.

17 113 S. Ct. 2786, 125 L. Ed. 2d 469 (1993). See also *Kumho Tire Co., Ltd., et al. v. Carmichael et al.*, ____ U.S. ____, No. 97-1709 (March 23, 1999).

18 See generally, §11.600.

19 See Brain, Robert D. and Daniel Broderick, *Demonstrative Evidence in the Twenty-First Century,* from "Winning - Trial Practice in the 21st Century" (John C. Tredennick, Jr., Editor), at 377, published by The Section of Law Practice Management of the American Bar Association.

Chapter 41

Models

§41.100 Introduction

There are many types, shapes, and forms of models that have been used as demonstrative exhibits; anatomical, architectural, chemical, electrical, geographical, and mechanical are a few. Models can be dynamic or static, solid or dismantled, scaled or distorted. Regardless of their type or construction, models, like other demonstrative exhibits, are governed by the general principles set forth in Chapter 40.

The decision of whether or not to admit a model is within the trial court's discretion, as is the case with other forms of demonstrative evidence.[1] "Clarification" and "simplification" are the key considerations.

§41.200 Foundation Requirements

The specific term of art used to insure that the model will serve the basic admissibility requirements is "Substantial Similarity." It might help to think of this standard as the "Substantial Similarity Test." It is the key foundation element for models.[2]

The model does not have to be mathematically perfect in every respect to be admissible, as long as inaccuracies are not misleading and are pointed out.[3] But where the differences between the model and the thing that it purports to represent are major or might tend to confuse the jury, admissibility will be denied.[4]

The proponent should remember that even if the model should fail the substantial similarity test, it may, nevertheless, be used for demonstrative purposes only, as long as it will not confuse or mislead the jury.[5] The best way to assure your ability to use the model would be to write a certified letter (return receipt requested) inviting the opposing attorney to inspect the model and advise about any objections or inaccuracies. That letter should be written as soon as the model is complete, i.e., well in advance of trial.

§41.201 Sample Foundation for Models

Q. (By Proponent's Attorney) State your name for the record.

A. (Plaintiff) Monty Modeler.

---

1 The trial court did not abuse its discretion when it refused to permit an injured motorist to use the model of a spine during the testimony of that motorist's doctor in *Haggerty v. Foster,* 838 So.2d 948 (Miss.App. 2002). Nor did a different trial court abuse its discretion in *State v. Farhood,* 844 So.2d 217 (La.App., 2003), when it *did* permit the victim in an attempted murder trial to use a doll during her testimony to demonstrate what happened to her on the day in question, even though the prosecution had planned in advance for this presentation. See generally Chapter 40; see also *Martindale v. City of Mountain View*, 208 Cal. App. 2d 109, 25 Cal.Rptr. 148 (1962).

2 To be admissible, the model must be substantially similar to the thing that it represents. *Detroit Marine Engineering, Inc. v. Maloy*, 419 So. 2d 687 (Fla. 1982); *Ferguson v. Chrysler Corporation*, 292 So.2d 791 (La. 1974).

3 *Martinez v. W.R. Grace Co.*, 782 P.2d 827 (Colo. 1989); *Dawson v. Mazda Motors of America*, 517 So.2d 283 (La. 1987); *Arkansas State Highway Commission v. Rhodes*, 401 S.W.2d 558 (Ark. 1966); *Finch v. W.R. Roach Co.*, 295 Mich. 589, 295 N.W. 324 (1940). *Preston ex rel. Preston v. Simmons,* 254 Ill.Dec. 647, 747 N.E.2d 1059, 321 Ill.App.3d 789 (2001). In medical malpractice action resulting from arm injuries that child suffered from shoulder dystocia during birth, skeletal model was admissible (in conjunction with physician's expert testimony) to demonstrate effect that pushing one leg of mother had on rotation of pelvic bone. Any distinctions between model and actual human female skeleton went to weight not admissibility and could be addressed during cross-examination. Key to using model for demonstrative purposes requires that medical expert testify that model accurately depicts movements in female's pelvis.

4 *Detroit Marine Engineering, Inc. v. Maloy*, 419 So. 2d 687 (Fla. 1982).

5 See *Hoffman v. Niagra Machine & Tool Works Co.*, 683 F.Supp. 489 (E.D. Pa. 1988).

Q. Please state your degrees and qualifications.
A. (The witness should provide such detailed information as degrees, seminars, certifications, experience, and licenses) I am an engineer specializing in...
Q. I call your attention to Exhibit 1 positioned to your right, and ask if you prepared (or directed the preparation of) it?
A. Yes, I prepared it myself but with assistants.
Q. Would you please briefly describe your preparation of the exhibit?
A. Yes... (Generally, the witness' preparation, or direction thereof, should be based upon facts established by eyewitnesses or other competent evidence.)
Q. Is it substantially similar to that which it purports to represent?
A. Yes, except for... (The witness should point out discrepancies and inaccuracies.)
Q. Will this exhibit assist your explanation of the subject event?
A. Yes, it will make it easier for me to explain what happened.
Q. Will this exhibit clarify the issues for the jury?
A. Yes, it will help the jury see what I am trying to explain.
Q. (Addressing the court) I ask that plaintiff's Exhibit 1 be admitted.
COURT: Any objections?
OPPOSING ATTORNEY: None.
COURT: Very well, it will be received.

§41.300 Use for Demonstrative Purposes Only

Q. (Addressing the court) Since the exhibit will aid the witness' explanation and will clarify matters for the jury, I ask that the court permit me to use the exhibit for demonstrative purposes only, with the clear understanding that no one is claiming that it is accurate.

Models and objects can be used to demonstrate an endless variety of propositions or points; indeed, it seems as if there are as many different "points" to be made as there are objects in the world.[6] And, with all due respect to the "substantial similarity" test (and other attempts to lay down some standard of admissibility), I have yet to see any two models receive the same precise foundation requirements for admissibility or use. It seems as if the courts follow an unspoken "common sense" test—Does the model fairly and accurately present a valid message or point (or does it mislead)? This sounds similar to the foundation elements required for a demonstrative photograph.

§41.400 Opposition

Opposition Checklist items 4, 5, 6, and 7[7] are potential candidates for spearheading an attack on a model. The opponent should always be prepared to attack accuracy, particularly where moveable parts are involved.[8]

6 *People v. Cook,* 216 Ill.Dec. 239, 665 N.E.2d 299 (1995), involved prosecution auto theft, where a steering column was permitted as a demonstrative aid to help an officer explain how such a column is "peeled." In *People v. Cummings*, 18 Cal. Rptr.2d 796, 850 P.2d 1 (1993), it was not error for the court to permit a mannequin to be used at a murder trial to demonstrate the paths of six bullets fired into the body of the victim. Nor was it improper in *Brady v. State*, 540 N.E.2d 59 (Ind. Ct. App. 1989) for the court to permit the use of anatomically correct dolls to assist a conviction for child abuse.

7 See Chapter 40.

8 See *Burriss v. Texaco Incorporated*, 361 F.2d 169 (4th Cir. 1966).

(This page intentionally left blank.)

Chapter 42

Maps, Charts, Graphs and Diagrams

§42.100 Introduction

Maps, charts, graphs and diagrams can all be very useful vehicles for clarifying a complex maze of events or complicated testimony. They are among the most basic and inexpensive presentations. But just because they tend to be simple and easy to produce does **not** mean that they are any less effective. The courts seem to favor such exhibits, recognizing their power to simplify and clarify issues:[1]

> It is a well established rule, applied in every day practice in courts, that maps, drawings, and diagrams illustrating the scenes of a transaction and the relative location of objects, if shown to be reasonably accurate and correct, are admissible in evidence, in order to enable the court or jury to understand and apply the established facts to the particular case.

Neither proponents nor opponents should lose sight of the distinction between exhibits that are inaccurate and those that are misleading. There is a significant and material distinction. A rough (inaccurate) map, drawn hurriedly during the presentation of testimony, for example, may be far off the mark by Rand McNally's standards; but, if its only purpose is to show some rough locations, the exhibit would not be misleading. No juror would likely mistake the intentions of the proponent with respect to distances. On the other hand, where boulevard size was significant in an auto negligence case, a Rand McNally map might be misleading, if offered to illustrate anything other than distances.[2]

§42.200 Maps

Maps are unique among our group of low budget items; generally, they are not created specifically for the purposes of litigation. Maps present a common frame of reference, recognizable to nearly everyone. They are particularly helpful in litigation involving natural disasters and boundary disputes, in addition to automobile, train, plane or water craft collisions. The major categories of maps are:

1. Those created by the U.S. Department of Agriculture.
2. Maps made by private companies.
3. Aerial photographs.
4. Hand drawn maps.

Maps created by the U.S. Department of Agriculture might be considered as something more than demonstrative exhibits; upon the laying of a proper foundation, they constitute official documents and may, therefore, be admitted for that reason.[3] Maps produced by governmental agencies or subdivisions are generally classified as official documents and, as such, are simple to authenticate.[4] This is particularly true if the map happens to qualify as an ancient document. [5]

---

1 29 Am. Jur. 2d, Evidence §802. See also *Gavoni v. Dobbs House, Inc.,* 164 F.3d 1071 (7th Cir. Ill 1999), a personal injury action (arising from an elevator accident), wherein a chart identifying gravitational forces for everyday human activity was admissible, even though the testifying expert only provided testimony for a portion of the information represented by the chart. With respect to admissibility of demonstrative evidence in general, also see *Preston ex rel. Preston v. Simmons,* 254 Ill.Dec. 647, 747 N.E.2d 1059, 321 Ill.App.3d 789 (2001).

2 Lines on maps vary in thickness and color to reflect the width of the streets. An older map might not reflect recent expansions or widening and may, therefore, be misleading, although otherwise accurate.

3 Official maps would come within the self-authentication provisions of Fed. R. Evid. 902(5).

4 *State ex rel. Columbia Reserve Ltd. v. Lorain County Bd. of Elections*, 855 N.E.2d 815, 111 Ohio St.3d 167 (2006). In an action for a writ of prohibition to prevent a county elections board from placing a referendum issue on the ballot, that county auditor's map was properly admitted. Even though the map was not self-authenticated, it was nevertheless authenticated by an affidavit executed by an appropriate party's attorney.

5 See *Buchheit v. Gillis*, 541 S.E.2d 441, 246 Ga.App. 838 (2000).

A map produced by a private company should be admissible if it can be verified by a witness with personal knowledge of its accuracy.[6] The witness does not have to be the map's preparer, but he or she must have had an opportunity to determine whether or not the map is correct.[7] However, an unauthenticated map may be admitted for a limited purpose with the proper instructions.[8] Caution must always be exercised with respect to any extraneous writing on a map which may be considered inadmissible hearsay.[9]

The aerial photograph is a cross between a map and photo. They should be authenticated by the person who actually took the photos.

Hand-drawn maps, despite their lack of accuracy, can be effective for demonstrative purposes. The offeror of such evidence would not, of course, pretend that such a map is accurate or drawn to precise scale.

§42.201 Sample Foundation for Maps

Q. (By Proponent's Attorney) State your name for the record.

A. (Witness) Mapp V. Ohio.

Q. For whom are you employed?

A. I am currently employed by Plaintiff Company.

[Ask that Exhibit 1 be marked, then place it in a position where it can be viewed by the witness, the judge and opposing counsel.]

Q. Can you identify Exhibit 1?

A. It is a map of the United States.

Q. Do you know who produced the map?

A. It's a U.S. Geological Survey map; there is an identifying mark in the lower left corner of the map.

[For unofficial maps, the witness will identify the map's producer and state whether or not the map was created for purposes of the litigation.]

Q. When was the map created?

A. The map is dated February 19, 1928.

[The proponent will want to point out that the map's creation predated the subject event.]

Q. Since its creation, are there any changes, deletions or additions that you are aware of?

A. No.

Q. Will this exhibit assist your explanation of the subject event?

A. Yes, it will make it easier for me to explain what happened.

Q. Will this exhibit clarify the issues for the jury?

A. Yes, it will.

Q. (Addressing the court) I ask that plaintiff's Exhibit 1 be admitted.

COURT: Any objections?

OPPOSING ATTORNEY: None.

COURT: Very well, it will be received.

---

6 *Albig v. Municipal Authority of Westmoreland County*, 348 Pa. Super. 505, 502 A.2d 658 (1985); *Sam Raine Construction Co, Inc. v. Lakeview Estates*, 407 So. 2d 542 (Ala. 1981); *Fountain v. MARTA*, 147 Ga. App. 465, 249 S.E.2d 296 (1978); *Bunting v. McConnell*, 545 S.W.2d 30 (Tex. 1976); *Cutts v. Casey*, 278 N.C. 390, 180 S.E.2d 297 (1971); *Crawford v. City of Meridian*, 186 So. 2d 250 (Miss. 1966). See also *CBS Inc. v. PrimeTime 24 Joint Venture*, 9 F. Supp. 2d 1333 (Fla. 1998) permitting the use of a "Longley-Rice" map (which demonstrated which of the satellite carrier's subscribers could receive a Grade A or Grade B signal).

7 *Bagley v. City of Alma*, 178 Ga. App. 474, 343 S.E.2d 740 (1986). *Gallery v. City of New York*, 699 N.Y.S.2d 266 (1999) involved pedestrian who was injured as result of slip and fall at crosswalk pothole. Map depicting defect in crosswalk was submitted to New York City Dept. of Transportation (DOT) more than one year before pedestrian was injured. Nevertheless, map was admissible in pedestrian's action against City, even though newer map had been submitted to DOT three months before fall. Earlier map was offered to show that city had notice of defect from date that it was submitted; map would thus rebut contention by City that it should not have been charged with negligence because it was inundated with street and sidewalk defects that needed repair.

8 *Id.*

9 *Chakos v. Illinois State Toll Highway Auth.*, 169 Ill. App. 2d 1018, 524 N.E.2d 615 (1988).

§42.202 Checklist: Opposition

Checklist: Opposition

1. The map is inaccurate and misleading due to topological distortions.
2. The map is inaccurate and misleading due to selective deceptive deletions.
3. The map is inaccurate and misleading due to scale distortions.
4. The map is inaccurate and misleading because it is outdated.
5. The map is inaccurate and misleading due to omitted obstructions.
6. The map is inaccurate and misleading due to inaccurate measuring devices.

§42.300 Charts, Graphs and Diagrams

Unlike "official" maps, demonstrative charts, graphs and diagrams are usually prepared specifically for litigation, although some may be contained in pre-existing reports or business records. There are endless varieties of charts, graphs and diagrams, ranging from a simple, single-line chart drawn by a proponent, to a complex, professionally prepared illustration.

Charts and graphs are most effective when used to reduce economic, financial or statistical data to a single, visual image that the judge or jury can quickly and easily understand. Diagrams are generally used to depict scenes, paths taken by vehicles, and the position of witnesses. While charts and graphs tend to show data for a fixed time period, diagrams are normally used to assist the trier of fact in understanding about dynamic witness testimony.

Charts, graphs and diagrams must all reflect, or be supported by, statistical or numerical data presented via witnesses or other competent testimony.

It is generally both proper and legitimate for a party to introduce diagrams for the purpose of explaining and clarifying testimony.[10] During a prosecution for violations of RICO (The Racketeer Influenced and Corrupt Organizations Act), demonstrative charts were permitted to show the movement of money into and out of the Cayman Islands.[11] In a products liability action against a tire manufacturer, plaintiff's expert was permitted to use a time line chart to clarify the sequence of relevant events.[12] And, in a personal injury action, the defendant was permitted to use computer-drawn diagrams of an accident scene.[13]

§42.301 Foundations for Charts, Graphs and Diagrams

The admissibility of charts, graphs and diagrams into evidence lies within the trial court's discretion, and will not be disturbed absent a clear showing of abuse.[14] Such items should be

10 *Mayfield v. State*, 848 S.W.2d 816 (Tex. Ct. App. 1993).

11 *U.S. v. Bertoli*, 854 F. Supp. 975 (D.N.J. 1994).

12 *Uniroyal Goodrich Tire Co. v. Martinez*, 928 S.W.2d 64 (Tex. App. 1995).

13 *Ladeburg v. Ray*, 508 N.W.2d 694 (Iowa 1993).

14 *Kimble v. Earle*, 830 N.E.2d 814, 358 Ill.App.3d 400, 294 Ill.Dec. 402 (2005); *Torbit v. Ryder Sys., Inc.*, 416 F.3d 898 (2005); *Strong v. State*, 805 S.W.2d 478 (Tex. 1990); *Schenck v. Ebby Halliday Real Estate*, 803 S.W.2d 361 (Tex. 1990); *McAuliffe v. Cashio*, 508 So.2d 1028 (La. 1987); *Libby v. Hill*, 687 S.W.2d 264 (Mo. 1985); *Petrich v. Hansen*, 204 F.2d 261 (9th Cir. 1953).

admissible if they are shown to be reasonably accurate and correct.[15] A proper foundation must be laid, and the exhibits should explain the witness' testimony and should not mislead or prejudice the jury.[16] Such a foundation may not be based upon guesswork or missing data.[17]

A graphic exhibit need not be drawn with mathematical precision in order to be admissible,[18] but if there are sufficient inaccuracies in such an exhibit, it may be denied even limited admissibility.[19]

Charts, graphs and diagrams that summarize other materials or testimony, in order to be admitted into evidence, must fairly represent, and be taken from, underlying documentary evidence which is too voluminous for convenient in-court inspection. Furthermore, the exhibit must be accurate and non-prejudicial.[20] Keep in

15 Illustrations and drawings used for demonstrative purposes should abide by a similar standard. See *State v. Torres*, 121 P.3d 429 (Kansas, 2005). In a murder trial, a doctor's use of artistic renditions showing the effects of the shaken-baby syndrome was a permissible use of medical illustrations as demonstrative evidence, even though the illustrations were not specifically of the victim. The illustrations were fair and accurate representations of the human body, and because the doctor used the illustrations in conjunction with actual photographs of the victim's brain to show where injury occurred, those illustrations were useful to explain her medical testimony regarding the shaken baby and the shaken-impact syndromes. See also *Torbit v. Ryder Sys., Inc.*, 416 F.3d 898 (2005); *Flah's, Inc. v. Richard Rosette Elec.*, 155 A.D.2d 772, 547 N.Y.S.2d 935 (1989); *Joynt v. Barnes*, 71 Ill. App. 3d 187, 27 Ill. Dec. 249, 388 N.E.2d 1298 (1979); *Vergott v. Deseret Pharmaceutical Co., Inc.*, 463 F.2d 12 (5th Cir. 1972) applying Texas law; *Kroeger v. Safranek*, 161 Neb. 182, 72 N.W.2d 831 (1955); *Sanders v. Walden*, 214 Ark. 523, 217 S.W.2d 357 (1949).

16 *Hinlicky v. Dreyfuss*, 6 N.Y.3d 636, 848 N.E.2d 1285, 815 N.Y.S.2d 908 (2006). In a medical malpractice action against an anesthesiologist and others arising from a patient's death from a heart attack shortly after an operation to clear a carotid artery, clinical practice guidelines consisting of algorithms and tables published by a medical association and used by the anesthesiologist to evaluate the patient's preoperative need for cardiac evaluation, were admissible for the defense as non-hearsay demonstrative aids; the guidelines were offered to explain the decision-making process of the anesthesiologist, who had incorporated the guidelines into his practice and who also testified, without objection, about his own use of them; the materials were not used to establish a standard of care by themselves.

Kilmer v. Browning, 806 S.W.2d 75 (Mo. 1991); *Zagaroli v. Pollock*, 379 S.E.2d 653 (N.C. 1989); *Elam v. Alcolac, Inc.*, 765 S.W.2d 42 (Mo. 1988).

17 *Clark v. Cantrell,* 504 S.E.2d 605 (S.C. 1998). See, supra, Chapter 11.

18 *Marsh v. Washburn*, 11 Conn.App. 447, 528 A.2d 382 (1987); *Griffin v. Gregory*, 355 So.2d 691 (Ala. 1978); *Jones v. Consumers Coop. Propane Co.*, 186 Neb. 629, 185 N.W.2d 458 (1971); *Stegall v. Wilson*, 416 S.W.2d 658 (Mo. 1967); *Mickelson v. Forney*, 259 Iowa 91, 143 N.W.2d 390 (1966).

19 *Mancuso v. Compucolor*, 172 A.D.2d 153, 567 N.Y.S.2d 694 (1991); *Libby v. Hill*, 687 S.W.2d 264 (Mo. 1985); *Barmeyer v. Montana Power Co.*, 657 P.2d 594 (Mont. 1983); *Feldsberg v. Nitschke*, 49 N.Y.2d 636, 427 N.Y.S.2d 721, 404 N.E.2d 1293 (1980); *Hamment v. Thompson*, 115 Ga. App. 752, 156 S.E.2d 190 (1967); *Hernke v. Northern Ins. Co. of New York*, 20 Wis.2d 352, 122 N.W.2d 395 (1963).

20 *Henry v. City of Tallahassee,* 216 F.Supp.2d 1299 (Fla. 2002). A chart that contains undue editorializing, offered as an exhibit under the exception to the Best Evidence Rule governing summaries, should be stricken.

U.S. v. Scales, 594 F.2d 558, 561-63 (6th Cir.), *cert. denied*, 441 U.S. 946 (1979).

mind that a chart or diagram that is part of an official report or document may, itself, depending upon trustworthiness, achieve "official," status and thereby be admissible.[21] And, by the same token, a chart or diagram may be part of a writing or record kept in the ordinary course of a private business.[22]

§42.302 Sample Foundation for Charts, Graphs and Diagrams

Q. (By Proponent's Attorney) Please state your name for the record.
A. (Witness) My name is Gary Grafo.
Q. What is your occupation?
A. I am a private investigator.
[Ask that the diagram be marked as plaintiff's Exhibit 1.]
Q. I show you plaintiff's Exhibit 1 and ask if you can identify it.
A. Yes, it is a diagram representing a stretch of road known as Stratford in Oak Park, Michigan, between the intersections of Avon and Marlow.
Q. Did you draw the distances to scale?
A. Yes I did. The scale is: 1 inch equals 200 yards.
Q. Does this diagram accurately and fairly represent what it purports to represent?
A. Yes, it does.
Q. Will this exhibit assist your explanation of the subject event?
A. Yes, it will make it easier for me to explain what happened.
Q. Will this exhibit clarify the issues for the jury?
A. Yes, it will.

---

21 The converse is also true. See *Pirolo v. DeJesus*, 905 A.2d 1210, 97 Conn.App. 585 (2006). In an automobile negligence action, a diagram of the car accident attached to the responding officer's police report (that depicted how the vehicles collided) did not fall within the business records exception to the hearsay rule; the diagram was based entirely on what a motorist, driver, and other witnesses told the officer about the accident. Moreover, while police reports are normally admissible under the business records exception to the hearsay rule, witness statements contained within those reports do not fall within any exception. To be admissible under the business records exception to the hearsay rule, a police report must be based entirely upon the police officer's own observations or upon information provided by an observer with a business duty to transmit such information.

Beckett v. Monroe, 548 S.E.2d 131, 249 Ga.App. 615 (2001). In auto negligence action involving rear end collision, police diagram of accident was admissible where driver testified that it was accurate depiction of accident; nothing in diagram indicated it reflected personal opinions of officer. Moreover, diagrams are admissible into evidence if based on testimony indicating that they are substantially accurate representations of what witness is attempting to describe. *Roy v. Missouri Pacific Railroad Co.*, 43 S.W.3d 351 (Mo.App., 2001). Generally, diagram of accident scene is admissible under business records exception to hearsay rule provided that it was part of that trooper's official report of subject accident. However, any statements made by officer which were not part of his observations cannot be admitted into evidence under that hearsay exception. Business records exception does not allow maker of report to testify as to anything in report that would otherwise be inadmissible. See also *supra*, §21.401.

22 *Sepulveda v. Wal-Mart Stores, Inc.*, 237 F.R.D. 229 (2006). In a lawsuit alleging that an employer had violated provisions of the California Labor Code (by classifying assistant managers as exempt from requirements regarding overtime pay in addition to meal and rest breaks), an employer's summary charts of point-of-sale data reflecting the total time spent by assistant managers at the cash register and time spent completing customer transactions were admissible as business records.

Kimble v. Earle, 830 N.E.2d 814, 358 Ill.App.3d 400, 294 Ill.Dec. 402 (2005) involved a negligence action wherein a truck driver was severely injured when a 4,000 pound steel bar being loaded onto the trailer of his flatbed truck came loose and rolled over his legs, severely damaging his feet and ankles. A diagram that described the accident which was made by an employee at the request of his supervisor was deemed to have been made in the regular course of business at or near the time of the accident, and thus, qualified as a "business record" and was therefore admissible pursuant to the business records exception to the hearsay rule.

Q. (Addressing the court) I ask that plaintiff's Exhibit 1 be admitted.
COURT: Any objections?
OPPOSING ATTORNEY: None.
COURT: Very well, it will be received.

§42.303 Use for Demonstrative Purposes Only

Q. (By Proponent's Attorney, following the standard introductory questions) I show you plaintiff's proposed Exhibit 1 and ask if you can identify it.
A. It is a graph that I drew for purposes of this trial.
Q. Will this exhibit assist your explanation of the subject event?
A. Yes, it will make it easier for me to explain what happened.
Q. Will this exhibit clarify the issues for the jury?
A. Yes, it will.
Q. (Addressing the court) Since the exhibit will aid the witness' explanation and will clarify matters for the jury, I ask that the court permit me to use the exhibit for demonstrative purposes only, with the clear understanding that no one is claiming that it is accurate.

§42.400 Opposition

Refer to opposition checklist items 1 through 7.[23]

23 The comprehensive opposition checklist is set forth in Chapter 40.

(This page intentionally left blank.)

Chapter 43

Documents

§43.100 Introduction

Documentary evidence and demonstrative evidence should not be confused; each has its own set of foundation requirements, rules, and strategies. This chapter is directed to those limited instances where a document, or a portion thereof, is to be enlarged, highlighted, framed, summarized, or otherwise used to create separate demonstrative presentations.[1]

If certain written words or phrases are significant in a party's position, they should be highlighted so that their importance may be displayed for the jury. The main reasons for using demonstrative documentary evidence are to:

1. Emphasize and highlight key words or phrases;
2. Magnify text;
3. Summarize more voluminous underlying text; or
4. Compare different portions of text.

The trial court has broad discretion with respect to the admission of summaries,[2] particularly where the underlying documents are voluminous and complex.[3]

Demonstrative use of a portion of a document might be considered as a "permissible distortion" that is used to help jurors visualize a given segment of a writing. For that reason, the proponent should explain to the court and jury that the segregation is not intended to mislead or distort the document but, rather, to permit a closer inspection and analysis.

Documentary exhibits are rarely admitted for demonstrative purposes unless the underlying materials upon which they are based also happen to be admissible.[4] But even if the underlying documents are accepted, admission of derivative exhibits based on those documents is not automatic.[5]

After the underlying document gains admission into evidence, counsel may attempt to have the demonstrative exhibits formally admitted. Occasionally, the proponent may try to ignore the distinction between documentary and demonstrative exhibits and forget to do this, hoping that the judge and opposing counsel will treat the exhibits as if they were actually the previously admitted documents. But the proponent should see to it that the demonstrative exhibits are formally and separately admitted into evidence if he or she wishes to use those exhibits in closing arguments, or have them taken into the jury room for use during deliberations.

A judge well versed in the best evidence rule, the hearsay rule, and the distinctions that we have been discussing, might issue the following ruling with respect to a typical documentary blow-up or enlargement:

> Since the underlying documents have already been admitted, there is no need to readmit them. Moreover, since they are offered only for purposes of clarification, I will permit them to be used, but for demonstrative purposes only.

---

1 Summaries or charts used as pedagogical devices or illustrative aids which organize or aid the jury's examination of testimony or documents in evidence may "in appropriate cases" also be formally admitted into evidence. See *Minebea Co., Ltd. v. Papst*, 231 F.R.D. 1 (D.D.C., 2005), which discussed at length the distinction between formally admissible documentary evidence and summaries or writings used for "demonstrative or pedagogical" purposes. Documentary evidence is covered in Part II (Chapters 20 through 25).

2 *Gomez v. Great Lakes Steel Div., National Steel Corp.*, 803 F.2d 250 (6th Cir. 1986); *Coates v. Johnson & Johnson*, 756 F.2d 524 (7th Cir. 1985); *United States v. Meriwether*, 486 F.2d 498 (5th Cir.), *rehearing denied*, 487 F.2d 1401 (1973), *cert. denied*, 417 U.S. 948 (1974).

3 *Bennion v. Utah State Board of Oil, Gas & Mining*, 675 P.2d 1135 (Utah 1983); *Ford Motor Co. v. Auto Supply Co., Inc.*, 661 F.2d 1171 (8th Cir. 1981); *Zenith Radio Corp. v. Matsushita Electric Industrial Co. Ltd.*, 505 F.Supp. 1190 (E.D. Pa. 1980); see also "Summaries" in Chapter 22.

4 *United States v. Johnson*, 594 F.2d 1253, 1255 (9th Cir.), *cert. denied*, 444 U.S. 964 (1979).

5 *Ferguson v. Williams*, 399 S.E.2d 389 (N.C. 1991).

Opposing counsel may present a blow-up of any portion of the document not already contained in the exhibit.[6]

§43.200 Foundation Requirements

The ultimate purpose of all demonstrative evidence is the **simplification** and **clarification** of other evidence for the jury. Such is the case with blow-ups and other demonstrative documentary presentations.

The proponent must take care that the offered exhibit is not taken out of context. If the segregation of a portion of text would mislead or confuse the jury, then it can be excluded as easily as any other type of demonstrative evidence.[7] Confusion, the antithesis of simplification, is a term to be embraced by the opponent.

In summary, assuming that the underlying documents have already been admitted, our one-word foundation for a blow-up of any portion would be "clarification." A very powerful argument in support of the exhibit might include a quotation from the court's opinion in the case of *Rowell v. Fuller's Estate*,[8] where Judge Russell S. Taft answered the opposition to an enlargement by stating that:

> ... (the opponent) may as well object to the use of an eye-glass by one whose vision is defective.

One might note the age of this particular case. As suggested, demonstrative evidence has been an accepted component of our trial processes for some time.[9]

How would you respond to the judge's tough stance if you were opposing the enlargement? Here's a try, assuming, of course, that the above statement was mouthed by counsel, instead of the judge:

> I won't resist such evidence as long as opposing counsel can show me an eye-glass that selectively enlarges and distorts chosen views while ignoring others.

---

6 This ruling would reflect the principles set forth in "The Completeness Rule," Chapter 20.

7 This principle, which guards against evidence taken out of context should, of course, apply to all forms of demonstrative evidence. It is best enforced early, at the discovery level. See *Tai Tran v. New Rochelle Hospital Medical Center,* 756 N.Y.S.2d 509, 99 N.Y.2d 383, 786 N.E.2d 444 (2003). A party seeking disclosure of relevant items that include "films, photographs, video tapes or audio tapes ..." is entitled to see the "out takes" regardless of whether or not they will be used at trial.

Beech Aircraft Corp. v. Rainey, 488 U.S. 153, 109 S.Ct. 439, 102 L.Ed.2d 444 (1988).

8 10 A.853, 861, 59 Vt. 688 (Vt. 1887).

9 A detailed history of demonstrative evidence, in general, along with a mention of the above case can be found in *The Derivative Relevance of Demonstrative Evidence: Charting Its Proper Evidentiary Status*, Robert Brain & Daniel J. Broderick, 25 U.C. Davis Law Review 957 (Summer 1992).

(This page intentionally left blank.)

Chapter 44

Photographs, Slides, Films and Videos

§44.100 Introduction

We might paraphrase a cliché by stating that a picture can be worth a thousand dollars. However, in light of today's verdicts, that can be quite an understatement. Photographic evidence permits each juror to see for himself or herself what so many confusing words otherwise try to convey; perhaps, that is why it has long been a recognized means for increasing the size of jury verdicts. And, few will dispute that it presents a very powerful method for strengthening arguments and clarifying issues during the course of trial. Moreover, it remains one of the most potent weapons in the practitioners'arsenal of jury-convincing devices.[1]

Photographic evidence can assume a variety of shapes and forms, and it can be used for many different purposes. It may highlight a key point of the controversy or provide important background information. It is difficult to conceive a presentation that would not be augmented by photographic displays.

Films and videos generally have a greater number of uses than still photos or slides. For example, a candid surveillance video can show an allegedly injured person doing hard, physical labor. In contrast, a self-serving, "day-in-the-life" video may show a seriously injured plaintiff struggling through a daily routine. And, animated motion pictures may permit us to view the inner workings of a complex piece of machinery.

The term "photographic," as used in this chapter, applies to any medium that is capable of recording and storing visual images. The most common are, of course, photographs, slides, films, and videotapes; but, those media are by no means exclusive. Cameras can now record directly onto compact discs, and computer hard drives. Moreover, it would be foolish to pretend that we might predict the different forms that such evidence might assume in the future. Nor is there any need.

As we shall see in the section that follows, for evidentiary purposes, the physical characteristics of the particular photographic medium are not nearly as important as the elements surrounding the creation of the images, particularly motive and timing.

§44.200 Major Types of Photographic Evidence

If we mention of the word "photograph," or "film," many would quickly jump to the conclusion that we are referring exclusively to demonstrative evidence, thereby implying that only a "clarification" type of foundation would be required. But such a conclusion would be no more correct than assuming that all photographs and videos should be treated as documentary evidence (a blatant error committed by the drafters of Fed. R. Evid. 1001[2]).

All photos and videos are not alike. Their foundation requirements and opposition strategies differ radically. And, those differences do not depend upon their physical structure or make-up. Rather, the foundation requirements and strategies depend upon their "type." Of the four major types of evidence,[3] we can eliminate only testimonial. Then, we need to inquire as to the motive or purpose for which the photographic evidence was created. The time of its creation will further assist that inquiry.

First, focus on the event which is the subject of the litigation. Then ask, "Was the photographic evidence created after the occurrence of that event, specifically for use during the litigation?" If so, you can stop there; it's demonstrative. This chapter applies.

If the photo, video, or film was recorded or created simultaneously with the subject event, the evidence may be classified as an on-site recording, which would be considered real[4] Surveillance films, such as those set in liquor stores, banks, Burger Kings, and kinky highway rest

1 Mnookin, Jennifer L. *The Image of Truth: Photographic Evidence and the Power of Analogy.* 10 Yale J. L. & Human. 1 (1998).

2 See The Best Evidence Rule in Chapters 2 and 20.

3 Testimonial, Documentary, Real, and Demonstrative (See Foundation Chapter).

4 See Chapter 36.

stops, should be considered as real; so too are those "candid" amateur offerings that capture fires, quakes, presidential assassinations, police beatings, and weddings.[5]

If photographs or films are created, handled, or archived, along with accompanying documents, they may be classified as documentary.[6] For example, those photographs that accompanied the Warren Commission Report on the Assassination of President Kennedy should be considered as documentary.

§44.300 Photographs and Slides

Visual images provide an excellent way to illustrate or emphasize a particular point clearly during trial, regardless of whether the subject image relates to a static or dynamic scene.[7] Photographs and slides are, ordinarily, inexpensive, convenient to produce, and easy to authenticate.

Photographic evidence is widely accepted.[8] Generally, as long as a photograph is relevant[9]

5 See Chapter 36.

6 See Chapter 20.

7 *Zolber v. Winters,* 109 Idaho 824, 712 P.2d 525 (1985). Photographs and videotapes taken approximately five years after an automobile accident helped a reconstruction expert demonstrate the impact on the plaintiff's forward visibility of other vehicles in the oncoming lane of traffic. See also *Fahringer v. Rinehimer,* 283 Pa. Super. 93, 423 A.2d 731 (1980); *City of Louisville v. Yeager*, 489 S.W.2d 819 (Ky. 1973); *Anderson v. Lippes*, 18 Mich. App. 281, 170 N.W.2d 908 (1969); *Kooyumjian v. Stevens*, 10 Ill. App. 2d 378, 135 N.E.2d 146, 151 (1956).

8 *Horne v. Vassey,* 579 S.E.2d 924. Generally, photographs may be used to illustrate anything that a witness might otherwise completely describe in words.

9 *Muniz v. New York City Transit Authority*, 30 A.D.3d 388, 816 N.Y.S.2d 561 (2006) involved a personal injury lawsuit prompted by the plaintiff's trip and fall while descending subway stairs. Photographs of the allegedly defective subway step on which the plaintiff claimed to have fallen were insufficient to demonstrate that the transit authority had constructive notice of the defect, even though the plaintiff testified that the photos were taken 12 days after the accident and that they accurately depicted the condition as of the date of the accident; also, there was some reddish-colored material underneath the concrete surface in the area of the step where the subject piece of concrete was missing; and there was no expert or other competent proof that the rust, rather than some other substance, was underneath the concrete surface, nor was there any proof indicating that the condition predated the accident. Generally, photographs may be used to prove constructive notice of an alleged defect if they are taken reasonably close to the time of the accident and there is supporting testimony that the condition at time of the accident was substantially similar as shown in photographs.

A photo that *fails* to show something might be relevant. See *Perryman v. H & R Trucking, Inc.*, 135 Fed.Appx. 538 (2005). An auto negligence action wherein photographs demonstrating that the subject vehicles involved in the accident sustained little or no physical damage were relevant to a determination of the extent of the personal injuries that could likely result in the absence of damage to the vehicles. *State v. Torres*, 121 P.3d 429 (Kansas, 2005). In a murder trial, two photographs of the 21-month-old victim after death were relevant to prove the manner of death and to explain the applicable medical testimony. The first photograph showed the victim's full body clothed in a diaper laying on a white sheet prior to the autopsy as well as the brain-pressure monitor attached to the victim's head, endotracheal tube, gastric tube, needle-puncture marks, and various catheters. A second photograph was taken during the autopsy and showed the victim's scalp. The doctor explained that the second photograph showed a large area of hemorrhage under the scalp and on the bone, indicating a deeper injury than just a surface bruise. Moreover, the standard of review for the admission of photographs requires a determination of whether they are relevant and probative.

Rittenour v. Gibson, 656 N.W.2d 691 (N.D., 2003); *Citrus County v. McQuillin,* 840 So.2d 343 (Fla.App., 2003); *Mason v. Lynch,* 822 A.2d 1281, 151 Md.App. 17 (2003). See also Rule 402 of the Federal Rules of Evidence. *Romeo v. Jones,* 144 S.W.3d 324 (Mo. Ct. App., 2004). In an abuse of process lawsuit, the trial court's exclusion of 14 photographs depicting the condition of various portions of drywall inside a homeowners' house was not an abuse of discretion; the photographs were not relevant since the specific condition of the homeowners' house was not at issue.

and properly authenticated,[10] it should be admitted.[11] In fact, there is no legitimate reason to prohibit the admission of a blowup of a properly authenticated photograph,[12] or a photograph that was made from the still frame of a videotape.[13]

When photographic evidence is mentioned, we normally think of a device for clarifying images in the minds of the jurors; but in reality, photographs can be used to show or present a wide range of matters.[14] But there are limits;

10 *Rivera v. New York City Transit Authority*, 802 N.Y.S.2d 247 (NYAD, Dept. 2, 2005). In a slip and fall action resulting from injuries that occurred on steps leading down to a subway, the admission of photographs which allegedly depicted the defective condition of the subway steps at the time of the plaintiff's accident was reversible error absent any proof as to when the photographs were taken. The accident occurred nearly eight years prior to the trial, and since the mishap took place on a heavily-traveled subway stairway, it could not be assumed that the photos (which may have been taken years later) accurately depicted the condition of the steps at the time of the accident. See §44.301.

11 *Castro v. Cammerino*, 186 S.W.3d 671 (Tex.App, 2006). In a personal injury action predicated upon a bus driver's liability, photographs of the bus, the accident scene, and the pedestrian's crushed leg were all relevant with respect to the victim's physical pain and suffering. The bus driver contested both damages and liability during the course of the trial and took the position that the victim did not look properly before entering and while walking in the crosswalk. The photographs showed that the victim was in the crosswalk and it also demonstrated just how far she had entered into the intersection when she was struck and dragged by the bus; the photograph of the victim's injured leg showed the extent of her injuries. But see Opposition Checklist, §40.500.

12 *Fournier v. Erickson*, 242 F.Supp.2d 318 (S.D.N.Y., 2003). But see *Citrus County v. McQuillin,* 840 So.2d 343 (Fla.App., 2003).

13 *Hendry v. Zelaya,* 841 So.2d 572 (Fla.App., 2003).

14 In *Russell v. Ramirez,* 949 S.W.2d 480 (Tex. App., Houston 1997), old photographs of the decedent were relevant in a wrongful death action brought by the decedent's mother in order to demonstrate a close personal relationship between the decedent and his mother, and to support the mother's claims of mental anguish from the subject death. In *Davis v. State*, 698 So.2d 1182 (Fla. 1997), during the penalty phase of a capital murder case, a photopack photograph which showed the defendant with long hair and facial hair was admissible during cross-examination of the defendant's grandmother (photographs of the defendant as a young boy had been admitted during the direct examination of the grandmother, making the defendant's appearance relevant); the photograph was proper rebuttal to show that the defendant no longer looked the same. *Gorman v. Hunt,* 19 S.W. 662 (Ky. 2000) involved personal injury action by pedestrian who was struck by vehicle while crossing street. "Posed" photo was taken of model against backdrop of actual scene of accident. Defending driver objected to admission of photo arguing that it showed model pedestrian blindly walking into path of driver's vehicle with her head pointed straight ahead as if she were oblivious to vehicle and other traffic. Photo was nevertheless admissible because defense expert did not use it to offer his opinion as to direction that pedestrian was facing, but only to show pedestrian's position relative to vehicle at impact. This case well summarized requirements for admissibility: 1) photo should be properly authenticated (verified by testimony as fair and accurate portrayal of what it is supposed to represent); 2) photo must be relevant by having tendency to make existence of any fact that is of consequence to determination of action more probable or less probable than it would be without photo; 3) trial court must determine that photo's probative value is not substantially outweighed by danger of undue prejudice, confusion of issues or misleading jury, or needless presentation of cumulative evidence.

admissibility may be denied where a photograph is unnecessarily cumulative,[15] confusing, or misleading;[16] or used to create improper inferences,[17] or where its prejudicial impact outweighs its probative value.[18] And, of course,

15 *Graney v. Ryan*, 796 N.Y.S.2d 496 (N.Y.A.D., 4 Dept., 2005). In a medical malpractice action, the trial court did not abuse its discretion by refusing to admit certain photographs offered by the plaintiff where the court had already allowed plaintiff to introduce other photos and drawings of a similar nature to aid the jury in assessing the medical evidence and testimony. But see *Leventhal v. Forest Hills Gardens Corp.*, 764 N.Y.S.2d 125 (N.Y.A.D., 2d Dept., 2003). In a personal injury action, three photographs showing the accident site in detail were not cumulative of other photographs that provided a general overview of the area; they should have been admitted. The photographs may have allowed the jury to infer, based on the appearance of the subject defect, that the condition must have come into being over such a significant length of time, and, therefore, the defendant knew or reasonably should have known about it.

16 See Rule 403 of the Federal Rules of Evidence. See *Clark v. Ill. Cent. R.R.*, 872 So.2d 773 (Miss. Ct. App., 2004).

17 *Davis v. Maute*, 770 A.2d 36 (Del.Sup., 2001). In auto negligence action, photographs showing minimal damage plaintiff's car had sustained were inadmissible to support inference accident could not have caused serious personal injury to plaintiff, who claimed to have soft tissue damage to her back, neck, and ribs. Generally, admissibility of photographs turns on whether improper inferences substantially outweigh their probative value.

18 *Perryman v. H & R Trucking, Inc.*, 135 Fed.Appx. 538 (2005). In an auto negligence action, photographs demonstrating that the subject vehicles involved in the accident sustained little or no physical damage were not substantially outweighed by the danger of unfair prejudice. The minimal damage was relevant to a determination of the extent of the personal injuries that could likely result in the absence of physical damage to the vehicles. *McKinney v. Brandywine Court Condominium Council, Inc.*, 830 A.2d 411. (Del.Super., 2003).

Schindler Elevator Corp. v. Anderson, 78 S.W.3d 392. Relevant photographic evidence is generally admissible unless it is calculated to arouse the sympathy, prejudice, or passion of the jury, as opposed to illustrating disputed issues or otherwise assisting the jury in understanding the matters presented in the case.

Squibb v. Century Group, Inc., 824 S.2d 361 (La.App., 2002). In a personal injury action by a motorcyclist for injuries sustained in a collision with a dump truck, photographs that depicted the accident scene were relevant and admissible despite the fact that the motorcyclist was not in the photographs. In fact, he had been propelled away from the scene of the collision. Nor did the presence of a sheet-covered body in the photographs render them unduly prejudicial; the photographs were not gruesome.

Henderson v. Fields, 68 S.W.3d 455 (Mo.App., 2001). In a wrongful death action based on auto negligence, photographs of the decedent's severely crushed vehicle were probative and therefore admissible. Defendant attempted to exclude the photographs by conceding that the crash caused the death of the decedent, but to no avail. The photos were admissible. The case provided a nice mini-checklist of reasons why the probative value of the photograph would, in such cases, exceed its prejudicial effect. In particular, the photograph was relevant with respect to. The speed of the vehicles, the position of the vehicles, the force of impact, and the point of impact.

Aka v. Jefferson Hospital Associations, Inc., 42 S.W.3d 508, 344 Ark. 627 (2001), involved medical malpractice and wrongful death action brought by estates of mother and unborn viable fetus. Admission of autopsy photograph of mother would not have been unduly prejudicial; physician who had performed autopsy testified as expert witness about resident physicians' attempts to rupture mother's membrane. Photograph was capable of authentication and had been previously supplied to all parties. *Belmont Homes, Inc. v. Stewart,* 792 So.2d 229 (Miss. 2001). In personal injury action by motorist against mobile home manufacturer, videotapes and photographs of highway were relevant and admissible to identify tortfeasor as mobile home manufacturer that had transported hundreds of mobile homes down subject highway causing deep rut to form that, in turn, contributed to motorist's accident; purpose was not to show subsequent remedial measures taken by Department of Transportation. But see *Boscia v. Sharples*, 860 A.2d 674 (R.I., 2004). In an automobile negligence action that resulted from a rear-end collision, photographs were offered by the rear-ended driver (i.e., the plaintiff), which tended to show that the defendants' vehicle became wedged underneath the plaintiff's vehicle. The photos supported the plaintiff's theory that the defendants' vehicle struck the plaintiff's car in such a manner as to force him to raise his elbow to protect his face, thereby hitting the dashboard and causing the subject injuries to his shoulder. The trial court could not exclude the photos on the ground that they were "unduly prejudicial," because there was no basis in the record for such a characterization.

let's not forget relevance,[19] and the ever-present possibility that the evidence might fall within the scope of the work-product doctrine or some other privilege.[20]

A common problem in the "prejudicial" versus "probative" equation involves photographs that are particularly graphic or gruesome.[21] However, as with all photographic evidence, the decision whether or not to admit graphic or even

19 *Brenman v. Demello*, 892 A.2d 741, 383 N.J.Super. 521 (2006). In a rear-end collision personal injury action, photographs showing minimal damage to the injured motorist's vehicle following the collision could not be used to infer that the accident was not the cause of the motorist's injuries in the absence of expert proof correlating the severity of the impact with the likelihood of injury. Generally, to qualify as relevant, evidence must have a tendency to establish the proposition that it is offered to prove a fact in issue, to make a logical connection between the proffered evidence and a fact in issue, or to render the desired inference more probable than it would be without the evidence. Absent facts that are supported by competent expert testimony, counsel may not directly argue to the jury that there is a correlation between the extent of the damage to the vehicles involved in an accident and the cause of personal injuries alleged from that accident, and may not rely on photographs of the vehicles involved to indirectly accomplish the same result. Generally, photographic evidence is not inherently relevant, but only as to a particular matter properly provable in a case when it makes the existence of a fact in issue more or less probable. The proponent of photographic evidence bears the burden of demonstrating its relevancy.

Rittenour v. Gibson, 656 N.W.2d 691 (N.D., 2003), involved a personal injury action by a tenant's guest against a landlord. Photographs of the exterior of a rental home were relevant but photographs of the interior were not; the subject accident occurred at the outside entrance to the home. See also *Tadlock v. Taylor*, 857 So.2d 20 (La.App., 2003).

20 See, for example, *Commonwealth v. Hetzel*, 822 A.2d 747 (Pa.Super., 2003). In a murder trial, photographs and bite mark tracings from the defendant's arm taken by a forensic odontologist did not constitute confidential attorney-client communications and, therefore, did not fall within the scope of the attorney-client privilege.

21 *Kimble v. Earle*, 830 N.E.2d 814, 358 Ill.App.3d 400, 294 Ill.Dec. 402 (2005). Photographs of a truck driver's injuries, though gruesome, were relevant to the issue of his pain and suffering and how that driver sustained his injuries. *State v. Torres*, 121 P.3d 429 (Kansas, 2005). In a murder trial, two photographs of the 21-month-old victim after death were relevant to prove the manner of death and to explain the applicable medical testimony. The first photograph showed the victim's full body clothed in a diaper laying on a white sheet prior to the autopsy as well as the brain-pressure monitor attached to the victim's head, endotracheal tube, gastric tube, needle-puncture marks, and various catheters. A second photograph was taken during the autopsy and showed the victim's scalp. The doctor explained that the second photograph showed a large area of hemorrhage under the scalp and on the bone, indicating a deeper injury than just a surface bruise.

Citrus County v. McQuillin, 840 So.2d 343 (Fla.App., 2003). In a wrongful death action against Citrus County for creating a dangerous road condition, the trial court did not abuse its discretion by admitting a photograph of the decedent being placed in a body bag at the scene of her one-car collision. The photo was relevant to the estate's argument that the decedent was a passenger as opposed to a driver. The assertion that the photograph was unduly inflammatory was offset by the fact that the jury already knew about the devastating, violent accident wherein the decedent's body had to be cut out of the vehicle. The photograph was not enlarged, nor did it exaggerate the decedent's lethal injuries.

In re Detention of Isbell, 268 Ill.Dec. 71, 777 N.E.2d 994 (2002). In a commitment proceeding, photographs of child sexual assault victims were admissible to establish the youth of the victims at the time of the assault; they were neither inflammatory nor prejudicial. See also *Squibb v. Century Group, Inc.*, 824 S.2d 361 (La.App., 2002).

See also *Estate of Iwanski v. Ray*, 44 Fed.Appx. 370 (10th Cir., Oklahoma, 2002). In a lawsuit brought pursuant to 42 U.S.C.A. §1983, alleging that prison officials violated a prisoner's 8th Amendment rights, the district court did not abuse its discretion by refusing to admit autopsy photographs of the prisoner to show the nature of his injuries and the dangerousness of the metal pipe that was used.

gruesome photographs lies within the discretion of the district court.[22]

With the advent of the relatively inexpensive camcorder, videos are, likewise, becoming less costly, easier to produce, and consequently, more common in the courtroom. It might be noted, even as we speak of photographs, that a motion picture or videotape is, generally, more effective than a photograph or slide when it comes to leaving a lasting and vivid impression on the jury.[23]

The cases cited in the footnotes are reflective of the courts' general attitude with respect to the admissibility of photographic evidence. In particular, it is more likely than not that a given photo will be admitted. But admissibility should never be taken for granted; there are several methods of attack.[24]

---

22 *Castro v. Cammerino*, 186 S.W.3d 671 (Tex.App, 2006). Generally, photographs that are merely calculated to arouse the sympathy, prejudice, or passion of the jury and do not serve to illustrate disputed issues or to aid the jury in its understanding of the case should not be admitted into evidence. Rather, to be admissible, photographs must illustrate disputed fact issues and must portray facts that are relevant to a material issue. The fact that photographs are gruesome does not render them inadmissible.

Mathes v. Sher Express, L.L.C., 200 S.W.3d 97 (Mo.App., 2006). In a products liability wrongful death lawsuit against a vehicle manufacturer, the probative value of a photograph showing the interior of a pickup truck cab at the scene of the traffic accident, which included the burned bodies of the deceased occupants, was not improperly cumulative and was not substantially outweighed by the danger of unfair prejudice. Moreover, the trial court has the discretion to decide the cumulative value of evidence, and to decide when the cumulative presentation of evidence should cease.

Kimble v. Earle, 830 N.E.2d 814, 358 Ill.App.3d 400, 294 Ill.Dec. 402 (2005). The admissibility of photographs normally rests within the sound discretion of the court. If a photograph has sufficient probative value, it should be admitted in spite of the fact that it may be gruesome or inflammatory. Moreover, gruesomeness alone is not enough to warrant the exclusion of photographs. See *Colon v. BIC USA, Inc.*, 199 F.Supp.2d 53 (S.D.N.Y., 2001).

23 *Lopez v. Foremost Paving,* 796 S.W.2d 473 (Tex. 1990). Because a videotape makes a more lasting impression on jurors than other forms of evidence, more caution is required in admitting videotapes into evidence.

24 See §44.600.

§44.301 Foundation Requirements

The decision of whether or not to admit visual evidence is within the sound and relatively broad discretion of the trial court.[25] And, a lower court's decision will rarely be disturbed on appeal; however, it may, nevertheless, be reversed if the court has abused that discretion.[26] It is not always necessary to have the photographer or laboratory technician authenticate a photograph or slide. If the authenticating witness has personal knowledge of the scene or image represented in the photo, then he or she need only tes-

25 *Tunica County v. Matthews*, 926 So.2d 209 (Miss., 2006). The admissibility of photographs is within the sound discretion of the trial court, and the trial judge has a wide latitude in admitting them.

Rittenour v. Gibson, 656 N.W.2d 691 (N.D., 2003); *Horne v. Vassey,* 579 S.E.2d 924; *People ex rel. Sherman v. Cryns*, 261 Ill.Dec. 655, 763 N.E.2d 904, 327 Ill.App.3d 753 (2002). The decision whether or not to admit a videotape into evidence is solely within the trial judge's discretion, and will not be reversed absent an abuse of that discretion.

Henderson v. Fields, 68 S.W.3d 455 (Mo.App., 2001). The admission or exclusion of photographic evidence rests within the discretion of the trial court, and the court's decision will not be disturbed absent an abuse of that discretion. And, an abuse of discretion will not be found unless the trial court's decision is clearly against the logic of the circumstances and involves a lack of careful and deliberate consideration.

Rose v. Jaques, 597 S.E.2d 64 (2004); *Segrets, Inc. v. Gillman Knitwear Co., Inc.*, 207 F.3d 56 (1st Cir. Mass., 2000); *ACTONet, Ltd. v. Allou Health & Beauty Care,* 219 F.3d 836 (8th Cir. Neb., 2000); *Gorman v. Hunt*, 19 S.W. 662 (Ky. 2000); *Merrill v. Sugarloaf Mountain Corp.*, 745 A.2d 378 (Maine 2000); *McFadden v. Winters and Merchant, Inc.,* 603 N.W.2d 31, 8 Neb.App. 870 (1999); *Cleveland v. Bryant,* 512 S.E.2d 360, 236 Ga.App. 459 (1999); *James v. Beauregard Elec. Co-op., Inc.*, 736 So.2d 353 (La.App. 1999); *Rawson v. Midsouth Rail Corp.,* 738 So.2d 280 (Miss.App. 1999); *Nelson v. McClintock,* 703 N.E.2d 829, 123 Ohio App.3d 139 (1997); *Aiello v. Southeastern Pennsylvania Transp. Authority,* 687 A.2d 399, reargument denied (Pa.Cmwlth. 1996); *Jordan v. Abernathy*, 845 S.W.2d 86 (Mo.App.E.D. 1993); *Nguyen v. Pausina*, 607 So.2d 675 (La. App. 4 Cir. 1992); *Washburn v. Beatt Equipment Co.,* 840 P.2d 860, 120 Wash.2d 246 (1992); *Kallgren v. Chadwick,* 589 A.2d 120 (N.H. 1991); *State Highway Dept. v. Snyder,* 570 N.E.2d 947 (Ind. 1991); *Miller v. Monongahela Power Co.*, 403 S.E.2d 406 (W.Va. 1991); *Hall v. Burns,* 213 Conn. 446, 569 A.2d 10 (1990); *Olympia Spa v. Johnson,* 547 So.2d 80 (Ala. 1989); *DiBuono v. A. Barletta & Sons*, 127 Pa.Commw. 1, 560 A.2d 893 (1989); *Berman v. Radnor Rolls,* 542 A.2d 525 (Pa. 1988); *Hale v. Firestone Tire & Rubber Co.,* 756 F.2d 1322 (8th Cir. 1985).

26 *Ferro v. Griffiths,* 836 N.E.2d 925, 297 Ill.Dec. 194 (2005); *Redfearn v. Huntcliff Homes Association, Inc.*, 579 S.E.2d 37, 260 Ga.App. 150 (2003); *Danbury v. Jackson County,* 990 S.W.2d 160 (Mo.App. 1999); *Allstate Ins. Co. v. Kidwell,* 746 So.2d 1129 (Fla.App. 1999); *Slaubaugh v. Slaubaugh,* 466 N.W.2d 573 (N.D. 1991); *Glusaskas v. Hutchinson,* 148 A.D.2d 203, 544 N.Y.S.2d 323 (1989); *Haddad v. Kuriger,* 437 S.W.2d 524 (Ky. 1968); *Reed v. Shelly,* 378 S.W.2d 291 (Mo. 1964); *Trammell v. Matthews,* 86 Ga.App. 661, 72 S.E.2d 132 (1952). In personal injury action arising out of low impact rear end collision, it was erroneous for court to exclude photographs and testimony pertaining to collision and lack of damage to vehicle; both were relevant as to whether or not accident caused plaintiff's alleged knee injury and, thus, should have been admitted. Note that neither MRI scan nor treating physician's notes indicated any traumatic injury to knee. See also *ACTONet, Ltd. v. Allou Health & Beauty Care,* 219 F.3d 836 (8th Cir. Neb., 2000).

tify that the photo fairly and accurately represents what it purports to represent.[27] But the photographer should be produced if there is any doubt as to whether the photograph technically provides a fair and accurate representation of the scene or image depicted.[28]

A lapse of time between the subject occurrence and the shooting will not, per se, render the evidence inadmissible.[29] But if material

27 *Cubeta v. York Intern. Corp.*, 30 A.D.3d 557, 818 N.Y.S.2d 136 (2006). In order to lay a proper foundation for a photograph, a competent witness with knowledge of the matter may identify the subject of the photograph and confirm that it accurately represents the subject matter depicted.

Barkett v. Gomez, 908 So.2d 1084 (Fla.App., 2005). In a negligence action brought by a pedestrian against a driver, who struck the pedestrian while he was delivering pizza flyers to vehicles in an intersection, a photograph of the driver's vehicle was not admissible because that driver was not able to testify as to whether or not the vehicle had been repaired in any way before the photograph was taken. Compare *Ferro v. Griffiths,* 836 N.E.2d 925, 297 Ill.Dec. 194 (2005). In a rear-end automobile negligence action, the trial court did not abuse its discretion when it admitted into evidence photographs of damage to a van (the struck vehicle), even though such an admission was without supporting expert testimony showing a correlation between the lack of damage to the vehicles and the injury to the van's passenger. The action (against the driver of the vehicle that rear-ended the van) was commenced by a passenger in the van who was being transported from a hospital following heart surgery. The passenger testified that the impact to the van was heavy and caused his body to hit an oxygen tank, and the physician who saw the passenger at the hospital shortly after the accident testified that the passenger did not have any additional bruising to his chest after the accident. Moreover, when the trial court makes a decision whether to admit photographs from a motor vehicle accident in a personal injury action, the court must determine whether the nature of the damage to the vehicles and the injury to the plaintiff are such that a lay person can readily assess their relationship, if any, without expert interpretation.

Platt v. Interstate Dodge, 843 So.2d 1178 (La. App., 2003). In an action by a car owner against a dealership, photos of the interior damage to the automobile, resulting from a leaking sunroof (after a dealership employee had disassembled and then reinstalled the gasket), were admissible. The owner's testimony established that the photographs were accurately taken and constituted a correct representation of the matter in controversy.

Kartychak v. Consolidated Edison of New York, 758 N.Y.S.2d 644 (1st Dept., 2003). In a personal injury action, photographs of a re-created work site where the plaintiff had fallen were admissible where three witnesses testified that the photographs fairly and accurately depicted the scene.

As long as this condition is satisfied, it doesn't matter if the photograph isn't perfect or that it might have been more "on target." See *APAC-Mississippi, Inc. v. Goodman,* 803 So.2d 1177 (Miss., 2002). In a personal injury action by a truck driver against a contractor resulting from a slip-and-fall accident, a photograph of the job site on the morning of the accident was both relevant and admissible despite arguments by the driver that the photo failed to show the specific spot where he fell.

On the other hand, a lack of personal knowledge on the part of the photographer can be fatal in the absence of testimony identifying the appropriate scene or "target." See *Kelly v. Housing Authority of New Orleans,* 826 So.2d 571 (La.App., 2002).

Nabisco v. Warner-Lambert Co., 32 F.Supp.2d 690 (S.D.N.Y.,1999); *Gibbs v. Abiose*, 508 S.E.2d 690, 235 Ga.App. 214 (1998); *Henson By and Through Lincoln v. Board of Education of Washington School District,* 948 S.W.2d 202 (Mo.App. E.D. 1997); *Tri-State Asphalt Prods. v. McDonough Co.*, 391 S.E.2d 907 (W.Va. 1990); *Allemand v. Zip's Trucking Co.*, 552 So.2d 1023 (La. 1989); *D.C. Transit Syst., Inc., v. Acors,* 293 A.2d 871 (D.C. 1972); *Toftoy v. Ocean Shores Properties,* 71 Wash.2d 833, 431 P.2d 212 (1967); *State v. Eilers,* 406 S.W.2d 567 (Mo. 1966); *Semet v. Andorra Nurseries,* 421 Pa. 484, 219 A.2d 357 (1966); *Miller v. Quaife,* 391 S.W.2d 682 (Ky. 1965); *Fox v. Martens,* 132 Colo. 208, 286 P.2d 628 (1955).

28 *Saks v. Yeshiva of Spring Valley, Inc.*, 684 N.Y.S.2d 560 (1999); *Vollert v. Wisconsin Rapids,* 27 Wis.2d 171, 133 N.W.2d 786 (1965); *Consolidated Furniture Co. v. Kelly,* 369 S.W.2d 53 (Tex., 1963).

29 *Davenport v. Albertson's, Inc.*, 774 So.2d 340 (La.App., 2000); *Rawson v. Midsouth Rail Corp.*, 738 So.2d 280 (Miss.App. 1999); *Ansani v. Cascade Mountain, Inc.*, 588 N.W.2d 321, 223 Wis.2d 39 (1998). In premises liability action against merchant, affidavits of witnesses who had seen toys and other objects in toy aisle since date of customer's fall, on same day of week, and at approximate time of fall, and photographs of toys laying in aisle, were admissible as relevant to issue of whether or not store had constructive notice that toy truck was on floor prior to customer's accident, even though evidence was collected 14 months after customer's accident.

changes have occurred, the evidence may be excluded.[30] On the other hand, if the changes are adequately explained and not unduly prejudicial, the changes should effect the weight not the admissibility of the evidence.[31] In some

30 *McKinney v. Brandywine Court Condominium Council, Inc.*, 830 A.2d 411 (Del.Super., 2003). In a pedestrian's slip and fall action against a condominium council, photographs depicting stairs at the accident's location five weeks after the incident and depicting the stairs at that location over three years after that incident were inadmissable. Any probative value that the photographs might have had was substantially outweighed by the risk of prejudice, as well as misleading jury. The photographs did not show the conditions at the time that the incident occurred.

DeGiacomo v. Westchester County Healthcare Corp., 743 N.Y.S.2d 548 (N.Y.A.D., 2002). In a premises liability action, photographs may be used to prove constructive notice of an alleged defect shown in the photographs provided that the photographs are taken reasonably close to the time of the subject accident. But there must be foundation testimony to establish that the condition at the time of the accident was similar to the condition shown in the photographs.

Saks v. Yeshiva of Spring Valley, Inc., 684 N.Y.S.2d 560 (1999); *Leahy v. McCain,* 732 A.2d 619 (Pa.Super. 1999); *Nelson v. McClintock,* 703 N.E.2d 829, 123 Ohio App.3d 139 (1998); *A-Cal Copiers, Inc. v. North American Van Lines, Inc.*, 180 F.R.D. 183 (Mass. 1998); *Satterly v. Louisiana Indemnification Company,* 704 So.2d 882 (La. App.,1997); *McFadden v. Winters and Merchant, Inc.*, 603 N.W.2d 31, 8 Neb.App. 870 (1999) involved injury that arose when trailer was rear ended by plaintiff's car. Photos of different trailer, offered by trailer owner, were irrelevant and thus inadmissible as demonstrative evidence; photographed trailer was parked southbound while trailer involved in accident was northbound; photographed trailer was shiny while one that was rear-ended was dirty, and there were other lighting discrepancies. Moreover, demonstrative exhibits are admissible if they supplement other oral testimony, clarify some issue in case, and are more probative than prejudicial. *Whiting v. Bella Vista Development Corp.*, 699 N.Y.S.2d 552 (1999). Photographs taken of loading dock area by delivery driver eight months after he twisted his ankle while exiting his truck were inadmissible in his personal injury action against landlord and tenant of building; it appears that affidavit of fellow deliveryman offered to authenticate photographs noted that area of disrepair in pavement, as depicted in photo, was larger than it had been at time of accident. *Saldana v. Michael Weinig, Inc.*, 766 A.2d 304. 337 N.J.Super. 35 (2001). Authentication of photograph requires verification by qualified individual who has made personal observations, thereby establishing that conditions depicted in photo existed at time of accident; in alternative, witness providing authentication should testify that depicted scene has not changed since time of incident in question. *Wilkinson v. Swafford,* 811 N.E.2d 374 (Ind. Ct. App., 2004) involved an automobile negligence action. Photographs that did not depict the injured motorist's vehicle in the condition that it was in immediately after the automobile accident were not relevant evidence. The photos showed the vehicle with its hood raised and with certain portions of the vehicle removed for repair purposes. Moreover, the admission of photographs into evidence is left to the sound discretion of the trial court, and the reviewing court will not reverse that decision except for an abuse of that discretion. This particular photograph was properly deemed to be irrelevant.

31 *Koch v. Mac Queen,* 746 N.Y.S.2d 229 (2002). In a landlord-tenant battle involving the condition of the premises, photographs taken by the tenants were admissible despite the fact that they were taken before the period for which rent was sought; the tenant testified that the photos showed the conditions of the apartment as they continued to exist during the relevant periods.

Ditto v. Stoneberger, 805 A.2d 1148, 145 Md.App. 469 (2002) involved a wrongful death action on behalf of a bystander who was watching the demolition of a building; a metal pipe fell off the roof of the building, striking and killing the bystander. The trial court did not abuse its discretion by allowing into evidence a photograph of the intersection adjacent to the demolition site, even though the photograph was taken a day or so after the accident, did not show the barricades, and did not show the "No Trespassing" signs. Nevertheless, during the course of the foundation, testimony was presented covering the missing items and explaining the changes.

instances, a limiting instruction by the court may be warranted.[32]

The recommended method for admitting a photograph is that which involves the least fanfare. The proponent should have the photograph marked for identification, hand it to the witness, ask a few preliminary questions (identifying the people and places), and then merely inquire "does this photograph, marked as _____'s Exhibit ___ fairly and accurately represent what it purports to represent?" After the document is shown to opposing counsel, the proponent should move for admission. If there is no objection, the more extensive foundation (infra) should not be needed.

REFERENCES

Admissibility of writings, recordings, or photographs. 50 A.L.R. Fed. 319.

§44.302 Sample Foundations for Slides and Photographs

(PROFESSIONAL PHOTOGRAPHER WITNESS)

Q. (By Proponent's Attorney) State your name for the record.

A. (Witness) Pee Wee Flasher.

Q. Please state your qualifications.

A. (The witness should provide such detailed information as experience, certifications, licenses and education.) I am a freelance professional photographer specializing in...

Q. Did you have occasion to become familiar with an accident that took place on Interstate 696 on April 15, (year)?

A. Yes, I did.

Q. What do you remember about that particular date and accident?

A. I was called out to I-696 by the City of Southfield to investigate a series of rear-end collisions and to shoot some photos.

Q. I call your attention to plaintiff's Exhibit 1 and ask if you can identify it.

A. Yes, it is one of the photos I took. It has my initials on the back.

[The proponent gives the photograph to opposing counsel, and then hands the photo back to the witness for identification. The witness examines it as he or she is being questioned; the examination avoids the appearance that the testimony was rehearsed.]

Q. Did you take this photograph?

A. Yes, I did.

Q. To the best of your recollection, does plaintiff's Exhibit 1 fairly and accurately represent the scene of the collision, on the date in question?

A. Yes, it does.

Q. (Addressing the court) I ask that plaintiff's Exhibit 1 be admitted.

COURT: Any objections?

OPPOSING ATTORNEY: None.

COURT: Very well, it will be received.

For most photographs, anyone who is familiar with the depicted scene can serve as a qualifying witness:

(Non-photographer Witness)

Q. (By Proponent's Attorney) State your name for the record.

A. (Witness) Larry Looker.

Q. Where were you on April 15, (year), at approximately noon?

A. I was on Eastbound I-696, driving to Detroit.

Q. Did you observe anything unusual at that time?

A. I came upon an accident scene.

---

32 *Green v. St. Francis Hospital, Inc.*, 791 A.2d 731 (Del.Supr. 2002) involved a medical negligence action against a hospital by a patient left unattended sitting on a bedside commode, just out of reach of the call button; the patient apparently fell while attempting to reach the bed. Photographs and videotapes of the patient's hospital room showing the call button to be within his reach were admissible for the purpose of showing the layout of the patient's room. The trial judge, however, properly gave limiting instructions that the jury was not to draw conclusions based upon the location of the call button as it appeared in the photograph and videotape since the location was disputed.

Q. I now show you plaintiff's Exhibit 1 and ask if you can identify it.

A. Yes, it looks like a photograph of the freeway.

[The proponent shows the photograph to opposing counsel, and then gives the photo back to the witness for identification. The witness examines it while being questioned.]

Q. To the best of your recollection, does this photograph fairly and accurately represent the accident scene as you remember it?

A. Yes, it does.

Q. (Addressing the court) I ask that plaintiff's Exhibit 1 be admitted.

COURT: Any objections?

OPPOSING ATTORNEY: None.

COURT: Very well, it will be received.

Notice from the preceding dialogue that it was not necessary for the qualifying witness to be a professional photographer; nor was it even necessary for him to have taken the photo.

§44.400 Films and Videotapes

With respect to films and videos, an individual with personal knowledge must establish that the images fairly and substantially represent what they purport to represent.[33] The witness should provide some testimony to show that the camera operator did not tamper with the film or videotape to the extent that the images fail to objectively portray the depicted scene.

Videos can be used to reconstruct an event,[34] such as a driver's view of an intersection prior to an auto accident. And, of course, a video may show an actual event, such as the Rodney King beating.[35]

Above all, a film or video made after a material event that purports to reconstruct that event, must pass the substantial similarity test, i.e., the place, object, or action depicted in the film or tape must be substantially similar, in

33 *United States Fidelity and Guar. Co. v. Hi-Tower Concrete Pumping Serf.,* 574 So.2d 424 (La. 1991); *Continental Concrete Pipe Corp. v. Century Rd. Builders,* 195 Ill. App.3d 1, 552 N.E.2d 1032 (1990); *Hodosh v. Ford Motor Co.,* 477 A.2d 77 (R.I. 1984); *Howard v. Stoughton,* 199 Kan. 787, 433 P.2d 567 (1967); *Kortz v. Guardian Life Ins. Co. of Am.,* 144 F.2d 676 (10th Cir. 1944).

34 The task might prove difficult, however, particularly if the subject of the reconstruction fails to consent. See *Czarnecki v. Welch*, 803 N.Y.S.2d 817 (N.Y.A.D. 1 Dept., 2005). The Trial court did not abuse its discretion when it denied the plaintiff's motion for an order directing a dog owner (in a dog bite case) to comply with the plaintiff's discovery demand that the dog be videotaped during a re-creation of events surrounding the biting incident so that it might be used for evaluation by animal expert

35 Where a videotape captures the very event which is the subject of the litigation, the resulting footage crosses the line from demonstrative evidence into the realm of real evidence. The notorious Zapruder film of the Kennedy assassination provides a classic example of such a crossover; see Chapter 36.

appearance and condition, to the actual place, object, or events involved in the action.[36] As is the case with all photographic evidence, any discrepancies or differences must be adequately

36 *White v. Consolidated Edison*, 33 A.D.3d 514, 822 N.Y.S.2d 533 (2006). In a personal injury action by a motorcyclist against a utility company to recover for injuries sustained when his motorcycle lost traction as an alleged result of pebbles or gravel in the street near the company's excavation site, a videotape depicting the motorcyclist on the day of the accident slowly riding a motorcycle at an event for motorcycle enthusiasts (at which time some of the participants were performing dangerous stunts) was admissible because it was relevant to the motorcyclist's credibility; there had been eyewitness testimony that the motorcyclist himself performed potentially dangerous stunts and that the subject accident occurred as he was performing such a stunt.

Black v. U-Haul Co. of Missouri, 204 S.W.3d 260 (Mo.App., 2006). In a wrongful death action brought against a truck rental company by the family of a passenger who was killed in a rental truck accident, a videotape of driving tests conducted by a rental company employee (which was offered to illustrate how a truck identical to the one in the accident would handle if a supporting nut was loose on the truck's front spindle) was admissible in evidence, even though the truck in the videotape may not have been driven at the same speed as the truck in the accident; the videotape was not offered to illustrate or recreate the specific events of the accident. Generally, videotape evidence may be admitted for two purposes: (1) to re-create events at issue in litigation; and (2) to illustrate physical properties or scientific principles that form the foundation for an expert's opinion. When a video submitted as evidence attempts to re-create an original event, the essential conditions must be substantially similar to those existing at the time of the event, but when the video is merely offered to illustrate the principles used in forming an opinion, the conditions need not be substantially similar.

Anderson v. American Limestone Co., Inc., 168 S.W.3d 757 (Tenn.Ct.App., 2005). In an action by a landowner for nuisance and trespass against the operators of a rock quarry and asphalt plant, the trial court acted within its discretion by excluding portions of the landowner's proposed videotapes on the grounds that the oral commentary on the videotape was more prejudicial than probative and that the perspective rendered by camera's zoom lens made the alleged nuisance from the rock quarry and asphalt plant appear closer to the landowner's property than it actually was. Moreover, a videotape is subject to the same scrutiny as a photograph in determining its admissibility. It must be relevant and not unfairly prejudicial and must be a true and accurate depiction of the events that it recorded. *Castille v. Wal-Mart Stores, Inc.,* 815 So.2d 973 (La.App. 2002). In a worker's personal action against a homeowner, a videotaped demonstration purporting to show a stove hood filter being set on fire had no probative value and was therefore inadmissible. The method of igniting the filter as portrayed on the videotape was unlike the method actually used to ignite the filter at the time when the worker was injured in the kitchen fire.

Stecyk v. Bell Helicopter Textron, Inc., 295 F.3d 408 (2002) involved a lawsuit brought against a military aircraft manufacturer by the relatives of victims of a crash. The defense introduced videotaped tests supporting a conclusion that a seal on the aircraft did not leak. The relatives asserted that the tests were too dissimilar because they lacked the normal vibration and centrifugal forces that the seal would normally experience during flight. The court, nevertheless, did not abuse its discretion by admitting the videotape since the only evidence pertaining to the issue of substantial similarity was introduced by the defendant; moreover, the relatives were provided with an adequate opportunity for cross-examination.

Kerrigan v. Maxon Ind., 223 F.Supp. 626 (E.D. Pa., 2002) involved a products liability action by a truck driver against the manufacturer and installer of a cement mixing bowl. A videotape showing a comparison between the actual agitator that was used and a related exemplar was admissible. The designs were similar enough to establish an appropriate foundation.

Loevsky v. Carter, 773 P.2d 1120 (Hawaii 1989). *Suanez v. Egeland*, 749 A.2d 372, 330 N.J.Super. 190 (2000) involved personal injury action arising from low speed rear end collision. Defendant sought to introduce videotape depicting crash-test dummy in automobile being struck at five miles per hour. Defendant, however, failed to show that videotape was accurate reproduction of that which it purported to demonstrate. He thereby failed to authenticate videotape for admission during expert's testimony during trial on issue of damages. Also, defendant provided little to explain circumstances surrounding videotape's creation; there were many differences between test depicted on video and actual accident. In addition, extreme slow motion of video was capable of influencing jury. Showing videotape was prejudicial error. To make matters worse, videotape was not provided to plaintiff during course of discovery; plaintiff saw videotape for first time on day of trial, nor was jury instructed as to videotape's limited purpose. *Tillis*

(Footnote 36 continued on page 44-14.)

explained.[37] As a general proposition, visual evidence should be no less admissible than testimonial evidence, provided that a proper foundation is laid and the evidence is relevant and

---

36 (Continued from page 44-13.) *Trucking Co., Inc. v. Moses,* 748 So.2d 874 (Ala. 1999) involved wrongful death action arising from collision between decedent's car and truck. Videotaped animation of accident prepared and presented by animation expert was admissible despite contention that expert was not properly qualified and that his animation was based on facts not in evidence. In fact, expert had participated in survey of accident site, had viewed photographs and videotapes made by police officers who inspected accident scene, and had talked with plaintiffs' experts with respect to accident reconstruction; in addition, animation was based on evidence and admissible opinions of plaintiffs' experts. Note that animated reconstruction was not inadmissible on ground that it showed one of truck's headlights and two of side lights as not burning. Those lights were not working after collision, and there was no evidence that lights were rendered inoperable due to damage sustained in collision. *Wilson v. Bradlees of New England Inc.*, 250 F.3d 10 (1st Cir., N.H., 2001). In product liability action pertaining to injuries resulting from flammable sweatshirt, videotapes containing flammability demonstrations, which were prepared by plaintiff's experts, were properly excluded because they purported to illustrate scientific principles, as opposed to re-enacting accident. Content of videotapes was not sufficiently close to actual circumstances of accident to avoid risk of confusion on part of jury. *Alice Leasing Corp. v. Castillo*, 53 S.W.3d 433 (Tex.App., 2001). In a survivor's negligence action against trucking company, videotape of simulated accident was admissible when it was used by experts during testimony to discuss whether or not safety screen would have prevented trucker's death. Defendant did not dispute expert's qualifications and expert testified that videotape represented fair demonstration of effectiveness of safety device. In particular, demonstration illustrated that safety screens, similar to types that had been installed by similar tracks would have prevented block assembly fragment from reaching driver. Witness also testified that demonstration matched speed which propelled block toward safety screen on date of accident. In addition, there was vigorous cross-examination of witnesses who provided opinions. But see *Grose v. Nissan North America, Inc.*, 50 S.W.3d 825 (Mo.App., 2001) holding that, generally, videotapes are admissible for two purposes: (1) To re-create events that are at issue in litigation, and (2) to illustrate physical properties or scientific principles that average layperson would find difficult to understand and which forms foundation for expert's opinion. When videotape is offered merely to illustrate principles used in forming expert's opinion, there is no requirement that conditions portrayed in video be substantially similar to those in accident.

37 *Broadbent v. Allison,* 626 S.E.2d 758 (N.C.App., 2006). In a landowners' lawsuit against a county for a private nuisance relating to the operation of an airport, the exclusion of a videotape showing airplanes flying over the landowners' property (based on the claim that the video allegedly failed to accurately present the subject events) was not warranted. The videotape condensed, into a period of six minutes, airplane fly-overs covering a several-month period; the jury, however, was told that the videos were edited from many hours of tape and had been recorded over a period of several months, and the videotape was time-stamped so that the jury could see exactly when each segment was recorded. Even if the shooting location of the footage was unclear and even if it was unclear whether the zoom lens was used, the jury was made aware that some of the footage was filmed in zoom mode, and there was testimony indicating the approximate altitudes of the planes as they took off or landed over landowners' property. Generally, in order to admit videotape evidence, three questions must be affirmatively answered: (1) whether the camera and taping system in question were properly maintained and were properly operating when the tape was made; (2) whether the videotape accurately presents the events depicted; and (3) whether there is an unbroken chain of custody.

Rosario v. City of Union City Police Dep't, 131 Fed.Appx. 785 (3rd Cir., N.J., 2005). A videotape was admissible in a wrongful death action arising from the death of an arrestee in order to establish the "ambiance" and set the scene at which the arrestee collapsed from an asthma attack despite the claim that the tape was of poor quality, depicted only part of the scene, was not taken in real time, and was never properly authenticated.

Daniel v. Indiana Mills & Mfg., Inc., 103 S.W.3d 302 (Mo.App., 2003). In a products liability action against a seatbelt manufacturer, videotapes pertaining to the disengagement of side-release seatbelts were admissible during cross-examination to rebut testimony from plaintiff's expert (who claimed that a prior study showed that inertial release was not a safety concern). The evidence was properly admissible even though the conditions involved in the videotapes and crash tests were different from those that actually occurred. Nevertheless, there was no claim

(Footnote 37 continued on page 44-15.)

material.[38] But like testimonial evidence, potential hearsay problems may be hiding in the wings.[39] This is particularly the case with respect to so-called instructional videotapes.[40]

---

37 (Continued from page 44-14.) that the rebuttal evidence was offered as a re-enactment of the driver's accident, nor was it represented that the proposed evidence explained how the seatbelt unlatched. Also, the defendant was able to show dissimilarities between the videotapes and the crash tests through additional cross-examination. Generally, videotapes may be admitted to: (1) recreate events at issue in the litigation or (2) illustrate physical or scientific principles that the average layperson would find difficult to understand and which form the basis for an expert's opinion.

Horn v. Hefner, 115 S.W.3d 255 (Tex.App., 2003) involved an action against a roofing company arising from a two-vehicle collision that occurred as the company's employee backed the company truck from a private driveway onto a street. A video of an out-of-court experiment performed by the roofing company was admissible even though there were differences with respect to the video and related testimony; most of the differences were, however, explained during the examination and cross-examination of the company's expert. Moreover, when an experiment is conducted out of court, in the absence of opposing counsel, there must be a substantial similarity between the conditions depicted on the video and the actual event that is the subject of litigation; however, the conditions do not need to be identical.

38 *People ex rel Sherman v. Cryns*, 271 Ill.Dec. 881, 786 N.E.2d 139, 203 Ill.2d 264 (2003). A videotape may be admitted as demonstrative evidence when it is properly authenticated and is deemed relevant to a particular issue in the case. In addition, a videotape will be considered as relevant only as long as its probative value is not substantially outweighed by the danger of unfair prejudice. To admit a videotape into evidence, a foundation must be laid by someone having personal knowledge of the filmed object, who is able to testify that the film is an accurate portrayal of what it purports to show. This verification may be furnished by the testimony of any competent witness who has sufficient knowledge to so testify.

Novosyolova v. Stephens, 850 So.2d 29 (La.App., 2003). In an action for damages brought by the widow of a pedestrian who had been struck and killed by a deputy sheriff's vehicle, a videotape of the accident scene was admissible.

Schindler Elevator Corp. v Anderson, 78 S.W.3d 392 (Tex.App., 2001). In an injury action against an escalator contractor that arose when a minor's foot became entrapped, an audio-muted videotape of a television news program was relevant to show the use of side-step safety plates on escalators, particularly since the defending contractor had suggested that such plates cause the steps to crash and lock up. Moreover, the videotape was not unduly prejudicial and it was admitted to explain safety precautions that could have been taken to avoid such accidents.

Los Angeles News Service v. CBS Broadcasting, Inc., 305 P.3d 924 (9th Cir. California, 2002). In a copyright infringement action, a videotape obtained by the copyright owner from a local television station, which allegedly contained a slate identifying the defendant's news service as the source of the owner's copyrighted footage, was adequately authenticated. Moreover, the slate itself was prima facie evidence of its own authenticity.

Smith v. Baker's Feed & Grain, 213 Ill. App. 3d 950, 157 Ill. Dec. 361, 572 N.E.2d 430 (1991); *Miller v. Monongahela Power Co.*, 403 S.E.2d 406 (W.Va. 1991); Burlington N.R.R. v. Whitt, 575 So.2d 1011 (Ala. 1990), *cert. denied*, 111 S. Ct. 1415, 113 L. Ed. 2d 468 (1991); *Nachtsheim v. Beech Aircraft Corp.*, 847 F.2d 1261 (7th Cir. 1988); *Bailey v. Valtec Hydraulics*, 748 S.W.2d 805 (Mo. 1988). See also *Saratoga Spa & Bath Inc. v. Beeche Systems Corp.*, 656 N.Y.S.2d 87 (N.Y.A.D. 3 Dept 1997), involving a breach of contract action by a seller of "hoppers." Hoppers kept inside the purchaser's plant, along with photographs and measurements of hoppers at the seller's facility, were held not admissible; the evidence was either not in substantially the same condition as when the alleged problem occurred or it did not constitute an accurate and fair representation.

39 For issues involving videotaped statements, see *Harris v. Morrow,* 63 P.3d 581, 186 Or.App. 29 (2003); *Hill v. Hill*, 634 N.W.2d 811, 10 Neb.App. 570 (2001); *Hawkins vs. Pathology Associates of Greenville, P.A.,* 498 S.E.2d 395 (S.C. App. 1998). Videotaped seminar on fibromyalgia was inadmissible when offered by wife in divorce action to show how her medical condition would affect her future employability. Videotape may fall within learned treatise exception to hearsay rule, but only if sufficient foundation is laid.

40 *Kmart Corporation v. Lee,* 789 So.2d 103 (Miss.App. 2001). In slip and fall action by customer against Kmart, videotape showing procedure used for implanting morphine pump in patient was relevant to assist jury's understanding of procedures endured as result of accident; and, thus, court did not err in admitting videotape into evidence. Moreover, videotapes or photographs should be only be excluded when primary purpose is to inflame jury.

In any event, the decision whether or not to admit demonstrative or real evidence is generally within the sound discretion of the trial court.[41]

This standard of discretion applies to films and videotapes in much the same manner as it does to photographs.[42]

§44.401 Sample Foundation for Videotapes or Films[43]

Q. (By Proponent's Attorney) State your name for the record.
A. (Witness) Sam Sinema.
Q. Please state your degrees and qualifications.
A. (The witness should provide such detailed information as degrees, seminars, experience and licenses). I am a private investigator.
Q. Before today, were you made aware of the subject accident that occurred on April 15, 19...?
A. Yes, you hired me to conduct an investigation of the accident and the accident scene... and to make a videotape of the area.
Q. I call your attention to plaintiff's Exhibit 1 and ask if you prepared (or directed the preparation of) it.
A. Yes, I prepared it myself. It has my initials on the label.
Q. Would you please describe, briefly, your preparation of the exhibit?
A. Yes... (Generally, the witness' preparation, or direction thereof, should be based upon facts established by eyewitnesses or other competent evidence.)
Q. Did you delete or cut any portion of the image or sound that you recorded?
A. No.
Q. Did you play back the images and sounds that you recorded immediately after creating the video?
A. Yes.
Q. Did you determine whether or not the video represented what you personally saw and heard at the scene on the date you made it?
A. Yes, I determined that the video accurately and fairly represented the scene that I personally viewed.
Q. Is it substantially similar to that which it purports to represent?
A. Yes, except for... (The witness should point out discrepancies or inaccuracies.)
Q. Will this exhibit assist your explanation of the subject event?
A. Yes, it will.
Q. Will this exhibit clarify the issues for the jury?
A. Yes, it will.
Q. (Addressing the court) I ask that plaintiff's Exhibit 1 be admitted.
COURT: Any objections?
OPPOSING ATTORNEY: None.
COURT: Very well, it will be received.

---

41 *People ex rel Sherman v. Cryns,* 271 Ill.Dec. 881, 786 N.E.2d 139, 203 Ill.2d 264 (2003). The admission of a videotape into evidence lies within the sound discretion of the circuit court and will not be disturbed absent an abuse of that discretion.

See *Floyd v. General Motors Corp.*, 960 P.2d 763 (Kan. App. 1998); *McGee v. Jones*, 499 S.E.2d 398 (Ga. App. 1998); *Shoemaker v. Ekunno*, 960 S.W.2d 527 (Mo. App. 1998); *Constans v. Choctaw Transport, Inc.*, 712 So.2d 885 (La. App. 1997).

42 See also *Castille v. Wal-Mart Stores, Inc.,* 815 So.2d 973 (La.App. 2002).

Our Lady of the Lake Regional Medical Center v. Helms, 754 So.2d 1049 (La.App.1999). The determination of whether or not certain photographs or videotapes are admissible is largely within discretion of trial court.

43 See Chapman, "*America's Least Funny Home Videos: A Critique of the Kephart v. State Authentication Standard for Videotape Evidence,*" 3 Tex. Wesleyan L. Rev. 71 (1996).

§44.500 Day-in-the-Life Videos

The day-in-the-life video is a very controversial form of demonstrative evidence. It is designed to take the viewer into the home of a severely crippled plaintiff and follow him through a day of torment. The goal is to permit the jury to see how difficult it is for the plaintiff to perform those everyday tasks that we consider "simple" and take for granted.

The day-in-the-life video is one of the most difficult types of evidence to classify. It is demonstrative, because it is self-serving, and is designed exclusively for use during litigation. But an argument can also be made that it is real. In particular, since "damages" is a material element of personal injury litigation, one might argue that a candid video depicting the trials and tribulations (i.e., material events) of the plaintiff as they happen, would constitute an "on-site" recording. In truth, however, since the whole "show" is really an event staged for the purpose of litigation, it could hardly be considered as "candid." Therein lies the problem.

The day-in-the-life film is really a piece of demonstrative evidence that pretends to be real. But unlike the holder of real evidence, a maker of a day-in-the-life film will likely resist discovery.[44]

Generally, courts are inclined to admit the day-in-the-life film because of its relevance with respect to injuries and treatment.[45] On the other hand, if the film is too prejudicial, too effective,

44 For a battle-royal over the right of defense counsel to be present during the filming of a plaintiff's day-in-the-life film, see *Cisarik v. Palos Community Hospital,* 144 Ill. 2d 339, 579 N.E.2d 873 (1991).

45 *Wakefield v. Reliance National Indemnity Company,* 845 So.2d 1238 (La.App., 2003); *Conrad ex rel. Conrad v. Alderwood Manor,* 78 P.3d 177 (Wash.App. Div., 2003); *Wagner v. York Hospital*, 608 A.2d 496 (Pa. Super. Ct. 1992); *Hahn v. Tri-Line Farmers Coop*., 478 N.W.2d 515 (Minn. Ct. App. 1991); *Burke v. Rothschild's Liquor Mart,* 209 Ill. App.3 d 192, 154 Ill. Dec. 80, 568 N.E.2d 80 (1991); *Lehmuth v. Long Beach Unified School District*, 53 Cal. 2d 544, 348 P.2d 887 (1960); *Pisel v. Stamford Hospital,* 180 Conn. 314, 430 A.2d 1 (1980). *Ocasio v. AMTRAK*, 690 A.2d 682, 299 N.J. Super. 139 (1997) involved a personal injury action, where the trial court was justified in concluding that the probative value of a "day-in-the-life" videotape was not substantially outweighed by the risk of undue prejudice, confusion of the issues, or misleading the jury; the tape would assist the jury in resolving the contested issue of whether the plaintiff required care at a long-term care facility. Even though the parties' medical experts both testified concerning their observations of the plaintiff's current condition and the kind of care he required, the videotape was, nevertheless, the only means by which the jury itself could observe his present condition. *Precht v. Case Corp*., 756 So.2d 488 (La.App. 2000). With respect to videotapes of injured persons, determination of whether motion pictures or videotapes are admissible is largely within discretion of trial court. Such evidence must be approached with great caution because its shows only intervals of activities of subject; it does not show rest periods, and does not reflect whether or not subject is suffering pain during or after videotaped activity *Long v. Missouri Delta Medical Center,* 33 S.W.3d 629 (Mo.App., 2000). Issue to be decided in admitting or rejecting "day-in-the-life" videotape involves determination as to whether or not videotape is practical, instructive and calculated to assist jury in better understanding case.

too self-serving, or too cumulative, it runs the risk of exclusion.[46]

Here are the key buzzwords for the plaintiff: relevance, damages, clarification, practical, instructive and informative. And, for the opponent: undue prejudice, self-serving acting, cumulative nature of the evidence, minimal probative value, inflammatory sequences, inability to cross-examine.

§44.600 General Opposition to Photographic Evidence

Any of the generic objections from the Opposition Checklist in §40.500 (excluding items #8 and #10) may be used to oppose visual evidence.

The most likely reasons for barring visual evidence include technical considerations such as poor picture quality,[47] the gruesome nature of

---

46 *Howard v. Holyfield Construction, Inc.,* 839 So.2d 0277 (La.App., 2003). Evidence in the form of films or videotapes must be approached with great caution because they only show intervals of the activities of the subject; they do not show rest periods, and do not reflect whether the subject is suffering pain during or after the activity.

See also *Patterson v. Central Mills, Inc.,* 64 FedAppx. 457 (6th Cir., Ohio, 2003); *Ocasio v. AMTRAK,* 690 A.2d 682, 299 N.J.Super. 139 (1997); *Foster v. Crawford Shipping Co.*, 496 F.2d 788 (3rd Cir. 1974); *Bolstridge v. Central Me. Power Co.*, 621 F. Supp. 1202 (D. Me. 1985); *Eckman v. Moore,* 876 So.2d 975 (Miss., 2004) involved a wrongful death action commenced by a patient's widow against a doctor and hospital arising from the treatment of that patient for a head injury. While wedding pictures could have been admissible to show the patient as he was before his injury, the proper place for those pictures was not in a "day-in-the-life" video of the patient (the pictures had also been admitted in photographic form). Moreover, the admission of photographs and motion pictures is a matter for the sound discretion of the trial court, and that court is afforded wide latitude in exercising that discretion. Scenes from a "day-in-the-life" video, showing the patient's stepson, who was not a party to the lawsuit, at a graduation ceremony and ball game served no other purpose than to elicit sympathy from the jury and also were not relevant to a "day-in-the-life" of the patient. Therefore, scenes were required to be deleted from the video. Portions of the "day-in-the-life" video depicting the patient engaged in physical therapy, the patient being visited by his wife and newborn son, and the patient being washed, clothed, and fed by the staff were typical and admissible portions of the video.

A second "day-in-the-life" video was cumulative of the first video and contained highly prejudicial scenes, such as one in which the patient's mother was sobbing, "Momma loves you, Momma loves you." This video should have been excluded by the trial judge. The proper purpose of a "day-in-the-life" video is to show an actual "day-in-the-life" of the victim and not elicit sympathy from the jury.

47 *Walker v. Fairchild Industries*, 554 F.Supp. 650 (D. Nev. 1982); *Short v. Jones*, 613 P.2d 452 (Okla. 1980).

an image,[48] or a finding that a photograph or video is likely to confuse or mislead the jury.[49] A videotape or film, in particular, may be rejected on the ground of undue prejudice, or because "undue" or "unfair" prejudice outweighs its probative value.[50]

48 *Fahringer v. Rinehimer,* 283 Pa.Super. 93, 423 A.2d 731 (1980); *City of Louisville v. Yeager*, 489 S.W.2d 819 (Ky. 1973); *Schueler v. City of Madison*, 49 Wis.2d 695, 183 N.W.2d 116 (1971); *Anderson v. Lippes*, 18 Mich. App. 281, 170 N.W.2d 908 (1969); *Hulsebus v. Russian*, 118 Ill. App.2d 174, 254 N.E.2d 184 (1969); *Darling v. Charleston Community Memorial Hosp*., 50 Ill. App.2 d 253, 200 N.E.2d 149 (1964), *aff'd*, 33 Ill. 2d 326, 211 N.E.2d 253 (1965), *cert. denied*, 383 U.S. 946 (1966); *Butler v. Pantekoek*, 231 Or. 563, 373 P.2d 614 (1962). *Cornelius v. Macon-Bibb County Hospital Authority*, 533 S.E.2d 420, 243 Ga. App. 480 (2000) involved wrongful death action brought against hospital by husband of deceased patient. Autopsy photographs of patient's bowel were properly excluded from evidence even though there was some question about viability of portion of bowel that remained after subject surgery. Moreover, autopsy photographs taken by pathologist are particularly likely to be gruesome and should be carefully screened for relevancy. They will not be admissible unless they are necessary to show some material fact which becomes apparent only after autopsy has occurred. As general rule, court is permitted to balance relevancy of photographs against their tendency to be inflammatory and prejudicial. *Huckaby v. AG. Perry & Son, Inc.,* 20 S.W.3d 194 (Tex. App., 2000). Fact that photographs are gruesome does not render them inadmissible. *Hooker v. Super Products Corp.,* 751 So.2d 889 (La.App. 1999). In products liability trial, photographs of plaintiff taken before, during, and after surgery were admissible even though some of them were unpleasant, though not necessarily inflammatory. In any event, photos were clearly relevant to issue of damages and they enabled jury to see severity of plaintiff's injuries.

It is important to remember that photographs of injuries are normally very probative and relevant to this issue of pain, suffering and damages. Therefore, unless a photograph is truly gruesome, it should not be excluded. See, for example, *Heath v. Makita Corp.,* 681 N.Y.S.2d 289 (1998); *Clement v. Griffin,* 634 So.2d 412 (La.Ct.App. 1994); *Rivera v. City of New York,* 160 A.D.2d 985, 554 N.Y.S.2d 706 (1990); *Paducah Area Public Library v. Terry,* 655 S.W.2d 19 (Ky.Ct.App. 1983).

49 *Smith v. Baker's Feed & Grain*, 213 Ill. App. 3d 950, 157 Ill. Dec. 361, 572 N.E.2d 430 (1991); *Hall v. Burns*, 213 Conn. 446, 569 A.2d 10 (1990); *Olympia Spa v. Johnson*, 547 So.2d 80 (Ala. 1989); *Mechanick v. Conradi*, 139 A.D.2d 857, 527 N.Y.S.2d 586 (1988). See also *Saratoga Spa & Bath Inc. v. Beeche Systems Corp*., 656 N.Y.S.2d 87 (N.Y.A.D. 3 Dept 1997), involving a breach of contract action by a seller of "hoppers." Hoppers kept inside the purchaser's plant, along with photographs and measurements of hoppers at the seller's facility, were held not admissible; the evidence was either not in substantially the same condition as when the alleged problem occurred or it did not constitute an accurate and fair representation. *Smalls v. South Carolina Department of Education*, 528 S.E.2d 682, 339 S.C. 208 (2000). In wrongful death action resulting from truck-pedestrian collision, photo of truck that hit pedestrian was properly excluded from evidence, despite claim that it showed how truck allegedly hit person on far left corner. Such conclusory argument did not indicate how photograph would demonstrate that driver could have avoided accident; and, proposed offering contradicted other testimony presented during course of trial that described location of damage to truck.

50 *Haselden v. Davis*, 534 S.E.2d 295, 341. S.C. 486 (S.C.App. 2000); *BE & K Const. Co. v. Will & Grundy County Building Trades Council*, 156 F.3d 756 (7th Cir. 1998); *Marsee v. United States Tobacco Co*., 866 F.2d 319 (10th Cir. 1989); *Loevsky v. Carter*, 773 P.2d 1120 (Hawaii 1989). For patient dying of breast cancer, videotape of her daily activities as she neared death was relevant to depict her condition and quality of life just shortly before death, and was, thus, admissible; its probative value was not outweighed by danger of unfair prejudice, confusion of issues, or misleading jury, nor was videotape particularly graphic or gruesome. And, any false impression that videotape may have caused concerning her swollen condition, was counteracted by records that documented her increase in weight prior to cancer diagnosis. *DiCarlo v. Keller Ladders, Inc.*, 211 F.3d 465 (8th Cir. Mo., 2000). In products liability action against manufacturer and vendor of ladder, arising out consumer's fall from allegedly defective stepladder, probative value of consumer's videotaped statement showing site of fall (and coincidentally, consumer's home) was not substantially outweighed by unfair prejudice, despite consumer's claim that statement distorted slope of ground on which ladder stood and introduced irrelevant evidence of consumer's wealth. *BD ex rel. Jean Doe v. DeBuono*, 193 F.R.D. 117 (S.D.N.V. 2000) involved lawsuit that challenged county's alleged policy of limiting availability of applied behavior analysis (ABA) therapy to children with autism and pervasive developmental disorder (POD). Probative value of videotapes of

(Footnote 50 continued on page 44-20.)

But photographic evidence, despite its seniority and wide acceptance in the courtroom, is also subject to the "unfair prejudice—probative value" balancing act.[51]

Delays between the time of the accident (or incident) and the shooting of the photograph (or video) may give rise to a valid objection. Material changes may occur in the subject scene or object over time.[52]

The self-serving nature of a film or video[53] might give rise to a successful objection, particularly where the production contains too much glitz or "Hollywood." For that reason alone, films should avoid looking as if they had been commercially polished.

Extraneous matter in the image, such as people who are not a part of the litigation,[54] or "other" injuries that are not at issue,[55] might also give rise to a valid objection.

With the foregoing in mind, it is apparent that every techno-legal advance has its limits, including the camera (which seems to be invading all of our lives). Consider the rather novel approach to discovery taken by the plaintiffs in *F.M. v. Old Cutler Presbyterian Church.*[56] F.M.'s parents brought suit against the church, alleging sexual abuse of F.M. while on church premises. During discovery proceedings, the church made a motion for an order that would permit it to videotape the child's therapy sessions. The plaintiffs argued that, at the very least, patient-therapist privilege would be violated; the trial court, nevertheless, granted the motion. The Florida Court of Appeals reversed

---

50 (Continued from page 44-19.) autistic children and children with POD outweighed their prejudicial effect. In particular, videotapes were relevant to show children's condition and to demonstrate manner in which ABA therapy was administered; they also served to demonstrate children's progress during ABA therapy. Moreover, tapes were made during ordinary course of therapy for purpose of assessing children's progress, and any undue weight that might be given to tapes could have been remedied by limiting instruction. *Gaines v. K-Mart Corp.*, 860 So.2d 1214 (Miss., 2003) involved a personal injury lawsuit against K-Mart that resulted when a customer fell from a stepladder while trying to retrieve a displayed item. The probative value of photographs of an allegedly defective ladder and testimony that the store allowed defective or damaged ladders returned by customers to be placed on the sales floor was substantially outweighed by the danger of confusion of the issues. The jury would be left to speculate about inferences that the ladder involved in the instant case was defective, and that the store knew of the ladder's dangerous condition. Also, the photographer had not identified the photographs.

51 *Allen v. Roberts Construction Co., Inc.*, 532 S.E.2d 534 (N.C.App. 2000). In action resulting from builder's alleged defective construction of home, photographs of cracks in foundations and floors of other homes constructed by same builder in same subdivision had sufficient probative value and were properly admitted. Owners' use of those photographs was not so expansive as to be unfairly prejudicial. See also *Hunt v. Long,* 763 So.2d 811 (La. App., 2000); La.App. 2 Cir. 2000; *ACTONet, Ltd. v. Allou Health & Beauty Care,* 219 F.3d 836 (8th Cir. Neb., 2000); *Macon-Bibb County Hosp. Authority*, 533 S.E.2d 420, 243 Ga. App. 480 (2000).

52 *Rivera v. New York City Transit Authority*, 802 N.Y.S.2d 247 (NYAD, Dept. 2, 2005). In a slip and fall action resulting from injuries that occurred on steps leading down to a subway, the admission of photographs which allegedly depicted the defective condition of the subway steps at the time of the plaintiff's accident was reversible error absent any proof as to when the photographs were taken. The accident occurred nearly eight years prior to the trial, and since the accident took place on a heavily-traveled subway stairway, it could not be assumed that the photographs (which may have been taken years later) accurately depicted the condition of the steps at the time of the accident. *A-Cal Copiers, Inc. v. North American Van Lines, Inc.*, 180 F.R.D. 183 (Mass. 1998); *Satterly v. Louisiana Indemnification Company*, 704 So.2d 882 (La.App. 1997). See *Wilkinson v. Swafford,* 811 N.E.2d 374 (Ind. Ct. App., 2004).

53 Day-in-the-life films are particularly susceptible, since they are self-serving from start to finish.

54 *Belluso v. Sunnyland Foods*, 142 Ga. App. 7, 234 S.E.2d 821 (1977).

55 *Repple v. Barnes Hosp.*, 778 S.W.2d 819 (Mo. 1989); *Bolstridge v. Central Me. Power Co.*, 621 F. Supp. 1202 (D.Me. 1985).

56 595 So. 2d 201 (Fla. Dist. Ct. App. 1992).

the order, finding that even though the defendant was entitled to confidential communications concerning F.M.'s state of mind, there was no precedent for permitting the videotape. If there is a lesson to be learned, it is this—an opposing attorney should not be timid about opposing video evidence, or nipping in the bud any proceedings that may spawn damaging evidence.

CHECKLIST: OPPOSITION

Because there is a profuse overlap among the various forms of photographic evidence (p.e. photographs, videotapes, film, slides, and digitized images), the items on the checklist should be carefully scrutinized for context:

1. The quality of the photographic evidence is poor or unintelligible.
2. The photographic images, as a whole, do not fairly and accurately represent what they purport to represent.
3. Extraneous prejudicial matter is contained within the photographic images.
4. The images are gruesome, shocking or otherwise disturbing.
5. The photograph or video contains irrelevant and immaterial portions that may be prejudicial.
6. The images are skewed, slanted, angled or otherwise unduly misleading.
7. The photograph or video lacks necessary reference points or measurement indicators.
8. The photographic evidence has been selectively edited, "staged" or otherwise modified.
9. There has been a significant lapse of time and change of scenery between the subject event and the shooting of the photograph or video.
10. Changes in lighting, sun position, haze, smog or cloud cover has effected relevant portions of the image.
11. Changes in temperature or humidity may effect or alter the size or appearance of the subject object or objects.
12. Captions or extraneous text images constitute inadmissible hearsay.
13. With respect to videos or films, voice overs constitute inadmissible hearsay.
14. The photographic evidence omits significant relevant material necessary for determining context.

(This page intentionally left blank.)

Chapter 45

Audiotapes

§45.100 Introduction

Audio evidence must be distinguished from ordinary "witness stand" testimony. Such evidence originates or is recorded outside the confines of the courtroom. As used in this chapter, audio evidence does not include tapes made by court reporters who parrot testimony into those funny little gas masks that we see every now and then.

Audiotapes are generally used for voice and speaker identification, or to allow the jury to hear the contents of a tape-recorded conversation; they may also be utilized for measuring sound intensity or pattern, or for gauging similarities between musical compositions.

§45.200 Foundation Requirements

As with all forms of evidence, the contents of a tape recording must be relevant in order to be admissible.[1] But a tape recording should, nevertheless, be admissible even if it contains some irrelevant matter, as long as the extraneous matter is not prejudicial.[2] And if hearsay is included, there had better be an exception to cover it.[3] Inaudible sections will not preclude admission of a tape if those sections are not relevant or material to the case.[4] Intentional erasures, however, are another matter.[5]

In order to authenticate a tape-recorded conversation, the proponent should be prepared to: (1) identify the evidence, (2) show the tape's accuracy and reliability, and (3) establish the tape's chain of custody.[6]

---

1 *Quinby v. Plumsteadville Family Practice, Inc.*, 907 A.2d 1061 (Pa., 2006). In a negligence action commenced by the wife of a quadriplegic patient, who died following his fall off of an examination table at a doctor's office, the audio portion of a videotape that the quadriplegic patient made 22 months prior to his fall from the table and the patient's videotaped deposition (which was taken after the fall) were both admissible for purposes of trial because they both related to damages. The patient's physical condition before and after the incident, including the quality of his voice, was relevant to the issues of damages and the cause of his death.

Saurini v. Adams County School District No. 12, 191 Fed.Appx. 628 (10th Cir., Colo., 2006). In an action by a middle school counselor alleging a claim for retaliation in violation of the First Amendment, the district court was within its discretion in allowing the defending school district and school district officials to play an audiotape of the school board meeting after denying the counselor's request to admit the tape, where, after hearing the counselor's testimony (that the school board had treated her rudely and cut off both her and her supporters while speaking), officials changed their position and offered to play the tape to refute the counselor's testimony.

KMS Restaurant Corp. v. Wendy's Intern. Inc., 194 Fed.Appx. 591 (11th Cir., Fla., 2006). In a tortious interference lawsuit by the purchaser of a Wendy's fast food franchise against the franchisor, the district court did not abuse its discretion by admitting tape-recorded conversations (within the deposition testimony of the franchisor's director), where the director identified his own voice on the recordings, verified that he had telephone conversations, and further verified questions asked and his responses thereto.

Rogers v. Unitrim Auto and Home Insurance Co., 388 Fed.Supp.2d 638 (W.D.N.C., 2005). An insured's tape recorded statement to an insurance adjuster may be used against him on a matter relating to coverage. *Diamond v. Howd,* 288 F.3d 932. (6th Cir., 2002). In an action for false arrest and use of excessive force against an hysterical, intoxicated arrestee, the admission of an audiotaped phone conversation between the arrestee and the police dispatcher was not an abuse of discretion; the tape's probative value was not outweighed by its prejudicial effect, particularly in view of the arresting police officer's account of the arrestee's drunken condition and behavior.

James v. State Farm Mut. Auto. Ins. Co., 810 P.2d 365 (Okla. 1991); *Philip Morris, Inc. v. Emerson*, 368 S.E.2d 268 (Va. 1988); *Muka v. Estate of Muka*, 164 Ill.App.2d 223, 517 N.E.2d 673 (1987); *Amco Ins. Co. v. Stammer*, 411 N.W.2d 709 (Iowa 1987).

2 *Paulson v. Scott,* 260 Wis. 141, 50 N.W.2d 376 (1951).

3 *Walker v. Board of Trustees,* 69 FedAppx. 953 (10th Cir., Colo., 2003). In a lawsuit by company retirees challenging a reduction in pension benefits, tape recordings and transcripts of two meetings of the board of trustees of a regional transportation district's pension plan were not hearsay, but, rather, were admissible evidence of the board's knowledge of certain facts that were material to the action.

(Footnotes 3 through 6 continued on page 45-3.)

3 (Continued from page 45-2.) *Union Carbide Corp. v. Montell NV.,* 28 F.Supp.2d 833 (S.D.N.Y. 1998). In an intellectual property action alleging antitrust violations and other claims, recordings of customer statements expressing concern about the negative effects of a particular venture, were not business records within the meaning of the business records exception and were, therefore, inadmissible. *Rivera ex rel. Rivera v. Eastern Paramedics, Inc.*, 702 N.Y.S.2d 724 (1999). In negligence action by brain-injured patient against paramedic service that allegedly failed to establish and maintain adequate airway for patient during post-accident emergency treatment, audio portion of videotape of patient contained description of patient's care and comments made by nurses, which were not subject to cross examination. Audio was thus inadmissible.

4 *Zhou v. Pittsburg State University,* 252 F.Supp.2d 1194 (D. Kan., 2003). In an employment discrimination action, an audiotape of a conversation between an employee and the employer's counsel was admissible, regardless of whether the audiotape included the entire conversation and regardless of whether it included all of the conversations between the parties for a specific period of time. The employee stated that he answered the phone and began recording shortly thereafter. Defense counsel confirmed his name and the date of the conversation on the tape, and did not claim that any portion of the tape was altered or that the transcript did not accurately reflect the conversation.

Seymour v. Gillespie, 608 S.W.2d 897 (Tex. 1980); *Lefort v. Meibaum Bros., Inc.*, 321 So.2d 824 (La. 1975); *United States v. Hall*, 342 F.2d 849 (4th Cir.), *cert. denied,* 382 U.S. 812 (1965); *Passantino V. Johnson & Johnson Consumer Products, Inc.,* 207 F.3d 599 (9th Cir. Wash., 2000). In Title VII Civil Rights action, plaintiff employee of defending company sought to introduce copy of her taped interview with employer's officer concerning particular job that employee inquired about. Tape recording was admissible, despite employer's claim that its copy of tape was unclear during critical portion of conversation in which officer lied to that employee about whether subject job was promotion, lateral move, or demotion. As a matter of fact, officer stated on different, uncontested portion of tape, that the job was on the "same level" as her current position, a statement that was false. *Iacobucci v. Boulter*, 193 F.3d 14 (1st Cir. Mass., 1999) involved lawsuit by journalist resulting from a claim of excessive force on part of arresting officers. Audio portion of partially erased videotape was properly authenticated and thus properly admitted into evidence. Several witnesses testified as to identities of speakers, and officers whose voices were allegedly captured on tape. Moreover, tape was not so unfairly prejudicial so as to warrant exclusion. *Pittsburgh Corning Corp. v. Walters,* 1 S.W.3d 759 (Tex.App. 1999), involved products liability action against manufacturer of asbestos-containing products to which victim was allegedly exposed. Probative value of audio portion of videotape, which depicted victim in hospital four days prior to his death, was sufficient to overcome whatever prejudice it created. Even if tape aroused sympathy of jury and was to some extent cumulative, victim's condition at or near time of his death was, nevertheless, necessary part of his widow's case, and even if there were some degree of repetition in tape, it was victim's only opportunity to inform jury about victim's condition. But see *Lauro v. Bradley*, 696 N.Y.S.2d 336 (1999). In breach of contract action involving auction of contents of hardware and painting stores, trial court properly exercised its discretion by refusing to admit audiotape recording into evidence on basis that recording was so inaudible and indistinct that jury would have to speculate concerning its content.

5 See *Cassetta Frank, Inc. v. P.G.C. Associates,* 694 N.Y.S.2d 102 (N.Y.A.D. 1999), wherein admitting surreptitiously-recorded conversations containing intentional partial erasures, was held to be reversible error. *McCormick v. Brevig,* 96 P.3d 697, 322 Mont. 112, 2004 MT. 179 (2004). In a family partnership dissolution proceeding, a taped telephone conference call among various parties included an admission by the mother of the partners that one brother should receive a salary as the ranch manager. The tape was inadmissible for lack of authentication; also, there was evidence that the tape had been intentionally altered to capture only certain phrases or sentences, and the original recording was no longer available. Moreover, the standards for admissibility of sound recordings are: (1) A showing that the recording device was capable of taking testimony, (2) a showing that the operator of the device was competent, (3) the establishment of authenticity and correctness of the recording, (4) a showing that changes, additions or deletions have not been made, (5) a showing of the manner in which the recording was preserved, and (6) an identification of the speakers.

6 *Larocque v. O'Connor*, 876 A.2d 1229, 90 Conn.App. 156 (2005). *Penguin Books, U.S.A., Inc. v. New Christian Church of Full Endeavor, Ltd.,* 262 F.Supp.2d 251 (S.D.N.Y., 2003). In a copyright infringement action, relatively old audio interviews were not admissible under the ancient documents exception to the hearsay rule. Even though the imperfections in the chain of custody could constitute a question for the jury, neither the integrity of the transcript nor the identity of the speakers had been established. Here are the factors to be considered for assessing the authenticity of proffered sound recordings: "[1] Was the recording device used capable of recording and taping the subject conversation?; [2] Was the operator of the device competent to operate it?; [3] Was the recording authentic and correct?; [4] Were any changes, additions or deletions made to the recording?; [5] Was the recording adequately preserved?; [6] Were the speakers adequately identified?; [7] Was the elicited conversation made voluntarily and in good faith?"

(Footnote 6 continued on page 45-4.)

A common battle ground involving tapes centers around the identification of the speaker, particularly where bugs are involved. Incriminating evidence has been obtained on tape from all sorts of people, ranging form mob bosses taking bribes to unsatisfied wives planning a "death do us part" divorce.

Where identification is a key issue, it is best to provide a witness who can identify the recorded voice by merely listening to the tape.[7] Some courts permit the speakers to be identified via the spectrograph. A spectrograph is a machine which separates the sound of human voices into three components: time, frequency and intensity. The machine then plots these variables across paper, resulting in a graph of the acoustical signal of the speaker.

Courts are likely to apply the chain of custody requirement more strictly to audiotapes than to other types of evidence simply because audio tapes may be manipulated or altered easily, without detection. The proponent should, therefore, be prepared to show the manner in which the tape was preserved, and should have available a record of any changes made to the original. The proponent should also have the original, unedited tape available in the event that opposing counsel, or the court, requests it.

REFERENCES

Admissibility of writings, recordings, or photographs. 50 A.L.R. Fed 319.

§45.201 Sample Foundation for Audiotapes

Q. (By Proponent's Attorney) State your name for the record.

A. (Witness) Sandy Snooper.

Q. Please state your degrees and qualifications.

A. (The witness should provide such relevant and detailed information as degrees, seminars, experience and licenses.)

Q. I call your attention to plaintiff's Exhibit 1 and ask if you prepared (or directed the preparation of) it.

A. Yes, I prepared the tape myself. It has my initials on the cassette.

---

6 (Continued from page 45-3.) *Moskowitz v Coscette,* 3 Fed.Appx. 1 (2nd Cir., 2001). In an action under 42 U.S.C.A. §1983 by a police officer alleging employment-related retaliation, the plaintiff officer taped conversations of other personnel in the police department without their knowledge; the taped statements concerned information that was testified to during the course of the trial. The police officer established proper foundation requirements by testifying to the manner in which he recorded, when the tape was made, and that it fairly and accurately recorded the subject conversations.

Hitt v. Connell, 301 F.3d 240 (5th Cir., Texas, 2002). In a civil rights action, audiotapes introduced by the defendant were properly authenticated, where those who recorded the defendant's statement testified as to how the recordings were made; moreover, the defendant did not dispute the identification of his voice on the tapes.

Aerotech Resources, Inc. v. Dodson Aviation, Inc., 191 F.Supp.2d 1209 (D. Kansas, 2002). The foundation for the admission of an audiotaped conversation was not established in this action for damages involving the sale of aircraft. And, the tape was not produced in accordance with the proponent's duty to update responses to pretrial discovery requests. See also *Skrmetta v. Bayview Yacht Club, Inc.,* 806 So.2d 1120 (Miss. 2002).

Cacciarelli v. Boniface, 737 A.2d 1170, 325 N.J.Super. 133 (1999) required a showing: [1] that the speakers can properly be identified, [2] that the recording device was capable of taping the subject conversation or statement, [3] that the operator was competent, [4] that the recording was authentic and correct, and [5] that no changes, additions or deletions occurred. See also *Ruggiero v. Ruggiero,* 737 A2d 997, 55 Conn.App. 304 (1999), a legal malpractice action by a client against an attorney who represented her during a divorce; the court monitor, who taped the marital dissolution proceeding, was not required to testify in order for the audiotape to be admissible. *Chianese v. Meier*, 729 N.Y.S.2d 460 (N.Y.A.D., 2001). In personal injury action by attacked tenant against her building's owner and managing agent based on lack of proper security, tape-recorded conversations between investigator and individual who attacked tenant were admissible; tapes were properly authenticated through foundation testimony indicating that tapes were credible and that they had not been tampered with. With respect to potential *Best Evidence* issues, see *Smith v. City of Chicago*, 242 F.3d 737 (7th Cir. Ill., 2001). See also Chapter 2.

7 See Fed. R. Evid. 905(b)(5).

Q. Would you please describe, briefly, its contents?
A. Yes... (The witness should provide a summary of the contents using the fewest words possible.)
Q. Please describe the circumstances surrounding the recording of this tape.
A. (The witness should briefly describe the type of tape recorder used and any other significant components, without getting too technical.)
Q. Has the tape been altered, erased or added to since the date on which you made it?
A. No.
Q. Has the tape continuously been in your custody since the date on which you made it?
A. Yes.
Q. (Addressing the court) I ask that plaintiff's Exhibit 1 be admitted.
COURT: Any objections?
OPPOSING ATTORNEY: None.
COURT: Very well, it will be received.

§45.300 Checklist: Opposition

Checklist: Opposition

Opposition may include any of the first eight items from the Opposition Checklist in Chapter 40, as well as the following objections:

1. The recording is inaudible.
2. The recording is confusing and garbled.
3. The recording contains other technical inaccuracies.
4. The recording contains inadmissible hearsay.
5. The recording contains irrelevant and immaterial portions.

(This page intentionally left blank.)

Chapter 46

Finger, Foot, and Palm Prints

§46.100 Introduction

It is interesting to think that all of the places we walk and are the things we touch may harbor little bits and pieces of demonstrative evidence. Though confronted with technologically superior identifiers (such as cameras and electronic bugs), these archaic telltale marks remain very effective, particularly in the criminal arena.

A fingerprint is an impression of the inner surface of the last joint of the thumb or finger. For purposes of identification, it may be compared to a similar impression made with ink.[1]

Foot or palm prints may be similarly defined with reference to the lines contained on the skin of the foot or the palm of the hand, respectively. Impressions made by shoes or boots have significance for identification purposes, but such comparisons are often inconclusive.

Evidence gurus might argue that the impression or print left at the time of the subject event would constitute real, not demonstrative, evidence. While such evidence does, in fact, constitute a component or piece of the subject act or crime, the print's existence as meaningful evidence, however, does not come into being until it is matched with another print taken, this time, after the fact. Moreover, it is the "match" that possesses probative value, not either print by itself, or both side by side. And, that match often requires some expertise.

But the "real" ingredient in this mixture is not without significance. It does suggest the presence of a chain-of-possession concern.

REFERENCES

Fingerprints, admissibility as business records. 36 Am. Jur. 2d Proof of Facts 285.

§46.200 Foundation Requirements

Finger, foot and palm prints often constitute important evidence in criminal cases. While they are rarely used in civil matters, there is always the possibility that such prints may be required to establish an identification in a civil case. Since such methods of identification are accurate enough to establish criminal guilt,[2] they should also be available to establish civil liability.[3]

Proper authentication is needed for finger, foot and palm prints.[4] Generally, expert testimony is necessary to compare and identify two sets of fingerprints,[5] although there are exceptions to this rule.[6] Also, a court may occasionally allow a jury to compare fingerprints.[7] Authenticated finger, foot and palm prints, or photographs of such

1 *State v. Kuhl*, 42 Nev. 185, 175 P. 190, 194 (1918).

2 *United States v. Roustio*, 455 F.2d 366 (7th Cir. 1972); *State v. Helms*, 218 N.C. 592, 12 S.E.2d 243, 245 (1940).

3 *Morgan v. Wilkinson*, 606 F. Supp. 564 (M.D. Pa. 1985); *Eastern Associated Coal v. Aetna Casualty and Surety Co.*, 632 F.2d 1068 (3rd Cir. 1980).

4 Authentication may require that compliance with the *Frye* standard (See *supra* §11.601 et seq. and §40.600); see also *Hutcherson v. State*, 677 So.2d 1174 (Ala. Crim. App. 1994), *rev'd*, 677 So.2d 1205 (Ala. 1996); *Jones v. State*, 482 N.E.2d 243 (Ind. 1985); *State v. Demouchet*, 353 So.2d 1025 (La. 1977).

5 *Coco v. State*, 62 So.2d 892 (Fla. 1953) (en banc), *cert. denied*, 349 U.S. 931, r*ehearing denied*, 350 U.S. 855 (1955); *Davis v. State*, 33 Ala. App. 68, 29 So.2d 877 (1947); *Grice v. State*, 142 Tex. Crim. App. 4, 151 S.W.2d 211 (1941).

6 See, for example, *State v. Bagley*, 39 N.C.App. 328, 250 S.E.2d 87 (1979) and *Scott v. State*, 434 P.2d 435 (Nev. 1967).

7 *United States v. Dressler*, 112 F.2d 972 (7th Cir. 1940). But see *People v. Peter*, 55 Ill.2d 443, 303 N.E.2d 398 (1973), *cert. denied*, 417 U.S. 920 (1974). The trial court correctly prohibited the jury from comparing fingerprints through a magnifying glass, since that required expert testimony.

prints, may be displayed to the jury via photographic enlargements.[8]

Logically, the requirements for foot and palm prints should be similar, if not identical, to that of fingerprints. Footprints, specifically, are recognized as a proper means of identification in criminal cases.[9]

§46.201 Sample Foundation for Fingerprints

Q. (By Proponent's Attorney) State your name for the record.
A. (Expert Witness) Lt. Dragg.
Q. State your occupation?
A. I'm a detective for the L.A.P.D.
Q. State your expertise, if any, with respect to fingerprint analysis.
A. (The witness should provide a litany of courses, seminars, degrees, and work experience relating to fingerprint matching and analysis.)
Q. Could you identify Exhibit 1?
A. Yes. It is a set of prints taken from the screen door of the subject house that was burglarized.
Q. Were you able to match those prints?
A. Yes.
Q. To whom?
A. The defendant.

---

8 *Collins v. State*, 415 N.E. 46 (Ind.), *cert. denied*, 451 U.S. 991 (1981); *State v. Cass*, 356 So.2d 936 (La. 1977).

9 *State v. Rogers*, 233 N.C.390, 64 S.E.2d 572 (1951), overruled on other grounds; *State v. Silver*, 286 N.C. 709, 213 S.E.2d 247 (1975). In a murder prosecution, the State's expert testified that the techniques used in identifying naked footprints were the same as those used to identify fingerprints. See also *State v. Abbott*, 654 S.W.2d 260 (Mo. 1983); *Chandler v. State*, 267 Ind. 610, 372 N.E.2d 465 (1978); *Commonwealth v. Bartolini*, 299 Mass. 503, 13 N.E.2d 382, *cert. denied*, 304 U.S. 565 (1938); *State v. Lapan*, 101 Vt. 124, 141 A. 686 (1928).

(This page intentionally left blank.)

Chapter 47

Computer-Generated Materials

§47.100 Introduction

Computer-generated materials can perform a wide variety of functions, cutting across the entire evidence spectrum. The computer, for example, can be used as a receptacle for business records, a generator of relatively simple statistics and graphics,[1] or, at the higher technological levels, as a complex simulator.

Analyzing the entire field of "computer evidence" from a single perspective has caused errors and confusion, both in treatises and in judicial decisions. A database containing corporate records, for example, has no business whatsoever being lumped in with computerized simulations or reconstructions. The basic nature, reliability, and foundation requirements bear no relation to one another. Yet they are too often discussed in the same breath.

A proper analysis of the computerized evidence generally requires that the subject matter be divided into at least five separate categories:

1. Computer-Stored Records
2. Computer-Generated Statistics
3. Computer-Generated Simulations
4. Computer-Generated Reconstructions
5. Computer-Generated Graphics.[2]

The last category relates more to the visual display of the output than to substantive content, as do the other four. Computer-generated graphics are often treated synonymously or confused with categories 3 and 4.

§47.200 Computer-Stored Records

Have your client (or a custodian) walk to his or her file cabinet, pull some business records, take them to court, and get them admitted into evidence; that is the process referred to in Chapter 22. That process remains essentially the same where the records happen to be stored in a computer's hard disk drive or on some floppy disk (or tape).[3] Under both scenarios, the writings end up in court, in readable form, ready to enjoy the special status that any records kept in the ordinary course of business enjoy.

The business records exception to the hearsay rule provides a large breach in the admissibility wall for computer-stored business records.[4] In *Transport Indemnity Company v. Seib*,[5] computer data was admitted into evidence even though it had been prepared specifically for the litigation. The court found that the system used to prepare the data, the repeated storage of information within the computer and the calculations based upon that information, were all done in the usual course of business.

1 In the face of a dramatic expansion of computer generated evidence into the realm of time altering, three dimensional displays and animations, it is easy to overlook some potent, though less dazzling capabilities for this relatively new medium. Simple charts and graphs can be less expensive without being less persuasive. See *Computerized Graphics Find Larger Role, Howard L. Nations and Douglas Filter, The New York Law Journal Guide* (Supplement to the New York Law Journal), p.S8, (July 27, 1992).

2 See Lipson, *The Art of Advocacy - Demonstrative Evidence* (Matthew Bender & Co., 1988).

3 See Fed. R. Evid. 1001(1); see also *Berkeley Federal Bank and Trust, FSB v. Ogalin*, 708 A.2d 620 (Conn. App. 1998).

4 *Doe v. Gunny s Ltd. Partnership,* 593 N.W.2d 284, 256 Neb. 653 (1999); *United States v. Miller*, 771 F.2d 1219 (9th Cir. 1985); *American Velodur Metal, Inc. v. Schinabeck*, 20 Mass. App. 460, 481 N.E.2d 209 (1985); *U.S. v. Croft,* 750 F.2d 1354 (7th Cir. 1984); *U.S. v. Sanders*, 749 F.2d 195 (5th Cir. 1984); *Brown v. J.C. Penney Co.*, 297 Or. 695, 688 P.2d 811 (1984); *State v. Bradley*, 17 Wash. App. 916, 567 P.2d 650 (1977); *King v. State*, 222 So.2d 393 (Miss. 1969). See also *Webster Bank v. Flanagan,* 725 A.2d 975, 51 Conn.App. 733 (1999) involving a mortgage foreclosure action, wherein a computer print-out of the mortgagor s loan history was deemed hearsay (since it was an out-of-court statement being used to prove that the mortgagor had a history of loan payments and had eventually defaulted on the subject loan). The printout was nevertheless admissible because it fell within the business records exception to the Hearsay Rule for the following reasons: (1) a bank employee testified that the records were kept in the regular course of business, (2) the bank was a business wherein the documents were regularly created, and (3) the records were prepared contemporaneously with the events that were recorded therein.

5 178 Neb. 253, 132 N.W.2d 871 (1965).

REFERENCES

Computer records proving bills as paid. 14 Am. Jur. 2d Proof of Facts 173.

§47.300 Computer-Generated Statistics

Computer programs are often carriers of hearsay. Any time that computer-generated (as opposed to computer-stored) materials are admitted into evidence, the court is relying upon the truth and accuracy of the computer program that was used to compile the data.[6] Computer programs, which are created by fallible humans, can contain errors. Often, the hearsay creeps into the code in the form of assumptions and opinions; the problem can be quite insidious.

Computer-generated statistics are not business records. Their ultimate credibility should remain a question for the trier of fact.[7] The proponent should always give the opposition adequate time to analyze the program and its output and should have an expert who is prepared to testify as to the program's function and its accuracy.

In a personal injury action, a computer printout interpreting psychological tests administered to a plaintiff, and the expert testimony predicated upon the printout, were inadmissible hearsay, absent a proper foundation under the business records exception to the hearsay rule.[8]

Important factors which may assist the admissibility of computer-generated materials include the following:

1. The program has a supporting expert who can testify to its accuracy, trustworthiness and reliability.
2. The opposition was given a reasonable opportunity to have its experts analyze and test the program.
3. The evidence would otherwise be admissible if it were generated without using the computer.
4. The underlying assumptions of the program are based on scientific, mathematical or otherwise accepted propositions.
5. Any potential for personal biases or subjective injections are explained to the court and jury.
6. The program has been adequately tested and debugged.

REFERENCES

Computer-generated calculations, challenge to proof of. 14 Am. Jur. 2d Proof of Facts 173.

§47.400 Computer-Generated Simulations

For the category of words that have used, abused, and confused more than any other, "simulation" and "reconstruction" should take the Oscar. I rarely see a treatise or article on the subjects without seeing them used synonymously.[9] But there is a difference.

6 *Duplissie v. Devino*, 902 A.2d 30, 96 Conn.App. 673 (2006). In a former employee's breach of contract action to recover unpaid commissions, a computer-generated record of job cost details for the subject construction project was admissible under the business records exception to the hearsay rule even though the record was not a complete statement of all costs for the project; the data entries were accurate, made in the regular course of business, and were contemporaneous with the specific events described in the record. Also, evidence is not inadmissible under the business records exception merely because a business record was created, stored, or produced by means of computer technology. When computer records are offered as evidence, however, the proponent must satisfy a two-part test; in particular, in addition to meeting the three requirements of the business records exception to the hearsay rule, the proponent also must establish that the basic elements of the computer system are reliable.

7 *State v. Ward*, 172 Conn. 163, 374 A.2d 168 (1976).

8 *West v. Martin*, 11 Kan.App.2d 55, 713 P.2d 957 (1986).

9 For some articles that use proper terminology, see Kreiger, *New Dimensions in Litigation, Computer Generated Video Graphics Enter Courtroom Scene,* 25 Trial 69 (Oct. 1989), and Turley, *Effective Use of Demonstrative Evidence, Capturing Attention and Clarifying Issues,* 25 Trial 62 (Sept. 1989).

A "simulation" is an artificially created continuation of events predicated upon a set of input data. It often purports to yield a result or climax to that continuation. A reconstruction, on the other hand, artificially determines the missing components that led up to the climactic event.[10]

The airplane crash seems to serve as the showcase for the forms of evidence under consideration.[11] Let us consider two hypothetical crashes:

In the first, a plane is missing somewhere in the Andes with a gang of noisy soccer players. The given data includes the time, date, and place of departure, along with the relevant wind velocity vectors (which include wind speed and direction); that information serves as input. The missing information is the location of the plane. That is the output we seek. Under these circumstances, the computer would perform a simulation, i.e., it would "continue" the flight to determine its possible location at any given time.

The second scenario involves a plane and a potentially drunk pilot who attempted, unsuccessfully, to land a 747 on Golden Pond. In this circumstance, the time and the location of the crash would be input elements (not output) because they are known factors. The missing elements might involve one or more of the components that served as input in our first example. But here, we want the computer to "reconstruct" those elements. In some respects, a reconstruction is really a reverse simulation.

§47.401 Sample Foundation for Simulations[12]

Q. (By Proponent's Attorney) State your name for the record.

A. (Witness) Mandy Microsoft.

Q. Please state your occupation.

A. I'm a systems analyst for a consulting company.

Q. Please provide us with your training and experience with respect to computer simulations, if any.

A. (The witness should provide such detailed information as college degrees, seminars attended, experience, and licenses; she should also indicate whether or not she passed any national examinations pertaining to data processing.)

Q. I call your attention to the monitor over there and ask its purpose and relevance to these proceedings.

A. It involves a computer simulation that I programmed and prepared in order to illustrate... (brief description.)

Q. What programming language did you use?

A. General Purpose System Simulation, or G.P.S.S.

Q. Is this particular programming language one that is susceptible to hidden biases or undetectable errors?

A. No. It is a very straightforward and simple language.

Q. Is G.P.S.S. recognized by the scientific and data processing communities as being reliable, trustworthy and accurate?

---

10 See Lipson, *The Art of Advocacy - Demonstrative Evidence*, §16.02 (Matthew Bender & Co., 1988).

11 See Marcotte, *Animated Evidence - Delta 191 Crash Recreated Through Computer Simulations at Trial*, 75 A.B.A. Journal 52 (Dec. 1989).

12 See *Bray v. Bi-State Development Corp.*, 949 S.W.2d 93 (Mo. App. E.D. 1997), where the defendant's expert laid a sufficient foundation for the validity of computer-simulation software that produced a chart depicting the light intensity levels in a parking garage. The expert testified that the software was a program which produced accurate results and was used generally by the lighting manufacturer's representative, and that it was relied upon by engineers to design lighting and make lighting decisions. The defendant did not need to affirmatively show the proper functioning of the computer hardware to establish a foundation for the admissibility of the computer-generated chart, because the plaintiff did not challenge the functioning of the hardware at trial or inquire about it during the voir dire of the defendant's expert.

A. Yes. Software based on G.P.S.S. is recognized as being capable of doing what it is designed to do.
Q. Would you please describe, briefly, your preparation of the exhibit?
A. Yes... (Generally, the witness should spell out the input factors, and they should, of course, consist only of previously admitted data.)
Q. (To the court) Your Honor, at this time I would like to represent to the court that I made the entire program and all of its elements available to opposing counsel more than three months prior to the start of trial.
Q. (To the witness) Does this simulation, in your opinion, represent that which it purports to represent, and nothing more?
A. Yes, except for... (The witness should point out discrepancies or inaccuracies.) I'm not claiming that the computer tells us, with one hundred percent certainty, the way real life would come out. It does, however, tell us with certainty the way the simulation would come out, based on the factors that were programmed into it.
Q. Will this exhibit assist the jury in understanding the subject event?
A. Yes, it will.
Q. Will this exhibit clarify the issues for the jury?
A. Yes, it will.
Q. (Addressing the court) I ask that plaintiff's Exhibit 1 be admitted.
COURT: Any objections?
OPPOSING ATTORNEY: None.
COURT: Very well, it will be received.

REFERENCES

Foundation for computer-generated evidence. 14 Am. Jur. 2d Proof of Facts 173.

§47.500 Computer-Generated Reconstructions

When computer-generated exhibits are offered, the "*Frye*" test may come into play. The test is derived from the case of *Frye v. United States*.[13] Under the *Frye* test, evidence derived from a new scientific technique is admissible only if the technique's reliability and its general acceptance in the scientific community are both established. Some courts apply the test to computer-generated materials,[14] while others do not.[15]

Note that the *Frye* standard has been significantly influenced by the Supreme Court's decision in *Daubert v. Dow*.[16] Also, those attorneys who have experience with new forms of evidence may appreciate that both "*Frye*" and "*Daubert*" standards are totally inappropriate for discussing or considering the admissibility of computer simulations and reconstructions (decisions to the contrary notwithstanding). In truth, there is nothing "new" or untested about computer-generated evidence.

The admissibility of a computerized reconstruction is not determined by the quality of the underlying software. Rather, it is the (1) the accuracy of the final product as displayed to the trier of fact (i.e., the "substantial similarity test") and (2) the manner in which that product is rep-

13 293 F. 1013 (D.C. 1923).

14 *Starr v. Campos*, 134 Ariz. 254, 655 P.2d 794 (1982).

15 *People v. McHugh*, 124 Misc.2d 559, 476 N.Y.S.2d 721 (1984); *Schaeffer v. General Motors Corp.*, 372 Mass. 171, 360 N.E.2d 1062 (1977); *Commonwealth v. Fatalo*, 346 Mass. 266, 191 N.E.2d 479 (1963).

16 113 S. Ct. 2786, 125 L. Ed. 2d 469 (1993). See also §11.603. For a more detailed discussion of this line of cases and the subsequent ruling in *Kumho Tire Co., Ltd., et al. v. Carmichael et al.*, ____ U.S. ____, No. 97-1709 (March 23, 1999), see §11.604.

resented that counts.[17] And even that two-prong standard, might be relaxed under the proper circumstances. Consider a case involving a civil rights action where a computer animation of an incident between a police officer and a person whom the officer shot, was held admissible, despite a claim that the animation failed to reflect conditions substantially similar to those existing at the time of the shooting. The jury understood that the conditions surrounding the shooting were disputed; and further, the court gave cautionary instructions that the animation was not meant to be an exact recreation of events, but rather a representation of the witness' evaluation of the evidence presented.[18]

§47.501 Sample Foundation for Reconstructions

Q. (By Proponent's Attorney) State your name for the record.

A. (Witness) Eric Assembler.

Q. Please state your occupation.

A. I'm an engineer for Animated Reconstructors Incorporated.

Q. Please provide us with your training and experience with respect to computer reconstructions.

A. (As with the prior example, the witness should provide such detailed information as college degrees, seminars attended, experience and licenses; he or she might indicate whether or not he or she passed any national examinations pertaining to programming or data processing.)

Q. I call your attention to the monitor over there and ask its purpose and relevance to these proceedings.

A. It involves a computer reconstruction that I programmed and prepared in order to illustrate... (brief description.)

Q. What programming language did you use?

A. I created my own software.

Q. Isn't there software on the market?

A. Reconstructions are a relatively recent development. For this particular case, I had to modify some software to match the particular facts of this accident.

Q. How can you be sure about reliability?

A. We tested the software repeatedly. And, I understand that it was even submitted to the opposition in this case to see if they could find any bugs.

Q. What does the program consist of?

---

17 See *Webb v. CSX Transportation, Inc.*, 364 S.C. 639, 615 S.E.2d 440 (2005). *Anderson v. Alberto Culver, USA, Inc.*, 273 Ill.Dec. 404, 789 N.E.2d 304, 337 Ill.App.3d 643 (2003). In a wrongful death action arising from a plane crash, computer-generated flight planning documents were admissible under the business records exception to the hearsay rule. An employee of the company (that provided pre-flight planning and weather services) testified that the company used a highly reliable form of computer considered standard for use in computing flight plan information. Information for the flight planning documents was received one hour prior to flight times, and, in addition, flight plans were generated in the regular course of business and transmitted to Federal Aviation Administration. If all the preceding steps had not been followed, the flight would not have been cleared for take off. Moreover, records that are generated by a computer are generally admissible as representing the tangible result of the computer's internal operations. In addition, absent an exception to the hearsay rule, printouts of computer stored records constitute statements placed into the computer by out of court declarants, and, therefore, cannot be tested by way of cross-examination. They thus constitute hearsay.

Clark v. Cantrell, 529 S.E.2d 528 (S.C. 2000). In automobile injury case, defendant offered computer-generated video animation which purported to show how accident occurred; however, it did not accurately reflect initial position of plaintiff driver's vehicle as defending motorist described it in her testimony; also, portion of animation made it appear that plaintiff's vehicle pulled directly in front of defendant's car, which contradicted defendant's expert witness (who testified that defendant driver could have first seen plaintiff's car some distance back from point where defendant motorist's car initially was positioned in animation).

18 *Hinckle v. City of Clarksburg, W.Va.*, 81 F.3d 416 (4th Cir. 1996).

A. As with all computer programs, the code consists of a series of rules or algorithms, similar to the solution of a math problem. This particular program is designed simply to take the numbers and data relating to the accident, apply some simple laws of physics, and then based on those laws, determine the missing elements of the accident.
Q. Is the software that you used reliable and trustworthy?
A. I believe it is. I have tested it thoroughly.
Q. Did you have to make any decisions involving personal opinions or bias?
A. No. It's all mathematical.
Q. Would you please describe, briefly, your preparation of the exhibit?
A. Yes... (As with a simulation, the witness should spell out the input factors, and they should, of course, consist only of previously admitted data.)
Q. (To the court) Your Honor, at this time I would like to represent to the court that I made the entire program and all of its elements available to opposing counsel more than three months prior to the start of trial, as the witness has correctly speculated.
Q. (To the witness) Will this exhibit assist the jury in understanding of your opinion about the subject event?
A. Yes, it represents only my opinion based on the facts and figures provided to me.
Q. Are the conditions represented by your reconstruction substantially similar to those of the subject incident?
A. Yes.
Q. Will this exhibit clarify the issues for the jury?
A. Yes, it will.
Q. (Addressing the court) I ask that plaintiff's Exhibit 1 be admitted.
COURT: Any objections?
OPPOSING ATTORNEY: None.
COURT: Very well, it will be received.

REFERENCES

Foundation for computer-generated evidence. 14 Am. Jur. 2d Proof of Facts 173.

§47.600 Computer-Generated Animation and Graphics

Those computer graphics that dazzle and mesmerize children and jurors are, likewise, mesmerizing more and more practitioners as the software gets better and cheaper. Animation is becoming a powerful courtroom tool; but its use in depositions and settlement conferences is also on the increase. There are those who see nothing less than a significant "evolution in evidence," attributable solely to this new medium.[19]

Keep in mind, however, that "graphics" are a tool for display, nothing more, nothing less.[20] It would be a mistake to assume that there is

19 See Mark C. Joye, *Computer Animations*, 34 Trial Magazine 47 (November, 1998). See also Roy Kreiger, *Sophisticated Graphics Come Of Age - And Evidence Will Never Be The Same*, 78 ABA Journal 92 (December 1992). The article provides an interesting discussion about some of the latest uses for computer graphics; but please ignore comments about the "more pedestrian forms of evidence" being doomed to extinction. Rest assured that the simplest charts, photos, and other "pedestrians" have their place. And, above all, remember that the media should be selected to suit the arguments and issues, not vice versa.

20 But see *Webb v. CSX Transportation, Inc.*, 364 S.C. 639, 615 S.E.2d 440 (2005). When a computer animation is admitted, the trial court should give a cautionary instruction that the video represents only a recreation of one party's version of events, and it may call attention to any assumptions upon which the recreation is based. Moreover, a computer animation is admissible if it is: (1) authentic, (2) relevant, (3) a fair and accurate representation of the evidence, and (4) more probative than prejudicial. The trial court has broad discretion in determining whether to admit a computer animation of an accident scene, and its decision will be reversed on appeal only for an abuse of that discretion.

microchip intellect producing the results. You have, no doubt, seen or heard about some of the fancy three-dimensional animations now being used in both civil and criminal trials alike. The computer is being used to create those potent images. But when it acts only as an animation tool, it does not generate them!

A human artist must render each basic cell and then "make" the moving sequence of images that conform to the living testimony presented during the trial. The images can be created or altered to serve the creator, much as a brush serves an artist.[21] The computer, when acting as a pure animation-tool, does not suck in a bunch of raw facts like some vacuum cleaner, and then spit out a completed animation. Yet, the distinction is not always clear, particularly when the animation function is combined with a simulation or reconstruction. The output produced by these different platforms tend to look alike. And, as we move down the road of the new millennium, where digital components are becoming intertwined with all media, the confusion may, indeed, increase.[22]

---

21 *Smith v. Kansas City Southern Ry. Co.,* 846 So.2d 980 (La.App., 2003). In a wrongful death action that resulted from a collision between an automobile and a train, a computer animation purporting to demonstrate what the motorist allegedly saw as she approached the railroad crossing was not admissible. The animation was created by an animator who used a computer program and specific information provided to him regarding the train, automobile, and the physical objects at, or near, the crossing to recreate what the motorist allegedly saw as she approached the crossing. Also, some of the information that the animator relied upon was not accurate.

See *Byrd v. Guess*, 137 F.3d 1126 (9th Cir. 1998), wherein facial expressions were removed from animated characters despite the complaint that it made them look like crazed androids (similar to a Jerry Springer guest).

22 *National Steel Car, Ltd. v. Canadian Pacific Ry., Ltd.,* 254 F.Supp.2d 527 (E.D.Pa., 2003). In a patent infringement lawsuit, a computer animation and accompanying illustrations offered by the defendants were at best confusing and at worst somewhat misleading. The evidence omitted several features of the underlying patents that they were intended to represent, and, in addition, used terminology that is not ordinarily employed with respect to patents.

Ramsey County v. Stewart, 643 N.W.2d 281 (Minn. 2002). The defendant was convicted of first-degree murder for shooting a bicyclist from a moving vehicle. During trial, the prosecution introduced a computerized animation containing sequences that depicted the shooting of the bicyclist from a moving vehicle. Portions of the animation accurately illustrated the witnesses' testimony with respect to the point of fire, the trajectory of the bullet, and the wound path; they were, therefore, relevant to an understanding of the cause of the bicyclist's death. Nevertheless, the court erred when it permitted the prosecution to use a portion of one sequence depicting events inside the car that did not express or illustrate the medical examiner's testimony. Those particular sequences contained depictions of defendant's face and eyes at the time of the shooting; such demonstrations amounted to original (i.e., substantive) evidence concerning the defendant's intent, a hotly contested issue during trial. Even though the presentation was improper, the error was, however, deemed harmless. The animation was not available to the jury during deliberations nor was it discussed by counsel during closing statements. Generally, proposed animations must be carefully scrutinized for proper foundation, relevancy, accuracy, and the potential for undue prejudice, and if there is a proper foundation for such evidence, the trial court should issue a cautionary instruction relating to the animation before playing it for the jury.

See also *Rub v. Consolidated Rail Corporation*, 771 N.E.2d 1015, 331 Ill.App.3d 692 (2002); *State v. Farner, Jr.,* 66 S.W.3d 188 (Tenn., 2002); *Commonwealth v. Serge*, 58 PaD.&C.4th 52 (2001).

Lally v. Volkswagen Aktiengesellschaft, 698 N.E.2d 28 (Mass. App. 1998), involved a lack-of-crashworthiness action against an automobile manufacturer. The plaintiff-motorist appealed from an adverse verdict, claiming that the trial court erred by admitting videotapes of a sled test along with a computer animation. The evidence was introduced by an engineer who had performed a complete accident reconstruction for the defense; he demonstrated the use of computers to reconstruct accidents, and included a brief movie excerpt of a complex automobile stunt accomplished with the assistance of computers. Contrary to the plaintiffs' assertion that the tape suggested that "Hollywood is in use to fix the gouge mark and the point of impact," the judge's conclusion was correct because the film most likely "assisted the jury in understanding the very technical nature of the testimony." See also *Clark v. Cantrell*, 504 S.E.2d 605 (S.C. App. 1998). For a crashworthiness case where a computerized animation was held to be inadmissible, see *Stamper v. Hyundai Motor Co.*, 699 N.E.2d 678 (Ind. App. 1998).

In the last analysis, it would appear that admissibility should depend upon the expressed purpose and accuracy of the presentation. Chances for admission would be enhanced where the offeror makes it clear that the proposed evidence is being used to help clarify or explain the facts underlying a material issue.[23]

REFERENCES

Foundation for computer-generated evidence. 14 Am. Jur. 2d Proof of Facts 173.

§47.700 Opposition

The number of possible objections to the use of computer-generated materials will increase along with the sophistication of the software used to produce the materials. The first eight items of the Opposition Checklist in Chapter 40 may come into play, along with possible hearsay objections with respect to the underlying computer programs.

Despite its age, the dissenting opinion in *Perma Research & Development v. Singer Co.*,[24] should be required reading for counsel preparing to oppose the admission of computer-generated materials. Here is a relevant portion:

> The possibility of an undetected error in computer-generated evidence is a function of many factors: the underlying data may be hearsay; errors may be introduced in any one of several stages of processing; the computer might be erroneously programmed to permit an error to go undetected, or programmed to introduce error into the data; and the computer may inaccurately display the data or display it in a biased manner.[25]

When analyzing computer generated evidence, review Chapter 44 (portions pertaining to videos), particularly where computer generated graphics and animation are involved; the presentations are similar and may give rise to similar objections, particularly with respect to matters involving substantial similarity.[26]

---

23 See *infra*, §47.600. See also *Lake Superior Center Authority v. Hammel, Green & Abrahamson, Inc.*, 715 N.W.2d 458 (Minn.App., 2006). In an architectural malpractice action commenced by the owners of an aquarium against an architect and tank design consultant (resulting from a defective concrete wall constructed for an exhibit tank), the trial court did not abuse its discretion when it admitted, for illustrative purposes, a computer animation showing the methods that the concrete subcontractor could have used to construct an exhibit tank. The owners claimed that the tank, as designed by the defendants, could not be constructed; the defending architect and consultant, on the other hand, claimed that the structure could have been erected using appropriate means and methods, and employed the animation to make their point. The owners did not suggest that the animation was inaccurate. As safeguards, the court did not allow the animation in the jury room during deliberations, and the court instructed the jury to consider the animation for illustrative purposes only. Generally, to be admissible, illustrative evidence must be substantially similar to the aspects being illustrated.

24 542 F.2d 111 (2d Cir.), *cert. denied*, 429 U.S. 987, 97 S. Ct. 507, 50 L. Ed. 2d 598 (1976).

25 *Id.* at 124.

26 *Kane v. Triborough Bridge & Tunnel Authority,* 778 N.Y.S.2d 52 (N.Y.A.D. 2 Dep't 2004). In an action by an injured passenger of a vehicle against the Bridge and Tunnel Authority, the plaintiff passenger failed to lay a foundation for the admission of a computer generated animation. The circumstances portrayed in the animation were sufficiently different from those which existed at the time of the accident, thereby rendering its utility questionable. In addition, the court failed to give a proper limiting instruction.

(This page intentionally left blank.)

Chapter 48

Live Demonstrations

§48.100 Introduction

Demonstrations and experiments are generally used to illustrate the proponent's theory of a complex case, or to explain the operation of an object or machine. Seeing a demonstration is akin to watching a mini-drama unfold. Such an offering can be very powerful where a material issue happens to be the focus of the show.

§48.200 Foundation Requirements

The trial court has very wide latitude to determine the admissibility of demonstrations.[1] Its decisions will only be reversed for an abuse of discretion.[2]

The proponent has the burden of laying a proper foundation for a demonstration.[3] Special knowledge or expertise should be provided by a qualified expert, in order to establish an adequate foundation.[4]

§48.201 Admission Checklist

To gain admission for a demonstration, the proponent must show the following:

ADMISSION CHECKLIST

1. The demonstration helps the jury understand an element of the case.[5]

1 In-court demonstrations clearly have their limits. In that regard, the ancient question that has plagued us from the beginning of recorded legal history has finally been answered. The question is "Can we strangle and choke a witness while he is on the stand?" The answer, unfortunately, is "No." Consider *Honeycutt v. State*, 56 P.3d 362 (Nevada 2002). During the cross-examination of the defendant, the prosecutor was deemed to have committed misconduct when he began to choke the defendant as a demonstration of what allegedly happened to the victim. Apparently Defendant Honeycutt testified on direct examination that an alleged sexual assault could not have occurred as the victim claimed and he gave an in-court demonstration with a neutral party to corroborate his story. Upon cross-examination, the prosecutor asked if he could do his own in-court demonstration. Upon receiving permission, he approached Honeycutt, placed his arm across Honeycutt's throat and began pushing hard. Honeycutt's eyes began watering after a few seconds and he began to choke. Defense counsel immediately objected and requested a mistrial. The district court judge sustained the objection but denied the motion for a mistrial. The misconduct was ruled "harmless."

2 *Naughton v. Bankier*, 691 A.2d 712, 114 Md.App. 641 (1997); *Monlux v. General Motors Corp.*, 714 P.2d 930 (Hawaii 1986); *Cooke v. Walter Kidde & Co., Inc.*, 394 N.E.2d 968 (Mass. 1979); *Fowler v. S-H-S Motor Sales Corp.*, 560 S.W.2d 350 (Mo. 1977); *Depositors Trust Co. v. Blanchard*, 377 A.2d 101 (Me. 1977). See also *Brown v. Ford Motor Co.,* 239 Ill.Dec. 637, 714 N.E.2d 556, 306 Ill.App.3d 314 (1999).

3 *Skelly Oil Co. v. Jordan*, 186 Okla. 130, 96 P.2d 524 (1939).

4 *Mehochko v. Gold Seal Co.*, 66 Ill.App.2d 54, 213 N.E.2d 581, 583 (1966). In a case involving out-of-court tests, the court stated: "In tests, the essential elements are the results, methods and qualifications of the tester. The method and qualification of the tester (to conduct the test and correctly read its results) give the results their veracity."

5 *Sewell v. McRae*, 52 Wash.2d 103, 323 P.2d 236 (1958). The court ruled that "the ultimate test for the admissibility of an experiment as evidence is whether it tends to enlighten the jury and to enable them to more intelligently consider the issues presented." See also *Monlux v. General Motors Corp.*, 714 P.2d 930 (Hawaii 1986); *O'Doherty v. Catonsville Plumbing & Heating Co., Inc.*, 269 Md. 371, 306 A.2d 248 (1973).

2. The demonstration is performed under conditions substantially similar to those of the subject incident.[6]
3. The demonstration is relevant and material.[7]
4. The demonstration will not confuse or mislead the jury.[8]
5. The demonstration will be performed by a qualified person.[9]
6. The materials employed in the demonstration are working properly and are the types which should be used.[10]
7. Any substances which are tested are properly identified.[11]

For each of the items listed on the preceding page, the proponent should take special care to assure that the demonstration passes the Substantial Similarity Test, which is vital to gaining admission for most forms of demonstrative evidence.[12]

6 *People v. Harold Oliver,* 306 Ill.App.3d 59, 713 N.E.2d 727, 239 Ill.Dec. 196 (1999); *Starter Corp. v. Converse, Inc.*, 170 F.3d 286. (2nd Cir. N.Y. 1999); *McFarland & Son, Inc. v. Basel,* 727 So.2d 266 (Fla.App. 1999); *Sears, Roebuck & Co. v. Kunze,* 996 S.W.2d 416 (Tex.App. 1999); *Naughton v. Bankier*, 691 A.2d 712, 114 Md.App. 641 (1997). See also *Krute v. Mosca*, 650 N.Y.S.2d 862 (1996), where Plaintiff, who allegedly suffered a serious injury, was caught on videotape carrying heavy rocks. The trial court did not abuse its discretion when it admitted into evidence a rock and scale to permit a test in order to determine, very generally, the weight of the rocks. It was held that any variation between the size of the rock received into evidence and those shown on the videotape was readily observable by jury; thus, objections went to the "weight" and not the admissibility of the demonstration and supporting evidence.

7 *Kehm v. Procter & Gamble Co.*, 580 F.Supp. 890 (N.D. Iowa 1982). See also *Krute v. Mosca*, 650 N.Y.S.2d 862 (1996), where Plaintiff, who allegedly suffered a serious injury, was caught on videotape carrying heavy rocks. The trial court did not abuse its discretion when it admitted into evidence a rock and scale to permit a test in order to determine, very generally, the weight of the rocks. It was held that any variation between the size of the rock received into evidence and those shown on the videotape was readily observable by jury; thus, objections went to the "weight" and not the admissibility of the demonstration and supporting evidence.

8 *Cooke v. Walter Kidde & Co., Inc.*, 394 N.E.2d 968 (Mass. 1979).

9 *Auto-Ion Chemicals, Inc. v. Gates Rubber Co.*, 33 Mich.App. 574, 190 N.W.2d 357 (1971); *Graves v. Wildsmith*, 278 Ala. 228, 177 So.2d 448 (1965); *Crecelius v. Gamble-Skogmo, Inc.*, 144 Neb. 394, 13 N.W.2d 627 (1944).

10 *Crecelius v. Gamble-Skogmo, Inc.*, 144 Neb. 394, 13 N.W.2d 627 (1944).

11 *Grogan v. United States*, 341 F.2d 39 (6th Cir. 1965).

12 *States v. R.D. Werner Co.*, 799 P.2d 427 (Colo. 1990). The conditions under which an experiment is conducted must be substantially similar to those present on the occasion of the incident at issue, so as not to confuse or mislead the jury. See also *Santucci v. Govel Welding*, 168 A.D.2d 845, 564 N.Y.S.2d 518 (1990); *Lopez v. Foremost Paving*, 796 S.W.2d 473 (Tex. 1990); *Foster v. Devilbiss Co.,* 174 Ill.App.3d 359, 529 N.E.2d 581 (1988), *appeal denied*, 124 Ill.2d 554, 535 N.E.2d 914 (1989); *Smith & Wesson, Division of Bangor Punta Corp. v. United States*, 782 F.2d 1074 (1st Cir. 1986); *Short v. Gen. Motors Corp.*, 320 S.E.2d 19 (N.C. 1984); *Kehm v. Procter & Gamble Co.*, 580 F.Supp. 890 (N.D. Iowa 1982); *State v. Philbrick*, 436 A.2d 844, 859 (Me. 1981); *Orwick v. Belshan*, 231 N.W.2d 90 (Minn. 1975); *Way v. Hayes*, 513 P.2d 1222 (Nev. 1973).

Substantial, not precise, similarity is the proper standard. Small differences will affect the weight, not the admissibility, of the evidence,[13] particularly when those differences are explained to the jury.[14]

If an in-court experiment involves matters of a technical or scientific nature, an expert's supporting testimony may be required. However, for most demonstrations, no such requirement will exist.[15]

§48.202 Sample Foundation for Demonstrations

Q. (By Proponent's Attorney) Please state your name for the record.
A. (Witness) Ellen Exhibitionist.
Q. Please state your occupation.
A. I'm an (electrical, chemical, mechanical, highway) engineer.
Q. Please state your area of expertise, if any.
A. (The witness should provide detailed information as to degrees, seminars, experience and licenses.) I am an expert in...
Q. Have you heard the testimony presented in this case thus far?
A. Yes, I've been present from the start of the trial.
Q. Is there an experiment that you could conduct for us that would resolve the dispute pertaining to...?
A. Yes, there is a way to settle it conclusively.
Q. Please briefly describe it.
A. (The witness' description should be very brief.)
Q. Will this demonstration assist the jury in understanding the subject dispute?
A. Yes, it will.
Q. Will this demonstration simplify and clarify the issues for the jury?
A. Yes, I believe it will.

---

13 *State v. Donesay,* 19 P.3d 779 (Kansas, 2001). The defendant was convicted of premeditated murder, aggravated robbery, two counts of felony theft, felony criminal damage to property, and criminal possession of a firearm. An in-court demonstration of the positions of the murder defendant, the victim, and the gun was permissible, despite discrepancies between the sizes of the models and the actual participants, and despite the claim that the jury's perception of the duration of the struggle would be distorted by a demonstration of the models' frozen positions. The purpose of the demonstration was to illustrate the pathologist's opinion as to the relative positions of the defendant and the victim when each shot was fired, not to recreate a flow of movement; the pathologist said that any differences between heights and weights of models and those of the defendant and the victim would not affect the accuracy of his opinion.

Kehm v. Procter & Gamble Co., 580 F.Supp. 890 (N.D. Iowa 1982); *Dritt v. Morris,* 235 Ark. 40, 357 S.W.2d 13 (1962); *Kling v. Denver*, 138 Colo. 567, 335 P.2d 876 (1959); *People v. Pfanschmidt*, 262 Ill. 411, 104 N.E. 804 (1914).

14 *Estate of Carey v. Hy-Temp., Mfg.*, 929 F.2d 1229 (7th Cir. 1991); *Short v. Gen. Motors Corp.*, 320 S.E.2d 19 (N.C. 1984); *State v. Jones*, 287 N.C. 84, 214 S.E.2d 24 (1975). See also *Hutchison v. Missouri Highway and Transportation Commission,* 996 S.W2d 109 (Mo.App. 1999) involving an automobile negligence action brought by the driver who rear-ended an escort vehicle. The defendant s in-court demonstration of the flashing warning lights on the escort vehicle (accompanying a weed-killer spraying rig) was admissible where the plaintiff first mentioned the evidence in his opening argument, explaining the difference between the courtroom conditions and actual conditions.

15 See *Strickland v. Washington,* 466 U.S. 668; 104 S.Ct. 2052 (1984), involving a death-penalty murder conviction. During trial, a witness testified about burns that she received during the perpetration of the crimes committed by Defendant. Defendant claimed that the burns were accidentally self-inflicted when the witness ignited lighter fluid that she had accidentally spilled on herself while filling her cigarette lighter. The prosecution, over the Defendant's objection, was permitted to have the witness demonstrate to the jury how she typically refills her Zippo lighter. The Prosecutor used this demonstration to show that it was unlikely that the burns occurred in the manner suggested by the Defendant. Defendant complained that the lighter used in the demonstration, while of the same type, was a new, as opposed to a used, lighter; he also claimed that this type of demonstrative evidence is inadmissible without the aid of an expert witness. The high court found that pouring fluid into a lighter is hardly a process shrouded in mystery; rather, it is a simple task within the ken of the ordinary juror.

Q. Will the demonstration assist your explanation of the more technical aspects of this case?
A. It's really the only way that I can explain things clearly.
Q. (Addressing the court) I ask the court for permission to conduct the demonstration (experiment) referred to by the witness.
COURT: Any objections?
OPPOSING ATTORNEY: None.
COURT: Very well, it will be received.

§48.300 Opposition

Any of the eleven Opposition Checklist items in Chapter 40 are possible candidates for objections. Claiming a lack of substantial similarity is often the best route through which to attack a demonstration.[16]

And, of course, there is always the Hamilton Burger assault: "Your Honor, Mr. Mason is trying to turn the court room into a circus." That attack rarely worked for Prosecutor Burger, and without a more substantial underlying basis, it will rarely work for you.

16 *Andrews v. State,* 811 A.2d 282, 372 Md. 1 (2002) involved a prosecution for homicide following the death of an infant. An in-court demonstration with a doll that was used to show the amount of force necessary to produce a "shaken baby syndrome" was irrelevant without a proper foundation establishing that the demonstration would be substantially similar to the events relating to the infant's death. Moreover, a foundation for demonstrative evidence must be laid through a witness's testimony indicating that the evidence fairly and accurately depicts what it purports to depict. Stated another way, in-court demonstrations are allowed with the court's permission if the pertinent conditions are substantially the same as at the time in question and if the procedure will not be unduly time-consuming, confusing, or likely to arouse unfairly emotional reactions in the jury. In this case, the trial court's decision to allow the state to proceed with the demonstration, despite a presumption and acknowledgment of dissimilarity between the child victim and the doll used in the demonstration, improperly relieved the state of its burden to establish the substantial similarity of the demonstration to the facts at issue in the homicide prosecution.

See *Naughton v. Bankier*, 691 A.2d 712, 114 Md.App. 641 (1997). A plaintiff, who was injured when the defendant used an eight-foot sling-shot toy to propel a water balloon through a window, was not entitled to demonstrate the toy in open court; the court found that it would be difficult or impossible to imitate the conditions under which the cause of action accrued. The toy was constructed of rubber and elastic, and it required three operators, and thus, the opportunity for variation would have rendered the demonstration scientifically unreliable. Moreover, If the demonstration is to occur, it must be conducted under circumstances and conditions similar to those that existed in the case at issue, and the trial court must, as a condition precedent to the demonstration, allow a full argument on the need for the demonstration and its fairness.

(This page intentionally left blank.)

Chapter 49

Internal Pictures

§49.100 Introduction

Medical procedures that produce "internal pictures" are used by physicians for a variety of reasons. The tests range from standard, well-accepted procedures, such as X-rays and surgical photographs, to new technologies, such as thermography and magnetic resonance imaging (MRI); the latter forms are currently on a rocky road to acceptance and admissibility. They are by no means automatically accepted by the courts.

§49.200 Foundation Requirements

Regardless of the level of sophistication of the subject test, it is important to remember that most internal pictures will be made for medical reasons (i.e., diagnosis and prognosis), not for the purposes of litigation. This fact lends credibility to the processes.

Internal pictures may be regarded as medical records and, therefore, may often qualify under the business records exception to the hearsay rule. But, in any event, the proposed evidence must be relevant to be admissible.[1] Generally, as always, admissibility lies within the trial court's discretion and will usually be reversed only where clear abuse is shown.[2]

With respect to X-rays, the proponent may introduce a print or an enlargement if it has a useful demonstrative function and the copy is properly authenticated.[3] Also, because X-rays are difficult for non-experts to interpret, a drawing of an X-ray may, likewise, be permitted.[4]

Authentication is generally made by the supervising physician[5] or the custodian of the hospital records.[6] The foundation requirements must show the following:

1. The X-ray or other internal picture is a picture of the person in question.
2. The picture was properly made.[7]
3. It is accurate.[8]
4. The picture represents the part of the body which it purports to represent.

---

1 *Roeder v. North Am. Life. Ins. Co. of Chicago*, 106 N.W.2d 624 (Minn. 1960).

2 *Atkins v. Graves,* 367 S.W.2d 372 (Tex. 1963); *Melford v. Gaus & Brown Constr. Co.*, 117 Ill.App.2d 497, 151 N.E.2d 128 (1958); *Kramer v. John Hancock Mut. Life Ins. Co.*, 336 Mass. 465, 146 N.E.2d 357 (1957); *Young v. Liddington*, 50 Wash. 78, 309 P.2d 761 (1957); *Quadlander v. Kansas City Pub. Serv. Co.*, 224 S.W.2d 396 (Mo.App. 1949).

3 *Aguirre v. Long Island Rail Road Co.*, 730 N.Y.S.2d 122 (N.Y.A.D., 2001); *Beauchamp v. Davis*, 309 Ky. 397, 217 S.W.2d 822 (1948). In suit by railroad employee against his employer, under Federal Employers Liability Act (FELA), X-ray of employee's lungs was not admissible because it did not conform to statutory requirements that X-rays be inscribed with name of patient, date taken, identifying number, and name and address of physician under whose supervision it was taken.

4 *Van Welden v. Ramsay's, Inc.*, 199 Kan. 417, 430 P.2d 298 (1967); *Slow Development Co. v. Coulter*, 88 Ariz. 122, 353 P.2d 890 (1960).

5 *Arkansas Amusement Corp. v. Ward*, 204 Ark. 130, 161 S.W.2d 178 (1942).

6 *Kovacev v. Ferreira Bros. Contracting, Inc.*, 779 N.Y.S.2d 204 (N.Y.A.D. 1 Dep't 2004); *Banks v. Bowman Dairy Co.*, 65 Ill.App. 113, 212 N.E.2d 4 (1965); *Allen v. St. Louis Pub. Serv. Co.*, 365 Mo. 677, 285 S.W.2d 663 (1956). In a personal injury action, Magnetic Resonance Imaging (MRI) films were not admissible because the plaintiff failed to show that the films fell within the scope of the business records exception to the hearsay rule or a statute providing for authentication.

7 *Howard v. State*, 342 N.E.2d 604 (Ind. 1976); *Texaco, Inc. v. Pursley*, 527 S.W.2d 236 (Tex. 1975); *Meade v. Belcher*, 212 Va. 796, 188 S.E.2d 211 (1972); *Hartman v. Maryland Casualty Co.*, 417 S.W.2d 640 (Tex. 1967); *Howell v. George*, 201 Miss. 783, 30 So.2d 603 (1947); *Eaker v. International Shoe Co.*, 199 N.C. 379, 154 S.E. 667 (1930).

8 *Howard v. State*, 342 N.E.2d 604 (Ind. 1976); *Howell v. George*, 201 Miss. 783, 30 So.2d 603 (1947).

Admissibility for other types of internal pictures is often based upon the same principles as X-rays,[9] or under the appropriate business records statute.[10]

Unlike X-rays, the accuracy of other medical tests may not be assumed simply because the machine's regular operator performed the test.[11] With new technical procedures, such as Magnetic Resonance Imaging (simply referred to as MRI),[12] expert testimony interpreting and explaining the test results may be permitted.[13]

With respect to new technologies, such as thermography and MRI, courts often apply the standards set down in *Frye v. United States*.[14] The "*Frye*" test allows admissibility for technologies which are sufficiently accepted in the relevant scientific community as reliable and accurate.[15] But *Frye* has not delivered a "consensus" test.[16] Thermographies, for example, have been accepted in several jurisdictions,[17] while being rejected in others.[18]

---

9 *Melford v. Gaus & Brown Constr. Co.*, 117 Ill.App.2d 497, 151 N.E.2d 128 (1958); *Kramer v. John Hancock Mut. Life Ins. Co.*, 336 Mass. 465, 146 N.E.2d 357 (1957); *Quadlander v. Kansas City Pub. Serv. Co.*, 224 S.W.2d 396 (Mo.App. 1949).

10 Where statutes exist to assist the admissibility of "medically" technical evidence, strict compliance may be required. See, for example, *Wagman v. Bradshaw* 739 N.Y.S.2d 421 (N.Y.A.D. 2nd Dept., 2002), declaring that in order to enter the results of X-rays, PET scans, electromylograms, sonograms, fetal heart rate monitors, and magnetic resonance imaging (MRI) without foundation testimony, there must be strict and literal compliance with statutory requirements.

Jezowski v. Beach, 59 Misc.2d 224, 298 N.Y.S.2d 360 (Sup.Ct. 1968); *Croll v. John Hancock Mut. Life Ins. Co.*, 198 F.2d 562 (3d Cir. 1952); *Freedman v. Mutual Life Ins. Co.*, 342 Pa. 404, 21 A.2d 81 (1941).

11 *Rhodig v. Cummings*, 418 P.2d 521 (Colo. 1966); *Quadlander v. Kansas City Pub. Serv. Co.*, 224 S.W.2d 396 (Mo.App. 1949).

12 *Pardodefigueroa v. Turner Const. Corp.*, 33 A.D.3d 601, 822 N.Y.S.2d 308 (2006). At a bifurcated personal injury trial on the issue of damages, the defendants seeking to exclude magnetic resonance imaging (MRI) films of the plaintiff's spine for lack of authentication made no showing that the films themselves failed to meet conditions for self-authentication, or that they were not otherwise admissible. MRI ia a diagnostic tool that produces distinct pictures of a body's internal organs without using X-rays. Instead, it utilizes magnetism, radio waves, and a microprocessor to obtain signals from the body which, in turn, generate an image capable of being translated into photographic images. In the forensic realm, see Diamond R. Fertilizer v. Davis, 567 So. 2d 451 (Fla. Dist. Ct.App. 1990).

13 *Flynn v. Mack*, 578 S.E.2d 488 (Ga.App, 2003). A physician relied on the results of an MRI to conclude that an injured motorist suffered a broken neck as the result of an automobile collision with the defendant's vehicle. The method by which that physician drew his conclusions went to the weight, not the admissibility, of his opinion.

Diamond R. Fertilizer v. Davis, 567 So.2d 451 (Fla. 1990).

14 293 F. 1013 (D.C. Cir. 1923); it should be noted that the *Frye* test, a strict one, is not without its critics. The test makes it difficult for the use of new technologies, such as DNA matching, because of its requirements.

15 For thermographic cases which cite *Frye*, see: *Kluck v. Borland*, 162 Mich.App. 695, 413 N.W.2d 90 (1987); *State v. Martin*, 101 Wash.2d 713, 684 P.2d 651 (1984); *State v. Maule*, 35 Wash.App. 287, 667 P.2d 96 (1983); *State v. Canaday*, 90 Wash.2d 808, 585 P.2d 1185 (1978).

16 The *Frye* standard will be significantly modified in nearly every jurisdiction due to a relatively recent case handed down by the United States Supreme Court; See the discussion of *Daubert v. Merrell Dow Pharmaceuticals, Inc.*, 113 S.Ct. 2786, 125 L.Ed. 2d 469 (1993) in Chapter 11.

17 *Cherico v. National R.R. Passenger Corp.*, 758 F.Supp. 258 (E.D.Pa. 1991); *Destin v. Sears, Roebuck & Co.*, 803 S.W.2d 113 (Mo. 1990); *Tenuta v. Heckler,* 606 F.Supp. 624 (E.D. Wis. 1985); *Grey v. Eastern Airlines, Inc.*, 480 So.2d 1341 (Fla. 1985); *Fay v. Mincey*, 454 So.2d 587 (Fla. 1984); *Procida v. McLaughlin*, 195 N.J.Super. 396, 479 A.2d 447 (1984); *Thornton v. United States Dept. of Agric.*, 715 F.2d 1508 (11th Cir. 1983).

18 *Kluck v. Borland*, 162 Mich.App. 695, 413 N.W.2d 90 (1987); *Burkett v. Northern*, 43 Wash.App. 143, 715 P.2d 1159 (1986); *Ferlise v. Eiler*, 202 N.J.Super. 330, 495 A.2d 129 (1985); *Crawford v. Shivashankar*, 474 So.2d 873 (Fla. 1985); *McAdoo v. U.S.*, 607 F.Supp. 788 (E.D. Mich. 1984).

§49.201 Sample Foundation (By Custodian of Records)

Q. (By Proponent's Attorney) State your name for the record.
A. (Witness) Sam Searcher.
Q. Please state your occupation.
A. I am the custodian of records at Providence Hospital.
Q. What are your job duties?
A. I keep all of the medical records for the hospital, everything, medically, which has to do with the patients.
Q. I call your attention to plaintiff's Exhibit 1 and ask if you can identify it.
A. Yes, it is the plaintiff's file from my hospital.
Q. I call your attention to plaintiff's Exhibit 1 and ask if you can identify it?
A. Yes, it is the plaintiff's X-ray.
Q. How can you be certain that this is the plaintiff's X-ray?
A. Because the patient's number in written on the X-ray. Patients at our hospital are each assigned a number. Every record, including X-rays and other medical tests, always includes the patient's number.
Q. Are records such as this kept in the ordinary course of business?
A. Yes.
Q. (To the witness) Does this X-ray represent what it purports to represent, and nothing more?
A. Yes, except for... (The witness should point out discrepancies or inaccuracies.)
Q. Will this exhibit assist the jury in understanding the subject event?
A. Yes, it will.
Q. Will this exhibit clarify the issues for the jury?
A. Yes, it will.
Q. (Addressing the court) I ask that plaintiff's Exhibit 1 be admitted.
COURT: Any objections?
OPPOSING ATTORNEY: None.
COURT: Very well, it will be received.

Notice the chain-of-possession elements in the preceding dialogue. They suggest the presence of some "real evidence" characteristics. X-rays taken prior to a patient's change in condition might actually reflect characteristics of real and documentary evidence, in addition to serving as a demonstrative tool.

§49.300 Opposition

The opponent may attack new technologies on the grounds that they are not accepted as accurate by the appropriate scientific community. Unfortunately, the emerging standard is one that greatly liberalizes the tougher *Frye* standard (*supra*). In particular, the United States Supreme Court, in the landmark case of *Daubert v. Merrell Dow Pharmaceuticals, Inc.*,[19] set down a new four-part test for new scientific evidence:

1. Whether or not the subject theory or technique can be and has been tested;
2. Whether the theory or technique has been subjected to peer review and publication;
3. The known or potential rate of error; and
4. The "general acceptance" of the theory or technique. Particular attention should be paid to the fourth element, which keeps *Frye* partially alive.

Attacks on more established technologies may include questioning the accuracy of the procedure, the working condition of the equipment, or the chain of custody of photos.

19 113 S.Ct. 2786, 125 L.Ed. 2d 469 (1993); see Chapter 11.

Appendix A

Responding to Objections at a Glance

§A.100 Introduction

The first twelve chapters of this book unleashed upon the world a new breed of attorneys who are fast and deadly when it comes to voicing objections. It is now, therefore, time to provide some rapidly deployable defensive maneuvers, to act as a shield in the event that you are on the *receiving* end. This chapter is designed to provide some simple, but effective responses to the most common objections.

§A.200 Objections as to Form

The so-called "form" objections are among the easiest to combat. You merely re-state the question. It is interesting to note that in many instances, opposing counsel will not even bother to voice a subsequent objection if you re-state the question incorrectly a second time. But some will. And that may make you look foolish. In any event, the fixes for these types of objections are often quite simple and should not be overlooked in favor of mere repetition.

A classy response, and one that can play well to jurors, involves a rapid restatement of the question, without shifting your eyes to the objecting attorney. This method keeps the attention focused in your direction.

§A.201 Objection! The Question Is Argumentative

The "fix" is normally quite simple. Lower your voice (assuming that you have raised it) and make certain that your question is, indeed, in the form of a question. Any other type of response may be perceived as a continuation of the argument.[1] Sometimes a pause may be warranted, particularly if you been engaged in a heated exchange with the witness. If, as opposed to *argument*, you have merely engaged in effective cross-examination, continue on with your next question as if you had not been interrupted, unless, of course, the court intervenes.

§A.202 Objection! Calls for a Conclusion

Experts may, of course, offer conclusions.[2] If you are trying to elicit technical or scientific information from a non-expert, lots of luck.[3] If your information is non-technical, you are permitted a bit more latitude today than the law traditionally permitted. The applicable federal rules set the standard.[4]

Response if witness is an expert: "He's an expert. He's paid to give conclusions!"

Response if witness is not an expert: "He's permitted to provide opinions and inferences based on his perceptions."[5]

§A.203 Objection! The Question Is Leading

Remember that every proper question (or statement, for that matter) can be put in a form that is leading. And likewise, every leading question or statement can be put in the form of a *proper* question.

Leading is generally not permitted on direct examination.[6] So be certain to avoid using the

1 See *supra*, §3.400.

2 See *supra*, §3.400.

3 See *supra*, §3.300.

4 See *Rule* 701(a) of *Federal Rules of Civil Procedure*; see also *supra*, §3.300.

5 This language flows directly from *Rule* 701(a) of *Federal Rules of Civil Procedure*. If tact fails, you might try laying foundation for question by employing *Rule* 701(b) and asking whether or not his "opinion" would "be helpful to a clear understanding of the witness' testimony" or helpful to "the determination of a fact in issue."

6 See *infra*, §7.300.

term: "Isn't it true..." to start your question. Such questions are per se leading. Also, avoid questions that start with contractions such as: "Didn't," "Shouldn't," "Couldn't," "Wasn't," etc. In any event, by the time you ask the question the second time, the witness will probably have received your message.[7]

§A.204 Objection! The Question Is Multiple (or Compound)

This is one of the easiest problems to rectify. Just break down your question into simpler components. The infamous "*and's*" and "*or's*" can create ambiguities that diminish the value of your transcript.[8]

§A.205 Objection! The Question Is Repetitive

Repeating a previously asked question is objectionable during both direct and cross examination.[9] If the two questions at issue are substantially identical, merely ask your next question with a change or twist. If, however, you are certain that the two questions were different in some material respect, request the court reporter read back the two questions. A third possibility is quite common; it involves a situation wherein the witness has not fully answered the question. In such a case, the response to the objection might be:

> "I'm repeating the question because the witness has failed to answer it." Or,

> "I wouldn't have to repeat the question if your client would answer it."

§A.206 Objection! The Question Is Vague

If your question was the least bit vague, ambiguous or subject to more than one interpretation, do not argue. Simply restate the question.[10] If however, the question was clear and the witness is being evasive, you might ask the follow up question: "Which word or term didn't you understand?"

§A.300 Objections as to Substance

The so-called "substance" objections are more serious. Failure to appropriately respond to such an objection may result in the exclusion of critical evidence. And, that may turn the course of the trial in an unfavorable direction.

§A.301 Objection! Best Evidence

The Best Evidence Rule is, to many, an evidentiary dinosaur with an abundance of exceptions. If a document is lost, stolen, destroyed or otherwise unable to be located upon a due diligence search, secondary evidence is permissible. In most instances a photocopy is admissible to the same extent as the original unless there is some issue concerning genuineness.[11]

Keep in mind that if a transaction has significance separate and apart from the writing itself, you can avert the objection entirely by merely asking the question without reference to the writing.[12] For example, instead of asking: "When does your birth certificate say that you born," you might simply ask: "What is the date of your birth?" or "How old are you?"

---

7 Intentionally "cueing" witness with a leading question and then repeating the question correctly (once thought to be clever) does not garner favor with judges, nor today's more sophisticated jurors.

8 See generally, Chapter 8.

9 See generally, Chapter 10.

10 See generally, Chapter 12.

11 See generally, Chapter 2.

12 See *infra*, §2.300.

§A.302 Objection! Parol Evidence

The *Parol* Evidence Rule applies only to contracts. More specifically, it is a narrowly construed objection that is **only** designed to bar attempts to introduce oral conversations for the purpose of contradicting the terms of a fully integrated, unambiguous contract.[13]

§A.303 Objection! The Question Assumes Facts Not in Evidence

Anyone voicing this particular objection must have been paying attention to every question and answer that preceded the objection. It is rare indeed that an attorney will not be distracted at some point during the question/answer process. If the objection has merit, then you are, in effect, attempting to inject evidence that has yet to be established.[14] If that is not the case, you should stand your ground and suggest that opposing counsel "review" his or her notes (or transcripts, if prepared daily).

§A.304 Objection! Hearsay

This particular objection occupies more than half of the entire body of the law of evidence. It is riddled with exceptions.[15] If all of the classic exceptions fail you, don't forget about the so-called "residual exception."[16] And, above all, unless statements are offered to prove the truth of the matters asserted in them, they cannot be considered hearsay.[17] My favorite response, therefore, starts with: "Your Honor, I'm not offering this evidence for its truth, but rather to show ..."

§A.305 Objection! Irrelevant

There are several types and degrees of irrelevancy. Some issues are deemed irrelevant as a matter of law by virtue of some special rule or statute.[18] Other questions draw an objection because their connection is not immediately apparent. Sometimes, this promise will solve the problem: "If I'm permitted to continue, the connection will become apparent."

§A.306 Objection! Privilege

Privilege is always a sensitive matter that transcends the trial itself and extends to all proceedings, including discovery. When confronting an objection based on privilege, do not lose sight of the fact that there are many ways that privilege can be waived, and those instances increase whenever one voluntarily takes the witness stand. But perhaps the only way to effectively counter a privilege objection is to become familiar with the various privileges and their limitations.[19]

§A.307 Objection! Speculative

Neither experts nor lay persons are entitled to speculate or guess.[20] Nevertheless, while a "guess" or "speculation" is inadmissible, an "esti-

13 See *infra*, §2.400.

14 See generally, Chapter 4.

15 See *infra*, §5.400.

16 See *infra*, §5.411.

17 See *infra*, §5.300.

18 See *infra*, §5.411.

19 See *infra*, §9.501 (Attorney/Client); §9.503 (Doctor/Patient); §9.504 (Therapist/Patient); §9.505 (Accountant/Client); §9.506 (Clergyman/Penitent); §9.507 (Husband/Wife); §9.508 (Parent/Child); §9.509 (Informant/Police); §9.510 (Journalist/News Source); §9.511 (Confidential Institutional Privileges); §9.512 (Self Incrimination); §9.513 (Self-Critical Analysis Privilege).

20 See *infra*, §11.300.

mate" is not. There is a difference between a guess and an estimate, though the distinction is not often appreciated or understood. Theoretically, at least, an *estimate* is predicated upon some substantive information that the witness possesses.

When questioning the witness, use the term "estimate." Do not use the term "educated guess" even though this latter term may be just as accurate.

§A.400 Foolish Objections

All objections must be dealt with seriously, even the ones that lack coherence or legal support.[21] There are, of course, as many improper objections as there are comedic attorneys to deliver them. Following are a few of the most common.

§A.401 Objection! The Question Is Prejudicial

Evidence is supposed to be prejudicial![22] If it has any value whatsoever, it will assist your case and prejudice the opposition.[23]

§A.402 (On Cross-Examination) Objection! The Question Is Leading

While leading questions are not generally permitted during direct examination, they are **always** permitted on cross-examination.[24]

§A.403 Objection! The Document Speaks for Itself

This particular objection, though improper, it one that will seemingly never die. It appears to draw its strength from some misguided interpretation of the best evidence rule.[25] A common response: "I've never had a writing speak to me yet."

§A.404 Objection! The Evidence Is Self-Serving

All good evidence *should* be self-serving! We certainly do not want introduce evidence for the purpose of helping the opposition. Nevertheless, though foolish, this objection remains alive and well.[26]

The objection most commonly arises from a misapplication of other appropriate rules of evidence. For example, when documents are to be admitted under an exception to the hearsay rule, trustworthiness is often a major factor. If the information contained within the writings happen to be self-serving, a serious trustworthiness issue might then arise to preclude admissibility.[26] But that is hardly a reason for denying *all* evidence that is "self-serving."

---

21 For outstanding discussion of subject, see Donald F. Paine, *Stupid Objections and Offers of Proof*, The Tennessee Bar Association, 1995.

22 This objection should not be confused with, "Objection! The proposed evidence is such that its prejudicial effect substantially outweighs its probative value."

23 *McCathern v. Toyota Motor Corp.*, 23 P.3d 320, 332 Or. 59 (2001). It is normal that relevant evidence should "harm" opposing party's position.

24 See *infra*, §7.300.

25 See generally, Chapter 2.

26 See *supra*, §21.400.

(This page intentionally left blank.)

Table of Cases

- A -

- B -

Bennion v. Utah State Board of Oil, Gas & Mining, 675 P.2d 1135 (Utah 1983), §43.100

Benson v. Honda Motor Co., Ltd., 32 Cal.Rptr.2d 322, 26 C.A.4th 1337 (Cal.App. 2 Dist. 1994), §20.400

Berger v. City of New York, 597 N.Y.S.2d 555 (N.Y.Sup. 1993), §5.408.1

Berger v. Sonneland, 1 P.3d 1187 (Wash.App. Div. 3, 2000), §9.503.1

Berger v. U.S., 295 U.S. 78, 55 S.Ct. 629, 79 L.Ed. 1314 (1935), §§1.300, 4.300, 10.300

Berkeley Federal Bank and Trust, FSB v. Ogalin, 708 A.2d 620 (Conn.App. 1998), §47.200

Berlinger v. Mt. Sinai Medical Center, 589 N.E.2d 1378, 68 Ohio App.3d 830, 569 N.E.2d 505, 58 Ohio St.3d 707, *reh. den.* 571 N.E.2d 136, 59 Ohio St.3d 709 (1990), §9.503.1

Berman v. Radnor Rolls, 542 A.2d 525 (Pa. 1988), §44.301

Berryman v. K Mart Corp., 483 N.W.2d 642, 193 Mich.App. 88 (1992), §5.408.1

Beto v. Stewart, 582 S.E.2d 802, 213 W.Va. 355 (2003), Overview

Bettius & Sanderson, P.C. v. Nat'l. Union Fire Ins. Co., 839 F.2d 1009 (4th Cir. 1988), §6.300

Betts v. Manville Personal Injury Settlement Trust, 167 Ill.Dec. 1063, 588 N.E.2d 1193 (Ill.App. 1992), §7.400

Bhatt v. Department of Health Services, 35 Cal.Rptr.3d 335, 133 Cal.App.4th 923 (2005), §21.426

Biggerstaff v. Nance, 769 S.W.2d 470 (Mo.App. 1989), §3.300

Bills v. Com., 851 S.W.2d 466 (Ky. 1993), §9.507.1

Birt v. Firstenergy Corp., 891 A.2d 1281 (Pa.Super, 2006), §§20.501, 22.100, 22.300

Bituminous Cas. Corp. v. Tonka Corp., 140 F.R.D. 381 (D.Minn. 1992), §9.501.1

Black v. U-Haul Co. of Missouri, 204 S.W.3d 260 (Mo.App., 2006), §44.400

Blackburn v. Richardson, 849 S.W.2d 281 (Mo.App. 1993), §22.419

Blacker v. Oldsmobile Div., General Motors Corp., 869 F.Supp. 313 (E.D.Pa. 1994), §21.421

Blackwell v. State, 818 S.W.2d 134 (Tex.App. 1991), §9.507.1

Blair v. State, 747 A.2d 702, 130 Md.App. 571 (2000), §9.501.1

Blake v. Pellegrino, 329 F.3d 43 (1st Cir., Mass., 2003), §20.300

Blake v. Southcoast Health System, Inc., 206 F.Supp.2d 174, (D.Mass., 2002), §21.409

Blanchard v. EdgeMark Financial Corp., 192 F.R.D. 233 (N.D.Ill. 2000), §9.501

Bloomgren v. Fire Ins. Exchange, 162 Ill. App. 2d 594, 517 N.E.2d 290 (1987), §21.413

Board of Trustees of Public Employees' Retirement Fund of Indiana v. Morley, 580 N.E.2d 371 (Ind.App. 1991), §9.501.1

Board of Trustees v. Schuyten, 326 P.2d 223 (Cal.App. 1958), §§8.300, 8.500

Bogan v. State, 426 S.E.2d 392, 206 Ga.App. 696, cert. denied (1992), §5.405.1

Bogdan v. Peekskill Community Hosp., 642 N.Y.S.2d 478 (N.Y.Sup. 1996), §§21.403, 21.416

Bolduc v. U.S., 265 F.Supp.2d 153 (D.Mass., 2003), §21.401(b)

Bolen v. Paragon Plastics, Inc., 754 F.Supp. 221 (D.Mass. 1990), §25.201

Boling v. Boling, 887 S.W.2d 437 (Mo.Ct.App. 1994), §21.419

Bolstridge v. Central Me. Power Co., 621 F.Supp. 1202 (D.Me. 1985), §§44.500, 44.600

Bonds v. State, 837 S.W.2d 881, 310 Ark. 541 (Ark. 1992), §9.506.1

Bondu v. Gurvich, 473 So.2d 1307 (Fla. Dist. Ct. App. 1984), §30.300

Boner v. Peabody Coal Co., 154 Ill.Dec. 662, 568 N.E.2d 883, 142 Ill.2d 523 (1991), §35.200

Borne v. Haverhill Golf Club, Inc., 79 N.E.2d 903, 58 Mass.App.Ct. 306 (2003), §22.403

Boscia v. Sharples, 860 A.2d 674 (R.I., 2004), §§22.420, 44.301

- C -

Chicago Firefighters Local 2 v. City of Chicago, 249 F.3d 649, (7th Cir., Ill., 2001), §24.203

Christenson v. State, 402 S.E.2d 41 (Ga. 1991), §9.504.1

Christian Health Care of Springfield W. Park v. Little, 145 S.W.3d 44, (Mo. Ct. App., 2004), §2.300

Cincinnati v. Bawtenheimer, 586 N.E.2d 1065, 63 Ohio St.3d 260 (1992), §9.512.1

Cincinnati Insurance Company v. Raymond Samples, 192 S.W.3d 311 (Ky., 2006), §22.421

Cirillo v. Davis, 732 So.2d 387 (Fla.App. 1999), §36.302

Cisarik v. Palos Community Hospital, 144 Ill.2d 339, 341, 162 Ill.Dec. 59, 579 N.E.2d 873 (1991), §40.100

Cisarik v. Palos Community Hospital, 144 Ill.2d 339, 579 N.E.2d 873 (1991), §44.500

Citrus County v. McQuillin, 840 So.2d 343 (Fla.App., 2003), §44.300

City of Austin v. Houston Lighting & Power Co., 844 S.W.2d 773 (Tex.App. 1992), §24.203

City of Bangor v. Citizens Communications Co., 339 F.Supp.2d 135, (D.Me., 2004), §§21.200, 21.426

City of Champaign v. Sides, 284 Ill. Dec. 634, 810 N.E.2d 287, (Ill. App. Ct., 2004), §§1.300, 10.300

City of Chicago v. Old Colony Partners, 364 Ill.App.3d 806, 847 N.E.2d 565, 301 Ill.Dec. 555 (2006), Overview, §§22.100, 22.300

City of Dallas v. Donovan, 768 S.W.2d 905 (Tex.App.- Dallas 1989), §5.408

City of Gulf Shores v. Harbert Intern, 608 So.2d 348 (Ala. 1992), §25.209

City of Louisville v. Yeager, 489 S.W.2d 819 (Ky. 1973), §§44.300, 44.600

City of Springfield v. Rexnord Corp., 196 F.R.D. 7 (D.Mass. 2000), §9.501

City of Tucson v. Superior Court In and For County of Pima, 809 P.2d 428, (Ariz. 1991), §9.400

Clark Construction Group, Inc. v. City of Memphis, 229 F.R.D. 131 (W.D., Tenn., 2005), §30.300

Clark v. Cantrell, 504 S.E.2d 605 (S.C.App. 1998), §47.600

Clark v. Cantrell, 529 S.E.2d 528 (S.C. 2000), §47.500

Clark v. Ill. Cent. R.R., 872 So.2d 773 (Miss. Ct. App., 2004), §44.300

Claussen v. State Department of Transportation, 750 So.2d 79, (Fla.App. 1999), §21.100

Clayborne v. U.S., 751 A.2d 956 (D.C. 2000), §1.300

Claypool v. City of New York, 699 N.Y.S.2d 363 (N.Y.A.D. 1 Dept.,1999), §5.300

Clear v. Missouri Coordinating Board for Higher Education, 23 S.W.3d 896 (Mo.App. 2000), §22.404

Clement v. Griffin, 634 So.2d 412 (La.Ct.App. 1994), §44.600

Clermont v. State, 704 A.2d 880, 348 Md. 419 (1998), §4.600

Cleveland v. Bryant, 512 S.E.2d 360, 236 Ga.App. 459 (1999), §44.301

Coal Resources, Inc. v. Gulf & Western Indus., Inc., 865 F.2d 761 (6th Cir. 1989), §11.300

Coates v. Johnson & Johnson, 756 F.2d 524 (7th Cir. 1985), §43.100

Coco v. State, 62 So.2d 892 (Fla. 1953), *cert. denied*, 349 U.S. 931, *reh. den.,* 350 U.S. 855 (1955), §46.200

Coho Resources, Inc. v. McCarthy, 829 So.2d 1 (Miss. 2002), Overview

Coker v. Hayes, 16 Fla. 368, 373 (1878), §7.400

Cole v. U.S., 327 F.2d 360 (9th Cir. 1964), §§3.300, 5.408

Coleman v. Fortner, 579 S.E.2d 792, 260 Ga.App. 373 (2003), §22.425(b)

Coleman v. Home Depot, Inc., 306 F.3d 1333, (3rd Cir., N.J., 2002), §§21.300, 21.401, 21.426

Coletti v. Cudd Pressure Control, 165 F.3d 767 (10th Cir. Wyo. 1999), §30.300

Collier v. Bradley University, 113 F.Supp.2d 1235 (2000), §23.412

Collins v. State, 415 N.E. 46 (Ind.), *cert. denied*, 451 U.S. 991 (1981), §46.200

Colon v. BIC USA, Inc., 199 F.Supp.2d 53 (S.D.N.Y., 2001), §44.300

Connors v. U.S., 720 F.Supp. 1258 (N.D.Tex. 1989), §36.304

Conrad ex rel. Conrad v. Alderwood Manor, 78 P.3d 177 (Wash.App. Div., 2003), §44.500

Consolidated Edison, Inc. v. Northeast Utilities, 332 F.Supp.2d 639, (S.D.N.Y., 2004), §2.400

Consolidated Furniture Co. v. Kelly, 369 S.W.2d 53 (Tex. 1963), §44.301

Constans v. Choctaw Transport, 712 So.2d 885 (La.Ct.App. 1997), §40.500

Conti v. Commissioner, 39 F.3d 658 (1994), §21.419

Continental Concrete Pipe Corp. v. Century Rd. Builders, 195 Ill.App.3d 1, 552 N.E.2d 1032 (1990), §44.400

Converse v. Ameritech Corp., 179 F.R.D. 533 (Mich. 1997), §25.201

Cooke v. Walter Kidde & Co., Inc., 394 N.E.2d 968 (Mass. 1979), §§48.200, 48.201

Cooper v. Kellogg, 42 P.2d 59, 2 C.2d 504 (1935), §3.700

Copeland v. Mr. B's Pool Centers, Inc., 850 S.W.2d 380 (Mo.App. 1993), §5.4041

Coppedge v. Missouri Highway and Transp. Com'n., 809 S.W.2d 164, (Mo.App. 1991), §§4.503, 4.600

Corbitt v. State, 596 So.2d 426, certiorari denied Ex parte Corbitt, 596 So.2d 430. (Ala.App. 1992), §9.507.1

Corcoran v. Sears Roebuck and Co., 711 A.2d 371 (N.J.Super. 1998), §25.210(A)

Corlett v. Smith, 763 P.2d 1172 (N.M.App. 1988), §5.410

Cornelius v. Macon-Bibb County Hospital Authority, 533 S.E.2d 420, 243 Ga. App. 480 (2000), §44.600

Cornett v. State, 450 N.E.2d 498 (Ind. 1983), §45.200

Corsie v. Campanalonga, 721 A.2d 733, 317 N.J.Super. 177 (1998), §9.506.1

Coscan Florida, Inc. v. Equiventure Florida, 567 So. 2d 17, (Fla. Dist. Ct.App. 1990), §2.400

Coscino v. Wolfley, 696 So.2d 257 (La.App.4.Cir.1997), §§4.300, 4.600

Costa v. Dresser Indus., Inc., 205 Ill.Dec. 33, 642 N.E.2d 898, (Ill.App. 3 Dist. 1994), §24.205

Costantino v. David M. Herzog, M.D., P.C., 203 F.3d 164 (2nd Cir. N.Y. 2000), §24.202

Countrywide Services Corp. v. SIA Ins. Co., Ltd., 235 F.3d 390 (8th Cir Mo.) 2000, §22.403(d)

County of Los Angeles v. Superior Court (Martinez), 274 Cal. Rptr. 712, 224, C.A.3d 1446 (Cal.App. 2 Dist. 1990), §9.501.1

Courteau v. St. Paul Fire & Marine Ins. Co., 821 S.W.2d 45, 307 Ark. 513 (1991), §9.501.1

Cox v. Oliver Mach. Co., 41 Ohio App.3d 28, 534 N.E.2d 855 (1987), §22.425

Coyle v. Kristjan Palusalu Maritime Co., Ltd., 83 F.Supp.2d 535 (E.D.Pa. 2000), §22.401

Crackel v. Allstate Ins. Co., 92 P.3d 882, 208 Ariz. 252, (Ariz. Ct. App., 2004), §22.428

Craft v. State, 764 So.2d 1253 (Miss.App. 2000), §§7.300, 7.400

Crawford ex rel. Goodyear v. Care Concepts, Inc., 608 N.W.2d 694, 233, Wis.2d 609, 2000 Wi. App 59 (2000), §9.503.1

Crawford v. City of Meridian, 186 So.2d 250 (Miss. 1966), §42.200

Crawford v. Dammann, 626 S.E.2d 632, 277 Ga.App. 442 (2006), Overview, §22.428

Crawford v. Hall, 531 So.2d 874 (Ala. 1988), §3.400

Crawford v. Shivashankar, 474 So.2d 873 (Fla. 1985), §§22.430, 49.200

Crecelius v. Gamble-Skogmo, Inc., 144 Neb. 394, 13 N.W.2d 627 (1944), §48.201

Creech v. Commonwealth, 410 S.E.2d 650 (Va. 1991), §9.507.1

Creger v. Robertson, 542 So.2d 1090 (La.App. 2 Cir. 1989), Overview

Crisci v. Sadler, 676 N.Y.S.2d 646 (1998), §22.420

Croll v. John Hancock Mut. Life Ins. Co., 198 F.2d 562 (3d Cir. 1952), §49.200

Cronier v. Cronier, 540 So.2d 1160 (La.App. 1 Cir. 1989), §9.504

- D -

Daymude v. State, 540 N.E.2d 1263 (Ind. 1989), §9.503

Deerhake v. DuQuoin State Fair Ass'n., 185 Ill.App.3d 374, 133 Ill.Dec. 508, 541 N.E.2d 719 (1989), §24.203

DeGiacomo v. Westchester County Healthcare Corp., 743 N.Y.S.2d 548, (N.Y.A.D., 2002), §44.301

Dellenbach v. Robinson, 642 N.E.2d 638, 95 Ohio App.3d 358, (Ohio App.10 Dist. 1993), §22.420

Delsack v. Cumella, 593 N.Y.S.2d 2 (N.Y.A.D. 1 Dept. 1993), §2.400

DeLuca v. Blanco, 31 A.D.3d 600, 819 N.Y.S.2d 86 (N.Y.A.D., 2 Dept., 2006), §21.401(b)

Demos v. Ferris-Shell Oil Co., 251 Ill.Dec. 179, 740 N.E.2d 9, 317 Ill.App.3d 41 (2000), §6.800

Denius v. Dunlap, 209 F.3d 944, 143 Ed. Law Rep. 736 (C.A.7, Ill., 2000), §9.501

Dennis v. Capital Dist. Transportation Authority, 711 N.Y.S.2d 836 (2000), §21.401

Denton v. Critikon, Inc., 674 So.2d 1169 (La.App. 1996), §24.206

DePalma v. Westland Software House, 276 Cal.Rptr. 214 (Cal.App. 2 Dist. 1990), §6.800

Department of Corrections, State of Fla. v. Williams, 549 So.2d 1071 (Fla. 1989), §25.201

Department of Economic Development v. Arthur Andersen & Co., 139 F.R.D. 295 (S.D.N.Y. 1991), §9.501.1

Department of Transportation v. Elm Land Co., 593 S.E.2d 131, (N.C. App., 2004), §6.300

Department of Transportation v. Taylor, 841 A.2d 108 (2004), §§21.300, 21.401(b)

Depositors Trust Co. v. Blanchard, 377 A.2d 101 (Me. 1977), §48.200

DeRosa v. Kolb, 90 Or. App. 548, 752 P.2d 1282 (1988), §40.500

Desai v. Blue Shield of Northeastern New York, Inc., 540 N.Y.S.2d 569, 146 A.D.2d 264 (N.Y.A.D. 3 Dept. 1989), §9.503

DeSoto Wildwood Development v. City of Lewisville, 184 S.W.3d 814 (Tex.App., 2006), §2.300

Desrosiers v. Flight Inter. of Florida, Inc., 156 F.3d 952 (9th Cir. 1998), §21.402

Destin v. Sears Roebuck & Co., 803 S.W.2d 113 (Mo.Ct.App. 1990), §§22.430, 49.200

Detroit Marine Engineering, Inc. v. Maloy, 419 So. 2d 687 (Fla. 1982), §41.200

Detroit/Wayne County Stadium Authority v. Drinkwater, Taylor & Merrill, Inc., 705 N.W.2d 549, 267 Mich.App. 625 (2005), §§22.100, 22.408

Diamond Fertilizer v. Davis, 567 So.2d 451 (Fla.Dist.Ct.App. 1990), §§22.423, 49.200

Diamond v. Howd, 288 F.3d 932. (6th Cir., 2002), §45.200

DiBuono v. A. Barletta & Sons, 127 Pa.Commw. 1, 560 A.2d 893 (1989), §44.301

DiCarlo v. Keller Ladders, Inc., 211 F.3d 465 (8th Cir. Mo. 2000), §44.600

DiCenzo v. Izawa, 723 P.2d 171, 68 Haw. 528 (Hawaii 1986), §9.501

Dickens v. Calhoun First Nat. Bank, 448 S.E.2d 237, 214 Ga. App. 490, (Ga. App. 1994), §22.402

Diehl v Blaw-Knox, 360 F.3d 426 (3d Cir. Pa., 2004), §6.703

Dillenbeck v. Hess, 539 N.Y.S.2d 707, 73 N.Y.2d 278, 536 N.E.2d 1126 (N.Y. 1989), §9.503

Dine v. Williams, 830 S.W.2d 453, reh. den. (Mo.App. 1992), §3.500

Ditto v. Stoneberger, 805 A.2d 1148, 145 Md.App. 469 (2002), §44.301

Diversified Telecom Services, Inc. v. Clevinger, 683 N.W.2d 338, 268 Neb., 388 (2004), Overview

Dixon Dairy Farms, Inc. v. Purina Mills, Inc., 601 S.E.2d 152, 267, Ga. App. 738 (2004), Overview

Dixon v. Internat'l. Harvester Co., 754 F.2d 573 (5th Cir. 1985), §3.400

Dixson v. Quarles, 627 F.Supp. 50 (E.D. Mich. 1985), §9.501

Doe v. Gunnys Ltd. Partnership, 593 N.W.2d 284, 256 Neb. 653 (1999), §47.300

Doe v. Puget Sound Blood Center, 819 P.2d 370, 117 Wash.2d 772 (1991), §9.503.1

Dole v. Service Employees Union, AFL-CIO, Local 280, 950 F.2d 1456 (9th Cir. 1991), §2.300

- E -

- F -

- G -

Ganske v. Spence, 129 S.W.3d 701 (Tex. App. Waco 2004), §§2.100, 20.200

Gant v. Novello, 754 N.Y.S.2d 746 (N.Y.A.D. 3rd Dept., 2003), §§24.202, 24.206

Gantt v. Whitaker, 57 Fed.Appx. 141 (4th Cir., N.C., 2003), §24.203

Garbincius v. Boston Edison Co., 621 F.2d 1171 (1st Cir. 1980), §22.414

Garden State Bank v. Graef, 775 A.2d 189, 341 N.J. Super. 241 (2001), §22.406

Garrison v. State, 589 N.E.2d 1156 (Ind. 1992), §7.400

Gastman v. North Jersey Newspapers Co., 603 A.2d 111, 254 N.J.Super. 140, (1992), §9.501.1

Gathers By and Through Hutchinson v. South Carolina Elec. and Gas Co., 427 S.E.2d 687 (S.C.App. 1993), §§4.503, 4.600

Gatto v. Mortgage Specialists of Illinois, Inc., 442 F.Supp.2d 529 (N.D.Ill., 2006), §22.300

Gavins v. State, 587 So.2d 487 (Fla.App. 1991), §6.400

Gavoni v. Dobbs House, Inc., 164 F.3d 1071 (7th Cir. Ill 1999), §42.100

Gelpi v. 37th Ave. Avenue Realty Corp., 721 N.Y.S.2d 380 (N.Y.A.D., 2001), §5.300

General Elec. Capital Corp. v. Ford Motor Credit Co., 149 B.R. 229 (D.Me. 1993), §2.400

Georgis v. Ashcroft, 328 F.3d 962 (7th Cir., 2003), §21.430

Ghere v. Industrial Commission, 215 Ill.Dec. 532, 663 N.E.2d 1046, (Ill.App. 4 Dist. 1996), §21.425

Gianfala v. State Farm Mut. Auto. Ins. Co., 615 So.2d 558 (La.App. 3 Cir. 1993), §§3.300, 3.700

Gibbs v. Abiose, 508 S.E.2d 690, 235 Ga.App. 214 (1998), §44.301

Gibbs v. Mayo, 591 S.E.2d 905 (N.C.App., 2004), §5.411.1

Gil v. Gil, 892 A.2d 318, §22.300

Gilbert v. Ireland, 758 So.2d 1050 (Miss.App. 2000), §22.416

Gilmer v. Carney, 608 N.E.2d 709 (Ind.App. 3 Dist. 1993), §21.409

Givens v. Lederle, 556 F.2d 1341 (5th Cir. 1977), §22.431

Glacier Tennis Club at the Summit, L.L.C. v. Treweek Construction Co., 87 P.3d 431, 320 Mont. 351 (2004), Overview

Glazer v. Lehman Bros., Inc., 394 F.3d 444 (6th Cir., Ohio, 2005), §2.400

Globe v. Sterling, 556 A.2d 731, 79 Md.App. 303 (1989), §3.400

Glotzbach v. Froman, 854 N.E.2d 337 (Ind., 2006), §30.300

Glusaskas v. Hutchinson, 148 A.D.2d 203, 544 N.Y.S.2d 323 (1989), §44.301

Goff v. Continental Oil Co., 678 F.2d 593 (5th Cir. 1982), §40.500

Goguen v. Textron, Inc., 234 F.R.D. 13, 69 Fed. R. Evid. Serv. 726 (2006), §§23.401, 24.203

Goings v. U.S., 377 F.2d 753 (8th Cir. 1967), §8.400

Gomez v. Great Lakes Steel Div., Nat'l. Steel Corp., 803 F.2d 250 (6th Cir. 1986), §43.100

Gonzales v. North Tp. of Lake County, 800 F.Supp. 676 (N.D.Ind. 1992), §23.401

Gonzalez v. Allstate Ins. Co., 615 So.2d 446 (La.App. 4 Cir. 1993), §6.800

Good Shepherd Manor Foundation, Inc. v. City of Momence, 323 F.3d 557, (7th Cir., Ill., 2003), §3.400

Good v. Bd. of County Comm'rs of Shawnee, 331 F.Supp.2d 1315, (D. Kan., 2004), §24.203

Goodloe v. Director of Revenue, 838 S.W.2d 506 (Mo.App. W.D. 1992), §21.406

Gordon v. State, 609 N.E.2d 1085 (Ind. 1993), §9.507.1

Gordy v. City of Canton, Mississippi, 543 F.2d 558 (5th Cir. 1976), §22.414

Gorman v. Hunt, 19 S.W. 662 (Ky. 2000), §§44.300, 44.301

Gould v. City of Aliquippa, 750 A.2d 934 (Pa.Cmwlth.App., 2000), §9.501.1

Gourley v. Nebraska Methodist Health System, Inc., 663 N.W.2d 43, 265, Neb. 918 (2003), §24.206
Government of Virgin Islands v. Dowling, 633 F.2d 660 (3rd Cir. 1980), §7.300
Grace United Methodist Church v. City of Cheyenne, 427 F.3d 775 (10th Cir., Wyo. 2005), §5.404
Graham v. McReynolds, 90 Tenn. 673, 18 S.W. 272 (1891), §4.300
Gramman v. Stachkunas, 750 So.2d 688 (Fla.App. 1999), §23.409(a)
Grand Jury, County of San Diego v. Superior Court (Harrison), 259 Cal.Rptr. 404 (Cal.App. 4 Dist. 1989), §9.501
Grandstaff v. Hawks, 36 S.W.3d 482 (Tenn.App., 2000), Overview
Graney v. Ryan, 796 N.Y.S.2d 496 (N.Y.A.D., 4 Dept., 2005), §44.300
Graves v. Atchison-Holt Elec. Co-op., 886 S.W.2d 1 (Mo.App. W.D. 1994), §23.412
Graves v. Graves, 531 So.2d 817 (Miss. 1988), §5.406
Graves v. Wildsmith, 278 Ala. 228, 177 So.2d 448 (1965), §48.201
Gray v. Brooklyn Heights R. Co., 175 N.Y. 448, 67 N.E. 899 (1903), §4.600
Grayson v. R.B. Ammon and Associates, Inc., 778 So.2d 1 (La.App., 2000), §22.401
Green v. Charleston Area Medical Center, Inc., 600 S.E.2d 340, 215, W.Va. 628 (2004), Overview
Green v. St. Francis Hospital, Inc., 791 A.2d 731 (Del.Supr. 2002), §44.301
Greene v. Bryant, 626 S.E.2d 185 (Ga.App., 2006), Overview
Greenfield v. Lykes Bros., S.S., Co., 848 So.2d 30 (2003), §20.100
Greenwood v. Greenwood, 596 N.W.2d 317 (N.D. 1999), §§6.300, 6.800
Grey v. Eastern Airlines, Inc., 480 So.2d 1341 (Fla. 1985), §49.200
Grice v. State, 142 Tex.Crim.App. 4, 151 S.W.2d 211 (1941), §46.200
Griffin v. Gregory, 355 So.2d 691 (Ala. 1978), §42.301
Grogan v. U.S., 341 F.2d 39 (6th Cir. 1965), §48.201
Grose v. Nissan North America, Inc., 50 S.W.3d 825 (Mo.App., 2001), §44.400
Gross v. King David Bistro, Inc., 84 F.Supp.2d 675 (D.Md. 2000), §21.100
Grossheim v. Freightliner Corp., 974 F.2d 745 (6th Cir. 1992), §21.421
Grossman v. Schwarz, 125 F.R.D. 376 (S.D.N.Y. 1989), §9.501
GTE Directories Service Corp. v. Pacific Bell Directory, 135 F.R.D. 187, (N.D.Cal. 1991), §9.501.1
Guild v. General Motors Corp., 53 F. Supp.2d 363. (W.D.N.Y. 1999), §21.425
Guillermety v. Secretary of Education of U.S., 341 F.Supp.2d 682, (E.D. Mich., 2003), §22.406
Gutierrez v. Albertsons, Inc., 824 P.2d 1058 (N.M.App. 1991), §2.300
Gutierrez v. State, 764 S.W.2d 796 (Tex.Cr.App. 1989), §6.400

- H -

Haddad v. Kuriger, 437 S.W.2d 524 (Ky. 1968), §44.301
Haffey v. Generac Portable Products, LLC., 171 S.W.3d 805 (Mo.App., 2005), §§1.300, 6.300
Haggerty v. Foster, 838 So.2d 948 (Miss.App. 2002), §41.100
Hagicostas v. Nat'l. Freight Sales, Inc., 641 N.Y.S.2d 365 (N.Y.A.D. 2 Dept. 1996), §21.401
Hagood v. State, 588 So.2d 526 (Ala.App. 1991), §7.300
Hahn v. Sterling Drug, Inc., 805 F.2d 1480 (11th Cir. 1986), §22.427
Hahn v. Tri-Line Farmers Coop., 478 N.W.2d 515 (Minn. Ct. App. 1991), §44.500

- I -

In re A.W. Lawrence & Co., Inc., 289 B.R. 20 (N.D.N.Y., 2003), §20.400
In re Agosto, 553 F.Supp 1298, 1325 (D. Nev. 1983), §9.508.1
In re Air Crash at Detroit Metro Airport, 791 F.Supp. 1204 (E.D. Mich.1992), §36.304
In re Air Crash at Stapleton Internat'l. Airport, 720 F.Supp. 1493 (D.Colo. 1989), §8.400
In re Arya, 168 Ill.Dec. 432, 589 N.E.2d 832, 226 Ill.App.3d 848 (1992), §9.510.1
In re Boelson Trust, 830 N.E.2d 37 (Ind.App., 2005), §2.400
In re Braun, 502 N.W.2d 219 (Minn.App. 1993), §9.512
In re Brink, 536 N.E.2d 1201, 42 Ohio Misc.2d 5 (Ohio Com.Pl. 1989), §9.503
In re Brittany L., 737 A.2d 670 (N.H., 1999), §§5.404, 5.404.1
In re Byington, 197 B.R. 130 (Bkrtcy.D.Kan. 1996), §24.204
In re Cain, 235 B.R. 812 (Bkrtcy.M.D.N.C. 1998), §24.206
In re Carmean, 153 B.R. 985 (Bkrtcy.S.D.Ohio 1993), §9.507.1
In re Columbia Securities Litigation, 155 F.R.D. 466 (S.D.N.Y. 1994), §24.203
In re Columbia/HCA Healthcare Corp., 192 F.R.D. 575, (M.D.Tenn.Nashville.Div., 2000), §9.501.1
In re Conservatorship of Smith, 655 N.W.2d 814 (Minn.App. 2003)
In re Contempt of Stone, 154 Mich. App. 121, 397 N.W.2d 244 (1986), §§9.510, 9.510.1
In re Criminal Investigation No. 1/242Q, 602 A.2d 1220, 325 Md. 740, 326 Md. 1 (1992), §9.501.1
In re D.M.C., 503 A.2d 1280 (D.C. 1986), §5.410
In re Daniel Z., 13 Cal.Rptr.2d 139, 10 C.A.4th 1009 (Cal.App. 1992), §5.408.1
In re Detention of Isbell, 268 Ill.Dec. 71, 777 N.E.2d 994 (2002), §44.300
In re Dow Corning Corp., 250 BR. 298 (Bankruptcy, E.D.Mich. 2000), §22.406(a)
In re Estate of Holmgren, 178 Ill.Dec. 569, 604 N.E.2d 1092 (Ill.App. 1992), §§5.406.1, 23.414
In re Estate of Love, 618 S.E.2d 97 (Ga.App., 2005), §6.300
In re Estate of Meyer, 747 N.E.2d 1159 (Ind.App., 2001), §22.404
In re Estate of Peters, 765 A.2d 468 (Vt. 2000), §5.408.1
In re Estate of Rennick, No. 82872, 286 Ill. App. 3d 318 (1997), §5.404.1
In re Fanaras, 263 B.R. 655 (Mass., 2001), §22.428
In re Fischer, 259 B.R. 23 (E.D.N.Y., 2001), §24.203
In re Grand Jury 90-1, 758 F.Supp. 1411 (D.Colo. 1991), §9.501.1
In re Grand Jury Investigation, 918 F.2d 374 (Pa. 1990), §9.506.1
In re Grand Jury Matter, The U.S. of America, 673 F.2d 688 (3rd Cir. 1982), §9.507
In re Growers Packing Co., Inc., 150 B.R. 82 (Bkrtcy.S.D.Fla. 1993), §9.512
In re Hillsborough Holdings Corp., 132 B.R. 478 (Bkrtcy. M.D.Fla. 1991), §9.505.1
In re Huffman's Estate, 349 Pa. 59, 36 A.2d 640 (1944), §22.300
In re Hunt, 153 B.R. 445 (Bkrtcy. N.D.Tex. 1992), §9.505
In re Interest of Andrew M., Jr., 622 N.W.2d 697, 9 Neb.App. 947 (2001), §§6.300, 6.800
In re Interest of Clifford M., 577 N.W.2d 547, 6 Neb.App. 754 (1998), §9.512.1
In re J.C.K., 143 S.W.3d 131 (Tex. App. Waco 2004), §2.300
In re J.M.V., 90 B.R. 737 (Bkrtcy. PA. 1988), §9.512
In re Jean Marie W., 559 A.2d 625 (R.I. 1989), §5.408
In re Johnson, 85 P.3d 1252 (Kan. App., 2004), §6.300
In re Joseph G., 87 Cal.Rptr. 25, 7 C.A.3d 695 (1970), §3.700

- J -

Jackson v. State, 270 Ga. 494, 512 S.E.2d 241 (1999), §§10.300, 10.500

Jacobs v. City of Neches, 7 F.Supp. 2d 829 (Tex. 1998), §21.401

Jacobs v. CNG Transmission Corp., 332 F.Supp.2d 759 (W.D. Pa., 2004), §2.400

Jacobs v. Yates, 27 S.W.3d 734 (Ark. 2000), §§20.200, 22.405

James v. Beauregard Elec. Co-op., Inc., 736 So.2d 353 (La.App. 1999), §44.301

James v. State Farm Mut. Auto. Ins. Co., 810 P.2d 365 (Okla. 1991), §45.200

James v. State, 580 S.E.2d 334, 260 Ga.App. 536 (2003), §1.300

James v. Texas Dept. of Human Services, 836 S.W.2d 236 (Tex.App. 1992), §§3.600, 3.700

Jaramillo v. State, 817 S.W.2d 842 (Tex.App. 1991), §11.700

Jean Doe v. DeBuono, 193 F.R.D. 117 (S.D.N.Y. 2000), §§22.428, 44.600

Jensen v. State of Wyoming, 116 P.3d 1088 (Wyoming, 2005), §§1.300, 10.300

Jesse by Reinecke v. Danforth, 485 N.W.2d 63 (Wis. 1992), §9.501.1

Jet Air, Inc. v. Epps Air Service, 194 Ga. App. 829, 392 S.E.2d 951, (1990), §21.413

Jezowski v. Beach, 59 Misc.2d 224, 298 N.Y.S.2d 360 (Sup.Ct. 1968), §49.200

Joel v. Weber, 581 N.Y.S.2d 579 (N.Y.Sup. 1992), §9.507.1

John Blair Communications, Inc. v. Reliance Capital Group, 582 N.Y.S.2d 720 (N.Y.A.D. 1 Dept. 1992), §9.501.1

John C. Lincoln Hosp. and Health Corp. v. Maricopa County, 96 P.3d 530, (Ariz. Ct. App., 2004), §22.428

John Cangelosi v. Capasso, Rockford Radiology Associates, 851 N.E.2d 954, 366 Ill.App.3d 225, 303 Ill.Dec. 767 (2006), §§9.501.1, 9.502

Johnson v. District of Columbia, 728 A.2d 70 (D.C. 1999), §21.404

Johnson v. Ellis & Sons Iron Workers, Inc., 609 F.2d 820 (5th Cir. 1979), §22.414

Johnson v. Herman, 132 F.Supp.2d 1130 (N.D. Ill., 2001), §§21.427, 22.300

Johnson v. Hoffman, 80 A.2d 624 (N.J. 1951), §4.300

Johnson v. Mountainside Hosp., 239 N.J.Super. 312, 571 A.2d 318 (1990), §24.202

Johnson v. Nickels, 66 N.M. 181, 344 P.2d 697 (1959), §24.204

Johnson v. People, 152 Colo. 586, 384 P.2d 454 (1963), §5.407

Johnson v. Piggly Wiggly of Pinetops, Inc., 575 S.E.2d 797 (N.C.App., 2003), §§11.500, 11.700

Johnson v. Washington County, 518 N.W.2d 594 (Minn. 1994), §23.408

Johnson v. Wilmington City Ry. Co., 23 Del. 5, 76 A. 961 (1905), §1.300

Jone v. Coleman Corp., 183 S.W.3d 600 (Mo.App., 2006), Overview

Jones v. Consumers Coop. Propane Co., 186 Neb. 629, 185 N.W.2d 458 (1971), §42.301

Jones v. Ford Motor Co., 320 F.Supp.2d 440 (E.D. Va., 2004), §21.430

Jones v. Halvorson-Berg, 847 P.2d 945, 69 Wash.App. 117 (Wash.App. Div. 3 1993), §10.500

Jones v. Industrial Commission, 169 Ill.Dec. 153, 591 N.E.2d 33 (1992), §9.503.1

Jones v. Jitney Jungle Stores of America, Inc., 730 So.2d 555 (Miss. 1998), §11.400

Jones v. Marcum, 197 F.Supp.2d 991 (S.D. Ohio, 2002), §21.401

Jones v. State, 482 N.E.2d 243 (Ind. 1985), §46.200

Jones v. State, 606 So.2d 1051 (Miss. 1992), §7.400

Jordan v. Abernathy, 845 S.W.2d 86 (Mo.App.E.D. 1993), §44.301

Jordan v. Tri County AG, Inc., 546 S.E.2d 528, 248 Ga.App. 661 (2001), §2.400

Joyce v. State Department of Corrections, 64 P.3d 1266 (Wash.App. 2003)__, Overview

Joynt v. Barnes, 71 Ill.App.3d 187, 27 Ill.Dec. 249, 388 N.E.2d 1298 (1979), §42.301

- K -

- L -

Lockett v. Bd. of Ed. for School D. 189, 555 N.E.2d 1055 (Ill.App. 5 Dist 1990), §3.400

Lockwood v. Baptist Regional Health Services, Inc., 541 So.2d 731 (Fla. 1989), §22.414

Loevsky v. Carter, 773 P.2d 1120 (Hawaii 1989), §§44.400, 44.600

Loftin v. Morgenstern, 60 So.2d 732 (Fla. 1952), §1.400

Lofton v. Kearney, 257 F.Supp.2d 1372 (S.D.Fla. 2001), §25.209

Long v. Missouri Delta Medical Center, 33 S.W.3d 629 (Mo.App., 2000), §44.500

Long v. St. John's Regional Health Center, Inc., 98 S.W.3d 601 (Mo.App., 2003), §22.420

Lopez v. Foremost Paving, 796 S.W.2d 473 (Tex. 1990), §§44.300, 48.201

Lopez v. Wal-Mart Stores, Inc., 700 So.2d 215 (La.App. 4 Cir. 1997), §32.200

Lorillard Tobacco Co. v. Reilly, 84 F.Supp.2d 180 (D.Mass. 2000), §21.100

Los Angeles News Service v. CBS Broadcasting, Inc., 305 P.3d 924 (9th Cir. California, 2002), §44.400

Loughnane v. City of Chicago, 188 Ill.App.3d 1078, 136 Ill.Dec. 626, 545, N.E.2d 150 (1989), §24.208

Louis Vuitton v. Spencer Handbags Corp., 765 F.2d 966 (2d Cir. 1985), §36.300

Louisiana Workers' Compensation Corp. v. Pro Source Roofing, Inc., 907 So.2d 113 (La.App., 2005), §2.400

Love v. Garcia, 611 So.2d 1270 (Fla.App. 4 Dist. 1992), §22.420

Lucas v. Christiana Skating Center, Ltd., 722 A.2d 1247 (Del.Super. 1998), §30.300

Lucas v. Love, 519 SE.2d 253, 238 Ga.App. 463 (1999), §11.400

Luebbert v. Simmons, 98 S.W.3d 72 (Mo.App., 2003), §20.200

Lugo v. State, 845 So.2d 74 (Fla., 2003), §1.300

Luke v. Spicer, 194 Ga. App. 183, 390 S.E.2d 267 (1990), §21.401

Lundquist v. Nickels, 179 Ill.Dec. 150, 605 N.E.2d 1373 (Ill.App. 1 Dist. 1992), §6.800

Lundy v. State, 596 So.2d 1167 (Fla.App. 1992), §9.512.1

Lunsford v. Laboratory Corp. of America, 568 S.E.2d 597, 256, Ga.App. 432 (2002), §22.420(a)

Lust v. Sealy, Inc., 383 F.3d 580 (7th Cir. Wis., 2004), §§22.300, 22.425(a)

- M -

Mack v. State, 432 S.E.2d 680 (Ga.App. 1993), §5.405.1

Mackey v. Irisari, 445 S.E.2d 742 (W.Va. 1994), §23.404

MacLean v. San Francisco, 151 Cal. App. 2d 133, 311 P.2d 158 (1957), §21.401

Macon-Bibb County Hosp. Authority, 533 S.E.2d 420, 243 Ga. App. 480 (2000), §44.600

Madden v. Creative Services, Inc., 646 N.E.2d 780 (N.Y. 1995), §9.507.1

Madden v. Dake, 30 A.D.3d 932, 819 N.Y.S.2d 121 (N.Y.A.D., 3 Dept., 2006), §22.408(b)

Madison v. Barnett, 601 S.E.2d 704 (Ga.App. 2004), Overview

Maffett v. Bliss, 264 Ill.dec. 741, 771 N.E.2d 445, 329 Ill.App.3d, 562 (2002), §21.425

Magar v. State, 826 S.W.2d 221, 308 Ark. 380 (1992), §9.506.1

Magill v. Edd Kirby Chevrolet, 627 S.E.2d 207 (Ga.App., 2006), Overview

Magill v. Superior Court, 103 Cal.Rptr.2d 355, 86 Cal.App.5th 61 (2001), §9.501.1

Magnolia Petroleum Co. v. Angelly, 306 P.2d 309 (Okl. 1955), §33.200

Maiden v. Rozwood, 597 N.W.2d 817, 461 Mich. 109 (1999), §21.401

Majdic v. Cincinnati Machine Co., 537 A.2d 334 (Pa. 1988), §24.202

McCathern v. Toyota Motor Corp., 23 P.3d 320, 332 Or. 59 (2001), Appendix, §A.401

McClard v. U.S., 386 F.2d 495 (8th Cir. 1967), §7.300

McClelland v. Ozenberger, 805 S.W.2d 264 (Mo.App. 1991), §9.503.1

McClelland v. Ozenberger, 841 S.W.2d 227, *reh. den.* (Mo.App.W.D. 1992), §7.400

McCollum v. McDaniel, 136 F.Supp.2d 472 (D.Md., 2001), §22.420

McCoo v. Denny's Inc., 192 F.R.D. 675 (D.Kan. 2000), §9.501.1

McCorkle Farms, Inc. v. Thompson, 84 S.W.3d 884 (Ark.App., 2002), §21.401(d)

McCormick v. Brevig, 96 P.3d 697, 322 Mont. 112, 2004 MT. 179 (2004), §45.200

McCormick-Morgan, Inc. v. Teledyne Indus., Inc., 134 F.R.D. 275 (N.D.Cal. 1991), §9.501.1

McDavid v. State, 594 So.2d 12 (Miss. 1992), §7.400

McDill v. Mark's Auto Sales, 626 S.E.2d 52, 367 S.C. 486 (2006), §11.700

McDonald v. Johnson & Johnson, 537 F.Supp. 1282 (D.C.Minn. 1982), §24.204

McDonald v. National Enterprises, Inc., 547 S.E.2d 204, 262 Va.184 (2001), §22.403(c)

McDonald v. State, 764 P.2d 202 (Okl.Cr. 1988), §6.400

McElhiney v. Mossman, 850 S.W.2d 369 (Mo.App. 1993), §5.404.1

McElroy v. Perry, 753 So.2d 121 (Fla.App. 2000), §22.300

McEuin v. Crown Equipment Corporation, 328 F.3d 1028 (9th Cir., Or., 2003), §22.425(b)

McFadden v. Winters and Merchant, Inc., 603 N.W.2d 31, 8 Neb.App. 870 (1999), §44.301

McFarland & Son, Inc. v. Basel, 727 So.2d 266 (Fla.App. 1999), §48.202

McGee v. State, 423 S.E.2d 666, 205 Ga.App. 722 (1992), §5.405.1

McGovern v. Attie, 30 A.D.2d 559, 291 N.Y.S.2d 167 (1968), §25.206

McGowan v. State, 188 S.W.3d 239 (Tex.App., 2006), §1.300

McGrath v. Nassau Health Care Corporation, 209 F.R.D. 55, (E.D.N.Y. 2002), §33.202

McGuire v. Walker, 423 S.E.2d 617 (W.Va. 1992), §23.401

McIntyre v. State, 571 So.2d 364 (Ala.Cr.App. 1990), §4.600

McKinney v. Brandywine Court Condominium Council, Inc., 830 A.2d 411, (Del.Super., 2003), §§44.300, 44.301

McKnight v. Johnson Controls, Inc., 36 F.3d 1396 (8th Cir. 1994), §11.500

McMunn v. Tatum, 379 S.E. 2d 908 (Va. 1989), §22.421

MCN Energy Enterprises v. Omagro de Columbia, L.D.C., 98 S.W.3d 766, (Tex.App. 2003), Overview

McPheeters v. Black & Veatch Corp., Inc., 427 F.3d 1095 (8th Cir., Mo., 2005), §23.405

McRae v. Echols, 8 S.W.3d 797 (Tex.App. 2000), §21.401

McVay v. State, 847 S.W.2d 28, 312 Ark. 73 (1993), §9.503.1

Meade v. Belcher, 212 Va. 796, 188 S.E.2d 211 (1972), §49.200

Mechanick v. Conradi, 139 A.D.2d 857, 527 N.Y.S.2d 586 (1988), §44.600

Meder v. Everest & Jennings, Inc., 617 F.2d 1182 (8th Cir. 1981), §5.410

Medine v. Roniger, 879 So.2d 706 (La. July 2, 2004), Overview

Mehochko v. Gold Seal Co., 66 Ill.App.2d 54, 213 N.E.2d 581, 583 (1966), §48.200

Melford v. Gaus & Brown Constr. Co., 117 Ill.App.2d 497, 51 N.E.2d 128 (1958), §49.200

Melville v. American Home Assurance Co., 584 F.2d 1306 (3d Cir. 1978), §22.427

Mendez v. Queens Plumbing Supply, Inc., 12 Misc.3d 1064, 820 N.Y.S.2d 707 (2006), §21.401(b)

Mendoza v. Mashburn, 747 So.2d 1159 (La.App. 1999), §31.200

Menendez v. Superior Court (People), 279 Cal. Rptr. 521, *reh. den.*, (Cal.App. 2nd Dist. 1991), §9.504.1

Menne v. Keowee Key Property Owners' Association, Inc., 629 S.E.2d 690, 368 S.C. 557 (2006), §23.408

Mercedes v. Amusements of Am., 559 N.Y.S.2d 252 (1990), §22.420

Merrill v. Sugarloaf Mountain Corp., 745 A.2d 378 (Maine 2000), §44.301

Message Center Management, Inc. v. Shell Oil Products Co., 857 A.2d, 936, 85 Conn. App. 401 (2004), §11.500

Methodist Home v. Marshall, 830 S.W.2d 220 (Tex.App. 1992), §9.501.1

Metropolitan Dade County v. Yearby, 580 So.2d 186 (Fla.App.3 Dist. 1991), §5.404.1

Michigan Department of Transportation v. Haggerty Corridor Partners, L.P., 700 N.W.2d 380, 473 Mich. 124 (2005), Overview

Mickelson v. Forney, 259 Iowa 91, 143 N.W.2d 390 (1966), §42.301

Mickens v. Robinson, 404 S.E.2d 359, 103 N.C.App. 52 (N.C.App. 1991), §3.700

Midstates Resources Corp. v. Dobrindt, 798 A.2d 494, 70 Conn.App., 420 (2002), §22.300

Mier v. Martin, 755 So.2d 958 (La.App. 1999), §36.301

Miller v. Hensley, 624 N.W.2d 582, 244 Mich.App. 528 (2001), 0-15

Miller v. Hometown Propane Gas, Inc., 167 S.W.3d 172, 86 Ark.App. 189 (2004), §5.200

Miller v. Monongahela Power Co., 403 S.E.2d 406 (W.Va. 1991), §§44.301, 44.400

Miller v. Neill, 867 S.W.2d 523 (Mo.App.,1993), §12.400

Miller v. Quaife, 391 S.W.2d 682 (Ky. 1965), §44.301

Miller v. Solaglas California Inc., 870 P.2d 559 (Colo.Ct.App. 1993), §21.421

Miller v. State, 410 S.E.2d 101 (Ga. 1991), §7.400

Miller v. State, 593 N.E.2d 1247, *reh. den.* (Ind.App. 1992), §9.505.1

Mills v. U.S., 363 F.2d 78 (8th Cir. 1966), §11.500

Milroy v Hanson, 875 F.Supp 646 (1995), §9.501

Minebea Co., Ltd. v. Papst, 231 F.R.D. 1 (D.D.C., 2005), §§40.100, 43.100

Minneapolis Pub. Housing Authority v. Greene, 463 N.W.2d 558 (Minn. 1990), §22.427

Minnehaha County, S.D. v. Kelley, 150 F.2d 356 (8th Cir. 1945), §24.208

Miranda v. Arizona, 384 U.S. 436 (1966), §9.512

Mirchandani v. Home Depot, U.S.A., Inc., 235 F.R.D. 611 (D.Md., 2006), §30.300

Miriam Osborn Mem. Home Assn. v. Assessor of City of Rye, 800 N.Y.S.2d 909 (2005), §21.300

Misek-Falkoff v. Internat'l. Business Machines Corp., 144 F.R.D. 48, (S.D.N.Y. 1992), §9.501

Miskin v. Baxter Healthcare Corp., 107 F.Supp.2d 669 (D. Md. 1999), §24.201

Missouri Highway & Transportation Commission v. Rockhill Dev. Corp., 865 S.W.2d 765, §44.301

Missouri Pac. R. Co. v. Haigler, 158 S.W.2d 703, 230 Ark. 840 (1942), §5.407

Mizell v. Glover 570 S.E.2d 176, 351 S.C. 392 (2002), §24.202

Modelski v. Navistar Intern. Transp. Corp., 236 Ill.Dec. 394, 707 N.E2d 239, 302 Ill.App.3d 879 (1999), §11.500

Monlux v. General Motors Corp., 714 P.2d 930 (Hawaii 1986), §§48.200, 48.201

Montanez v. State, 592 So.2d 650 (Ala.App. 1991), §9.507.1

Moore v. Chesapeake & Ohio Railway Co., 340 U.S. 573, 95 L.Ed. 547, 71 S.Ct. 428 (1951), §11.300

Moore v. State, 755 So.2d 1276 (Miss.App. 2000), §1.300

Moore v. Swoboda, 157 Ill.Dec. 37, 571 N.E.2d 1056, 213 Ill.App.3d 217 (1991), §12.400

Moran v. Pittsburgh-Des Moines Steel Co., 86 F.Supp. 255 (D.C.Pa. 1949), 183 F.2d 467 (3d Cir. 1949), §22.427

Morfesis v. Sobol, 567 N.Y.S.2d 954 (1991), §24.202

Morgan v. Massachusetts General Hospital, 901 F.2d 186 (1st Cir. 1990), §§22.424, 25.201

Morgan v. Wilkinson, 606 F.Supp. 564 (M.D. Pa. 1985), §46.200

Morse v. Colombo, 31 A.D.3d 916, 819 N.Y.S.2d 162 (N.Y.A.D., 3 Dept., 2006), §5.402

Morvant v. Construction Aggregates Corp., 570 F.2d 626 (6th Cir. 1978), §7.300

Moskowitz v Coscette, 3 Fed.Appx. 1 (2nd Cir., 2001), §45.200

Mowen v. Holland, 270 Ill.Dec 605, 783 N.E.2d 180, 336 Ill.App.3d 368 (2003), Overview

Moyer v. Moyer, 602 A.2d 68 (Del. 1992), §9.501.1

Mueller v. Abdnor, 972 F.2d 931 (8th Cir. 1992), §22.426

Muka v. Estate of Muka, 164 Ill.App.2d 223, 517 N.E.2d 673 (1987), §45.200

Mullican v. Transamerican Ins. Group, 773 So.2d 207 (La.App. 2000), §22.401

Mullins v. State, 721 N.E.2d 335 (Ind.App., 1999), §9.506.1

Muniz v. New York City Transit Authority, 30 A.D.3d 388, 816 N.Y.S.2d 561 (2006), §44.300

Munley v. Carlson, 125 F.Supp.2d 1117 (N.D., 2000), §5.400

Murphy Tugboat Co. v. Crowley, 658 F.2d 1256 (9th Cir. 1981), §11.500

Murray v. Shanks, 27 Wash. App. 363, 618 P.2d 102 (1980), §21.403

Musgrove Construction, Inc. v. Malley, 912 So.2d 227 (Ala.Civ.App., 2005),Overview

Myers v. State, 133 P.3d 312, 2006 OK CR 12 (2006), §10.300

Mykytiuk v. Stamm, 143 Ill.Dec. 570, 554 N.E.2d 505, 196 Ill.App.3d, 928 (Ill.App. 1 Dist. 1990), §§31.400, 32.200

- N -

Nabisco v. Warner-Lambert Co., 32 F.Supp.2d 690 (S.D.N.Y.1999), §44.301

Nachtsheim v. Beech Aircraft Corp., 847 F.2d 1261 (7th Cir. 1988), §44.400

Nanda v. Ford Motor Co., 509 F.2d 213 (7th Cir. 1974), §3.400

Nat'l. Steel Products Co. v. Superior Court, 164 Cal.App.3d 476, 210 Cal.Rptr. 535 (1985), §9.502

Nat'l. Sur. Corp. v. Fast Motor Service, Inc., 157 Ill.Dec. 619, 572 N.E.2d 1083 (Ill.App. 1 Dist. 1991), §3.700

Nat'l. Utilities Service, Inc. v. Northwestern Steel & Wire Co., 426 F.2d 222, (7th Cir. 1970), §22.432

National Congress for Puerto Rican Rights v. City of New York, 194 F.R.D. 105 (S.D.N.Y., 2000), §9.501

National Football League Properties Inc. v. Superior Court, 75 Cal.Rptr.2d 893 (Cal.App. 1998), §9.501.1

National Freight, Inc. v. Snyder, 191 S.W.3d 416 (Tex.App., 2006), §36.301

National Pub. Co. v. Hartford Fire Ins. Co., 892 A.2d 261, 94 Conn.App. 234 (2006), Overview

National Steel Car, Ltd. v. Canadian Pacific Ry., Ltd., 254 F.Supp.2d 527, (E.D.Pa., 2003), §47.600

NationsBanc Mortgage Corp. v. Eisenhauer, 733 N.E2d 557, 49 Mass.App. 727 (2000), §5.400

Naughton v. Bankier, 691 A.2d 712, 114 Md.App. 641 (1997), §§48.200, 48.201, 48.300

Neal v. State, 805 So.2d 520 (Miss. 2002), §7.300

Neher v. Kauffman, 242 P. 713, 197 C. 674 (1925), §12.400

Nelson Morris & Co. v. Columbian Iron Works & DryDock Co., 76 Md. 354, 25 A. 417 (1892), §24.204

Nelson v. McClintock, 703 N.E.2d 829, 123 Ohio App.3d 139 (1997), §44.301

Nelson v. Waxman, 9 S.W.3d 601 (Mo. 2000), §§10.400, 10.500

- O -

- P -

People v. Garcia, 273 Cal.Rptr. 666, 224 C.A.3d 297 (Cal.App. 4 Dist. 1990), §5.405.1

People v. Garwood, 106 P. 113, 11 C.A. 665 (1909), §10.300

People v. Gerace, 568 N.Y.S.2d 833 (N.Y.A.D.2 Dept. 1991), §10.500

People v. Goodridge, 674 N.Y.S.2d 24 (N.Y.A.D. 1 Dept. 1998), §10.500

People v. Gorman, 542 N.Y.S.2d 225 (N.Y.A.D. 2 Dept. 1989), §9.507

People v. Govan, 701 N.Y.S.2d 474, 268 A.D.2d 689 (2000), §9.507.1

People v. Greenberger, 58 Cal.App.4th 298, 68 Cal.Rptr.2d 61 (Cal.App. 2 Dist. 1997), §10.500

People v. Grey, 100 Cal.Rptr. 245, 23 C.A.3d 456 (1972), §7.400

People v. Guerra, 37 Cal. 4th 1067, 129 P.3d 321, §1.400

People v. Gutierrez, 78 Cal.App.4th 170, 92 Cal.Rptr. 2d 626 (2000), §23.415

People v. Hamacher, 402 N.W.2d 484, 428 Mich. 844 (1987), §9.507.1

People v. Hamacher, 438 N.W.2d 43, 432 Mich. 157 (1989), §§9.507.1, 9.502

People v. Hamilton, 30 N.Y.S.2d 155 (1941), §7.400

People v. Harold Oliver, 306 Ill.App.3d 59, 713 N.E.2d 727, 239 Ill.Dec. 196 (1999), §48.202

People v. Harris, 706 N.Y.S.2d 392 (N.Y.A.D. 2000), §§6.800, 10.300, 10.500

People v. Hatfield, 18 P.2d 366, 129 C.A. 162 (1933), §1.400

People v. Hawkins, 121 Cal.Rptr.2d 627, 98 Cal.App.4th 1428 (2002), §31.200

People v. Hayes, Cal. 802 P.2d 376, 276 Cal.Rptr. 874, 52 Cal.3d 577 (1990), §5.401.1

People v. Hirschmann, 124 Ill.Dec. 779, 529 N.E.2d 760, 175 Ill.App.3d 150 (Ill.App. 1 Dist. 1988), §7.300

People v. Jenkins, 768 P.2d 727 (Colo.App. 1988), §5.405

People v. Johnson, 111 Mich.App. 383, 314 N.W.2d 631 (1981), §9.503.1

People v. Johnson, 568 N.Y.S.2d 611 (N.Y.A.D. 1 Dept. 1991), §10.500

People v. Johnson, 683 N.Y.S.2d 681 (1998), §§1.300, 1.400

People v. Johnson, 999 P.2d 825 (Colo. 2000), §9.501.1

People v. Karelse, 143 Mich.App. 712 (1985), §2.200

People v. Kelly, 17 Cal.3d 24, 130 Cal. Rptr. 144, 549 P.2d 1240 (1976), §45.200

People v. Knapper, 594 N.Y.S.2d 210 (N.Y.A.D. 1 Dept. 1993), §9.507.1

People v. Knuckles, 165 Ill.2d 125, 650 N.E.2d 973 (1995), §9.501.1

People v. Kosters, 438 N.W.2d 651, 175 Mich.App. 748 (Mich.App. 1989), §7.300

People v. Krawitz, 542 N.Y.S.2d 824 (N.Y.A.D. 3 Dept. 1989), §9.501

People v. Lamb, 167 Ill.Dec. 179, 587 N.E.2d 61, 224 Ill.App.3d 950 (1992), §9.512.1

People v. Landis, No. A391-583 L.A. Sup.Ct. (1987), §35.200

People v. LaPlanche, 598 N.Y.S.2d 877 (N.Y.A.D. 4 Dept. 1993), §9.507.1

People v. Leahy, 8 Cal. 4th 587 (1994), §11.700

People v. Lee, Cal.App. 5 Dist. 281 Cal.Rptr. 9 (1991), §6.800

People v. Lindsey, 805 P.2d 1134 (Colo.App. 1990), §9.400

People v. Lloyd, 5 Mich.App. 717, 147 N.W.2d 740 (1967), §10.50

People v. Love, 762 N.Y.S.2d 162 (N.Y.A.D., 2003), §1.300

People v. Lustig, 206 N.Y. 162, 99 N.E. 183 (1912), §1.400

People v. Machado, 63 P. 66, 6 C.U. 600 (1900), §12.400

People v. Mackey, 185 Colo 24, 521 P.2d 910 (1974), §5.407

People v. Malkin, 250 N.Y. 185, 164 N.E. 900 (1928), §1.400

People v. Manning, 182 Ill.2d 193, 695 N.E.2d 423, 230 Ill.Dec. 933 (1998), §5.411.1

People v. Marshall, 534 N.Y.S.2d 623 (N.Y.A.D. 4 Dept. 1988), §7.300

People v. Martinez, 575 N.Y.S.2d 938 (1991), §11.700

People v. Mather, 4 Wend. 229 (1830), §4.600

People v. Matthews, 150 Ill.Dec. 310, 562 N.E.2d 1113 (Ill.App. 1 Dist. 1990), §§1.400, 10.500

People v. McHugh, 124 Misc.2d 559, 476 N.Y.S.2d 721 (1984), §47.500

People v. Miles, 286 Ill. Dec. 827, 815 N.E.2d 37 (2004), §§7.300, 7.400

People v. Mincey, 827 P.2d 388, 6 Cal. Rptr.2d 822, 2 C.4th 408, *reh. den.* and op. mod. (1992), §9.501.1

People v. Miner, 197 Ill. App.3d 1078, 136 Ill. Dec. 626, 545 N.E.2d 150 (1989), §21.407

People v. Moore, 260 Cal.Rptr. 134, 211 C.A.3d 1400 (Cal.App. 1989), §4.400

People v. Mulgrave, 558 N.Y.S.2d 607 (1990), §9.507

People v. Ogg, 66 Cal.Rptr. 289, 258 C.A.2d 841 (1968), §3.700

People v. Palacio, 180 Ill.Dec. 862, 607 N.E.2d 1375 (Ill.App. 4 Dist. 1993), §9.510

People v. Pegram, 124 Ill.Dec. 525, 529 N.E.2d 506, 124 Ill.2d 166 (Ill. 1988), §5.405

People v. Peter, 55 Ill.2d 443, 303 N.E.2d 398 (1973), *cert. denied*, 417 U.S. 920 (1974), §46.200

People v. Pfanschmidt, 262 Ill. 411, 104 N.E. 804 (1914), §48.201

People v. Pickett, 339 Mich. 294, 63 N.W.2d 681 (1954), §5.407

People v. Pohl, 507 N.W.2d 819, 202 Mich.App. 203 (1993), §9.507.1

People v. Prevo, 302 Ill.App.3d 1038, 235 Ill.Dec. 950, 706 N.E.2d 505 (Ill.App.4.Dist. 1999), §§1.300, 1.400, 10.300, 10.500

People v. Quick, 236 Ill.App.3d 446, 177 Ill.Dec. 272, 603 N.E.2d 53 (1992), §§1.300, 1.400

People v. Ramos, 535 N.Y.S.2d 663 (N.Y.Sup. 1988), §5.402

People v. Resendez, 15 Cal.Rptr.2d 575, 12 C.A.4th 98 (Cal.App. 4 Dist. 1993), §9.507.1

People v. Riel, 998 P.2d 969, 96 Cal.Rptr.2d 1, 22 Cal.4th 1153 (2000), §§10.300, 10.500

People v. Ruiz, 244 Cal. Rptr. 200, 749 P.2d 854, 44 C.3d 589, *cert. denied* 109 S.Ct. 186, 102 L.Ed.2d 155 (1988), §11.700

People v. Sammons, 478 N.W.2d 901, appeal denied 480 N.W.2d 103 (Mich.App. 1991), §1.300

People v. Sammons, 91 Mich.App. 351, 478 N.W.2d 901 (1991), §§1.300, 1.400

People v. Schnurr, 151 Ill.Dec. 674, 564 N.E.2d 1336 (Ill.App. 2 Dist. 1990), §§1.400, 10.500

People v. Shirley, 31 Cal.3d 18 (1982), §21.422

People v. Sifford, 429 N.Y.S.2d 270, 76 A.D.2d 937 (1980), §4.600

People v. Slover, 232 N.Y. 264, 133 N.E. 633 (1921), §4.600

People v. Spain, 201 Cal.Rptr. 555, 154 C.A.3d 845 (App. 3 Dist. 1984), §7.400

People v. St. Joseph, 276 Cal. Rptr. 498, 226 Cal.App.3d 289 (1 Dist. 1990), §9.512.1

People v. Stack, 184 Ill.Dec. 583, 613 N.E.2d 1175, 244 Ill. App.3d 166 (Ill.App. 1 Dist. 1993), §§4.300, 4.600

People v. Stiles, 692 P.2d 1124 (Colo. App. 1984), §5.405

People v. Sul, 652 N.Y.S.2d 57 (N.Y.A.D. 2 Dept. 1996), §10.500

People v. Tarsia, 67 A.D.2d 210, 415 N.Y.S.2d 120 (1979), *affirmed* 50 N.Y.2d 1, 405 N.E.2d 188, 427 N.Y.S.2d 944 (1980), §§11.601, 21.419

People v. Tenner, 157 Ill.2d 341, 193 Ill.Dec. 105, 626 N.E.2d 138 (1993), §§10.300, 10.500

People v. Tobey, 401 Mich. 141, 257 N.W.2d 537 (1977), §45.200

People v. Trottie, 582 N.Y.S.2d 31 (1992), §§6.400, 6.800

People v. Vermeulen, 438 N.W.2d 36, 432 Mich. 32 (1989), §9.507

People v. Visciotti, 825 P.2d 388, 5 Cal.Rptr.2d 495 (1992), §7.400

People v. Von Villas, 13 Cal.Rptr.2d 62, 10 C.A.4th 201 (Cal.App. 2 Dist. 1992), §9.510

People v. Walker, 282 Cal.Rptr. 12, 230 C.A.3d 230, op. mod. (Cal. 2nd Dist. 1991), §9.511.1

People v. Ward, 226 Mich. 45, 196 N.W. 971 (1924), §9.509

People v. Weber, 86 P. 671, 149 C. 325 (1906), §11.700

People v. Wheeler, Cal.App. 2 Dist. 281 Cal.Rptr. 758, 230 C.A.3d 1406 (1991), §6.800

People v. Witt, 169 Ill.Dec. 915, 592 N.E.2d, 402 (1992), §6.600

People v. Wright, 552 N.Y.S.2d 285 (1990), §10.300

People v. Zak, 457 N.W.2d 59, 184 Mich.App. 1 (1990), §9.507.1

Perma Research & Development v. Singer Co., 542 F.2d 111 (2d Cir.), *cert. denied,* 429 U.S. 987, 97 S.Ct. 507, 50 L.Ed.2d 598 (1976), §47.700

Perryman v. H & R Trucking, Inc., 135 Fed.Appx. 538 (2005), §44.300

Peters v. Johnson & Johnson Prods., 783 S.W.2d 442 (Mo. 1990), §23.403

Peterson v. BASF Corp., 657 N.W.2d 853 (Minn.App. 2003), Overview

Peterson v. National R.R. Passenger Corp., 618 S.E.2d 903, 365 S.C. 391 (2005), §6.300

Peters-Riemers v. Riemers, 624 N.W.2d 83 (N.D. 2001), §6.300

Petrich v. Hansen, 204 F.2d 261 (9th Cir. 1953), §42.301

Pettus v. Louisville & N.R. Co., 214 Ala. 187, 106 So. 807 (1925), §1.300

Phelps v. Provident Life and Accident Insurance Co., 60 F.Supp.2d 1014 (CD.Cal. 1999), §36.301

Philip Morris, Inc. v. Emerson, 368 S.E.2d 268 (Va. 1988), §45.200

Phillips v. K-Mart Corp., 588 So.2d 142 (La. App. 1991), §21.418

Phillips v. State, 728 So.2d 681 (Ala.Crim.App. 1998), §§4.300, 4.600, 6.800

Phipps v. Skyview Farms, Inc., 610 N.W.2d 723, 259 Neb. 492 (Neb. 2000), §21.401

Phoenix Services Limited Partnership v. Johns Hopkins Hospital, 892 A.2d 1185, 167 Md.App. 327 (2006), Overview

Phyfer v. State, 577 S.E.2d 56, 259 Ga.App. 356 (2003), §6.500

Piatz v. Austin Mutual Insurance Co., 646 N.W.2d 681 (N.D., 2002), §40.500

Pickett v. Detella, 163 F.Supp.2d 999 (N.D.Ill., 2001), §25.211

Pierce v. Central Maine Power Co., 622 A.2d 80 (Me. 1993), §3.400

Pieszak v. Glendale Adventist Medical Center, 112 F.Supp.2d 970 (C.D.Cal. 2000), §5.402

Pilgrim's Pride Corp. v. Smoak, 134 S.W.3d 880 (Tex. App. Texarkana 2004), §§21.300, 21.400, 21.401(b)

Pilkington v. Peking Chinese Restaurant, Inc., 596 So.2d 586 (Ala. 1992), §1.300

Pirelli Armstrong Tire Corp. v. Titan Tire Corp., 4 F.Supp.2d 794 (Ill. 1998), §24.203

Pirolo v. DeJesus, 905 A.2d 1210, 97 Conn.App. 585 (2006), Overview, §42.301

Pisel v. Stamford Hospital, 180 Conn. 314, 430 A.2d 1 (1980), §§3.700, 44.500

Pittman v. Pittman, 139 S.W.3d 134, 84 Ark. App. 293 (2003), §2.400

Pitts v. Bode, 403 S.E.2d 66, 198 Ga.App. 787 (Ga.App.1991), §1.400

Pittsburgh Corning Corp. v. Walters, 1 S.W.3d 759 (Tex.App. 1999), §45.200

Platt v. Interstate Dodge, 843 So.2d 1178 (LaApp., 2003), §44.301

- Q -

- R -

Ravary v. Reed, 163 Mich.App. 447, 415 N.W.2d 240 (1987), §9.501.1

Rawson v. Midsouth Rail Corp., 738 So.2d 280 (Miss.App. 1999), §44.301

Read v. Ellenville National Bank, 20 A.D.3d 408, 799 N.Y.S.2d 78 (N.Y.A.D. 2nd Dept., 2005), §36.301

Reagan v. Brock, 628 F.2d 721 (1st Cir. 1980), §§8.400, 12.300

Recer v. State, 821 S.W.2d 715 (Tex.App. 1991), §§1.300, 1.400, 10.500

Recreational Developments of Phoenix, Inc. v. City of Phoenix, 220 F.Supp.2d 1054 (Arizona, 2002), §24.203

Redfearn v. Huntcliff Homes Association, Inc., 579 S.E.2d 37, 260 Ga.App. 150 (2003), §44.301

Redmond v. Breakfield, 840 So.2d 828 (Miss.App., 2003), §21.401(b)

Reed v. Reed, 44 P.3d 1108, 137 Idaho 53 (2002), §22.428

Reed v. Shelly, 378 S.W.2d 291 (Mo. 1964), §44.301

Reed v. State, 283 Md. 374, 391 A.2d 364 (1978), §45.200

Regan v. Garfield Ridge Trust and Savings Bank, 163 Ill.Dec. 605, 581 N.E.2d 759, 220 Ill. App.3d 1078 (1991), §9.501, 9.501.10

Regent Corp., U.S.A. v. Azmat Bangladesh, Ltd., 686 N.Y.S.2d 24 (1999), §21.425

Rehab Project Inc. v. Sarno, 80 Ohio App.3d 265, 608 N.E.2d 1188 (1992), §36.301

Rehling v. City of Chicago, 207 F.3d 1009, 10 A.D. Cases 589 (C.A.7, Ill., 2000), §9.501

Rehm v. Weiss, 28 N.Y.S. 772 (1894), §7.400

Reichenberg v. Davis, 846 So.2d 1233 (FlaApp., 2003), §§21.300, 22.300

Reid v. Pyle, 51 P.3d 1064 (Colo.App., 2002), §25.201

Reid v. Sledge, 224 Ill. App.3d 817, Dec. 541, 587 N.E.2d 1156 (1992), §44.301

Repple v. Barnes Hosp., 778 S.W.2d 819 (Mo. 1989), §44.600

Resolution Trust Corp. v. Diamond, 773 F.Supp. 597 (S.D.N.Y. 1991), §9.501.1

Reuther v. Smith, 926 So.2d 9 (La.App., 2006), §25.201

Reyes v. Wyeth Laboratories, 498 F.2d 1264 (5th Cir. 1974), §22.431

Reynolds v. Green, 184 F.3d 589 (C.A.6 Mich. 1999), §5.400

Rhodig v. Cummings, 418 P.2d 521 (Colo. 1966), §49.200

Rice v. C.I. Lanning, 97 P.3d 580, 322 Mont. 487 (2004), Overview

Richardson v. Calderon, 713 N.E.2d 856 (Ind.App. 1999), §24.203

Richardson v. State, 130 P.3d 634 (Montana, 2006), §6.704

Richardson v. State, 581 S.E.2d 528 (Ga., 2003), §§5.405, 6.300

Richey v. Chappell, 594 N.E.2d 443 (Ind. 1992), §9.501.1

Richwind Joint Venture 4 v. Brunson, 625 A.2d 326, 96 Md.App. 330 (1993), §§11.500, 11.700

Rieker v. Kaiser Foundation Hospitals, 96 P.3d 833, 194 Ore. App. 708, §24.205

Riggs National Corporation & Subsidiaries v. C.I.R., 295 F.3d 16, (D.C.Cir., 2002), §21.100

Riisna v. American Broadcasting Companies, Inc., 219 F.Supp.2d 568 (S.D.N.Y., 2002), §§22.403, 23.405

Riley v. City of Chester, 612 F.2d 708 (3rd Cir. 1979), §9.510

Rinehart v. Schubel, 794 A.2d 73, 2002 ME 53 (2002), §35.200

Rittenhouse v. Superior Court, 1 Cal. Rptr.2d 595 (Cal.App. 1991), §§9.503.1, 9.504.1

Rittenour v. Gibson, 656 N.W.2d 691, 2003 (N.D., 2003), Overview, §§44.300, 44.301

Rivera ex rel. Rivera v. Eastern Paramedics, Inc., 702 N.Y.S.2d 724 (1999), §45.200

Rivera v. City of New York, 160 A.D.2d 985, 554 N.Y.S.2d 706 (1990), §44.600

- S -

State v. Francis D., 815 A.2d 191, 75 Conn.App. 1 (2003), Overview, §6.500
State v. Freeman, 378 S.E.2d 545 (N.C.App. 1989), §7.300
State v. Garcia, 83 N.J. Super 345, 199 A.2d 860 (1964), §5.404
State v. Girouard, 561 A.2d 882 (R.I. 1989), §9.512
State v. Gomes, 764 A.2d 125. (R.I. 2001), §7.300
State v. Gonzalez, 853 P.2d 526 (Alaska 1993), §9.512.1
State v. Gooding, 989 P.2d 304, 296 Mont. 234, 1999 MT 249 (1999), §9.506.1
State v. Grays, 856 S.W.2d 87 (Mo.App.E.D. 1993), §9.512.1
State v. Green, 609 N.E.2d 1253, 66 Ohio St.3d 141 (1993), §§1.300, 10.500
State v. Guffey, 39 S.D. 84, 163 N.W. 679 (1917), §5.404
State v. Guthrie, 428 S.E.2d 853 (N.C.App. 1993), §23.408
State v. Hardy, 651 A.2d 322 (Me. 1994), §24.203
State v. Harris, 839 S.W.2d 54 (Tenn. 1992), §§1.300, 1.400, 10.300, 10.500
State v. Hatcher, 524 S.E.2d 815 (N.C.App. 2000), §§1.300, 1.400, 10.300
State v. Hawkins, 572 So.2d 108 (La.App. 1 Cir. 1990), §1.400
State v. Helms, 218 N.C. 592, 12 S.E.2d 243, 245 (1940), §46.200
State v. Hennum, 441 N.W.2d 793 (Minn. 1989), §9.512
State v. Hill, 823 S.W.2d 98 (Mo. App. 1991), §5.404
State v. Hotoph, 750 So.2d 1036 (La.App.5.Cir.,1999), §§7.300, 7.400
State v. Humphrey, 36 P.3d 844 (Kan.App. 2001), §7.300
State v. Hydock, 725 A.2d 37 Conn.App. 1999, §7.300
State v. Ireland, 773 P.2d 1375 (Utah 1989), §7.300
State v. Jackson, 655 N.W.2d 828 (Minn.App. 2003), §5.405
State v. Jacobs, 616 S.E.2d 306 (N.C., 2005), §1.300
State v. Jaynes, 464 S.E.2d 448, 342 N.C. 249 (1995), §10.500
State v. Johnson, 573 A.2d 1218, 21 Conn.App. 291 (1990), §10.500
State v. Jolley, 656 N.W.2d 305 (2003), Overview, §6.500
State v. Jones, 287 N.C. 84, 214 S.E.2d 24 (1975), §48.201
State v. Jones, 587 So.2d 787 (La.App. 1991), §9.512.1
State v. Jones, 593 So.2d 1301 (La.App. 1991), §7.400
State v. Kellner, 103 SW.3d 363. (Mo.App., 2003), §5.405
State v. Knight, 378 S.E.2d 424 (N.C.App. 1989), §9.504
State v. Knowles, 946 S.W.2d 791 (Mo.App., 1997), §§11.300, 11.700
State v. Kuhl, 42 Nev. 185, 175 P. 190, 194 (1918), §46.100
State v. Lankford, 775 P.2d 593 (Idaho 1989), §9.512
State v. Lanz-Terry, 535 N.W.2d 635 (Minn. 1995), §10.500
State v. Lapan, 101 Vt. 124, 141 A. 686 (1928), §46.200
State v. Lesane, 528 S.E.2d 37 (N.C.App. 2000), §7.400
State v. Lindesy, 543 So.2d 886, *reh. denied* (La. 1989), §10.300
State v. Loazia, 829 S.W.2d 558 (Mo.App. 1992), §7.400
State v. Locke, 502 N.W.2d 891 (Wis. App. 1993), §9.504.1
State v. Lozia, 829 S.W.2d 558 (Mo.App. 1992), §7.300

State v. Makerson, 52 N.C.App. 149, 277 S.E.2d 869 (1981), §§11.601, 21.419

State v. Marlow, 432 S.E.2d 275 (1993), §7.400

State v. Marr, 536 A.2d 1108 (Me. 1988), §§5.404, 5.405

State v. Marshall, 105 Iowa 38, 74 N.W. 763 (1898), §4.300

State v. Martin, 101 Wash.2d 713, 684 P.2d 651 (1984), §§9.506.1, 49.200

State v. Maule, 35 Wash.App. 287, 667 P.2d 96 (1983), §49.200

State v. Mayer, 589 So.2d 1145 (La.App. 1991), §9.506.1

State v. McClaugherty, 64 P.3d 486 (N.M. 2003), §5.405

State v. McCoy, 414 S.E.2d 392 (N.C.App. 1992), §7.300

State v. McNeil, 613 So.2d 752 (La.App. 4 Cir. 1993), §10.500

State v. Moore, 575 So.2d 928 (La.App. 2 Cir. 1991), §7.400

State v. Moore, 598 N.E.2d 1224, 74 Ohio App.3d 334, dismissed, jur. mot. ovrld. 580 N.E.2d 1099, 62 Ohio St.3d 1469 (Ohio App. 10 Dist. 1991), §7.400

State v. Moore, 877 So.2d 1027, 38 (La.App., 2004), §§7.300, 7.400

State v. Morgan, 608 N.E.2d 1114, 80 Ohio App.3d 150 (Ohio App. 1992), §5.409.1

State v. Murillo, 349 N.C. 573, 509 S.E.2d 752 (1998), §10.500

State v. Murphy, 394 S.E.2d 300 (N.C.App. 1990), §7.300

State v. Ochalla, 285 N.W.2d 683 (Minn. 1979), §§11.601, 21.419

State v. Odom, 878 So.2d 582 (La.App., 2004), §7.300

State v. Oliveira, 882 A.2d 1097 (R.I., 2005), §§1.300, 10.300

State v. Orwick, 790 N.E.2d 1238, 153 Ohio.App.3d 65 (2003), §9.504

State v. Parsons, 612 A.2d 73, 28 Conn.App. 91 (1992), §7.400

State v. Patino, 502 N.W.2d 601 (Wis. App. 1993), §§9.512, 9.512.1

State v. Perolis, 398 S.E.2d 512 (W.Va. 1990), §7.400

State v. Peters, 534 N.W.2d 867 (Wisc. 1995), §21.410

State v. Pharr, 430 S.E.2d 267 (N.C.App. 1993), §1.400

State v. Phegley, 826 S.W.2d 348. (Mo.App. 1992), §9.507.1

State v. Philbrick, 436 A.2d 844, 859 (Me. 1981), §48.201

State v. Poullard, 532 So.2d 327 (La.App. 3 Cir. 1988), §5.405

State v. Quintero, 823 P.2d 981, 110 Or.App. 247 (1991), §9.507.1

State v. Rapp, 585 N.E.2d 965, 67 Ohio App.3d 33 (1990), §§10.300, 10.500

State v. Reynolds, 824 A.2d 611, 264 Conn. 1 (Conn., 2003), §6.500

State v. Rice, 184 S.W.3d 646 (Tenn., 2006), §1.300

State v. Richmond, 590 N.W.2d 33 (Iowa 1999), §9.506.1

State v. Rodriguez, 839 So.2d 106 (La.App., 2003), §7.300

State v. Rogers, 233 N.C.390, 64 S.E.2d 572 (1951), §46.200

State v. Rogers, 674 A.2d 1364, 41 Conn.App. 204 (1996), §4.600

State v. Ross, 604 So.2d 1036 (La.App. 1 Cir. 1992), §7.400

State v. Rouselle, 559 A.2d 779 (Me. 1989), §7.300

State v. Rupp, 614 So.2d 1323 (La. App.3 Cir. 1993), §9.504.1

State v. Sanchez, 815 A.2d 242, 75 Conn.App. 223 (2003), Overview, §6.500

- T -

Tona, Inc. v. Evans, 590 A.2d 873 (R.I. 1991), §9.512.1

Torbit v. Ryder Sys., Inc., 416 F.3d 898 (2005), §42.301

Tracy v. Cotterell, 524 S.E.2d 879 (W.Va. 1999), §22.408

Trademark Research Corp. v. Maxwell Online, Inc., 995 F.2d 326 (C.A.2 N.Y. 1993), §§11.500, 11.700

Trammell v. Matthews, 86 Ga.App. 661, 72 S.E.2d 132 (1952), §44.301

Transonic Systems, Inc. v. Non-Invasive Medical Tech., 192 F.R.D. 710 (D.Utah, 2000), §9.501

Transport Indem. Co. v. Seib, 178 Neb. 253, 132 N.W.2d 871 (1965), §47.200

Travelers Cas. & Sur. Co. of Am. v. Wells Fargo Bank N.A., 374 F.3d 521, (7th Cir. Ill., 2004), §25.201

Travelers Indemnification Co. of Illinois v. CDL Hotels USA, Inc., 322 F.Supp.2d 482 (S.D.N.Y., 2004), §2.400

Triple A Machine Shop, Inc. v. State, 261 Cal.Rptr. 493 (Cal.App. 1989), §9.501

Tripp v. Anderson, 1 Conn. App. 433, 472 A.2d 804 (1984), §40.500

Tri-State Asphalt Prods. v. McDonough Co., 391 S.E.2d 907 (W.Va. 1990), §44.301

Tritek Technologies, Inc. v. U.S., 67 Fed.Cl. 727 (2005), §40.500

Trolley Square Assoc. v. Nielson, 886 P.2d 61 (Utah App. 1994), §22.300

Trotti v. Estate of Buchanan, 706 N.Y.S.2d 534 (N.Y.A.D. 2000), §22.403(b)

Troyan v. Reyes, 855 N.E.2d 967, 367 Ill.App.3d 729, 305 Ill.Dec. 451 (2006), §22.420

Tuchscher Development Enterprises, Inc. v. San Diego Unified Port District, 132 Cal.Rptr.2d 57, 106 Cal.App.4th 1219 (2003), §20.100

Tunica County v. Matthews, 926 So.2d 209 (Miss., 2006), §44.301

Turner v. Board of Aviation Commissioners, 743 N.E.2d 1153 (Ind.App. 2001), Overview

Turney Media Fuel, Inc. v. Toll Bros., Inc., 725 A.2d 836 (Pa.Super. 1999), §§6.300, 6.800

Tveraas v. Coffey, 818 F.Supp. 75 (D.Vt. 1993), §21.420

Tyrrell v. Wal-Mart Stores Inc., 719 N.Y.S.2d 163 (N.Y.A.D., 2000), §5.408.1

- U -

U.S. Fidelity and Guar. Co. v. Barron Indus., Inc., 809 F.Supp. 355 (M.D.Pa. 1992), §9.501

U.S. Fidelity and Guar. Co. v. Hi-Tower Concrete Pumping Serf., 574 So.2d 424 (La. 1991), §44.400

U.S. v. 91.9 Acres of Land, Etc., 586 F.2d 79 (8th Cir. 1978), *cert. denied* 441 U.S. 944, 79 S.Ct. 2162, 60 L.Ed.2d 1045 (1979), §11.500

U.S. v. Abascal, 564 F.2d 821 (9th Cir. 1977), §5.300

U.S. v. Addison, 498 F.2d 741 (D.C. 1974), §45.200

U.S. v. Allery, 526 F.2d 1362 (8th Cir. 1975), §9.507

U.S. v. Allison, 474 F.2d 286 (5th Cir. 1973), §6.300

U.S. v. Anderson, 446 F.3d 870 (2006), §7.300

U.S. v. Anderson, 532 F.2d 1218 (9th Cir. 1976), §24.204

U.S. v. Audsley, 486 F.2d 289 (5th Cir. 1973), §6.400

U.S. v. Bailey, 327 F.3d 1131 (10th Cir., Kansas, 2003), §6.704

U.S. v. Baller, 519 F.2d 463 (4th Cir.), *cert. denied*, 423 U.S. 1019 (1975), §45.200

U.S. v. Baptista-Rodriguez, 17 F.3d 1354 (11th Cir. Fla. 1994), §10.300

U.S. v. Barletta, 652 F.2d 218 (1st Cir. 1981), §5.404

U.S. v. Berg, 178 F.3d 976 (8th Cir. Mo. 1999), §7.300

U.S. v. Thomas, 571 F.2d 285 (5th Cir. 1978), §5.403

U.S. v. Two Bulls, 925 F.2d 1127 (8th Cir. 1991), §21.410

U.S. v. Upjohn Co., 600 F.2d 1223 (6th Cir. 1979), §9.501

U.S. v. Ware, 247 F.2d 698 (7th Cir. 1957), §22.427

U.S. v. Weinstock, 153 F.3d 272 (6th Cir. 1998), §22.300

U.S. v. Wheeler, 444 F.2d 385 (10th Cir. 1971), §3.300

U.S. v. White, 974 F.2d 1135 (9th Cir. 1992), §9.507

U.S. v. Williams, 583 F.2d 1194 (2d Cir. 1978), *cert. denied*, 439 U.S. 1117 (1979), §45.200

U.S. v. Wyant, 576 F.2d 1312 (8th Cir.1978), §22.300

Uhr v. Lutheran General Hosp., 168 Ill.Dec. 323, 589 N.E.2d 723, 226 Ill.App.3d 236 (1992), §10.500

Ulm v. Ford Motor Co., 750 A.2d 981 (Vt. 2000), §22.401

Union Camp Corp. v. Daley, 374 S.E.2d 329 (Ga.App. 1988), §32.200

Union Carbide Corp. v. Montell NV., 28 F.Supp.2d 833 (S.D.N.Y. 1998), §45.200

Uniroyal Goodrich Tire Co. v. Martinez, 928 S.W.2d 64 (Tex.App. 1995), §42.300

United States v. Mandycz, 447 F.3d 951 (6th Cir., Mich., 2006), §23.401

United States v. Wood, 171 Fed.Appx. 534 (8th Cir., Ark., 2006), §10.300

United Technologies v. Town of East Windsor, 807 A.2d 955, 262, Conn. 11 (2002), §6.300

Upjohn Co. v. U.S., 101 S.Ct. 677 (1981), §9.502

- V -

V.D. Anderson Co. v. Helena Cotton Oil Co., 117 F.Supp. 1932 (E.D.Ark. 1953), §22.432

Van Dusen v. Petty, 709 N.Y.S.2d 791 (N.Y.A.D. 2000), §22.406(a)

Van Hattem v. Kmart Corp., 241 Ill.Dec. 351, 719 N.E.2d 212, 308 Ill.App.3d 121 (1999), §31.200

Van Steemburg v. General Aviation, Inc., 183 Ill. Dec. 496, 611 N.E.2d 1144, 243 Ill.App. 3d 299 (Ill.App. 1993), §§5.410.1, 21.402

Van Welden v. Ramsay's, Inc., 199 Kan. 417, 430 P.2d 298 (1967), §49.200

Van Westrienen v. Americontinental Collection Corp., 94 F.Supp.2d 1087 (D.Or., 2000), §5.404

Vance v. Vance, 784 N.E.2d 172, 151 Ohio.App.3d 391(2003), §§1.300, 10.300

Vargas v. Lee, 317 F.3d 498 (5th Cir., La., 2003), §11.600

Vargas v. Retail Clerk's Union Local 1428, 260 Cal.Rptr. 650, 212 C.A.3d 319 (1989), §5.300

Vaughn v. Ems, 744 S.W.2d 542 (Mo. 1988), §§23.403, 25.211

Vaughn v. St. Helena Parish Police Jury, 261 F.Supp.2d 553 (M.D.La., 2002), §30.300

Vazquez v. National Car Rental, System, Inc., 24 F.Supp.2d 197 (D.Puerto Rico, 1998), §5.407

Velasco v. Commercial Bldg. Maintenance Co., 169 Cal.App.3d 874, 215 Cal.Rptr. 504 (1985), §30.300

Vergott v. Deseret Pharmaceutical Co., Inc., 463 F.2d 12 (5th Cir. 1972), §42.301

Via v. Commonwealth, 590 S.E.2d 583, 42 Va. App. 164 (2004), §23.408

Viens v. Lanctot, 144 A.2d 711, 120 Vt. 443 (1958), §10.300

Vigorito v. Ciulla Builders, Inc., 783 N.E.2d 883, 57 Mass.App.Ct. 446 (2003), §30.300

Vining v. Enterprise Fin. Group, Inc., 148 F.3d 1206 (10th Cir. 1998), §6.500

Visconti v. Hollywood Rental Service, 580 So.2d 197 (Fla. 1991), §22.420

- W -

- Y -

-Z -

Index

-E-

-F-

-G-

-H-

-I-

Federal Trial Evidence by Howard O. Boltz. Tactics, illustrations, key cases and simplified restatements of the Federal Rules of Evidence. Dozens of checklists and a quick reference guide. 626 pages, CD-ROM included. **$99**

Federal Trial Objections by Judge David F. Levi and Magistrate Judge Peter A. Nowinski. Evaluate admissibility, object and respond quickly, preclude trial objections with motions in limine, and draft briefs on evidentiary objections and motions. Pattern objection language, responses, comments, tactics, practice tips, cautions, foundational elements, case citations and synopses for over 100 objections. 876 pages. Includes condensed softcover edition and CD-ROM included. **$99**

Is It Admissible? by Ashley S. Lipson. Fast answers and solid principles on how to propose and oppose virtually every form of evidence. Divides the universe of evidence into four categories — testimonial, documentary, real and demonstrative — providing extreme detail in a concise, organized manner. Instant access to cases, statutes and checklists help you lay solid foundations, make accurate objections, and effectively examine. 840 pages, CD-ROM and courtroom softcover included. **$99**

Preparing for Trial in Federal Court by Phillip J. Kolczynski. A unique task checklist that provides the what, why, when, and how for structuring the case, discovery techniques, admitting and excluding evidence, using experts, settlement strategies, trial tactics, cost-saving measures for smaller cases, and more. 880 pages, CD-ROM included. **$99**

Qualifying & Attacking Expert Witnesses by Robert C. Clifford. Disqualifying, cross-examining, and impeaching your opponent's expert. Controlling expert witness costs. Effectively presenting your expert. Includes pattern questions by expert type. 540 pages, CD-ROM included. **$99**

Small-Case Litigation Forms by Lawrence Klemin. 315 task checklists, referral agreements and letters, pattern interrogatories, deposition checklists, requests for admissions, records requests and authorizations, trial preparation documents, settlement analysis forms and releases, collection letters and forms, and more. 478 pages, CD-ROM included. **$99**

Trial Evidence Foundations by John A. Tarantino. The rule, elements, tactics, and key cases are provided for 60 frequently-needed foundations. Helps you anticipate and avoid objections and provides alternate admission procedures. Contains a 30-page quick reference guide. 760 pages, CD-ROM included. **$99**

Trial Hearsay: Objections & Exceptions by John Conlon. Raise and oppose hearsay objections. Understand and remember exceptions. Accurately apply the rules. Provides the rule, elements, discussion, illustrations, tactics, and cases. 768 pages, CD-ROM included. **$89.98**

Trial Objections by Rogge Dunn and Karen Hirschman. When and how to make and meet objections more successfully. This quick-reference book covers the full range of objections, complete with over 100 pattern objections, tactics, forms, suggested responses, necessary foundations and hundreds of state and federal cases. 628 pages, CD-ROM included. **$99**

PERSONAL INJURY

Determining Economic Damages by Gerald D. Martin, Ph.D. Use proven procedures, checklists, samples and tables to value economic loss in wrongful death and personal injury cases. Learn how to calculate damages, what to ask a forensic economist, which tables to consult for current information on damages and more. 644 pages, CD-ROM. **$99**

How Insurance Companies Settle Cases by David H. Frangiamore, Thomas McGreal, and Clinton E. Miller. A behind-closed-doors look at how insurance cases are valued, what the adjuster needs to settle your case, and how to keep your case moving. Scope runs from estimating bodily injury damages and investigating coverage to claims denials and action letter outlines. 692 pages, CD-ROM included. **$99**

Insurance Settlement Handbook by Kevin M. Quinley and Kenneth A. Satin. Insider's guide to the insurance settlement process. What adjusters look for, how to arrive at a demand figure, reviewing medical reports, valuing common injuries, building damages, pain and suffering, and more. 90 forms, 1,232 pages, 2 volumes, CD-ROM included. **$129**

Litigating Neck & Back Injuries by Michael J. Morse and John A. Tarantino. An accomplished trial attorney explains in detail the medical and legal aspects of common neck and back injuries, focusing on how to win larger settlements with better discovery, negotiation and trial techniques. 702 pages, CD-ROM included. **$99**

Maximizing Damages in Small Personal Injury Cases by Ellsworth T. Rundlett III. Learn how to choose small to medium-sized personal injury cases with the best chances of success, and how to efficiently deliver the biggest results. Includes pattern responses to adjusters, case-screening rules, cost-reducing techniques, sample letters, discovery, motions and more. 702 pages, CD-ROM included. **$99**

Medical Evidence by Thomas H. Quinn and Jeffrey S. Morris, M.D. Support your claims with medically accurate illustrations. Handle medical topics with confidence. You receive: 442 detailed and labeled medical illustrations (most in four-color) in print and on CD, anatomy in plain English, case studies of common injuries, questions and answers for experts, and other sources of additional information. 666 pages. **$129**

Medical Proof of Whiplash by Michael R. Melton and Steven R. Young. Overcome insurer suspicion and juror skepticism with scientific studies and PowerPoint exhibits. Includes summaries of more than 400 medical and engineering studies, and four-color medical illustrations suitable for enlargement as exhibits. The full-text CD contains a color PowerPoint presentation perfect for trial. 782 pages. **$99**

Personal Injury Forms: Discovery & Settlement by John A. Tarantino. Discover hundreds of tested forms, plus detailed check-lists and practice guides for client contact, case evaluation, experts, discovery and settlement in any personal injury case. Track critical topics in specific cases, such as automobile, medical negligence, slip and fall, and others. 962 pages, CD-ROM included. **$99**

Proving Mental & Emotional Injuries by John D. Winer, Dr. Richard B. Pesikoff, and Dr. Richard T. Goldberg. If you are not aggressively and knowledgeably pursuing the mental and emotional injury elements in your cases, you may be selling your clients and yourself short. This complete practice guide shows you how to work up the mental and emotional injury component of physical and psychological injury cases to dramatically increase settlement and verdict value. 1,164 pages, 2 volumes, CD-ROM included. **$129**

Slip & Fall Practice by Charles E. Turnbow. Receive expert guidance from the leading authority on proving notice and breach, investigating the accident scene, determining the coefficient of friction, dealing with experts, preparing for trial and more. Expanded index, building code references, comprehensive table of authorities and CD-ROM included. 626 pages. **$99**

SOCIAL SECURITY DISABILITY

Medical Issues in Social Security Disability by Dr. David Morton. Explains the SSA's unwritten medical rules and how to best present your claimants' impairments. Shortcomings in submitted medical records, the types of mistakes adjudicators are most likely to make, where generous allowances are provided claimants, ailments and tests frequently overlooked by treating doctors, and more. 55 medical opinion forms. 1,648 pages, 2 volumes, CD-ROM included. **$129**

Social Security Advisory Service by Peter Young and Kevin Morton. An accessible and compact quarterly reporting service used by many OHA offices. Recent SSA transmittals, new rulings, and precedent-setting cases. A quick-reading newsletter contains hard-to-obtain details about policy changes, pending legislation, cost of living increases, coverage changes and more. 1,378 pages, CD-ROM included. **$149** for a year's service (regularly $175)

Social Security Disability Advocate's Handbook by David F. Traver. Knowledgeably and effectively challenge vocational testimony with this book's pattern questions and supporting data. Problems with the DOT. How to attack other data sources used by vocational experts. Vocational information and analysis at Step Four. Vocational evidence at Step Five. Transferability of skills analysis. Includes a unique, 82-page annotated index/summary of the rulings. 702 pages, CD-ROM included. **$119**

Social Security Disability Medical Tests by David A. Morton, III, M.D. Were your client's medical tests properly performed? By the right person? Interpreted correctly? What is the chance of a false negative result? Find the answers in this plain-English guide to 457 medical tests frequently encountered in SSA disability determinations. Real-life examples and explanatory drawings accompany many tests. 1,216 pages, CD-ROM included. **$129**

Social Security Disability Practice by Tom Bush. What to do and how to do it, with 150 custom-drafted forms. This popular work walks you step-by-step from interview through hearing and appeal. Loaded with valuable tips and model questions. "Worth buying solely for Mr. Bush's more than 46 valuable RFC questionnaires." "The book to get if you can only afford one." 1,224 pages, 2 volumes, CD-ROM included. **$149**

Social Security Issues Annotated by Sarah Bohr. A brief writer's guide to the law on the key issues. Pre-researched language and up-to-date citations you can import from the disk into your supporting papers. Contains (1) a case update summarizing recent cases, (2) an outline of the law of the last six years, and (3) digests of the regulations, rulings and cases organized by 44 issues. Includes 86 complete briefs. 1,826 pages, 2 volumes, CD-ROM included. **$129**

CRIMINAL

Attacking and Defending Drunk Driving Tests by Donald Bartell and Anne ImObersteg. Voir dire strategies, cross-examination questions, and science to convince the jury that your DUI case deserves an honest review. Strategy and arguments found nowhere else. Includes pattern motions and trial tactics. 450 pages, CD-ROM included. **$119**

Defending Drinking Drivers by Patrick T. Barone and John A. Tarantino. Tactics, motions, case law and sample examinations you need to help your client prevail. Cross-examining cops, challenging test results, sample arguments, new case law, and more. 40 forms, 1,300 pages, 2 volumes, CD-ROM. **$99**

Federal Criminal Practice by Barry Boss and Edward F. Marek. Pretrial release strategies, alternatives to prosecution, discovery angles, plea bargaining and agreement suggestions, sentence negotiation tactics, recent case-based examples, dozens of pretrial motions with memoranda, hundreds of practice tips, and much more. 740 pages, CD-ROM included. **$119**

Federal Forfeiture Guide by Eric Honig. Keep up with forfeiture law with the Guide's fact-heavy summaries and analysis of federal forfeiture cases, including all circuit court and Supreme Court decisions and leading district court cases. Includes a 786-page digest of civil and criminal forfeiture cases decided since 1989, an annual cumulative case digest, monthly newsletters, quarterly indexes and a 3-ring storage binder, CD-ROM included. **$195**

Federal Sentencing Guide by Roger W. Haines, Jr., Jennifer Woll, and J. Douglas Wilson. Quick access to every federal sentencing guideline case published since the guidelines became effective. Includes six hard-bound volumes, twice-annual cumulative supplements and biweekly newsletters, indexed bimonthly, in a 3-ring binder. This service also includes a key word-searchable CD-ROM of the entire 15-year text. **$269**

Ninth Circuit Criminal Law Reporter by Roger W. Haines, Jr. and J. Douglas Wilson. All Ninth Circuit and U.S. Supreme Court criminal cases decided from 1983 to the present. Includes four hard-bound volumes, an annual cumulative supplement, a 3-ring binder, bimonthly cumulative indexes, biweekly newsletters and a CD-ROM. **$199**

EMPLOYMENT

Age Discrimination Litigation by L. Steven Platt and Cathy Ventrell-Monsees. Forms, arguments, and strategies. Tested documents, heavily-annotated arguments, step-by-step procedures, novel strategies, and well-supported discussions of frequently recurring legal issues. 85 custom-drafted forms, 1,030 pages, CD-ROM included. **$99**

Employment Evidence by Eugene K. Hollander. Admit and exclude with these strategies, forms, and cases – past sexual conduct, after-acquired evidence, discriminatory remarks, missing documents, medical and psychological history, employee disciplinary records, and more. Foundational elements, objections, responses, tactics for plaintiff and defendant, jury instructions, motions in limine, checklists of arguments, and supporting cases and statutes. 87 forms, 562 pages, CD-ROM. **$99**

Federal Employment Jury Instructions by Todd J. McNamara and J. Alfred Southerland. Forms, authorities, and strategies to evaluate your options and plan for trial, get better settlements, set out the factual and legal elements juries consider, present proof necessary to establish liability, and deliver winning closing arguments. Includes outlines of all elements necessary for claims brought under federal statutes, 780 current jury instructions, interrogatories and verdict forms, 1,100 citations and a CD with forms. 800 pages. **$99**

Litigating Employment Discrimination Cases by Andrew H. Friedman. A practical work for experienced plaintiff and defense lawyers. Proven tactics, pattern arguments, common mistakes, and 97 forms for evaluation, discovery, summary judgment, trial preparation, and mediation. 1,724 pages, 2 volumes, CD-ROM included. **$149**

Litigating Sexual Harassment & Sex Discrimination Cases by Elizabeth Hubbard. Chronological step-by-step format for everything from workplace investigation and the administrative process, through pleadings, discovery and trial. Practical information for employers and human resource departments on avoiding these claims. Includes a case digest and a CD with 70 forms — policies, demands, complaints, answers, interrogatories, requests for production and admission, motions, memos, and jury instructions. 706 pages. **$99**

§1983 Civil Rights Digest by Richard Rosenstock. Quick access to 2,000 civil rights decisions in employment discrimination, police misconduct, public employee conduct, sexual harassment, and more. Determine who is liable, what legal theory applies, how to structure your case, how to maximize damages, and defenses, including an expansive list of immunity provisions. 974 pages, CD-ROM included. **$99**

FAMILY

The Determination of Income for Child Support by Nicholas L. Bourdeau. This practical, groundbreaking guide walks you through the areas where income adjustments are most likely to be found. You receive: guidance to Form 1040 and its supporting forms, completed tax forms keyed to footnoted spreadsheets, and detailed illustrations highlighting common adjustments. Use it to win courtroom points, save on experts, guide your clients, and understand more. 338 pages, CD-ROM included. **$99**

Divorce Taxation by Melvyn B. Frumkes. This plain English manual walks you step-by-step through the most commonly arising trouble spots in property distribution, support, and more. It is intelligently organized and indexed, well supported with citations, and most important, loaded with practical advice. 526 pages, CD-ROM included. **$99**

OTHER NATIONAL BOOKS

Bankruptcy Courts & Procedures by Pamela Everett Nollkamper. This is a comprehensive guide to the entire bankruptcy process, including involuntary, creditor, and adversary proceedings. The book also lists fees, filing requirements, names, addresses, and telephone numbers for every bankruptcy court. 712 pages, CD-ROM included. **$99**

Legal Secretary Federal Litigation by Pamela Everett Nollkamper. How to file federal pleadings and papers, document completion and filing requirements, and a directory of names, addresses, telephone numbers and more for each federal court. 612 pages, CD-ROM included. **$99**

The Limited Liability Company by James L. Leet, James Clarke and Pamela Everett Nollkamper. Model formation and operation documents, drafting tips, sample client letters, comparison charts, IRS revenue rulings and more. The authors discuss each state act separately in a detailed state-by-state analysis that includes checklists and forms. 898 pages, CD-ROM included. **$99**

MAGAZINE

Legal Assistant Today. Turn to the voice of the paralegal profession to find out if you're making what you're worth, to avoid the most common paralegal mistakes, and to plan your future. Every other month you'll receive practical, problem-solving articles written by veteran paralegals, computer experts, paralegal managers and other legal professionals. **$28**

CALIFORNIA

California Causes of Action by Mary E. Alexander, Kevin Lancaster, and Stanton T. Mathews. 125 pre-researched causes of action written by specialists in 19 separate legal fields. Draft better and quicker complaints, cross-complaints, answers or demurrers with up-to-date coverage of areas such as employment, intellectual property, negligence, contracts, real estate and much more. 826 pages, CD-ROM included. **$99**

California Courts and Judges. Provides biographical information on state and federal judges in California and candid attorneys' comments about many judges. Also includes a comprehensive statewide court directory containing important addresses, phone numbers and contact information. 1,184-page softcover, 2 volumes, CD-ROM included. **$149**

California Drunk Driving Law by Ed Kuwatch, Paul Burglin, and Barry Simons. Hundreds of creative decision-based defenses, dozens of artfully-drafted and heavily-supported motions, answers to 95% of the questions arising in day-to-day DUI practice, and authoritative interpretation of 1,500 cases. 1,270 pages, 2 volumes, CD-ROM included. **$129**

California Legal Secretary by Marlene Hazlewood. Complete and comprehensive guide to California legal procedures. Definitions, background information, step-by-step guidelines, statements of procedure and sample forms. In-depth coverage of nine practice areas: civil litigation, federal proceedings, family, real property, corporations, landlord/tenant, wills and probate, and adoptions. 892 pages, CD-ROM included. **$99**

California Lien Claims by Judge Pamela W. Foust. Step-by-step coverage of the law and procedure of lien claims in workers' compensation cases. This book comes complete with common fact patterns, resolutions recommended by the top authority in the state, and effective arguments. Pattern forms and over 400 citations support the text. Full-text CD, 662 pages. **$119**

California Objections by Judges Gregory Ward and James Byrne. 125 objections are covered with: pattern language, how to respond when faced with the objection, comments on how the rules apply, practice tips and cautions with detailed advice from the bench, arguments and strategies to support your objection, tactics and arguments to counter your opponent's objection, and relevant case cites with a synopsis of each case. 598 pages, CD-ROM included. **$99**

California Pretrial Practice & Forms by Judge Owen Lee Kwong, Robert F. Kane and Donald G. Rez. Step-by-step procedures, practice-proven strategies, 175 digital forms, and 3,600 recent case citations. Delivers quick and reliable answers with its outline format, tight writing, superb scholarship, and extensive supporting authority. Focused on pleadings, motions, and discovery. 1,604 pages, 2 volumes, CD-ROM included. **$129**

California Workers' Compensation Law and Practice by Judges David G. Marcus, Richard L. Newman, Sheldon C. St. Clair and Alexander Wong. Contains advice from the bench, step-by-step procedures, practice proven strategies, 6,000 case citations, and 78 forms. Considered by many to be the number one authority on the subject. 1,762 pages, 2 volumes, CD-ROM included. **$149**

FORECITE California by Tom Lundy. How to challenge and modify CALCRIM and CALJIC. Critically annotates both the plain-English and the old standard California criminal jury instructions with more favorable replacement language, issues, practice notes, and thousands of cases. Relied on by major county Superior courts, appellate courts, public defenders and more since 1990. Includes twice-annual newsletters and full-text website access. **$295**

FLORIDA

Florida Causes of Action by Arthur L. Berger. Elements for over 100 causes of action, complete with differences by District Court of Appeal, defenses, issues, and references to other texts. 592 pages, CD-ROM included. **$99**

Florida Criminal Cases Notebook by Kurt Erlenbach. The best single source for Florida criminal law citations. Quickly find your on-point case with over 8,000 annotations and citations of cases covering the full panoply of Florida criminal law. Compiled and summarized by one of the leading criminal specialists in the state. Includes a comprehensive subject matter index. 1,500 pages, CD-ROM included. **$125**

Florida Criminal Trial Procedure by Clayton R. Kaeiser. Arguments, law, and forms for arrest, indictment, arraignment, bail, pretrial detention, discovery, pretrial motions, notices, speedy trial, jury selection, proof and argument, verdict and judgment, and more. 766 pages, CD-ROM included. **$99**

Florida Family Law & Practice by Judge Renee Goldenberg. Provides techniques, law, and forms to improve your effectiveness and efficiency in everything from client preparation through entry of evidence to closing argument. The book is heavily annotated with over 3,000 case citations, dozens of practice tips, and 180 forms. 1,374 pages, 2 volumes, CD-ROM included. **$129**

Florida Family Law Trial Notebook by Roberta G. Stanley. Summaries and citations of key cases for: trial procedure, documentary evidence, testimony, privileges, objections, witnesses, hearsay, substantive family law, and family law rules. 752 pages, CD-ROM included. **$99**

Florida Legal Secretary by Kathleen J. Hill. Prepare Florida documents more efficiently in seven major areas of Florida law: civil litigation; estate administration; guardianship; marital dissolution; real estate; business organizations; and criminal law. The comprehensive two-volume set includes more than 900 forms on CD-ROM. 1,198 pages, 2 volumes. **$129**

Florida Objections by Judge Paul Siegel. Over 100 objections are covered with: pattern language, how to respond when faced with the objection, comments on how the rules apply, practice tips and cautions with detailed advice from the bench, arguments and strategies to support your objection, tactics and arguments to counter your opponent's objection, and relevant case cites with a synopsis of each case. 618 pages, CD-ROM. **$99**

Florida Pretrial Practice by Judge Amy Steele Donner, Robert D. Peltz, and Linda F. Wells. Focuses on drafting pleadings, preparing and presenting motions, conducting discovery, resolving discovery disputes, and negotiating settlements. Annotated with advice from the bench, case-based illustrations, practice-proven strategies, 1,450 recent cases, and 90 forms. 1,514 pages, 2 volumes, CD-ROM included. **$129**

ILLINOIS

Illinois Objections by Judges Daniel M. Locallo and Gerald F. Grubb. 130 objections are covered with: pattern language, how to respond when faced with the objection, comments on how the rules apply, practice tips and cautions with detailed advice from the bench, arguments and strategies to support your objection, tactics and arguments to counter your opponent's objection, and relevant case cites with a synopsis of each case. 454 pages, CD-ROM included. **$99**

Illinois Pretrial Practice by Judge Jennifer Duncan-Brice, Timothy W. Kelly and Kevin G. Owens. Advice from the bench, step-by-step procedures, practice proven strategies, dozens of digital forms, and thousands of citations. Delivers quick and reliable answers with its unique outline format, tight writing, superb scholarship, and extensive supporting authority. Focuses on pleadings, motions, and discovery. 1,194 pages, 2 volumes, CD-ROM included. **$129**

NEW YORK

New York Civil Practice Before Trial by Michael Barr, Burton Lipshie, Sharon Stern Gerstman, and the late Justice Myriam Altman. Step-by-step procedures, answers to knotty questions, tips from the bench, 3,200 citations, and 120 forms. Quickly find detailed and authoritative answers to difficult questions concerning pleadings, motions, discovery, and more. 1,564 pages, 2 volumes, CD-ROM included. **$129**

New York Fire District Officer's Guide by Raymond S. DiRaddo. This helpful guide includes: (1) 150 forms and resolutions and (2) quick answers to your day-to-day operating and legal questions such as officers' functions and duties, formation and operation, personnel, financial, and contracts. CD-ROM included. 780 pages. **$125**

Practical Tools and Techniques

YES! Send my James title(s) to examine for 30 days. If I am dissatisfied for any reason, I may return the undamaged materials with the invoice marked "cancel" and receive a full refund. Updates will also be sent to me on a 30-day review basis. I may cancel the update service at any time.

QUANTITY	TITLE	PRICE
QUANTITY	TITLE	PRICE
	CA residents add 7.25% sales tax	
	TOTAL	

FOUR EASY WAYS TO ORDER

Call: (800) 440-4780 • **Fax:** (714) 751-2709 • **Online:** WWW.JAMESPUBLISHING.COM
Mail: James Publishing / P.O. Box 25202 / Santa Ana, CA 92799

CAT07

PREPAY AND SAVE SHIPPING CHARGES

❑ My check for $ __________ is enclosed. ❑ Charge to my credit card: ❑ VISA ❑ MC ❑ AMEX

(Make check payable to James Publishing.)

Card # ______________________ Expires __________ 3(or 4)-Digit Security Code: ______

INVOICE OPTION:

❑ Bill Firm ❑ Bill Me *(I do not wish to take advantage of the free shipping offer.)*

Please complete all blanks, providing a street address for your office.

Printed Name: ______________________ Telephone: (______) ______________

Firm Name: ______________________ Fax: (______) ______________

Office Address (Including suite number, city, state, zip): E-mail: ______________

______________________ Bar #: ______________

______________________ Signature: ______________

New James Law Books

Attacking and Defending Drunk Driving Tests. Proven DUI cross examinations, motions, and trial tactics. *Page 4*

Deposing and Examining Doctors. Pattern medical depositions and examinations for the injuries you are most likely to encounter. *Page 1*

Deposition Checklists and Strategies. Pattern questions, outlines, and alternate approaches for common or thorny scenarios, disputes, and deponents. *Page 1*

Florida Causes of Action. Elements, authorities, circuit variations, defenses, and related issues for over 100 causes of action. *Page 6*

Texas Criminal Forms. 430 forms supported with step-by-step procedure, case and statutory citations, and advice from the bench. *Page 7*

Texas Small-Firm Practice Tools. Summaries of law, practice checklists, tax considerations, forms, and detailed procedures for 16 practice areas. *Page 7*

Customer Favorites

Our customers rave about these books…

- Building Trial Notebooks. *Page 1*
- Determining Economic Damages. *Page 2*
- Divorce Taxation. *Page 5*
- Federal Criminal Practice. *Page 4*
- Medical Evidence. *Page 3*
- Model Interrogatories. *Page 1*
- Social Security Disability Practice. *Page 3*
- California Causes of Action. *Page 5*
- California Drunk Driving Law. *Page 5*
- Florida Criminal Cases Notebook. *Page 6*
- Florida Legal Secretary. *Page 6*
- Florida Family Law and Practice. *Page 6*
- New York Objections. *Page 7*
- Texas Criminal Lawyers' Handbook. *Page 7*
- Texas Estate Planning. *Page 7*

Publishing practical and affordable law books since 1981.
We give 1% of revenues to needy youth.

James Publishing's

KIDS

Helping kids around the world.

Every year James Publishing gives at least 1% of its revenues to James Publishing's Kids. This private charitable foundation supports education and health projects for needy youth in the United States and in less developed countries. For more information, visit our website (www.JamesPublishing.com/foundation.htm).

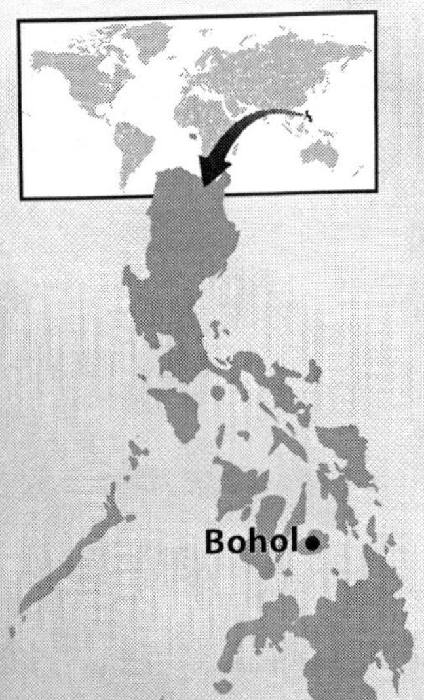

Homes and support for street kids.

We are teaming up with **Arms of Love** to build additional homes and take in more orphaned, abandoned, and abused children in developing countries. Our first steps are to finish and furnish a home in **Bohol, Phillipines** and sponsor one child. Next we hope to build a home in Brazil or Nicaragua and support some children there.

Bohol is one of the poorest and most underdeveloped areas of the Philippines archipelago. To learn more about Bohol, and how Arms of Love is helping the region, visit their website, **www.ArmsOfLove.org**.

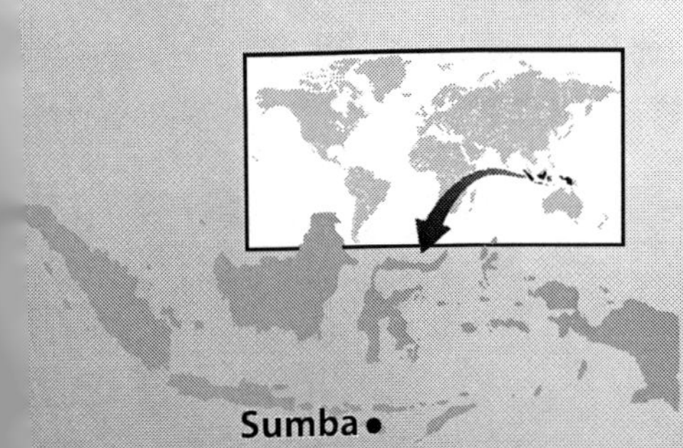

Clean water in Indonesia.

We provided money for the **Sumba Foundation** (www.SumbaFoundation.org) to dig water wells and lay water pipe for the village of **Paholo** on the island of **Sumba**. Our well and pipe provide clean water for 145 students and 800 villagers.

A clean water source is important during the Indonesian monsoon months of December–March. The springs become polluted with runoff, causing dangerous outbreaks of diarrhea that kill many young children. Our wells will eliminate this cause of death.

College scholarships in California.

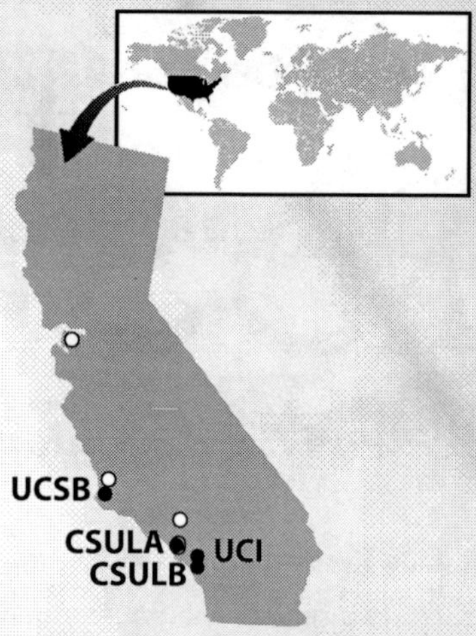

We have directly provided full scholarships (tuition and living expenses) and guidance to five inner-city students who were accepted to good universities, but could not afford to attend. Our scholarship recipients attend **UC Santa Barbara, Cal State Long Beach, Cal State Los Angeles**, and **UC Irvine**. Several are nearing graduation.

We also found sponsors for six additional needy scholars. Thanks to generous providers of full scholarships, these students now attend UC Berkeley, USC, Cal Poly San Luis Obispo, Cal State Los Angeles, and Cal Poly Pomona.

New school in Afghanistan.

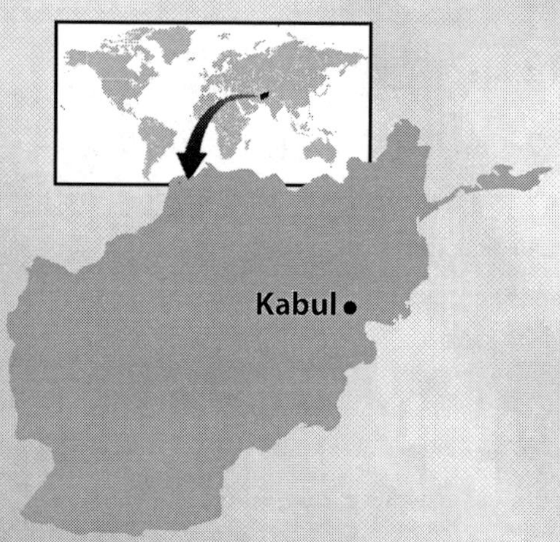

We provided the startup money and contribute 80% of the annual budget for the **Helping Hands School** in **Kabul**, which educates and feeds 195 students. Helping Hands started as an elementary and trade school for orphans and widows, and still contains many students who have lost a parent or spouse. Its doors are now also open at no charge to others in need.

Helping Hands differs from the public schools in that:

- Our student-to-teacher ratio is 25:1, half the public-school ratio.
- Our classes are co-ed, which is unusual in Afghanistan.
- English is taught as a second language beginning in 1st grade, compared to 7th grade elsewhere.
- We teach science, history, and art. Religion is not taught.
- Our class day is twice as long.
- Meals are served. Many of our students come to us malnourished and unable to concentrate, but after a few months of our fare, they fill out and are able to focus.

For more information on

James Publishing's
KIDS

visit our website: www.JamesPublishing.com/foundation.htm.